The House on Via Gombito

THE HOUSE ON VIA GOMBITO

Writing by American Women Abroad

Second Edition

Edited by
Madelon Sprengnether
and C. W. Truesdale

A New Rivers Abroad Book

NEW RIVERS PRESS 1997

"The House on Via Gombito" originally appeared in *Clinton Street Quarterly;* "Friends of the Teatro Colón" originally appeared in *Revista/Review Interamericana;* the "Venetian Winter" section of "Italian Two-Part Invention" originally appeared in the *Minneapolis Tribune Travel Magazine;* the "Umbrian Spring" section originally appeared in the *Los Angeles Times Travel Magazine.* Our thanks to the editors for allowing us to reprint these stories here.

Support has been provided by the Beim Foundation, General Mills, Liberty State Bank, the McKnight Foundation, the Minnesota State Arts Board (through an appropriation from the Minnesota Legislature), the Star Tribune/Cowles Media Company, the Tennant Company Foundation, the United Arts Council, and the contributing members of New Rivers Press. New Rivers Press also wishes to acknowledge the Minnesota Non-Profits Assistance Fund for its invaluable support.

New Rivers Press
420 North Fifth Street, Suite 910
Minneapolis, MN 55401

www.mtn.org/~newrivpr

*This book is dedicated to all great
women travelers, especially
Eurydice, Margaret Fuller, Martha Gellhorn,
Nor Hall, Mary McCarthy, Mary Morris,
Kate O'Neill, Persephone, Kate Simon,
and Fanny Trollope.*

CONTENTS

INTRODUCTION TO THE SECOND EDITION

C. W. Truesdale

When *The House on Via Gombito* appeared in 1991 it was a first in contemporary travel writing by women, and since then it has become the best-selling anthology New Rivers Press has ever published. We are proud to say it filled a gap in publishing that is very large—so much so that New Rivers has followed it with a second anthology of writing by American women abroad called *Tanzania on Tuesday,* and will publish still a third volume in the spring of 1998, *An Inn Near Kyoto.*

I think it is entirely appropriate that the third volume will take the name of an essay by Michelle Dominque Leigh, because the whole idea for the series was generated many years ago by a discussion we had at the Small Press Book Fair at the Loeb Student Center in New York.

When it first appeared, *The House on Via Gombito* received many excellent comments from both local and national reviewers. They ranged from such publications as the *Minneapolis Star Tribune,* the *St. Paul Pioneer Press,* and *City Pages,* to *Glamour* magazine and *Publishers Weekly.*

Mary Ann Grossman, for instance, wrote in the *Pioneer Press* that "The best travel experiences teach us geography, patience, foreign words. They disappoint, make us giddy, make us ill, show us some gorgeous sunsets, and give us peeks at other cultures. But most of all, as the forty-six writers in *The House on Via Gombito* show, travel teaches us about ourselves. . . . And what a variety of voices. Some of the contributors are experienced poets and writers; others are being published for the first time."

The Bookwatch said that "Over forty women writers are represented in a strong literary collection which probes North American women travelers' experiences abroad. Letters, diary entries, essays, and short stories use varied formats to describe experiences ranging from the comic to the deadly serious. The result reflects not only cultural encounters, but the contributors' personalities and observations."

Chris Faatz, formerly of Graywolf Press, recommended this book as "a beautiful collection of fine writing." *The Launch Pad* had this to say: "From a journeywoman's notation of various men's crude pick-up attempts . . . to a mother's concern for the special dangers—and benefits—a foreign land holds for her children, these tales get their life breath from a singularly feminine experience and consciousness. These women are bold, courageous risk-takers and leaders, and their narratives can teach us what it means to face life with all its variety and challenge, and carry on."

Dave Wood, writing in the *Minneapolis Star Tribune*, also recommended *The House on Via Gombito* in his "On Books" column. He said that it "is a very diverse collection of stories, some fictional, by North American women about their travels abroad. Dedicated to women travelers from Eurydice to Frances Trollope, *Gombito* covers the globe—Central and South America, Africa, the Middle East, India, Eastern and Western Europe, with a whole chapter devoted to Italy."

Helen Antrobus, in a piece called "Kerouac's Sister" published in *City Pages*, reflected on how unique a collection of travel writing by women really is:

A woman traveling alone in this culture is disconcerting because she goes against the grain of Western tradition. Our culture is built on the hero's journey, on men's experience traveling. The first collection of travel writing by men was called the Bible. One of the earliest written documents (in cunieform on a stone slab) is the Epic of Gilgamesh, a story about a guy traveling. The Quest for the Holy Grail was basically a bunch of road stories. Gilgamesh, Beowulf, Sir Lancelot, Columbus, Lewis and Clark, all those British guys in Africa and India, Jack Kerouac, the astronauts—the history of the world as we've been taught it is one long string of travel writing by men. And all of those stories have in common the assertion of control—frequently through violence, whether slaying the dragon, shooting the wild boar, converting the "savages," or conquering outer space. Our heroes all basically filled the same formula: if it looks different, conquer it, kill it, or enslave it, and then name the area where you found it after yourself, thereby establishing ownership. But what if someone reinvented that formula? What if *women* traveled, following entirely different rules, and then told their stories? Wouldn't that turn the entire body of Western history on its head? Yes, it would, and that's just what New Rivers Press has done by publishing *The House on Via Gombito*, . . . an incredibly diverse collection of stories of women's journeys, . . . powerful stories about transformation that, taken as a whole, reinvent the tired old formula of the Western Hero's conquering journey.

Comments such as these—and many more—told the editors that this undertaking was unique and worthwhile. New Rivers Press is pleased to present to readers a second edition of this strong and inspiring anthology.

INTRODUCTIONS

I HAD MY first airplane ride sometime in the late 1940s, in a small private craft owned by one of my parents' adventurous and somewhat eccentric friends. What thrilled me about this experience was not only the new perspective I gained on the earth hundreds of feet below, but also the rush of wind against my face, the pitch and roll of the aircraft, the generally precarious sense of riding on air. To my mother's acute dismay, our pilot even cut the engine at one point in order (as he said) to demonstrate the utter reliability and hence safety of his machine. Flying was like being on the highest of all possible roller coasters. It was the greatest fun I had ever had, and the most scary.

Later, in the 60s, when I flew back and forth to college from the midwest to the east coast, I was disappointed that the large propeller planes which routinely made this run didn't reproduce my earlier sensations. Instead the fear and excitement I felt came from geographical dislocation, from leaving home and being for the first time alone in a new environment. That my family supported me in traveling so far didn't alleviate my homesickness that first semester, nor the feeling of being out of my element. Many of my new friends, for instance, not having any clear picture of the midwest, talked about St. Louis (where I had grown up) as though it were part of the deep South. Yet I had not really come so far after all. I had not crossed any oceans or international borders and was perfectly comfortable speaking my native tongue.

When I went abroad the summer after my junior year to live with a French family for six weeks and study in the south of France, I nervously boarded a jet. While the ride was smoother than the ones I was used to, I was frightened by the thought of being so high up. At 30,000 feet, I couldn't imagine how, if there were any trouble, we would ever get safely down. Yet, I did find a comfortable niche for myself where I landed, in the sleepy French provincial town of Avignon. I remember wanting, above all, to fit in—to look, dress, think French, in particular to refine my accent to the point where I could sometimes pass as a native. One of my moments of greatest pleasure was when my hostess, a shrewd and capable mother-hen of a woman, deliberately used the familiar "tu" form in addressing me.

Then I fell out of the habit of travel and stuck to the relatively safe paths of graduate school, marriage, and motherhood until I was well into my thirties. Somehow I lost my confidence and lapsed into a state of anxious dependence. I date my recovery from this condition from my decision to go places again by myself, taking on the risk, along with the promise and excitement of travel.

It is now so easy (for those with money at least) to have this experience that we sometimes forget how much anxiety it can also generate. Especially for women, who not only must confront the internalized voice that says this is not proper, this is not ladylike, but often real physical harassment as well. For those of us who have grown up with such fears, the choice to step off of one's familiar ground (whether alone or in company) in order to encounter the new, the strange, or simply the unexpected, can be a significant act of courage. Perhaps this is one of the reasons I responded with such enthusiasm when Bill Truesdale first raised the possibility of our co-editing a collection of writings by North American women traveling abroad. But I was also curious; I wanted to see how other women felt, what experiences they had had and how they understood themselves.

I was stunned by the diversity of responses we received—not only in geographical terms but also in the different styles of writing and reflection. I read about spiritual journeys, quests for ancestral origins, psychic jolts and dislocations. I also read about culture shock, confrontations with contemporary history and politics, negotiations between first and third world realities. I read about the sheer exhilaration of travel, about the comedy and terror inherent in accident, about the differences between a child's and an adult's perspective on leaving one's homeland. Travel (not anatomy), I decided, is women's destiny.

In *Nothing to Declare: Memoirs of a Woman Traveling Alone,* Mary Morris says "It was my mother who made a traveler out of me, not so much because of the places where she went as because of her yearning to go." I like this idea that a woman's desire to travel can act as an inspiration to other women. Later, in the same essay, Morris describes a costume that her mother once devised for a Suppressed Desire ball. "On her head sat a tiny, silver rotating globe. Her skirts were the oceans, her body, the land, and interlaced between all the layers of taffeta and fishnet were Paris, Tokyo, Istanbul, Tashkent. Instead of seeing the world, my mother became it." What I read in this passage is a statement about a woman's proper sphere, which, far from being confined to home and hearth, encompasses the globe.

When I first went to France, it was my mother (who had yet to travel abroad) who most urged me to go. Later, she had many opportunities to realize her own wanderlust. I remembered this when my eighteen-year-old daughter announced that she wanted to buy a Eurail pass and travel around Europe the summer after her graduation from high school. My first thoughts were about her safety, my awareness of all the things that might possibly go wrong. But I basically approved of her desire and was proud of the responsible way she planned her trip. I really wanted her to go. I wanted her to explore different cultures, to test herself against adversity, and to have a wonderful time. Most of all, I wanted her to be able to find her own footing in the world. The essays in this collection tell us, richly and abundantly, how other women have done, and are doing, just that.

—Madelon Sprengnether, co-editor
Minneapolis, Minnesota, June 1990

THE IDEA for this anthology came about a long time ago at the Loeb Student Center in New York City. I had come in from St. Paul that Easter to display an array of New Rivers books at the annual book fair in that crowded, stuffy, but exciting environment.

One afternoon, a young woman came up to my table carrying a large black portfolio full of interesting drawings and a few essays she had published accompanied by her own art work. She identified herself as Michelle Anderson. I was struck immediately by the quality of her work and the degree of craftsmanship it displayed. But what really fascinated me was the stories about her wanderings in Africa she began to tell me. I asked her to leave some stuff with me and come back the next day.

Much as I liked her art work, I was intrigued and excited by her story and by its potentialities. She began telling me how she had gone to Europe and Africa on her own when she was barely twenty and had spent two or three years moving from place to place as her spirit led her. She had lived, she told me, on an island off the coast of Kenya and had explored among veiled Muslim women the mysterious world of African magic and ritual. I knew that some day I would try to get her to write out those stories for me and that I would publish them in one form or another.

It was then that the idea for a travel anthology began to form in the shadows of my mind—a natural one for me, since I love traveling myself when I can afford it and the perspectives it has always given me on my own country. Over the years since that meeting in the early 80s Michelle and I have become good friends—an occasional dinner or lunch when I came to New York, illustrations for a book, and occasional letters (some of them very long). In the meantime she married Bruce Leigh, had two children, and moved to Japan (where she has lived for two or three years now). Michelle Leigh's contribution to *Via Gombito* includes meditations on some of those early travels.

In the spring of 1989, New Rivers Press received special, generous funding from the now beleaguered National Endowment for the Arts for this anthology. We gratefully and warmly thank the NEA for that support and wish it godspeed in its own difficult travels through Congress.

At that time I invited another old friend and New Rivers author, Madelon Sprengnether, to join with me as principal editor of *The House on Via Gombito* because I knew that Mimi herself is a gifted traveler, a brilliant teacher and critic, and a thorough and discriminating feminist. I also knew that we would work very well together.

What I didn't know was that we would be almost overwhelmed by contributions so rich and varied and of such high quality that we would have to turn away many excellent pieces or that the volume you have in your hands would assume such large dimensions. Early on Mimi and I decided to ignore arbitrary space limitations and let the volume grow as it would and find its own shape. I also could not have anticipated how eagerly so many of these writers took to the process of being edited and would produce just stunning revisions/transformations of their original pieces. At New Rivers we are committed to publishing bold, new writing but we also believe in strong, old-fashioned editing. As more and more of these amazing revisions poured in I became increasingly enthusiastic about this project.

There are many, many unique and individual journeys in *Via Gombito,* ranging from a few weeks or months abroad to a ten-year sojourn on the Greek island of Mykonos. What most of them share is some sense that the journey abroad is also an intense, if sometimes light-hearted, journey within. And taken altogether, this anthology is witness to the vitality of the creative spirit among American women and to the fact that the women's movement in America is alive, healthy, eclectic, and powerful. If *Via Gombito* is any evidence, the future of first-rate writing in this country will be a very happy one.

Like most New Rivers anthologies *The House on Via Gombito* is a blending of much-published writers like Patricia Hampl, Kathleen Coskran, Sharon Mayes, Catherine Stearns, Helen Degen Cohen, Monica Ochtrup, Diane Glancy, and Sharon Chmielarz with a great many superb writers who have seldom or never been published before: Rhiannon Paine, Gretchen Legler, Katherine Maehr, Jennifer Ochtrup, Melissa Sanders-Self, Emily Meiers, Vivian Vie Balfour, Nancy Raeburn, Sharon Brown, and many others—all of whom you should keep a look-out for!

We have begun this anthology with a piece about flying written by Beverly Baranowski who was for a number of years a flight attendant on domestic and overseas jet liners. Unlike the Charon who ferried the souls of the dead across the River Styx in Greek mythology, we take her as companion and shepherd not to Lethe or oblivion but to the warmth, intelligence and remembrance of these many journeys. Alive to the dangers and the exhilaration of travel, she is a fit attendant to the spirited flights of imagination that make up the body of this book.

We hope that you will enjoy this immense collective journey as much as we have in putting it all together. For us this has been a real trip, an adventure of discovery in itself.

— C. W. Truesdale, co-editor
Minneapolis, Minnesota, June 1990

Beverly Baranowski

FLYING

Beverly Baranowski worked as a flight attendant for Northwest Airlines from 1965 to 1983. Twelve of the eighteen years were spent flying international trips to Tokyo, Osaka, London, Munich, and Glasgow.

THE WINDOW IS open and I hear an airplane far away. I hear the voices of all the people I served in eighteen years, a soft murmur in my life, a pool to drink from, a soothing. I remember the fire at the Hilton in Chicago, coming down nineteen flights of stairs on the outside of the building in November. The whole thing a joke until the seventh floor and people crying with blackened faces, two lives gone up in smoke, two deaf mute boys dead in their beds. A dalmatian on the corner ran back and forth as if looking for them. The bar across the street served us coffee until our hands shook and we remembered our names and how to walk.

Someone called their parents. Two mothers woke to hear those words while we flew on to Seattle and the next hotel. Always checking the back of the door now, follow the red route with your eyes, count the doorknobs to the exit, stay on your left. Don't open the door if the knob is hot, never open your window. Never, never close your eyes.

The red sun rides along the wing of the airplane, blue sky and sun always above the clouds. There is a buoyancy in the morning and the climb into the sky is effortless, silent, dreaming the way children do, without envy and greed. As if someone held our lives on strings, tangling and untangling us, the known and the unknown, glancing off each other in those sparkings between human beings. Dancing light patterns in the sky above Anchorage shoot an avalanche of memory out of the sky.

An airplane breaks up on takeoff and the smell of a 747 rushes back: the smell of people, the odor of fear and of plastic burning, the great intake of the last breath before the burning light. Escape of souls into the sky, still wearing seat belts, the earth unable to hold them any longer. We take off and land so many times during one lifetime. Sometimes we should stay rooted, grounded without being buried.

But I flew for a while. I watched the sun rise through the cockpit, carried meals as if it meant something to feed thousands, patted the hands of strangers and let drunks kiss me goodbye.

And so I was with them, even though I've quit flying, I was with them when the airplane took off over the blue bridge of the sky, out over the water and into the deep reverie that is the long flight to Australia. I was with those nine people who were sucked through the rushing hole to death. They've given up the search; they won't find their bodies. There aren't any bodies any more.

Imagine if two of them were your parents. They belong to you; you are made up from them. Retired now, they are traveling a little and you are happy for them, and relieved. Think of your mother sitting next to the window looking for the turquoise water even though it's night. She watches the lights of Diamond Head fall away, turns, and says something to your father. He leans toward her, to listen, to see what she sees. She is always the one to point things out: Points of Interest. As a child, she was very serious, memorizing facts to please the nuns. Depth of the Pacific Ocean, names of clouds, how an aircraft stays aloft. Her hair is dyed blonde and cut short, but fluffy around her face, girlish. She wears pink lipstick and powders her nose, the only woman you know who still carries a compact.

Today she wears a blue pantsuit with a white blouse, and they both wear running shoes, although neither of them has run anywhere in a long time. She loves navy blue; her eyes are blue. She loves the ocean but they've always lived in the middle of the country. When she's near the ocean, she gets dreamy and seems to lose her everyday self. It's as if she could be anyone.

The terror. They must have felt it. Did she scream? Did she reach for him? Did they hold one another as they went down? Or were they ripped apart? Were the "many small body fragments found in the crippled engine" part of them: eye, tooth, fingernail? How is any one of us safe again, flying, wondering about the fragile skin of an aging aircraft, peering into our own mirrors at our hundreds of cracks of age. I think about the smallest thing: where are they floating now? If you die in an airplane engine, does your spirit inhabit the clouds, the air around a star? If you die in the ocean, does it wave like a small fist around the bones of your old body?

Even if it happened very fast, I don't think it can be fast enough not to know that you're about to die, that you are being torn apart, that you are dying and that now, surely, you are dead. I'm sure they felt something. Cold. They felt the cold wind first, heard the cracking, the sound of their own voices, their eardrums popping. Then I'm not sure. Maybe you die of fright first.

The FAA is going to protect us from the thin skinned airplanes; there will be inspections and grounded flights and serious looks at cargo doors. You can't use things like we use them, nonstop, back and forth across the ocean like that. The aircraft should rest too, like a tired elephant should be hosed down, watered, allowed to stay in one place for a few days. A few nervous passengers will joke about how we all have to go sometime, just don't seat me in row eight through eleven. Those who don't say anything will be thinking about it on every takeoff. There are people praying at 30,000 feet right now.

I remember another time. The DC10 window cracked, blew out and sucked a passenger half out while the man behind him hung on to his feet as the pilot aimed the plane down. Finally he couldn't hold on anymore and the stuck man was gone. When they interviewed him he said, "I held on, tight as I could. I had him. Then he was just gone." Shaking his head, the pilot said later that holding on to him through the window saved everyone else. It kept the aircraft partially pressurized until they reached a safe altitude. It kept more people from being sucked out. "The man was dead when you were holding on to his feet," the pilot said, "no one could survive. The temperature at that altitude is -70." But the man who held on still believed he could have saved him, still believed that one human being can save another.

The next time you fly, smell the shape of the person sitting next to you. See the gold hairs on the back of the hand, realize you both have knees. Taste the wind and roll it around in your mouth. Put your seat back before you turn the pages of your book and pretend this is real. Eat whatever they serve knowing you are just another flock of birds.

Flying is not winging over the earth alone. It is breathing and believing that we'll all arrive together. In a cold place with no light, it is someone holding you.

CENTRAL
& SOUTH
AMERICA

Barbara Abel

VIA POCHUTLA

Into our consciousness come giants with empty hands. They put a star in our palm and say: keep this forever.

Tomás Borge

I HAVE ONLY been to Mexico once. Unfamiliar with the culture, not speaking the language, I came to this land ignorant and left knowing little. I was there only two weeks, but it was long enough to recognize a place close to its mysteries.

* * *

The plane descends over the Sierra Madre del Sur, the Mother Mountain of the South, one arm of the Sierra Madre chain that encircles the central Mexican plateau. The smell of cigarettes and a.m. cocktails permeates the stale air of the cabin. Most of the passengers are drinking and have grown louder through the morning. The captain's reference to the mountain is drowned out by laughter and jests of protest to the last call before landing.

The mountain below is unspeakably old. Gnarled peaks reach toward the sky, with crevices etched in them, telling stories of volcanoes, of old rivers, of veins full of silver and gold. If the mountain reaches toward us, the gesture goes unnoticed. Her beauty barely brushes the underside of our perceptions as the plane descends into Acapulco de Juarez, a port in the curve of one crooked knuckle.

Customs is the last egalitarian act before we divide into layers. The big buses of the luxury hotels swallow the bulk of the passengers. Private taxis take up another layer. Those left board the airport vans, mostly Mexicans, all men, and they laugh when I name the hotel I've chosen.

The van winds its way along the glitz of the costera where large resort hotels boast matching hot pink jeeps and uniformed, good looking staff. When we reach the center of the old port town that flourished before the resorts sprung up things suddenly change. The dazzling shops are gone; we pass an open market. Chickens hang by scrawny legs in the midday sun. Dogs run down the streets with no one in particular, and there are people begging. Beggars with canes and crutches, beggars with metal cups, beggars with beers in their hands. And children, many of them, begging with gestures that make them appear already old.

* * *

The hotel is a miserable place run by beautiful women. The smile of one of them makes the glitter of all the costera seem dull. The room, clean, has a plastic grease bucket under the trapless sink, the biggest cockroaches I've ever seen, and a second adjoining bedroom that I worry may be rented while I sleep. There are broken glass louvres on the screenless windows and spring locks on the flimsy doors. The big engines of tour buses roar up the hill, their exhaust drawn up into the room by the clattering blades of the ceiling fan.

I sleep uneasily on the ticking covered springs, and in my dreams I'm back in the −30° I left early that morning. I soar above the Nevada, the sibling of the Sierra Madre. Her limbs are also old, but stiff with cold, a beauty different from her sister's. Outside it is 90° and the smells of frying fish, of spice, of diesel fuel and salt water fill the late afternoon.

In the evening I walk to the old town square, the *zócalo*. Such a whole, round word, with room for the old banyans, the grandfathers gathered beneath them like ancient birds, the shy couples hand in hand, the river of children that pours from the school, the babes in the arms of venerable women, the men who drink and talk in long melodic lines at orange cafe tables.

* * *

Vendors and hawkers work the beach all day, trudging under their heavy bags of carvings or fruit, baskets of peanuts, stacks of woven blankets, racks of leather belts, hats piled twenty, thirty high upon their heads. Indian women with pieces of brilliant cloth braided into their waist-long hair move across the burning, shifting sand, their necks erect with trays of pineapple, papaya and melon balanced on their heads.

There is also the begging, hunched over, with a burning light somewhere back behind the eye, protected.

* * *

Anxious to leave the city and see the countryside, I head to the bus depot, a three-sided building swarming with people and crowded with boxes, bags and goods. I move to the end of one of the many groups standing three and four abreast in ticket lines. When my shoulder is tapped from behind I assume it's someone cueing me to move up, but it's a uniformed driver who indicates that he is driving the next bus to Puerto Escondido and will sell me a ticket so I can board now. I'm glad not to stand in line, and better yet to find an empty seat remaining in the back, to sit and watch the aisle fill, tighter and tighter, bodies packed close.

The bus backs out of its cramped space, creaks and groans with the weight of its load, and makes its slow way through the congested city streets. A man leans over my seat from the aisle and speaks, pointing to his ticket. I take out my ticket and hand it to him. He goes on talking, waving the tickets, then points to the rack above, so I get up and push my pack as far as it will move to make more room. He shakes his head, sighs and speaks more slowly. People around us smile at each other, comment and laugh. He hands back my ticket, throws up his hands and shoves his way toward the back.

It's then I realize the number on my ticket is not the number on the rack above, which must be for this seat. I make my way to where he stands, point to the empty seat. His wife forces her way to the seat with an infant and young child. I push my way back to move my bag for her, and tell her what I suddenly remember from the phrases at the back of the guidebook: I'm sorry, I'm very sorry. She waves it off, her quality of voice telling me not to worry about it. Her husband stops me from moving my pack, and the people in the back make room for me to sit among them on the floor.

I sit between a young woman whose young man is pleased that they are squeezed yet tighter, and an old campesino who tries exceptionally hard to maintain a fraction of distance. Every time we turn a corner, downshift on a steep grade or come to a quick stop we are thrown against each other. I feel as uncomfortably aware of my privilege in the world as the old man is of my proximity.

A few villages later there are seats open. The bus wheezes along in the fierce heat, past dusty crossroads and shrunken rivers where women do wash. We roll past scrubby trees hung with USDA boxes that track the migration of killer bees. Buzzards dive into the path of the bus for their food, flattened on the pavement. The woman in the seat beside me crosses herself, her hands like soft brown birds.

In every available patch of shade, someone takes cover. A campesino draws his legs up into the shade of a roadside shrine. A small child lies curled in the shadow of a sign. The old woman beside him shades her eyes and gazes down the empty road.

Further on the federales stand against the trunks of trees, their lean bodies fit easily into the columns of shade. Their uniforms blend with the shadows, leaving them nearly concealed. The sun is too dazzling to make distinctions within the shadows between the dark skin, the deep navy uniforms, the black hair and eyes. Only the glint of their automatic rifles slung across one shoulder in a slim line of captured light catches the eye.

Until they step from those slender columns and flag the bus down. Two of them spring onto the bus, waving their arms and issuing commands in rapid Spanish. The rifles slap against their backs with the ease of heavy woven hammocks or burlap bags of peanuts on the hawkers at the beach. But the similarity ends there — these men are like well-oiled machines, ready to kick in at a moment's notice, able to perform in high temperatures. Their faces and bodies and uniforms and guns are impressive, whether I want them to be or not. Part of me, like a child watching fire fighters hop a roaring engine, is caught in the power of the clothing, the glint of the equipment, the sheer readiness of them.

People file from the bus. Outside I notice it is only men who get off and line up to be frisked. As I get back on the bus the women laugh, some loudly and with comments to each other, some shaking their heads silently, all of them between me and my seat in the back. But many meet my eyes as they laugh, and several say things to me as I pass. What I understand is the cadence of their speech and the spark in their eyes, and at that moment I feel very safe.

Suddenly I realize how much I have been cautioned: by friends and fellow travelers, at the airport before leaving, in the brochure that came with the tickets, in the pages of the guidebook. I've been warned of very real dangers; but I've also been made wary and fearful. As the bus rolls through the villages and fields, as people board it not with luggage but with goods, I feel myself grow calmer, more curious and comfortable, until even the wiry federales look less like guns and more like men.

* * *

About halfway to Puerto Escondido the bus empties out and the driver eats and rests. When he returns I am the only passenger. He motions me to come sit up front. As we drive on the road changes to sharp, surprising curves. He drives faster, with skill, and we race through jungle-like sections of vegetation and burst out the other side into the fading light.

The bus fills again quickly, stopping in every village. As we get closer to Puerto Escondido a group of girls gets on. They wear fashionable jeans and amazingly white blouses. Some have their gleaming hair cut short, which makes their eyes look even larger. Their nails are brightly painted.

When they board the bus their heels click hard on the metal floor, and the old campesinos avert their eyes.

* * *

The guidebook's hotels are full in Puerto Escondido. The cabby drives from place to place and does most of the talking. We move farther up the hill away from the sea, the shops, the places catering to travelers. Near the top, by the highway that divides the village from the tourists, are two hotels across the street from one another. One, mentioned in the book, is all white stucco and fresh paint and paved, lit walkways. The driver goes in, and I cross to the other, a brown plaster facade with a dim cavernous entrance. At first I can't quite see the man in the back, but his white hat bobs as he nods his head and calls out. I assume he speaks to me so I begin to ask for a room. A girl appears in the dark. She crosses the floor in silence, slips behind the desk and turns on a small, heavily shaded lamp. The counter is of thick, nearly black wood, as is the wall behind it hung with silver keys. The walls are umber plaster hung with weavings and the floor is cracked, dark granite the color of a dried rose.

There are rooms available upstairs. I find and pay the driver, and sign for my stay. As I turn from the desk clutching my key, uncertain how many nights I've paid for, I see the man more clearly. He is very, very old, and lies in a huge rope hammock in the back of the room. He stares through me with the unfocused, steady gaze of the blind as he grumbles and points to the curved granite stairway whose steps have shifted with time.

I climb two flights of the odd stairs, past open courtyards hung with ghostly wash, past potted palms and walls crawling with bougainvillaea to a door at the very end of the walk on the top floor. The room is the same plaster, dark wood and granite, cool on the soles of my feet. A large iguana lies across the curtain rod.

Later, after eating and walking, I find gates of wrought iron closed across the yawning entrance. They are locked, and there is no light on and no bell. I call out until the old man shuffles from the dark, disheveled, and opens the gate. A child out too late, I slink up the crooked stairs not daring to stop for water from the big jar on the desk. I wake with my mouth dry and find him in the hammock, waving off my hoarse apology before it's even spoken.

* * *

The beach is long and clean, and I swim throughout the morning. When the sun is high I cross the burning sand to the palapas up the slope. The vendors work hard; I buy peanuts and bottled water, donuts and wooden combs. A young boy comes by with paintings to sell. I remember seeing him in town, early, while the street was still cool. He was working on pieces of pressed bark laid out before him, his paints in a perfect half circle. He stands directly in front of me, displays his twenty or so pictures one by one, asking with each turn, "You like?"

I like them all, but there is one that rivets me. It is a small picture of a wedding party moving toward a church. Halfway across the painting the sky changes abruptly from light to dark, the day a deep pumpkin orange, the night the grass green of a crayon. At the vertical line where day turns to night is a crescent moon, its center pierced by the green dark. The convex side of the moon crosses the axis, cutting a small groove into the sky of day, which the tongue of night fills like a well made joint. Both skies are full, brimming with stars, a few of them falling, shooting long tails. Flat bottomed clouds reach up with long white fingers as if combing the heavens for treasure.

The people in the painting are clearly of the earth: the brown, mustard, orange, beige, dotted curve of land they travel. Even the tall, rounded hats of the men do not rise above the horizon. In the foreground is the bride. Her white dress stretches over the landscape, across the orange skirts of the women, across the white pants of the men in sombreros. All of them point with raised arms to the triple spired church with three dark doors; and the bride moves ahead, urged on by her entourage, by the dotted curve of earth, by the hinged skies themselves.

I suppose it is a common sort of painting, not hard to come by. More seasoned travelers might have smiled at its obvious appeal and passed it by. But in it I see something whole, as if the elements of the universe were balanced in this piece of painted bark, endlessly revolving.

* * *

As the afternoon wears on the fishermen come out and pull their boats from shore. I walk further down the beach away from town. Horses are led down hillside paths to the sand, where their owners sell gallops, bareback, through the surf. Pelicans soar and wheel, then dive across the surface of the water.

By sunset huge waves heave themselves from the sea, catch bands of hot pink light on their crests and carry them to the disappearing sand. Sheets of water crash to shore, forcing those of us who watch to move to higher ground. I sit mesmerized as wave after wave throws its rib of light at land and people shift position like the other bits of stuff cast upon the beach. A group of boys lie on their surfboards out where the water heaves and swells. A few at a time choose waves, move skillfully into their curves and ride balanced inside the massive walls that thunder to shore. I try to track them with the more powerful lens of the camera, entranced by the pitch and force of wave upon hungry wave. The growing darkness prods at me to leave, but I sit on and on, caught in the web of the scene. I watch until there is no light left and the last of the boys, like a slick young otter, lifts his body from the sea.

In darkness I walk back to town, up the long hill, slip through the open iron gates and up the cool stone stairs to sleep. I wake abruptly in the middle of the night with knowledge: the water has changed, the undertow sucks with far greater urgency to take what it finds back to the deep. Though I am too far up the hill to hear, I listen hard, certain I've been wakened by the sound of waves, sure that the sea, as it throws itself into this port, has changed.

In the morning I go to swim having forgotten this middle of the night awareness. As I enter the water the undertow grabs my legs away from me, and what might have been left as some dream-spawned fear resurrects itself as warning. I keep feeling I am learning to recognize myself here.

* * *

The next day I check out at dawn. The old man is in the hammock. I stop to thank him, to tell him in my broken, memorized Spanish that his hotel is good. His smile is like the glint of the breakers I'd sat and watched so long. You see it coming, watch it reach its peak and then it's gone, back into the sea that you can never really know.

* * *

The guidebook warns that the bus ride to Oaxaca is long and exhausting, winding up through the Sierra Madre del Sur on mostly dirt roads. Dead center on the dash of the bus, just below the worst of the windshield cracks, is a statue of Jesus, one creamy plastic hand raised toward the passengers in blessing. Taped to the wall at the driver's left is a picture of the Virgin surrounded by paper flowers and streamers. At the top of the windshield hangs a long, multi-colored fringe of crocheted yarn to shield the driver from the glare of what promises to be a killer day. A plastic Barbie in a metallic mini-dress straddles the shift.

When every seat is filled and the ticket taker has collected all the stubs, the driver boards the bus, takes a stern look down the aisle, adjusts the Barbie so that one pale, elongated arm is raised toward the passengers, and pulls out onto the road. After a few minutes we reach the coastal highway, paved and smooth, which will last about an hour. I doze on and off as the bus rolls through the growing heat.

* * *

The bus to Oaxaca goes via Pochutla, a village of a few constricted streets. Vendors, dogs and children scatter slowly, dream-like in the noon heat as we round the tight bend to the station. The ticket man makes a fine leap off the moving bus and directs the driver forward and back repeatedly, changing the angle by inches until the bus backs from the narrow street into the yard at last.

The village must thrive on this joining of roads. From the street, the buildings, and the bits of shade in the yard come vendors and hawkers. The first of them burst into the bus with huge trays of cooked food. Their cries ricochet off the metal walls, and the clink of change-filled pockets rings in counterpoint. As they fill the aisle others gather outside, claiming space at the windows and reaching inside with burritos and enchaladas and cold fruit slush in plastic bags tied tightly around straws.

Outside the bus the day stands full height. Dogs and small children huddle wherever a shadow is cast, waiting. The sun is harsh and undiluted, with lessons for all who enter its path. I wonder if anything escapes illumination in light this strong. Inside the bus seems dark by contrast, all hot, stifling shade and noise and movement. I am overheated, overwhelmed, pressured to buy and eat and drink what is almost certain to make me sick. I'm anxious for the bus to move on, up, away from the coastal lowland and into the mother mountain.

Arms move in and out of every window now, hands laden with pungent food cradled in coarse brown paper. They push through the empty window frames; fingers open fast to release goods, close around coins and drop them into pouches hidden from the sun. Hands spread and grasp, arms thrust and pull, working rapidly in and out of light so strikingly different that it seems as if they move between the elements. It is the reaching, the way there is all at once a perfect row of arms stretching through the windows as if by some instinct of form, that makes me think of geese. The fingers spread, the paper lifts, and the row of hands becomes a line of soft brown birds. The neat, rapid movements turn to slow grace, the opening of wings, the stretch of neck and breast, the sudden appearance of head and beak. The air filled bodies lift, unbound, poised in the elongated moment of flight I've witnessed once before — rounding the bend of a wild river as a great heron spread its wings and left the water, but for one round moment went nowhere.

The bus is filled with sound, the tones and half tones words unknown to me, full ruby vowels all forward in the mouth. They echo off the metal walls and roof, the language multiplies from speech to music, and the quick, reverberant song becomes the call that these birds make. Amidst the ringing clamor is the sound of beating wings, the softest imaginable percussion.

Like the hinged skies in the little painting, I am flush with the moment. For just this heat-stroked second, mystery pushes its tendrils up from land and through these lives, these limbs, into the deft spread of fingers turned to wing, poised on a nonexistent wind. A curtain parts in the breeze. It takes but an instant, and it refuses explanation.

There is one rest stop on the nine-hour trip to Oaxaca, a scenic overlook with enough space for the bus to pull most of its creaking width off the narrow road. The old wooded mountains lumber off into the distance. Like a chameleon on a slow turn in the sun, they change from bright green to hunter to forest to black, from deep blue to grey to great rolls of smoke on the shadowless horizon. A corrugated tin privy is suspended from the overlook on a small platform of wooden slats with nothing beneath it but the view.

Across the road the mountain rises, clothed in a wild mix of broadleaf, pine and palm. A tiny vine-covered cantina clings to the steep incline. The driver holds a coke bottle to a trickle of water running down a section of exposed rock, crosses the road and empties it into the back of the bus, over and over until the radiator is full.

The bus chugs on, higher into the Mother Mountain of the South. The load grows heavier with every village. Men emerge from shadowed doorways and pour water down the engine's throat. Higher still, and the engine labors louder. The Barbie falls from the vibration of the shift. People board with bills the driver cannot change, and he waits while they run to the village cantina. A woman with two young children can't quiet their cries, and he waits while she runs to a roadside stand for cakes and soda. No one complains and no one rushes. The bus again climbs up the Mother. The air grows thin.

A man with a bucket of fish sits on the armrest of my seat, reaching up and holding the overhead rail, the pit of his hard-working arm a steady few inches from my face. Each switchback in the road brings him closer to my lap. Even after the aisle has cleared he remains perched there. His butt shoves my arm with every rut and ridge. He does not look at me; he does not speak. Yet everything about him seems to say, to me: be aware, this is my space, my land. I think of the old campesino, our bodies thrown together on the cramped floor of the bus as we left Acapulco. There is a persistent dignity to both these men, one intent on maintaining an empty fraction of an inch between us, the other on filling it.

* * *

Poised on the western edge of the continental divide at the convergence of three valleys lies Oaxaca, the jewel in the Mother's navel. The air is cool, the pace crisp, and mountains encircle the city. Traffic is barred from the cobblestone square filled with large trees with white washed trunks, bougainvillaea, fountains, sculpture and elaborate benches of white wrought iron. In the middle of the square is a two-tiered white bandstand with intricate lattice work all around and a slate grey dome on top.

The place is ringed with cafes and shops, peopled with students, beggars, travelers, families and vendors. Vendors with huge bouquets of multi-colored balloons that look like stained glass orbs, vendors with poles toting cages of parrots, cockateels, and lovebirds, their cries and colors raucous and soothing by turns. Vendors with hundreds of roses in every imaginable color.

At one end of the square is a massive cathedral of weathered stone that glitters in the sun. Thick doors of reddish wood are open, waiting. Inside is a world secluded by thick stone walls from the bustling scenes outside. The altar is graced with dozens of white lilies, and the votive alcoves all along the sides are lit by candles in tall blue glasses and filled with all kinds of flowers, lush, bright, delicate, stunning bunches of blossoms on every available surface. It is good to rest in the cool, smooth pew, breathing in the scent of them.

* * *

Twelve hundred feet above Oaxaca lie the ruins of Monte Alban. Inside the leveled mountain top, hidden from the Spaniards who marched within sight, is a great plaza of monolithic buildings, sunken courts, elevated platforms, palaces and tombs. The hulking stones of the ruins, the scrub brush that grows up their bases, the sand of the expansive courtyards, and the grasses in between are all the neutral color of dried wheat. People are dwarfed here, our movements made small, our comments muted. There is no sound but light footsteps and soft voices and the barely audible click of a camera.

When the sun has come down to the height of the mountain all this changes. An invisible arc rises above the ancient city, marked by the pale of a three quarter moon. Into the monochromatic hush comes a swift, articulate wind, and the sound of it moving through the plateau gives the ruins voice. The air fills with whispers, with chants and incantations. The footsteps multiply in unfamiliar rhythms. The grasses turn a deep burnt brown, the scrub brush deeper still, the color of black olives. The buildings cast long shadows, extending the bulk of their bases like massive paws. Upon these come the ghosts of dancers, priests, magicians. Figures appear in the arches of tombs. The courtyards fill with players. The ancients wait for nightfall.

A lonely horn sounds, the signal to leave. High above the ghostly scene a guard stands on a once great wall. Flooded with late red light, he leans into the speaking wind. His body appears rooted in the ancient wall itself, as though his head and neck, arms and trunk, legs and feet had sprung perfectly formed from the ancient rock to scan the city as darkness descends.

* * *

Back in the square the cafes fill and the night grows crisp and starry. A band plays in the gazebo. People spill from the heavy cathedral doors, giving coins to the beggars who sit on the steps with cups and baskets. Girls sell wooden utensils, combs and trinkets. Boys sing for money, shine shoes, do both at once.

An old woman with shawls to sell pins me with eyes set deep inside the broad bones of her brow and cheeks. She is clearly Indian, her features strong and clear, her hair in braids that trail her hips, probably never cut. She wears a gathered skirt embroidered at the hem with big bright flowers and tied at the waist with a bright piece of twisted cloth. She wears a shawl much like the ones she works to sell. Its colors are the landscape's blend of subtle contrasts, wheat and rose and russet brown, pale blue and moon white.

Sure of herself, she ignores my refusal and begins to drape the shawl around my shoulders. The veins in her hands and arms remind me of the mountain's reach, what seems like months ago when the plane descended into Acapulco. I notice the streaks at the top of her hair, not grey but gleaming silver, like metal fibers drawn from the range receding around us in every direction. Broad silver hoops hang from her ears and she must wear twenty strings of black ceramic beads around her neck.

She fingers my nylon anorak, shakes her head, makes disapproving clucking sounds and nails me again with those eyes. What landscape does this coat reflect? Not hers, not even mine. Certainly not the Oaxacan Valley. Not the northern forest or the prairie. I forget, under the slight weight of her hands, the times it's kept me warm and dry, cut the worst of the wind, let the sweat evaporate in winter. It is her sense of beauty that matters; it is this landscape I am to mirror.

She takes her time expressing her disdain, adjusting the thick woven landscape she prefers about my shoulders. Exhausted from travel, giddy from the altitude, I feel as though she lifts some essence from the mountain top, from the roll of the surrounding land, from the transformative light itself, and there in the cool high air, drapes spirit on my shoulders and then steps back to look.

* * *

It takes less than an hour to return to Acapulco by air. It is my last night in Mexico, Ash Wednesday. The zócalo is a riot of paper. Paper flowers wave from every corner. Paper birds hang from shop awnings. The old banyans are woven with paper chains like strands of bright cloth in black braids. The paving stones are swathed in sheets arranged with paper hats and masks, whirligigs, wands, pinwheels and flags.

Everything is streaming: the children from the school gates, the faithful from the church, the strings of light and twisted strands of paper from the trees, the tinted waters mixed with fruit poured into paper cups, the folds of deep-dyed blankets that sway across the hawkers' backs returning from the beach. A duo sings a liquid song to the men at cafe tables who nod in murmured consensus, sip beer and pat each other's backs.

The first morning home I look out my window and see clean, well-ordered streets in muted winter colors, the houses all so visible on every side, so square, straightforward and alone — and suddenly they strike me as being without mystery. *Mi casa*, I whisper to myself, *mi casa*, and the movements of my tongue and lips describe odd angles, cracked marble floors, stairways open to the stars, courtyards strung with wash and rows of palms, all hidden behind a plaster facade that seemed so without promise.

A few months later I have this dream. I'm on the street at night, outside my house, a flashlight in my hand. On the sidewalk is a woman with cloth in her braids, long full skirts, broad chiseled features. She is beautiful like the land, and entirely out of context on this urban residential street with its smooth walks, right-angled lawns and lonely box-like houses.

I shine my light on her. I want to make her visible, but the way I train the beam of light is like a guard, a reporter, a cop. She looks like an animal frozen in the path of headlights. I shine the beam in her eyes. She parts her lips in a drawn back show of teeth and hisses at me, cornered by my stupid, frightened light. I hold the beam steady and scream at her, full, wordless, from behind the false safety of the light.

The strength of her trapped energy is palpable. The effort of my scream and the power of her anger collide, and the space between us cracks and buzzes like an electrical field in a great storm. I wake in shock, my breath knocked from me, the knowledge of her fresh in my mind.

Gretchen T. Legler

JUAN MINA

AUDREY WAS TRAPPED in the dugout canoe until some of the boxes around her were unloaded. She was uncomfortable. She'd worn shorts for the ride from Balboa and her thighs had burned crab red. Sticky sweat trickled down the back of her neck where her hair lay in dark clumps. She drew a bandana across her forehead, pulled her shirt away from her breasts, fanned herself, and surveyed her surroundings. So *this* was Panama.

All around her were walls of wet green. Upriver, downriver, across the river. Green. Floating mist, flashes of parrot wing, vines winding up tree trunks like snakes. A crooked sign nailed to one of the dock posts read, "No Trespassing. University of Minnesota Chagres River Research Station. Juan Mina." Audrey sniffed the air. It smelled like a sewer.

"It's those," her husband Robin said. He pointed to cream-colored flowers hanging in the trees. "They attract flies with the smell, and then eat them."

The flowers looked to Audrey like open mouths with long tongues.

"Sun lotion. It's the one thing we forgot. You put everything else in the world in this canoe," she said, stepping over bales of mosquito netting and boxes of all sizes, finally able to move.

"Thank God I didn't let you talk me out of this at least," Robin said, buckling a holster to his belt, unsheathing a pistol, waving it once in the air. "It's a damn smart thing to have in the jungle." He grabbed Audrey's hand and steadied her as she stepped out of the rocking boat. At the same time, his left foot went through a rotten board and Audrey watched as he flapped his arms like a tightrope walker in trouble and catapulted over the edge of the dock, the gun roaring and brown-yellow river water spraying in all directions.

Henry Boulez, the research station overseer, lept across the piled up boxes on the dock, reached into the river, grabbed Robin's shirt collar and hauled him from the water. "You must not go in the water again," Henry said to both of them. "There are crocodiles here. It's very dangerous."

Audrey heard laughter. She scanned the half circle of grass huts set back from the dock and saw a man and two boys in one of the doorways, watching. Henry waved at them. The man's unbuttoned shirt billowed behind him as he jogged down to the dock.

"Here are Doctor Robin and Mrs. Audrey Smith," Henry said, handing the man a box from the canoe. "They're here for three months to study monkeys. . ."

"And butterflies," Audrey added. She saw Robin roll his eyes. "It's only a hobby, of course," she said. "I'm not a scientist."

". . .and butterflies," Henry continued. "They're from St. Paul." Nodding, the man passed the box to one boy who passed it on to the other who put it in a cart at the end of the dock. "And here," he said to Audrey and Robin, "are Lorenzo, Juan and Elias, and over there, or somewhere else, you'll find the rest of this family — wife Sophia and four other children." Lorenzo patted his stomach. It was tight and ribbed with muscle. Audrey looked away. "Oh, and one on the way. Sophia has one on the way," Henry laughed. "Lorenzo lives here," Henry told Robin. "He's sort of a handyman. My assistant, if you will. He'll help you with most things, as long as you pay him. He's useful and friendly and knows enough English to get by. But you must not try to cheat him." Robin frowned at Henry, as if the idea had never occurred to him.

Audrey fell exhausted onto a box in the shade of the dock roof. She was still dizzy from the heat. About 100 yards from the dock, set among the grass huts, was a huge blue cottage raised high on stilts. It was Henry's house. In front of the house was a patch of trampled grass and hard-packed red dirt. On one side of Henry's house a white bull with a humped neck was tethered. Audrey saw a woman in a turquoise dress come out of Henry's door, walk around the back of the house then reappear a minute later with vegetables.

"Is that your wife, Mr. Boulez?" Audrey called out as Henry hoisted a box of toilet paper and sent it down the line. He looked up and waved at the woman who smiled and waved back.

"Her name is Leticia. She's just a friend," he said.

Audrey knew they were lovers and she was inexplicably bothered by it. She had expected Henry to be tall, black and big-chested. Instead he was shorter than Robin, flabby and loose-jointed and hardly dark at all. His brown hair was kinky and cut close enough to his head so Audrey could see a scar above his left ear. He had grown up in New Orleans, he said, and came to Panama with the Army when he was 19. He was hired by the university to manage Juan Mina a few years after that, he said, and since then he had lived in the jungle. He had pulled Robin from the water so easily, Audrey thought. His strength was hidden. It surprised her.

Robin had peeled off his wet bush jacket. Compared with the

brownness of Lorenzo and his sons, Robin was blue. He looked gangly, sick. She guessed she looked that way too, only shorter and softer. She watched Lorenzo. His hair, kept back from his face with a yellow rag around his forehead, was a dusty black. He wasn't older than 30, Audrey guessed, but his face was hard, the skin tight against every bone. His body was well made; his shoulders broader than his chest, chest wider than hips. His calves bowed to the back and sides with muscle. Lorenzo lifted a crate of canned fruit cocktail and carried it to the cart. Passing Audrey on his way back he smiled, showing small teeth stained with tobacco juice. "Welcome to Juan Mina," he said.

* * *

"The house we're in is on stilts to protect against floods and animals. On every side, jungle. Out front are the hills where Robin will do his work. Henry teased Robin about it. We invited him up for Scotch. "Monkey pheromones, eh? Making aphrodisiacs?" Robin's trying to see if howler monkeys have the same chemical sex scents as rhesus monkeys. They can be copied and added to perfumes. Robin says it's not commercial. "We can learn a lot about mating behavior, including that of humans, through this research," Robin told Henry. Henry told me not to wear red around his house. "That's a myth that bulls charge red," I said. He leaned back in his chair and winked at me. The first thing Robin wanted to do last night was make love. He likes to mark beginnings and endings this way. I can't until I'm settled somewhere. He said he just wanted to put his head on my stomach, but if I let him, I knew he'd start kissing me between my legs and he'd run his hands over me and they'd feel like spiders. Withholding is my only power, the only way I can match him. We lay a long time listening to mosquitoes in our ears. Robin says he'll fix the screens. We started taking malaria medicine a month before we left. "What'll you do while I'm working?" he asked me. "I'll collect butterflies and write," I said. He said, "If you go out there stay on the paths." I said, "Don't worry about me." Already saw a Eurybia lycisca. *It landed on Lorenzo's shoulder at the dock. I reached for it, but it got away. A speedy flier. I may be wrong, but the dark brown forewings and metallic shine seemed unmistakable. This one specializes in imitating other inedible butterflies, a common defensive strategy. Cryptic mimicry."*

* * *

"Why are we putting up a fence?" Audrey asked. She stood in the doorway watching Lorenzo string barbed wire. When Lorenzo worked he tied his shirttails in a knot at his belly and unbuttoned his shirt to the knot. Audrey's shoulder and neck muscles tightened each time Lorenzo stretched a piece of wire, each time he pushed down on the increasingly resistant ratchet handle. With each click of the toothed wheel Audrey anticipated that the wire would spring loose and, like a snake, whip back and rake Lorenzo along his bare chest.

"To keep things out," Robin said, looking up for a moment then returning to the hole in the porch screen. Audrey wiped her forehead. She rolled up the sleeves of her white shirt. Lorenzo clipped a piece of wire, set his cutters down and, in turning back to the pile of wire at the other end of the yard, looked up momentarily at Audrey as she stood, hands in the pockets of her long khaki pants. She swatted a mosquito on her neck and swore. Robin looked up at her again, squinting, and said in a voice that only thinly veiled irritation at being watched, "If you put on shorts you'd be cooler. If you'd put on repellent the bugs wouldn't bother you." Audrey continued to watch Lorenzo, who was now pounding u-shaped nails into the fenceposts. Lorenzo turned again and glanced up at her standing behind the screen. In the darkness of his eyes she thought she saw herself reflected; static, watching, white, angular in a particularly Western way, uptight, hips cocked, hair pulled back.

✳ ✳ ✳

"Lorenzo brought his family up. Sophia, pregnant and due any week; the littlest boy, Buster, 2, and then, Armando, 3, Angelina, 4, Gracie, 5, Juan, 7, and Elias, 8. He introduced each one stepping along behind them and putting a hand on their heads as they stood in line in the yard at the bottom of the steps. Robin and I sat on the steps in the grandstand. "How do you do?," we said to each one. They all giggled and looked down at their bare feet. They were all dusty brown with round brown eyes and black hair, except for Angelina, whose hair was somewhere between black, red, and blonde. The boys all wore tiny ripped shorts and singlets. The girls wore little flowered dresses. Sophia's black hair is tied back in a braid that reaches to the small of her back. Her face is the opposite of Lorenzo's; soft and flat. The whole family looked so ragged. Angelina had a sore on her ankle and I brought out our first aid kit and put some antibiotic salve on it. Sophia was concerned. "It's the latest thing," I told her. "It will help it heal." All the kids crowded around me while I put the salve on. We looked like a football huddle. Robin and I have wanted children. Robin thinks now is a good time since he is almost done with his work. His motive is simple. He says, "We should have a family!" I told him I would leave my pills at home, that conceiving a child in Panama would be a romantic foundation for a kid's life. But in the end I packed enough cycles to last me until we get home. I am preoccupied with butterflies. Today I netted an **Adelpha serapa***, also called a spider web, or stained glass window butterfly. Walking around the jungle (on the paths!) with my butterfly net and book I reminded myself of the Butterfly Lady, Margaret Fountaine, a Victorian who chased all around the world after*

butterflies and men. Slight pressure of the thumb and forefinger on the thorax paralyzes them, then I put them in a jar I've fixed with cotton-soaked chloroform in the lid, which kills them, but keeps them moist and elastic so when I pin them later I can move the wings and antennae around."

* * *

Audrey thought Lund's in St. Paul might have carried plantains, but she wasn't sure, since she didn't buy exotic fruit anymore, only wheeled her cart past the mangoes and kiwi fruits, which Robin didn't care for, and some of which he was allergic to, on the way to the apples and oranges. Lorenzo had hauled a bunch of the strange fruit out of the forest and stood with them on the front steps.

"You can bake them. They are starchy, like potatoes," he said, smiling.

"They look like bananas. Don't they taste like bananas?"

"They only look like bananas. They are not. You bake them. They taste more like a potato."

"They certainly don't look like potatoes."

The long stem was too unwieldy for her to handle, so Lorenzo lifted the fruit to his shoulder, stepped inside the kitchen and set the plantains on the counter. A furry black tarantula dropped out on the linoleum with a soft thud. Audrey jumped backward into Lorenzo who put out his arms to steady her and keep them both from toppling over. She wheeled away from him, throwing his hands away from her waist. Lorenzo smashed the tarantula with his bare foot. Audrey heard it collapse with a pop. Its yellow fluid oozed out upon the floor.

"What an accident," he said, cheerfully, shyly, eyeing Audrey, who now was standing in a far corner. She looked from the mess on the floor to Lorenzo with a mixture of disgust and fear. He waited, knees slightly bent, elbows bent, hands at waist level, in a posture as benign as an upright rabbit, but that looked to Audrey like a jump-ready crouch. Caution welled up in her and she fixed her eyes on his hands with their slightly pinkish palms, long, thick fingers and tan backs lined with veins. She could still feel where they had been at her waist. She was alone, she realized suddenly, and felt Lorenzo's presence fill the kitchen with an uneasy power. Anything could happen. "Take that out of here," she pointed at the green-yellow bunch of plantains. "Never bring any more fruit. Never come here again when Robin is gone."

* * *

"I am ridiculous, disgusting. The ugliest American. I had an idea that Lorenzo would hurt me. Lorenzo rape me. This is a filthy idea. I am afraid of it. Of myself.

I tried making bread. Robin says if we want fresh bread we (I) have to make it. We're not going back to Balboa unless Henry makes a trip. First, there are beetles in the flour. Second, the yeast is dead. The bread doesn't rise. I don't know what I am thinking. I can't make bread even at home. This is important for Robin, whose mother made bread. Big round loaves of rye that filled the house with sweet spiciness. I am ashamed that I cannot do this. I'm crying now. The ink is smeared."

✳ ✳ ✳

"You're embarrassed that he caught you being afraid," Robin said. When he got home Audrey's eyes were red and her hands were gloved with flour. He held her. "Actually, tarantulas aren't significantly poisonous."

"You might be afraid too if you were here with no one to talk to, thinking up recipes for foods you've never seen and making bread with flour full of beetles." She sniffled and wiped her nose and smeared flour on her face.

Robin paused. "I got Lorenzo's dog back for him today."

"Torka?"

"His half brother, Carlos, stole him to fight in Panama City. He was chained up behind Carlos's shack downriver."

"What did you do?"

"I showed him this," Robin said, pulling the pistol out of his front belt. "He understood this."

"I suppose he would," Audrey laughed.

"This is the one thing in the world everyone understands. Maybe you should have it around here."

"Maybe," Audrey said.

"You didn't even want me to bring it, remember," he said.

"I didn't know what it would...feel like...here."

"Don't go blowing your foot off," he said, pushing the gun across the table to her. "I discovered something interesting today."

"What?" Audrey said.

"You really want to know?"

"Of course."

"Sometimes I think you don't care about my work."

"Tell me what you found."

"Howlers have been considered strictly arboreal and non-territorial. But this bunch seems to only wander a home range and comes down to the ground regularly to gather other foods, including fallen mangoes and even some tubers." He paused. Audrey nodded. "I think you should go apologize," he said.

As Robin and Audrey walked down the path to Lorenzo's they paused to watch a wobbling trail of army ants carrying triangles of green leaves on their backs. Robin stuck his boot into the middle of their parade and they marched over the toe, oblivious, not missing a step.

Lorenzo's hut had one room, a thatched roof and a mud floor, hard as baked clay. There was a rough-built bamboo table in the middle, grass mats piled in the corner, one bed and a fire pit alongside which sat several blackened tin pots.

Robin and Audrey heard giggling as they approached and, sure it was the children playing a game inside, both stuck their heads unself-consciously around the door frame, then as quickly jerked them back. Sophia lay on the bed, her dress up past her bulging belly and far enough up on one side so that a breast showed. Lorenzo, on his knees beside the bed, ran his hands down each side of the shining mound of Sophia's stomach.

"Sorry," Robin yelled after he and Audrey had walked a few paces away and turned their backs.

"Who's there?" Lorenzo called out, just as Buster, the most curious of Lorenzo and Sophia's kids, ran up from the river to see what was going on.

"It's the butterfly lady and the scientist," he cried and ran away again to find his brothers. In a moment, Lorenzo and Sophia stood at the front door of the hut.

"Sorry," Robin repeated.

"No need to be sorry," Lorenzo said, holding out his hand to Robin and nodding to Audrey. Robin pushed his hands deep into his pockets and looked at Audrey. She felt like a little girl again, her father accompanying her to the neighbor's house where he would cue her in the same way when it was time for her to say she was sorry for giving the neighbor boy a black eye. She summoned up as much dignity as she could.

"I didn't treat you well this afternoon, Lorenzo. Thank you for bringing the plantains."

She might have said more — she might have told him she was crazily afraid of him, that the jungle had set her senses all haywire, that she admired his children, his tight belly, the way he effortlessly was a part of the earth — but he cut her off, interrupted her by ducking back into the shade of the hut, breaking off a bunch of plantains from a long stem hanging in the rafters, handing it to her and saying, "Don't worry. We have scientists like you here all the time."

* * *

"I'm moving hesitantly, the way I move when I swim Square Lake at home. Even though the water is clear and I see the sandy bottom and the sunfish, the weeds

that touch my thighs are grasping hands and the black clam shells on the bottom are the eyes of unfamiliar, dangerous creatures. Robin is out. I'm eating the last of the oranges we brought from Balboa. We've agreed he'll leave me the gun now. I resisted at first, resisted the way Robin deals with things; guns, fences, screens, repellents. Added another specimen to my collection. Ascalapha odorata. Black Witch. *From the* Noctuidae *family. About five inches from wing tip to wing tip. Violet/pink bank with undulating margins cuts through the middle of the fore and hind wings. Two eye spots on the forewing. Outer margin of the hind wings black with violet and blue, double-arched crescent. Rest of wings is silvery, powdery gray/brown. Caught it in a pheromone trap. Robin's idea. We captured females by hanging a white sheet in front of a lantern at night, then put the females in a small cage with an opening the male could get in but couldn't get out. This one has been drying for four days and was stiff, until Robin suggested I inject some ammonia in the thorax to soften the wing joints. As Robin progresses with his work I see less of him. We're sleeping separately because he stays up late writing. I tried to kiss him last night. He was stooped over some papers. He said, "What are you doing?" I found a centipede in my bed this morning. What do other people do with their anger? I want to break things. I realize I am too sensitive. I have no confidence. I don't think I was like this before I married him. Sometimes I wonder why I married him. This is frightening to write. I have started out each day since we have been at Juan Mina with every intention of being a well-mannered, giving, confident wife. But each day without fail I have been petty, humorless and selfish. I apologize and sleep without guilt and wake with intentions of goodness, then fail again. I think often of darkness enveloping me, and partly relish it. Someone is at the door."*

✳ ✳ ✳

Audrey eased open the kitchen drawer and drew out the pistol. It hung down low, almost to her knee. Lorenzo clung to the door frame, his normally brown, leathered face was white and shining with sweat. He was stinking drunk.

"Hello," he said, swaying, grinning.

She thought again of his hands on her waist on the day of the tarantula. "What are you doing here?"

"No plantains today," he said, leaning closer to the door, reaching for the handle. In one hand he held a wide-bladed machete, the sharp edge smeared with blood. He was breathing heavily, exhaling whiskey. Audrey stepped back from his face pressing against the screen and raised the gun. Lorenzo made a great effort to stand straight, pushing himself away from the door frame, dropping the machete. Audrey saw his adam's apple bob as he swallowed hard. His eyes were deep, swimming brown, bordering on panic. Then, she realized, horrified, why he had come.

High on his right thigh near the hem of his shorts was a six-inch gash, spread scandalously open, both sides of skin hanging limply, and the inside glistening like a fresh cut of beef. He had covered the wound with a large green leaf, but the leaf had soaked through with blood and fallen around his ankle. "I was clearing the canal for Henry. . .," he said, woozily.

"Don't move," she ordered. "Stay here on the porch." As if in a trance, Audrey turned her back and began walking slowly down the narrow hallway for the first aid kit when Lorenzo fell, crashing through the screen, pulling down the thin wood frame and letting loose a guttural moan. She came back with the black box, bent to touch him and pulled back, bent down again, and again pulled back, then grabbed him firmly under the armpits and dragged him, remarking to herself that he was surprisingly light, from the rubble of the door onto the wooden floor of the front hallway and propped him against the wall. She cut the outer seam of his shorts up to the waist and the inseam up to the crotch, then peeled the bloody material away from his right leg, exposing a linen loin cloth that barely covered him. She set the gun beside her as she worked, methodically, following instructions for "Large, Deep Wounds," in the illustrated first aid pamphlet.

She doused the gash with iodine. Lorenzo's eyes flared open, he growled through clenched teeth and grabbed Audrey's wrist, spilling iodine over both of them and the floor. His fingers grew white as he held her. She leaned into him, her breasts pressing against his chest, and looked into his now glassy, almost black, eyes. "Let me go," she said. He dropped her arm and let his hand fall to the floor.

Audrey daubed the wound with cotton, holding the flaps of muscle and skin apart, reaching deep into Lorenzo's body. Then holding the flesh together, she began to stitch the slash closed with black thread and a small, sharp needle. Each time Audrey touched Lorenzo's leg his body jangled in pain, every muscle reaching out, then trying to draw back into itself. Each time Lorenzo moved Audrey recoiled. His eyes began to fade in and out like a blinking light. She realized he was going into shock. She imagined Robin returning with Lorenzo in a heap in the hall, a bloody machete on the stairs, his pants wide open. She smeared the stitched gash with antibiotic salve, then wrapped Lorenzo's thigh carefully and tightly in three layers of white cotton gauze. Then she covered him with a blanket and turned into the kitchen.

Anticipating the soothing effect it would have, she tried to mix herself a gin and tonic, spilling ice cubes, splashing gin on the counter. Fleetingly, she felt the lazy fans and coolness of the Balboa Country Club. She sliced a lime she picked from the tree in back, barely missing the tip of her finger. Inside, the lime was black and mushy. A green worm wriggled out onto the cutting board. Audrey clamped her eyes shut and in that moment of calm darkness tried hard to balance herself. Something sour rose in her as Lorenzo moaned and Robin's loose, booted footsteps made their way up the stairs. She met him at the door and pulled him past Lorenzo to the cutting board. "All I wanted was a gin and tonic. That's all." She shook her head, gripping his arm. "All I want is a gin and tonic and there's a worm in the lime."

Robin shook Audrey by the shoulders. "Did you shoot him? What's going on?"

"I sewed it all up. Here's his blood on my hands," Audrey said, holding her fingers in front of Robin's face and seeing, for the first time, that they were smeared with Lorenzo's blood.

Lorenzo moaned again, still propped against the wall.

"Where did he hurt you? I should never have brought you here. I knew this wasn't the place for you." He drew her up to him.

"He didn't hurt me. Not at all," Audrey said. "I thought he might, but he didn't. I helped him."

* * *

"Robin took Lorenzo home in the two-wheeled cart. Then he came home and fixed the door and then fixed dinner. He said Henry paid Lorenzo a fifth of Old Crow to cut the jungle away from the canal, but Lorenzo drank too much before he started the job. I am exhausted. Robin is asleep. As I write a beetle buzzes around the lantern. Every morning the door is plastered with beetles and moths that stick themselves to the wire trying to get to the light of the kerosene lamp. It's a hot blue night and outside toads as large as footballs are creeping out from the bush, filling the yard. I hear their liquid thumping. Just now I stood at the screen door tracing the new mesh Robin put up. As I watched, the dark green of the jungle turned purple black and the moon came up red. An elephant with a harness of rubies and emeralds knelt in the forest. Around one of its front legs a snake curled. The elephant tumbled over and a man fell off. It was only those funny bugs with red taillights and the big leaves that Robin calls elephant's ears, and the vines, the thick green vines that wind themselves around the tree trunks. I heard music. Eerie, mournful music coming from deep in the trees. High notes sailed across the face of the moon and worked their way under the yard fence and up the steps to where I stood. In my chest I felt a fluttering, as if something there was beginning to grow. I have a thousand things to say but no direct route. So far I have been safe in silence."

* * *

"Lorenzo's fine," Robin said, walking in his robe from his bed on the porch into the lamplight where Audrey bent over a notebook. He rubbed his eyes. "You did a good job on his leg. Come to bed."

"While you were asleep I heard music. It sounds like an oboe," Audrey said, looking up.

"It is. It's Henry," Robin said, yawning. "He's on his front porch by the dock. When it's not raining he plays outside."

The haunting, rich sound wrapped itself around the mango trees and around the white house. It crept slowly through Audrey's body and inside of her the fluttering started again. She shivered.

"It's just Henry," Robin repeated. He stretched an arm out, touched her shoulder, cocked his head to one side and raised his eyebrows. Audrey stared at his face and saw disbelief in it. Misunderstanding. She knew he felt his practical explanation should satisfy her. She knew he felt she should nod and thank him for clearing up this mystery.

"You think I'm crazy! Say it." She shot from her seat, her pen and journal flying across the table, the lantern almost tipping.

"Sit down," Robin said, quietly, as if to avoid a scandal. He moved toward her and she backed up to the bookshelf.

"I don't know what you want," he said. "What *do* you want?" He hunched his shoulders and put his hands in the air. "I married you for this, because you were mysterious. But you scare me now."

"Here's scary," Audrey said, pulling Robin's *Principles of Biology* from the shelf and assuming a pitching stance, aiming for the screen door. In mid forward motion she stopped short.

"Shh," she held her breath. "Listen. There it is again." The music was rising. While Audrey was off guard Robin grabbed her wrist and took the book from her hand.

"Let me go," she said. He dropped her hand. "Next time you see Henry, tell him to. . . ," she whirled around and grabbed another book from the shelf, ". . .play louder." The volume ripped through the screen door and sailed out onto the porch, leaving another ragged hole. Immediately, in fluttered a confused gray moth followed by several beetles. And then there was silence. Audrey moved toward the door, opened it, and stepped into the night. She turned back to Robin, his face greenish white in the propane light.

"What do *you* want?" she asked. "Can you tell me that?"

Robin paused for a moment, then said, "I know exactly what I want. I want you to keep helping me be myself."

"You've never done that for me," she said. She began to let the door close behind her.

"If you go out there I'm not coming after you," he said and walked back to his bed. Audrey watched his back until it disappeared in the shadows.

"I'm only going out to get your book," she said.

* * *

"I've decided to quit collecting butterflies. I looked at my rack this morning. The rack is two wide pieces of cork glued to another thin sheet of cork that sits on plywood. The thoraxes are pinned to the cork in the middle with a long pin. The wings are fastened down to the upright cork with strips of paper pinned at each end. I didn't want pin holes in the wings. I was pinning down a Dynamine gisella. *I looked at its small dark blue wings with the white dots on the margins of the forewing. The deep blue reminded me of a Minnesota midnight sky with stars. While Robin was at Henry's last night I set up the sheet and lantern again. I took off my shirt and my shoes and stood in front of the sheet with my naked arms stretched out in front of me. At first they came slowly. Their soft wings batted my face and their tiny legs crawled up and down my neck, my belly. One landed on my nipple. They were in my hair. I just let them come. As many as wanted to be on me, I allowed. I whispered to them to come to me, press against me. As soon as I stepped from the light, they flew back into it. They left silvery powder on my skin. I don't want to collect anymore. I can go out the front door, walk two dozen steps into the jungle and watch all the butterflies I want. They are creatures whose life is ruled by instinct; not conventional, unaltering behavior, but, depending on the group, instinct that enables them to adapt to the needs of unforeseen situations. The* Geometridae *are particularly good at it. They can erase their own shadow by pressing their wings to the ground."*

* * *

Audrey found Sophia and Leticia sitting on the floor of Sophia's hut. She rapped on the door frame and was invited in. Sophia was weaving a grass basket with long strips of blonde bamboo interspersed with dark pieces. Leticia sewed the hem of a blue dress. Loose spots in the thatch let in beams of yellow sunlight, warm and thick with dust. The tight fullness of Sophia's belly made Audrey feel there was a great emergency at hand, that she should move carefully and keep quiet, but she wanted to talk; to talk to Sophia and Leticia about babies, about baskets, about the weather, gardens, anything. She sat self-consciously, her hands in her lap. She watched Juan, Elias and Buster in the yard. They teased Henry's bull, waving red handkerchiefs at it, giggling and darting out of the way when the bull pawed the ground and pulled at its thick rope.

"It would be nice to take some of your baskets back to Minnesota. I don't have time to make baskets."

"Why?" Leticia looked up from her work.

"I teach school."

"What age?"

"Kids Juan's age."

"You like children?" Sophia asked, passing a dark piece of bamboo through her basket frame.

"Of course."

"Where are your children?"

"We don't have any of our own," Audrey said. "You have so many."

"They come easily to me," Sophia said.

"Don't you worry at all?" Audrey asked her.

"They grow inside me and when they are ready they come out. I have little choice."

"You make it sound simple."

"Yes," Sophia said, her head bent to her basket. "It's the simplest thing."

Audrey suddenly rose to her feet. "I've got to go," she said. Leticia and Sophia kept working.

"Stop by Henry's for cucumbers," Leticia said. "So many grew in the garden we have more than we need."

* * *

"I thought I could find company with other women, with two women who are so good at being women, two women who are fertile, desirable, beautiful. Leticia was smiling, making tiny stitches with red thread in blue fabric. Sophia wove the bamboo. Simple, she said. Simple. Independent natural rhythms. I've spent my life thwarting them, controlling them. I felt accused, defensive. It wasn't them. It wasn't Sophia and Leticia who pointed at me, who pointed at me with straight arms and long fingers and said, 'We can read your mind, we can see in your heart, you are not true, you are not devoted.' It was another part of myself."

* * *

Audrey climbed the wooden stairs to Henry's open door and knocked. Inside was a half burned candle on a small wooden table and a cord of chicken wishbones strung from one wall to the other. Henry came to the door without a shirt. His waist curved over the edge of his pants and his nipples rose from pectoral muscles that had turned into half full breasts. Audrey turned her face away.

"I was with Leticia this morning. She said to stop by. For cucumbers."

"Give me a minute," Henry said and stepped into the room to get a shirt off the back of a chair. A small, dark woman poked her head around the corner from the bedroom. She wore only a white sheet and her long dark hair was curled with the damp heat. It was Leticia. She smiled at Audrey.

"It's silly. I don't need them now," Audrey said, starting down the stairs, her face reddening.

"It's perfectly fine, Mrs. Smith. No need for embarrassment."

"I'm not embarrassed, Henry. What's there to be embarrassed about?" she said, laughing, stuffing her hands in her pockets.

"I'll bring them to the house," Henry said.

"It's best that way," Audrey called up to him from the bottom of the steps.

Instead of going home, she went down to the dock. She never caught fish to eat there, she only caught the fish, as small as a child's hand, to see their colors — the *Badis badis*, only three inches long, that could change color from yellow to brown to red to green or blue; the Firemouth Cichlid with its red eye and purple back; and prettiest of all, the tiny Blue Acara. She fixed a grub to the end of a hook and dropped the line over the edge of the dock.

She paddled her feet in the water, making circles that repeated themselves out and out and out into the river until they disappeared. "Wishbones," she whispered. "What's Henry doing with all those wishbones?" Audrey remembered a dinner guest once in St. Paul, a biologist from Haiti, who asked to keep the chicken wishbone from dinner, saying it had powers. She kicked at the water hard, raising white foam. She let it settle again. A man's reflection appeared in the stillness around her toes. In the wavering mirror of the water the man wore a long white caftan and strings of chicken wishbones hung in long loops from his neck. In his hand was a basket full of green eggs. She looked up to see Henry, clean-shaven, brown-eyed, white-shirted Henry, wearing khaki pants and carrying a basket of cucumbers.

"Mrs. Smith, have you seen something strange?"

"This isn't you in the water, Henry," she said, pointing. "It doesn't make sense."

He laughed. "You know, because a thing doesn't make sense doesn't make any difference. Not here." He set the vegetables on the dock then squatted beside Audrey. "Are you catching anything?"

Audrey suddenly wanted to cry. She wished that Henry would hug her, put his hand on her back and rub up and down. She wanted comfort.

"My mind works so strangely, Henry," she said, shaking her head.

"You shouldn't have your feet in the water," Henry said. "Remember, crocodiles."

She drew up her feet. "Why have you stayed so long at Juan Mina?" she asked him.

"It has become my home," he said.

* * *

"I have no home. No desires that are my own. But I can answer his question. Robin asks what I want. I want to be what I am. A woman with large hands. Contradictory. I am full of voices. Robin has no clues to this. He has said that if I get any worse (Worse? What does he see when he sees me?) he'd like me to leave. Go home. No. I want to explore the jungle. I want to say to the jungle, 'Come into me. Give me pleasure. Fill me with joy.' Where is my bravery now? I want to say to the jungle. . .'Make love with me.' This disgusts me. And it delights me. Until now I have been frozen in the ground between the two, between delight and repulsion, thinking I cannot go after what I desire, ashamed of this idea, fearing myself. Now I don't care. This is something I have dreamed of. I have dreamed of this forever. He asks me what is wrong. I want to say that I want to be loved so that parts of me are not murdered. The only way to do this is through myself. I never saw it before. Never tasted it or heard it before coming here, this cage I am in. This cage. I want to dance my way out of this cage, forget every way he has taught me, open every gate, every window."

* * *

Audrey sat on a log. Behind her was a small clearing in the jungle. In front of her was the river. Her feet were crossed over one another, a straw hat was tilted back on her head. She held Robin's pistol in her hand. Just as the red tip of a wooden canoe eased around the curving bank downstream, Audrey tensed her shoulders, drew her right hand behind her then arched forward, sending the gun sailing away from her in a high arc, spinning barrel over grip. It landed squarely beside Lorenzo's canoe, sending a cascade of muddy water over him. He laughed and paddled toward her, close enough to say without shouting, "Sophia will have her baby soon. Come and watch it be born." As he looked up at her from the water she saw in his eyes a funny woman, arms crossed over her breasts, a fierceness in her face.

* * *

"I can't find Audrey," Robin said. He leaned against the dock post watching Henry unload a turtle trap, a tube-shaped net on a metal frame, baited with sardines.

"When she comes back, give her one of these," Henry said, tossing a dark, plate-shaped turtle onto the dock. "They make good soup." Henry paused. "I told your wife I'm going to Balboa tomorrow. She said she didn't need anything. How about you?"

"There's nothing I need," Robin said. He fidgeted. "Henry, I'm worried. The gun is gone, the sun is setting and I walked around the paths by the river and I can't find her at all."

Henry straightened up and wiped the sardine oil from his hands with a rag. "Has Lorenzo seen her?"

"Can't find him either," Robin said, looking away from Henry, squinting downriver. Henry laughed. Robin smiled at Henry and then his eyes filled with tears. "I know what you're thinking about and there's nothing to it. She hasn't been well."

"In heart or head?" Henry asked.

"I don't know; malaria, the food, something in the water."

"This place can do that to some people," Henry said. "Some adjust better than others. In my mind she was doing pretty well."

"It's more than that," Robin said.

Henry suddenly was waving. He was waving at Lorenzo who was paddling up the river in his dugout. "Have you seen Mrs. Smith?" Henry called. "Dr. Smith can't find his wife. Have you seen her?" Lorenzo nodded and pointed downstream, indicating it was quite a distance.

"What's she doing?" Henry called.

"Just sitting," Lorenzo said. "Sitting in the trees throwing rocks into the water."

* * *

On their way down the path in the direction Lorenzo had pointed, Henry and Robin ran into Leticia carrying a basket of clothes on her head. She did Audrey's laundry once a week, pounding pants and shirts with rocks in the river, sewing the smashed buttons back on for an extra twenty-five cents.

"Dr. Smith's wife is missing," Henry said. "We're looking for her."

Leticia put down her basket and fell in step with Henry. Robin had started to walk very fast. He was sweating through his shirt and breathing shallowly and quickly. "I'm thinking the worst case scenario," Robin said. "Henry," he suddenly stopped, turned around, and cried, "She didn't belong here. It's all my fault." Henry swung his arm around Robin's shoulders and propelled him down the path.

"Let's see what we find," Henry said.

* * *

In the clearing, with wet green all around her, Audrey's naked skin glowed like a white candle with a flame deep inside of it. Her pants, shirt, underwear and shoes were folded and piled on a rock. She lay on her back, feeling soft, cool mud and thick grass against her skin. An ant crawled across her stomach. She stared up into the darkening, brightening evening sky, watching pink coming on, gold coming on. She stared past the tops of the tall trees falling inward above her until she was dizzy. She turned onto her stomach then arched her back, making a bridge of her whole body, an arc of flesh. Her bones strained against her skin, her shoulders shook, her hair fell over her head into the dirt. She kicked high and flipped her legs into the air, walked on her hands, came back down, did it again and again. She stood and laughed. She had never been able to walk on her hands. She flung her arms above her head, waving them back and forth like a tree in the wind. She spun around and around, her face to the sky, grabbing vines and tall leaves, tearing at them and putting them all, cool, smooth and green, to her body, to her arms, to her thighs, to her belly. She spoke quietly at first, then louder, her face tilted upward, her neck stretched tight, then louder still until she screamed, "I Am Here. I Am Here. I Am Here. I Am Here."

* * *

"I hear her. I hear her," Robin said, grabbing Henry's hand and pulling him toward Audrey's scream. "She's calling us." The search party arrived at the clearing as Audrey was buttoning her shirt. Her feet were still bare.

"What's she doing?" Robin asked Henry, astonished. Robin stepped toward her but Henry held onto his arm.

"Just let it go," he said. "Let Leticia go to her."

"Look at you. You're a mess," Robin said to Audrey. "What did you do with my gun?"

"I threw it in the water. I didn't need it anymore."

"What is this madness?" Robin said, grabbing her arm and squeezing it between his thumb and fingers.

"Crazy fool," Henry said, wrestling Robin away. "Let her be for now." He held Robin by the elbow, letting Leticia and Audrey walk ahead.

Audrey walked quickly, her arms swinging by her sides, making Leticia hurry to catch up. Audrey took the stairs to the house two at a time, lit a lantern and carried it with her to the bathroom mirror. Leticia followed and stood beside her.

Robin and Henry went to the far end of the house. Audrey heard a cupboard door squeak open, the rattle of ice and glass, the slosh of liquor from a bottle, the first dull, low, indecipherable murmurs of their conversation. Outside, she heard the hum of insects rising, a great dark pulse for the jungle night. Next to her the lantern hissed white light.

In the mirror her face was striped with mud. Rivers of dirt ran from her forehead to her chin. Her hair was thick with clumps of clay, pieces of grass, tiny pebbles. She poured water from a bucket into the sink and began to wipe away the dirt with a washcloth. Leticia slowly began pulling a brush through the long red strands of Audrey's hair.

"It was easier than I ever thought," Audrey said.

Leticia untangled a yellow butterfly wing from Audrey's hair and held it out to her. Audrey took it in the palm of her hand and began to laugh. Leticia embraced her and for a moment the laughter of the two women nearly covered the rumbling noise of the men in the other room.

Audrey pulled her hair back into a ponytail and walked down the hall to the room where Robin and Henry sat with glasses in their fists, leaning forward in their chairs, their faces strained. She stood in the doorway and they turned toward her.

"Now it doesn't matter what I do," she said.

Robin shook his head. "No," he said. "Not anymore."

"Then Henry, when you go to Balboa for supplies tomorrow, I'm leaving," Audrey said. As she spoke she rolled the yellow butterfly wing back and forth in the fingers of one hand, sprinkling iridescent powder over her pants.

Linda Mathiason Norlander

THAT SUMMER IN CARACAS

THE LETTER NOTIFYING me of Uncle Harry's death in Venezuela came exactly twenty years after that summer in Caracas. I read and reread the
carefully worded letter while the sticky onion-skin paper crackled in
my hands. Uncle Harry had died under "unfortunate circumstances"
but no details had been given by the lawyer.

As his niece and only survivor, I knew I had a responsibility to do
something, but I felt as helpless now as I had when I'd stepped off the
plane into the heavy-sweet mugginess of the Maiquetia airport twenty
years ago.

Mother had taken me to the airport chattering the whole way about
what a unique opportunity this would be to explore the world and learn
a new language. I had sulked as only a sixteen year old could — eyes
staring straight ahead, lips set in a thin line. Why was she sending me
away? Because she had caught me that Saturday night in April heaving
my guts out after an evening with Vince Springfield and a bottle of sloe
gin? Or because of the confrontation we'd had after someone slipped
me an anonymous note in study hall that said, "Did you know you were
a bastard?"

"Yes," my mother had said, her jaw tensed to hold back the tears,
"Your father left shortly after conception."

"But you lied. You said he was dead."

"He was to me."

I had said a few choice words to her and stormed out the door to nurse
my wounds. I was too young then to realize that her wounds were greater
than mine. I was still angry with her when she announced in May that
I would be spending the summer in Caracas.

Caught up in my anger and resentment, I drew inward, failing to
notice how gaunt she had gotten and how sallow her complexion had
become over the wet spring. No. I was sixteen and I had been wronged.
Being sent to Caracas was to be a long and cruel punishment.

Mother was not close to her family and I knew very little about Uncle
Harry. I had a vague memory of him coming to visit one Christmas,
bringing me a book about horses written in Spanish. I couldn't read

Spanish and I had stuck it on my shelf with a flourish of selfish disgust.

Uncle Harry worked for an oil company in Venezuela. Mother said he was always the one in the family destined to be successful and to be nice to him because he was a rich bachelor. His money meant nothing to me because it wasn't in my pocket.

My plane was late getting in due to a storm and when I walked down those steps into the evening heat I was sure that no one would pick me up. The tarmac was wet as the steam of the day's heat rose up through the soles of my shoes. By the time I reached the terminal, the sweat of heat and fear rolled in big droplets down the inside of my arms. Noise surrounded me all through the line. Staccato Spanish words that I couldn't understand, braying laughter, the sounds of people being greeted and clapped on the back. The smell of human dampness mingling with perfume in the sticky air made my head reel.

I hated Maiquetia. When Uncle Harry finally picked me out of the crowd, I was near tears.

"Jane?" His voice had a disconcerting soft, almost whisper-like quality. When he tried to pull me in for a Venezuelan *abrazo*, a kind of half hug, half handshake, I stiffened and jerked away from him, my eyes stinging.

Uncle Harry looked a lot like Mother except that his features were softer and rounder. He didn't have her faded color or the worn lines that etched her face. And there was a sensuousness about his mouth that fit in with the smooth texture of his skin.

He ushered me through all the formalities, speaking an easy Spanish and never looking directly at me. I noticed even then how readily he touched the men around him and how close he got to them as he spoke.

Once we were settled into his little Volkswagen, the first thing I remember saying was, "I didn't know it was going to be so hot here."

The words were edged with an automatic sarcasm that I instantly regretted.

"Caracas is up higher, over the mountain. It's very nice there."

I don't think he said another thing to me as we climbed our way up from sea level, through exhaust-choked mountain tunnels and into the city. My first impression of Caracas was total disappointment. I think I had expected to see exotic buildings or primitive grass huts. Instead, I saw freeways, high-rises, and giant, lighted billboards advertising American brand cigarettes and soft drinks.

"Do you speak Spanish?" he inquired as we turned onto a narrow climbing street off the congested freeway.

"I had it in school last year."

"Oh."

My head was pounding from pressing it so hard against the window and I felt like throwing up. What was I going to do when I got my period? How could I ask Uncle Harry to please buy me some sanitary napkins? My eyes filled with tears.

I hardly noticed when he pulled into a little driveway and snapped up the emergency brake.

"We're here. This is *Quinta Maria*. All houses in Caracas have names."

In the dark, all I could see was a low, narrow building with an orange tiled roof surrounded by a high hedge. When we stepped out of the car, the air was filled with a chorus of crickets. We had left the mugginess of the airport behind. As the cool evening air caressed my face, I finally relaxed.

The floor in the house was tiled and polished to a high, cool gloss. Uncle Harry's little *quinta* was sparsely but tastefully furnished, with an air of precise order. I liked the contrast from Mother's clutter at home.

"You'll sleep here." Uncle Harry showed me a small room with gleaming white walls and a low, short bed. The bed looked brand new. There were no curtains on the window and I suspected that the hedge provided complete privacy.

I sat in the living room and watched as he brought in my suitcases. Though his features were soft, his body was firm and he carried the bags with ease.

When he was done, he stood over me, clearing his throat. Now we were going to have the serious talk. I expected that he would lay down the rules of the household, then ask politely how I liked school and what I planned to be when I grew up. The tension was already crawling up my shoulders.

"Would you like a drink?" he asked.

I nodded thinking about the billboard with the tall, dripping bottle of Coca Cola. Uncle Harry walked into the kitchen, opened the refrigerator and tinkered around for a few minutes. When he came back, he handed me a gin and tonic.

Surprised, I tipped the glass to my lips. It tasted bitter and lemony. Within two sips I felt warmth creep up to my cheeks.

Uncle Harry sat down across from me and stared as I downed the drink. His expression was amused. When I set the glass down my head was already spinning. I noticed how his long slender fingers curled around his drink. The nails had been manicured.

"So, Jane. We have each other for the summer."

The rules were coming. I felt like giggling.

"When you go out of the house, make sure you lock the door. I can't let you drive here, you're not old enough and the streets are filled with *Latino* maniacs anyway. Soledad comes during the week to clean and cook. She brings her son Rafael to take care of the hedge."

With this, Uncle Harry smiled and finished his drink, "I'll see you in the morning."

That night, with my head still buzzing, I curled under the rough textured sheets, breathing their foreign scent, and wondered why he hadn't mentioned Mother at all.

I woke up early in the morning to the sound of a woman crying out through a bullhorn.

"*Huevos! Huevos!*" Her voice was singsong like an auctioneer's and soon faded down the road.

The clarity of the blue sky that morning was one of the most vivid memories I kept of the summer in Caracas. I stared at it until little spots started floating in front of my eyes. Outside the *quinta* the city hummed. Cars rumbled by on the patched concrete street and horns honked with every screech of brakes. I lay in bed, listening to all of this wondering if my friend Chrissy would be jealous. Probably not. She was involved in heavy petting with Carl Otis for the summer and I doubted if she would spend much time thinking about me.

Slipping on a light cotton shift, I padded into the kitchen. Uncle Harry had already made a pot of coffee. I could hear his chair scraping against the cinderblock patio floor just out the side of the living room. I fixed a piece of toast and walked out to join him.

He was reading a tabloid newspaper that had a huge picture of a man in a coffin on the front page. In the bottom corner was a grainy picture of the same man lying face down in a pool of blood.

"Yuck," I said, pulling up a chair.

"*Buenas dias,*" Uncle Harry smiled. "You get used to the newspapers over here after awhile."

Somewhere out of our line of vision I heard the rhythmic clip clip of the hedge trimmer.

"Your person is here working on the lawn?" I was trying to be polite. I really didn't care.

"Rafael," Uncle Harry replied, not looking up from the paper. I liked the rolling sound of the "r" in his name.

As if he had sensed our conversation, Rafael came sauntering toward the patio. He wore khaki pants and a white T-shirt that contrasted with his deep tan complexion. His hair was a shiny black and long enough so that a hank of it fell over one eye. I couldn't take my eyes off him, off the boyish swagger in his walk, off the pearly white teeth, and off the frank way he looked me up and down. I felt the flush of my cheeks almost immediately.

"*Hola, Rafael,*" Uncle Harry looked at him and then at me with a curious expression.

"*Como esta, Señor?*"

The whole time he talked with Uncle Harry, he kept his eyes on me. I felt myself straightening, hitching my skirt up a little. I think I was even holding my breath.

Uncle Harry was silent for a moment, as if weighing something, then he beckoned Rafael over and introduced us. My one year of high school Spanish was enough to get me through the introduction and nothing more.

I laughed as he struggled with my name and finally settled on calling me *Shane*. He grinned back when my tongue stuck trying to roll the "r" in his name.

"Perhaps you and Rafael could spend some time together. You need your Spanish and it wouldn't hurt him to learn a little English."

At first, I thought Uncle Harry was teasing, but he looked very serious as he explained his proposal to Rafael. We both nodded and smiled at each other while the flush on my cheeks deepened. Uncle Harry gave Rafael a slight nudge on the arm and pointed back to the hedge.

"His family is poor. *Campesinos* from the country — peasants. He could use a little head start. I think he is a bright boy."

"Oh."

So began our relationship. For an hour every day Uncle Harry sat back and watched as Rafael and I struggled to communicate. At first we looked to him to interpret but he would only lean back with his arms folded and shrug. As the days passed and we started to find some common words like *Beatles* and *musica*, we learned to ignore him entirely.

After Uncle Harry left for work in the morning, I would watch Rafael work on the lawn. His movements were slow, and deliberate as if he savored every contact with the earth. When he walked by me he smelled of fresh clippings and the sharp pungent odor of sweat. I could feel his heat across the white metal table and it sent shivers up my spine.

During the afternoon when the sun was high and hot, Rafael would join some of the other *campesinos* working on other yards on the palm lined boulevard in front of the house. The men were older, paunchier in their white T-shirts. They clumped together squatting under the palms, smoking cigarettes, and touching each other as they joked around. I would watch through the hedge, noticing that Rafael always kept a little distance from them, always watched the hills that surrounded the city, as if he were yearning for something beyond what the other men had.

I took long walks during the afternoon *siesta* because the streets were quiet and I felt comforted by the wall of heat. Caracas was a city of contrast, not a light-grey, dark-grey contrast, but a black and white one. In Uncle Harry's neighborhood of well kept *quintas* nestled up to the mountainside stood little pockets of *barrios*, slums made up of corrugated tin-roofed shanties. The poor came in the middle of the night, setting up their squalid dwellings on vacant lots between the expensive fenced-in, hedged-in houses.

I would walk past these, always uneasy with the smell and with the poverty. Once a peasant woman approached me talking rapidly in a staccato Spanish. At first I could only stare at the shiny black hair that grew like fur on her bare legs. Then, as her voice rose, I noticed that a small child lay in her arms, listless and glassy-eyed from a fever.

She wanted something from me and I had nothing to give her. I could not understand her words so I backed away from her gesturing with my arms and saying, "*No hablo espanol. No intiendo. No intiendo.*"

The baby's eyes haunted me all the way back to *Quinta Maria*. I wished that I was home with Mother and Chrissy worrying about whether the new mascara I'd bought would run if it got wet.

When I asked Uncle Harry about the woman, he shrugged it off. "There is less poverty here than in most of Latin America. She'll find help."

Several days later, with a pocket full of *Bolivares*, the Venezuelan money, I walked back to the little *barrio*. It was gone. The cardboard houses had been broken and scattered. All that remained was rubble. I never knew if the child survived.

When I asked Uncle Harry where they had gone, he made a sweeping gesture, "They come to the city because it promises riches, but their heart is in the interior. They go back to the land."

Uncle Harry generally ignored me except for the sessions with Rafael. I spent much of my time reading from his collection of pulp novels. It was a summer filled with John D. MacDonald, Mickey Spillane, and Ross MacDonald. Occasionally, he would take me out for supper to a little Chinese restaurant down the street. We had no other social life.

Then, one Friday, while Rafael and I were trying to talk about an American movie he'd seen, Uncle Harry interrupted and said, "Let's go to the beach tomorrow. A friend has given me a pass to his club."

He repeated this to Rafael in Spanish, who responded by furrowing his brow, scratching his head, then nodding pensively.

"Rafael is a peasant. He's a little afraid," Uncle Harry confided to me later. "I'll pick up some suitable clothes for him this afternoon."

I'll never forget the wide grin on Rafael's face when he tried on the blue jeans. They fit him snugly and perfectly. As I watched him parade across the patio my breath came in delicate little pants. When I looked over at Uncle Harry, to share the moment, I was struck by the strange expression on his face. His eyes glistened, and his lips formed just a hint of a smile.

On our way out of town, Uncle Harry pointed out the neighborhood of rundown high-rises from the freeway.

"They call them the *superblockes*. Someone, filled with infinite wisdom, decided that if you built giant apartment buildings for the poor, you'd eliminate poverty. So the peasants moved in with their chickens and their goats and their squalor and turned the beautiful buildings into slums. The police won't even go there now. It's too dangerous." His voice was filled with contempt and I never did know whether it was for the people who built the buildings or the people who lived in them.

I saw a chicken roosting on a broken-out third story window and shuddered. When I glanced back at Rafael, he was chewing his lip and looking sadly in the other direction.

The day at the beach was filled with sun, the lull of the warm Caribbean Sea, and Rafael. Though Uncle Harry seemed to be with us everywhere as we explored the beach or clambered out onto a rocky point filled with sunbathers, we still managed a brief touch, a surreptitious caress, a shared wink.

I felt heavy from the awareness of my own body. With my long blonde hair wafting in the breeze, I stood out among the darker skinned, darker haired sunbathers. Rafael seemed to stand tall and protective next to me. I wanted him to hold me and run his fingers down my breasts but Uncle Harry was always there.

The charm of the day wore off quickly, though, because I sunburned so badly I had to spend the next three days in bed. Uncle Harry ministered to me in a kind, but stand-offish way. Soledad clucked and shook her head everytime she came into the room.

"*Gringa*." Her voice held a whisper of contempt that I did not understand. For the first time, I missed my mother.

I lay in a fever going over and over the feel of Rafael's body next to mine. In the afternoon silence of the *quinta* I prayed for him to come to me.

I saw nothing of him for the whole time I was in bed.

When we were able to resume our language lessons, though, a new awareness had blossomed between us. Under the table his knees brushed against mine. When he walked by, his hip would bump into my shoulder. With every touch my body would go slack.

All the time, Uncle Harry watched.

Mother wrote irritating little letters filled with non-news. The garden was growing well. Mrs. Simpson had her gallbladder taken out. The car broke down in the middle of downtown. She never said anything about herself and though my anger was ebbing, I never asked.

One evening while the rain poured outside the *quinta*, Uncle Harry fixed gin and tonics and sat down beside me on the couch. His expression was serious and I fully expected that he was about to tell me he knew something was going on with Rafael. I tensed, ready to snap back at him if he tried to give me any advice. I was sixteen. I knew everything.

"Jane," he pressed his lips together trying to find the words. I gathered myself to spring. "I got a letter from your mother today. It's not good."

"What's not good?" My tone was irritable, more out of habit than anything else.

He seemed surprised at the question. "You mean she didn't tell you?"

"I don't know what you're talking about."

Uncle Harry's look sent an aching chill up my arms. I set down the drink. "What . . . what are you talking about?"

"The cancer."

What word could be more stunning than "cancer"?

"She has cancer?" He must be talking about someone else. I felt panicked. When I grabbed for the gin and tonic it spilled onto my hand.

Uncle Harry sighed and looked away. "God, Jane, I didn't know she hadn't told you. She sent you here because she said it was too hard on you to watch her go through the treatments."

"Oh my god," I whispered. I felt no warmth from the gin. "I need to go home."

I cried and Uncle Harry patted me on the knee. At that moment, I wanted Rafael's warmth, but mostly I wanted to be with mother. I wanted to apologize to her.

Uncle Harry made the arrangements so I could fly home three days later. The day before I was to leave, I sought Rafael out.

He was leaning against a small tree in the back of the *quinta*, slowly smoking a cigarette. When I approached him, saw the way he looked at me, my halting Spanish left me. He dropped the cigarette, mashing it with his foot, and held his arms open to me.

It was the first time we had truly held each other. All the weeks of heavy anticipation, of daydreaming, of putting together our touches were tied up in this embrace. Yet, I felt the sadness in the way we clung to each other. His lips were warm and sweet and experienced. I didn't care that Soledad prowled somewhere inside.

How long we stood locked together, I'll never know. We were interrupted abruptly and forever by the sound of Uncle Harry's Volkswagen in the driveway. Rafael lept away from me. I grabbed his hand and gave him a clumsy kiss and nothing more.

That night, Uncle Harry invited Rafael to stay for supper. Soledad cooked a delicious *paella* and left it for us. She said *"adios"* to me with no kindness in her voice. At nine, after an uncomfortable evening where Rafael sat well away from me, Uncle Harry beckoned to him.

"I'll take him home. You go to bed because we have to leave early."

Rafael nodded to me but I could not read his expression as he walked out the door. My thoughts turned to mother and why she had tried to save me from her illness. Perhaps she thought I wasn't mature enough to deal with it. Perhaps she wanted to give me one chance to experience myself without the lingering sadness of grief.

Sometime in the middle of the night, a groaning noise from Uncle Harry's room woke me from a light sleep. I climbed out from under the sheets wondering if he had gotten back yet from taking Rafael home. The moon was high in the sky casting a bright twilight across the glossy tiles of the *quinta* as I padded to his room.

Uncle Harry's door was open about four inches. I peeked in.

He stood naked in the moonlight with his back to me. His white flesh contrasted deeply with Rafael's burnished brown. He held Rafael in a tight embrace, his hips swaying and his chest heaving. Rafael just stood, arms down at his side, unmoving. I think he saw me, but I'll never know. In the moonlight, his eyes seemed to lock into mine and the expression was mournful, but resigned.

After he took me to the airport the next day, I never saw Uncle Harry again.

Mother greeted me with enthusiasm that covered her pain, "Jane, you've matured so. I can see it."

She managed to live long enough to get me through high school. Even during the depths of her illness, every once in a while she would look at me and smile.

"I knew a summer in Caracas would be good for you."

The onion-skin letter brought back a vivid picture of Rafael lingering over the hedge, his face glossy with sweat. He was a *campesino*, a farmer, and his love was the land. I know now that Uncle Harry used me as a lure, as a bait to keep Rafael for the summer. Without me, he would have disappeared, like the little *barrio*, back to the land.

I decided to make no effort to find out about the "unfortunate circumstances" that took Uncle Harry's life. I don't think he would have wanted me to know. Instead, I placed the letter in a drawer and mixed myself a tall glass of gin and tonic. Alone, I savored its tangy bitterness, so remindful of that summer long ago.

Nina Barragan

FRIENDS OF THE TEATRO COLÓN

"And how do you find the Argentine, *un poco caída*, a bit fallen, yes?" The voice comes in small bursts, crackling sparkles sifting to the floor. Olga asks but answers herself, not having the heart to hear the awful truth from the mouth of an outsider. And yet, her small, intense eyes are hopeful, her mouth nervous. Olga is dark, with tiny limbs and a rather large head. Her proportions are nearly dwarf-like.

I, the outsider, visitor from the north, fumble for a discreet phrase, something polite about Argentina's wretched state of affairs in the months following the Falklands' War. I've come to Argentina in search of a past I never knew, a family I've never met. My aunt Eva, in turn, has brought me to the Colón theater, so that I might see what is still fine and grand in this country, so that I might meet her three dearest and oldest friends.

Olga drops her eyes to her coffee cup. To her right, the poet Madalena sighs. To her left, the still beautiful Felicia shakes her head. Friends since infancy, they have remained inseparable. Together they have celebrated their milestones, together they have weathered their storms.

Endless rows of crystal and gilt chandeliers sparkle along the high ceiling of the Salón de Té. Waiters rush among the crowded tables. The noise level is high; talking, peals of laughter, even the occasional shout of recognition. Smoke drifts in the room as people light more cigarettes, shifting in their chairs, engaging in new topics of conversation.

"Like Lautrec, is it not?"

I look across the table towards the voice. It is not Olga, but Magdalena, the poet.

"I'm sorry, I don't —"

"The scene, the whole Salón," she waves her arms. "I saw how you were observing. Does it not seem like Lautrec? The crowds, the elegant evening clothes, the smoking and drinking — you know his work?"

"Of course, you're quite right."

Magdalena nods approvingly, smoothing the white tablecloth with her dry palms. She wears no make-up. She lives simply, alone.

I have the feeling it's not the first time she's said this about Lautrec. I had been told about her disastrous marriage and the suicide attempt, the two slim volumes of poems and her yearly readings. Earlier, while my aunt Eva prepared dinner, she talked and talked about her three friends I would meet at the theater. She had spoken of their similarities and diversities, marriages and jobs, successes and failures. 'As for Magdalena's poetry,' her voice had quieted with hesitation, 'I think it's very controversial, but to tell you the truth, I don't keep up with those things.' Aunt Eva walked around the dinner table, offering flowered dishes as though they were afterthoughts. 'Not that it matters you understand, because our closeness, our friendship, is uppermost for all of us.'

During my brief visit, I have come to love my aunt's poignant efforts at cheeriness, despite Buenos Aires' pervasive atmosphere of uncertainty and self-preserving denial. She's a steadfast optimist, a true romantic. I find myself flipping back ten, twenty, a hundred years, and then relocating her in an unknown, impressionist painting, something that might have been called "The Picnic." A plumpish young mother — abundant, reddish hair, beautiful skin — is caught in a moment of tranquility and observation. She watches as the sun's rays sift through the trees and dance on the white of her small childrens' stockings. If there are realities beyond the sun's rays, she is not destined to see them.

"A bit fallen, to be sure. Argentina, as you Americans say, is 'down in the heels.' Is this not how you say it?"

The third voice, Felicia's, soft and fluid, draws me back to the coffee table and the four friends, the Salón de Té.

I nod, smiling.

"But she will rise again, just you wait and see! Argentina will rise again!" Felicia, of the long suffering eyes and aristocratic bearing, elegantly dressed, raises her cup in mid-air, her hand quivering. Tragedy haunts this woman's life. Clearly God has put her on this earth to receive and store pain.

Olga, Magdalena and Eva join her, raising their cups, clinking, toasting their country like chimes on a summer night. Forty years of companionship, forty years of meeting twice a month at the Colón, attending opera, concerts and plays with their subscription tickets. There had been phone calls back and forth. A trip to the box office by Olga who worked close by, and finally, a shift in their seating arrangements. Olga went up to the next balcony, alone. All this, so that I might attend, so that I might sit next to my aunt Eva.

"Do we dare hope?" Eva pipes up brightly, her eyes twinkling, her cheeks flushed. She's excited, pleased I'm meeting her friends, pleased they're meeting me. For the moment, this engrosses her far more than Argentina's depressing circumstances.

"Yes — once again girls — Argentina will rise again!" Now it's Olga who leads the toast; but this time, somehow it sounds hollow, without vigor. The four sip their coffee silently.

"The theater is so beautiful," I offer. "And the music, it's breathtaking!" My aunt smiles approvingly.

"And the chorus, it must have close to a hundred voices." I continue.

"Exactly one hundred," Olga confirms.

"Would you like to stay for the second half? Mind you, it's long! We won't be out until after mid-night." My aunt warns.

"Yes, please. I had no idea that I'd want to stay, quite the contrary, I —"

"Of course she wants to stay! How often do you get to hear St. Matthew's Passion in the Colón?" Despite what must be an unbearable burden of grief, Felicia manages a smile. "Right?" She looks me in the eye.

"Absolutely," I assure her.

"So, after all we too have *hermosura*, beautiful things?" Her voice is confident, almost reprimanding. She finally relinquishes her hold on an obedient, silk scarf and waves the air around her, indicating the Salón de Té, the marble halls and the theater beyond. I find her difficult, unyielding, hard.

"Argentina does have beautiful things," she repeats.

"Certainly, " I smile. I have to give them that.

For indeed, Buenos Aires has the Colón. Its splendor and pomp and glitter eases the pain. It's one of the few public places not affected by the last forty years, its stateliness little changed since its first opera in 1908. The people still flock to it, eager to escape the reality of their time. The continual economic inflation and political subversion do not enter its doors. Felicia rides into the Colón on the waves of her time; elegant clothes and silk scarves, impeccable make-up on a face aged by anguish.

* * *

Sometimes he wails, for no apparent reason. The nurse on duty rushes to his side, but she can find nothing physical to cause the pain. The straps of his bib are not too tight, he has not soiled himself, nor has he dropped his crayons. A simple, plaintive wail, and for eight years Felicia has learned to accept it as his mode of communication. It has been eight years of caring for and listening to his miserably desperate soul, trapped in a healthy body, with a brain that has turned to mush. Total mush, all on a Sunday afternoon. It had been a bright sunny day that he had gone out to play the usual round of cards with his friends at the cafe. On his way home, he had paused long enough to drop all his money down a street drain, again for no apparent reason. Shortly after that, his friends started complaining that there must be something wrong with Don Carlos, because he was cheating at cards, and he had never cheated before. That was only the beginning. The doctors called it premature senility. Felicia called it hell. One morning, shortly after he became ill, the doctor came to visit. He told Don Carlos he would have Felicia, his wife, get him some medication that would help him sleep. Don Carlos looked up at Felicia and winced.

"That woman is not my wife. I would never have married such a miserable soul."

Felicia wept, and then dried her tears. Although not her first, he had certainly been her finest lover, and he had always made her completely happy.

In the years that followed, Felicia took pride in the fact that she was able to keep him comfortable. He spent his mornings on the great, sunny, patio-porch, with the sliding glass doors that open out onto a garden of large leafed, tropical plants, palms and eucalyptuses. The gardener kept a bird cage in the far back, and for some time he'd been in the habit of bringing his two pet parakeets up to the porch on his arm. The birds sang out to Don Carlos, asking him repeatedly if he was better. But not long ago, one of the birds learned to imitate his wail. Naturally it was shriller than Don Carlos', but nevertheless, disturbingly accurate. Felicia had the birds destroyed.

Every morning they set Don Carlos out with his coloring in front of the television. They keep it on for him constantly. The incessant garbage of noise drowns out his small, animal-like sounds. Only the wails can be heard echoing through the long, old corridors. Felicia is glad now that she has decided to keep the house. She had considered selling it when her husband became ill, toyed with the idea of an apartment. But how confining that would have been for him. At least in the house he can be comfortable and private. He is exposed to no one, and no one is exposed to him. Their son, the architect, now lives in Rio. He comes to see his father twice a year, no longer bringing his wife and children with him. It is of course, too depressing for them. So Felicia is not only deprived of a husband, but of grandchildren as well. She does not travel to Rio to visit, for she would never leave him, whether he knows it or not.

Every night before she goes to bed, she thanks God that there is enough money to hire the staff necessary for his well being.

* * *

"To tell you the truth, Argentina *está muy baja*, very low right now." Another burst of words. Olga looks up at me. "It would be ridiculous to deny it," she adds.

I nod, understandingly, but I sense it is not my place to ask political questions. I watch as Olga begins to stack the cups and saucers, obviously driven to keep busy, either for the waiter's sake, or her own. The others watch her.

An active socialist all her life, Olga is the voice of the people. As a student she had joined the young university socialists, and within a few years, she rose to the rank of leadership. Although somewhat unattractive, she was an intelligent, committed girl, and she had the good fortune of being kind and unselfish. She fell desperately in love with another young socialist, who later went on to become the national socialist candidate. All her life she held secretarial or office-type jobs, just enough to maintain her, but nothing so demanding that it would involve her emotionally or intellectually. She held out for the party. As the years went on, her lover submitted to family pressures and married a wealthy girl, a union arranged by the two families. The marriage proved to be disastrous. Olga never married. She continued to live for the party and her lover. Both relationships were steadily maintained throughout the years. And yet, never once did she utter his name to her friends. It was for the good of his political career. But in her heart, Olga knew it would not have mattered. The other girls were not political animals; they did not care about all the factions of all the parties. They would not have searched the newspapers for his name; nor would they have followed his career, nor would they have told the butcher and the grocer that they knew his mistress. But Olga needed her privacy, and she respected theirs, and for this reason, she hardly ever spoke politics with her Colón friends.

"I don't believe our country has ever been so low." Olga says, staring sadly at the pile of cups and saucers.

"*Pero como*, Olga, how can you say that? What about a few years ago, when the military took over from Isabel Perón. What about the terror and disappearances, have you forgotten already?" Magdalena asks indignantly. "You know I lost a nephew," she lowers her voice, "you know my sister still marches in the plaza."

My aunt reaches over to pat Magdalena's arm. Concern shows on Felicia's forehead.

"Magdalena, none of us ever forgets those years," Felicia offers gently.

"Such depressing talk!" My aunt Eva straightens up. "We should all be ashamed of ourselves. This poor niece of mine will go back with a black view of Argentina!"

"Magdalena is right. The people suffered quietly, now they suffer out loud," Olga states.

They all nod seriously.

"She was once a great and fine nation." Olga looks at me. "In your schools, *amor*, do they teach the children about the history of Argentina? About Sarmiento, and all of his reforms?" She looks hopeful.

"To tell you the truth —" I begin.

"From what I understand, they don't even teach the children the history of their own country. How are they going to teach them the history of ours!" Magdalena states bitterly.

The lights begin to flicker on and off in the Salón. Women pull out their cosmetic bags and quickly dab and brush at their faces. Men put out their cigars. Intermission is over.

"Shall we?" Felicia asks, already standing.

We walk slowly through the Salón, the crowd pushing and swaying around us. It is several flights of stairs up to the third balcony, and my aunt clings to my arm as we climb the marble staircase.

"I hope you weren't upset by what Magdalena said about your schools." Her voice is low, almost a whisper. She knows Magdalena and Felicia are close behind us. "Sometimes she tends to be a little harsh."

"Not at all," I assure her.

"She really has had a miserable life, poor girl. Here we are!" My aunt steps forward and leads me into our aisle. We ease our way slowly, inching towards our seats.

"Don't you love the crowds?" My aunt asks cheerfully. "It's wonderful seeing people appreciate music, appreciate the Colón!" She speaks lightly, gayly.

"I've always wondered how those ladies with their big skirts ever managed to sit in these chairs. They're the same ones you know, the very same." She smiles, lowering her plump body into a tight, hard velvet seat.

"Look, 1909," Eva says, pointing up at the ceiling, and the date painted in at the foot of the fresco. Can you imagine the clothing of that time? Those enormous silk and velvet skirts, what a bother they must have been!" Eva adjusts herself in the seat and picks up her program. "The soprano is wonderul! I must say, though, I don't care at all for the tenor." She puts on her glasses and begins reading the program.

I watch as people enter and sit in their seats, adjusting, preparing, readying themselves. A comforting, quiet hum rises from the audience. An older couple enter our aisle and begin working down towards their places. All those sitting have to stand to let them pass.

"You know," Eva says, easing herself up, "It's really a shame you can't stay in Buenos Aires just another few days."

"What will I be missing?"

The couple passes, Eva lowers herself again.

"Magdalena will be reading her poetry."

* * *

Once a year Magdalena was invited to read her poetry at the Society of Women Poets. She read at the San Martin Cultural Center. Chairs were set up in the lobby-like space, and Magdalena, in flowing charcoal chiffon, sat with the other poets. When it was her turn, she rose and moved to the podium like a ghost. Her voice was shrill, but she read with passion and conviction. She wrote about love.

The Colón friends always went, naturally. They arrived together, sat together, and left together. They never discussed Magdalena's poetry, nor did she with them, anymore than Olga talked politics. Merely their love and support for one another was enough. When my aunt Eva was periodically hospitalized for weeks on end with her back problem, they all came faithfully to visit, as often as they could. Two years ago, when Magdalena finally decided to leave her husband after twenty years of marriage, they all supported her completely. Of course, with her suicide attempt just weeks before her decision, what else could they do but support her?

* * *

Emilio Esquilache was a tall, dry man who spent most of his waking hours totally engrossed in his legal practice, and in the management of his inherited acres of ranch land. He was far too busy for children, or for that matter, for love and poetry. He awoke, ate breakfast and left for work at precisely the same time every morning. The only occasion their paths were sure to cross was at breakfast, when Magdalena sat opposite him at the long table. She daydreamed as she stared at Emilio's rings and watch and cuff links. His nails were always immaculate, his collar stiff, his hair perfect. The silver gleamed, the napkins, snowy white. She had never seen him shave; she had never seen a tarnished knife nor a stained napkin. That was the problem. She had never felt in control of her life in this house. It had never been her house, but rather his family's. Not that his mother lived with them anymore. She had been in a home now for several years, but somehow she was still present. Whenever Magdalena gave the servants orders, they frowned and mumbled something about how Doña Clara would not do it that way.

For God's sake, Magdalena thought, as Emilio tapped at his soft boiled egg, it had been twenty years, and still, nothing in the damn house was of her doing or choice. It always amazed her how Emilio could remove the egg's cap so neatly, precisely. The pantry door swung open, the flash of gleaming white tiles on the wall, and the cook entered the dining room with Emilio's coffee. She placed it gingerly in front of him. He nodded, without looking up from his paper.

"Cafe, Señora?" The cook asked.

"Yes, please." Magdalena watched her disappear again through the swinging door. Every morning she played a game to see how many tiles she could count before the door closed.

"Have you plans for the day?" Emilio asked, not bothering to glance at her.

"I haven't thought about it yet."

"I do wish you could find something to do with yourself Magdalena." Emilio wiped his mouth and stood up, glancing at his watch.

"Yes."

"I will have clients until late tonight. Do not wait to dine."

A perfunctory kiss, and he was off, the scent of Spanish lavender trailing behind.

She had plans, but in the end, they didn't work. She didn't take enough pills, and the maid found her semi-conscious at four in the afternoon.

* * *

"Did you enjoy it, my dear?"

My aunt Eva, her cheeks flushed and eyes red around the rims, wrestles with her short fur jacket that has slipped down behind her back. I reach over to help.

"Very much so."

"Good. Now let's see how quickly we can get out and find cabs."

It's a long, slow descent. People are tired and crowding, eager to be home. The marble floors and stairs seem harder than they did before. I can no longer see Magdalena and Felicia ahead of us in the crowd. I feel the weight of my aunt's weariness, as she leans towards me for support. Her back must be hurting, I realize. It was probably too long a time to be sitting. Finally, the huge, impressive doors, and cold air.

Magdalena, Felicia and Olga are waiting for us, huddled together under one of the street lights in front of the theater.

"*Otra noche en el Colón!*" My aunt says, approaching her friends. She turns to me, about to explain.

I nod, understanding.

They shiver and yawn and embrace good-bye. Magdalena and Felicia leave together in one taxi, both living in the same district, and Olga alone in another.

My aunt hails a cab. As we climb into the back seat, I ask if they've really been attending performances for the last forty years.

"Since we were sixteen!" She smiles and leans forward to give the driver directions.

"And during all those years — the Perón era, and when he returned with Isabel, the military governments — didn't you talk about what was going on?"

Aunt Eva reaches up and gently taps a finger to my mouth, making the same hushing sound one utters to a restless infant, unable to sleep. "We tried not to."

I ask no more.

As the taxi pulls off, she snuggles up against me, sighing happily.

AFRICA,
MIDDLE EAST,
INDIA

Catherine Stearns

ICARUS IN AFRICA

Selly Oak Colleges
Birmingham, England
November 11, 198-

Dear K.,

Just got back from a weekend in London where I went to an exhibit of Fabergé jewelry at the Victoria & Albert — beautiful stuff, though it does give one a certain sympathy for the bolsheviki. The first thing I saw when I got back to my room was a magpie dancing on the lawn. They really do seem to dance. Such a blinding black and white — and I gather they have a rather nasty disposition at times, just like your mother.

I spent most of last week working at the library on a paper I'm doing on the development of Zambian education. It's wonderful to be writing again, when I'm not sidetracked by my duties as an American tourist. I will miss you all at Thanksgiving, too, if I have time. Thursday is my busy day: five lectures, language lab, then back to the library for a few hours. Tell S. I'm glad her divorce is final at last, and that I decided long ago not to disapprove of my children's first mistakes. Your loving conscience and

Ma

Telegram
Christmas Eve, 198-

Check coming STOP Bouvez une libation pour moi STOP Preferably bourbon STOP Ma

Selly Oak Colleges
Birmingham, England
January 7, 198-

Dear K.,

You asked me why I decided to go to Africa in the first place, and I'm assuming you don't mean why at the preposterous age of 60. First of all, as you know I've suffered — and that is the right word — all my life from what your father used to call my Icarus Complex. Anywhere I haven't been I'd like to go. After your father died, I decided to yield to my deeper impulses, and the teaching offer in Zambia seemed the perfect opportunity. Besides, I'm adventurous, and one of these days I'll be too old to be adventurous except, I hope, in spirit. Last week I went to see some slides taken by a woman who used to live near Lusaka, the captial of Zambia, and her pictures reminded me of the small town I grew up in: McClure, Illinois, 50 years ago. Perhaps I'm just going through the proverbial second childhood?

I've learned that Zambia, of all the African countries, has been very forbearing in its attitudes towards whites. And from all accounts their treatment there before Independence was just as wretched as anywhere else. Africans have been dragged into the western world by whites without being consulted about it; the least we can do is help. I suppose you'll try to psychoanalyze me now, that's one of the troubles with your generation.

Anyway, as my daughters are wont to tell me, I've had a soft life. Good, but soft. I could say more but I've run out of something to drink. Last night I dreamt I was in the Cape house braiding your hair. Do you realize my next letter — fingers crossed — will be from Africa? Your loving and impatient

Ma

Kafue Secondary School
Kafue, Zambia
January 19, 198-

Dear K.,

I wish you could see it. The rainy season makes everything sparkle: yellow wattle trees with bright orange flowers, a flamebush with scarlet candle-shaped blossoms, jacaranda, hibiscus, frangipani. . . . Blue wax-bills as common as sparrows at home, paradise flycatchers with spindly golden tails. I don't have enough words for this place, especially its colors, or know which hurts my eye more: its beauty or its poverty. Driving from Lusaka I saw the thatched-roof huts, rondavels, where squatters and tribal people live. Their children's bellies puckering down like balloons. I kept remembering how both of you looked like little Buddhas.

I finished my last week of classes yesterday, and I think the kids are beginning to believe I'm human — if colorless. I'm learning to cope with the African names; my favorite so far is Happiness Hampango.

All the boys are willing and work very hard. They have to, because there are lots of others out there ready and eager to take their places if they don't. Fewer than half the students who finish elementary school go on to secondary school — there isn't enough room. This week both kids and staff have been busy cleaning up the place, slashing weeds and grass, working in the gardens. I was just settling into my Wednesday afternoon class when the announcement came that we were needed to plant beans. I guess that happens often. Before I forget, I have a request: would you send me once a month or so a package of instant coffee, tea, and dried milk? I didn't know enough to bring supplies from Birmingham, and my fellow teachers tell me some things are available only once or twice a year. Send them air mail, or they'll take forever. I've decided I can be lonely for particular people but not for people in general. Take care of your cold, my dear. Your newly-bandannaed

Ma

Kafue Secondary School
Kafue, Zambia
January 27, 198-

Dear K.,

Today I had a bath! I now have a tub in my house, though my bathing ritual isn't nearly as elaborate as you might remember it when I took oils and bubble-bath and at least an hour. Here, after I filled the tub, I had to skim the surface with a pan to get rid of locusts, mosquitoes, and these strange winged-ants — quite a delicacy, I understand. The bath was cold and quick. Not having water or electricity regularly makes you feel both careful and grateful...

The rains continue, but somewhat abated. Mornings and evenings are becoming distinctly cool, though it's still between 70 and 80 during the day. I suppose you might say autumn approaches.

I had lunch the other day on a houseboat in the middle of the Kafue River. My host was an agricultural expert for the Family Farms project of the Zambian government, trying to settle Tonga farmers on government land. The Tonga tribe have been farmers for centuries, but when the whites came they took all the good land along the river and drove the Tonga back into the mountains where the soil is poor. At Independence the whites who didn't want to stay could sell their farms to the government, and most of them did. So now the Tonga are being re-settled on this rich ground — which once belonged to them. The houseboat was fascinating; he'd mounted a wheel-less house trailer on a sort of walled raft. I don't suppose you remember that I once wanted to live on a houseboat? Your father and I flipped a coin: that was the first summer we rented the Cape house.

Looks like rain any minute — have to take my clothes off the line. By the way, tell S. I have no intention of telling either of you whether or not I ever had affairs. Both of you should mind your own damn business. Mwapoleni — your mysterious, clean, and ever-loving

Ma

Kafue Secondary School
Kafue, Zambia
February 9, 198-

Dear K.,

Went into Lusaka this afternoon to get my National Registration card, required of anyone planning to stay in the country more than three months. It's a little plastic square with a number and the usual fat-faced picture. But at least I'm legal now. When I got back to school, I could hear the drums from the bush. "Inside the bush you'll find your hidden heart" is an African proverb. Maybe that's what I heard.

Your description of the blizzard reminded me of Halliburton's famous last cablegram to a friend in London, just before he disappeared in the China Sea about 1938: "Having a wonderful time; war going on; storm coming up; food running low; wish you were here instead of me."

I'm sending you a copy of my paper on Zambian education, which should answer some of your questions about the system here. The main problem is, of course, money. Zambia is a poor country, especially since the price of copper has declined. The mines are now operating at a loss, but the government won't close them down because that would put a lot of people out of work, and Zambian humanists say that people are more important than the government making money. I can't see Uncle Sam deciding that.

Thanks very much for the milk, etc. If there's room in the next parcel, any dried soup would be appreciated, especially mushroom or oxtail. Tell S. to write me a vivid description of her new boyfriend, if you think he merits it. Some of the boys just killed a python behind my house; they're saying it was after rabbits. Better them than me,

Ma

Kafue Secondary School
Kafue, Zambia
March 4, 198-

Dear K.,

Only five more weeks to go before the end of term when I'll be going down to Livingstone to see one of the wonders of the natural world, Victoria Falls. One whole week at a place called the Intercontinental Hotel where I imagine myself watching the sunset, evening drink in hand, almost close enough to dangle my toes in the Zambesi River. — Almost is as close as you get, unless you want one of several disgusting-sounding diseases. I'll spend most of the last week of term giving exams because we have no more mimeograph paper, and the school can't afford to buy more, so instead of having a typed exam, they'll have questions we can write on the board. The Ministry of Education is very nearly broke — the school hasn't received its government grant for the term, and money to feed the kids is running short. We all need a vacation.

I believe I have a new reputation for intrepidity. One day last week I was going into a History class, usually a rather quiet group, who seemed to be making an extraordinary amount of noise. When I got to the door, there was a student clasping an upraised axe. (For a minute I thought studying had pushed him over the edge.) I said, "Matado, what are you doing with that axe?" "Killing a bat, madam," he replied, although he wasn't. Being unwilling to come within three feet of the thing, he missed it entirely, and the bat was quivering before him on the floor. I decided I'd better intervene before Matado chopped a hole somewhere. I told him to put down the axe and kick the bat out the door. But he — and all the other boys — looked at me, their feet, the bat, their feet, me. Finally, I was the one with the quick glissade. Since then they've been extremely respectful: the white lady has chutzpah after all.

Ma

Kafue Secondary School
Kafue, Zambia
March 23, 198-

Dear K.,

I now have a gardener. Two hours a day, Monday through Friday. I share him with a doctor at the clinic; he keeps us trimmed, mown, weeded, and dug. I'm hoping to plant a garden of my own as soon as the beds are finished. Seems you can plant any time here, you just have to keep things watered in the dry season. The more food we grow ourselves, the better — so many things are hard to come by. And the prices are at least equal to Boston, which is very high indeed for the average Zambian. I can pay my gardener about $16 a month, which means if he has three other customers, all he could handle, his monthy income is $64. And he has two boys at the school. I feel strange having a gardener, it seems so upper-crust, but various people urged me to, and it's true I don't have time for a garden without him. Everybody calls him George, although that's not his real name, and he promises to show me how to make mango chutney.

(I put this away for a few days; let me add a bit.)

I suppose it's not strange in a country where there is so much hunger that the green beans and cucumbers aren't harvested until they're as big as they can grow and are, to my taste, overripe. George and I argue all the time about gardening. He's become my companion in culinary investigations these last few days, and I share most of my meals with him and his boys. I was trying to describe a Cuisinart of all things the other day when his eyes lit up and he said he wanted to go to America and become a great chef. Then his sons started to give their reasons: to wear blue jeans and buy Cadillacs and hear Michael Jackson live. I said a few things about poverty at home, too, but then decided to shut up. Just because having a Cuisinart didn't change my life doesn't mean I have the right to deny others. You learn things like this when you have children. If you still want to send me something for my birthday, how about 102 Michael Jackson T-shirts? Or my *Joy of Cooking* and a picture of snow?

Ma

Postcard of the Falls
Victoria Falls, Zimbabwe
April 13, 198-

If you ever decide to get married, take him to Victoria Falls — or *Musio Tunya*, thundering smoke in Tonga — it makes Niagara look like a millstream. All the water in the Zambesi, gathered from tributaries for nearly a thousand miles inland, comes rushing down the river and suddenly falls 350 feet in a boiling sheet of water. (I'm paraphrasing my guidebook.) For miles from the train I could see what looked like a huge white cloud in the sky — mist rising from the falls, thundering smoke in the air. There's a perpetual rainbow on sunny days because of it. Yesterday, I went on a sundown cruise along the river: the sky turned orange, red, gold, all the colors in your hair, and finally, gray, mine. I miss you.

Intercontinental Hotel
Livingstone, Zambia
April 15, 198-

Dear K.,
I sip my drink and watch an old vervet monkey with bright blue testicles leap from table to table trying to filch the marmalade. Last night a Mr. Daraas, originally from Beirut and married to the Englishwoman who owns half the shops in Kafue, showed up at the hotel and flirted outrageously with me. He drives tours into the game parks in Zambia, Tanzania, and Kenya. He told me that in five years there won't be any animals left, so I'd better come with him now while there's game enough and time. Apparently poaching is a problem since there's still such a lucrative market in hides and tusks. Even in the puny game park here in Livingstone, I saw a lot of bloody carcasses by the paths.
There is a woman here — I can see her out of the corner of my eye as I write this — who keeps coming up to me. Just close enough for me to know she is there. She's obviously very poor and walks with her hands outstretched — not to beg, I think, but as if to tell me to touch her. Or to say *Here, take them, they do me no good.* The first time I saw her I was walking back from the falls, and before I could think one of the waiters ran up and shooed her away, just as he does the monkeys. The African family behind me made faces at her and told me to ignore her because such beggars are hurting the tourist trade, "driving away the money," they said. But you should see the way she looks at me and walks toward me, as if she had no right to the ground.
Are you done with your exams yet? I am very tired today, and it seems strange and cruel to be past 60. I used to think I could change the world,

did you know that? Well, perhaps we still can. I love you, your future-shooting

Ma

Kafue Secondary School
Kafue, Zambia
May 3, 198-

Dear K.,

I got your parcel yesterday. Chocolate! You are delightful daughters. Thanks to an influx of several items from Romania, of all places, shopping has improved since I've come back.

I've been working more and more at the clinic these days when I'm not teaching. I'm not sure whether it's to expiate that vision of the woman at Livingstone or what. I can't seem to forget her face, her hands. She has made me feel that even the smallest thing I do must matter. Does matter. Do you see? This is what I always wanted to show you, but so often I forgot it myself.

Bear with me — I have another request: would you send me half a dozen cans of Sterno, airmail? I think I can make a burner out of an old fruit tin, and then at least we can boil water when the current goes off.

As always, it was good to get your letter, although it's strange to hear about spring when I'm finally needing a blanket at night. It's been a beautiful day today, the sky's that blue the Renaissance Italian painters used to make the virgin's robes. No smoke, no smog, what the world was meant to be. I should tell you that I've decided to spend part of my next vacation here, so I won't be home as soon as planned. But tell S. I should be home in time for the wedding, that no I don't have anything "teal," whatever that is, and that I refuse to wear high heels. In fact, I think I'll go barefoot. Love,

Ma

P.S. I wonder whether you'll recognize me; I'll be the one with her hands out.

Sarah Streed

A MOROCCAN MEMOIR

For Nadia, in enduring friendship

Settling-in

The eleven week training period was held in Morocco. With the other Peace Corp volunteers, I studied Classical Arabic, the spoken dialect, Teaching Methodology and Cultural Adaptation. At the end, almost all of the fifty that had arrived as a group were invited to the Swearing-In.

We rode by bus to the resort/hotel poised on the edge of the Mediterranean Sea. It seemed lavish after the summer's hardihood; I was in a celebratory mood and swam in both the pool and the sea. Cocktails were served, followed by dinner and speeches. We signed pledges to uphold the Constitution of the United States of America. I stood in line — my turn came — I was sworn in as an official Peace Corps Volunteer.

In a corner, I opened the sealed envelope containing the name of my post — the spot in Morocco where I was going to live and serve for the next two years. I looked; the name meant nothing. Later, I looked it up on a map and found it was a large village — actually a town — on the train line between Casablanca and Marrakesh. Because it was the only education for miles around, there were two high schools: one of "Letters" or Humanities, and the other "Science." I was relieved that I had been assigned to the School of Letters; the students would probably be receptive to English teachers.

* * *

A few weeks later, the train ejected me at my town in the evening. I halted on the platform, checked for the equivalent of $400 in my pocket (settling-in allowance), gripped my straw basket and travel bag, then looked around. Everything was dry dust. The dark spread from the train station, swallowing the yellow flatness of the desert.

Men, all around me, alone or in groups, were walking toward a paved road with a landscaped median of palm trees. I didn't move, just shook my head when the men called to me, until I saw a pretty, modern woman flanked by two men. I stopped this group and asked the way to the hotel in town. They were friendly — one of the men took my travel bag — and we set forth.

We walked down the paved road that stretched off into the night. I didn't see any cars. At one point, a street light lit up a billboard with the King's portrait and a few yards of sand beyond. Then two uniformed *gendarmes* appeared. They barked fast words in the Arabic dialect and my companions scattered, leaving my travel bag on the road.

The *gendarmes* switched to French to ask for my passport and papers. I was angry and handed them over with a lot of rustling. They examined them, then one asked, still in French, "So what are you doing in our town?"

"I'm the new English teacher," I said, "at the High School of Letters."

"Do you want to come to dinner sometime?" the same *gendarme* continued.

"Sometime would be fine," I said, lying.

They handed back my passport and left, diappearing into the night as fast as my companions had previously. I was alone on a dark road, and cursed them, but picked up my travel bag and continued walking. After a few yards, the man who had carried my bag popped out from the night. In French, he explained the couple had thought it best to go on but he had waited for me.

We walked together. After a long time I could see the town — a clump of yellow stucco buildings behind a red sign advertising Coca-Cola in Arabic.

"What are you here for?" he asked me.

I told him.

"I teach biology at that same school," he said, "I live with the other man you saw — he's an engineer here — and that was his girlfriend. We were picking her up at the train station."

We arrived in the town proper, but there weren't any streetlights, so I felt, rather than saw, the shadow of buildings. The dense blackness was eating the town. We stopped at a two-story building with a neon sign at the top spelling "OTEL" with the "H" missing. I thanked my companion and walked inside — safe for the night. It was a few days until school began, so I decided to stay in "OTEL" until I could find a place to live.

The next morning my companion came back to "OTEL." He introduced himself as Najib and offered to help me find a real estate agent. I worried that perhaps he was helping me because he wanted an American girlfriend, but I hadn't detected any signs of this in his body language; he was very stiff and distant. I also knew that I couldn't find a real estate agent by myself.

So we left to seek the *simsar*. Daylight images of the town banged at my eyes: a robed woman shrieking at a man behind a cart, a ragged boy swatting at a hunk of meat hanging in flies.

We entered a narrow alley flanked by adobe mounds. Each mound was a cave with an entrance hole. Najib stooped at one, stuck his head in and called. He motioned me to follow with his hand.

The room was four feet by six feet. A large man wearing a white cotton robe and pointed yellow slippers sat on a ripped vinyl chair. I heard Najib explaining that I was the new American schoolteacher and needed a place to live. The man heaved to his feet, belly shaking, and we followed.

The first stop was the traditional Moroccan landowner's house: large, spacious, even a tiled courtyard with a fountain that was presently turned off. I gasped. The *simsar* assured me that the fountain could be turned on at any time.

"It's very nice," I said, "but it's too much." (I waved my arms around). "Much too much. I wish to live like most Moroccans. Even though I'm American, I don't have enough money for this house."

The *simsar* looked at me with something like disgust, then turned on his leather slippers and slapped out. Najib and I again followed.

For such a large old man, he could walk very fast, and we didn't stop until we were on the other side of town. Then he halted before a house that was in the process of being built; some young boys were sawing wood, an older man was pouring cement, and only a framework stood.

"So," the *simsar* said to me, "you don't like an old house. Here is a brand new house."

"Yes, I see that," I said, "but it isn't finished."

The *simsar* turned and talked with the man pouring cement.

"They can finish it in a month," he said.

"I need a house NOW," I said.

The *simsar* shrugged his shoulders. He took off again, white robe flying.

He next stopped before a pretty second floor apartment with a balcony. It was clean and the rent was in the category of what I had been thinking.

"Yes, yes," I said to the *simsar*, "this is perfect."

He smiled.

Najib pulled me aside.

"I don't think you should take this house," he said to me.

"Why?" I asked, "It's clean. It's small but pretty. . . ."

Najib leaned close to whisper, "This is a street where all the prostitutes live. I don't think it would be good to have the new American teacher living on the street with all the prostitutes."

"Yes," I said, "I see what you mean."

I turned to the *simsar*. "I'm sorry," I said, "I don't think I'll take this apartment after all."

He threw out his hands in a gesture of exasperation, shook our hands abruptly, and left. Najib and I walked towards the center of town. I was discouraged.

"There is one thing," said Najib, "There is a top floor apartment available in the building we live in."

I looked at him, considering.

"You don't have to worry," he said stiffly, "My roommate and I are moving to another building in a month."

I felt a little sad — but relieved. Just past the *Marche*, we turned off the main road onto a dirt alley. Two little boys were winding thread — loops of green and blue went back and forth — and Najib bent under these and ducked into a tiled doorway. I did the same. We climbed two flights of stairs and waited. One of the little "winding" boys must have gone to fetch the landlord, for soon a thin man with glasses came up panting. He explained that he owned the building, including the shop on the first floor where he sold appliances, and I should drop off my rent there each month.

He pulled out a key and let me in. It was small — two rooms connected by a closet-like kitchen and a chamber with a squat toilet — but it was clean and cheap, about $50 a month.

"Great," I said to him, "I'll take it."

Najib had slipped out. The landlord and I began discussing the terms of the agreement. I gave him two months' rent on the spot, one month to reserve the room, and one month to rent. He handed me the key and left.

I walked back to the hotel, paid my bill, then carried my travel bag and straw basket the few blocks back.

Inside my new apartment it was getting dark, so I examined the rooms, taking stock: the smaller room could be the bedroom, next to that was a cubicle with two footpads on either side of a hole — the "squat" as we affectionately called it. There was a sink in the entryway, but I suspected there was water only in the morning and evening. There was a tiny kitchen with another sink, and a small tile counter — I could buy a small gas burner. The larger room I would use as the living room, or a sort of salon.

I opened the shutters of this room. By then it was fully dark. The street below had emptied with the night, but I could hear noise everywhere, murmurs, snatches of music, men talking. Dust drifted in and settled on my skin. I lit a candle and laid out my sleeping bag on some plastic heaped in the corner.

I took off my sandals and got in the bag. I began to read part of a travel book by candlelight, but then it seemed absurd. I was living in North Africa! This thought was so vigorous and vibrant compared to the typed words on the page, that I grew agitated and blew out the candle.

I lay in the dark listening to the noises and after awhile, fell asleep that first night in my new apartment.

The Baths

The next day I met my neighbors: Amina, wife and mother, her son Karim, the maid, Halima, and a few hours later, the husband, Hassan. That first day I learned that they were a progressive Moroccan family because, although Hassan's family lived a few blocks away, they had their own place.

Amina took me shopping for a Butagaz burner and pointed out the women's public bath, or *hemem*, just down the street from our building. At one stop, she bought a *kis* — a washcloth mitt — for me to take along with my bucket and soap.

A day later — the day before school was to start — I went to take my first public bath.

The outer room of the *hemem* was a sort of antechamber where all the women were stripping down to their panties and leaving their clothes in a basket. I did the same, feeling uncomfortable with my breasts exposed. I followed the woman in front of me who grabbed her bucket and approached the front of the chamber where a lady with gold teeth and earrings guarded the door. The woman then set down a coin and went through a door. I stepped up.

The *"hemem* lady" held out a coin.

"*Dirham*," she said to me in Arabic, "It costs a *dirham*."

I went back to my basket and fetched the right coin. When I returned and gave it to her, she pocketed it. Just as I was about to slip past, she reached out and tweaked my right nipple.

"I can see you don't have any children," she said, laughing.

Stunned, I walked through the door and into the first empty sauna-like cubicle I could find. I filled my bucket with steaming hot water from the spigot, added some cold, and bathed. I washed my hair with another bucketful, rinsed it, and was finished in fifteen minutes, similar to what I would spend taking a shower in the States.

The *"hemem* lady" regarded me with surprise as I walked back into the antechamber. As I was dressing, a young woman came up and asked, "Why don't Americans have the little things?" and pinched a black roll of skin off her arm. I shrugged, but when I got home I asked Amina if the next time I could go to the *hemem* with her, which I did three days later.

The *hemem* lady nodded when she saw me with a Moroccan woman. Amina and I stripped, paid, and found an empty cubicle. Then we washed our hair, combed it through and washed it again. Then we scrubbed every inch of our bodies with the *kis* and homemade soap. We repeated this three times, and on the third time the little rolls of black skin came off my body. We cleaned our ears, pumiced our feet, rinsed off completely and finished it all by eating an orange in our own steam.

* * *

The thought of going through this process more than once a week exhausted me, so I began attending only on Fridays. The *hemem* lady knew when to expect me and we became friends.

After a few weeks, I noticed another lady hanging about the antechamber. She was old, without teeth, dressed in a skirt pulled up about her waist. When she ran about the room, her thin breasts hit against her protruding stomach. Once, she came up to me and garbled something in Arabic. I backed off, afraid. The *hemem* lady explained that she was the "scrubber" and would scrub me for a small fee.

"No thanks," I said. The scrubber looked disappointed, but then led me to a cubicle, swinging the door open with a flourish. I laughed and gave her a coin.

As the year wore on, I learned more and more of the Arabic dialect, and began to understand the conversations around me as the women dressed and undressed in the antechamber.

"Yes, teacher of English in our school."

"Oh yes, very nice. Speaks Arabic and lives near here, by herself."

"Wears the traditional *djellaba* robe, but a bright red one! Can you imagine?"

* * *

Slowly, as my *hemem* day — Friday — became known in the town, students and their families began to use this fact to their advantage.

One afternoon, as I was walking to my cubicle, a girl student came quickly out of hers and greeted me with a kiss on both cheeks. I felt that it was inappropriate to chat with a student in my panties, and broke off after the greeting. Later I heard her bragging to a friend that she had seen me in the *hemem* and talked with me.

Another afternoon, just after the first semester grades had gone out, an older woman rushed at me. She grabbed at my free hand — the one that wasn't holding the bucket — with her two hands and clutched.

"Please, please," she implored, bending her face to kiss my hand again and again. I was completely confused.

"Please," I said back to her, pulling my hand away, "What is it?"

Grabbing my hand again: "My daughter is failing in your English class. Please give her a passing grade."

I took my hand away for the second time and left her weeping.

During summer vacation, I traveled, and thus bathed elsewhere. But with my return in the fall, I resumed my regular *hemem* days. On the first *hemem* of my new school year, the *hemem* lady gave a cry and kissed me on both cheeks. From then on, I greeted her in this manner first thing when I came in the door, just as the other women did. It made me think of the previous year when I had stalked in — oblivious — taken my bath, and gone home without a word to anyone.

The *hemem* lady began bantering with me in Arabic. She asked if I knew how to make Moroccan tea — a sweet mint drink involving a ritual preparation.

"Of course I do," I said, "I've been living in Morocco for over a year."

"Well then," she said, "Why don't you make some and bring it here for me."

I had a vision of transporting the pots of boiling water and sugar in cones and fresh mint leaves and tiny glasses on the proper silver tray, and I said, "Oh no, that would be much too difficult."

Her face fell.

"But," I added, "I'll bring you a Coca." (Coke was sold in bottles and used only on special occasions.)

The *hemem* lady laughed, showing her front gold teeth, and told the scrubber what I had promised.

After that bath, when I was home, I sent Amina's live-in-maid — a nine year old girl from a poor family — to buy bottles of Coke for all of us. Then I added some money and told her to buy two extra bottles and deliver them to the *hemem* lady and the scrubber. The girl returned after a while and told me she had done as instructed.

The following Friday, the *hemem* lady laughed when she saw me and thanked me for the Coca. I started undressing and as I folded up my clothes I could hear her chatting to the other women in Arabic.

"That's Sarah, she's the teacher. Yes, you'll never believe what she did. I told her to bring me some tea from her house, and she said that was too difficult but that she would give me Coca instead. . . ."

The Abuse of Women

Whenever out in the streets of my new town — shopping at the market, walking to and from school, going to the post office — I noticed an aggressive disdain in the manner of the Moroccan male toward all women. The Moroccan women responded to this by scuttling; eyes cast down, veils covering three-quarters of the face, *djellaba* hoods pulled up to cover most of the hair and neck, they crept around outside until they were safely back home.

I also noticed that men continuously lined the streets; they lounged in doorways shaded by the sun, smoked at outdoor cafes facing the *marche*, chatted with friends at the entrance to the baths. And while standing and watching, they softly, almost absent-mindedly, poured out a stream of abuse.

One time I asked a very Westernized Moroccan male why Arabic men treated women in such a degrading fashion. He replied, quite seriously, that according to the Muslim religion men can't speak directly to women so they must resort to oblique harassment and insults to get attention. Whatever the reason, I was an easy target: female, white, single and blond.

On a certain morning I was walking to school, dressed to teach in skirt, pumps, and lipstick. I went my usual route, past the old man stuffing pallets with straw, past the bread man selling fresh round loaves, past the little boy who sat on a mat in the doorway of his father's store and sold drums — big bongos to baby drums the size of a saltshaker.

As I reached the last block where the boys and men loitered in order to watch girl students approach, I saw three or four men gather in a huddle. I walked faster. A few yards past the group, I distinctly heard my name chanted in accompaniment to an intricate rhythm of clapping: Sarah, Sar-ah. Clap, clap-clap.

It couldn't be. I turned to look and the men smiled widely and chanted louder. People turned their heads to watch; I felt a hundred eyes waiting for my reaction. So, deliberately, I grimaced and flicked my outspread hand back and forth by my ear in the Moroccan gesture of being crazy. The crowd laughed, the men laughed — and then stopped.

* * *

During my term I had many conversations with Moroccan women about their status — or lack thereof. One of these took place in a compartment of a train. I was travelling to Rabat when suddenly, without any preliminaries, an older Moroccan woman sitting directly across me began speaking.

"In all Arabic countires, we women are the slaves of men," she said.

I glanced at the only other occupant of the compartment — male — sitting in the corner.

"Yes, I know there are ears," she continued, "but I must say it. Not just in Morocco but in all Arabic countries, women are slaves. Look at my case." (Her voice was rising.) "I was married to my husband for thirty years when he left me for a young girl of twenty-nine. Now I am fifty-two and what have I got? Nothing. So I am going to try and find work in a foreign country because of what he did to me."

The man rose to his feet and left the compartment. The woman looked at him with a blank face. My stop came shortly after.

"Good luck," I said.

"Good luck to you too," she replied.

* * *

Once, when I had a long weekend off, I went to stay with my friend Rachida and her family in the country. On the first night, just before the horn from the local mosque rang out to signal the evening meal, Rachida and I went for a walk in the dusty fields with her older brother.

"Rachida is happy tonight," said the brother, "Because you are here as a guest, she does not need to help with the cooking, but can walk with us."

"Why must Rachida usually help with the cooking?" I asked.

"Because it is the custom, especially for the eldest girl," her brother said, "I think it is different here from America."

"Yes," I said, "there are women in America who, if their husbands tell them to go make a cup of tea, they say 'Go make it yourself.'"

The brother laughed. Rachida put her hand to her face in a gesture of dismay.

"Well," I said, "why should a woman work all day for no pay just because she is a woman? For example, why does Rachida do everything for her brothers, while her brothers spend all their time at the cafe or the cinema?"

The brother thought.

"When I go away to University in Marrakesh," he said, "I wash my own clothes and my roommate and I share the cooking."

"There you are," I said. "Why must women cook just because they're women? Why do men not cook just because they're men?"

The horn blew for dinner so we returned to their home. The parents and four children lived in an enlarged hut made of stones, dirt and mortar. At night, the children grabbed blankets and slept on the sponge cushions in the main room, while the parents took the only bed in the other room.

For dinner, Rachida's parents joined us, and we knelt around the table and ate with our fingers from a common bowl. As we ate, Rachida's brother began to relate how I had said things were different in America. The mother listened, nodding. After we had finished the meal, she called to the youngest son, about ten years old, "Hey, you, clear off the table tonight. Didn't you hear how things are in America?"

This boy grew red in the face and ungraciously slammed a few wooden bowls around.

Rachida said to me, "If my mother makes my father do anything like that, you'll cause a divorce."

Rachida's eldest brother lay back on the couch.

"I have started the Revolution here in Morocco," he crowed, "From now on, wherever, I will plant the seed of this new thought."

* * *

A more sobering scenario occurred one day when I was at the local police station renewing my "green card" that allowed me to work in Morocco.

I sat in the lobby while the paperwork was going through — a process that went on indefinitely, with or without a bribe. After I had waited about an hour, a weeping, distraught peasant woman dragged in a cowering girl. They went straight to the reception desk and the woman — whom I assumed was the mother — raged and screamed at the man behind it. Occasionally she shoved the girl toward him as if to say, 'See. Look at her.' The girl stood silent, her face removed and vacant, her eyes blank.

The man spoke platitudes — yes, we will look, I will report — and soothed the mother to the point where he could lead both of them to the bench where I was sitting. The girl crouched down while the mother put her head in her hands and wept.

The man at the reception desk left to talk to some police officers in the corner. One of the officers nodded, then came over to the mother. He spoke in a low voice. Jerking her head up, she listened, and then grabbed the girl's arm. As she pushed up one sleeve of the dirty and ripped dress, I could see huge purplish bruises, three or four, leading from the wrist to the shoulder. The policeman nodded and left.

A servant brought my green card up to the desk. The man behind it called my name. I went up, troubled, and glanced back at the woman and the girl.

"Do you know what this is?" he said in French to me, bobbing his head in the direction of the mother and the daughter.

"No," I said.

"*C'est un viole*," he said, and grinned. ('It's a rape.')

Then, continuing in harsh French, "Do you know what a *viole* is?"

"Yes I know what it is," I said, enraged at his horrible grin.

"Oh yes," he said, "They're peasants and work in the fields outside of town. This morning the girl was on her way to a field and a man attacked her. Because he is married already and has children, he denies it, and refuses to marry her. That is the usual punishment in our society: if a man rapes a virgin he must marry her because he is the first man to sleep with her."

I turned away in disgust, but he hadn't finished and reached for my arm to keep me listening. I drew it away before he could touch it. He perceived the insult and grew loud.

"You saw the bruises," he sneered, "Everyone knows she was held down by force, that she had nothing to do with it, but because they are poor, no one can accuse the man, who is rich. That is why the mother is carrying on so — she knows that it will all end with her daughter marked for life as a whore, defiled and never being able to marry, because she is not a virgin."

Suddenly he was finished.

"You like that story?" He grinned and handed me my green card.

I walked out.

A List

I began to write down the comments shouted at me in the streets:

—We don't want you foreigners.

—You speak the Arabic.

—Ah, you walk back and forth seeing people. You are making a tour?

—I'm going to come to your house. Will you open the door for me?

—Ah my gazelle, you please me.

—Money!

—Lucky, lucky, you American. You have everything.

—Shame on you — you won't give your books away.

—Whore!

—One can sleep with you?

—My blond!

—You have blue eyes, Madame.

—Oh you English speakers. You never say the truth; all is twisted and lies.

—Hey nice teacher, give me English lesson?

—Beauty of America; Welcome to Morocco.

—CIA. Are you a spy?

—We know you — you aren't a tourist; you live here.

—I don't like girls.
—A fine day.
—I love you.
—Fish-and-chips. Fish-and-chips. Fish-and-chips.
—Good Morning, America.
—You think you're doing well in Morocco, don't you. Well, watch out!

Sex and Relationships

As my stay in Morocco continued, the exotic sheen wore thin and disclosed dark stains of anger, poverty and ignorance on the underlying fabric.

Earlier in the year, Amina had approached me about hiring her friend as a maid. This woman, a widow supporting two children in a hut outside of town, badly needed the money. After thinking it over I had agreed and Hajiba began cooking my meals, cleaning, and washing for me.

One night after dinner, I was correcting lessons while Hajiba washed up in the kitchen. Suddenly there was a loud smashing sound in the apartment next door followed by cries and screams. I went out on the stairwell where the landlord's apprentice joined me. We rang the doorbell and, as we waited, we heard thumps, then more screaming.

Finally my neighbor Hassan stuck out his head. I could hear Amina sobbing in the backround.

"Nothing is the matter," he said vaguely, and shut the door in our faces.

The apprentice muttered, "Drunk, drunk" and went back downstairs. I went back to my correcting.

Ten minutes later there were louder screams and thumps that seemed to go right through the wall. I went over and knocked on the door again.

This time Amina opened the door — crying hysterically — and grabbed my wrist to try and pull me inside. Hassan appeared and tried to shut the door to keep me out, while still keeping his wife in. Amina wouldn't release my wrist. I called to Hajiba to come help, and she came out of my apartment. All four of us wrestled together for a few minutes, and then we were all inside.

Hajiba put her arm around Amina and tried to soothe her as a mother would; I couldn't see their little boy. I approached Hassan who was pacing around the room.

"Hassan," I said, "Please sit down. Just sit down so we can all talk about this."

"It will be fine now, Sarah," he said, "I'm fine. It's all right now. You can leave."

He stopped pacing and went to stand by his wife. I motioned for Hajiba to leave with me. Just as I was closing the door, I looked back, and Hassan was hitting Amina on the cheek with a closed fist. I pulled Hajiba back in.

This time I pulled Hassan into another room, and pushed him down on a couch. Amina peered in.

Hassan stood up.

"I'm going to my mother," he said, pulling on his jacket over his pajamas, "I've got to get to my mother."

I stopped him before he reached the door.

"Hassan," I said, "You're not a little boy; why do you want your mother? You're acting silly. Just calm down."

He sat down again and took off the jacket. I sat down at the other end of the couch.

Hassan leaned forward and said to me, suddenly sober, "Sarah, you don't understand the Moroccans. They are. . ." (he made a circle with his forefinger and thumb) "They are zero."

Hajiba and I stayed five hours longer, until Amina tucked Hassan into bed. Then I returned to the correcting, Hajiba to the supper dishes.

* * *

Sometimes Najib, his roommate and I would spend Saturday afternoons together, drinking mint tea and talking about Morocco. One afternoon, Najib was trying to explain the sexual tension between Moroccan men and women.

"You see, every Moroccan man needs to have sex at least twice a week," he said, "When a man isn't rich enough to get married and support a household, he has to settle for something else. Prostitution is expensive, so sometimes men from the poorer quarters of the city — like where I grew up — get together in a pack and go out to find a younger boy to have intercourse with."

"But that's rape," I said.

Najib paused.

"Well, it is quite brutal," he admitted, "That's why I never participated. But it's not considered wrong. It's only the younger boy who has done wrong."

"How so?" I asked.

"Because he is the one on the bottom," Najib said, "It's only shameful if a boy, or a man, takes the female role."

His roommate nodded.

"But you foreigners are responsible for a lot of it," Najib added.

"Responsible for what?" I asked.

"For this kind of activity," Najib said, "The rich foreigners come to Morocco interested in the cheap and available young boys. I myself have seen cars drive in from Casablanca and Americans dressed in fur, wearing gold chains. They drive right to the middle of our town and offer the young boys a pencil for sex. I have seen them hold out a pencil to a young boy, in order that he get in the car with them."

* * *

Sometime after this conversation, I unwittingly observed the making of a prostitute. Out of all my students, male or female, Fatiha was especially insolent, but also pretty and appealing. Her classmates admired her spunk and daring on the one hand, but on the other, thought she was a bit too much.

She was the first girl in town to cut off her long hair — traditionally pinned up in a bun — and wear a Western-style pageboy. The day after the change, she came into the classroom and asked how I liked it. When I answered that it was very modern, her eyes gleamed.

Later on, in the middle of a lecture on the present continuous tense, she raised her hand and asked, "Miss do you make sex?"

"Close your mouth," I said, in English she could clearly understand, "Besides, I don't answer personal questions in class."

She smiled, irrepressible.

By the middle of the second semester, I realized that Fatiha hadn't been to class in a long time. I wondered if she had stopped for good, or if, like others, she would show up in the same seat months later, with a sheepish smile. I waited to see as the weeks passed.

One afternoon I was "promenading" with some friends along the main street — it was a town custom to get dressed up and parade up and down the streets on Saturday, watching everybody else and maybe shopping. A few of us were tired and sat down on a bench to rest. Immediately, I spotted Fatiha. She was strolling by, swishing the material of a new turquoise *djellaba* with a defiant swing.

She spotted me watching her and paused, unsure of whether to speak or simply pass by.

So I asked, in Arabic, "Where have you been?"

"Oh, around," she sassed.

"Well, not in the classroom," I said.

She shrugged. We stared at each other for a moment and then she turned. I watched her walk away.

One of the friends who had been listening said, "You understand she's a prostitute now."

I said, "Are you sure?"

"Yes. She first started sleeping with the Saudis. You've heard how the Saudis come to Morocco to get all the pretty virgins. Well, now she's walking the street."

"Oh," I said.

Then I knew for certain that Fatiha wouldn't return to school.

* * *

At the end of the school year, Nadia invited me to be a guest at her cousin's wedding. It was to be a traditional celebration of an arranged match — and it was an honor for a foreigner to be invited. I accepted with pleasure.

Nine o'clock on Friday evening, we began dressing at Nadia's house. She put on a heavy brocade robe edged in gold braid and gave me a white chiffon gown with silver sequins. After applying heavy make-up, we walked over to a big garage designated for the women guests. The men were in a similar structure down the street.

The room had been whitewashed, then hung with huge banners. It was crammed with women — maybe fifty or more — all dressed in their finery. We chatted together quietly.

After an hour, two sisters carried the bride in on a huge silver platter. All but her face and hands was hidden under a heavy robe, and they were painted with make-up and gold dust. Only her eyes moved — looking about fearfully. A gold necklace, spanning chin to chest, hung below the headdress of jewels. Nadia whispered to me that the outfit had been rented for the occasion.

The women sang and danced as she was held aloft, songs about the bride leaving her parents and going to a new home. Then the bridegroom and his brothers entered. The crowd of women, growing festive, shouted for him to dance. The bride was taken off the platter and the groom put in place. He attempted to dance on the platter as his brothers pushed him in the air. Afterwards, he and the bride were led to thrones at the front of the room where they sat and held court, talking to the various women who approached, before the brothers took the groom back to the men's place.

Four plump women wearing long, loose hair came in. They sang songs about the more ribald aspects of marriage and gyrated seductively. Nadia whispered that these were the *shirets* — singing prostitutes imported from another town to provide wedding entertainment.

The *shirets* alternated between the male and female buildings all night long, because they were the only women who would dance in front of the men. I asked Nadia why they were called prostitutes if they were only dancing. She said that the *shirets* wrote their addresses on small slips of paper to give to men who tucked money into their gold belts, and the men made contact at a later date.

Nadia tied a scarf around her hips — low down — and got up to dance using the pelvic undulation that every woman in the room knew. The *shirets* began to sing a song with my name in it, so I got up and tried to imitate Nadia, but couldn't. Instead, I put a ten *dirham* note in the leader's belt and sat down again.

A few hours later, the *shirets* sang a song with a different, penetrating, rhythm. The sister of the bride — who was wearing a filmy, siren-red dress — fell down on the floor in a fit, jerking and crying. Her mother and aunts surrounded her so she wouldn't hurt herself, but let her continue the thrashing. When the song ended the girl fell exhausted into a deep sleep and the older women carried her off to a side room.

"What happened to her?" I asked Nadia.

Nadia was excited. "You saw how she had on a red dress? Well, that last song contained the name of a *Gnouoa* spirit in the lyrics and the *Gnouoa* like red. So when their song was sung, one of the spirits entered her and she had the fit." (The *Genouoa* are spirits in an ancient Muslim cult.)

Refreshments were passed; we ate cookies and drank Coke while watching the dancing. A while later Nadia poked me: the sister in red was coming out of the side room, refreshed and smiling. Nadia told me that her mother and aunts had asked her about the fit but she had no memory of what had happened.

During the early morning hours the guests began to grow subdued.

"You realize what happens at the end," Nadia said, "They consummate the marriage and exhibit the blood."

"But what if there isn't any blood?" I asked.

"But she's a virgin," Nadia said.

I thought of the bride's frightened eyes and the potential disaster.

"But what if the hymen is already broken — even if she's a virgin — say if she fell on a bicycle when she was little?"

Nadia disappeared. She reappeared a few minutes later.

"I asked the bride," she told me, relieved, "and she has never ridden a bicycle."

Around ten o'clock a.m. — thirteen hours after the festivities had begun — the guests formed a parade and escorted the bride and groom to their new home. We wove through the streets banging tin pans, singing, clapping and shouting their names.

Only the relatives — and myself — entered the house; the other guests went on home. The bride and groom entered the bedroom and we waited in the salon. The mother stood post by the bedroom door. Once she looked in and then told us how things were going.

Twenty minutes later, the youngest sister was sent into the bedroom. She came out bearing something white on a silver platter. She danced and sang around the room. Then she lowered the platter to show us: a pair of bloodstained white bloomers. All the relatives around me clapped and cheered. Later the bride came out in her robe to have breakfast with us. We congratulated her and she smiled — happy that everything had gone well.

For weeks afterward, I remembered the bride's frightened eyes. I thought of her passive acceptance of the wedding ritual. When I spoke of it to Nadia, she said that some modern couples — usually the ones that had chosen their own mate — dispensed with the elaborate ceremony and got quietly married in order to save money.

"It's nothing," Nadia said, "My cousin and her husband are good together. Sometimes things don't work out so well."

Then she sang a popular song to illustrate to me how difficult — even impossible — a love relationship could be in Morocco. She translated the words to French for me, and later I translated the French to English. So, roughly paraphrased, the song goes like this:

(*Two men are walking down a road.*)

She passed by us, me and my friend.
She smiled at us, me and my friend.
I smiled back, and smiled back,
Until she was gone.
I forgot the incident.
But then I recalled it.
Had she taken the sun with her and disappeared?

I was preoccupied.
But before my preoccupation could prolong itself,
I asked myself:
What are you thinking of?
And why are you so preoccupied?
How was I going to find out what pursued me?
How was I going to find out if the smile was for my friend?
And if it wasn't, why me and not him?

A second time,
By chance, in the summer, both my friend and I were on another
    road.
We saw a pretty step,
And a third shadow that tried to pass by.

I turned,
And I saw that it was her.
Unbelievable that it was her!
She smiled that same smile, and then she was gone.
How life arrives in one moment,
And goes away again in another.

I looked for my friend, next to me,
But he wasn't next to me.
He had wanted to say something,
That was already said in my heart.
I wanted to ask him,
If he too had perceived it and had been preoccupied.
He too, he too, he too.

(Time passes.)

Now I find my friend talking,
I say, surely she has heard these words.
And if I notice a complaint in his eyes,
I say to myself, surely he has disputed with her.
I don't have any other road before me.
I have been acquainted with his road.
I have had sorrow before making the acquaintance.

I sent two messages.
No more than two.
I wrote to her:
Ease my pain; and tell me what I mean to you.
I received the answer.
And it was the answer I had been expecting.
She wrote to me:
From the beginning,
I smiled at you, my dark one.

Religion
While living in Morocco, I observed that Muslim believers seemed to
fall into two groups. One group, the nominal Muslims, didn't pay the
least attention to religious requirements, like the shopkeeper who, one
day when I was buying some shampoo, pulled out a bottle of vodka
from beneath the counter. "But," I said, knowing that alcohol was forbidden, "Aren't you a Muslim?" "Oh," he answered, "Just a little."

The devout ones took literally the name of "Islam," which means "The Submission." They rigorously followed the five pillars of the faith: Profession of Faith, Prayer, Almsgiving, Fasting and Pilgrimage to Mecca, if possible. In my mind, I thought of this group as "extremists," the believers who accounted for every happening by saying, "It's the Will of Allah."

One day a cluster of my more religious students cornered me after class and said, "Please, Miss, just repeat after us that Allah is God and Mohammed is his prophet."

"I can't do that," I said to them.

One girl took my hand and looked at me with imploring eyes. "Please Miss, or you'll go to hell," she said.

I said, "Don't you realize that all over the world, people of all different religions feel only they are going to heaven. Think of where I came from — it's a whole nation of Christians — *Nazzerani* — who believe they won't see any non-Christians in heaven."

I could tell she didn't believe me. Muslims in my village had no conception of a world past Tangiers, much less of different religions, each with its zealous converts.

"Just do it for me, Miss," said the girl. She was so sincere.

"I'm sorry," I said to her, gently, "I can't."

In my school, the faculty referred to these students and others like them as future "fanatics" — that is, political Muslims who refuse to follow the King's edicts because they obey the higher Law of Allah, represented by his Prophet Mohammed.

There was a fanatical Muslim on the faculty. He scared the other teachers because he had power. It was whispered that he had been in jail for a couple of years and hadn't repented under torture, so now he was free to teach whatever he pleased in his classes. I saw him occasionally, dressed in the simplest of robes and a white turban, silently moving about the halls.

The townspeople referred to me as "The *Nazzerani*" or "The Christian." Usually I managed to avoid clashes about religion, but sometimes I couldn't — or wouldn't.

Take, for example, the time that Nadia and Asma and I decided to travel to Fes, the traditional Holy City of Morocco and the current religious center. There was a *moussem* scheduled — a fantasia of lights and music and shooting horsemen.

We crammed into the cross-country bus with everyone else going to Fes, luggage and sheep strapped on top. As soon as we arrived, we reserved a hotel room, left our bags, and then walked to the dusty field on the outskirts of Fes where the fantasia was taking place.

Forty men in full dress — turbans, pointed slippers, robes, brocaded vests and guns — lined up on horseback at the end of the field. At the sound of the horn they raced, full gallop, guns held in the air. Halfway across the field, they shot in the air without slacking the speed and then reined sharply into the finish.

After watching the performances for an hour or so, Nadia, Asma and I wandered toward the tents set up around the perimeter. Everywhere there were lesser shows: snake charmers, acrobats, dancing ladies with tambourines, even sellers of *kif*, the Moroccan hashish.

We arrived at a huge tent encircled by a crowd. Maneuvering our way past open-mouthed gazers, we reached the front. I heard frenzied music. Nadia and Asma were staring at the scene intently. I slipped in front of a large man and saw — all at once — the sawdust ring, little boys playing drums, and a man with a lolling head making an incision in his bare stomach with a knife. It bled and then he made another one. After the fourth incision, he fell to the floor in a swoon. Another man with glazed eyes and matted hair danced in to take his place.

A row of bleeding men were lined up off to the side in various stages of exhaustion. One had ten to twelve cuts up and down his arm, the freshest just beginning to clot. Another sat humped forward so that the crowd could see the huge gashes on his bare back.

After several minutes I grew sick. I muttered something to Nadia and Asma and they followed without a word. Once outside, we agreed that it was too much mutilation. We left the *moussem* and walked back to the hotel.

Perhaps because of what we had seen we didn't walk around the city that night. Instead we stayed in our hotel room. We were lounging in pajamas on the beds, chatting, when the subject of religion came up — the bizarre sect of flagellation in the back of our minds.

Nadai asked me, "What is it exactly that Christians believe?"

"Well," I said, "I guess mainly that Christ is the Son of God and that He died on the cross for our sins and then rose again from the dead." I was being careful because I knew that in Islam, Jesus was just another prophet superseded by Mohammed.

Nadia jumped up from the bed. "Oh no Sarah," she cried out, "That's a trick. Jesus never rose; that's not right."

I said, "We're just discussing our religions. You have explained to me what it is that Muslims believe; I'm explaining what it is that Christians believe."

But she was disturbed by the thought of God having a son. She knelt on the small hard bed in her yellow pajamas — body bowed in submission — and began to reel off long clumps of the Koran in classical Arabic.

As the minutes passed, her voice got more and more sing-song and she rocked back and forth.

When I glanced at Asma out of the corner of my eye, I could see that she was moved by this exhibition of faith. I thought of the small boys I had seen in the Koranic schools in the village, chanting and rocking for hours. Suddenly, I was angry. What right did Nadia have to quote me verses from her holy book in a language I couldn't even understand? Did she think that just the act of saying them would make me aware of the error of my ways and come to see the light of the true Islamic religion?

This anger made me rash. I began to recite — loudly and in English — all the Bible verses I could dredge up from Sunday School Memory Contests. For several minutes Nadia and I refused to stop. We knelt on our beds yelling out verses from the Koran and the Bible.

Soon Asma had had enough.

"Stop, stop," she said.

Nadia and I paused for breath.

"We can't resolve this," Asma said, "We are all devout believers and can't convince each other because we believe too strongly."

Nadia and I both nodded.

"Now Sarah," Asma said, "even in your religion you agree that God is never wrong."

"That's true," I said.

"So," she continued, "that means either you are wrong, or we are wrong."

I shrugged; as far as I could tell, there was no way Christ could be the son of God and *not* be the son of God at the same time.

"So," Asma said, "We won't know until after death and the Judgment who has been wrong all this time."

And that's where we left it; each of us confident that the other would eventually see the unreasonableness of her position.

✳ ✳ ✳

While living in Morocco, I was the underdog — a Christian living in an Islamic country, an infidel heathen residing in the land of the true believers. Part of the fault of that night lay in my desire for Nadia and Asma — two intelligent, talented, Moroccan women — to view their religion from a global perspective, one religion among the many of the world. But this was impossible; they had never been out of the country, had never lived away from their families, had never had a chance to view their life from another perspective.

The three of us never discussed religion again. Whenever Nadia stayed overnight, she continued to wash herself in my squat and then kneel on a shawl facing east to pray. I ignored this, just as she ignored my Messiah tapes at Christmas, after I once translated some of the words.

* * *

Out in the country, religion got inextricably mixed with sorcery and folk tales. One day a peasant boy told me a story:

"Norredine the villager went to the *hemem*. He was bathing himself and rubbing vigorously with his *kis* when he realized he couldn't reach his back, so he looked around for someone else to do that part for him. The only other bather was a silent, sullen man in the corner, so Norredine asked him politely if he wouldn't mind scrubbing his back.

"The man came over and took the *kis*. As he was scrubbing, Norredine looked down and noticed that the man had cloven feet like a camel. Even though he was in the steaming bath, Norredine grew cold all over and began to tremble. The stranger finished, handed Norredine the *kis*, and returned to his spot without saying a word.

"Norredine finished his bath as quickly as he could, and dressed — mixing up the sleeves of his robe in his haste — and scurried out blinking into the bright sunlight. He went to his usual cafe on the corner and sat down with his friends. After his glass of mint tea arrived he began telling his story.

"When Norredine got to the part where the stranger had cloven hooves like a camel, his best friend sitting next to him, stood up and said, pointing at his own feet, 'Were they like this?' Norredine looked down and where his friend's pointed slippers should have been he saw the cloven feet of a camel. He screamed and fell out of his chair, spilling his tea. He never recovered, but remained a babbling idiot and spent the rest of his life in the insane asylum."

The boy finished the story and looked up at me with eyes wide at the horror of it all.

"That's not true," said his older brother, who was home on vacation from university, and had advanced further than peasant *jinoon* tales.

"It is too," said the little boy, fierce and bright, "It is very true."

The Cheating

While in Morooco, I considered myself first a schoolteacher, and secondly a Peace Corps Volunteer. Most of my waking time — just as it would be in the States — was spent on the job. I taught two junior classes and one senior class of English five days a week — Tuesdays and Sundays off — at the town High School of Letters.

In the beginning, when I wasn't accustomed to classes of fifty students with barely a book between them, or blackboards without chalk or erasers to go with them, I made many mistakes. They were insignificant errors that were humorous to all. As the months wore on, however, and I persisted in taking my job seriously, mistakes were made — both by me and the students — that had larger, more encompassing consequences. Let me illustrate by recounting four incidents, two that happened at the beginning of my first year, and two that happened well into my term.

During my first year I found it difficult to pronounce the students' names correctly in Arabic, so there was general snickering every time I took roll. This snickering extended into class time, and I didn't get very far in the lesson.

To counteract the problem, I arranged a seating chart that split up the loudest snickerers. On a chosen day, I walked into class, took roll (in order to establish who was actually present) and walked around the classroom tapping each desk and pronouncing the name of the student supposed to be there.

"Now," I said, "Move to your correct seat."

Wails and complaints assaulted me. I stood firm.

"Move," I repeated, "From now on you will sit according to the seating chart."

A few of the girl students timidly went to stand by their new desks but the boys — men really — already sitting there wouldn't move. I recognized one of them, a boy with dark curly hair and a sullen face called Hamid.

The class teetered on the edge of chaos. I knew that if just one of the difficult boys moved, everyone would move and I would be able to get through a lesson. I looked at Hamid and he stared back at me, arrogant, scowling, defiant.

Suddenly a rage filled me: I was their teacher, trained, qualified, smart. How dare a bunch of schoolchildren refuse to do what I, their teacher, had asked?

"Get up!" I screamed at them in English, not caring that they couldn't understand such a furious torrent of foreign words, "Move immediately. I won't have it. I'm the teacher and you do as I say or you are out."

I slapped at the desk nearest me. "Right now — fast. Get to your correct seat. I'm sick of you defying me and not doing as I ask. Hamid, get out of that seat and move to your desk, NOW!" and I pointed at him, finger shaking.

There was a stunned silence as the class took in my anger and the screaming of English words. Then, perhaps in admiration of my fine show of authority, or perhaps simply in admiration of a fine performance, they all raised their hands high in the air and clapped, whistling and cheering. And then, cheerfully, with a rustling of robes and papers, they found their new seats, not one student out of place.

This class was more productive after the new seating chart, but there were still problems. They didn't learn fast and couldn't keep up with the assignments. After a few weeks I noticed that even though I had assigned the textbook in the beginning, there were only a few copies around the classroom. When I referred to a certain page, most of the students got up and clustered around the student nearest them who had the book.

"What does this mean?" I asked one day. "I assigned you the textbook." (I held up my copy that I had purchased at 12 *dirhams*, or approximately $1.50.) "Why haven't you bought the book?"

There was a low growl from all sides of the room.

"What is it?" I asked again. "How come most of you haven't bought the book?"

The muttering increased, and then one student, one of the poorer ones in a wooly brown peasant robe, stood up.

"Miss," he said, trying his best in English, "You understand the book is too expensive."

"Oh," I said. Then I thought. "But some of you spend more money on other things. You buy cigarettes." (I made the motion of smoking.) "A packet of black-market Marlboros is as much as two-thirds of this book. Or if you didn't go to the cinema for three weeks you could buy the book."

There was open arguing back and forth. The one of the wealthier students — a stylish young man who sat in the back wearing store-bought shirts, narrow trousers and leather shoes — stood up.

"You are right, Miss," he said, "It's not too expensive."

All over the room students leaped to their feet. Screaming, shouting, pointing at him, they forced him back down into his seat with their obvious resentment of his wealth. Two boys began fighting off to the side; a girl's desk was pushed and she fell onto the floor. The roar grew louder and out of the corner of my eye I could see a boy throwing the textbook at the wall.

"Stop it," I shouted, "Sit down all of you."

I waded into the middle of it all, slamming my teacher's manual against desks to make loud CRACKING sounds, and trying to push boys back into their seats.

"Now," I said, as I walked back up to the front, "This is what we will do. Two students share each desk. One of these students must have a book. Some of you have books already, some of you must buy one. But tomorrow, I want every desk to have a book."

They nodded their heads, understanding and approving. This was reasonable.

* * *

Things were serene for months afterward. Then I began to be aware of larger, less-easily solved problems beneath the surface.

For one, no matter what threats I uttered, or what vigilance I gave to catching the offenders, the majority of the students cheated on tests, exams, and homework assignments. I understood that the Moroccan school system fostered this temptation, because only an educated person could hope to get one of the few available jobs, even with some palm-greasing. But I also felt that if I couldn't give each student an accurate grade, I might as well not teach. For the sake of academic integrity alone, I had to grade according to knowledge and merit, rather than according to which student was the most cunning in his efforts to avoid an accurate grade.

At the end of the semester, I gave the final exam, graded it and then averaged out semester grades. During class, I called each student up to my desk to show the final grade. Grades were calculated on a scale of one to twenty. A Moroccan saying has it that twenty is for the Prophet Mohammed, nineteen for the King, eighteen for the best student and so on, all the way down to zero, with the *moyenne* — or average passing grade — being ten.

I called Hamid — the well-dressed one — up to my desk. His final grade was a number eight. He was extremely upset.

"But look," I showed him the line of figures in my gradebook, "These are all your scores, and they average out to an eight."

"You can't give me a below-average grade," he said to me, genuinely shocked, "My father is the richest man in this town."

"This will be your grade," I said, "It's the grade you deserve. Now leave."

After school, he and a friend were waiting. They followed me back to my apartment chanting, "Miss, Miss, please change the grade, just to a ten, just to the average, please." I never said a word, just shut the door in their faces.

The next morning I was organizing my materials in the classroom, waiting for the bell, when I noticed another teacher of English — a young Moroccan man I had seen at teacher's meetings — beckoning to me from the hall.

"Sarah," he said, "I understand you are going to give Hamid a below-passing grade."

"It's an accurate grade," I said.

"Oh, I'm sure it is," he said, "It's just that his father is the wealthiest man in our town, and his father doesn't want him to get low marks."

"I don't care what his father wants," I said.

"There's just one more thing," the teacher said, visibly embarrassed, "I share a house with Hamid's brother. I've been sent by the family, to you as a fellow teacher, to change his grade."

Suddenly, I understood. I had passed his house. It was a nice little bungalow with a yard — much more than a teacher could afford.

"Please," he said, appealing to me directly, "Will you change his grade?"

"No," I said, and walked back in the classroom.

I ignored the whispering and walked up to the blackboard. I was very angry, but determined not to show it to the students, all of whom by now knew what was happening.

"Turn in your books to page 23," I said.

After school Nadia came to my apartment. Her family lived in a village a one-hour bus ride away, so on the days when she had classes back to back she spent the nights with me. I told her about the incident. She wasn't surprised.

"It's very difficult Sarah," she said, "To fight against the corruption. I try to, but am not always successful. Just be sure to mark down his grade in the gradebook as '08' instead of plain '8' because he might try to sneak in and put a '1' in front of your '8' and change it that way."

"Thanks for the warning," I said.

The next morning instead of going to my classroom, I went to the teacher's salon to record my grades. Each student had one gradebook, and the teacher marked down the grade in the space next to the proper subject. When I came to Hamid's English slot, I carefully penned in "08." As I left, I nodded good-bye to the *shaoush* guarding the door; his sole responsibility was to let only the teachers in and keep the students out.

Nadia came over about suppertime.

"Sarah," she said as I let her in, "You'll never believe what happened with Hamid's grade." Her voice was shaking with anger. "Sometimes I cannot stand it. I was in the salon marking my grades, when the History teacher came in — you know her, she's very wealthy and is friends with the *moudir*. Well, she began marking her grades and she came to Hamid's name, who is a student of hers in history. She told us that she had been instructed to add five points onto his History grade to make up for his

English grade. So she gave him a '17' in History, instead of the '12' he was supposed to get."

It was hopeless.

"Oh Nadia," I said, "Don't you be upset. It's too bad but it's my problem."

"But that's just it," Nadia said, "I told her she shouldn't change the grade – that it was too corrupt, even here in Morocco – and another teacher who was listening, sneered at me and said, 'Do you think you are in the United States or something?'"

We ate our dinner in silence and listened to the street noises coming through the open window. All I could think was that Hamid had won; when his grades were averaged together, he would do fine, because his History grade would make up for the English one. He had swerved around me and was speeding down the path of academic success without obstacle.

*   *   *

The school year wore on. The cheating abated somewhat, but I suspected that the worst students had been told to stay out of my classes, because I wouldn't be bribed. Toward the end of the year, when the tension was at its highest because only a small percentage of students were allowed to pass, and those who failed would have to drop out of school forever, something happened that made the "Hamid Incident" seem trivial.

I was collecting my books and materials after class – including the sponge I carried to erase the board – when I realized my gradebook was missing. I searched underneath the desk, looked around the room, even went through my bag, although I knew immediately that it had been stolen. There was nothing to do but report it to the *moudir*.

"Are you sure?" The *moudir* was skeptical. He was an intimidating man who had achieved his powerful position by means I sensed rather than actually knew; he emanated an air of corrupt ambition and cruelty.

"Of course, I'm sure," I answered, keeping my words precise and clear in French, the second language for both of us.

"Well, why do you bring your gradebook to class in the first place?" asked the *moudir* and looked at me angrily.

I stared blankly for a moment.

"Because I have to write down attendance and grades and extra-credit assignments."

"Well, you shouldn't, you know. The temptation is too much for these students. If the gradebook is there in front of them . . ." He let the sentence trail off.

"Anyway, you go teach your next class," he said, "And leave the problem to us."

By "us" I knew he meant the three Moroccan bodyguards he surrounded himself with. In my mind, I had referred to them as the "Goon Squad" ever since they had come into the classroom one day to push around some troublemakers. I had watched as they had lifted students out of desks and threw them against the wall. I had cringed as one had raised his huge boot and literally kicked a student out of the seat. I didn't want to think about the "Goon Squad" and its methods of finding my gradebook, so I nodded and left.

At the end of the day, I was called back into the *moudir*'s office. Cowering in the corner was one of my poorest, slowest, and generally, weakest students.

"Here," said the *moudir*, handing me my gradebook, "This one took it."

I flipped through until I got to the right page. Sure enough, about eight students had changed their grades. They had used the same color of pen, so it was hard to tell at first glance, but looking closely, I saw that a consistently "6" and "7" student now had "16's" and "17's" and that some had even changed "0's" to "8's" by putting a line through the circle, and a few had blatantly crossed out old grades and written in new ones.

"Listen," I said to the *moudir*, "This boy is just a scapegoat. The more assured, smarter students got him to change the grades so they couldn't be traced."

I showed him the changes.

"All right," he said, "I'll take care of these students." He wrote down some names. I noticed that he didn't write down the names of the daughter of the Police Commissioner or the son of the man who hosted the national soccer team.

I knew that he was going to punish the boy and have done with it.

"Fine," I said, "And I'll put a zero in place of every grade that has been changed."

"And I'll expel this boy for good," said the *moudir*.

"Don't do that," I said.

"Why not?" asked the *moudir*, "I thought you'd be happy with that punishment."

"For the right person, yes," I said, "But this boy is just stupid. He's not mean or malicious like the other, smarter students who talked him into stealing the gradebook. They're the ones who should be expelled."

"Tell you what," said the *moudir*, irritated that I wasn't going along with his plan, "I won't expel him, just suspend him for a few days. But then, you don't change the grades to zeros — that's too hard on the others."

I wondered how it was that I had gotten into the position of bargaining. "All right," I gave in.

As I left, a ragged woman with a dark scarf covering her face ran up to me. She grabbed my hand and kissed, then got down on her knees and garbled out some plea.

"She doesn't want you to expel her son," the *moudir*, watching, called.

I pulled my hand away and went back to my apartment where I was safe, where I didn't have to face another Moroccan student or administrator until the next day.

Peace Corps Aftershock

Six months before my two-year term was due to end, I was medically evacuated back to the States. The evacuation came suddenly. I had been sick with a variety of intestinal ailments for a long time, but then, it seemed as if all the volunteers were sick. On the Paris-New York plane flight everything became bigger, whiter and brighter. The business of living — for the first time in months — seemed manageable and desirable.

After landing in New York, I flew on to Washington, D.C., where I underwent a three-week battery of physical and psychological exams. Once again, I was living in the U.S. I began to try and re-assimilate into the culture to which I had once belonged. I quickly found that I had underestimated the changes that had taken place, changes that were a result of my experience as a Peace Corps Volunteer.

First, and most obviously, my behavior toward men in public places had become extreme. Whether walking to an appointment in the streets of Georgetown or at a restaurant, I reacted to the presence of strange males by cowering and shrinking back in fear of being harrassed. My sensitivity was made clear one Sunday morning when I was touring the sights of the Capitol alone. As I walked past the White House gate, a guard said, "hello" and I fled back to my hotel room, certain that he thought I was a whore and was propositioning me.

Then, the abundance of material things — especially food — shocked me. Every trip to the grocery store was pure confusion at having to choose between so many options or seeing a steak looking obscene in its redness and blood. To celebrate my return, a cousin took me out to dinner. While perusing the menu, she remarked on an item containing cheese. Startled, I blurted, "Cheese? You can get cheese here?" As she looked at me blankly, I froze — completely lost in distance and perspective.

Things that might have seemed a pleasure upon returning from a more

ordinary kind of trip became a kind of torture for me. For example, taking a hot shower every day if I wished. I had gone to the *hemem* once
a week for so long that I only felt bewildered, and had a kind of disgust
when I turned on the "H" spigot in the bathroom. Somehow it was all
too easy and convenient. Every time I put on shoes, I stared at the henna
dye Amina had put on my feet for a celebration preceding my departure. For months, my rust-colored toenails stayed a reminder of my past
life when what I wanted was to wipe out all traces of a disturbing
experience.

After the three weeks of testing were completed, it was recommended
that I not return to Morocco. The reasons for this were partly physical:
several nodules (probably stress-related) had been discovered on my
small intestine. More important, however, was that I was diagnosed as
suffering from acute psychological distress. I flew back to my parents'
home in Minnesota, and, during the months of alienation that followed,
I tried to sort out what had happened. It was during this time that I
had to acknowledge some drastic changes: my personality presented
as confused and defensive; my mind was disoriented, and conflicting
emotions kept me a shattered wreck. In short, I wasn't functioning.

A few months later, I received a letter from one of my students, sent
on to my parents' address. It read:

Dear Miss:
I was sorry, with all affliction and despair to hear of your leavetaking.
The administration told us you are ill with "SIDA." Please write and
assure me that this is not true, as you are the best teacher of English of all.

Sincerely,
Your student.

SIDA is the French acronym for AIDS. I understood that someone —
possibly even the *moudir* himself — had started the rumor flying that
I had gone back to the States because I was dying of AIDS. I didn't feel
angry, only a bitter amusement, that this was the Moroccan interpretation of the ending of my career as a Peace Corps Volunteer.

I sat down to answer my former student's letter. First, I wrote that
I appreciated being called the "best teacher of English of all." Then I told
him that he was a very good student and should be sure to continue
his studies. Finally, I wrote that I did not have "SIDA" and that I was
in no danger of dying. At this point I faltered; how could I explain my
sudden departure? I thought and then wrote: "I'm sorry I left so suddenly, but it was necessary for personal reasons."

A few months before leaving, an old friend had visited me in Morocco.

During his visit we had become engaged to be married. Certain that my former student would read "personal reasons" to mean "fiancé" and, although not accurate, satisfied with this interpretation, I signed my name and sealed the letter. As I dropped it in the airmail box, I knew this information would be relayed to anyone in Morocco who truly cared about my whereabouts.

* * *

The post-traumatic stress seemed to center around one particular incident that had happened a few months before I had been evacuated. I could remember it vividly:

Nadia and I were on our way to the market to buy eggs and vegetables for supper. It was the dusky time of day, when the robed women bustled around the stalls, purchasing food and screaming for better bargains. The children played without clothes in the dirt while the men leaned against the buildings and smoked. Everyone was moving fast to get business done before the dark deepened into another black, airless, desert night.

I had slipped my *djellaba* over my jeans and T-shirt and was carrying the straw basket to hold the food. Nadia and I wove around the boys spinning thread in the alley. We reached the main street. Nadia took hold of the basket to propel us through the crowd; I was on the outside, Nadia was further in toward the wall of shops.

Some stones thudded behind me; I felt grit and dust swirl around my bare ankles. I didn't look back, not wanting to react in case the stones weren't meant for me — it was so crowded they could have been meant for someone else. Then a bigger stone — it felt about the size of a ripe olive — hit me square on the back of the calf. Another followed, going slightly wide of the mark, and just brushing my waist. I cried out and stopped.

My calf stung viciously (I was to have a bruise that lasted for a week) but mostly I was scared — and angry. The crowd jostled against me. No one gave the slightest sign of noticing the incident, other than stepping around me as I stood, not moving.

"Sarah, let's go," Nadia was tugging at my arm, "Don't stop in the middle of the street."

She was speaking in French, a sign that she didn't want the people around to catch what we were saying.

"Do you know what they did?" I said, "They threw stones at me. One hit me — what if it had been my head? — I could have been badly hurt."

"It's nothing, Sarah," she said, "Just keep walking; don't stop."

"What do you mean it's nothing?" I asked, "They're throwing stones at me for God's sake. It's not nothing."

People flowed by. I tried to catch someone's eye. Had no one seen the stone or heard my cry — or was even wondering why I was stopped in the middle of the street arguing with Nadia?

"Please Sarah," Nadia was begging now, "You've got to keep walking. You can't do anything."

Suddenly, I sagged inside. I knew she was right. Even if I had seen who had thrown the stone. . .I raised my head and by some instinct looked straight across the street. In a gap in the crowd I could see a group of young men, well-dressed, exuding strength. They were looking at me and laughing.

I recognized one — he had been my student once, a serious, respectful student. As I was looking he slapped another on the back, as if saying, "Well done." He looked up, met my eyes for the barest of instants, then turned away. The group huddled, arms around each other's shoulders. The crowd closed in, I couldn't see them anymore, and Nadia led me away.

I completed the shopping trip in a daze. My mind convoluted on the possibilities: Had the stones been meant for me? Why? Why my student!? Nadia selected peas and tomatos for our omelette. I automatically held the basket as she dumped in the packages wrapped in newspaper. I followed her back to my apartment.

In my living room, I slumped down. Now Nadia was willing to talk.

"Forget about it, Sarah," she said, sitting down across from me, "It's different here. It's no good to think about it because you can't do anything."

"Has it ever happened to you?" I asked.

"Well, no," she admitted, "but I have heard of stonings. It used to be a punishment — it was an old Arab custom to stone bad women — but that has changed."

"Not so very much," I said.

"Sarah, you are not a bad woman," she said to me.

"But everyone thinks I am a bad woman," I said, "Because I have blond hair and am American, and live by myself without a brother or a cousin or an uncle to take care of me."

"Yes. . .," Nadia's voice weakened; she didn't want to agree with me, but couldn't think of anything else to say.

"I hate them," I said to her.

"Shh, Sarah," she said, getting up to cook our meal, "Just forget about it."

* * *

But I hadn't been able to forget about it. Originally, I had blamed myself: I shouldn't have been walking in the street/maybe it had happened because I had previously caught one of the boys cheating on an exam/I had always been conspicuous with my blond hair so I should have been more aware of the danger. Then the blame had shifted to the boys — after all, I had seen the congratulatory-slap-on-the-back — and lastly, it veered over to the Peace Corps Organization, and there it stayed.

The fault, I felt, lay in the lack of preparation for volunteers. Peace Corps officials had never acknowledged the enormous difference in lifestyle and esteem any American woman would have to face in an Arabic/Muslim country. They had not accounted for the Koranic system of learning — memorizing and recitation — that confronted teachers trained in the Western, Socratic system of question and answer. And they had not emphasized the sacrifices (beyond time and money) required of volunteers to Morocco: health, well-being, and safety.

Reeling from the violence I had encountered, I felt the Peace Corps hadn't prepared volunteers for the risk and the danger. Sure, they admitted a risk — even to the point of glorifying it in their slogan: "Peace Corps — the toughest job you'll ever love." But this risk was never defined. It was left vague — perhaps contracting hepatitis? Having to evacuate your post in case of political turmoil? Never was it specified that — especially in the case of white American women in Arabic countries — the risk might come in the form of personal violence.

I began to compile a list of volunteer casualties in Morocco during my term alone:

—A volunteer couple living in a small town were forced against the wall of their house by a mob throwing stones. The man stood in front of the woman who covered her head with her hands and crouched against the house. When the mob ran out of stones, the man had a deep cut below one eye and the woman's hands were bruised and cut.

—One woman volunteer was assaulted during daylight — while at her post — and raped.

—A volunteer was walking in his city one night when a Moroccan man he didn't know accosted him with a razor and cut him across the cheek before he could fend him off.

—Another volunteer confiscated the exams of several students he had caught blatantly cheating. The next day he received death threats. When they continued, he changed locations.

—A volunteer posted in a big city was riding his bicycle home from a party one night when a group of men — apparently waiting for him — stepped out and forced him off the bicycle, then attacked him with broken bottles, leaving him cut-up and bruised.

—One volunteer was driving when he had a fatal car accident. There were rumors of suicide, although no one knew for certain. A Peace Corps "official" — the only one I had ever met who seemed to know what went on outside of Washington, D.C. — escorted the body back to the States. Later I found out this person was leaving. I asked why. He said to me, "There are a lot of reasons. One is that this is not the first time my job has included accompanying a body back to the family. I fly with the casket on the plane. Then I meet the parents. And you know, it's just getting to be too hard to do."

And every year a new batch of volunteers is sent to Morocco.

I asked someone in Peace Corps Washington why at least the women weren't warned before being posted in Morocco?

"Well, the Peace Corps doesn't want to be sexist," was the answer, "If they admitted a certain country was unsafe for women volunteers, in order to avoid being sexist, they would have to stop sending the men too. Then there wouldn't be any volunteers in Morocco, and that, of course, wouldn't be acceptable."

I knew why "of course" it wouldn't be acceptable. The U.S. currently enjoys a friendly relationship with King Hassan of Morocco. In official language: "The U.S. cannot turn a blind eye to the fact that Morocco has historically been a good friend and indeed, in a practical sense, an ally. . . .we need to nurture our relations as never before with all Islamic and non-aligned states, but we particularly need to stand up for and support our avowed friends and supporters."*

Translated, this means that the U.S. cannot afford to offend a politically sensitive country by the cessation of peace offerings, i.e., volunteers.

Questions filled my mind. Had I asked to be used as a peace offering? I recalled a conversation I had once had with a Belgian who was in Morocco for his two years of civil service.

"You realize why we're all here," he had said to me, "All of us, the Americans, French, those of us from Belgium, even the British. We're all here for the attention. As foreigners, we're given attention in Morocco whether it's good or bad. Even if the natives stare at you and make nasty remarks in a language you can't understand and spit as you walk by, you are at least noticed. Your existence matters, even if it is acknowledged in a negative way. Whereas if you work in a big city — let's say New York — and travel with a mass of humanity on the subways each day, you are given no indication of your existence whatsoever. If you dropped dead, people would step around you to catch the right line for their suburb. It's addictive to stay here; it's addicting to be given

* Harold J. Saunders, testifying as U.S. Assistant Secretary of State for Near Eastern and South Asian affairs before the Africa subcommittee of the House of Representatives Foreign Affairs Committee.

attention all day long, every day, in a thousand little ways. And it's devastating to return to a society where you are completely ignored. No wonder we tolerate anything, take any kind of job in order to keep on."

His words to some extent, were true. But that hadn't been the whole reason for my wanting to be a volunteer in Morocco. I had wanted to help. I had wanted change things. I had wanted to participate in a cross-cultural interaction that wasn't tainted by idealism or colonialism. And so I taught English, in a village, on the train line between Casablanca and Marrakesh.

Dreams of Students
Six months after my return, I was going through my belongings in preparation for getting married and moving to Arizona. Stuffed in the back of my closet was a leather satchel from Morocco that I had never unpacked. Inside were teaching materials: English texts, gradebook, lesson plans and a folded batch of students' papers. As I rifled through these, I caught the title "My Dream" on one, and recalled the circumstances. Once a month or so, I had assigned a creative essay so that my students could practice writing down their thoughts instead of copying textbook compositions.

"Write an essay about your dreams," I had said, "Write in your best essay form about what you dream of having in life, what kind of person you dream of being." I took the essays and began to read:

"Last week I had a dream, and a nice dream it was. I was very happy because I won 8,000,000 *dirhams* and then I built a long Factory and I bought a new car for my dad. 3 weeks ago I traveled to New York to get married to an American woman, and to get very rich. Then I bought a villa in Florida. So I was living in it, near the American people with my wife. The villa was named 'KHADIJA' (who is my mother). A minute ago, when I got up, I didn't find anything. Oh, it was a good dream but it was a dangerous dream, because it made me think foolishly."

* * *

"When some one dreams while sleeping he dreams about what keeps his mind during the day especially the things that are out of his power to reach like happiness and a good house. As I'm a hopeful person I always dream about good things that always make me imagine having a wonderful life. Once while I was sleeping I saw myself as an important person working in an office in a great company and with the wages that I got from it I could buy a good house and marry a pretty girl who was a rich man's daughter. The people became jealous of my unusual situation, but unfortunately when I woke up I found myself in a poor room and on an old bed. If only I hadn't dreamed this kind of dream."

* * *

"I can remember my last dream because it was a very good and nice dream.

In my dream I saw a beautiful and a nice young man who told me 'let's get married,' but my father refused because the gentleman wasn't very rich and I must finish my studies.

I started to shout and cry 'No. I love him. You can't refuse' when all my family woke-up.

I was very ashamed because all my family heard what I said.

From this dream I hope never to dream.

What a lovely dream!"

* * *

"Last night I dreamed a funny dream. I hadn't any money and I wanted to do something to get some money. Then when I was walking down a street I saw a purse under a little car. I took it then I opened it. I found so much money! I decided to go to the pub, and I asked the waiter to give me one drink. While I was drinking, a drunkard came, and sat near me, but I didn't say anything to him. A few minutes later he told me to buy him some more glasses of wine. I refused and I told him to let me alone but he didn't want to and he began to insult me. I couldn't bear being that near all the people. Then I took a bottle, and hit him on his head and then the blood began to trickle. I was afraid and I escaped."

A Postscript

It is winter now, almost four years to the day, after my return. I'm working on some pieces about Morocco. As I write, it gets chilly in the study. For some reason, instead of a sweater, I go and get my black leather jacket from the back of the closet. I slip it on and smell it; that odor making the place perceptible: Casablanca, Morocco.

Nadia and her brother have taken me to the leather shops in the medina to buy a jacket. We go in and out and finally settle on one that is displaying all sorts of leather goods — footstools, book covers, slippers, drums, belts, jackets. I look at the row of jackets. Some are fancy, with designs handstitched in contrasting colors for the tourists. I try on a plain, black one. It is good, strong leather with a leather collar and sleeves — not the ribbed knit — and has both front zipper and snaps to keep out the cold. I try it on and look in the mirror: Does it make me look tough enough? I think so. In the back corner I whisper to Nadia that it is the one I want. She motions to her brother. They bring the jacket and confront the store owner on my behalf.

"No, that's too expensive."

"She can't afford that; she's not a typical American tourist."

"No, she's with Peace Corps — they live like beggars — give her a good price."

"Well, that's better, but I tell you, it's too expensive."

"Now listen, I know you paid one-fourth of that to the leather worker."

"You think I don't see what you're trying to do?"

"Still too high, and don't think she won't know it, but we'll settle for that."

"If you throw in one of those leather bookcovers."

I continue at the computer, wearing the jacket that still smells of those years, redolent of a place and a people — an odor of a former life: heavy, acrid, stark.

After several hours, I turn off the computer, tug the jacket tight over my slumped shoulders, and weep.

Kathleen Coskran

THE COOK'S CHILD

"I'M GETTING ONLY floribundas this time, Angel Face and Orangeade. They're tougher than the teas and relatively free of disease. Guaranteed to make it in Africa." I was flipping through the Burpee catalog. It was our fourth year in Addis Ababa. "No more roses named after people. Last year was a wasteland, what with the Madam Hardys and Mrs. John Laings getting black spot and dying all over the place. I couldn't bear that again."

Felix put his finger in the journal he was reading and looked at the picture of the cook's child on the wall behind him, my beauty, Hannah, at twelve months, taking her first step, wearing the daisy nightgown from Sears. "I thought you spent your days printing old negatives of that child," he said.

"I've been known to do two things at once," I said. "Sometimes three." He was chief surgeon at Haile Selassie Hospital. I was gardening and trying to have a baby, but my roses never lasted a year and I was definitely not pregnant. So I'd ordered new catalogs, books on roses, and photography manuals. There had to be something I could do.

I wanted an old world rose garden like Mama's, and was charting, soil testing, and fertilizing as recommended because the previous year's bushes hadn't taken hold — the air was too thin, too hot, or too cold, there was too much rain or not enough. The seasons weren't normal in Ethiopia. It was either raining or not raining, with no regular spring, summer, fall, winter. *The Rose Diet* said to fertilize in the spring, but I could never decide when that was.

"Your mama was the rosarian, sweetheart. Give it up." He went back to his reading.

"I can't." He had no idea what I was going through, planting roses that died all around me and loving a child who didn't belong to me, whom I hadn't seen in fifty-seven days.

I needed to keep busy. As the roses withered, my photographs got bigger. "I'm cultivating the odd angle," I said, later, showing Felix a sixteen by twenty of Hannah that bisected her at the ear.

"Your picture is skewed," he said.

"It's all preparation for the Cosmic Photo." I was planning a shot of the stars wheeling across the sky and figured that all I had to do was to position the camera in the back yard with the lens open and pointing up on a clear night.

I'd tried it a couple of times since Hannah left, but something always ruined it. The first time, Abebe, the night watchman, shone his flashlight in the aperture. "There are spirits in your machine, Madam." At the next attempt, high cirrus clouds blurred the path of the stars. And, on the last moonless night, Flea Trap, in heat, lured an African mutt under the compound wall for a bit of canine passion beneath the tripod. So I was still waiting.

I'd photographed the child daily, until the cook snatched her away. I think I was trying to preserve her on film, as if pictures could protect her. She was so fragile, with her velvet braids cupping her smooth, cameo face, the butterfly mouth under luminous eyes, her tiny feet, doll hands.

She was born in our house the same year I lost Elizabeth. "Miscarried," my husband, the doctor, said. "You don't name a fetus. It's easier to forget."

That was January 1967, and Hannah was born in December, just before the new year, on the floor in my bedroom. I was in the studio, hanging the black curtains for the dark room and the cook was sweeping. I heard a funny sound and went to the door. She was slumped against the wall with a startled expression on her face.

"What is it?" I said.

"Baby coming," she said.

I craned my neck. "Baby coming? Where?"

"Here," she said, patting her belly. "I go home now." She was a broad-beamed, country woman with tatoos ringing her neck — too fat for the pregnancy to show — but it was her fourth child and she didn't make it out of the room. The baby was born on the throw rug, received by my clammy hands. A girl.

"I call her Sissy, for you, Madam," the cook said.

I held the child, glistening in her own birth sweat. She opened her black eyes and looked right at me. "No," I said, "Elizabeth."

The cook shook her head. "What is your mother's name?"

"Anna."

"Ah," she said. "Hannah. I call her Hannah."

"Hannah Rose," I said.

"Is good?"

"Yes," I said, lifting Hannah Rose's damp body to my lips. "Is good."

* * *

The cook and I raised her together, me reading Dr. Spock aloud, her fixing dinner. Sometimes she laughed so hard, she had to stop peeling the potatoes to wipe her eyes on the corner of her apron. When I told her Dr. Spock was a man, she laughed until tears came. "He know baby like all man do," she said.

Felix paid no attention to Hannah until she began walking, and then he was continually annoyed. She learned to tiptoe and whisper when he was home.

One morning she and I were playing hide and seek. "Peek-a-boo," I said and she dashed away from me, knocking his humidor on the floor. Tobacco billowed around her.

"Ah," she said, raising her eyebrows and sucking in her breath. She glanced at Felix, then began scooping double handfuls of tobacco back in the humidor.

"Stop her," Felix said.

Hannah filled her hands again.

"Wait, Honey. I'll get the broom," I said.

The cook appeared at the kitchen door just then, with a tray in her hands.

Felix waved his journal at her, before she was all the way in the room. "I can't work with that child racing through my house," he said. "I don't want her here again. Do I make myself clear?"

The cups clattered on the saucers. "Yes," the cook said. She put the tray on the table, then gave a sharp order to Hannah in Amharic.

I had picked Hannah up, but she kneed me in the stomach, crying and struggling to get down. "It's okay. It's okay," I whispered in her ear.

"Madam?" The cook held out her arms.

I let Hannah slide down my leg and the cook swooped her up. The two of them backed toward the swinging kitchen door until they disappeared.

"The child is terrified of you. I won't have it," I said.

He threw his hands up. "What won't you have? This girl racing through the house at will, upsetting my things? Why not the whole family? We are not paying this woman to raise her children in our living room. We are paying her to cook our food and clean our house."

The cook reappeared with a broom to sweep up the tobacco.

I forced myself to smile. "She belongs here, near her mother," I said quietly. "Since her father died, we're all the family she has. It's the right thing to do."

He fumbled for a pipe from his rack, pulled out his favorite Arusha meerschaum, and tapped the bowl against his palm before facing me. "That was Balkan Sobranie. Do you know how much half a kilo costs?" He tossed his head in the direction of the cook. "I didn't come ten thousand miles to live with her child. I have a right to my own home." He picked something out of the bowl of the pipe with the tip of his little finger and looked around for the humidor. The cook was just backing through the kitchen door with a dust pan full of tobacco. "You really have no idea, do you? You don't see what I see in the hospital every day. These children have scabies, tuberculosis, rabies, the plague, for god's sake."

The room was heavy with dust and the smell of tobacco. "Sugar, you only see sick children," I said. "Hannah is perfectly healthy."

"Maintaining *my* health and equilibrium is essential to my work."

"She means a lot to me," I said. "A lot."

Felix sighed. "I should be able to relax in my own home. That's all. She's not our child."

"You only think of yourself."

"Do you know how tired I am of hearing those words in your mouth, the refrain of every minor disagreement between us?" His voice was barely audible. He didn't look at me. He clamped the empty pipe between his teeth and stepped backward, fading into his study.

"This is not minor," I whispered, but he was gone. I lived in a house of ghosts, Hannah and the cook and Felix moving backwards through doorways until they disappeared.

* * *

When I opened the kitchen door, the cook stood at the counter, tenderizing thin slabs of meat with a wooden mallet.

"I'm sorry about Felix," I said. "Is Hannah all right?"

The cook nodded.

"Where is she?"

She pointed at the back door with her chin. I grabbed a banana from the bowl and opened the door. Hannah sat on the steps, her head in her lap, her arms tight around her bare legs, holding her body to keep from trembling. She glanced up at me, then buried her head in her knees again.

The thumping of the steak stopped behind me. "No banana," the cook said. "We are going home early. Hannah will stay with Konjit."

Hannah's sister, Konjit, was only eight years old, too young to take care of my girl. I let the door swing shut and put my hand on the cook's shoulder. "Don't pay any attention to Felix. You know how he is."

"Yes, Madam. He is right."

"Don't you worry about him. I want Hannah here. I've raised her." I thumped the copy of *Baby and Child Care* on the shelf next to the cookbooks. "You, me, and Dr. Spock," I laughed. "This is her home. Don't worry, now."

The cook glanced at the book and frowned. "Yes."

I opened the back door and Hannah moved over to make room for me. I pulled her into my lap and she nuzzled her head between my breasts and put her thumb in her mouth. I stroked her soft hair and kissed the top of her head. She smelled like smoke. "Don't be scared, sweet Hannah Rose. It's okay."

She raised her wet lashes. "I don't like him."

I nodded.

She trembled once, then sighed, closed her eyes, and sank into my body.

"That's my girl," I whispered. I peeled the banana but she pushed it away.

"No," she said and stuck her thumb in her mouth again.

It was quiet on the back porch. The leaves of the Madam Hardy under the mimosa tree had rolled up like pale green cigarettes and dropped off. The bush bloomed anyway, but the white roses drooped, broken-necked, as soon as they opened. I bit into the banana. A kite floated overhead, raising its wings at the last minute to catch the wind and circle again, like the vultures at slaughtering time home in Georgia. Hannah's lips smacked against her thumb. I swallowed the banana and curved my hand around the small body, slowing my own breathing to match hers. The kite's shadow swept over us again and the heavy thud of the tenderizing mallet echoed from the kitchen.

* * *

Hannah's third birthday was the next week. I ordered a cake, made her a birthday girl crown with three stars, and Cook prepared the two of us a special lunch on a day that Felix was detained at the hospital. As I lit the candles, I said, "Darling, you should live here with me, my own little girl." I'm sure I said *should*, just an idea, you know. But the kitchen door slammed open and the cook appeared, gasping, and snatched Hannah off the birthday chair. The crown with three stars slid to the floor as Hannah wrapped her legs around her mother's hip. They were out of the compound gate before I got to my feet. "But we'll send her to all the best schools," I called, stupidly. It was all I could think of.

* * *

The cook was a widow with four mouths to feed, so she continued to place shirred eggs and coffee with cream in front of us at seven o'clock every morning, but she kept Hannah Rose at home. If I asked about her, she showed her teeth and laughed.

"Bring her back," I demanded.

She shrugged and wrinkled her brow. "No English."

I continued to read Dr. Spock out loud, but she pretended she didn't understand when I said things like "the child needs a stable, sanitary environment."

I ordered special paper and blew up all my pictures of Hannah, posting 16x20 prints in the living room and plastering the narrow hallway with them. I taped the one of her reaching out to me when she was learning to walk, on the refrigerator door. The cook ignored me when I begged her to let me see the child, so I stopped speaking to her, concealing my despair like thorns. We shall be madam and servant, I thought, and took to leaving the illiterate woman written menus each day that she had to take to the shop keeper across the road for interpretation.

"We could get another cook," Felix said.

"No, this is perfect," I said. "Just what you wanted. No family. We won't fire her." There was always the chance that she would bring Hannah Rose back.

*   *   *

I hadn't seen Hannah for fifty-eight days when the witch doctor rumor hit. We had heard there were sorcerers in Ethiopia, pagan priests who routinely sacrificed sheep, burning the horns, bathing themselves in the contents of the intestines, making oblations of the stomach, heart, and liver, magicians who imbibed warm blood and ate choice bits of flesh, gibbering at one another, in an unintelligible stream of incantations, leaving a harmless trail of amulets and exorcised souls. In fact, most of the children we knew, Hannah Rose included, wore some kind of charm around their necks, little leather pouches with bat dust or some such thing inside. I never thought much about it, a normal part of the exotic landscape, but in early April, when a witch doctor killed, ate, and drank the blood of an eight-year-old child, it wasn't considered normal. The *Ethiopian Herald* decried the primitive ritual "that hinders the achievements of His Imperial Majesty and the Ethiopian people and is an obscenity before the Church." There was excited debate and general disapproval in the streets and the wizard was scheduled for public strangulation in the Market within the week.

Felix, predictably, was spurred to action.

Whenever anything untoward happened, Felix announced that we were leaving. He'd make reservations with Alitalia —"Can't trust Ethiopian Airlines during a national crisis" — and give all our electronic possessions to Dr. Faisal, his colleague at the hospital. My role was to calm him until the crisis passed. The witch doctor rumor occasioned the eighth transfer of the transistor radio, the short wave radio, the tape to tape and the electric mixer to Dr. Faisal.

"You're overreacting," I said. "You know how rumors are in this place. For all we know, nothing at all happened and, even if it did, it has nothing to do with us."

"That's where you're wrong. A foreign doctor is vulnerable here, related in the minds of the people to this witch doctor. Both of us *hakim*."

"Hoodoo voodoo. An isolated incident," I said. "You don't understand these people like I do. Relax."

"I've promised Faisal the blender."

"We need the blender," I said.

"It's the wrong wattage for the States."

I poured him a cup of tea. "Look. The cook made *Hindi chai*. Your favorite." I held the cup under my nose and breathed in the sweet carda-mom and cloves, then set it in front of him. "We're not going home. This witch doctor stuff has nothing to do with us." These departure scenes with Felix were predictable. He had come to Ethiopia to study what he called the endangered diseases — he wanted to see a case of small pox before he left. On the other hand, he was terrified at being caught in the middle during the inevitable revolution. The Emperor had ruled for fifty years and couldn't last much longer. "How can I take you seriously when you do this every time Haile Selassie turns over in bed?" I said.

"Wake up, Sissy. It's all around you. Don't fool yourself just because we can get the Beatles on the radio here. Your night watchman believes in ghosts; your cook in the evil eye."

"You exaggerate everything," I said. "The cook is too sensible." I put my catalog aside and got up from the table. "It's going to be a clear night. Perfect for the Cosmic Photo."

"They're hanging this so-called *hakim*. I'm tainted by association, *hakim* and American, perfect target for the revolutionary enraged at the United States for propping up His Imperial Majesty. I'm doomed."

"You always say that."

He bit his lip; the freckles across his nose protruded like smallpox scars. "Every once in a while, the generated lights fail and, in the darkness, we see. This is one of those times. Mark my words."

"Consider yourself marked," I said and leaned into him, flattening my breasts against his back and massaging his chest. "Think of it as ex-perience. Travel is so broadening. There are no witch doctors home in Clintock."

He shuddered under my hands. "Exactly," he said. "And no human sacrifice. No cannibalism."

I dug my thumbs into his trapezius. There was no give to the man. "You could tie off the Queen Mary with the cords in your chest. Loosen up." I pressed my fingers into the occipital muscle and he moaned. "It might never have happened. You know how they love rumors here."

He rotated his head from side to side as I worked on his neck. "It's no rumor. They're hanging the man tomorrow."

"We can't go anywhere," I said. "I've already sent in the Burpee order."

He twisted away suddenly and stood up. "This is no place for a rose garden." He stared past me for a minute, then looked at his watch. "I have to sort my books for the sea freight."

I had to laugh "I know," I said. "You always pack the books first."

"I'm warning you, Sissy. The darkness of ignorance surrounds us."

"Fear makes you eloquent," I said. "There's something to be said for that."

When he left, I slipped into his warm chair and tasted his sweet tea, letting the milky steam coat my face. "I'm married to a crazy man," I called, but he was already in his study, dragging boxes out from under the day bed.

He appeared a moment later. "If it's all right with you, I'm giving Faisal both transistor radios this time."

"Sugar, we're not going anywhere," I said, as I always did, but he was gone again. I held the warm cup against my face and leaned back. It was a quiet evening. The only sound was the regular thump of medical books against the cardboard box.

When I finished the tea, I grabbed my camera and took the cup out to the kitchen. The cook was drying dishes.

"Thanks for the *chai*," I said, but she pretended she didn't hear me.

I stretched across her to pull back the curtain and look outside. "Great sky," I said. "I'm going to get the Cosmic Photo tonight."

She unplugged the teapot, still pretending she was alone in the kitchen, and poured scalding water over my empty cup. Her brown arm, smooth and hairless as a newborn, stopped me. I thought of Hannah squatting in her mud hut, picking flies out of her eyes, drinking unboiled water. I stared at the cook's beautiful hand for a minute and considered asking how Hannah was doing, but my tongue thickened as I tried to form the words, the hand disappeared in the dishwater, and the moment passed. I would ask her nothing.

I went out on the back porch. It was a clear night, perfect conditions for my picture, but too early to set up the shot. Abebe was still padding around the compound with his torch and the cook would be another twenty minutes in the kitchen. I didn't want either of them sticking their face in the lens after I set it up. I sat on the steps with the camera in my lap and Flea Trap clicked over and sagged against me.

"I've got to clip your toenails, Trap."

The dog dropped a heavy paw in my lap and pressed its long nose against my leg.

A chicken screeched on the other side of the compound; Trap lifted her head and barked. A minute later, the bird fluttered against the bottom of the steps with the watchman at its heels, shouting, *"Hidj!"* The old man flashed his dula.

Some things don't change when everything has changed, I thought. My first Ethiopian picture was of the watchman, limping after a rooster, his dula raised, gargling obscenities.

"Abebe, what's going on?"

The old man stopped, clicked his heels together, and saluted. The chicken dove behind a lone rose bush, scattering its petals, and squatted as if it had eggs to incubate. Abebe stole a glance at his prey.

"Good morning," he said, in English.

"It's evening," I said. "Whose chicken is that?"

He bowed and nodded but didn't answer. I repeated the question in Amharic.

He smiled broadly. "It is your chicken," he said, raising his stick to me.

"Then why are you chasing it?"

He clicked his heels together and tucked his robes around his slight form, waiting for me to say it in Amharic, but I couldn't get the words together. He bowed suddenly, wrapped his gabi tightly around his body and marched to the gate, where he took up his post for the night, as if he had just realized that chasing chickens was beneath his dignity.

Trap stuck her nose under my hand and I scratched the bony head. The dog quivered with pleasure. I sighed and leaned against the railing, massaging the soft dog neck. Trap's tail hammered the wooden porch — whap, whap, whap — then stopped suddenly. The dog laid its ears back and left its tail suspended in the air.

"What is it?" I said.

A light went on in the back bedroom. I turned around and saw Felix's silhouette, walking slowly, bent over, carrying something. Books.

The light cut across the corner of the porch, just short of the broken rattan bench against the house. I heard a low whistle, like a balloon exhaling, but couldn't see anything.

I shoved the dog off my lap and staggered up. "Who is it?"

I heard a breathy "peek-a-boo" and stumbled over the bench but still didn't see until two small hands grabbed my fingers and pulled me down. "I see you," she whispered.

Hannah.

I lurched at her touch, losing my balance and cracking my knees on the floor.

"Oh, baby." I wrapped my arms around the small body and she bent her head to mine. She smelled sweet, sweet, sweet, butter, cotton, smoke.

Her hand flickered on my hair. "Peek-a-boo," she said and giggled.

I scooped her up and twirled with her in my arms, stumbling over the bench, the dog, a stool, an old rug.

"Hannah, Hannah, Hannah, Hannah Rose," I said, inhaling the sweet musk of her smooth, brown skin. Tears spread across my cheeks. I kissed her face, her neck, her hair. She kissed me. "I've missed you terribly," I said. I didn't know how much I'd longed for her until I held her there in my arms with her little legs tight around my waist and her head on my neck. I couldn't stop crying.

"I have missed you also," she said, enunciating each English word precisely, like a language tape.

I stopped dancing and leaned back to gaze at her face. "Oh, let me *look* at you."

She reared back too and wrinkled her nose. "I see you," she said, then lay her head on my shoulder and pulled my thumb into her mouth, the way she used to. The sucking of her wet lips on my thumb, the movement of the small head against my chest and the flicker in my ears made me stagger. I looked up and the stars in the clear sky dived for me. I had to brace myself against the side of the house to keep from falling. My baby was home.

✳ ✳ ✳

An arc of light cut across both of our faces. The cook was at the back door.

Hannah shifted against me, adjusting the position of her head, sucking her own thumb.

"Why didn't you tell me?" I asked.

A ripple passed across the cook's face, but she continued drying her hands on the apron. "Is good?"

"Oh, yes." I kissed the child's hair.

The cook bit her lip, twisting her hands in the apron, as if they were still wet.

Slowly, slowly, I thought. I won't ask if she can stay the night. I won't offer her ice cream, won't carry her about the rest of the evening. Not yet. "Will you bring her tomorrow?" I asked, casually, as if I didn't care.

"Yes, Madam, if . . ."

I lowered my voice and stepped closer. "Felix is so obsessed with the witch doctor rumor these days, he'll never notice."

The cook's chestnut eyes glazed over. Her sallow face sagged. She's lost weight, I thought. Her black dress was stained. The longer I stared at her, the less familiar she seemed.

"Why didn't you tell me Hannah was here today?"

She wrung her hands and said something quickly, in Amharic, to the child.

Hannah slipped to the floor.

"I am sorry to bring her, but I have no place. She is here two days."

They were both dressed in black. I had been so consumed with punishing the cook, that I hadn't noticed she'd been in mourning clothes all week.

"What is it?" I stretched out my hand for Hannah but she didn't move.

The cook wiped her forehead with her thin hand, clicking her tongue. "Konjit die."

"Hannah's sister? That Konjit?"

The cook shuddered and covered her face. Hannah buried her head in her mother's skirts, picking up the rhythm of her mother's cries; a tiny ululation escaped the child's throat, the funereal wail. I took another step towards them, but the cook turned so Hannah was just out of reach.

"Tell me," I said.

She pressed the child's face into her legs and looked over her head at the compound, watching the dog nose among the ashes of Abebe's cooking fire. Then she took a deep breath and began to speak. "My boy, Bekele, he sick. Very sick."

"I thought you said Konjit."

"No. Konjit never sick. Bekele. He lie in bed crying all day, all night. Konjit and Hannah are taking care of him, but he does not eat. We are afraid. He is sick like his father." She spread her hand across her face and turned away.

"Why didn't you tell me?" I said. "Felix could have helped. He's a doctor. A *hakim*."

"I get one. Ethiopia *tanquay*, stronger than *hakim*. Bekele is too sick. The *buda* eat him," she said, lowering her voice.

"*Buda*?"

She nodded and cupped her fingers around her right eye, as if she were removing it. "Devil eye," she whispered.

"Evil eye?"

"Yes. Bekele need blood from his sister. Is all that can help him, so. . .*tanquay* take knife. . .he tell me to leave my house, but Konjit, she stay. I make her stay with *tanquay*." She stopped speaking and looked up quickly, then turned away, as if she expected me to know the rest.

"What is *tanquay*?"

She drew a long breath and picked up Hannah. "You know, Madam, what he do to Konjit."

She was speaking so softly I could hardly hear her. She continued the twisting and wringing motion with her hands, even as she held Hannah. I stepped closer.

"You know. He is in the newspaper. I see him on your table. That *tanquay* — witch doctor." Hannah tried to cover her mother's mouth, but the cook held the tiny hand away. "He not eat Konjit like they say. He not eat her. No." She pressed the child's hand to her lips and mumbled something into the hand, a rapid throb of Amharic words.

I stared at them stupidly for a minute, then lifted my leaden arms around them both and pressed my eyes and nose and mouth against the cook's shoulder.

When I straightened up and opened my eyes, I was surprised that we were still standing on the back porch. The dog's toe nails clattered on the steps. Felix's silhouette moved across the bedroom window again. Abebe's torch flashed.

"And Bekele?" I said.

"The boy is well." The cook's face softened and she smiled. "The *tanquay* made him well." Then she pressed Hannah against her chest and began backing away, towards the kitchen door. "Hannah is coming tomorrow," she whispered and stepped inside. The door snapped behind them.

I was alone on the porch. Through the curtains I watched the faint outline of the cook's body moving in the kitchen, putting my pots, pans, knives, forks, plates away.

Felix dropped a box of books in the house. The dog's tail slapped the porch; a lid clanged against a pot in the kitchen.

There had been a witch doctor, as real as the gravel-voiced old man I heard shouting Leba! Thief! in the street; as real as the woman singing falsetto in the bar on the other side of the compound wall; as real as Felix boxing up the blender and transistor radio for Faisal. I crossed my arms and leaned against the house, listening to the tidy clicks of the cook moving in the kitchen. I hadn't said a friendly word to her, hadn't asked about her family, since the day she stopped bringing Hannah. I could have helped her.

Through the window, I saw Felix enter the bright kitchen to give some order.

It came down to the same thing. I wanted the cook to give her child to me — like the *tanquay*. He took a daughter to save a son. The evil eye. I wanted her for myself.

I turned to the yard. My dress was drenched with sweat and I was shivering. I walked to the end of the porch and down the steps so I couldn't see the cook's shadow in the kitchen. It was a clear night, not a drop of moisture in the air. Still. No moon, but I couldn't see in the dark. White rose petals littered the yard, like a reflection of the stars wheeling overhead, waiting to be counted. I reached for my camera, pried open the diaphragm with my fingers, and pointed it up. I didn't need a tripod. I wanted to hold it myself.

Sharon Mayes

MAPUTO: A WRITER'S DIARY

Mozambique is a long, narrow country on the Indian Ocean on the southeast side of the African continent. Its population is estimated at 14,000,000. A decade of war and famine has taken the lives of 4 to 5 million people. Maputo is the capital of Mozambique. Beira is a port city with rail links inland to Zimbabwe.

The "bandits," as they are referred to by the Mozambican government are also known as RENAMO, Movimento Nacional de Resistenica de Mocambique, and the MNR, Mozambique National Resistance. They are an anti-government force created by the Rhodesian security services in the mid-seventies and later, after Zimbabwean independence in 1980, were supported by South Africa.

FRELIMO, Frente de Libertacao de Mocambique (Front for the Liberation of Mozambique) is the party that led the revolution against Portuguese colonialism first led by Eduardo Mondlane who was assassinated in 1969. Samora Machel led FRELIMO to independence in 1975 and became the first President of Mozambique. In 1984 Machel signed the Nkomati Accord, a non-aggression treaty with South Africa. Machel agreed to close the African National Congress (ANC) bases in Mozambique in return for the South Africans withdrawing military support for RENAMO. It is widely known that Machel kept his part of the bargain while Botha, the South African President, did not. In October of 1986 Machel was killed in a mysterious plane crash just inside the South African border. Joaquim Chissano is the current President of Mozambique.

* * *

February 18, 1987

We're waiting in the Harare airport for the Air Mozambique plane to come back from Beira. In Africa the pilot can change his schedule at will. Our flight was to leave at 11:30 this morning, but too many people were waiting to go to the capital city, Maputo. The pilot decided to take the passengers to Beira and return for others. Never mind that we'll wait six hours — such is life here. One must bend to necessity and learn how to wait.

Our group, Peter, Ahmed, Gladys, David and I, are in good spirits. We're off to the Indian Ocean, to the tropical breezes of a once plush seaside resort. Maputo used to be the winter playground of Europe, but for a decade Mozambique has been ravaged by war. My husband and his colleagues are on war-related business. They are medical professionals, and their job is to find out what Zimbabwe can do to help Mozambique with their beleaguered health-care system. I am going in search of a story. The Zimbabwean newspapers are filled with reports of shortages and massacres in Mozambique, but I've read very little in the Western press about the war. I want to see for myself.

While we wait, Ahmed, an Indian doctor born in Zimbabwe, makes jokes and entertains us with Africa stories: tales of mishap and misadventure in boiling heat and monsoon rains, in dirty, crime-ridden cities, "not like Harare," he stresses, "in the real Africa." In his "real Africa" people beg and steal and die of horrible diseases on the sidewalks. People are bartering to stay alive in a state of permanent anxiety. Raw sewage runs down the main streets. Buildings crumble in disrepair. Cars are swallowed by potholes.

Peter and Gladys laugh. I smile. We've lived in Zimbabwe a year and have never seen this "real Africa."

We are on an aging Boeing 707, having fought for our seats in the absence of seat assignments. I'm taking a Valium. This is, after all, Air Mozambique, and I can't help thinking of Samora Machel's plane crash four months ago. I try not to think about whether or not the bandits have anti-aircraft guns, or whether or not they would shoot down a passenger plane. But I can't stop myself. I try to concentrate on the book I'm reading. I wonder if I brought enough paper; there could be a lot of time to kill. The men in front of us are passing around a bottle of whiskey from the Duty Free. Peter says they are from the Zimbabwean-Mozambican Friendship Association.

The plane shakes violently as we lift off, but soon we're high over the lush, green hills of eastern Zimbabwe. The drink cart is coming down the aisle. They have coke, beer or water. The lunch is two pieces of bread with a thin square of dried egg in the middle. "It's food." David says. I laugh half-heartedly.

We arrive without mishap. Rebecca, an American doctor who has been in Mozambique for three years, has come to meet us. She seems "burnt out," explaining in a tired voice about the currency problems, our schedule, and where we will stay. This said, we ride silently through the dark streets to the hotel, the Andalucia. To my surprise, the hotel, one of two functioning in Maputo, is lovely. Dark wood paneling and enormous totem-like carvings decorate the lobby. Frayed wing-backed chairs sit next to small tables in alcoves, most with a telephone that isn't connected. Marble stairs lead to a fern-laden outdoor terrace. Everything is immaculate. Light from the lobby spills across the terrace and into the street. Except for a few people entering and leaving the hotel, the street is quiet, as if abandoned. We take our key and go to the sixth floor.

The room is adequate. Furnished in the same heavy wood as the lobby, it reminds me of Mexico. The tile bathroom is large with tub, shower and bidet. The water runs and the lights work. The bed is a sore point. The mattress is constructed of material that lumps up over thick wire springs. But we have an air conditioner, the only one in the hotel, the desk clerk said. A small balcony looks out over palm trees to the harbor. A strip of scarlet rims the horizon, the dying sunset. With the binoculars I see a few fishing boats anchored in the bay.

No one is hungry after a day of eating as we waited in the airport, but a peculiar animation remains. After looking over our rooms and freshening up, we meet for drinks on the terrace. No waiter comes. I notice that no one on the terrace has drinks. Everyone is chain smoking and talk is rapid. Ahmed goes off to find a waiter and returns with the news that there are no drinks served on the terrace or in the lobby. David suggests we go to our room and break into the Duty Free whiskey. Without discussion we follow. Around midnight everyone scatters to their rooms. I stand on the balcony, staring into the warm black night, wondering what tomorrow will bring.

* * *

February 19, 1987

Gladys woke me up knocking on the door.

"What time is it?" I stumble over my nightgown.

"Six. Rebecca is picking us up at seven. I don't have any water. Can I use your shower?"

"Sure." I let her in, then fall back on the torture device they call a mattress. I'd tossed and turned most of the night, unable to get comfortable. Relieved to hear the water running, I drift back to sleep. This time I sleep deeply. When I wake up Gladys and David are gone. I'm feeling grumpy, drenched with sweat and hungry. I open the heavy red drapes to a blazing hot sun, then close them and go to the shower. The shower is refreshing, and by the time I'm dressed, my mood has improved considerably.

Downstairs I go into the dining room and no one is there. I try out bits of Spanish on the desk clerk, but he speaks only Portuguese. With sign language I manage to communicate that I'm hungry. He shakes his head and leaves. Another man who speaks a little English returns and says he regrets breakfast is served only from six to nine. "You regret it?" I reply, knowing my sarcasm is lost in translation. "Never mind. Just tell me where I can get some coffee?"

"You can have coffee in the bar." He points down a small staircase behind the counter. They didn't tell us about the bar the night before.

I go into the windowless bar in the rear of the hotel. At ten in the morning several men are drinking and smoking. They are not talking. I order coffee and take out my notebook. The men are indifferent to me. They gaze into space through thick cigarette smoke and stare into the drinks, as if they were crystal balls. I'm unnerved. I make a list of things to do. I will go to a grocery store and buy bottled water.

The coffee is terrible, but I drink it anyway. The bartender gives me a check for $1 US or the rand equivalent. I offer to pay in the local currency, but he refuses to take the meticais. "What country won't take its own currency?" I say to him, but he doesn't understand English. He waits for me to give him the right money. I take out a hundred dollar traveller's check. He shakes his head no. "This is all I have," I protest.

A Mozambican man who speaks English explains my predicament to the bartender. The bartender relents and lets me sign for the coffee. The man tells me I must go to a bank and get rands or dollars. In Maputo foreigners must use rands or dollars in the hotels. I write, 'go to bank,' on my list.

The clerk who speaks English gives me directions to a bank and tells me about the Loia Franca, a store where I can buy water and food. When I leave the lobby the heat hits me in the face like a blast furnace. I'm not annoyed or unnerved anymore; I'm determined. Perhaps fear is nipping at my heels like the emaciated dog following me, but I quiet my emotions and concentrate on the task at hand.

As I walk along the street, the 24th of Julio, I forget my task. I forget myself. On this main street the stores are empty. Signs say "pastellaria" or "cafe," but under the signs and in the buildings there is nothing except shiny glass and chrome shelves. The nakedness of the shelves is shocking. At a cafe two men sit at a table without anything in front of them. They lean towards each other and whisper. A few old-looking women with babies on their backs sit on the ground along the sidewalk, selling tinned cans filled with coal. Children in rags linger in doorways, staring wide-eyed as I pass by. Several scramble to their feet and follow me with their hands out, begging in Portuguese. Some are too listless to beg.

In this city of well over a million people the streets are quiet and empty like the stores. The petrol station is closed. The vehicles that are on the road are marked with the logos of various AID agencies. It's too hot, I think, everyone must be staying inside. I stop to look at a poster in a store window, a photograph of a dead child with an orange-sized hole in his chest. The caption says "Never Again — Death to the Bandits." I see this FRELIMO poster repeated in store after store. Farther along I come to the headquarters of FRELIMO. The white wall has "The Vanguard of the Proletariat" painted across it in bright red letters. The door stands open and no one seems to be there. A strong smell of urine emanates from the building. I stand there watching, surely someone is in the headquarters of the party. A sleepy looking man appears and takes a seat on the steps by the door. I take a photo of the wall. He looks at me with listless eyes. I wonder why he isn't curious.

The Loia Franca is a two story store, selling food and liquor on the bottom floor, clothes, radios, toys and the like on the second floor. I take a basket and go down the aisles. Most of the food is in bulk and very basic, but they have sardines from Portugal and olive oil from South Africa, two products unavailable in Zimbabwe. Shoppers speaking different languages fill their baskets with sacks of rice, boxes of crackers and canned goods. There is almost nothing fresh. I find the water and get several bottles. I don't buy any food. I'm too depressed. The checkout lines are marked: Rands, U.S. Dollars, American Express and Traveler's Checks. I stand in the Traveler's Check line. The woman speaks rapidly in Portuguese when she sees my hundred dollar check and waves her hand to a man standing inside a glass office nearby. A friendly manager comes to the counter and directs me to a bank down the street. I leave the basket full of water and go back outside.

Several little boys crowd around, jabbering in Portuguese, pulling at my clothes and my camera bag. I back away. They hold out their hands. I don't have any change to give them. "No comprehende," I lie, walking away. The bank is on the next corner. The teller is very nice. We speak in bits of English and Portuguese, as if we understand each other. She tells me the bank has no money. I think she says it's over a hundred degrees today. She points out directions on my map of Maputo to a Barclays Bank. Back on the street, I follow her route, but come to no bank. I give up and go back to the Andalucia. I ask the clerk about the Barclays Bank. He smiles, his eyes sad. "There is only one bank in Maputo. The Bank of Mozambique."

The others return for lunch. Ahmed insists we will find a restaurant, if we walk down the street. I am skeptical, but go along, happy to be with the group. "That is a restaurant," Ahmed says. I don't know how he can tell. Curtains are pulled across the windows, and there's no sign. The door is locked. Ahmed knocks on the door. A man wearing a turban answers. He eyes us suspiciously. "We want to eat." Ahmed is adamant, "we have meticais." The man let us into a dark anteroom. At the end of this room is a guarded door, and behind the door people are eating lunch. We are given the last table. Eating behind a locked door is so strange I'm not hungry anymore. On the other hand, not eating is foolish. How do I know when I'll get another chance?

The restaurant has no choices. We are brought a meal of chicken broth, rice, and a piece of meat that tastes like shoe leather. The discussion is a welcome distraction. Peter, Ahmed and David are impressed with the Mozambican Ministry of Health. They have well-planned, sound programs and policies. They want to meet the health care needs of the people and are open to suggestions. The problem is the dire shortage of supplies and trained personnel. Gladys talks about the medical laboratories. They need everything, but most of all they need trained technicians. The grave reality is that 4.5 million people are starving to death. Severe malnutrition is taking its toll on the population, along with tuberculosis, malaria, all the diseases that cannot be combated without adequate sanitation, nutrition and medicines. David says he asked the nurse at the tuberculosis hospital how often the patients get meat. She said they hadn't had meat since 1983, but they give them a glass of milk twice a day. I'm staring at the piece of meat on my plate. I don't want it, but when the waiter comes to take away my plate I feel guilty. I force myself to eat.

We walk toward the Ministry of Health for a meeting on infant mortality. The others are looking in the shop windows. A "Galleria" on the corner displays one crude piece of pottery. Another small store has a heartrending inventory of two avocados, two ears of corn, two limes, and three bottles of ketchup spread across a long shelf. I photograph the windows, using my camera as a defense. We come next to a shoe store with four pairs of poorly constructed leather shoes in the window behind the dead child poster. Two canvas bags, one with crooked stitching, the other with a dirt stain, are placed below the shoes. My heart is sinking. Peter stays away from the windows. His face is drawn and downcast. This is not easy to see. The next plane to Harare is in a week.

Soldiers take our passports at the Ministry of Health. An Australian doctor, Julia, greets us and leads us upstairs to the meeting. I have to pee, but the water is not on in the building. The smell drives me away from the bathroom. I'll wait. The meeting is beginning. Most of the doctors are expatriates from around the world. They conduct their meeting in Portuguese. Translations are whispered to us by the English speakers in the audience. I can read the charts. The infant mortality rate is the same as Nicaragua and Gaza, about 101 per 1,000 babies die before the age of two, 350 die before the age of five. Maternal health is hard to maintain because of the scarcity of food. Child malnutrition creates brain damage and other problems. An argument erupts over the reliability of the statistics. I look out the window, trying not to think about my bladder, thinking instead how dedicated these people are.

After the meeting Julia takes us to the Polano Hotel in her car, even though it's only a few blocks away. I ask her about the missing front window. She explains Mozambique has no glass for repairs. Fancy cars fill the parking lot of the Polano Hotel. I am jolted into another reality:

uniformed doormen, women in pretty tropical dresses, men in tailored business suits, red carpets, display cases filled with art, waiters carrying platters of food and drink. I remember I need to change my traveler's check. The desk clerk says it is too late in the day; the dollars are gone. David tells me not to worry and pulls out his American Express card. This is the first time we've used the card.

We go through the well-appointed lobby and bar to the outdoor tables by the pool. Julia orders cokes. I'm bursting with questions. "How do the ordinary people survive here without rands or dollars?"

"They aren't surviving very well. They're just hanging on; they've been hanging on for years. They just do."

"How did FRELIMO land in this disastrous state?"

"It's the war with South Africa, of course." Her tone is angry. The "of course" is exasperated. I should have better sense than to reveal my ignorance. I shut up; the questions run around in my head, forming themselves, regrouping, rephrasing. I know a bit about the situation. RENAMO was created by the Rhodesians and Portuguese in the mid-seventies, and after the Zimbabwean revolution in 1980, the South Africans took over their support. I wonder if our government has a hand in this, knowing about our "freedom fighters" in Angola and Nicaragua. I want to ask her more questions. I want to know what's going on here.

Ahmed stands up to leave before the cokes arrive. He has to give a talk on sexually transmitted diseases. Peter, Gladys and David go too, leaving me with Julia and four cokes. We watch the children of diplomats splash in the pool. "The food shortage is much worse than has been reported, isn't it?" I'm determined to make friends with her.

"Yes." She finishes a second coke and seems on the verge of leaving.

I gesture toward the sea. "Why don't they eat the fish?"

"The fish is exported." She leans back and sighs.

"I'm sorry for asking so many questions. I'd like to understand this situation. Who's taking the fish? Is it the Russians?"

She smiles. "Many people come to Maputo for a few days. They look, they ask questions, they go, and they do nothing to help us. Who told you the Russians are taking the fish?"

"Nobody. I just . . ."

"The fish is exported to Europe. Mozambique has very few exports left. The economy is almost destroyed. I have to go. Can I give you a ride?"

"No. Thank you. I'll walk back. I just want to say I'm impressed by what you're doing. It seems very difficult."

"Thank you." Her eyes narrow into strips and she says, "Who are you? Why are you here?"

I'm taken aback. The implication stings. "I'm a writer. I came with my husband. To see, you know."

"A writer? What do you write?" She sounds skeptical.

"Fiction. I'm writing a novel."

"I see. Maputo is good material?" Her tone is cordial. She turns to go not waiting for a reply. "Ciao."

After she leaves I try to think about what was said. Why do I feel the culprit? I haven't done anything wrong. Does she think I'm a spy or something like that? A crowd is gathering around a group of men to my right. I notice the men from the Zimbabwean Mozambican Friendship Association are sitting on the terrace. A welcome breeze is coming off the ocean. A group of Mozambican men are singing songs and dancing to the lyrics. They are miners I hear from the conversation at the next table. I listen and take some pictures. The songs are sweet and sad, the dance a tale of work and woe. Everyone applauds for a long time. The sun is falling low in the sky, casting a blanket of pink over the white stucco hotel. I leave the Polano and walk back down Patrice Lumumba Avenue to our hotel on Julius Nyerere Boulevard.

I pass more empty stores with taped broken windows. Once magnificent houses and apartment buildings fill the neighborhood, now occupied by AID workers. This feels like peeping at other peoples' dirty laundry. The people on the street don't have desperation, fear or panic in their expressions. Their faces are depressed and resigned. In the dark, white people stand out — they can be seen coming or going — but not black people. The streetlights don't work and darkness falls fast. I am a foot or two away from a silent black man before I realize he is in front of me. We collide. I look point blank into his eyes. In the moment before we each avert our gaze I see indifference, fatigue, but no hatred. I expect to see hatred.

Beside the ramshackle buildings and around the large potholes, groups of laughing children play with wire toys. I watch them pull pieces of wire and cloth from a torn awning and mold it into a ball they can throw. Fires burn in open areas between buildings. Electric lights glow from some windows, but women are cooking outdoors, talking in soft voices. "They've been hanging on for years." Julia's words echo in my mind. Yes, this is what people do when they have no other choice. They hang on like survivors of a ship wreck. They wait for rescue. Everyday life continues. Men are coming home from work toting briefcases. Mothers shout at children. A lecture is being given in a school. Students with notebooks under their arms are going in the door.

I arrive at the hotel bedraggled and blue. I want to eat dinner and go to bed, but the others have not come back from their lecture. I have a shower and drink a glass of whiskey. By the time everyone assembles for dinner the head waiter informs us no more tables will be served. They have run out of food. We take turns haggling with the waiter but to no avail. We are competing with the other foreign currency holders in the city for a seat in one of the two restaurants. The desk clerk suggests we telephone the Polano Hotel. As time passes I get hungrier and realize I might go to bed without dinner a second night. To be refused food is not the same as refusing it oneself.

The Polano Hotel has food, but they are about to close. We are a thirty minute walk away. Taxis no longer exist in Maputo. Ahmed telephones a friend in the city who, minutes later, turns up in a barely running car. We cram ourselves into the car and drive to the Polano. Twice the engine dies, the second time a few hundred yards from the hotel. We are giggling hysterically as the car sputters into the driveway.

The dining room is brightly lit. White linen table cloths and flowers are on the tables. The diners have plates of food and chat gaily, as if eating dinner is a perfectly normal thing to do. This is the world I understand. I am at home in a fancy restaurant. Yet, going back and forth from nothing to plenty is disorienting. We order too much food. I eat more than I need of the sumptuous meal: curried prawns on rice, filet mignon with peas, carrots on artichoke hearts, cauliflower, wine. I don't think about the starving people during dinner. The warm rush of wine makes the conversation lively and silly. We joke about the perils of travel in a war-zone, having escaped peril up to this point. At midnight we stumble back along the deserted streets. Giant cockroaches are strolling along in droves. In a debris-filled office a hungry rat runs back and forth.

* * *

February 20, 1987

It's Friday. Beastly hot again. Everyone says it's never this hot in Maputo. I awoke from a bizarre dream about being pursued by soldiers with machine guns. I was involved in a plot to conceal soldiers' underwear for resale. A man gestured for me to run and led me to a hiding spot in a bathroom. The clothing was stacked on shelves in the anteroom outside the toilet and the soldiers were hot on our trail. He left me there to be caught. I was trying to escape through a tiny window when the soldiers opened fire with machine guns.

I decided to stay in bed and read Jack Kerouac's *On the Road*, one of the novels I brought. After last night I have a burning sensation from my neck to my thighs and a stomach ache.

The day is passing, but I don't want to get out of bed. David just came back from the morning rounds. "Let's have lunch," he says. "Peter and Gladys are waiting for us in the bar."

"I have a stomach ache. You go ahead."

"Come on, you can't stay in bed all day. I insist."

In the bar Gladys and Peter are drinking beer. Gladys recounts the morning activities. The bartender says our table is ready. We are eating in our hotel dining room for the first time. At the door the head waiter says David can't enter. Through some funny sign language we discover it's because he is wearing sandals. The restaurant can run out of food, but the customers must have proper shoes! The morning of reading Kerouac has put me in a strange mood. Bums in America lived in luxury compared to Mozambicans today. Auntie sent money. Booze flowed freely. Kerouac seemed flippant and fancy-free, searching for the Truth with a capital T, not Reality like this with a capital R.

I refuse to order lunch because I won't be able to eat everything on my plate. David frowns, but doesn't say anything. The portions they're serving are large. I can't waste food here. The waiter serves soup to the others. We wait for the main courses a long time. Gladys has to leave before her meal comes. I glance at David, feeling vindicated in my decision. I'll eat Gladys's food. Nothing will be wasted. The waiter offers ice cream for dessert. I love ice cream and accept with gusto. His face lights up in a wide grin. He is making as much as he can out of what little they've got. Unfortunately, the ice cream is granular and melted. I eat every bite, wanting the waiter to think I like it, feeling miserably sad. Food. Shoes. Ice cream. These people are tough. They endure. Appearances are maintained. Pleasure is taken in simple things. I'm not as tough as they are. I want to hide in the room.

After lunch I follow David and Peter to visit the children's hospital. Lord Have Mercy! If I were religious I'd pray. Forty to fifty children, two or three to a bed, are crowded into several open wards. The nurses and doctors move swiftly. Dozens of pairs of glazed little eyes follow us from bed to bed. Some of them stare into space. They are already dead. The doctor says many of the children are in such advanced stages of malnutrition they can no longer focus or hear or eat. They concentrate on the ones who can be helped; the others they make as comfortable as they can. "Yes," she says, "the childhood diseases take their toll, but it's malnutrition that does the worst damage. Enough food would have saved many of these children. The simple truth." She speaks in a matter of fact way. I think of my daughter when she was a child; I loved her madly. How much pain is it for a mother to watch her child starve? I can't write about this. I'm getting angry. Who are the people that cause children to starve?

David and I are getting ready to go out to dinner. We are going to the apartment of a Swedish AID worker, a friend of Gladys. I start raving. "How can you stand seeing children starving like that?"

"I don't like it." He says. "It's bad."

"Why did I come here? I can't stand it." I'm angry with him for inviting me on this trip.

"You have to write it down." He ignores my anger.

We walk to the building where Margaret lives. The elevator isn't working so we walk up to the tenth floor in a dark, dank stairwell. Her apartment overlooks the Indian Ocean. It's large and comfortable and decorated with modern furniture. She has books on philosophy, music and art. Three novels and several recent magazines are on the coffee table. Candles burn, the flames blowing in the warm ocean breeze. Gladys mixes the drinks and passes around bowls of cashew nuts. Except for the buckets of water around the apartment we could be in Acapulco or New York.

Margaret is the head of a Swedish AID group that organizes workers' cooperatives. She supervises over a hundred volunteers in Maputo. The Swedes are giving a lot of aid to Mozambique. They believe they are doing good works. Margaret is nice, very dedicated like the others I've met, but she doesn't talk about politics. I don't mention it either. We talk about architecture and history, movies and fashion. Margaret has been in Maputo several years, but she is as cosmopolitan as anyone you can imagine. I ask her how she manages to keep up on everything. She travels to Swaziland and Lesotho, she says. She buys supplies there. South Africa is up on everything, the "first world" of this continent.

* * *

February 21, 1987

Saturday. We are going to the beach today with Julia. Tonight Rebecca is having a dinner party for us.

The Indian Ocean is gray and calm in the still heat of mid-day. Julia has gone across the street to the lone remaining beach front restaurant, the Costa del Sol. She's arranging our lunch and meeting two friends she wants to introduce to us. Peter, David and Ahmed are swimming. I'm guarding the cameras and clothes, although we're the only people on the beach. A small boy is coming towards me. Here we go again. His wide eyes survey the clothes and camera. He talks. "No. No comprehende," I shake my head in the negative and shoo him away with my hand. He's not moving his eyes from the clothes. I take off the long-sleeved shirt I brought to keep the sun off and give it to him. He grabs it and runs away fast. Far down the beach he turns to stare at me, clutching the shirt in his fist.

Julia's friends, Derek and Simone, are engaging. I like them instantly. When we come in from the beach they order pitchers of beer and wine and two dozen steaming pink prawns. I sit next to Derek, across from Simone, and listen to the conversation already underway. At last someone is talking politics. "He bloody well was murdered." Derek is saying to Julia in a loud voice.

"Are you talking about Samora Machel?" I jump into the conversation.

He nods his head. "Of course. The South Africans brought that plane down. They engineered the crash, but we'll never know the whole truth. They destroyed the evidence."

"Why do you think they did it?"

"Why? It's obvious. Even though Machel signed the Nkomati Accord he wasn't pliable enough. They gave him a death sentence a week before the crash."

"I remember wondering why Machel signed that treaty in 1984. I couldn't believe then he would stop the ANC from operating in Mozambique."

"He didn't have much choice at the time. South Africa controls the electricity here, you know. They employ eighty thousand miners who bring in foreign currency. Machel needed that treaty to stop RENAMO. That's where he was mistaken, to think that the South Africans would abide by the treaty."

"Does South Africa want to take over Mozambique?"

"Not exactly. They want to control what happens here. This country is rich in resources, swarming with cheap labor. We have strategically important ports, direct routes to Harare and Lusaka. If imports and exports went through Mozambican ports Durban and Capetown would lose business."

"What do you think of Chissano? The Zimbabwean press portrays him as a clone of Machel."

"Is he?" Simone interjects. She'd been listening intently. "I don't think so. He's going to turn to the West. He has to end the war or everyone is going to starve to death."

We continue with this conversation through several dozen plates of prawns and pitchers of beer. Time vanishes. When no one can eat another bite Derek suggests we retire to his house for coffee. Being able to ask questions and hear forthright opinions puts everyone in an exuberant mood. Derek and Simone believe the government is composed of decent people, and their priorities — agriculture, veterinary science and medicine — are sensible. The irony is that their programs can't be implemented because of the war. The war drains the foreign currency. Refugees flock to Maputo putting a tremendous burden on scarce services in the city. The industrial sector doesn't function, even with the hundreds of expatriates trying to get the old factories going. Workers can't work when they're hungry. A long-range orientation is fading from the peoples' consciousness. The upshot of the conversation is that the government can't be blamed. The Portuguese raped the country when they left after the revolution of 1975, leaving FRELIMO with few resources. RENAMO is supported by external enemies. In the early eighties natural disasters — droughts, floods, famines — wreaked havoc.

But, but, but. . .I feel like a cheerleader at a football game with too much enthusiasm for the losing team. I'm sweating. Bob Dylan whines "Mozambique" on Derek's aging record player. I'm thinking, can all these problems be attributed to external forces beyond their control? We're having such an agreeable afternoon I'm reluctant to criticize, but I do. "Listen, don't misunderstand, I'm an admirer of Machel and FRELIMO. But how is pouring in food aid going to build up the economy and create a basis for growth? The revolution was twelve years ago, the government has made a few mistakes. The point is what can they do to turn it around?"

The questions meet with sympathetic smiles. Derek wipes the sweat from his forehead and says, "The government is treading water, waiting."

"For what?" I push. His comment is like Julia's "hanging on." No one answers. Julia stands and says we have to go back to the city. Expatriates are in a peculiar position. They are desperately in demand and appreciated, but they may serve the same interests they oppose. Maybe we are all unwitting agents of the white, Western world view? I don't dare say this.

As we are thanking Derek for his hospitality and saying goodbyes, Simone pulls me aside. "I have a friend who was captured by RENAMO and lived with them for three months." She whispers, "I think you're sincerely interested. He's coming to my apartment on Monday night. Do you want to meet him?"

"Yes. Of course, I want to meet him." I'm elated. I can speak to a man with first hand experience of the bandits. We agree she will contact me at the Andalucia to make the arrangements. I leave feeling less adrift, satisfied. I have a mission in Maputo. I have someone to interview.

The dinner party at Rebecca's is completely opposite to the afternoon luncheon. The atmosphere is strained, awkward. Questions meet with silence, and uncomfortable silences dominate the evening. Nobody wants to discuss Mozambique. A pretty British nurse talks about her work in refugee camps in Pakistan and Nepal. Her stories are fascinating, far away from Africa, but obliquely relevant. Later when most of the guests have left, Ahmed and David pursue a heated discussion of amoebic liver abscesses.

It's midnight. Still hot. I'm sitting on the balcony, writing by the moonlight. I can't sleep. When I close my eyes I'm flooded with thoughts, questions, answers. Maybe, there is a way to understand this, but I don't.

February 22, 1987

Sunday. Ahmed has gone to visit his friend. Peter went to the beach with Rebecca. Gladys is with Margaret. David is sleeping. I've finished reading another novel, *Waiting To Live*, by a South African. I'm running out of reading material, and we have three days left.

When David wakes up we go to the bar for the icky coffee. He observes. "Have you noticed? Women are operating most of the services in Maputo. In the hospitals the Mozambican doctors are women. The majority of expatriate doctors and AID workers are women."

"The men are probably in the Army, or in the provinces." I conjecture. "You're thinking of working here, aren't you?" I ask him, even though I already know it's true. I've asked myself several times, should I stay here and work?

"Yes." He admits. "But we'd have to learn Portuguese." After coffee we walk downtown toward the Botanical Gardens and the Independence Plaza. The sun is fiery. Almost no one strolls in the beautiful gardens. Two old men are playing a board game on a bench. A tourist photographer leans against the entrance gate, displaying his tattered photos. He looks at us as if he has forgotten what tourists look like. The daze of inactivity has sapped his spirit. We continue through the lush tropical garden to the eery and unnaturally deserted Independence Plaza. I close my eyes and imagine the crowd that recently filled the Plaza at Samora Machel's funeral.

Downtown, in the commercial center, stand skyscrapers and large department stores. Modern malls and sidewalk cafes line the unoccupied streets. There are no sounds. No traffic. It is like walking through a futuristic movie: The bomb has destroyed human life and left the buildings intact. I don't expect people to be here, but a few are. I trip over a skinny leg poking out of a doorway. A ragged man lies on the concrete in the shade of the building with his arms covering his face. A thin girl with wild eyes, scampers alongside an equally thin woman. A teenage boy sits, elbows on his knees, chin in hand, watching the girl. Life is in present-time-only. The heart of the city is exposed. I have no energy. I want to go back to the hotel.

David points out a Soviet travel agency with bright enticing pictures of snow in the window. "Look at that ancient Russian camera equipment." He's trying to distract me from depression.

"Why haven't the Russians sent more aid to them? They're supposed to be allies." I'm annoyed at the Russians.

"The Soviet economy isn't doing so hot. I don't think they have as high a stake in this part of the world as the State Department likes us to think. I've only met one Russian doctor. Seems like a decent fellow." David examines the contents of each store window. What might have been a sophisticated art gallery has prints of Mickey Mouse, Donald Duck and Goofy in the window. Experience is surreal, I think. Reality doesn't exist.

"Doesn't this make you angry? They have to do something. They have to fight back." I'm furious.

"Yeah." He takes my hand. "It gets to you."

We retreat to the promenade by the sea and walk under the coconut palms, heading toward the Polano Hotel where we can swim. We hike past several extravagant embassies built to overlook the sea: The Cubans. The Bulgarians. The West Germans. They have mansions with transmitters and receivers on the roofs. The Vietnamese have a palace. We Americans have a fortress. The luxurious embassies make me sick. They are immoral.

We are hungry by the time we get to the Polano, but they won't let David in the dining room because he's wearing shorts. He's having a real problem with proper attire in Maputo. The head waiter says they will serve us by the pool. After an hour I put on my bathing suit and dive in the dirty, but refreshing water. When I get out lunch still hasn't come. David's angry and about to complain. The waiter arrives with two stale cheese sandwiches. I joke. "This is the perfect place to diet. We could start a fat farm: ABSOLUTE GUARANTEE — LOSE TEN POUNDS A WEEK IN SUNNY MAPUTO. Think we could sell it in the *New Yorker, California Magazine,* or *The Nation?*"

On our way back we stop at the Museum of Natural History, crowded with stuffed animals — elephants, rhinos, giraffes, zebras. The galleries are dark and cool. Cobwebs of dust cover the exhibits. The caretaker is snoozing in the corner. Three children stand with their noses pressed against the glass staring at jars of preserved elephant embryos in different stages of development. Will human beings soon be stuffed and displayed here as examples of an endangered species?

* * *

February 23, 1987

Today I'm 'waiting for Godot.' Thirty-six hours until we leave. Earlier this morning I finished my last novel, then slept through lunch. I'm sitting in bed, smoking cigarettes. They make me nauseous and dizzy, but I don't care.

Simone left a message to come to her apartment at six this evening. Like the other expatriates she lives in the quadrant between the Andalucia and the Polano Hotel. I'm going to the Loia Franca to buy some beer for her. David is coming too.

The sun is going down. Simone has put chairs on the terrace and distributes the beer. Adolpho is sweet and self-effacing. He's a veterinarian and was trained in Zimbabwe and Zambia. As a result he speaks English reasonably well. In 1985 he was in charge of 1,800 head of cattle at a sugar plantation in the province of Zambezia. He tells his story. "RENAMO attacked the plantation at dawn with lots of guns. Me and two friends were running away when they captured us. We were marched into the bush. They told us to sit and wait. The next day RENAMO bombed the sugar factory, then burned it down. They took my money, clothes, shoes and other possessions and gave me their old clothes. They didn't harm me or my friends, but I heard them killing the villagers who didn't cooperate. They said they would take us North to their base. Perhaps, to train as soldiers."

"Did they say why they were fighting the government?"

"No. They said they wanted to get rid of socialism and bring back private enterprise. They said they didn't harm the local people, but I knew it wasn't true. I was afraid. They slaughtered the cattle and stayed near the village until the food began to run out. I cooked my own food over a fire in the bush."

"Who are they?" I interrupt.

He smiles. "They spoke many languages. Most were black, but some were mulatto, one or two whites sometimes came. They were not from our province." He stops a moment, remembering. "I tried to escape twice and both times the villagers took me back. They were afraid to be punished if I escaped. But one night a small boy came and led us out of the bush. We ran for three days and nights without stopping, then the boy left us. We went on alone for three more days. We met many lions on the way. I was very frightened. My body shook, but the game was plentiful. They didn't need to eat us. At Quelimane, near the sea, we found the Army. The soldiers were very glad to see us. They had orders to find us. They didn't want to meet with RENAMO." He laughs.

"What do you think RENAMO wants? Do they have a program?"

"I don't know. I want nothing to do with politics. I hope the war is over soon. I don't want to see RENAMO again. Next time they will kill me."

Simone smiles and says in her soft voice. "Adolpho is on his way to be the chief veterinary officer in Gaza."

"Gaza? Isn't RENAMO still operating there?"

Adolpho shrugs his shoulders. "I have to do my job. I like taking care of the cattle. Politics is too complicated."

The conversation turns to the effects of the droughts and the floods of the early 1980's on agriculture. Adolpho thinks a lot of the current scarcity goes back to these natural disasters. A considerable number of cattle died in the floods. We carry on talking until Adolpho says he must return to his family for the evening meal. The evening had faded into a clear, starry night.

I invite Simone to have dinner with us, but she has to teach an English class. David and I walk back, talking about Adolpho. Ahmed and Peter are in the dining room. I tell them the story. Ahmed says his friends know an Indian family who lived with RENAMO for a year before they were released. It is a relief to hear these stories. They don't kill everybody. Peter looks gloomy and doesn't talk. It occurs to me he hasn't said anything in three days. I'm worried about his mental state. "Is this depressing you, Peter?" I blurt out. He nods his head. A few minutes later he leaves a half-eaten dinner and says he's going to the bar.

* * *

February 24, 1987

The expatriates here have never heard of yuppies. America is not the whole world, yet I am surprised. I have conducted a small survey, asking everyone I've met, and no one has heard of yuppies.

Gladys invites me to come with Margaret and her to the open air market. The market is downtown and I'm glad to see the downtown during the week. It's not nearly as deserted as it was on Sunday. The stalls have seasonal vegetables and fruits, not a wide variety and not a large quantity, but more than nothing. One side of the market is reserved for food, the other for wood carvings and sundries. Margaret comes to buy her weekly vegetables, but she's grumbling about the prices. One kilo of tomatoes cost a third of an average worker's monthly salary. Now I understand why the place isn't jam packed with shoppers. I walk past a display of ugly black crabs. An old woman is waving them at fascinated children who jump back in fright.

Margaret wants to go to another market on the other side of town. The vegetables are too expensive here, she says. We walk out through the stalls of wood carvings. The Indian merchants are not aggressive. They don't try to sell us anything. I study the expressive carvings of emaciated African figures. They tell stories of pain and suffering. I want to buy one, but feel too depressed as I did in the Loia Franca. The money in my pocket feels hot against my skin. I don't want to have it, but I don't want to let go of it either. In the parking lot we push through a crowd of beggars waiting beside Margaret's Landrover. "Don't give them anything." She instructs. "Begging is not a solution."

The next market is on the beach road. They have fresh fish and eggs. Eggs cost about twenty U.S. dollars a dozen. As we are looking a white woman buys several dozen to the astonishment of everyone in the market. Margaret examines the fish and complains the price is too high. She doesn't buy. A Mozambican woman she recognizes calls to her from behind a stand, and they enter into some negotiations. Gladys and I walk to where three old women are cooking ears of corn (mealie) over an open fire. She buys one and eats it. Margaret has bought her fish and is ready to leave. A beautiful, black-eyed boy about five years old stands on the passenger side of her car. He holds out his hand to me and pats his belly. I open my purse to give him some money. Margaret says, "don't give him money," and yells at him in Portuguese. He stares at me pathetically. All the way back I regret not giving him anything. His eyes will haunt me forever.

In the evening we take Julia and Rebecca to the Polano for dinner. The food is not very good, but both women have warmed up and treat us less like CIA agents. I sympathize with their anger, suspicion and fatigue. It must be frustrating to have the same questions asked by every set of visitors. Questions with no answers. They have difficult jobs in pathetic circumstances and carry on for their own reasons. The suggestion that all is for naught is cruel and unfair. At least they are trying. "What does RENAMO want?" I ask at a moment when we're getting on quite well. "What would they do if they were running the country?"

Julia answers. "This is the crux of the problem. They have no program. I saw one document that supposedly explained their position. It was written in such archaic, flowery Portuguese I couldn't understand it. They only want to disrupt, to destroy. They don't want to see Mozambique thrive as an independent country."

* * *

February 25, 1987

We leave the hotel for the airport very early. Rebecca has to stop for gas. I'm edgy, anxious that something will interfere with our departure. Three times Rebecca is refused gas. "Today gas is reserved for diplomats only," she explains, "but I know the manager at a station downtown." After some discussion the friend gives her gas.

We drive in daylight past the shanties on the outskirts of the city. This is where the majority of Maputo's citizens live, in shacks made of cardboard, corrugated metal, thatch or whatever material they can find. These last glimpses underscore the poverty of the refugees. We come to a traffic island with a white pyramidal structure in the middle of it. "What is that?" I ask Rebecca.

"That is where Eduardo Mondlane and Samora Machel are buried."

"You're kidding. They are buried under a traffic island in front of the airport?" David squeezes my knee.

"Yes." She has no emotion in her voice.

Peter is not on the list of passengers. Rebecca says this is normal; someone is always left off the list. Peter is nervous. She sorts it out with the immigration people and Peter is added to the list of passengers. She walks with us to customs where she says goodbye. We wait in the Duty Free lounge. I buy some fabric and watch mechanics take apart an airplane engine. In an hour we are on the plane. I fall asleep as soon as we're in the air.

We are driving home. Harare seems to have turned into a city of opulence. The roadside stands are busy. The shops are full. Buildings are going up. Workers in blue and green overalls work alongside the roads. It's lunchtime. Children in their school uniforms stand around cafes eating cornish pasties and drinking soft drinks. Women carry baskets of food home for their dinner.

I wonder if Zimbabwe could end up like Mozambique. Mugabe says, "Zimbabweans will fight to the last person to protect the sovereignty of Mozambique. Their fate is our fate." How far will South Africa go to control the region?

We are home. Our lovely house and swimming pool has been kept in pristine condition by the man who works for us. The stereo is still there. The food is on the shelves. We have fuses and batteries. I'm overwhelmed at the luxury I take for granted. I go to the computer. I'm burning to write it down, to get it out of me. I can't write a word. I put music on and burst into tears. I've never had a writer's block. I don't feel well. I cry off and on all afternoon.

Maputo. What can I say for you? Empty. Drowning under a blazing sun. Starving in tropical splendor. Close to nothing.

Apathee Ananke

MIS EN ABYME

GANESOMAI. I shall become. Ashes to ashes. Dust to dust. The professor wrote the Greek letters in chalk.

Like Ganesa, Apathee interrupted, the Hindu god with the body of a man and the head of an elephant....

Ganesa! Yes yes you're quite right....Although I've always pronounced it Ganersa.

Everybody says it differently. Anyway he's the king of trolls in Hindu mythology. I knew that if Ganesa showed up on the test I'd do alright.

It's amazing how the mind is wired, isn't it? Mine is rather like one of those old cloth covered heating cord contraptions, all frayed at the ends, throwing sparks...

* * *

The rooms of the Singapore Station Hotel opened around a central space overlooking the high church-ceilinged waiting room. Large grey bomb-shaped lights hung dimly from cords high above, as if to remind passengers of impending holocaust. Everything seemed to have happened forty or fifty years ago, pluperfectly preserved by the eternal rains. The pipes had burst and water was cascading down the stairs. A bent old Chinese woman attempted to rectify the situation with a wispy broom.

Thick dark wood double doors shielded long narrow rooms from the hum of the station. The interior might have been any cheap hotel in London, but at a fraction of the cost. A sinking mattress spread across the floor beside the sagging bed frame patched with plywood. The soothing rattle of the six a.m. train. Wires stretched over the aluminum tile roof outside the window. Wires stretching on and on.

The shopping mall was large and modern, across the street from a famous hotel with the names of celebrated writers on plaques outside the bedroom doors. *Joseph Conrad. Somerset Maugham. Maxine Hong Kingston*... The red tile hotel reminded Apathee of The Breakers in Palm Beach. Only dead authors could afford to sleep there.

The names were like the names of people Apathee had known over the years who had shared one or two of her interests. A man in an advanced analytical training seminar when she was twenty now lived in a mansion and charged $75 an hour to talk to people. A friend of hers who was living on welfare went to him and was always telling her about "the transference." The friend thought the analyst was intrigued by her bohemian lifestyle. Maybe...

Apathee had been kicked out of the training seminar for barefeet and a bad attitude. She was the only one in the group who had read all of Jung's collected works and everything else then available. More important, she was the only one in the group with any real inner life. The training analyst had lectured her for an hour on how she reminded him of his daughter, which apparently wasn't a compliment. There were no more buses running when finally he finished yelling at her. She hitchiked home past midnight. He was dead now, thank the gods. She had wanted to kill him herself.

There had come a time when she could no longer stand to open a magazine or look at a bulletin board for fear of seeing someone she had known in writing or photography, art or astrology, making it in the big world or capitalizing on some exotic ethnic background. She had spent three weeks in a little town by the ocean in Thailand where no one really spoke English and the light melted like ice cream. A palimpsest of staples, fading headlines and cheshire smiles.

The shopping mall in Singapore sold chocolate honey frozen yogurt and curry puffs. The air-conditioning sucked the heat off the street. People changed inside the mall. The men no longer peeled her skin with their eyes. They became cool, civilized. Sometimes there was free jazz in one of the overpriced bars. She watched the tall flashy African businessmen with their shiny gold watches in the lobby of the hotel that opened into the mall. Fascinating, but she knew that her loneliness had already reached the stage of no return. Once you let yourself get this bad, you could only go in and hope to come out the other end. She opted instead for the fan cooled red checked table cloth omelette and chips joint around the corner, where ale on tap was a fourth the price in the famous hotel.

She had found a novel in the shopping mall that afternoon en route to buy an air ticket to Bali. She had begun reading Askar Muhammed after her breakdown in London. His novels seemed to recreate for her the universe of the Ethiopian whose rejection had inspired her short circuit. There was a certain similarity of language and allusion. Are you sad for me or sad for you? I'm just sad, she said. She had often spent afternoons in the little walled garden full of former tenants' garbage, hypnotized by the grey cat dancing in the shadows of PreRaphaelite green, sipping rum and reading Schnitzler and Askar Muhammed. Her chair sank six inches into moist black earth.

Baedeckers, Muhammed's new novel, was playing with Jungian interpretations of the legend of Solomon and Sheba, reified onto Horn of Africa politics. Muhammed had been reading *The Wise Wound*, Sheba as Kali, a menstruating woman who had snuck into paradise. Her dream in the garden had been of splicing Muhammed's feminism onto Solomon's terrible beauty, thus solving the riddle of the sphinx from whom Sheba was descended. All these years she had sought healing in the hermetic world of Muhammed's novels and now Muhammed too was writing of Solomon and dreams, writing from the point of view of a woman passing through strange men's eyes, evil eyes penetrating.

She held the book like a shield against the spikes of hibernating umbrellas through the narrow covered streets of old Chinatown. She was going to tell Muhammed everything. She told him of Solomon, her former college advisor years ago in a small Midwestern town. She had shared her journals with Solomon for nearly four years. One day he had come to her apartment and started hugging and kissing her. She had asked if he wanted to make love and he had backed out the door, promising to call her. She had sent him a love poem and he had become very angry, apparently thinking his wife might have read it. She moved to London and had a breakdown. Then she had begun studying the myth. . . .

No no no. . . One could not go on writing crazy letters to people one didn't know. How many strange-ears had she accosted with this tale of woe? Muhammed was no analyst. His knowledge of Jung was a brief guided tour. She had left the standard maps behind decades ago, hitchhiking with no destination. Something told her he wasn't the kind of man who would understand. He might take offense at her questions about Islam and women. The letter was long. She had wasted several hours and more than a few years. She tore it up.

Someone was beating Hell out of the door — short sharp knocks. Who is it? Silence. More loud pounding. Who is it? Silence. . .and a third time. She cracked the door. A tall dark man with an oil slick on his head peeked inside. She slammed the door in his face. She had been in her room for a long time. He must have seen her pass through the station earlier. He might have been watching her for days, even weeks. She saw him disappear around the corner to the hall toilet as she ran to report the incident to the desk.

It would have been her fault if he had raped her. She apologized even as she complained to the receptionist. She was wearing shiny turquoise skintights and a turquoise silk shirt with nothing under it. She had even cracked the door for him. The receptionist was full of the usual stories about Scandinavian women sleeping in the station who got men to buy them rooms and then found queues forming outside the door. He wasn't local, the woman told her — a merchant seaman from Kuala Lumpur. He had been hanging out it the bar for roughly a week now.

The knocking resumed an hour or so later just as she sat down to pee. Evil people always disturbed one on the toilet. Like viruses, they sensed when one was weakest. She jumped up and grabbed the telephone, but the switchboard was dead as usual. He heard her moving around and knocked even louder. Her hair was still wet from the bath and she had been naked inside her sleeping bag. Her mildewed laundry was hanging all over the room and on the wires outside her window. Nothing ever got dry in Asia. The shiny turquoise skin was the only thing not damp. She had seen other women dressed that way, both in Singapore and Malaysia, especially on trains and airplanes. But those were local women. They had brothers and families. They were not immoral foreigners like herself.

She stepped through the waist of a long-rose printed skirt and ran for the desk. He was sauntering around the corner back to the bar as she emerged from her room. He is not going to quit. I think we should call the police. The manager was a tough mellow old Chinese man. He led her into the bar where men were shooting pool and throwing darts. The sailor from KL made up a story about how his friend had told him his room was number 11. You're lying! she yelled as hysterically as the heroine of *The Insulted and Injured* by Dostoyevsky, which she had been reading when again so rudely interrupted. If you were looking for your friend why didn't you answer when I asked who is it? I didn't hear you. If you didn't hear me why did you keep pounding and pounding on my door? You knocked three times! I didn't knock three times. I only knocked once. You knocked three times and then you came back an hour later and knocked again. I thought my friend was there. Do I look like your friend? Are your retarded or something? Couldn't you see when I opened the door that I wasn't anybody you knew? You only opened the door for a minute and then slammed it in my face. Then why did you come back again? Do you have a brain? Why didn't you ask at the desk if you were looking for your friend? You're lying! You're taking this much to seriously. Why don't you just calm down? And why did you run away and hide when I came out of the room? Because you were staring at me. Wouldn't you stare at someone if they were pounding on your door? I was just trying to have some fun. You're spoiling my evening. (That humiliating grin in his eye. . .she might win this one, but he was sure of his ultimate victory. . .because there were millions and billions of others just like him. . . .) I'm spoiling your evening! Have I been pounding on your door all night? Why are you making such a big thing of it? I told you I was looking for my friend.

She's absolutely right, said the manager. Why don't you just admit it and apologize instead of making up stories about your friend? Alright I'm sorry. You know what you are, she said.

The summer Apathee turned 19 she had hitchiked for three months with an old friend from summer camp in the North Woods, old friend from the horse show circuit, double jointed in the knees, always leaping over fences. Every man who picked them up had wanted her friend. She had no money and was living off free dinners and hotel rooms. Her friend was insanely naive and still a virgin at twenty. Apathee was beginning to feel like a pimp. She watched innocence turn to cunning in the eyes of the child she had always tried to protect against the cruelty of those with greater intellectual endowments. She had found that this strange childwoman had understood as the more sophisticated did not when she talked of Dostoyevsky with sixteen year old seriousness.

No one cared and no one understood. The road and the sky went on forever. She had fallen into love with an acid dealer, street musician, Vietnam burn-out in Boulder where she was supposed to be studying beatific history with Allen Ginsberg. The dealer had been living under a tree. She had taken him in. He had teamed up with a little Cajun who had robbed a bank in Oklahoma. They had invested the money in drugs. He announced that he didn't need her anymore, then glanced up from a biker rag with a fleshy cover to tell her she was too fat. Their knees remained touching side by side on the couch. She was taking more and more speed and acid, ignoring the parasites in her belly which caused chronic diarrhea and occasional vomiting, hoping that she too might have long skinny legs like her friend. Although never going anywhere in particular, she was always in a tremendous hurry to get there, afraid even a moment's delay might cause her to sink into unfathomable pain. The point was to keep on keeping on no matter what.

A car had dropped them on the beach just north of Santa Cruz — blue sleeping bags washed ashore like jelly fish in the early morning fog. He stood by the rust carved archway in the cliff, leaning on his cane. A nail had pierced his foot to the bone. His trembling hand held a joint between perfect square nails. Are you the guardian of the gate? she asked, having not yet dreamed of reading Dante. They smoked in silence, lulled by waves. He wore sandblown denim and a shirtless vest with pearl buttons. Long black hair streaked prematurely gray cascaded over stooping shoulders, determined chin thrust forward. Sad brown laughing eyes like Siamese fighting fish about to meet in mortal combat. Long straight nose and delicate nostrils slightly flared like a horse scenting water. Stubborn pouting lip and fu manchu. High round hollow cheeks and a smile like a gold mine. He was a painter turned car thief, a Mexican wino with no I.D. He never spoke beyond necessity. The other tourists avoided him and chased him away from their schoolbuses and vans.

One day he saw Apathee's friend high jumping to show off her long skinny legs and she knew that he wanted her friend too. She wrote a thirty page doggerel rhyme about him and gave it to Tara as an assignment for a class on feminine psychology. Tara knew that beach near the University of California where she had done her Ph.D. Apathee had often hitchhiked to the "country club," as the beach people called the campus, for free showers in the gym. Tara didn't quibble about the poem's lack of redeeming academic value or amphetamine leaps of consciousness.

The poem had been the beginning of Apathee's analysis with Tara. She returned to that beach many times over the years, walking along the shore to the little cave at the end of the peninsula where she had once eaten peyote with Michael the Archangel Wino, but he never made another epiphany. One freezing Easter Sunday, wrapped in old blankets someone had lent her, she dreamt that she looked over the cliff and saw the back of his head on the beach below. He wore a beautiful embroidered oriental silk robe, but when she leapt over the edge to join him, he turned towards her and she saw that his face was covered with rotting flesh, psyche leaping to her marriage with death. That day she met another Mexican also named Michael in a stolen van who took her as far as Vancouver. Her writing amused him and he never kissed her. She read aloud from *Wuthering Heights* as he drove through the winding fog. He hadn't even bothered to peel off the Grateful Dead stickers.

A decade later Tara stood upon the stage in her tight black tights and said, "I didn't realize how aware of body I've been in my analytical work all these years." Aware of body my ass! Those tights make you aware of your body alright! I bet they make your crotch itch under all those spotlights, make you long for a long flowing Muslim robe or a Hindu Sari, cool and anonymous in the bustling city streets and skintight buses. Not hot and tight like Shakespeare — like a culture just verging on the painted word. You want to be cool as a shopping mall, an air-conditioned daydream in that hour just before the afternoon rains when everyone starts mumbling to themselves and picking their noses in the corner of subways. You want clothes as loose as the big puffy domed clouds that hang low above the mosques merging seamlessly with the minimal mirrored lines of ziggurats suspended from the "sheltering sky."

Kuala Lumpur in that hour just before the dawn when strangers seem to sense you're awake and begin phoning your room to ask if you want any company and your stomach gnaws and burns with a rage and a hunger that forbids sleep as the birds commence chirping, the deep sad male voice with the infinite chanting vowels calls the faithful to prayer and the traffic sweeps the streets of fading dreams.

Are you a religious woman? asks the Indian waiter in the station restaurant. Railway stations. Terminals. Acupuncture points. Stations of the cross. He says that your pink silk skirt and tight shiny lilac danskin are traditional Hindu colors, but you have just arrived and know nothing about Hindus. You hadn't known, had never thought about it, had wanted only to blend into the beauty of this incredible city viewed from the stone arched balcony of the mosque shaped train station hotel. Your stomach has ulcered from the fear of fear, the fear of strange men's eyes. All night through the jungle on a second class train from Thailand packed full with Chinese New Year. Waiters balancing a half dozen plates of curry on each arm to the tune of "La Bamba." You drive the tip of your capped pen deep into the aching acupuncture point just below the navel while the other hand holds *Travels in Hyperreality* by Eco, pushing tongue to roof of mouth in Taoist circular breathing and trying not to phart too loud as the train stalls for another hour in the humid chirping darkness. You step over someone vomiting on his foot in an attempt to reach the toilet, which is also full of passengers. The year of the dragon has begun. You are trapped in its belly. You have stopped for two weeks to take acupuncture for your stomach at the small local Chinese hospital in Kuala Lumpur. The Chinese doctor is teaching you to laugh with a belly full of needles. Dark eyes glow with compassion from the corners of the night.

March 3rd, 1988
There's one in every country. He's usually of the upper class, but almost invariably of mixed blood. He speaks better English or knows a little more about the outside world than his fellows. He works in a place that gives him easy access to every new face that comes into town. You're traveling alone, have hardly talked to anyone in weeks or months. So tired of rude come-ons from boys on the street. He seems polite, helpful. It's a dead set up. He's hopelessly sincere, has been dreaming of you for years before you walked in the door. He mentions marriage in his third sentence. You feel guilty. Loneliness is your native land. You can imagine how he feels. Have you really led him on so badly? He seeks the other world in you — a link to the outside, something bigger than himself. You try to make him realize that you are only a means and not an end, a womb not a tomb. If he were a cold-blooded hustler, you could tell him off and be free, but he really means it. It's no use just being friends. He is drawn to your complexity, feeling at last he's found

someone who can see him, confirm his sense of being different, his superior potential. . . . He may be in his thirties, but is usually still dependent on his family in some way, living in their house or receiving money. He has had a few tragic adventures himself and one big disappointment with a woman in some other country where he traveled. When you speak, he never listens. He says all your lines for you. He has turned down many a worthy woman while he waited for you. Sometimes he moves you to great pity and often to rage. It's too much like seeing a part of yourself.

* * *

Kumar is sitting beside you in the railway station. He wants to get up to your room. He is telling you about at Scandinavian woman who once walked into the restaurant where you have just met him. She dragged him up to her hotel room and nearly raped him. Her kunt was full of heroine. You realize he has probably never seen an Edward Munch painting, bordered in drops of sperm and blood forming fetus. His discourse is punctuated by formulaic Americanisms like, "No joking, Amnesty!" (another feature of this type of male is that he will always call you Amnesty or Atrophy or Anomie and it's useless to try to convince him your name is Apathee. He knows better.) As Kumar talks, a Muslim woman with a headscarf resembling a Catholic nun's habit is glancing over his shoulder at you with pleading shocked eyes. She obviously thinks this whole scene is the product of some gross immorality on your part and leaves in disgust when she realizes that you are impassively hearing him out. You have told him that you need to be alone, that your ulcer makes you tired, that you have to rest, that you find his company uncomfortable, that it makes your stomach raw and miserable. You want him. You want to be wanted, but only if he can really see you first. The riddle of the sphinx. You want to be understood. He wants to know if you have been to see the Batu caves yet. . . .

April 1988
Askar Muhammed was trying to write from the point of view of a woman being raped by men's eyes. Apathee had written a letter to Askar Muhammed asking how there could be anima development if one was always in the womb, the collective, the Umma. Did this not guarantee an idealized distant feminine and an abhorred earthly woman threatening incest? Hadn't that been what happened with Solomon? Hadn't it cost her much more than her life? Wasn't it wrong? Not questions, Apathee, opinions. You're animus possessed. He won't listen. He won't

understand. The letter lay shattered in the garbage. She dreamt of a man with an elephant's head.

A strange man with the head of an elephant was hugging her in a dream just before waking. He gave her the most wonderful sensation, detached, yet personal, like the hands of a blind masseur. Like a dream she had had as a teenager reading *Love's Body*. A little round man had hugged her and somehow communicated the term "parasensual," which she had sought the next morning in a dictionary. She had had a similar dream years later after visiting the Villa of the Mysteries.

Walking down to breakfast with her journal, she remembered that her father had laughed through the entire movie of the elephant man. He had been the only one in the theatre laughing. She had been very sad for him, but also embarrassed.

The restaurant had black vinyl booths and dull coffee stained red checkered tablecloths. It was serviced by a blind and senile Old Chinese man with kohl shaded eyes and a young boy who could barely reach the tables standing on his toes. The old man spoke less than a dozen words of plausible English or perhaps just didn't want to be bothered. She had managed to convey to him that she ate no meat and he had smiled and nodded approval. He charged arbitrarily, was very nervous about being paid, and cleared things while you were still trying to eat them or else stood nearby staring. If you wanted anything, he was invariably buried deep in a book, which he pretended to read by mumbling and giggling to himself. He also answered imaginary phone calls. There was not another restaurant for miles.

It was Apathee's last day before leaving for Bali and she felt obliged to visit the museum to which she proceeded directly after breakfast. . . . A strangely familiar face smiled at her through the glass — a man with the head of an elephant. GANESA, read the inscription, THE ELEPHANT GOD OF WISDOM WAS DESCENDED FROM SIVA, THE AMORAL CREATIVE DEITY. . . .

Dear Tara,

You've got to admit it's strange. All these years reading Muhammed in attempt to heal my Solomon wound. Then finally in S'pore I write him a letter and tear it up only to return from China and find Muhammed has flown all the way from Cairo to teach at the University fall quarter. Can you believe?

I see patterns in what he says in class. I've begun to weave a web around him. I wrote him a long letter. He never mentioned it, never acknowledged receiving it. Is this meglomania as usual or does he actually spend almost our entire three hour class time responding indirectly to my letters — never meeting my eye? And is he conscious of this? That's been my big mistake with Solomon all these years — assuming he was perfectly aware of the conversations behind conversations. It turned out he hadn't understood one word of what he'd been saying to me all those years. It was all in my head.

Now Muhammed is becoming Solomon. He told a story in class last night about a man in a bar in Colon who threatened to punch him out for claiming to be Askar the Prophet. The man had a photograph of a much younger Askar in his briefcase. He told Askar that Muhammed was a famous author, hence he must be lying. The story was meant to illustrate "Borges and I" — the great Homeric cliche of the double. Je est un autre (Rimbaud). The two brothers fighting for the love of the Moon goddess, which Graves claims is the perennial theme of all poetry. It was exactly the kind of story Solomon would have told, exactly as Solomon would have told it.

So you see, I've decided I have to give Muhammed the poems about Solomon. I'm so scared that I've decided I'm going to do it tomorrow no matter what — tomorrow or never. The way I see things isn't really real and yet . . .

* * *

The Moon was going void at 12:14. She had been afraid to make an appointment, afraid of disappointment. Still she might just make it if she went directly after Greek class. She might just make it to his office before the Moon went void. Astrologers said it was bad luck to do anything when the Moon was void, making no major aspects before entering a new sign, not translating the light of any other planet down to Earth. Zeus had swallowed Metis and Pallas Athena had not yet burst forth from his head as the new crescent. They said anything could happen when the Moon was void of course. Anything could happen and nothing would come of it.

12:12 according to the digital clock in the basement of the English Department. She might just make it yet except that she was going the wrong direction. Damn these buildings! She might just make it yet. . . . His office right around the corner. . . . She was rushing like a woman pursued by trolls.

She had been to his office once before. She had forgotten her headphones after class and gone back to find him alone in the hallway, acting guilty as if he thought she thought he had stolen the damned things. Her $12 headphones. I wanted to talk to you anyway, he said. Have you got a minute? I have to get my bicycle. It's not London, she said, as he led her to his office in the basement. Bicycling in the winter here is Hell. Ah yes, he smiled, the weather. . . Do you suggest I invest in a car? No, not that! If I could do one thing I'd destroy all the cars.

I read the writing you submitted. . . . Is that what you want to use for the class? I . . .don't know. . .I thought I might give you a bunch of poems and let you decide.

You seem different than the others, he said. What do you think of all this? She was different because she heard voices on her headphones like Joan of Arc. He had picked up her headphones. She couldn't speak and stood staring at *Beloved* by Toni Morrison on his desk. I'm teaching that in the other class, he smiled. I loved *Song of Solomon*, she said softly. Beloved beloved be-loved. Did he know? Had she maybe actually sent that letter from Singapore? Goodday to you then, he said suddenly.

* * *

Yes, he said, in the tone of someone who didn't like being disturbed. I brought you something. The door opened. She handed him a sealed manilla envelope with a tarot reading recorded on its surface in lieu of an address. It had been a very positive reading, especially considering she used the Crowley deck, which tended to call a spade a spade. Her final outcome was the Queen of Wands, a maenad in a long flowing robe bathed in golden light, holding forth the pine cone thyrsus of Dionysus. A leopard reclined at her feet, unable to change its spots.

Sit down, he said, squeezing the envelope until the stick-em popped open. Somehow for all her calculations she hadn't counted on such a peculiar development. She had thought that if she could make it to his office by 12:14 and hand him the envelope. . . He began to remove the sixty page manuscript and cover letter scribbled in various shades of magic marker. Don't read it while I'm here! Ah. . .yes, he smiled.

Have you read any of the other writers in the African series? Her head shook sideways. Because it's strange when someone tells you they found one of your books at. . .you said in your letter that you took one of my novels out of Swiss Cottage Library in London? Um hum. . .One wonders why. . .It was well written. What's your racial background? Are you slavic? Eastern European? She kept her coat tightly buttoned and stared at the bookcase while reciting: German, English, French, Danish, and Welsh.

Muhammed said he had written part of a novel in Denmark living at the home of some lesbian friends. They were out all day. He didn't want anything to do with the Danes in the village so he wrote. . .She had bicycled in Denmark — a good place to bicycle. . . .

The door knocked. Muhammed looked confused. Slowly she twisted the knob without moving from her chair. Open sesame and enter Prince Hamlet! A tall thin bearded Ethiopian was leaning over her chair. Apathee, this is Solomon.

The Ethiopian smiled. You know each other? Yes, we know each other.

Hello Apathee! Solomon added kindly, bowing ever so slightly. He volunteered to step outside and let them finish, backing out so gracefully, just as he had done a decade ago when she had asked if he wanted to make love. I think I saw a chair out in the hallway, he said diplomatically. Like her father he had started his career in foreign affairs and ended up a provincial petty bureaucrat. Like her father he seemed to thrive on obscurity.

The manila envelope lay unsealed atop Muhammed's desk. Solomon had been furious with her for sending him a love poem ("No Deposit/No Return — Compassion, One Size Fits All") in an unsealed envelope. She had been poor and had always recycled old envelopes like the prostitute in Muhammed's first novel restitching her sealed vagina to resell herself as a virgin. The stick 'em was worn out, but the metal clasp still closed firmly enough. She understood nothing about marriage (or mirage as she called it), but she had assumed that wives weren't supposed to read their husbands' mail. . .and if they did. . .well then that was their problem. . . . Wasn't it?

We have very different ideas of what art is, young lady. You'd better learn not to write about your friends! We have very different ideas of what art is. And this after all those years of telling her to read Henry Miller! Trapped behind glass, his eyes criticized her like paintings. You'd better learn not to write about your friends.

She had been so careful to seal the envelope this time, but the genie had gotten out of the bottle again. Muhammed continued to speak of Denmark, but his voice had lost all sense of its own importance. Goodday to you then! he said suddenly.

Sharon Brown

BORDERS:
THOUGHTS AND IMAGES

Friday Morning
This morning I went down to the Wailing Wall or the "Cottel" in the
Old City of Jerusalem. The first time I was there was three weeks ago.
I was with three other Americans from the group I had been volunteering with on an army base in the Negev Desert. They had always dreamed
of being in just this spot. One of my friends started to cry, and later talked
about the flashbacks he had as he began to pray. They concerned his
family's journey out of Russia. They moved from Russia to Italy, and
from there, to Canada before settling in the United States, a real odyssey
that took over six years between the time they left Russia until they
reached their final destination.

The Wall symbolized for him and his family the endurance of Jews
as a people, and the security of a Jewish nation which many Jews dream
of making their final resting place. He described the memories of this
journey as if they came forward out of some deep rooted part of him,
and it seemed as if the tears welled up from that same place he had not
known existed before: like an ancient treasure just uncovered in himself.
It was his strong sense of identity to a land and to a culture that perhaps,
to be honest, I envied; that ingrained belief he had in belonging.

This time I came to the Wall by myself. I wanted to be a participator
instead of distancing myself through the lens of a camera, as I had done
on my first visit. I wanted to see if I could capture that same feeling —
that I could experience "my Jewishness." I never understood what that
really meant. Both my parents were Jewish, but I was never brought up
with the religion and always felt myself a fraud when I claimed to be
Jewish. Like my parents, I was born Jewish, but that's the only reason
why I have adopted Judaism as part of my heritage. Now I believe that
being a Jew is more than that. "Jewish identity" becomes tangible and
meaningful through living according to specific values and allying
oneself to Jewish communities all over the world. Judaism is an entity

that encompasses the spirit, the intellect, and culture, and I have come to realize that all these aspects are a part of me in some way I hadn't been willing to explore before, and it was no longer enough to call myself a Jew without questioning what that meant to me. I remembered a conversation I had when I was younger with my parents which still has a powerful impact on me. I was wondering whether I had the right to call myself a Jew if I never practiced the religion. They told me that wasn't the issue. Calling yourself a Jew was only important if another Holocaust-like event occurred. They said, "The fact is, in that situation, it doesn't matter whether you are religious or that you don't identify with being Jewish. You will be labeled a Jew whether you like it or not. So you better accept that you are a Jew now." My interpretation of their comment was that someday, the choice could be taken away from us, and we will be forced to acknowledge that being Jewish is a basic identity that none of us can dismiss. I didn't want to wait with my hands over my eyes until some awful event forced them away from my face. Visiting Israel was, for me, a place to start. And part of my reasons for going there was not only to find out if I could connect with the spiritual component of Judaism, but, also, with the community, and, through the community, the culture. There is a special connectedness that other Jews have talked about regarding being in a country filled with people who are of "their own kind" and experiencing the intense emotions that are brought forth by visiting holy places which are so personal and significant to Jews.

I wanted to know if I could feel this way too. So, I went down to the Wall, and I placed my hands and forehead flat on the surface. The stones were cool even under the hot sun. I closed my eyes to try to pick up the energy that everyone else around me seemed to be absorbing. I'm not sure what I expected to feel. It was a peaceful moment. I could hear murmers and clothing rustle as the Hassidim rocked back and forth in prayer. But there was nothing else. I suppose a quiet moment is all I should have expected. And I have the feeling that no matter how many lectures and courses I take, or religious and historically significant landmarks I visit, that sense of belonging is going to elude me, because finding an identity is not like buying some ready-made cake from a store. It's not something that is going to "happen" to me just because I go through the motions of looking for one. It's just not that easy.

Friday Afternoon

I was a little nervous about traveling to the West Bank from Jerusalem all by myself. I had heard horror stories about ambushes and stonings which had occurred on the route to the settlements through Arab villages. And it was true that each window on the bus had the telltale web of cracks spraying outward from one specific center. This is what happens when a small object is thrown with some force at a piece of shatterproof glass. It cracks — and the refracted image cracks too and becomes jagged and edgy, but the disfigured window very rarely breaks. And, I have been thinking that this image seems to be a kind of analogy to the trials of Jews everywhere. It is a particularly powerful one in the Arab-Israeli conflict, because Israel, like the resilient window, continues to stay intact despite the incredible disparity between its small population and the volume of its Arab neighbors. However, there are lasting traces, because the violence leaves fragments of hatred and distorted images both sides have towards each other, which, inevitably, spread down to succeeding generations.

I am baffled by the depth of this enmity these people feel for each other. It seems to me that the most ironic and tragic aspect of this situation is that violence and hostility are just as psychically harmful to the perpetrator, because they leave their ugly residue on the creation of that individual's own sense of self. In the end, bigotry and vindictiveness towards others is like spitting on one's own image. So, everyone is destined to lose.

Saturday Afternoon

It's Shabbat, and I'm sitting behind a trash can dumpster outside hiding, so no one can see that I'm writing on a Saturday. It is a time Jews set aside for rest, reflection and prayer. Prayer and the study of the bible is the only "work" that is allowed in religious households. It is considered a holy day purposefully separate from the everyday duties that can cause clutter in the minds and souls of people during the rest of the week.

But, despite my guilty conscience for breaking the letter of the law during Shabbat, I felt I had to record some of my impressions of the family with whom I'm spending the weekend. I'm staying with an American-born family who have made "Aliyah" — which means becoming an Israeli citizen — in an orthodox settlement called Bet El, situated in the West Bank. I was set up with this family by a doctor I became friends with at the army base where I have been volunteering. He was doing his reserve duty and invited me to spend Shabbat with him and his family, however, at the last minute he and his family had to leave town, so he arranged to have me stay with another family in the same settlement. Being a typically reserved, somewhat insular American, it continually surprised me how easily Israelis invited virtual strangers into their homes for Shabbat. The only criteria for the hospitality was that the individual was Jewish. It is a way for Israelis to make visiting Jews feel at home, because they believe that Israel is the true home for all Jews.

The Frankels are a large family: two parents and six children. The parents were originally from New York City, and when their oldest child was three months old, 19 years ago, they moved to Israel. Both are teachers, and David Frankel is in the midst of negotiating an offer to become principal at one of the high schools on the settlement. I think that both had always planned to move to Israel. When they first moved to Israel they lived on a kibbutz for many years and loved it. Mrs. Frankel told me how helpful it was for them to be able to step into a ready-made community. They were also enamored with the ideals kibbutz living represented. These ideals worked for Israel for a long time. They were based on the belief that all Jews should feel they had a personal investment in building the country through a cooperative system. In addition, Jews needed to work together very closely: to build up the land, much of which was swamps; to protect that land; and to develop an economic system and government from scratch. However, according to Mrs. Frankel, kibbutz life, after awhile, began to promote mediocrity because of the communal structure. They also wearied of having no privacy. Settling in the West Bank satisfied their need to build something new, to have a secure community, but to retain the integrity of their family as a separate unit.

So, for the most part, this weekend, I have been a true observer: sitting out of the way on the perimeter of whichever room they are occupying at the moment. The Frankels live out their Shabbat as they always have, and my presence does not change the tone of the performance of the weekend rituals, because they are truly interwoven within the fabric and the meaning of their lives. They are a cohesive, closely-knit family, and the strength of the relationships creates a feeling that they are a whole entity: completely dependent only on each other. And they are so comfortable with each other and their own roles within the family that watching them prepare for Shabbat is like viewing an expertly choreographed dance.

That sense of enclosure and completeness is reflected in a fleeting way as I observe a silent, loving moment between Mrs. Frankel and her youngest son, Aron, at the kitchen table. No others are needed. It also occurs to me that the belief that "no others are needed" is reflective of Israel as a whole. There is constantly that division between Jew and Gentile. Being a Jew automatically makes one extended family. But, anyone else is considered an outsider. I am a Jew, but am disconnected from the religion and the culture, so I hover over the border: not quite family and not quite stranger.

Saturday Night

Shabbat is now officially over. We have just concluded the third meal of Shabbat and the final candle lighting prayer called "Havdalah" meaning making separations. During "Havdalah" everyone cups their hands so that the light of the braided, multi-wick candle is reflected on the fingernails and casts shadows onto the palms. What is so beautiful about Judaism is that every part of life has another meaning. Thus, even the mundane is imbued with significance, so that nothing is ever taken for granted.

In this case, God is thanked for the gift of the light. Because using light is prohibited from sundown to sundown, the "Havdalah" is the first use of the light, and, also, an acknowledgement that illumination is needed for any creative work. But, this tradition has a whole other level of interpretation. This is where the term "Havdalah" becomes so signifcant. "Havdalah" refers to the image of light casting shadows which signifies many divisions in the life of a Jew. It separates the light from the dark, the holiness of Shabbat from the mundane duties of the week, and the division between Israel and all the other nations. It commemorates a history of building boundaries which many Jews feel is integral to surviving as an entity. I am not sure that I agree with that belief. I think that concentrating on differences rather than similarities amongst people perpetuates the "us against them" philosophy. What I do know is that all people have the same basic needs: for life; for growth and love; and they need each other to fulfill them.

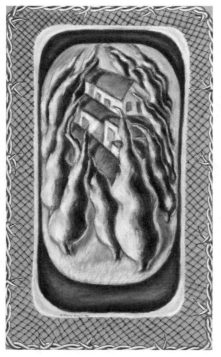

Sunday Morning

On my way back to Jerusalem from Bet El, the bus stopped at another settlement. As the bus wound around the curved road, I looked out the window and saw that all of the buildings were built on a central plot encompassed by the road. Tall poplar trees had been planted so that they completely encircled the buildings: leaning inward towards them as if to enfold them lovingly. I could barely see the roofs of the buildings. It seemed that the people living there had enclosed themselves first by the buildings, then the trees, the road and, finally, the barbed wire fence: squares inside three concentric circles to mark their territory. In addition, there were men guarding the settlements twenty-four hours a day. In fact, during Shabbat, David Frankel had to get up at three in the morning to take his turn at guard duty. All of the men rotated shifts even on Shabbat or holidays. And as I watched the cars leaving and entering both this settlement and Bet El, I saw that most had metal grids attached to the windows to protect drivers from stonings like those which were used to protect ground level floors from someone breaking into the building.

This is normal life for Jews who live in the occupied territories. Apparently, the Frankels and others I spoke to would not live anywhere else. They feel comfortable in their protected little community where all the faces around them are known and the values are shared. I'm not sure that I could live that way. I have strong doubts about living within borders that are so impregnable, because I would need to feel I could go out, and that other, non-Jewish people would be welcomed in, too. But, another part of me longs to wrap myself up in a circle of people who are like family to me, like the Bet El residents are to each other, and to set myself securely among them.

Jane and Katherine Maehr

THE SEARCH FOR BLIND
CAMELS AND BALLOONS:
A MOTHER-DAUGHTER MEMOIR

I was five when we lived in Iran. My mother was 35. Our memories are drastically different. While she was concerned about the social, cultural, economic, religious, and language differences, which brought exhilaration and fear, I concentrated on my Barbie dolls, people who touched my hair, and six-foot tall rose bushes.
—Katherine Maehr

MOTHER: When we decided in the spring of 1973 to take our family of five to Iran for a year's sabbatical, the fears began. At that time there was already much concern about airport security and unaccompanied luggage. But the real terror was having to explain and justify to my parents just why we were going.

Try it. Try to explain why it would be a wonderful opportunity for your three children under age 12 to accompany their parents halfway around the world to a Muslim country. Explain this to grandparents who had grown up, courted, married, raised their family, attended church and lived ever after in the same county in central Nebraska.

DAUGHTER: I want to go back to Teheran. But I can't. It doesn't matter who is ruling the country, or what the political situation is. I know if I go back, I will be struck by sights and sounds which I was not aware of when I was five. My memories allow Iran to be a time, a series of emotions, and epiphanies. I don't want to see the mosques and ancient ruins, and learn more about the culture. I want to find an old man with a withered face who sold balloons on Sunday afternoons.

MOTHER: We rented our house in the States, furnished with bedding and linens, the china and silver that we received as wedding presents. We went to Teheran, and found a small, unfurnished apartment, without central heat, and plumbing that amounted to little more than a tiled hole in the floor. We bargained for kerosene and learned to pronounce words we did not understand.

We gave up dependable food sources like Safeway homogenized milk, chickens already separated into fryer parts, homegrown potatoes and Kellogg's cereals. In exchange, we had to encourage the children to try bread which was not white, meat which wasn't wrapped in plastic, and beets which were roasted on carts and kept hot in old newspapers. Lambs were selected for butchering "on the hoof" and fresh vegetables needed to be soaked in an antiseptic solution before serving.

DAUGHTER: We didn't have too many friends. In all of our school, I think that we were the only American kids who didn't have parents who served in the military. And I realized that the very first day of school. I had never been to school before, but I wasn't too nervous. I didn't have any experience to make me nervous, or frightened. But my brother Mike stayed by me, and made sure that I found the line for Mrs. Kelly's first grade class. When he went to find the line for fifth grade, I turned and started talking with the girl behind me in line. I still remember her name. Heather Bluett. She had the strangest voice, a southern accent, I realize now, and wore the prettiest, laciest dress, white socks, and black shiny shoes. Her blonde hair had a wonderful soft ribbon in it.

"What did you bring for lunch?" I opened up my brown paper bag and showed her. A flat pita, filled with sausage, and some fruit. She crinkled her nose. "I have peanut butter and jelly, and some chocolate pudding." I can remember explaining to my Mom the importance of having something more prestigous than salami and pita bread. I needed to have chocolate pudding in my lunch. She explained that we couldn't buy any chocolate pudding because it wasn't in the neighborhood stores. "But Heather Bluett had some today." And then it was explained that Heather Bluett lived in military housing, they had a commissary where they could buy American food. I wanted to shop there. But we weren't allowed. After that, school made me more nervous.

MOTHER: There were a few other things to be confronted. The language was Farsi, and the little German I knew from college had not prepared me for that. Mail often took as long as six weeks to arrive from the States, and even then, had often been opened. We had been told there were good pediatricians who spoke English. And when the children got sick despite all of the shots they had been given, we learned that, in fact, the doctor did speak English.

DAUGHTER: We didn't have many toys. Space was limited, so a lot of our things had to be carried. I was small, and couldn't carry much. I had a few Barbie dolls, and a friend we met in Iran made clothes to fit Barbie and Skipper. She must have used an old scarf. All of the dresses were the same yellow and black batik pattern. I wanted to have a "real" baby doll. One that was life sized. For the first half of the year I used pillows, and our cat Shah, and paraded around the apartment pretending I was a mom, with a baby. The cat ran away soon after. I never told anyone that right before Shah disappeared, I had punished her for being a bad little girl. I made her sit in the closet. Then she was gone. I don't know how she got out.

In the winter we had snow days. And if the snow was wet enough, my brothers and I would make big forts, and throw mushy snow balls at each other across the court yard. Mike made his fort in one corner of the court yard. Marty made his in the opposite corner. Then the snowballs just flew. They had some sort of point system about who was winning each battle. At the end, the winner got me. It operated something like a handicap. While my teammate was busy defending the fort, I'd lie down and make snow angels, or small snowmen, which would be stepped on when my brother took a step back. A truce would finally be called, and I'd wander back towards our steps. And then someone would whizz one of those snowballs, and I'd go face down in the snow. It happened every time.

On weekends we went skiing. I remember the weekend Mike hurt his leg while skiing down the mountain. We had to leave early to get back to Teheran. And Mike got to have the whole backseat of the car, because his leg was in a cast.

MOTHER: According to our visa, I wasn't allowed to have a work permit. But when we arrived in Teheran, and enrolled our children in the American school, we learned that the tuition had been raised $500 per child. To ask the parents —who felt we were irresponsible for being in Iran— to lend us the money was not an option. So I went down to the superintendent's office, filled out an application, and three weeks later I was hired to teach the third grade. I rode the school bus with the children, and was just down the hall from them during the day; that was comforting. I hadn't planned to go back to work, especially not in Iran. But back to work it was.

One morning, on a day that school had been cancelled because of snow, there was a knock at the door. It was a policeman, checking passports and work permits. Since I was at home, as far as I know the Iranian government did not find out that I unexpectedly had resumed my career.

DAUGHTER: We had every Monday afternoon off from school. My Mom was a teacher at the American Elementary School, so my brother Mike and I went home alone on those days. For months, every Monday as we got off the bus Mike said "Aw! I forgot the house key!" And every time he was kidding. One time he said that, and I just laughed. But he had forgotten it. For an hour or so, we just sat on the front stoop of our apartment building. We skipped rocks off the pavement of the alley, and watched the workmen who were building a mosque across the street. Then Mike decided to climb over the walls to our courtyard. When he came back, he had some empty Coke bottles. We went down to the corner market, and the man gave us money for returning the bottles. We each got an ice cream cone with the change. We went back to our stoop, and sat, eating ice cream. My Dad came home a while later, and was really upset that we had been on the stoop. I think Mike got in trouble because he had forgotten the key.

MOTHER: Everything about going to Iran was potentially frightening to me. But I knew when we first had the opportunity, that if we didn't take it, the results would be more disturbing than a new language and different kinds of food. I was acknowledging that I wanted a lifestyle that valued change and growth. I was announcing that I wanted a life and lifestyle different from my parents. I wanted to be able to claim opportunities and memories that were less predictable than ironed linen table cloths and being home, safely, every Sunday. I dreamed of the Caspian more than windows which sparkled with Windex. I wanted to touch the blue tiles of Meshad's domed mosques. And, I cared more for the romance of Joshaghan carpets than sensible blue/green shag. I knew that for me, there was more to be feared in staying home, serving fried chicken on wedding china, than there was with bargaining in unkown Farsi for an unplucked rooster.

I knew that I needed to acknowledge my dreams. But it was hard. To admit that I wanted to travel, to see and do different things implied that I wanted more than I had. To explain that I wanted to see strange sights and unfamiliar architecture somehow implied that corn fields and bungalows were not enough to satisfy me. It undoubtedly suggested to my parents that I questioned the lifestyle they had adopted.

DAUGHTER: On Saturdays we went to a Persian carpet market, owned by two men named David and Rubin. The rugs were piled almost to the ceiling, with ladders propped against them. My brothers and I climbed to the top, and David brought us hot tea, with lots of sugar cubes. My parents would exchange news with David and Rubin, perhaps show interest in a carpet. I pretended I was the Empress Farah, sitting on a throne. My parents have a photograph of me, wrapped in a big white bath towel, with a paper crown on my head. The caption in the photo album says "Katie, age 5, pretending to be the Empress Farah." I don't ever remember dressing up in that towel, or making the crown that was on my head. I guess that I don't remember being the Empress, except for when I sat on top of all those carpets, and felt so much taller and could see so much more than when I was on the ground. I do remember that feeling, and because of the photo in the album, I think that the feeling of sitting on top of all of those carpets, being so high up is the feeling of wanting to be an Empress. Even today, I'll climb up ladders, stop and look around, and for the slightest second, I'll have that feeling of being in charge, of seeing all the things that other people can't.

MOTHER: I had read about a place, deep in the darkened, inner maze of the bazaar in Isfahan, where a blinded camel was hitched to a stone grinding wheel. For as long as anyone could remember, this camel had plodded in a rutted, never-varying path, crushing to meal whatever grain was provided. I wanted to see that camel. I wanted to explore that bazaar. I wanted to experience Isfahan.

But suggesting to my parents that I felt it was important to search for Isfahan's blind camel, implied that those who long ago stopped looking for adventure were as blind as the ancient beast who simply walked in circles.

DAUGHTER: After Christmas we went on a trip. We went to Isfahan where we stayed in a big hotel. And we went to see the ruins of Persepolis. The stairs of the ancient, ruined palace were still intact. My Dad explained why the stairs were as shallow, and odd-sized as they were. They had been designed for horses to climb up, so the animals could enter the palace, as part of a great procession. I tried to imagine what event would ever be significant enough to allow horses to walk inside of the house.

A little later, as my family walked ahead, I saw something on the ground. It was blue. I crouched down, and began to dig. After a while it came loose. It had rounded edges, and was hard, like a rock. I put it in my coat pocket, and kept it until third grade, when I got a new coat. After four years of Art History classes in college, I know that it must have been a pottery shard of some sort, and feel a sense of guilt about removing the piece from the site. But it was a very pretty color, and no one else in my family had seen it.

MOTHER: The holidays brought special challenges. The children missed the food they had grown up with, so birthday gifts meant special trips to a market that imported American products. We closed our eyes to the cost and bought jars of peanut butter and boxes of Captain Crunch for birthdays. We closed our eyes several times when we bought a baby doll, imported from China for Katie's Christmas. Somehow, a five-year-old just had to have a Christmas doll.

DAUGHTER: For Halloween we carved squash. I got to wear a costume, but I can't remember what I was dressed up as. I waited as my Mom put candles in each of our squashes. Then I got my coat and waited. Then my parents told me that we couldn't go trick-or-treating. I throught it was because we were in trouble. Both of them tried to explain that the people who lived in Teheran didn't know about trick-or-treating. That was the craziest thing I had ever heard. Everyone knows about Halloween and trick-or-treating. For Christmas, we hung our socks on the *bokari*, or heater. I got roller skates, and a real doll, which was life-sized. Since I couldn't rollerskate outside, my brothers and I pretended that the spaces between the carpets were streets, and we played "taxi" with one of us pulling the other down whatever streets the passenger on skates asked to drive on. Usually I was the driver, and Mike and Marty were the passengers.

MOTHER: Iran was, even in the 1970's, a place of unbelievable contrasts. Women of wealthy families were educated abroad, expressed concern for better health care and less government control, wore beautiful clothes and exquisite jewelry. When they worked at challenging jobs they were supported at home by a host of servants and members of an extended family — often illiterate, and almost certainly still under the impression that women should be veiled in the presence of all men except their husband, father and brothers.

Nowhere were the contrasts more observable than on the streets of Teheran. Traffic on Eisenhower Boulevard was clogged with push carts, donkeys, camel caravans, herds of sheep — all competing with Mercedes Benz busses and imported cars. The irony was that the busses and cars were being driven by the same impatient young men who last month had herded the sheep and camels.

The rush to gain western style and use American products was made more poignant by watching the *jubes*— the ribbons of water that flowed along all city streets. While this system had once represented a value as a source of running water for washing and ritual cleansing, city traffic, animal waste and urban pollution had all but obliterated it. Still, more than once a young man was seen dipping water from the *jube* to rinse his mouth after brushing his teeth with American produced Colgate toothpaste.

DAUGHTER: We didn't have a car. So there was this man, who worked at the University with my Dad, who drove us, when we wanted to go anywhere. His name was Mr. Zabbah. He was really tall, and whenever he came over, he would pick me up and put me on his shoulders. And he always touched my hair. A lot of people did that. Mike and I were the only people in the neighborhood who had blonde hair. But I didn't like it when strangers in weird clothes, who smelled, touched my hair. It was only okay if Mr. Zabbah did it, because he was nice. When we went skiing, he helped me build snow men.

MOTHER: Zabbah loved our children. When Mike hurt his leg on the ski slopes, Zabbah bargained with the ski patrol to get him to bring Mike off of the mountain. And when he finally brought Mike down, Zabbah bargained with the doctor who wanted money up front before he would look at Mike's leg. I couldn't understand what they were saying. I knew Mike was in pain, but I didn't know what was wrong. And no one would tell me.

DAUGHTER: There were these really big rose bushes in the courtyard, but we weren't allowed to cut any of the flowers off, because they belonged to the man who owned our building. His wife would come out and put soggy tea leaves on the plants. Once I went over and smelled the flowers and she came out onto her balcony and screamed at me. I got scared, and never went too close to the bushes again. But when I close my eyes now, and think just hard enough, I can still remember the way the bushes smelled, and that smell, which is different from other rose bushes, still makes me a bit scared.

MOTHER: My parents still don't really understand what it was we were doing in Iran. They saved our letters and mentioned it to their friends, most of whom seemed more interested than they ever did. We brought them gifts of copper pots and a small Persian carpet. My mother vacuumed the carpet, kept it in a back bedroom, and finally encouraged us to take it back to our house. There really was no place for it with wall-to-wall carpeting, she said. The copper pots are in the basement.

DAUGHTER: The balloon man came down our alley every Sunday. We lived on Kouchi Hasht, Neelafar, Abassabad. My Mom and Dad made me remember that. I had to repeat it over and over again. Hasht was the name of the alley, Neelafar was the big street, and Abassabad was the neighborhood. Every Sunday the man with balloons rode his donkey down Kouchi Hasht. He had balloons like I hadn't seen before. There were balloons inside of balloons, shapes of animals, balloons that looked like donuts, striped and polka dotted balloons. And they all had sticks attatched to them, instead of strings.

MOTHER: Isfahan was "half-the-world" as people had always declared. The sand along the Caspian Sea was finer and blacker than any I had ever seen, and the roses, long cultivated in old Persia, fragrant beyond believing. The beauty of carpets we watched being woven on primitive looms in sun-drenched village huts would never be matched.

DAUGHTER: I can only remember two things about our visit to Isfahan: a big hotel, and a camel that walked in circles, while roaring like a lion.

MOTHER: We walked the winding and narrow pathways through the bazaar in Isfahan and we saw the blind camel. A year or two later, we heard that the camel was gone.

DAUGHTER: Every so often pictures of Teheran will be on the news. The images are unfamiliar, a far-away place that I'm not sure I was ever in. David and Rubin are dead, their carpet store, undoubtedly gone. After the Revolution, no word was ever received from Mr. Zabbah. War and upheaval have probably changed what landscape I can remember, forever. But I always watch those pictures of Teheran carefully, and hope, that maybe, for a brief second, I'll catch a glimpse of an old man, hunched over, with one hand leading a donkey, and the other hand holding a bunch of balloons.

Nora Reza

AHAR

A dissident poet from Russia whispers to me
I whisper back
We smile. We depart
Soft pieces of ice pass between us———

from A Double Mask, Our Mission in Arras
by Reza Baraheni

MANY RELATIVES and friends came to welcome Lara and her father to Teheran. Among them Lara was happy to see Dr. Azadi and his wife, Pam. Dr. Azadi glanced around the crowded room. "But where is your dear mother? Why didn't she come?" he asked.

When Lara answered with a vague smile and a shrug, the doctor persisted. "Your mother should have come, the country is different now."

He pointed to the view of concrete and glass buildings and to the shining doorways of the Bank Melli. "Now we have everything. Before, when your mother was here, Iran was a poor country. You must write and tell her to come. You must make sure!"

Lara promised to make sure. She would write her mother and tell her that she had made a mistake leaving Iran in the first place. The country had changed. The empty desert had been replaced by tall verticals of glass and concrete and the roar of a million cars. What was not modern, machine-driven, or made of bright steel, was pushed away to slums and poor dilapidated villages. Now the city had running water, indoor plumbing, chic restaurants, even discotheques. Americans were emulated in this Iran. They were not infidels, like her mother, whose food the servants had prepared separately.

"Iran has changed so much," Dr. Azadi continued. "I tell Pam that it's unrecognizable, even to me...."

Lara's father and the other men sighed in agreement. *Yes, the old Iran had drifted away. Like a bare brown tumbleweed blowing through dust...You could never catch up with it. You could never find it again. The ancient towns and cities were gone, spoiled by neglect and greed. The heart of the country lived on only in people's laughter, stories, and memories.*

Outside on the balcony Pam lit up a cigarette and leaned against the railing. Her blond hair was longer than Lara remembered and she had lost her pixie-like expression. Lara recalled how Dr. Azadi's mother, a tall thin woman dressed all in black, had come to Buffalo in order to prevent Dr. Azadi from marrying Pam. But the dignified old mother had been unable to persuade her son not to marry an American woman, with a child from a previous marriage. Now Pam flicked away her cigarette and shielded her face from the sun. Her blue eyes seemed far away.

"Mrs. Azadi," Lara's father called. "Don't look so sad, I hear that tomorrow you are going on vacation."

Dr. Azadi laughed gently, "She doesn't like Ahar."

"I understand. Next time tell your husband to take you to the Caspian."

"Where's Ahar?" Lara asked, disappointed to learn that the Azadis were soon leaving.

"The Russian border," Dr. Azadi answered. He was an easygoing man, always ready to laugh. Lara enjoyed being around him. "I spent many summers of my childhood there. . . . Will you come with us?"

"Yes, yes I will."

"Wait a moment, my girl!" Lara's father laughed. "You've only just arrived. Besides, Dr. Azadi is making *taraf*."

"I swear it's not *taraf*. Lara is like a daughter to us. It's settled. Lara will come with us tomorrow, won't she, Pam?"

Pam leaned over the railing. She didn't say a word.

The next day Lara and the Azadis flew to Tabriz. They stayed for a few hours, long enough to have lunch, buy supplies, and hire the jeeps that would take them to Ahar. On a newsstand Lara spotted a *Time* magazine and bought it, along with a worn paperback of *The Bad Seed*. The title and the cover drawing of a young girl surrounded by an eerie light attracted her.

They drove out of the city, leaving behind the elegant tree-lined central squares and the vast northern slums. They wound up a road leading to higher and higher elevations. The earth turned red. They stopped and put on heavy canvas tents to protect themselves from the dust. The tents were standard clothing for these parts, but donning them in the back of the jeep with Pam, Lara felt excited, as though the tents were robes of initiation to another world.

For a long time they ascended the bumpy clay road. They saw no one, nor any signs of life. Wrapped up so that only their eyes were visible, they did not speak. As the dust fell on them, caking their throats and tongues and eyes, Lara sensed Pam's anxiety. Lara too felt uneasy. After a few hours, they seemed to have exhausted all there was to say.

There were no towns, no trees, only the red mountains above them and the red canyons far below. At last they ascended to a plateau and the air began to cool. Scrub appeared and gradually the colors changed from red to gold. No words, just the constant whine and jostle of the jeep. Now and then a peasant working in a field would look up and stare at them until they were out of sight. They passed through hazily marked fields and birch groves, gold and gold-green grasses. The doctor smiled and pointed to the wooded fields where he planned to hunt quail and partridge. Lara understood. This was his country and his vacation. Pam was the dutiful wife to accompany him. That Lara understood also. Pam had to be dutiful. She had married a Persian.

Riding for hours in the dust seemed extraordinary to Lara, but not to Pam. When they entered the village Lara peered around for any signs of life. Pam said abruptly, "It's not worth looking at." Lara looked anyway. To the right, along a mud road she saw a few veiled women and a police or army vehicle. The villagers too turned to stare, before the Azadi jeep headed away.

The mud walls lining the shabby mud street seemed not much different from villages elsewhere in Iran. The door in the adobe wall was so modest one might pass it by and never know it hid a garden and a stately house. Inside the garden they walked along the grassy path of overgrown blackberry bushes, dusty roses, quince and apple trees.

Parts of the house were wooden and their woodenness in that land of clay and stone and dust struck Lara as fabulous. Three walls of the sitting room were made of leaded glass windows. Interspersed among them were panes of amber stained glass, in the Russian style. Bowers of overgrown grape vines obstructed the view and even crawled in among the broken panes. It was to this house that Reza Shah, the present Shah's father, had come for hunting parties. Everywhere among the decay there were traces of what had been an era of elegance.

The days were clear. Far from the heat of Teheran, the leaves of the birch and poplar turned gold and the quince gold. The house suited Lara's idea of "the district mansion" and she wondered when they would hold the first ball.

Several days passed, but there was no ball, nor any social activity whatsoever. Lara never saw outside the garden walls. Pam said it would be unwise to go unveiled into the street, and she did not offer Lara a veil or company. The doctor went hunting. The others disappeared inside the house. But perhaps it was Lara who disappeared. She wandered the large overgrown garden and read *The Bad Seed*, a book about a girl who was born demonic and possessed the terrifying power of thinking others dead.

Hens and roosters scattered at the sound of Lara's footsteps in the dry leaves. Once she whirled around, certain she heard someone. There was no one, only the sharp edge of the blue sky above the yellowing grape arbor, the blowing leaves and light. She wanted to grasp this light, the way a child clutches a favorite toy. All the preceding months when she had wandered through school corridors, or secretly met Richard, and greedily sought his kisses, she had held away from her, like a painted mirror, this upcoming voyage to Iran. In this way she had kept September a distant reflection. And when the morning finally arrived, and her mother had waved a yellow telegram and had said, "Tomorrow you are going to Iran," Lara had not wanted to believe it. Now, seated in this unimagined garden, on a mouldy wicker chair, she drank tea and yearned for a turning point, for some magical release to another reality.

The kisses and gold coins of her new acquaintances in Teheran were gradually replaced by a conviction of complete isolation. Sometimes Pam came out and brought her a package of *Petit Beurre* biscuits. Perhaps Lara was meant to help her with the children, but she was not conscious of their presence. The fact that Pam was American, a friend of her mother's, no longer made any impression on Lara. Lara's mother didn't know where she was.

In the morning tea was served from a large brass samovar on a glassed-in porch. In the evening they sat at a table laden with dishes. The room was a mass of shadows, dark corners and flickering flame light. It took a long time for Lara to notice that she was being enticed with food. She had convinced herself that if she ate more than a biscuit she would get sick. Everything around her receded into dimness. Outside the house all was silent. Even the sounds of the river, the cries which only the poets heard...

One night, in the middle of the meal Lara unexpectedly came to life. She began a conversation with the youth who was serving the food. He was large, and his broad shoulders reminded her of Richard. Ordinarily Ahmad, for soon she would learn his name, would stand behind them passing dishes and waiting on table while they ate. Now, with a nervous smile about his lips, he came forward and politely tried to answer Lara's questions.

"What are you studying?"

"Calculus and physics."

Lara was impressed. In this mud village they were taught such things! "Oh, really," she smiled, drawn out of herself for a moment.

But her plate remained empty and in that dark room with the flickering kerosene lamps she did not notice what others said or how they looked. "What year are you?" she continued.

"Last year." His answers were short but understandable, and Lara laughed.

"I'm second year." She looked up at him dreamily.

For a couple of nights Lara carried on these conversations, showing some signs of animation. Ahmad's eighteen-year-old masculine presence had, it seemed, aroused her dejected spirits. She began to look forward to meals, although she still refused to eat anything but the biscuits and tea. She might get sick, she told herself.

There was a hallway leading upstairs. From it were doors to the servants' quarters, the kitchen and the rest of the house. Intuition, calculation or chance seemed to bring Lara close to this young man's path. She brushed against his body as often as she dared. His touch stirred her dreams. She looked up at him, her eyes lit with meaning and desire. She wanted him to put his arms around her, to hold her close.

One night Lara waited for him at the top of the stairs. She watched his shadow go back and forth under the eaves, past the lamp. Were there so many dishes to carry? Didn't he know she was waiting? "Ahmad," she whispered. He looked up at her warily, the flame of the lamp flickering beside him. Lara stepped down to the landing, close enough for him to touch her. He backed away. "Is there tea?" she asked nervously. He went into the kitchen. In a moment the old woman servant, her long silver braids tied together at the tips, came bearing a tray. Lara took the cup and continued up the stairs, her heart beating fast.

She looked forward to seeing him each night at dinner. During the day she walked about the garden, carelessly dressed, lost in a blur of shadowy thoughts, until startled by the color of a ripening apple, a falling leaf, a corner of sky. In the evening she put on a dress or a skirt. She applied small amounts of lipstick, imagining that she might thus inflame him.

One evening Pam came to her room while Lara was dressing. She looked at Lara shyly. Hesitantly, she said "I'm not used to teenagers." An image of Pam's son, far away in the United States, crossed Lara's mind. "My own children are so young," Pam explained. Lara nodded. Somehow she had managed to ignore them.

"Be careful," Pam said.

"About what?" Lara asked.

"The servant, Ahmad."

Lara blushed. Did she dare feign ignorance? "Why?" she asked ingenuously. She wanted to convince herself that she was innocent. She had forgotten that her emotions were often transparent. She was afraid then that Pam knew her fantasies, knew how she wished to be touched by that large, clumsy youth.

"This is Iran. That kind of thing isn't done, you know. Azadi asked me to speak to you." Like Lara's mother, and most Persian wives, Pam called her husband by his last name.

Lara angrily wiped off the lipstick, picked up *Time* and pretended to read. That night she made a point of not speaking to Ahmad. He served silently, as usual. Lara looked down at her empty plate. Her stomach had grown very small by then, her nerves jangled on a diet of *Petite Beurre* and tea.

For the remainder of the week Lara avoided looking at Ahmad. She stared straight ahead at the wall where the tiny old woman with the silver braids, his grandmother perhaps, stood ready to clear the table. The shadows of the lamp flitted across the granny's wrinkled face and her eyes gleamed with an intensity that embarrassed Lara. The old woman looked directly into Lara's eyes. Perhaps she guessed what Lara was feeling.

On their last night they were served a large meal of chicken in pomegranate and black walnut sauce and yellow saffron rice. "*Fes in joon* is the specialty of the region," Dr. Azadi said, "that and the delicate quail." He pointed to the basket of the birds he had hunted and brought home to be baked. They were tiny creatures, no bigger than the palm of Lara's hand, their bones small as an infant's fingers. Lara looked at the others, at the shoulder of the youth whom she desired, at Pam, whose hair in the lamplight was as transparent as the wings of a flitting moth, at the balding, good-humored doctor, and lastly, at the feast spread before her. She decided to taste something, after all.

Nora Reza

THE ERRAND

LARA LOOKED UP from the *Time* magazine she was reading. She was in a part of Teheran that was new to her. The modern glass buildings, wide boulevards, and the view of the mountains had disappeared. Everything was a dusty clay color. Busses streaming black diesel smoke screeched around a circle. "Where are we?" she asked, but Mr. Ali, who was going very fast, did not answer except to mutter under his breath. Most likely he had planned to have the morning to himself, and was disgruntled about having to deliver Lara to her aunt. "Madame Leila?" she reminded him.

"Yes, yes," he nodded. "Soon." He turned the car into a cobbled street, one with a *jube* of dirty water running right down the middle. "Five minutes," he said, holding up spread fingers. Lara watched him slip into an alley decorated with the droppings of donkeys and half-starved dogs. Mr. Ali was so skinny and bent, he resembled his shadow as it crept along the wall, wavered and disappeared.

Instantly the Mercedes was surrounded by a band of children, who touched the windows, fenders and antenna, regarding Lara with filmy eyes and faces caulked with dust. Five minutes passed. The car grew hot. She fanned herself with the magazine, smiled at the children, looked for Mr. Ali to return at any moment and grew impatient when he did not. Some women clad in black veils sat in doorways and watched her. She grew uncomfortable under their gaze. The children clamored. She tried to read her *Time*, which contained a short article about the Shah's "White Revolution," how he was giving his land away to the poor. The children, dressed in tattered rags, stretched out their hands for change. Soon she was shrugging and saying she had no more. One boy wanted to wash the windshield and she said no, fearing Mr. Ali's wrath. A couple of older boys came down the street and looked her over. They made lewd smacking sounds with their lips. Lara ignored them and they went away.

She was, it appeared, in one of the slums of south Teheran, far from her aunt's house. She looked at her watch. An hour had passed. Her thin dress was wet with perspiration. The children stepped back when she opened the door. The boys whistled. One threw a small stone near her foot. She glared at him. He covered his face laughing. The other children began laughing too. They danced around her. Lara suppressed a smile. She wanted to remain as irate as possible for Mr. Ali. He had no right to bring her here and leave her to swelter in the hot car. She planned to scold him in the same way she had heard Mrs. Aram scold him. She saw herself standing imperiously before him. "Take me to my aunt's house this instant!" she would say.

There was a cistern nearby where women were washing clothes. As she passed them they stopped their chatter and stared at her bare arms and legs. The children followed her. Their tiny sticklike shadows criss-crossed her own. She felt more and more angry with Mr. Ali. Facing the twisting alleyways she didn't know which way to turn. She walked confidently ahead, thinking to fool the children. She knew where she was going. All of the windows and doors were now shut against the noon sun. She turned a corner. The alley looked the same. Where was he? The stupid man! Soon she was lost in a maze of alleyways. The children followed her, laughing and pointing, "Miss, go down here. Miss, try this one." She refused their directions, knowing they were trying to trick her. The sun was unbearable and she longed to be back in Shemiran, beneath the mountains, on the Arams' cool, flower-strewn patio. She wanted a glass of water or coke. She turned into a dead end street and came back without seeing Mr. Ali.

The little boy who had thrown the stone at her stopped before a door. Shyly he pointed at it. Lara knocked. The door was opened by a girl, about twelve, with a checkered scarf wrapped around her head. She stepped aside to let Lara in. Lara peered into the dark. She was relieved to see Mr. Ali's scullcap, in a backroom, among a crowd of others. His heavy pinstripe suit, which had once belonged to Mr. Aram, hung ludicrously on his scarecrow body. She entered. On her left, against a wall, two boys were stretched out asleep on a wooden bed, made up of rough boards. To her right a table was piled with dry clay figures and pots. On the floor was a naked child. Among the child's bare legs and the folds of a dirty blanket some slimy furred creatures moved. Lara pulled back. Then she saw that the animals were kittens, recently-born. The child, his nose running, smiled up at her.

She stood there, wondering what to do. She looked at the figures and pots on the table more closely. The figures depicted couples in intercourse. The freestanding ones were phalluses and vulvas. She looked away, amazed that there were such things in Iran.

Mr. Ali saw her and called, "I've come," which meant "I'm coming."

The girl with the checkered head scarf said, "Please enter, Miss." She led Lara to Mr. Ali. Several people stood up and bowed, clearing a path for her. Lara nodded to them, and made little bowing gestures as she stepped through the small crowded room. "You're welcome, Miss," they murmured. "Please. . ." Mr. Ali was near a bed, where a girl was lying. The girl's hennaed hair was tangled, a scarf had fallen down around her neck. Her skin was pale and streaked. There were deep blue shadows under her eyes. The cloth that covered her was spattered in blood. Oh, God, Lara thought. She's sick. She's dying. Near the bed was a pan filled with more flesh and blood. When Lara saw this she felt scared. There was a heavy sick odor in the room. It was hot and flies were everywhere. An old woman was on her knees cleaning up. She called, "Miss, dear, come here," and gestured for Lara to come closer. Obediently Lara stepped forward, averting her eyes from the bowl of flesh and blood and the bed. The woman lifted up a cardboard box, which Lara recognized as one of Mr. Aram's wine cartons. Lara looked into it. "This hour," the old woman said, smiling.

"Beautiful," Lara answered, although the baby, born while she sat out in the car, looked not much different from the wet rags in the bowl. The others closed around Lara, regarding her with expectant eyes. She had no idea what to do. Then the girl who had let her into the room appeared with a glass of tea. "Thank you," said Lara, and accepted the tea, which was so hot she could barely hold it. Lara turned her eyes again to the new mother, a girl who looked not much older than herself. "Boy?" Lara asked, pointing to the box. The mother regarded Lara dully, and made no answer.

"*Na, dauktar,*" the old midwife said. "Next time, boy."

"Congratulations," Lara said. The midwife lifted the ugly wet creature out of the box. For a moment Lara feared that she would be asked to take it. Instead the midwife put the baby at the mother's breast. The mother turned her head away and moaned, "*Na. . .*" The baby made a few miserable sounds. The midwife grinned, as though all was going well.

Lara took a step back. She turned to Mr. Ali. "Yours?" she asked, indicating the mother and the baby.

He shook his head, but the midwife understood. "*Pedare buzurg,*" she said. Mr. Ali was the grandfather, but of the girl or the baby Lara wasn't sure. The mother was Lara's age, sixteen. This was her first child. Her labor had ended with the birth of a daughter, which perhaps accounted for the subdued atmosphere.

Lara said goodbye and walked through the path they had cleared for her. In the front room she followed Mr. Ali past the table of clay objects, which, in the yellow light of the open door, looked grotesque and lifeless. The little boy still lay on the blanket, squeezing a kitten that desperately sought to get away. In the car, Mr. Ali did not speak. Lara wanted to convey to him that she would not get him in trouble, she would not tell anyone where he had taken her.

"Your daughter is pretty. The baby is pretty," she said after awhile. Mr. Ali grunted and wiped the sweat from his face, and continued to speed and curse his way through traffic. Perhaps he thought that by delivering Lara to her aunt instantly she would forget the little errand he had kept her waiting for.

Mimi Albert

RAIN OF FLOWERS

BECAUSE WE ARE associated with the Gandhian movement, and are living and working with Gandhians at the Swadhyaya Ashram here in the impoverished province of Haryana, one of the female workers has invited us, the six European women, to visit a small primitive village, about an hour's drive from our ashram.

The inhabitants of the ashram, most of them social workers in the tradition of Mohandas Gandhi and Vinoba Bhave, have been doing as much as they possibly can to help people in this poverty-stricken area. They've already helped put in tube wells through which water is pumped and distributed through the arid fields. There are plans for developing the growth and distribution of village crafts, like weaving and dyeing, and a paper-making plant already exists near the ashram living quarters. Also, for years, the head woman at the ashram, whom everyone calls Mata-ji — "honored Mother" — has been speaking to local village women about health and sanitation. Now that we are living and studying there with the Gandhians, she has asked us for our help.

"If you would come to spend a day in this village, how much influence you might have on the women here, especially if you talked about the lives you led in the West," she tells us.

"Besides, they would so much like to meet you. You know, they've never met women from any other country. They know nothing but the lives they themselves lead, so much like the lives of their mothers and their grandmothers before them. There's so little change, especially among the women, who live most of the time at home and go nowhere. Some of them have never been on a bus, or even seen the Grand Trunk Highway."

It takes very little to convince us. The only questions concern setting a time and hiring a car to bring us there. At last, on a warm March Sunday, the six of us set out with Mata-ji and one of the ashram men to drive and guide us. All the other men are left at home. Driving over the unpaved roads, miles back into the country, we hardly know what to expect. Something dull, perhaps; a few wary women from the outlying villages, which are no more than a cluster of brick and mud houses, who may sit and listen to us with suspicious faces before going their ways on the treeless lanes. Speeches through the hot afternoon. An exchange of greetings, probably mostly only with the men of the village, as Indian women tend to be curious but shy.

The six of us living here — Anthea, Edythe and Margot from England; Gayle, Tanya and myself from the United States — are probably the only Western women in this area for hundreds of miles. To remain as inconspicuous as possible, we always dress in what we hope is unremarkable clothing; simple saris, well-pleated and just the proper length, hair combed back from the forehead with oil as Indian women usually wear their hair, no jewelry or only a pair of small golden earrings. Careful expressions on our faces.

Instead, we're so conspicuous that when we take the bus from Sonepat, the nearest city in this dusty, rural area, we find ourselves surrounded by crowds. Dozens of silent men with nothing else to do make a ring around us at the bus station, standing still and just staring.

Now, crossing the wide plains in the car that was sent for us, we notice women stopping their work of picking and weeding in vermillion fields of chillies to fold their hands and look, men pausing for a moment behind the white bullocks that pull their plows, watching us as they might watch the setting sun. The large car is itself a rarity on these back roads.

At last, in the distance we see a mass of sandstone buildings, open to the sky. The buildings are low and blend into the flatness of the earth with sameness and the color of dust; they have a peculiar look of abandonment and habitation at the same time, like a Greek ruin.

These low, sandstone buildings are the destination of our journey. Waiting for us before the buildings that house the kitchen and the school is a small, laughing cluster of women, mostly heavily veiled and dressed in their newest pants suits (*salwar kameez*); our hostesses. They've been expecting us and they don't stare. But when we skid to a stop on the rutted path and step out of the car, they hurl things at our chests and faces. For a moment I'm astonished, almost scared. Then I reach up and catch one of the things they've thrown, crushing its fragrance with my hand. A bright, thick marigold. Flowers. They're pelting us with flowers. Marigolds fall into the road like stones. The huge pigs roll over in their puddles on golden flowers, nosing pedals and stems. Then we're hung with garlands, like those placed around the shoulders of the gods. My garland smells of sun and fresh earth and homage. I want to keep it on all day, but after a few minutes we're asked to hand them back.

The women who come to greet us are led by a small figure completely draped in navy blue. She comes forward and raises her hands in a gesture of welcome. We can't see the expression of her face because she's in *purdah*. What this means is that above her very plain dark blue trouser suit and over her head, she had draped a dark blue veil. The veil covers her hair and face, completely obscuring her. All the married women are covered in the same way, so we feel as if we're being greeted by an army of faceless phantoms. Only widows, unmarried girls, children and men, who wear muslin shirts and *lungis*, have uncovered faces. Most of the women are bodies topped with swirls of chiffon.

"I've tried so very hard to get them to give up the *purdah*," Mata-ji says, indicating to them. "But it is hard for them to change. They will not do it."

She herself has always gone proudly bareheaded. In her homespun sari with bare feet and her strong dark tired eyes, she's well-known to the villagers. She wraps her arms around the dark blue woman now, and brings her forward to us.

"The women say they couldn't live in this village with the men if they didn't cover their faces. They say it's not the men who force them to do this, it's their own choice. Even this wonderful young woman, who is a college graduate and now teaches the children and is so much respected, even she cannot remove the veil."

As she says this, Mata-ji laughs and tugs gently at the young schoolteacher's veil. The younger woman resists, but she, too, is laughing, and the two embrace.

These aren't Moslem women, but Hindu. There are no Hindu strictures against women baring their faces: this is probably a result of the influence of the great Islamic Mughal empire, which completely dominated Northern India for two centuries. Like so many faiths and customs, those of the Mughals have been swept into the daily life of village India and thrive as if they've always existed here. Customs are like the buildings themselves, the archways and parapets of this remote village; they are soon blended softly with the earth and turned the color of dust, the features of different times and cultures gone blank, erased.

Now there's a kind of procession for us through the village. We're pressed into the center of a crowd of villagers and marched slowly through the twisting alleyways. We go past a jumble of houses, doorways leading onto wide private courtyards, stairways of rotting stone. Under the sharp blue sky there are domes and minarets, small pointed windows, windows shaped like six-pointed stars. In the hottest weather everyone sleeps on the rooftops or in courtyards, trying to drain a little coolness from the night air.

Women wait for us before each of the houses. There are two or three women in front of every house; they watch in silence as we pass. Some have drawn their veils across their cheeks, but as our male escorts have stayed behind with the car and there are no men with us, most have let their veils fall to reveal remarkable, dark, high-boned faces and burning eyes. There is not a dull or ugly face among them.

At the corner of one tiny, rutted, lane I almost trip over a baby. What is it doing here, lying in the gutter all alone, wrapped in rags, flies covering its hands and eyes?

Mata-ji sees it at the same time. Our glances meet. I move forward and her eyes flash; I feel that she is prohibiting me from touching it. Her eyebrows lift and she motions with her chin; without her saying a word I realize that if I lifted this baby in my arms or moved it in any way I might offend many people . . . the women I'm walking with, the woman who left it behind. . . It might be a beggar-woman's child left here for some reason, it might be sick, it might be Untouchable. There are strictures of caste and custom here I haven't even dreamed of. I turn away from the child and continue walking forward, lifting the end of my sari against my cheek, as if to shield myself from the impact of this neglect. I've never before understood so much about what it is like to live in this place. How often must people here turn their eyes away from a sight like this in order not to feel the pain of another's suffering?

I don't give myself the chance to answer this question. We're rushed on swiftly. No one else has noticed and the baby is left behind, untouched.

Near the village square where we were greeted is a large cool room which is the community's public kitchen; next to this is a small whitewashed room in which we're seated at last. The young schoolteacher comes forward and slips her veil from her head, revealing coarse black hair, blue eyes, round-featured prettiness. She reads a poem to us in excellent English. Then she sings, off-key but lustily, Mata-ji responds by singing back, and after her song, also off-key but sung with feeling, all the village women join in singing a reply to her. The songs are invariably devotional, religious; they are the hymns or bhajans of Kabir, Mira Bai and Tulsi-das, some of which the six of us are already learning, with the help of a music master.

It doesn't make any difference whether or not anyone can carry a tune; Mata-ji's voice is droning and tuneless. The important thing is the message of the song, the words, and the feeling with which each song is delivered.

When the singing and the welcomes are finished, the women replace their veils and leave the room. The men will serve us our food, as the women have done the cooking. This is quite a sight: a squadron of Indian husbands bearing trays and plates. I wonder whether they've ever served women before, or if this is the kind of extraordinary role reversal that comes about on special occasions, as during the spring festival of Holi when staid adults become children and hurl dyes at one another while laughing hysterically at stained hair and ruined clothes.

As usual, there's too much food. There are the puffy round *chapattis*, *dal* or lentil soup, and vegetables cooked in clarified butter and spices. There are pickles and yogurt. At the end of the meal there's the great delicacy, *kheer*, a pudding of rice cooked in buffalo milk, loaded with nuts and raisins, so sweet it makes my mouth burn. I try to leave a little on my plate but Mata-ji again looks at me with blazing eyes and I finish everything. We fight torpor with the powerful village tea mixed with milk, *chai*, and then, after using the one flush toilet in the village, recently installed and revealed to us with incandescent pride, and being allowed to wash with a single bar of pink soap, we're brought to a large open hall which buzzes with women and children. No men are allowed, so once again the veils are removed. We're now supposed to speak about how much we like India and what life is like for women in America and Europe. How it is different from life here, life in village India.

How is it different? But how can we possibly tell them? For one, small thing, in America there's usually more than one flush toilet per village. When infants are left on streetcorners someone eventually notices; at least social workers or the police will come to take them away. I left my father's house, unveiled, in my late teens, to find an apartment and live alone; I chose my own husband and later, I chose to leave him. Can I even mention any of this without shocking them? I'm not at all sure, and for the sake of diplomacy I decide to remain silent on all topics that might be controversial.

But I can say that in America, no one ever welcomed me with a rain of flowers.

I sit next to a very old woman in a very white sari, a widow. Widows wear white in India and cut their hair short. At one time they were persuaded to commit *suttee*, probably in an attempt to keep the non-productive population down: that is, they placed themselves, or were thrown by obliging relatives, onto their husbands' funeral pyres and were burned alive. This is no longer commonly practiced, and groups of widows are frequently seen traveling to holy shrines and cities like Benares, having what looks like a pretty fine time. And why shouldn't they? They've risen above the social order. In the Northern villages they no longer have to cover their faces. If they're really lucky they get enough to eat and can boss their daughters-in-law shamelessly until they themselves die.

This particular widow is extremely spry and happy. Her sari is so white it's almost blue. She talks to me at a rapid clip, telling me how to wash a sari and what shrines she has visited. I listen. She speaks Hindi laced with a little English. I can almost understand her. I catch complaints against her daughter-in-law.

Anthea stands up and begins to make a speech, in her excellent Hindi. She speaks about each one of us — what kind of work we did in the West, why we came here — and about how much she herself loves India. As usual she's extremely discreet and tactful; she'd make an excellent diplomat. As she speaks I look at the yellowed walls of the meeting place, which is probably the schoolroom for the whole village. I can see the radiant sky, brilliant through the columns, the sun lighting the strong faces of the crowds of women, bareheaded now.

A stillness seems to gather itself about me. For almost the entire bitter winter, I've longed for the jewel-like memory I had of America; warm houses, white bathrooms, kitchens that worked. How odd, I think, that just a few weeks earlier I felt so homesick that I even wanted to go back right away. And now all those longings have fallen away, and what is left is only this wide schoolroom, flat sandstone columns, open sky. Only these seated women with their veils hanging down around their shoulders and their bright faces, oddly not coarsened by years of work and hunger. Only the streets outside that curve into the shapes they have taken for centuries and been stained the color of dust.

* * *

At the end of the day we're invited to the house of the richest man in the village. For years he was a merchant in Delhi; he was married to a city woman. When he retired, he decided to move back to his family's original home, in this village, to take up his responsibilities for his father's household.

We go into a shadowy courtyard and are greeted by the rich man and his wife, an extremely fat woman who sits us down to tea and more vast trays of food; spicy nuts and fried dough, English biscuits and slices of spongy white bread, which is considered a great luxury.

I cough into my hand, not knowing how I'm going to stuff any of this into myself. This time Anthea shoots me a look, so again I force myself to eat, slowly chewing biscuits and slices of fruit.

After tea we tour the house. The rich man's wife has her own private shrine for devotional services, many servants, many sets of drapes, many pillows and sofas. She has empty rooms, almost unheard-of in this land of extended families packed into tiny huts and crowded flats.

"But you see," she sighs, "I'm so terribly lonely. Yes, it's true. No one will come and visit me. And I can't even go out of the house. There's no one to talk to. I was happy when I lived with my husband in Delhi. This is such a very different life."

Loneliness has made her ill. She's happy only when she must travel back to Delhi for surgery or medical treatment.

"So many operations I must have." She nods and shakes her large head at the same time in the Indian fashion, agreeing and commiserating with herself at the same time.

"When I first came here I would go out. I was dressed as usual in my sari but the people looked at me with such horror. 'Why you are not in *purdah*?' they would say.

"You see, a married woman must be in *purdah*, especially in the village of her husband. Everywhere else, so long as she does not meet her husband's relatives or men from the husband's village, she may show her face. But in this village there are all my husband's family and the friends he grew up with, who are like his brothers. And especially with a woman's brothers-in-law and father-in-law, with these especially she must keep her face covered, by the customs of these villages. Always. And you understand, in my whole family no woman ever wore a veil. And here I find that if I do not wear a veil over my face I cannot walk into the street. So I go nowhere. I only sit at home."

She throws her arms wide apart as if to reveal herself, and looks at us with a shrug.

"And eat. And grow ill."

Twilight comes. Back in the communal kitchen where our car and driver wait for us, the women are now cooking for the men. They uncover their faces while they work together, rolling *chapattis* between their flattened palms, slapping them back and forth before cooking them on round pans and setting them to puff beside the coals. There are five women cooking, five pans going at once, *chapattis* puffing magically at the bottom of the huge adobe stove. As it grows dark, the kitchen is lit by lamps and by the reflections of the stove's roaring flames.

When we say goodbye, women come to touch our feet. I try to prevent this, but find myself a little overwhelmed.

"No. Please don't."

I lift a woman by her shoulders, which are sharp and thin. Her dynamic face confronts me. Her eyes are bright and fierce, her skin dark, her features straight and even. She has white strong teeth and a fearless smile. She looks directly into my eyes.

"What is your name? *Apke nam kya hein?*"

She asks this in Hindi. I answer in the same language. Then she slaps herself on the solar plexus.

"As for me, I'm Sherti Devi. Sherti Devi, *Harijan*."

It was Gandhi who named her people *Harijans*, the Children of God. Generally they're called Sweepers, but this is just another euphemism for "Untouchables." People of higher caste still won't touch them, won't eat out of the same dish or even cook with them in the same kitchen. The *Harijans* clean the streets, houses and toilets, cart away the trash, do the most menial jobs. I've seen three women walking in the road in Dalhousie, with a single sweeper-woman two paces behind them. She's their friend, they'll gossip and laugh with her, but she may not walk beside them or touch their hands.

To me this seems painful and strange, but then I, like all foreigners, am considered an outcaste and therefore also untouchable in this society, at least in the strictest households. Nor has political reform yet created the great , expected changes, although Western technology has begun to transform India in interesting ways. Movie posters bloom and peel on the walls of dilapidated open-air tea shops, men in *lungis* and *kurtas* mill tirelessly in front of the movie houses, and the young covet motor scooters, tractors and transistor radios. But caste and the dowry system persist, called by other names.

Now Sherti Devi, *Harijan*, looks at me with intelligence and challenge. She knows who she is, in this strong formal order of things. She also knows who I am, in this order. We embrace. She seems to be measuring the distance between us. We both know it's enormous. But in another sense, it doesn't exist at all.

Our driver is ready. Night falls. We get into our hired car and drive away from Sherti Devi's village. We drive up the narrow dusty pathways she knows well and turn finally into the Grand Trunk Highway which cuts down the length of India and which she hardly knows at all. We will travel into a distant landscape which exists for her only as a repetition of this flat land, wide sky, sparse foliage. Someday, to my regret, we will get into a plane and vanish out of India, and cease to exist altogether, except in some unknown world where rain comes at regular intervals and women show not only their faces but their thighs. Sherti Devi, *Harijan*, stands with the others beside the road to watch us leave. She turns back towards her village and her work before we're even out of sight. She has too much to do to say goodbye.

EASTERN EUROPE

Maureen Hurley

NIGHT TRAIN TO MOSCOW: WAGING PEACE

"Though this land is not my own I will not forget it."
—Anna Akhmatova

WE RIDE ACROSS the limitless snowbound Russian steppes by train in Car #17 to Moscow from Cherkassy. Once reserved for high-ranking Communist officials, the car with its russet wooden paneling reveals an earlier era. In fact, one still can't officially buy tickets for this well-appointed carriage at the train station. We get them through a friend. Connections mean everything in the USSR: in a country of perennial shortages, anything is available for a price. Out of the grimy window blanketed with coal soot, a monotonous landscape rhythmically repeats itself. My partner, Oleg Atbashian, says, "Siberia is like this; only it goes on forever."

We are leaving the Ukraine, where few villages have survived the many wars. Instead, industrial high-rises now punctuate the landscape, holding the low cloud ceiling aloft. Battered about for eighteen hours by train, we see that it could be any city — the curious sensation of *déjà vu*, and of arriving without ever having left. In frozen fields, haystacks hibernate like slumbering mastodons under a coat of snow. Poet Nazim Hikmet was right: No European hills or chateaux skirt the rivers here. There is nothing lovelier than birch trees in winter. Birch trees are as Russian as vodka. We eat small dark Ukrainian cherries steeped in liquor, and I hum "Moscow Nights," but not much is left in the way of onion domes to inspire me. Not much is left of the Oriental architecture of the Tatars, the Golden Hordes that once taxed the Slavs of the steppes into submission. In the morning, the *dezhurnia* brings us sweet amber tea in delicate lead crystal glasses confined in flowery brass holders.

I visited the USSR twice; during August 1989, and again the following December and January to set up a poetry and art exchange. I met with artists, writers, and publishers in Moscow, Leningrad, and Cherkassy, a Ukrainian town near Kiev. Armed with a crazy dream and a Macintosh computer, printer, and modem to revolutionize the cultural exchange with Cherkassy, the sister city of Santa Rosa, California, I met poets and artists everywhere: in cafés, video bars, and homes. Impromptu gatherings formed on street corners and trolleybus stops. We read poems, shared art, sang, made toasts, and talked of everything under the sun until late into the night. Sleep was often forsaken as we demystified the myths. Summer was sultry — lingering sunsets followed by incredibly long twilights, the white nights that lasted until dawn. Long walks along the Dnieper River, a wide expanse that moves without hurry through the drowned valley.

At home in California's wine country, people doubted my sanity when I made a return visit to the USSR in the dead of winter. Winter solstice. Then the dark that stretched past forever, a hungry tiger following us. Spectacular dawns and sunsets followed in rapid succession, and the long curtain of night beating against window panes announced its Arctic origins. To understand another culture, we must forsake fair-weather travel; we must see it even in winter. I came to the Soviet Union by accident, but I'm not an accidental tourist. As a writer, the world is my teacher, my inspiration. Stripping away acculturation, like so many layers of clothing, we discover we are alike in the flesh, after all.

"We Americans and Soviets are sentenced to understand one another," someone said. It was easy to begin. I was impressed with the openness and generosity of these people — most of whom had never met an American. I was part of a home-stay program, living with Soviet families in small crowded flats where I was treated like a long-lost relative — in a country where suspicion and distrust are inbred after generations of government terror, and repression is as common as the borsht we ate three times a day. It was not always easy. Misunderstandings arose — and required careful translation even from English to English. From this, I learned what "détente" really meant. Distrust sometimes went to funny extremes. At a birthday party, Oleg's grandmother thought I was a spy, but when — after politely parroting *chut-chut* too many times — I nearly slid under the table, she decided I was all right. *Chut-chut* is not a national toast as I first thought (since everyone was saying it) — it means "a little more!"

Glasnost, which literally means "open door," has done much to tear down the walls of misunderstanding on both sides of the American/Soviet power equation. Like many, I too was a product of the Period of Stagnation, raised in the ignorance and misinformation of our McCarthy era, and of the Stalin/Breshnev periods in the Soviet Union. Another reason I went to the USSR was to banish ghosts. When I was a child, my best friend's mother, a Russian translator for the United Nations, blacklisted during the Red purges, took to drink for solace, and died, branded by fire. Coming home from school, we were moths circling the blazing house. An accident, they said — blaming a crossed wire in the dryer. But our political climate killed her — surely as if they'd set the fire themselves. . . . Because of *glastnost*, I was able to move in relative freedom around the country and discover what Citizen Diplomacy, a natural grass-roots evolution based on personal contact, friendship, and sharing — is all about. When we shared the stories about our fears during the Cuban Missile Crisis, and the Bay of Pigs — the stories were identical, only our nationalities were different. The Russians have only one word, *mir*, for both world and peace.

* * *

A question most often asked by Soviets was, "What do you think of the Soviet Union?" Often it's hard to know where to begin — the hospitality, the incredible warmth of the people. I've literally come from the opposite side of the earth to find a community that has become like a second home. I expected darkness but found music and laughter instead. The tenacious dedication to the quality of life in this land of fabled shortages and inevitable lines is nearly incomprehensible to an American. Soviets have to spend far too much time to accomplish even the simplest tasks; hours and hours are squandered by useless procedures and layers of bureaucracy. I'd go crazy if I had to face such obstacles day after day. Life is hard enough as it is.

In the West, we watch the news daily with open-mouthed amazement. Gorbachev has truly revolutionized Eastern Europe, but I wonder when the quality of life in the USSR will improve. *If not now, when?* With the drastic devaluation of the ruble coupled with galloping inflation, to save the worn red, blue, and brown banknotes is, literally, a waste of money. Long lines at the jewelry stores; Soviets buying up gold as a hedge against inflation. People carry satchels everywhere in case something's for sale. It doesn't matter if they need it or not. To shop for dinner may take some strategic planning. *What line, where?* No small wonder the black market thrives; there's nothing like dedicated consumers when so little is available. In this context, "shop till you drop" takes on a whole new level of meaning.

"Now you know our problems, to be a common person in a common grave here. Our *perestroika* consists of pairs; good news/bad news. This is what they mean by the word 'dialectics.' Like others, I don't know where to apply myself," said Oleg, my translator, who is also a writer and an artist. "They say, previously people had faith; they believed in communism and life was easier. Now life is so much harder because nobody believes in anything. People must have hope. Russian history tells us the best people spent their lives trying to fill the bottomless vessel, but with no qualitative changes. The quantity of the best people has never affected the quality of the nation. Dialectics doesn't work in Russia. It's not a dialectical country. Evidently the only thing that has ever driven people to do anything is hope and faith. So that's where I am now."

As a child, my imagination was fired by Russian fairy tales lavishly illustrated with snow queens bundled under fur lap robes in troikas with bells, *baba yaga* witches in three-legged spinning huts, and personified winds. The Cossacks riding across the steppes, the very words *Russia* and the *Ukraine* conjuring up a fantasy world of onion domes, black bread, and borsht. But though the myths shattered when I arrived in the 20th century (no black bread — but *plenty* of borsht), I was not willing to give up the childish notion of a dream to build a bridge for peace through the exchange of poetry and art.

* * *

Novelist Boris Pasternak wrote that those who love poetry love poets and nobody loves poetry like the Russians. My worn copy of *Dr. Zhivago* was immediately snatched from my hands by a literature student from Moscow State University. Turning it over like a rare manuscript, he said excitedly, "I've heard of this book." From him I learned that Pasternak's novel had been banned for decades because it was critical of the Russian Revolution and of official censorship. "Now, under *glasnost*," my friend said, "it is allowed, but no one can find it anywhere." Pasternak is much revered in the USSR. His poems are taught and memorized in Soviet schools, but few even know of the existence of his autobiographical novel, *Dr. Zhivago*. By contrast, in the States, we are familiar with the book or a least the movie, but not the poetry. Through the eyes of the fictional Zhivago we see the horror of a world war followed by civil war in Petrograd, Moscow, in the Urals, the Ukrainian front, and the birth of communism. One form of tyranny was followed by another. After the 1917 revolution, Pasternak's poetry was considered self-indulgent and petty-bourgeois and was banned by the Communist Party, as was the novel. Underground copies of his work filtered through the populace. *Dr. Zhivago*, written after World War II, and published in the West in 1957, was a mirror chronicling the roots of artistic censorship in the Soviet Union. Official pressure compelled Pasternak to refuse to accept the Nobel Prize for Literature in 1958. But censorship, which is cyclical, began much earlier in the USSR — now we face it too in the United States, e.g., fundamentalist Christian politicians labeled the controversial Mapplethorpe photographs as obscene, and their legislative actions threaten both funding for the National Endowment for the Arts and our First Amendment rights.

Russia has made great contributions to literary tradition: Tolstoy, Dostoyevsky, Turgenev, Gogol, Chekov, Pushkin, Blok, Mandelstam, Akhmatova, Solzhenitsyn. In August 1989, Solzhenitsyn's work was allowed to be published for the first time in the USSR. Previously, his writing, like that of other banned writers, was clandestinely published and distributed by *samizdat*, or smuggled in from the West, as were the pacifist writings of exiled scientist and Nobel Laureate Akademician Andrei Sakharov, which dared to criticize the state. Sakharov, also known as the father of the Soviet bomb, was not allowed to go to Stockholm to receive his prize. His essay, *Reflections on Progress, Coexistence, and Intellectual Freedom*, published in the West, led to his exile in the city of Gorky. In his memoirs, Sakharov wrote: "We should apply ethical standards to all our actions, no matter how large or small, rather than rely on the abstract arithmetic of history."

Ironically, in autumn 1989, the death of Sakharov was turned into a state holiday. We watched hours of footage in tribute to him — including excerpts from the movie, *Sakharov*, starring Jason Robards — on the small T.V. perched on the refrigerator in the miniscule kitchen of a friend's flat. "A circus," Oleg growled. "Patronizing patterns are typical in our country. It's hard to tell if patronization has national roots or was formed by 72 years of socialism." He jokes: "In Russian, the word for advice, 'soviet,' is close in meaning to 'Soviet' [council, the giving and taking of advice]. When someone says, 'I don't need your advice [soviet]', the reply is: 'We all live in a country of Soviets; what did you think?'" He concludes: "We're accustomed to letting society's patterns guide us, and have vague ideas of privacy — the boundaries are always moving, like the golf game in *Alice in Wonderland*."

In a recent article in Milwaukee's *Shepherd Express*, Leningrad writer and guitar-maker Yuri Dmitrievski described Social Realism as "a monster nobody has actually seen with the naked eye. . . It has worked to sever any support an individual or collective creative effort might receive from society. Today, though the monster's nearly dead, we joke about it. . . . One of Stalin's first work camps bore this slogan, above the gate through which all entered: 'With an iron hand we shall lead humankind to happiness.' If you weren't killed, survival was agonizingly hard for anyone banished from the obedient herd. Consequently, there's scorn among Communists for anyone who is independent and, worst of all, creative."

Some U.S. artists and writers complain about the lack of public support for the arts. Often they say that, even in the Soviet Union, artists have salaries, a place to work, and publishing/display opportunites. This is only half-true, for it applies to officially approved "professional artists," but certainly not to younger artists on the "cutting edge," who until recently had to display work illegally or in underground publications. To become a "professional," a writer must join the Writers' Union — but most of the professional writers I met were old men in their 60s — very few women. The powerful Writers' Union controls more than just publishing: housing, studio space, and medical and food coupons are issued by the union. It also dictates what is an "acceptable" form of expression in the arts. Likewise for the Artists' Union. I am both an artist and a writer, and while I was touring artists' ateliers, Soviets kept asking me if I was a professional artist (it took me a while to catch on). They assumed I was an officially approved and government-sponsored artist because, as an artist in residence, I've received several grants from the California Arts Council and the National Endowment for the Arts. And I was whisked through yet another studio replete with canvasses out of the 19th century. Social Realism: the glorification of the worker, industrialism, Lenin, the Great Patriotic War, the October Revolution, May Day. . . Wearily I squeaked for help, having seen enough "acceptable" art and learned too much of Russian history through this rhetoric. Besides, I'd seen enough Lenin portaits to last a lifetime. When I told them I was not a government-sponsored artist and was visiting on my own, they relaxed their regime and allowed me to view the work of artists outside the system.

Frustrated with rhetoric either for or against the system, I kept asking where the avant-garde artists and poets were. Renegade artists are alive and as well as could be expected in the USSR. No one is starving, exactly, but they're supporting themselves at menial jobs so they can do their art. With no support from the government, they can't show their works in public places, and publishing houses won't touch their writings. "Entire bodies of literature disappeared with the Communist consolidation of power in the 1920s (after the presses and publishing houses became the organs of official opinion)," wrote *Macworld* editor Jerry Borrell, who brought some Macintosh computers to Moscow. He continued, "Writers have vanished from (or never appeared in) government-sanctioned bookstores. Putting Macs into the hands of Soviet technocrats will accomplish what *samizdat* has only aspired to do." I figured placing Macs into the hands of Soviet *writers*, not technocrats, would be more appropriate — which is exactly what I did. (When Gorbachev visited San Francisco in June of 1990, CEO John Scully gave him two Macs, so Macs are already in the hands of the technocrats. Whether more writers will see their works in government-sanctioned bookstores remains to be seen.)

Even with a Mac in the Soviet Union, I learned first-hand the problems of publishing without government approval. Everything is state-owned. Officially there's no censorship, but for those outside the system there is no access to printing presses. This also means one can't purchase ink, paper, or equipment for printing. In Cherkassy there are no public photocopying machines, just carbon paper. My own project — to co-produce a bilingual book of poetry by children and adults, to be published simultaneously in both countries, is in serious danger of foundering because I don't have governmental sanction. The Kiev printing houses turned down the work, not because the poetry is risky, but because they were waiting for a law to go into effect the following summer that would allow publishing without strict censorship. Fortunately, networking in the USSR is honed to a fine art. Everyone seems to know everyone else. And so I went to the heart of the culture, Leningrad, in search of a publisher.

I didn't have a visa for Leningrad, and the local OVIR (tourist and internal passport) office, where I had to register my passport, wouldn't grant me official permission to visit. So we took the night train to Moscow in private luxury on Car #17, and from there, on to Leningrad. On the Leningrad train we rode like cattle, sleeping on stained bedrolls, because I couldn't show my passport to get better tickets, and I was so tired I didn't care. In the bunks below, en route to a funeral, an elderly sister and brother stashed flowers in all the luggage compartments, including ours. She and I nearly came to blows. Oleg, my partner, told me, *"You're a real Soviet citizen now."* I pelted him with a carnation.

Once the capital of the USSR, Leningrad is the second largest city, with 5 million inhabitants. Leningrad, with her mosaic of 101 islands wrested from the marsh, is said to be built on a foundation of human bones. By the canals, the Church of the Spilled Blood and the Fields of Mars were dressed in winter-white, common graves invisible under a blanket of snow. I can't help but think of the half-million who perished during the 900-day seige — *No one is forgotten; nothing is forgotten.* And the poet Anna Akhmatova wrote of censorship in Leningrad, "Like white stones in a deep well / one memory lies beside me. . . / I remember how the gods turned people / into things, not killing their consciousness." Akhmatova later committed nothing to paper: Akhmatova's poems, including her famous "Requiem," survived, because friends memorized sections of them for her. "Requiem" is a chronicle of her wait in line outside the prison walls to see her son. An old woman asked, "Can you describe this?" Akhmatova said, "Yes, I can." The Writers' Union refused to publish Akhmatova's work.

The transcript of a recent film (co-translated by Maryna Albert and Yuri Dmitrievski) by Leningrad filmmaker Semyon Aranovitch, *The Personal File of Anna Akhmatova*, states: "Akhmatova has become the symbol of courage and endurance for the Russian people. The words of Akhmatova come down to us in letters, memoirs, poems, fragments of her life guarded by friends. . . . She stayed in Russia, and became the voice of her people." Later in the film, Anna says, "Solzhenitsyn gives us back our native languages and loves Russia with a 'deadly insulted love.' Two years before her death, she was reinstated into the Writers' Union. Solzhenitsyn fled to the West to publish freely. Akhmatova was later "rehabilitated" after her death. Semyon Aranovitch, who filmed archival footage of Akhmatova's funeral in 1966, risked arrest and was unable to show these images until now, under *glasnost*.

On Nevsky Prospect I schuss down the frozen sidewalk in late afternoon. The low winter sun bathing Leningrad with a pale orange hue glints a binary code off windows. Neat pyramids of grapefruit stacked in the display windows hold captive long lines of silent, bundled people; only their breath commingles. Mortified and amused by my peculiar form of locomotion, Oleg says, "Akhmatova, Pushkin, Tchaikovsky — they all walked down this street, but I don't think they ever schussed down it." He is referring to the unwritten Soviet code, "Keep silence; don't attract attention." The water in the narrow canals, the Grivoyedov and the Moika, has already stopped flowing; ice everywhere. Beneath the bridges mallard ducks relentlessly circle the shrinking puddles of open water. When World War I and then the Revolution battered Russia, Akhmatova wrote, "Even the birds have stopped singing. . . Everything is plundered, betrayed, sold. / Death's great black wing scrapes the air. . . ." On the green walls at the Literature Club, a list: many of the world's greatest artists lived here and, during the Period of Stagnation, smuggled their work abroad. *Is that what's in store for us?*

Oleg tells me Russia is like a great abbey full of monks of both sexes. "Humbleness and patience are the most useful virtues for survival. Though things are improving, the past will haunt us for decades. Moses kept his people in the desert for 40 years so that a new generation, unused to slavery, was born. It will take us at least that long to reverse the damage as well."

From the Leningrad publishing offices I watch a tugboat break a trail of ice up the main channel of the river Neva. Someone is ice-fishing; a small punctuation mark on the frozen expanse. The publisher is more hopeful, but after offering the usual instant coffee, chocolate, and stale cookies, he suggests we return to Moscow. Oleg helps me with my coat. We stumble out into the wet snow to yet another editorial board meeting. I feel despondent. "There is a certain hour every day / so troubled and heavy. . . ," wrote Akhmatova, "I sense the unavoidable darkness coming near. . . I can no longer tell beast from man." Strolling women push swaddled babies in enormous black prams toward the Winter Palace.

After Hitler bombed the city, refugees lived in the Hermitage, where empty frames hung on bleak walls, the paintings removed. Ghosts from another time. We can't comprehend the multitudes, more than 27 million slaughtered in World War II alone, and the count continually rising; the desire for peace runs deep as water, deep as blood. Anna did not wash the blood of Russia from her hands; she stayed to chronicle the events. At first, I hated the war memorials everywhere like Verdun, but I came to realize, slowly, that they serve as a fitting reminder to wage peace. A friend told me that, inside the museum at the base of the statue of Mother Russia overlooking the Dnieper River in Kiev, are bars of soap made by the Nazis from human fat. He drolly added, "But they had to give it up, since there wasn't very much fat."

We visit the Tikhvinsky cemetery. The stone angel holds sheet music and frozen red carnations above Tchaikovsky's grave. I sweep snow from nameplates: Dostoyevsky, Borodin, Mussorgsky (I'd just seen the paintings that inspired his *Pictures at an Exhibition*). The crescendo of inner music drives me out of the graveyard and into the refuge of the Church of Alexander Nevsky Lavra. Monks take handwritten prayers and offer them up to the saint. Oleg translates, "One must light a beeswax candle, pay the monks to say the prayer, and next morning eat a special cookie to make it all come true." The lines are too long. I steal a candle nub and write my own prayer for peace. We both sign it and leave it in the wooden box filled with neat rows of notebooks inscribed with handwritten prayers. I tell him this church is very much like those of Oaxaca, Mexico. The statues of saints wear mirrors; the worshipper sees only himself. The church ravens, more like monks than birds in their grey and black cowls, hop ahead of us, mumbling to themselves. There are only a handful of working churches in Leningrad. The fairest of all the churches, Our Lady of Kazan, with her classic facade, is not one of them. It houses the Museum of Religion and Atheism. Another is now a library. Seeking warmth, we head downtown to the Café Sever on Nevsky Prospect for tea and pastries. I can't shake the unstable frenzy of Tchaikovsky's *Violin Concerto in D* from my head.

Why I came to the USSR had something to do with a student, who, unhappy with presidential election results, yelled out on election day, "We oughta nuke those commies!" Then and there we dealt with stereotypes. It also had to do with facing my own lack of knowledge, my fears and prejudices. Not satisfied with the mass media, I wanted to see for myself if it really was as awful as we'd been led to believe. But my journey began in Latin America, not the USSR. I began to doubt my own government's sanity when I saw how the Cold War was being fought. I didn't see democracy, I didn't see communism; I saw a fertile land devastated by war. I saw no men of rifle-bearing age in the fields of Guatemala during the planting season; only women and babies feeding an entire nation. *It no longer mattered who was right*. The Soviets see themselves, as they say, in typical mixed-metaphoric fashion, "We are microbes on the pawns in a gigantic game of world chess."

I was in the USSR when the National Endowment for the Arts (NEA) Helms censorship controversy made Soviet prime-time news. I was struck by how much America and the USSR have traded places on so many levels — including censorship. Sometimes, it's embarrassing to be an American traveling the globe — especially when asked why we do what we do. The news looks very different mirrored from a Latin American, European, or Soviet perspective. The United States looks oddly phobic and aggressively silly. (My Soviet visa was suddenly denied after the United States invaded Panama. I spent Christmas morning in the San Francisco Soviet Consulate pleading for a visa.) I was in the USSR also when the United States confiscated Noriega's tamales. I was in the jungles of Guatemala when the United States invaded Honduras; backpacking in the Andes when the United States' heat-seeking missile shot down an Iranian commercial airliner over international airspace, and when the war on drugs escalated in Peru and Ecuador.

When soldiers stopped the train to Puno, Peru, to search our baggage for coca leaves, I was really scared — more so than when we had to hitch out of Tikal, Guatemala, when our jeep was stopped at three military road blocks. At the military installation, two young soldiers practiced kick-boxing, their Uzis swinging like sticks. A toy war in a banana republic. At their feet, the campesinos, with studied indifference, feigned sleep. Like a border patrol, a crocodile patrolled the pond where they attended to KP duties. I was living in Switzerland during the Vietnam War. And from all this I've had to learn I am not my government, but a cultural ambassador. People do not make policies, governments do. Lincoln's famous proclamation, once a rallying cry for freedom ". . .a government of, by and for the people" — has lost its power over the years, particularly during the Cold War, which saw the rise of secret government and uncontrolled surveillance — even in this democratic society.

The reason I write is to heal something in myself. I am one voice in the chorus, the multitudes of artists who make up the moral consciousness of humankind. I write poetry because I'm ashamed of the unbidden tears that come so easily. To bear witness is to see with one's own eyes. Like a sponge, I absorb it all and wring it out in my poems. When I think of that man on the Berlin Wall with a sledgehammer raised in jubilation, it reminds me of the poets and artists I've met in Peru, Mexico, and the USSR — *we've been tearing down the walls all along*. Someone gives me a piece of the Berlin Wall for Christmas. A splash of red paint. McCarthyism is not dead. It again raises its ugly head in the form of Senator Jesse Helms and of other religious right-wing fanatics. Throughout history more people have been killed under the auspices of religion and politics than by any other catastrophe.

To paraphrase the doctor-poet William Carlos Williams: It's difficult getting the news from poetry but men die every day for lack of what is found there. It is hard getting the news from art, but art's the most explicit conscience we have and sometimes we are not even allowed to witness it. Picasso's famous painting about the devastation of the Basque village of Guernica by the Nazis during the Spanish Civil War could not even be exhibited in Spain until after the death of Franco. I remember the Lincoln Brigade veteran Ed Balchowski, a poet and painter, weeping as he played the march on the piano with his one good hand. The stream of martyrs.

Public Law 101-121-a — a diluted version of Senator Jesse Helms' original amendment — reads like a cultural loyalty oath. Under its provisions, NEA funds can't be used to support "obscene" or "indecent" art. This is a direct violation of the freedom of expression guaranteed to us under the First Amendment. Not only that, but the law does not identify who is qualified to judge whether or not something is obscene. The art police? The FBI? Shades of J. Edgar Hoover! Having seen the Mapplethorpe photos ten years ago, I knew the Helms judgment legislating morality to be subjective and, therefore, dangerous. Like other writers, I submit my yearly manuscript in the hopes of receiving a coveted $20,000 NEA Fellowship — not just for the money, but also for the recognition it brings. But this year, I wondered if it was ethical to ask for federal support — the law, so poorly reproduced as to be nearly illegible, was stapled like a filthy bandage inside the application book. Do I submit the poems that have the words *piss* or *shit* in them? What comes next? State-approved Realism? The NEA reauthorization is not just about obscenity, it's about setting the cultural agenda for the United States.

The opening poem about my experiences in the USSR is, appropriately, about censorship — Solzhenitsyn's gulags — though I didn't consciously plan the content. In "Country of Origin" I wrote, "Stalin's been dead nearly as many years as we've lived. / America is also an experiment, / an armed song singing itself / toward extinction like all the rest." I wrote this before the controversial amendment authored by Senator Helms hit the Senate floor. I spent a long time debating whether or not to send these poems, or to change to words into something more innocuous and decided "Fuck it!" — thankful for those artists whose works have paved the way for all the rest of us. The literary world would be poorer without Ginsberg's *Howl*, Joyce's *Ulysses*, Kazantzakes' *Last Temptation of Christ*, or Marquez's *One Hundred Years of Solitude*. Or for that matter, Solzhenitsyn's *Gulag*, Pasternak's *Dr. Zhivago*, Nabokov's *Lolita*, and Akhmatova's poems. In our public schools today, many fairy tales, including "Little Red Riding Hood," and such classics as Twain's *The Adventures of Huckleberry Finn* and Salinger's *Catcher in the Rye* are routinely banned from school libraries by various groups for all kinds of reasons — from alleged racism to alcohol abuse. In "Little Red Riding Hood," Granny's glass of wine was reason for censorship. The list is long: There are 174 court decisions banning books in the United States.

My friend Libby Maynard, printmaker and director of the Humboldt Arts Council, who testified at the House of Representatives subcommittee's NEA hearings in Los Angeles that began March 5, 1990 (the anniversary of Stalin's death), told the committee, "Art is a mirror. You can't make problems go away by breaking mirrors." She was not only reflecting the sentiments of a large population of northern Californians who happen to be artists, she was also echoing a speech made earlier by the formerly exiled Chilean-born novelist Isabelle Allende, who now lives in Marin County, California. In a keynote address at the California Confederation of the Arts Congress in November 1989, petite Allende, fiery in a red dress, opened with these words, "Art is to humankind what dreams are to individuals. In dreams we wander in no man's land, where all rules are abolished. . . . Art is a revelation of the collective human soul." Allende, niece of the slain Chilean president, Salvador Allende, held us spellbound as she recounted the powerful role art plays in defining what it means to be human — both in the remote past and in the future. "Every civilization has understood the power of the arts, and, in different ways, has tried to use it. Fortunately, art is a rebellious child, a wild animal that will not be tamed. . . . When it has defied authority and the prevailing morals, when it has denounced, protested, or searched for some forbidden truth, it has been brutally repressed."

Now, in America, reactionary politicians want to legislate morality by censoring artists by refusing to renew funding for the 25-year-old federally sponsored NEA (whose annual budget, $171.3 million, is less than the cost of one Stealth bomber, or $22 million less than the annual military band budget). Artists are now required to sign a consent agreement — what amounts to a loyalty oath — stating they promise not to use federal funds for "obscene or pornographic purposes." Almost every artist and arts organization benefits directly or indirectly from NEA funding. If we lose NEA support, we'll be plunged back into the Dark Ages. How loud will our free voices be then?

We cannot afford to keep silence when it comes to censorship. Every day, little by little, our rights are stripped from us; we let it happen. I am reminded of the story of Khrushchev addressing the Supreme Soviet and the Party Congress. When asked why he kept silent during the Stalinist purges, Khrushchev asked the speaker to please identify himself. And was met with silence. Khrushchev said, *"You see how it was? On that note, my case rests."*

When Allende recounted the horrors of Santiago, Chile — the soldiers rounding up piles of books, burning them "in shameful bonfire...Books don't burn easily. It takes them a long time to die" — I knew what was coming. A name. A poet: Victor Jara, whose hands were cut off by the junta in September 1973. Jara, with his bloody stumps, sang to thousands of prisoners at the National Stadium until the military shot him down. We are sobbing. There are some atrocities the psyche can never heal. I am reminded again of what poet Carolyn Forché wrote, "There is nothing one man will not do to another." Allende momentarily stopped her onslaught to smile at the bereft audience waving truce flags — a sodden sea of handkerchiefs — but ruthlessly continued, "The oppressors know there is a mysterious force in art. What is that power? Art is a mirror where reality is reflected.... Often we can't see and understand our own reality until it is reflected in a mirror." When she mentioned the photograph of the naked little Vietnamese girl running in napalm rain, I was pulled back into time. I can't escape the image burned onto my retina — even after all these years.

Cinematographer Semyon Aranovitch of Len-Film studios in Leningrad shows us that Stalin systematically silenced the poets (and most of the intelligentsia) who, since Pushkin's time, have been critical of the government. Like many writers, poet Osip Mandelstam, Akhmatova's friend, was sent to a Siberian prison camp and died in a common grave somewhere near the seaport city of Vladivostok — below the most eastern Russian peninsula, Kamchatka. He wrote, "Only in Russia is poetry respected. Is there anywhere else where poetry is so common a motive for murder?" Mandelstam's wife, Nadeshda, wrote: "A poet, painter, composer, or any other kind of artist cannot belong to an elite, because they know that men are created equal. An artist therefore is a deeply social being. Not setting themselves up against the crowd, though they refuse to accept the order in the society they live in."

Ironically, the USSR houses the world's largest collection of art. Peter the Great, founder of Leningrad, knew the value of art and used the Dutch Masters as a propaganda instrument in his struggle for the modernization of Russia. A pastime of Russian aristocracy was to purchase Western art. Catherine II bought European art for art's sake, though it was not available to the public until the reign of Nicholas I in 1852. Catherine II had the Hermitage built to house her private collection of 3,926 paintings. After the Revolution, these collections were taken over by the state. Today, the largest body of Impressionist and Post-impressionist works or artists, including Monet, Gauguin, and Van Gogh, can be seen only in the USSR — a country that made dubious art history in 1974 by bulldozing an unofficial Soviet modern-art exhibition hung on Moscow fences. I saw slides of the work of those bulldozed exhibitors, who are still painting 20 years later in spite of governmental repression, but it is difficult for them to exhibit anywhere.

Do we also want to take a giant step backwards? San Francisco poet David Meltzer wrote, "Poetry is a two-way mirror. . . The outside looking in; the inside looking out." All art is a two-way mirror.

In 1453 an unknown monk scribed, "Two Romes have already fallen, but the third remains standing, and a fourth there will not be." The fire of 1812 nearly razed Moscow, the former capital city, which didn't fare too well during the revolutions either, but the city is still standing. All roads lead to Moscow, the third Rome. Founded in 1411 by Prince Yuri Dolgorvky, she is the capital once again. Everything is centralized. Eleven million strong in what was once the sacred city of white walls, *Matrushka Moskva* is now the drab grey hub of an enormous empire. Sparrows huddle on the Kremlin wall. On Arbat Street (once Stalin's private thoroughfare), we pass a frozen sparrow, and a dead pigeon, feet up, a question mark in the snow. *Who lined up the birds in the sky?* Misha, a Muscovite, who for 25 years has been a translator for the State Committee for Television and Radio, and who teaches Spanish at the university, said, "When I was four, I asked Stalin's guard if he was a sparrow. An informer. My mother was paralyzed with fear." Luckily, nothing happened. "She could have lost her life because of this."

Misha says he was hounded by the KGB because he made the mistake of complaining about substandard living conditions. He explained, "It began slowly. I lost my job. I couldn't get another. Finally I had to lie." He shook his head and said, "Now it's a little better." We passed along the Moscow River, whose banks were "made with the bones of the worker. Now that he's dead, the dissident Sakharov has been elevated to the status of God. Everything is free of charge here, but first you have to pay for it with wooden rubles," Misha ironically commented. "Not worth the paper it's printed on."

We passed by an old woman bundled in a black overcoat who sat feeding pigeons in the snow. Misha said she was Marina Tsvetayeva's sister, also a poet. Not as fortunate as Marina who emigrated to Paris in the '20s, she was sent to forced-labor camps during the purges. Stalin was especially distrustful of poets who were traditionally notorious for criticizing the government. Blacklisted Marina, whose father founded the Pushkin Museum in Moscow, returned to the Soviet Union in 1939 to join her husband, who was later shot as a "counterrevolutionary spy," and she found her daughter and sister in concentration camps. Deprived of family and friends, and denied publication, Marina was exiled to the provincial village of Elabuga, and hanged herself on August 31, 1941.

"All signs of me, all traces / all dates rubbed out by some hand . . . my country has not saved me," she wrote in despair. Right before her death, Pasternak introduced Marina to Anna Akhmatova, who wrote, "You and I, Marina, walk the capital this midnight. . . ." We are all shadows walking the night. I recalled Marina's lines from "Versus to Blok," "Your name is a bird in my hand, . . . a kiss of snow, / an icy blue swallow. . . ."

On Gorky Street, someone sells red carnations in glass houses heated with votive candles to keep them from freezing. Relics of saints. I get a minute taste of the frustration they must've suffered; the Moscow editorial boards break appointments and don't answer phones.

Spassky Gate; a stream of black Volgas with tinted windows barrels across Red Square, or *Krasnaya Ploshad*, by St. Basil's Cathedral. The old Slavonic root-word of modern Russian *krasnaya* means both beautiful and red. Snow falling in large constellations. The liberation of snow is an illusion through lace curtains. As a rule, the Soviets are very obedient people. It is said Ivan the Terrible had the architect's eyes put out after St. Basil's was built so there'd never be another church to rival it. With snow falling from the night onto what looks like hallucinogenic ergot-inspired onion domes, St. Basil's is truly the epitome of the heart of czarist Russia. Byzantium's imperial double-headed eagle was replaced by the red star in 1917, but the two-party system of the "haves" and the "have-nots" remains the same in spite of all the talk of reform. *Perestroika* and *glasnost* have not yet penetrated to the worker's level.

With the latest political events sweeping Eastern Bloc countries, things are changing at an alarming pace. It didn't take a lot of brains to predict a brewing revolution in many of the fifteen republics as well. In January 1990, I attended a concert in Cherkassy commemorating a dead exiled Ukrainian poet's music and poetry. The mother of the poet Vasily Simonenko, who died in exile in a Siberian hard-labor camp — like so many writers and intelligentsia — was a babushka like any other Soviet grandmother. She was dressed in black, and wore the ubiquitous floral scarf. The babushka, so much a part of the Russian landscape, like the statues of Mother Russia, is seen a thousandfold — in summer sitting on park benches, sweeping the streets with handmade brooms or chipping ice from the curbs with crowbars in winter. This grandmother sat stoically on the stage, surrounded by pompous party officials who presented her with plaques, bouquets, and a thousand rubles (a half of a year's salary for the average worker) to a standing ovation as T.V. cameramen stumbled over each other to get the best angle. Her moment of crowning glory; a dead son. Perverse patriotism. Too much like IRA mothers who gloated in the glorification of martyrdom as if it were a blessed sacrament.

Militia by each door. That the concert is allowed is a revelation unto itself. *Glasnost* in the flesh. But the packed house is in a pitched fervor; clapping in unison, singing anthems, lighting candles, and holding red carnations aloft, unfurling the blue and yellow Ukrainian flag from the balcony, its Cyrillic letters, a trident stabbing the sky. The Ukraine is more crucial to the Soviet economy and stability than the Baltic states. Gorbachev can afford to let them go. But the Ukraine, a region larger than France, with a population of 50 million, is the kingpin of the Socialist states; it produces most of the food, heavy industry — especially steel — and nuclear power for the entire Soviet Union. If the Ukraine secedes, there's nothing to prevent the other 14 federated republics from revolting, and the USSR as we know it will cease to exist. "Death sends patrols into every courtyard," wrote Akhmatova. "Wild honey has the scent of freedom. . . / but we have found out forever/ that blood smells only of blood." I'd been in enough political demonstrations and riots in the United States during the '60s to see the writing on the wall. We slip out into the lobby before the concert is over; the stomping and clapping echo our footsteps as if we were inside a huge drum.

I dream of finding two dead eagles in the snow. A soldier intercepts me, asking for a trespass fee. Death in the trees, on the ground. Oleg says the double-headed eagle is Russia. Oleg, a journalist who is Armenian and Ukrainian, writes, "Irritated and angry, those of us stuck here, half-sunk into this dirty mess of snow, go on living — wasting time and energy hating each other. Last night the snow fell again; it was white, then it mixed with the dirt. Russian Nazis shouting anti-Semitic phrases, national socialism, like Berlin 1933. Hatred mirrored again. The snow fell so pure. Azerbaijanians killing Russians and Armenians. Refugees crying; nowhere to live, nowhere to go." Dostoyevsky wrote: "There are only three forces that can hold the weak and the unhappy captive, and these are miracle, mystery, and authority." Even inside the house, snow collects, migrating toward death. "The political winter is over, everything melts," Oleg writes. "There are some people, poets and writers among them, who are afraid of the dirt, who sing only of the white sparkling snow, the pureness of winter. They say Russia is a country of winter, and those who spoil the snow, they spoil Russia."

Our last night together in Moscow, Oleg and I go to the Tretyakov Gallery on the Krymsky Embankment across from Gorky Park to see Soviet political art. Vuchetich's famous sculpture "Swords into Ploughshares," presented to the United Nations by the USSR — but still here — is dusted with snow. In the church at the Novodevichy monastery, nuns are singing in Old Church Slavonic from behind an ornate panel. Incense. In the cemetery, Gogol, Chekov, Stalin's wife, and Sakharov under the great equalizer, snow. I am crying, I don't know what for. Oleg feels it, too. We are no closer to saying goodbye than before. Leaving the sanctuary, I wonder who will kiss the relics when all the old women are gone. He asks, "How would you like to become a citizen of Cherkassy?" I answer, "Even you dream of escaping." He zips my coat up against the cold. Pigeons dance in the gutters and peck at the small curtains of snow. The thirsty ground will not drink, the snow cannot enter; the heart of winter, indifferent.

Red Square is closed to the general populace and tourists alike. Militia check each person's white invitation card and internal passport; bundled delegations of diplomats lay red carnations in the snow at the graves of patriots buried in the Kremlin Wall near Lenin's tomb — the red granite comes from the Cherkassy region. Someone says they removed Stalin's remains from the wall. A squadron of spruces stands at attention. We press against the guard rails, a sodden conspiracy punctuated by the red glow of a cigarette. Someone spits. The guard's heel grits on ice and sand as he makes an about-face in front of us. He ignores our questions, staring through us as if we weren't there. In less than a week, the streets will be filled with protesters, Soviet President Gorbachev will denounce the one-party system. "We cannot turn back. The path forward is difficult, but it promises to be a very interesting route.... We are entering a world of greater trust, of greater understanding," said Gorbachev. Communism as we know it will fall. No longer keeping silent, they are challenging the repressive behemoth. Shouldn't we be doing the same? Or will we become like the Soviets, who often quote a popular saying, "Freedom has come a lifetime too late?"

Helen Degen Cohen

RETURN TO WARSAW

Maria Szumska in 1981

MAJKA (PRONOUNCED MAYKA), modern as a young Shelley Winters, is trying to be patient with her overly religious Catholic mother. The mother who is looking at me with those same eyes — though not as deep, not as foggy any longer — as she did when I was eight years old, when she had me in hiding among the wheatfields. She is eighty-five years old now, sitting in a house dress that covers her sagging weight, her bad legs. Her gray hair is brushed back into a bun, and deep in her still smooth face, her eyes twinkle. She is staring at me with a slight smile. Mocking? Scrutinizing? Without any loss to her dignity, hands quietly in her lap, like a Mona Lisa. She is asking me questions, though not the ones I would have expected. She is entirely flesh-and-blood now. No. Not entirely.

If Maria Szumska were entirely of this world now, her daughter would not be so impatient. It's a habit, the way Majka reacts to her mother, to everything her mother says. She shifts in the chair, flushes, perspires. As if to say, oh *please*, they *know* already, why don't you leave them alone. And yet she is her mother's daughter. She herself has just made a pilgrimage, to Wilno (pronounced Vilno), as I am making mine, to Poland. Majka knows that this is my pilgrimage, she has made every conceivable accommodation for us, but this *is* her mother, this *babcia* (bahb-cha — granny) who will not leave the little three-room apartment on the fourth floor, who insists on sitting in the corner of the room —

where she literally lives, eats, sleeps, watches television, and writes letters to missionaries.

Maria Szumska sits at her table facing the window (and me, now), writing meticulous letters in a nearly perfect hand. The hand was perfect a year ago, but now it is less steady, the lines don't run as neatly across, nor do the letters stand as regally. But God forgives what can't be helped. Her stationery is precious. I know it so well. It has a red rose on each sheet. (There are huge red roses on a dark gray tapestry on the dining room wall, roses the size of lions. She has kept that tapestry since her youth in Wilno.) She addresses the envelopes just as carefully, an ingrained European habit, developed when correspondence was a matter of life and death, when packages and letters carried, or asked for, vital help or information, when telephones rang only in the movies. Written communications in Europe are still precious. Addresses are precious. When after the war my mother wanted to bring her family to America, she had to recall the address of an uncle in Chicago. There were four digits in the street number, and try as she might, she couldn't get them quite right, until one day she was close enough, the letter was somehow delivered and — that is why I am here today. When I'm in Florida I see my mother addressing packages to Israel, to Iowa, to Poland, I see how carefully she prints each name, every digit.

The table is up against the window. Maria Szumska sits facing the gray buildings of the suburb Ursus in the window, pen in hand. A few feet to her left, nearly touching the swung-open window-frame, is the television set, and on its screen the politics of Poland. She is writing a letter to a missionary and watching the changing fate of Poland, as we come in.

Maria Szumska is a super-patriot. She is passionately involved in what happens on the television screen. It is a gray meeting of the government officials, in a huge hollow assembly hall. It lacks the spunk, the showmanship, the confrontations, the play, of U.S. hearings on television. This meeting is dead serious, the room seems gigantic, the men lost within it, talking in gray, somber voices. It goes on and on for hours. She doesn't take her eyes off it. Her daughter Majka is extremely annoyed.

"You can finish later," she tells her mother, and shuts off the television set. Maria Szumska acquiesces. She begins to talk about Poland, about its patriots, its martyrs, one after another. She pulls out pictures of saintly heroes, of Holy Mary, of the Pope. They seem to appear out of nowhere, since there are no files to be seen. They are postcard-sized, most of them, depicting heads with sharply pointed haloes. She is not senile, she repeats herself out of her intense preoccupation, repeats stories of her heroes day after day, which I still can't absorb fast enough — I am still getting re-acquainted with the language. I try, I bring tapes,

Maria Szumska in 1940

I hang on every word. I want to listen with everything I've got. This is my pilgrimage, after all.

On the table are a bowl of red currants, bread and sausage, a vase of flowers. Majka brings meals to her mother two or three times a day. And now that Majka has left us for a bit, her mother leans forward to ask me a favor, a secret. She wants to know if I could get her some milk chocolate. She accents the *milk*. *Milk* chocolate. But don't tell Majka, she would get angry. I say of course, looking around. I am always looking around, as if she were made of the room itself. My back is to the window, and I'm looking into the room, at her bed along the wall on my right, at the picture of the Madonna high on the wall, beyond the television set. Szumska is facing me, to my left, penetrating me with her stare. It is not a spiritual stare, as I expected. It is a worldly (bemused?) stare.

She has just talked about the glory of Poland, and now she stares at my American athletic shoes. Nods with approval. Her granddaughters should have such shoes. Majka comes in at that point and her face goes red. I wish it didn't amuse me as it does, this trip was supposed to be all sacred.

When I was almost eight years old, we stood at a train station in Lida, my parents and I, about to be shipped to the Camps. My mother gave me a cup and told me to pretend I was going for water at the pump — and to keep on walking until I found the house of a woman we knew. I asked for directions from house to house. I walked across the town until I found the woman's house. But because it was too dangerous for this woman to take me into hiding, she searched for someone else, and found Maria Szumska.

It is a much longer story, of course. The woman my mother told me to find was a cook at the town prison, where we had been hiding in a room over the guard house, my mother, my father, and I. Because my father had made himself indispensible at the prison (by barbering, distributing food supplies, and supervising all the plumbing), he was permitted to move us from the Ghetto — where living conditions were miserable and hundreds of thousands of people were marched into the fields to be shot during "selections" — to live, discreetly, at the prison. In the end, though, we too were rounded up, with the rest of the remaining Jews in town, and placed on trucks headed for the train station and the Camps. That is when my mother handed me the cup and told me to find the prison cook, Waclawska (Vahtzlavska). When I was out of sight, she and my father boarded the train, and later joined an escape party: while the train was speeding, they had a small boy squeeze out of a tiny window and unlatch the door from the outside; whereupon 11 people (out of 500) jumped, four were shot immediately, and seven survived and joined the underground — my parents among them.

After several failed efforts at finding me a safe place with someone else and having appealed to the Mother of God, Szumska decided to do it herself. She sold her clothes, and with the money rented a cabin in the country. She was an educated, striking young woman, and her clothes too must have been attractive. Before the war her husband loved taking pictures of her, one of which is now displayed on the wall — a picture of a beautiful, dark-haired young woman seated on a lawn, her romantically ruffled white dress spread out around her.

Maria Szumska left her husband in Lida, and came to live with me in the country. She would walk twenty-five kilometers from our cabin in the country back into town, to do her husband's laundry and get food to him. It occurs to me that I still don't know how she got all our food, even after all the questions I've asked her. We picked some of it wild, like spinach and chamomile and stray carrots, and poziomki — tiny wild strawberries. (*Truskavki* is the word for normal strawberries; these tiny ones are *poziomki*.) She made potato dumplings which we ate in hot milk, with boiled carrots. She baked some of our bread herself, in a makeshift oven. She walked me to the forest and lake. She left me with what I call "The Cousins" in a novel I have written about the war, though now it seems that they may have been "neighbors." They were farmers, I am almost sure of that. That was in 1943.

Szumska was in her thirties then, with prematurely milk-white hair — it had turned suddenly white soon after that romantic picture on the wall — and a pure, doll-like porcelain face with haunting eyes — liquid, moonstruck eyes, as I remember. In the pictures she shows me now they are sad, melancholy; to me, then, they were only mysterious, only otherworldly. I have moved onto a chair on her left, shoulder to shoulder, and she turns to look at me more closely, and tells me that my teeth could be whiter. The surprise that goes through me amuses me — I am disconcerted, I accept everything. I look straight through her, into her, trying to see the young woman, the one who sleepwalked and prayed, prayed and sleepwalked, who crossed her hands on her chest beside me, when we lay down to sleep, in the cabin in the country. The young woman who showed me a world my parents never knew, though they survived the war and are alive and well in Florida.

* * *

What else did we do in Poland in July? We toured Warsaw; we were taken to both northern and southern Poland. Majka and her husband Jacek (Yahtzek) had met us at the airport and brought us to the house they were building out of concrete. They put us up in an upstairs room which belongs to their then nineteen-year-old daughter, Dorota, since both daughters (the other was twelve) were staying at their rented cabin in the northern country ("on the Mazuras"). Several days later we took the opportunity to get into that northern vacation countryside by accompanying Jacek on his trip to pick up the girls at the cabin and bring them home (at which point Dorota would share a room with someone else, and continue to let us use her room.) It was our first trip out of Warsaw.

Jacek drove us there in his fifteen-year-old Mercedes. We reached our destination, near the Russian border, hours later. (Lida and the cabin where Szumska had had me in hiding were just across the border, but we had no Russian visas with us). It appeared to us a primitive, somewhat depressed country, and their cabin was a shack; but the girls loved it, it was summer camp, it was freedom to them. They'd become housekeepers, were perfect hostesses when we arrived, cooked meat and potatoes and made us tea. We picked wild strawberries and blueberries in the forest.

* * *

In my book we are spirits, Szumska and I; in July of 1989 we are encased in concrete. Literally. We are seated in one of the many gray concrete buildings in a suburb of Warsaw. They don't have the paint with which to cover the dirty-looking ugliness of concrete. When you land, the entire city looks gray. When you land, you smell the odor of war. I am not exaggerating. We looked out the windows, as the plane rolled it, and saw several Russian military men in green capes strolling around the bleak airport, the flat, overcast gray city behind them. Outside, my friend asked me, "What is that odor?" I said, "It's the odor of the war." Months later, in a book on Poland, I found that another writer had characterized it exactly the same way. My friend wondered, later in our trip: "What did they do with all the rubble?" We had just finished seeing a film on the demolition of Warsaw by Hitler. It was shown in an upstairs room of a museum, with the windows wide open, overlooking the rebuilt Old City square, painted in colorful pastel shades, with tourists and artists wandering around below in the heat, or sitting under ice-cream umbrellas. The scene below us, through the wide-opened windows, was in such contrast to the crumbling, black-and-white Warsaw on the screen, that I think we both wondered: what happened to the rubble?

It must have been recycled. It smelled to me — initially, at least — like recycled war. And yet when we got into it, the ordinary life of the city made us forget the smell, all our initial impressions, just a week into our stay. By the time we left Poland, two weeks later, we'd forgotten it entirely. You can imagine what happens to permanent residents.

* * *

In *The Book of Laughter and Forgetting*, Kundera says that "the struggle of man against power is the struggle of memory against forgetting." But it seemed that the struggle in Warsaw was in both directions — to forget on the one hand, and not to forget on the other. To forget — in the form of building new houses, questing for jobs, American shoes, rock music. To not forget — in the form of Jacek, as he stood in back of his house looking around at all the land that once belonged to his family; of Szumska, reviewing her pictures; of Majka, making her pilgrimage to Wilno, when it was finally allowed, in May of 1989. Many such freedoms are only a few months old, in July of 1989. What was the black market currency exchange rate only three or four months ago is now the legal rate at any of a number of public currency exchanges. One can choose whether to buy meat at a state-run store, or at a private booth at the market. Women in babushkas sit on the sidewalks of Warsaw selling raspberries. There are long lines at the "dollar" stores — where one can use dollars or marks only — for Western goods. Everything is all mixed up. In July, 1989, it is practically impossible to forget, though there is little time to remember.

The ghosts of Jews are everywhere, though I realized it only gradually. One begins to forget the odor in the air; one begins to remember the Jews, in time. It's a story I don't want to get into here; not at this time. It is too big, too complex. But what is curious, is that the more the Jews dwindle here, the more their ghosts are felt. Poland is a country dotted everywhere with death camps, and yet people live all the way up to their edges — new and old developments are immediately adjacent, children play along their fences — without acknowledging them. Jacek had never 'been to Auschwitz and didn't want to go with us at first. "It is too macabre," he said. Though he did decide to go in the end, even shed some tears, and was glad for it. Majka had been, before. I didn't cry at all. I wanted to write the story of the tour guide, a Polish native of Auschwitz (*Oświecim*) who as a child had been exiled with his family from his town, while they were building the camp. He returned in middle age, to do tours of the camp — every day, day after day, year after year. "Six million Polish citizens died here," he says, day after day. "Three million of them were Jews."

The Jews and the Gentiles had lived like two countries intertwined, co-dependent as Siamese twins. Three-quarters of the world's Jews once lived in Poland. There were 3.5 million at the start of the war, about one tenth after the war, and only 5,000 by the mid-1980's. Two post-war occurrences, one of them a pogrom in 1946, and the other a government-encouraged wave of anti-Semitism in 1968, account for the two mass emigration of Jews from Poland. I had never known this. *No one I've asked since knew anything about it.* When I returned home, I read it in a book called *Remnants*, given to me three years earlier by a Catholic ex-nun. Strange, that I hadn't read the text till now. It is in a way a history of my people. It interviews a handful of the handful of remaining Jews in Poland, most of whom are old or sick. I picked up other books, with similar accounts. There is much more I have to read.

Majka and Jacek drove us south to Krakow during the second week of our stay, and there — at a museum across the road from our hotel, advertised in bold letters — was the exhibit "ZYDZI-POLSCY" ("The Jews — of Poland"), paintings of Jews and their life in Poland — predominantly portraits from centuries past, young and old, some with flowing Jesus-like hair. From the book *Zydzi — Polscy* which accompanies the exhibit: "...the few thousand Jews still living in Poland can by no means carry on life in the social structure which belonged to their fathers and grandfathers. A thriving graft has been cut off; its oral transmission has been reduced to single stereotyped phrases....Those of us who are quick to blame others, including Jews, for our misfortunes, and who worship our poets and artists, will be reminded by the exhibition of how high a regard for the Jews those poets and artists had. The Jews in turn, historically made sensitive to everything that concerns them, will sense sympathy and even admiration in the works of Polish painters, the artists of a nation at whose hands they have suffered in the past." The few people in the museum were staring at depictions of a vanished culture. It was haunting, as are the suppressed attitudes towards Jews.

After dinner, back on the third floor of the Hotel Cracovia, I heard some singing, in Hebrew — songs I had known in West Germany after the war, at a D.P. camp, where our common language had been Hebrew. The sound was incongruous with the setting. This was Krakow, 1989. I had been an impressionable kid, I had loved those songs and dances. I followed the sound down the hallway, toward our third floor lobby, where I found a group of high school students from Israel, singing. I asked if I could join them, and two girls made room between them on a couch. They weren't just singing, they were making a statement: it was blatantly exuberant singing. They were laughing, singing, clapping. It was their version of "We Shall Overcome." The director said they were here studying the Camps, (Krakow is near Auschwitz), that otherwise they wouldn't know anything about them.

Upon my return to the U.S., I was told by a Pole who has lived here several years now that people on buses in Warsaw, as well as Polish cleaning women in the U.S., are still overheard saying, "It's a good thing Hitler took care of the Jewish problem." When Majka took us to Grójec, the town where I was born, just south of Warsaw (a thriving "shtetl" prewar, like the one in *Fiddler On the Roof*, but now a rough-looking place) and asked, at a tiny tourist office, whether there are any Jews left in Grójec, she was told that yes, there are a few, but they wouldn't own up to it. The famous Warsaw Ghetto (famous for its uprising against Hitler) is a large, square, empty park surrounded by apartment buildings. Where so much had happened, there was nothing, not even visitors. We were the only ones there, standing before the monument to the heroes of the uprising, the ghostly emptiness palpable around us. The neighborhood where my father had been born was nearby.

The subject is overwhelming, and I am open. All my pages are open. I don't want to write on the white till I know what to say. I was in Poland in July, 1989, to see, to ask questions of, the woman who had risked her life for my sake. She is Polish, and Catholic.

There I stand, overwhelmed in the indoor tourist market, Sukiennica, trying to buy Babcia a present. Strange that we call her Babcia, or Granny, the woman who once haunted the countryside like a saint. What can I buy her? We can't find slippers. We can't find chocolate. And besides, I want to get her something meaningful. I've come all the way to Poland and I can't give her anything. What would you give her? A Polish doll? A Polish wooden plate? A necklace of amber beads? And then I see some plaques, upon which are painted madonnas. They are cheap. Too cheap. But what else in the world can I give her?

She is disappointed that I haven't converted. My son married a gentile, she says — did he convert? No, I tell her. She looks at me. It is a great surprise to me, the greatest surprise of the trip — that she'd wanted me to convert back then. She had asked the priest, and *he* had told her to wait, that perhaps my parents would return. I always thought it had been her idea. That she was all spirit, all noble. She is smiling at me. Her eyes twinkle. There is dignity in the way she is sitting. I feel thankful, in a way. I feel peaceful. Everything is as it should be, in a way. I love her, in a way.

This is not the spiritual trip I thought it would be. This is an earthy trip. It is loaded with raspberries, sour cherries, black and red currants, strawberries, tomatoes such as we remember in dreams; home-made sausage and fresh white cheese for breakfast, along with a platter of sliced cucumbers, onions and tomatoes, four kinds of bread and sweet rolls. We have ice-cream at mid-morning almost every day on our jaunts to Warsaw, we look into every window for amber, the streets are full of ordinary people. I see nothing especially spiritual, no one straining to remember or forget. The crowds are in the streets as they are in Chicago, impersonal, shopping. They look Western. What can I bring back to Szumska?

Her daughter, Majka, is our hostess, our joy. Working at the sink in her modern kitchen, she turns to smile at us. Warm, demonstrative, motherly, with plenty of flesh on her, and blood that keeps rushing to her face, she cooks for us day and night, like crazy. Cakes and "ushki" (fried pierogi stuffed with mushrooms), and soups, and cutlets and borscht, and potatoes. There's fresh berry juice instead of water (which she boils). The only thing they can't give us − anywhere − is ice. It's strange all right, to have nothing cold, no Coca Cola (which is served everywhere, but warm, and in lieu of water), no beer, not even cold ice-cream (nearly all melted and topped with berries), nothing cold whatsoever, but then what is ice? Majka drives us everywhere, she won't let us out of her sight, afraid that we may be treated rudely, be cheated, be − who-knows-what. We see palatial Łazienki Park with its roses, sculptures, and princely buildings. Churches, cathedrals. We take us all out to a restaurant and can't spend more than a dollar. And throughout it all, Babcia is sitting at her table, with her pen, indelible.

Behind the concrete house they've been building for three years, Jacek's brother Mihal has his greenhouses and his outdoor flower and vegetable nurseries. Behind them is Babcia's apartment building, rising gray, with its flower-boxes. We cut through the planted field each day, to visit her, passing Mihal's wife Yola in the field. We enter the bleak elevator building, ride the rickety elevator up, and find Babcia in precisely the same spot, at her table by the window, the television set on her left. She turns toward us, slowly, happily, waiting for me to hug her. There's a Friday in each month when a priest comes to see her, for a private mass.

I take out my present, loosely wrapped in paper. It is from Krakow, I tell her. She didn't want us to go to Krakow. It was too hot, and she was afraid for Jacek, with his bad heart. She looks at the present suspiciously. Oh, it costs too much, she says, without having seen it. She smiles uneasily. I unwrap it. She stares at my plaque with the painted Madonna. What do I need it for, she says, I have one already. We both look at the Madonna on the wall, and I feel my embarrassment, my inadequacy. She looks at the present again, kindly. I thank you very much, she says, but you take it. Here it will be soiled. Not quite "soiled" − the word is untranslatable. It will be damaged, disrespected, trashed. I know what she means. Halinko, she says to me, my life is an infinitesimal minute. I am gone. This must not be soiled. Take it. She hands it to me. I don't know what to do.

She stands up laboriously, walks toward a drawer, and extracts several more items. A gray, tinny cross on a chain. Some dresser covers, which she herself has crocheted, years ago. Hand-crocheted doilies in several sizes. She returns laboriously to her chair, and places the items neatly before me.

By the time I have returned I will have half a dozen books, a peasant skirt, earthenware bowls, holy pictures and objects, home-made jams and dried mushrooms, vodka, and of course all the store items: dolls, garlands, beads, wooden plates — folk art sold at the state-run Cepelia stores. Most of the presents will have come from Majka, one of the books from Mihal and Yola. It is *Pan Tadeush*, Poland's most beloved book of poems. A large, hard-cover book, it must have cost them a pretty penny. Mihal has been treating us to vodka in the back yard adjoining his flower nurseries, amidst sunshine and roses growing among weeds. Yola has baked a cake for us, brought me flowers.

Flowers and berries are dirt cheap around Warsaw. When it comes to roses, I have never seen so many in my life. They seem to grow like weeds, among the unmowed grass along the sidewalks, behind fences, in the parks. Łazienki Park has square, formal gardens of the same red roses as far as the eye can see. The king had his mistresses and bath-houses there, and an outdoor theater, now in ruins. On one side of the river lived the royalty, on the other was the poor (then Jewish) neigh-borhood, with its huge outdoor market, still there. When we come home from sightseeing, a friend of the family, a stranger, greets us with flowers, for me — for my name day. We were met at the airport with flowers, and sent home with flowers.

In 1943, when I was in hiding, I lived intimately with a wheatfield, and even more intimately with habri (hah-bree, plural for "haber") — what we call here the cornflower. But there, beside the floppy orange poppies, the fragrant blue cornflower is radiant. I wish we had a different name for it, since in Poland it grows along the wheatfields, not cornfields. I've never seen a cornfield in Poland. Habri are on Polish postal stamps. Habri are my madeleine, the intoxicating whiff of my year with Szumska.

Pansies are the whiff of my earlier childhood, when I could formulate no thoughts about pansies. Or sunshine. Or wars. Habri have become more generic, are the sun and the moon turned into a flower, the sum of everything I've named beautiful.

I was dazzled, while in hiding with Szumska. And mystified. I'd been lifted out of the heat of the war and set down in a wheatfield — where the sun was cool as glass and the Holy Family lived with us in the dark cabin. Seeing that I liked to sketch, especially when she left me alone at night, she bought me a pencil for my birthday. It's the most important present I have ever received. One pencil. Would the soul be happier with twenty? Never. The soul is happiest when it isn't abandoned. The pencil was and is my surrogate mother and father.

She brought branches into the cabin and stuck them in the ceiling, for decorations. We brought in wildflowers and placed them on plates on the floor, as decorations. She brought in a fir tree for Christmas, and I made paper chains, angels, Saint Nicholases and stars. When on one occasion she left me with the "Cousins," and Nazis came in to interrogate the family, and me too — since they'd heard a rumor of a Jewish child in the vicinity — when one of them came up to me and asked me, "Are you Jewish?", I was dumb. The farmers were so genuinely stunned, that the Nazis had to believe them and leave. How could anyone ask such a question of the child, of Szumska's niece, Szumska, who was holy. At least that's the way I remember it.

I am trying to leave a hundred-dollar-bill for her. She protests, mildly, glancing at Majka. Majka is beet red. No, she says. And to me, You have brought enough, we have enough. But it's for *her*, I tell her, in case something goes wrong, and you need it. We can take care of her, says Majka. While her mother begins to calculate, Well, the pension comes to. . .Majka is livid. Don't take it!, she orders. I know what a hundred dollars means. One dollar is 5,000 zlotys, a large head of cabbage at the city market is 100 zlotys. A pound of meat at the state-run store is 1,000 zlotys; at a private stall in the outdoor market, 6,000 zlotys. We bought the girls Puma athletic shoes, and Agatka slept in them all night.

It has occurred to me to wonder who has the richer life, Majka or her mother. Majka, with her busy suburban household, with her husband (Jacek's workshop is in his house) and their workers, the children and their friends, Mihal and Yola, guests and neighbors. Maria Szumska, alone in her room, her mind flooded with the distant work of missionaries, the entire kingdom of the Holy Family, the nobility of Poland's heroes. What makes Maria Szumska unique is the largeness of the world within her mind. Were she to be moved into her daughter's house, the noise would disturb her world. The sorrow she feels toward her daughter's lack of the spiritual is matched only by Majka's sorrow. And yet their names are the same: Maria. Majka is a nickname. And I felt like a bridge between them. We've all suffered and tried.

Even the suburb at first seemed drenched in the worn-out odor of its history. It came in the open window of our room — Dorota's upstairs bedroom. The bodies, the buildings, the manikins in the windows, the Ghettoes and castles. The walls. It's not like your normal industrial smog, said my friend. We were silent. Majka's friendly voice intruded. The trees intruded, the forest was unreal. Each time we drove into Warsaw, it seemed hotter. We noticed the strangeness less, and the shoppers and the heat more. Trying to find parking. The lines for vodka and meat. Communist government buildings, street-names. People (*quiet* people, speaking in undertones), an underground of people, sidewalks full of people, museums, Stare Miasto (Old City), lody, (lawd-y, ice-cream); hushed, harrassed waitresses. People in a corner of a square, along a wall, hushed in the strange light. In one upstairs room, a film about the destruction of Warsaw. Clips of survivors wandering among the ruins, looking into holes.

These people could never be American, much as they would like to be. *Nowoczestno*. Modern. Be Nowoczestno, and come work for us, says a sign on a state-owned streetcar. It seems to be moving through a fog, to our left and behind us, as we ride in Jacek's car, as if it'll never catch up. It passes us, into a new fog.

Dziecinko (my child), says Babcia Maria Szumska, we must be thankful for what God has given us. She points to the features on her face, saying, *The mouth speaks, the eyes see, the ears hear.* Often she complains about how difficult times are, how empty the stores are, echoed by Majka. She goes through her litany of sighs, how weak she is getting, how much she has lived through, how difficult it is to die. Then her face changes, she wants me to buy the books of a missionary, to contact certain people in the States, to repeat after her: *The mouth speaks, the eyes see, the ears hear.* What more can we ask for, Dziecinko?

* * *

This wasn't a spiritual journey. Nor was it a temporal journey. It was a door I have walked through. Everything begins here. There's a weight to it. It's as if I've built my own concrete house and then walked through it — in the front door and out the back, or in the back door and out the front. I am looking at the new landscape. The door is like the Arc de Triomphe — around it, through it, comes the air of possibility. When I crossed the threshold, I left nothing behind. There is no wall between the past and future.

There's nothing sentimental about actual returns. Nostalgia is only a place in the mind. When you literally touch the past, it disintegrates. It will not let you stay there; and because you can't stay there, it propels you into the future — it is a door.

Childhood has nothing to do with smallness. As a child, I was a genie, I created the biggest world in the world. When childhood, the biggest dream of all, reverts back to reality, it vanishes, turns into a door.

* * *

She smiles.

We are smiling at each other. We are seeing each other through the mirrors of our past. She *is* the young woman I knew. I *am* the child who liked to draw, whom she left in a cabin at night, in the light of a kerosene lamp. She *is* the woman with white hair, who prayed to the other Mary day and night.

* * *

She was supposed to receive the award with which Yad Yashem (in Israel) honors gentiles who helped Jews during the war. The letter she had received confirmed it. I have written to Yad Vashem again, their bureaucracy is like any other, I have told them, she is *eighty-five*. It would mean a great deal to her.

* * *

"Can you tell me what flowers we had there? I need their names, for my writing, and I don't remember."

"Flowers?"

"Yes."

"Well, you see it was so long ago. We had roses — "

"No, I mean in the fields."

"In the fields?"

"Yes."

"In the fields we had habri, and maki (poppies). We had chamomile flowers, and those small, tiny ones. . . niezapominayki (forget-me-nots).

* * *

Unless you return to the past and touch it, you stand in place. The fear of returning is the fear of the future. My God, what will happen to me, I had thought. Going back is different from remembering. Remembering is gilded, going back is facing impoverishment. The nourishment of the dream disintegrates; one has to reexperience hunger, to proceed. In order to survive death, we must die.

I am no longer here, says Szumska, the serious look of a child on her face. When I was a child, she was not my mother. When I was a child we were spirits together. Majka is mother to the child Szumska. Maria Szumska was never just a mother, her soul has a revolutionary bent.

She smiles.

The secret between us is as deep as the lake she took us to, when I was eight.

Martha Roth

IN THE VERNACULAR

HER PEOPLE *chose to fight and of course they lost to the Romans, who simply slaughtered them and flung the wounded into a stockade. She herself had clubbed a sleeping Roman soldier when she and her twin daughters crept past the sentry post in the early dawn, grasping the club firmly and bringing it down across his eyes because she knew the skull would be more vulnerable where there were holes in it. Hearing the nose bone crack, feeling the face bones break. His big-muscled arms twisted and his feet kicked as she raised the club and hit him again with all her force. The girls made no sound. As soon as she could be sure he was dead they headed up the slope to the top of the ridge, scrambling through oak and pine to where the cypresses stood like black fingers poking into the sky. It was more honorable to fight than to surrender but by the Mother! It was better to flee than be taken captive.*

They journeyed ten days through the forests, keeping as high as they could because it was dry and because it gave them an advantage over the Romans whose bodies and weapons were too clumsy to slip easily up the uncleared slopes. Her wounds were not healing. She and her daughters slept in pairs, one always keeping watch, for they dared not light a fire. They ate roots and grubs and they suffered from lack of water, sucking the dew from the meager undergrowth.

On the eleventh morning they stumbled out of the forest into a steep meadow, where a flock of long-haired goats grazed. The goatherd spoke a language not unlike their own, and he brought them milk to drink and led them to a hut where women cleansed her wounds. When she could speak she told them about the Romans. Her twin daughters watched her, their big eyes dark and round, tearless.

* * *

The tea in Yugoslavia is sweet and strong, *čai,* comforting to drink after a long flight. But the language sounds like coal dumping down a chute. I recognized a lovely Argentinian poet on the plane from New York. She smiled at me, but I don't think she realizes we are going to the same place.

Several men who might be poets got on the shuttle in Belgrade. I think one of them is Chris, he is only a little drunk. She smiled dazzlingly at him. He looks good, I suppose, if you don't know him.

The Belgrade shuttle was late arriving in Split (spectacular light on the water), and we missed our ferry connection to Hvar, the island where this conference is being held. By the time the late ferry landed, the moon was high. A couple of old Mercedes taxis met the boat and brought us across the island. Hvar looks like desert under the moon: few trees, all scrub. Olives grow here, and herbs. The mild night breeze carries fragrance.

Our taxis followed a winding road, up what felt like a spine of mountains, then down the other side. The sea shimmers black under the moon. "*Succeso,*" murmured the Italian poet when our taxis pulled into the town square.

The conference hotel, the Palace, is absurdly splendid, a new building behind the facade of a Venetian governor's palace, built about 1610. Hvar is pronounced Hhhwaaar. The Italian poet wears a rusty black derby and striped black-and-yellow socks. La Argentinita, I think her name is Paola, wears a smart leather suit, and Chris wears jeans. He nodded curtly to me in the lobby, muttered, "Thought I might find you here."

Now it's very late, and I sit in a bar on the loggia level writing these notes and drinking slivovic and listening to a most unmusical organist wurlitzing away — "O Sole Mio," "I Get Ideas." Around me sit people speaking French, German, English, Srpsko-Hrvatski. Tomorrow some of them will be revealed as poets but for now they are just background.

People travel in order to find reflections of themselves. Travel's broadening, we say, because it lets us spread ourselves over the big or the beautiful or at least the famous structures of another world. A man who studies Roman brickwork makes himself a Roman and a bricklayer, not just a tourist.

Women go shopping when we travel, because only in shops can we see ourselves reflected. Everything else gives back the masculine image or the masculine gaze. Peaches and rugs and shoes and lace we recognize. A convent of nuns on this island makes a special lace, more delicate than spiderweb, from fibers of the agave plant. I wish I could afford to bring some back for Matilda.

This conference could be a holiday. Time slows down; each day a delicious gift, bland and fat, asks to be pulled apart and slowly, voluptuously devoured.

Next morning the sun shines hot on the sea front. The water is so clear, a magical blue-green, I can see starfish and sea urchins. Aquamarine! It bursts on me like a nova. It's the color the Sears Roebuck catalogue gave as aquamarine, when I was a child. How vivid those catalogue colors are to me still: aquamarine, pink, yellow, powder blue. Slightly off-register to memory's eye, on flimsy coated paper that smelled of something between sawdust and nail polish. The pink my mother called Polish pink. Would she call this Adriatic aqua? *Aqua adriatica; voda jadranska.*

I was out on the front by six this morning, along with the housewives of Hvar who carry long breads in their net bags and plastic sacks. Two English poets were out, too, feeding the gulls. I wished them good morning. I think they're gay. The gulls have black heads. Along with the fresh iodine stink of the sea I smell myrtle, rosemary, and something else — I'll have to ask what it is.

Just outside the hotel dining room is a smart little bar, and against its walls stand two amphoras, giant crusted things that must have been reclaimed from the sea. The old economy of the Adriatic ran on oil and wine, didn't it — and slaves, wheat, salt, iron ore.

At least four centuries before Christians started to count time forward, this island had tribal settlements. The Greek geographer Strabo says Greeks from Pharos landed here and called it Pharos — Hvar. This town faces Italy. When the Romans took over the job of colonizing the known world from the Greeks, they occupied this island. Then they spread over the whole Dalmatian coast. Some mysterious weight shifted and Dalmatia became the center of the empire. Perhaps Rome had become too crowded, too dirty, too corrupt. They began to pick their emperors from the new center, and they called it Illyria. . . .

Our Yugoslav hosts convene us after breakfast in the sunny dining room. They are two men and a woman: Mirko, Darko, Zlata, all tall, all charming. We are eleven: three women, the smiling Paola, me, and a thin elegant Frenchwoman named Stéphany, and eight men — Charlie and Julian, the two Brits, Chris, who is Canadian, Valdo from Chile, a Palestinian named Mahmoud who seems very young, the Italian, a Hungarian, and a Belgian. . . .

Zlata, very pretty in a flowered sundress, leads us on a brief tour of the town, including a magnificent sixteenth-century theater. It is a little treasure of a place, ringed with boxes stacked one above another from the loges to the gods, with a flat space in the center where the groundlings stood, only now the space is filled with folding chairs. The walls are paneled, the panels prettily carved and painted with garlands, and the boxes are draped in real velvet. "Was here given first play written in vernacular — in Slavic tongue," Zlata tells us. "Is written by great national poet from Hvar, name Petar Hektoróvic. We have brought you here to Hvar because of Petar, because of tradition here of vernacular culture. For conference on translation, you see?. . ."

* * *

At our afternoon session the sociable, peace-loving official poets of the Croatian republic swarm cordially over their sleepy, cotton-mouthed guests. "We have gift for you," says Darko, and Zlata passes out copies of a slim paperback volume, issued by the state publishing house especially for this conference, containing poems by all of us, in three versions: one in the original language, one in Croatian, and then — looking so strange, so official — one in the Cyrillic alphabet of Serbian.

Of course, I turn at once to my poem, "The Daughter," "Ćerka," "Ћерка." I'm used to the way it looks in Croatian. "My friend Matilda translated this," I tell Mirko, who sits next to me and peers over my shoulder.

"Is very fine, I think," he says. "It's against male chauvinism, correct?" He pronounces it chow-vinism. "This would not be possible to write in Croatian at this historical moment."

I point to Matilda's text. "Looks to me as if it's written in Croatian."

He shrugs. "I mean, originally."

"You mean, it's not a Croatian poem?"

"Precisely."

"Is it a Serbian poem?"

"Even much less so."

My poem is written in the Serbo-Croatian ballad style, and it has a woman hero, the daughter, who vanquishes the ancient spirits of evil and violence. It's unrhymed and full of my own language tricks; still, I thought Matilda's version looked like a real poem.

After several extemporaneous speeches of thanks to our hosts, we deliver our prepared remarks, some of which turn out to be at cross purposes. Stéphany flings names about — Lacan, Irigaray. She says, "The words are always already there. In one sense, all writing is quotation."

Francis the Belgian speaks of spiritual hunger, "the need for God." Paola mentions the need for an international community of artists. Julian salutes the rich traditions of the Adriatic — Greek, Roman, Venetian, Slavic, Turkish, Austro-Hungarian. The Hungarian Joszef comments acerbically that this is "a catalogue of colonial exploiters"; then he gives a conventional speech about the importance of vernacular writing for a poet's sense of identity. Mahmoud follows him and says much the same thing. Guli, the Italian poet in the striped socks, recites two stanzas of Dante.

I try to deal lightly with the irony that the official language of this conference is English; smiling at Julian and Joszef, I mention cultural imperialism. I can't yet say that as a woman writing, I feel I must always translate.

But Valdo takes me up. "Language itself is imperialism," he says, "colonization of the infant consciousness. The process of socialization is also one where the dominant fraction subdues the savage. Everyone must always translate. Language, whether Spanish or English or Chinese, is always only a gesture, a system of *correspondances*."

When he has understood what Valdo is saying, Joszef disagrees. "The vernacular tongue much more puts together than drives apart. This is a unifying force."

"Desire," says Guli, shaking his head. "All poetry is merely clothing for naked desire."

"If that were true," says Charlie, "then translation would be easy — like changing last season's coat for this. Only it's not."

"The American Chomsky has described quite well what happens," says Stéphany, who has put on her dark glasses because she is sitting in a patch of sunlight. "Language gives shape to thought."

Chris is drunk and waives his turn, and then we read some of our own translations. Paola has translated a poem of Chris's into Spanish. It is one of his awful ones where the earth is dark and female, but in Spanish it sounds fine.

In the late afternoon I go for a walk with Zlata, Charlie, Joszef, and Mahmoud. Every other doorway seems to open into a wineshop. Zlata leads us away from the front, up steep streets toward an old fortress overlooking the town. "From Napoleonic time," she tells us. "Is now a video disco. Unfortunately, right now is closed for repairs."

Outside every wineshop a few tables have been set on the narrow pavement. Old men in black with seamed faces sit at them, and tourists, Anglo-Saxons mostly, wearing beige or khaki poplin with cameras close at hand. We all smile and nod at one another. Between the shops we look over low walls into gardens. The streets are so steep that dwellings are terraced and the gardens sit on the roofs of houses in the street below: orange and lemon trees, flowering aloes, palms and oleanders in huge pots, camellias, roses, alyssum, yucca, cannas, salvia, jade trees nearly as tall as palms, grapevines twisted like old women, bougainvillaea, brilliant geraniums. Bright flowering sprays nod over the shoulders of tourists drinking Coke or Fanta from thick wineshop glasses.

Mahmoud pulls his kefiyah over his head and draws a lot of attention. Children speak to him, laughing, and he smiles. Some of his teeth are missing. Soon we have picked up a little entourage of children. Mahmoud smiles, shrugs, passes out candies. Zlata nods. "These are poor children," she says. "This island lives on tourism, and fishing. They don't get too much sweets. They follow after you now."

"Everyone here makes a living from the tourist trade? Or fishing?"

She shrugs. "Some live on lavender."

This is the scent I've been trying to identify.

After dinner some of us stroll to a bar down on the front. We drink beer and slivovic and listen to John Lennon and the soft corrupt babble of Italian rock. The walls are hung with fishnets and cork bobbers, like a bar in any seaside resort. I could get used to this place.

"You realize, don't you," says Charlie, "that our hosts don't give a flying fuck what we do now?"

"As long as we don't get hurt," says Francis.

"Barring that. Right. But they've done their job just getting us here. We don't even have to go to their silly sessions. Decent of the Yugos, I call it."

"Jolly decent, " says Julian. "How do you suppose they feel about decadent Westerners laying seige to their official poets?"

"Darko is very nice," Charlie agrees.

"Sexual entrepreneurialism," I shake my head. "A fine old tradition in this part of the world."

"In every part of the world," says Stéphany. "*Il y en a partout.*"

"Why here especially?" asks Julian.

"Oh — I was thinking of Byron. You know — *Don Juan. The Corsair.*"

"Of course-air!"

"Byron is one of few English poets I know well," says Joszef, leaning in on me. "He translates well into German, also Magyar. Like Shakespeare."

"So I've heard."

The door is open and under the buzz of conversation, the keening of John Lennon, "Imagine all the pee-pu-u-ul," the lapping of water can be heard against the harbor pilings. "What do you think about translating?" Joszef murmurs. "Desire, for instance. From Magyar?"

I laugh and shake my head.

"Aren't you a romantic? Don't you believe in two people?"

"I'm not a romantic."

"All poets are romantics." He gazes into my eyes, not trying very hard, but hey! what's he got to lose?

"Me, I'm a realist."

"I don't believe you."

Yet I manage to sleep alone.

* * *

Every woman I know, lesbian or straight, picks people up — especially traveling. My English friend Betty told me about a romp with a man in a train: going into an empty first-class compartment and locking the door, unscrewing the light bulb from its wire cage. "We were sort of half on the floor when the conductor comes by with his passkey. 'I'm very sorry, sir, but I'm afraid you'll have to leave.' 'Just let us alone a bit, hey?'

says my bloke, with his hand in my crack, for god's sake. 'Newlywed couple, y'know,' and he slips him a wink and some lolly.'"

Another friend had an affair with her woman guide on a raft trip down the Colorado. Another went sailing in Barbados and had it off with someone else's husband; they snuck down to the cabin when their spouses weren't noticing and squirmed together on a narrow bunk with the swell of the sea beneath them. "We couldn't make a sound, it was absolutely the most exciting — "

I haven't had such adventures. Perhaps I look too prim. It's not as if I were such a heterosexual enthusiast. Or sexual enthusiast. I like it fine with the right person, if everything else is all right, too; but I've never just wanted to make love, just for its own sake. "Don't you ever get horny?" my friend Arabella asked. "When I have to travel alone, I get so horny I could hump a doorknob. Literally."

"So what do you do?"

"Usually I pick up some croupier or something, some dumb tourist trap. And it's okay, you know? I mean, he knows what I want. There was this hairdresser in Mexico, a little Greek guy, great muscles. I was there for a whole month, and we paced everything just right — the flowers, the first time this, the first time that."

"No," I told her. "I don't get horny."

"Fantastic!" said her voice, but her eyes said, "Poor you!"

Maybe I should get one of these lovely Dalmatians into an elevator — or a closet. One of the bellboys — one of the chambermaids. It could be like a tip, quick and neat. Maybe Zlata. Maybe Mirko. I like that better than fucking some cold sentimental fish like Joszef.

Refreshing as a cup of tea, perfunctory as a nod. The blood thickens, the flesh swells and parts, a quick rub dissipates the tension. One feels more like oneself afterward: confirmed. What you want isn't love — breakless union of body and spirit, tender slow rising of desire, flowering of pleasure, ebb and return. What you want is Dr. Feelgood's hot starch injection.

It sounds nice, but I can't talk myself into it.

Yet there is something in these men's faces — the high bones, the soft mouths — some calm assumption that they will please. And many of the women do seem pleased. Perhaps their bodies are a gift. Remarkable people — noisy, sociable, strong, well made. I like to think of them as people who have conquered no one. . . .

* * *

Her people called her the mother, and they prayed to her as the chief of spirits, the source of all things. Their life was hard, filled with birthing and dying, storm and drought, but they had a great capacity for joy, and they thanked her for it. Certain nights in every moon they drank the sacred drink and danced the spirals that pleased her. She was the mother of creation and destruction, of the owl and wolf and headless infant as well as the fertile olive and the blessed serpent that coils down inside the hardest rock.

She made the bodies of men and women, birds and goats and fish, and she provided them with the uses of pleasure as well as increase. Women are her praise-givers. Women have made the great calendar of moon cycles that shows when the rains come, when the herbs regain their fragrance. Women understand feeding, blood, and healing. Women rule the tribe, and in good years the people prosper and hold many festivals in thanks to the mother. In bad years the old people die; newborn kids and babies die; the great-winged eagle and vulture draw their circles lower and lower in the sky.

The mother speaks to her women in their dreams. When they need to hear from her, the wise women and the queen will breathe the sacred smoke and drink the sacred drinks and sleep long nights until the mother sends them messages. Don't snare any more rabbits, she told them once, until you pluck the feathers from a hundred owls. A hard winter is coming; salt down twice as much fish as you think you will need. Once, she sent two wise women the same dream — that goats died from eating the long silver fish, so the people didn't gather that fish. The long silver bodies heaped up on the shingle of an inlet, and the birds wouldn't touch them, either.

Women dreamed the coming of their babies, and they dreamed of taking joy with one another and also with the men. The mother spoke in the men's dreams too, but not so importantly. They dreamed of mounting the goats or of eating them roasted, or they dreamed of each other or of being chosen by powerful women during the time when the people planted their babies. The women always looked at a man's hands carefully. Many of the men's jokes had to do with scrubbing their nails in water and sand to get rid of the grime and goat smell. "Whose flanks were you gripping yesterday?" they greeted each other.

All joy celebrated the mother, even the men's joy with the goats, even the rams' and nannies', the birds' quick flutters and the flowers' opening and the insects' lightning couples in the air. All beings praised her when they released their fragrance, when their bodies shivered in delight. All twining couples worshipped her. All hands and mouths and genitals in any combination offered their gladness to the mother, and she beamed upon her people in her person as the sun.

* * *

Whew! Febrile enough. That's what comes of not writing prose habitually — when you do do it, you go over the top.

We are on a day trip to Split to see "the palace from Diocletian time." "How do you say 'Diocletian'?" I ask Mirko.

"*Dioklecìjan*. Was first Illyrian emperor, you know. Later were many. He build great palace, *Dioklecìjan*. Others make palace even greater." He spreads his arms and for a moment seems vulnerable and young, a bragging boy. "Center of empire shifted. *Dioklecìjan* ruled from Rome, had retirement here. Later emperors ruled from here — Spalata, Split."

The ferry from Hvar is a small boat, dirty and hot. I stay on deck while the other poets club together in the bar, drinking beer, slivovic, and *loza*, the cruel pear brandy. Mirko stays with me, either to keep me from jumping overboard or to figure me out. "You are not like other women," he says at last. "I watch you. You are quiet. You do not flirt."

Paola and Chris have definitely paired off. Joszef and Stéphany are approaching an understanding. Guli the Italian has acquired a bevy of blondes who surround him on the island like a swarm of gnats. Mahmoud gazes at the young girls. Julian keeps on at Darko.

"You've got it, Mirko," I say. "I want to do it differently, and I want to find reflections of this difference — of my own vernacular culture." We have to holler these words at each other, the sun and the wind snatching sound out of our mouths.

"My friend Matilda, who translated my 'Daughter' poem — she showed me a poem about heroic women. It was a ballad, a folk poem. I don't remember the name, but it had something in it about the old warrior queens of Illyria. The brave women — that appealed to me."

"Bravery in women appeals to you."

"Yes."

"But not in men."

"Oh — " The gulf of culture yawns between us. "Look, Mirko — I think that men's meaning of heroism is too close to death. Too much involved with destruction. I want to find some other way to be heroic. A woman's way."

"But the warrior queens of Illyria — they were not killers and killed?"

"I don't know. That's why the poem appealed to me. I thought maybe there might be a meaning of courage I could find — and say — that is directed to life, not death."

"So there is your reflection — in an Illyrian queen?"

"What do you know about them? Tell me what you know," I shout into the wind, in Mirko's direction.

"Is a place in Crne Gore, in Montenegro, name for one old queen. Old Illyrian queen name *Téuta*. Is a legend that she die in prison rather than surrender to Romans. Her tribe was last one on this coast."

"The last?"

He shrugs. "Last tribe ruled by a queen. This is legend, of course, is not history." He squints into the sun. Seagulls scream over our widening wake, where the ferry's screw churns up glassy chunks of aquamarine.

On the water the breeze always feels cool, though I'm sure it will be hot in Split, as hot as it was on the front at Hvar where the long blonde women bare their breasts on the shingle and slap and pinch their thighs, thighs that are flat and hard as the oars of a galley.

We are sailing into the wind. The Greeks would have sailed in this direction, putting out in their little boats from the *pharos*, the lighthouse, and heading for the mainland. Sun presses down on us with crushing brilliance, and the glittering water forces us to blink. Shading my eyes, I glimpse other islands dotting the sea. Wait, wait. Stop the boat, give me time to be here, time to slide myself into the real Adriatic. I need to feel in my own body the sun the water the salt.

Humans have coaxed a living out of these rocky islands for a long time. The first mapmakers must have had quite a job, there are so many; one would grow confused, mistake one shape for another. Zlata told us, "There are eight hundred islands in this Adriatic, but only fewer than one hundred are inhabited."

Darko said, "There are more than one thousand islands in the Adriatic. Less than one percent are settled on."

Mirko now tells me, "Are about twelve hundred islands in this sea, one thousand, two hundred, yes? You can see, clear on map, was once part of coast. Long ago, sea came up over mountains. Islands now are tops of mountains what once were. Volcanic. Whoosh." He waves his arms again, and again he is a boy. "Most have no water."

In the strong light the islands are purple, blue, dark green. The littlest ones float on the water like a child's toys in a bathtub, but the bigger ones look like continents, their slopes bristling with scrub like the flanks of a show-cropped poodle. When we pass close to an island we see slow waves lapping up against the land. The roar of our engines is the only sound. In a small boat I would hear clearly the cries of the gulls, the slap of the gentle swell. Perhaps dolphins would break the surface and gleam silver in the sun.

It's frustrating, not to know for sure how many islands lie off this coast. If I lived here, I would have reference books, atlases with aerial photographs that would tell me authoritatively. Connaissance maps. The phrase amuses me, and I smile. "You like this passage," says Mirko, leaning against the rail, looking at me looking at his sea.

The Slavs must have traveled this way. The Romans sent their galleys prowling out here. Suppose the settlements along this coast — the whole peninsula, the broken-off part of the mainland all the way down to Albania, all the way to Greece — suppose they were once a matriarchal civilization. Suppose they were ruled by tribal queens. The mountains rise right out of the sea; when the Yugoslavs built a coastal highway after the war, they had to blast it clear. The Romans would have had trouble with those tribes. . . .

* * *

A small shaggy man clambered up the rock face from the beach to his queen's long hut. He wore skins on his body and his feet were bare, the soles almost as tough as the hooves of the long-haired goats he tended. Goats could graze up and down the steep incline, clinging to the rock and cropping the gray-green succulents that grew in the crevices. "My queen! My queen!" he gasped as he approached the stone-and-timber hut. "A huge boat approaches, and another, and another, like fish with many fins! Men walk on its back! Come and see for yourself, my queen!"

One of the queen's attendants met him in the yard of the hut, a bare swept space laid out in a maze of paths intended to deceive the spirits of drought and sickness. "What is worth such an expense of breath?" said the attendant, an old woman wearing a shift woven of goats' hair.

"Men! On the water! I saw them from the harbor!"

"I believe you, my mother's son, but the queen is taking joy with her favorite and I can't disturb them."

"She should try a man, if she wants to harvest fruit," sniggered the goatherd.

"I'll tell her."

"Only a joke, my mother. What of the men on the water?"

The old woman sighed. "We have seen them before. Since your mother was a suckling. We hope they don't see us — or if they do, we hope they can't climb the rock face."

He nodded sagely.

"Thanks, my mother's son. You do well to look around you. The queen will hear your message."

He scrambled back down among his beasts.

* * *

We land at Split and make our way to Diocletian's palace. Julian has bought a gold chain for Darko, and Mirko is scandalized. "But you're a poet," we tease him. "There's a fine old poetic tradition — Catullus, Verlaine, Rimbaud, Auden, Spender, Cavafy, Sappho — "

"Oh-ho!" he pounces on me. "You are Sapphic. Is that it?"

I smile and shrug, trotting after him into the cool darkness of the palace cellars. He whisks us through the chambers, where I would like to linger. The cellars are immense. "Was many years in cleaning," he snaps at us over his shoulder. "In Middle Ages people living above threw down their garbage here. Was a midden."

During the long centuries after the Romans and before the Austrians, people lived in the galleries and peristyle of the palace, building their little dwellings between the columns that the emperors had raised. They blurred the clarity of Diocletian's plan, his foursquare design for a palace-temple-garrison-fort. Crooked alleys took shape, decade by decade, it must have been, as the big houses broke down into little apartments. The monuments of imperial caution and vainglory decomposed slowly into spaces for ordinary life.

I see it as a kind of digestion, the big primary substances worked on by the catalyst of time, crumbling gradually into heaps of usable stuff. Bubbles of vitality rising from among the crumbs, the lives of ordinary people crept along, over the centuries, spilling out across the thresholds of rooms, cutting against corners, uncoiling into open spaces, hooking onto other lives.

They dug the simplest sewers: holes in their floors where they poured their refuse. Did they know of the palace cellars, the great connecting chambers underneath? Or did they trust in the awayness of what they couldn't see to protect them from their own filth? As the level of garbage rose, thousands must have died of various plagues, miasmas, pestilence. When the palace was excavated finally — and Mirko is unclear about the date — the middens of a milennium and a half had to be cleared. The Roman brickwork was restored. Wreckage, garbage, human shit; they mucked it all out of the underground rooms.

The surface of the palace has gone on changing. Now between the walls are kiosks where Arabs sell scarves and purses. Five thousand people still live within the original walls, but the old formal structure has been brushed up and restored so that its lines can be admired by poets like Mirko and tourists like me. "Wouldn't it be wonderful to live up that flight of stairs?" I point into a courtyard.

"To live there with your Sapphic lover," he sneers. "Was once Baldessare family palace, in Venetian time." The courtyard opens off a tiny square that sits crosswise on the field where retired emperors drilled their legions, hoping for the call back to Rome. Sitting out their retirement, until they were murdered.

"I want to go back to the cellars," I tell him.

"Impossible. We visit market now, then we have lunch. Then we go to Meštrović gallery."

"*Molim*. Please. I'm very moved by them. Please, Mirko — fifteen minutes. I'll go alone."

"Impossible." He holds a rapid consultation in German with Francis,

Valdo, and Joszef. *"Nema problema.* I take you." He sets off angrily, fast as a heel-and-toe walker, and I follow.

The gate must be unlocked again. I give the guard five hundred dinars. Slow drips collect in puddles under the vaulted ceilings. "This masonry is amazing," I say, wanting him to know I really am impressed. The pillars are built out of huge chunks of limestone quarried from hills, he tells me, three miles to the east of the town. My shoulders ache with the strain of transporting them: ropes, block-and-tackle, ox-drawn carts. High in the walls are cut the recessed shelves where Diocletian's household stored their imperial supplies.

"Is here granary." Tall stone jars must have held grain, oil, wine. At one end stands an oil press, grand, symmetrical, like an altar. Bare electric bulbs probably give as much light as torches did, when slaves poured olives into that press seventeen hundred years ago and strained the first pressing from the square stone trough.

On the deep shelves, the restorers have placed bits of sculpture rescued from the chaos. Some of them are sphinxes. "Much was brought from Egypt," Mirko says again, "as we have seen above in peristyle. Pink stone, from desert. *Dioklecìjan* was proud of Egyptian conquest. He built temple to Jupiter but put sphinxes to show he was also lord of Egypt."

The dankness of the cellars is refreshing after the heat of the surface. They are a warehouse not just of time but of intentions. When the German occupying army was driven out in the Second World War, while they were fighting their own struggle for independence, the Yugoslavs excavated these rooms, teams of archeologists and helpers sifting through the shit. This has something to do with national identity, perhaps as much as language. The chamber we are in looks as high as a circus tent. I wonder how many women could stand on my shoulders before one touched the vaulted ceiling.

"Thanks for bringing me back. I'm ready to go now."

He strides ahead of me, through the swarming life of the present day. To the west of the palace an open market flourishes: clothes, toys, jewelry, pottery, flutes, cheeses, nuts, eggs, chickens — alive and dead — bloody hunks of meat, vegetables with earth clinging to them, fruit like the cheeks of children, grain in metal scoops, honey in jars topped with paraffin, flowers, red, blue, mauve, pink, yellow, misty white, tough brown roots of grapevines, little cherry trees with their balls of earth like scrotums bound around their trunks, fig trees, almond trees, tomatoes, cabbages, lettuces, peaches, apricots, spinach, oranges, lemons, quinces, onions, garlic, figs, pears, carrots, bunches of herbs, rosemary, sage, lavender, spilling and sprawling over stone terraces on trestle tables and packing boxes. Old countrywomen sit on overturned plastic buckets. Old men with heavy thumbs squint and weigh out the cheeses and grain with lead weights — "Same like in *Dioklecìjan* time," says Mirko with a nod. The meat and cheese draw flies; the old women fan them away with leaves, gossiping to one another or staring straight ahead.

We pass a group of gypsies who call after us in shrill, husky voices. Their mouths gleam with broad gold teeth. A young gypsy man stands behind a table full of carved wooden spoons, playing a one-stringed wooden instrument. I can't hear what sound it makes. "Are there many gypsies in Yugoslavia?" I have to shout because Mirko is striding fast again, looking for the other poets.

"Gypsies go where money is." He barely turns his head.

Francis has bought a wooden crucifix. "I am lonely without one over my bed," he says, smiling. The sun cooks odors out of all the market stuff, blending lavender with the juice of crushed fruits, blood, sour cheese. "We go to lunch now," says Mirko.

In the nice restaurant he does not speak to us. Joszef taunts Francis. Julian and Darko sit very close. Most of the others have stayed on the island; they are having lunch elsewhere, now, with Zlata. We are hot and dusty and don't feel much like eating. Mirko has a long, chummy conversation with the waiter. . . .

* * *

After the final session there is to be a formal dinner, but first we go for a swim, Stéphany, Joszef, Charlie, Mahmoud, and I. And Mirko. "We go to workers' club where is good beach," he says. The late afternoon heat lies on the seafront like a carpet, as Mirko loads us into an old VW van. In spite of our brief political rapport, Stéphany ignores me, as before. Joszef smokes, Mahmoud whistles.

The workers' club has doorless cabanas that face the water. I can practically dive from my changing room into the lively, ancient sea. Sunset is happening on the other side of the island. The Stone Age people of Illyria would have loved their sunsets.

My arms and legs feel delicious in the water. Thanks to the mother who transforms one shape into another: the bark and bole of cypress trees into flame; flame into ash; the thin soup of love into mewing, clinging children; the sea's brilliance into danger, into plenty. Enemies into friends, imperial palaces into tenements; magic into words and words into plain speech.

"Fuck!" splutters Charlie, his head surfacing a few yards away. "I hate bathing costumes. Why are southerners such bloody prudes?"

"Beats me." Mirko approaches, treading water, spraying droplets through his curly moustache. His shoulders are roundly, massively muscled. He looks like Meštrović's portrait bust of the Serbian hero Branko Krsmanović. "Do you see that island?" he snorts, nodding his head to the left, the south. "Is kilometer and a half away. Do you want to swim there?"

"Not me, mate," says Charlie. "See you at choir practice."

But I strike off after Mirko, trying to match my stroke to his longer one, loving the way I slide through the Adriatic. *Jadransko, more Jadransko more*, I say over in my head. Breathe out, gulp, kick, kick, kick, out, in, kick, kick, kick, kick, *more, Jadransko more*. When my head is above water the sea is liquid pearl, or milk, but when I look down and open my eyes in the water I see a deep, translucent green and the suggestion of waving branches. Of a forest deep below my body that glides and dances over it. Straight as a bird's flight through the cool dark greenness.

It must be after six o'clock. The sponge fishers are coming in, their little boats holding a man and a boy each, nets, bobbers, and a pile of creatures. Did the Illyrians swim for pleasure?

The light begins to wane. The humped back of the island floats nearer with every stroke. Finally my fingers scrape a pebbly bottom. I stand up in shallow water. The light is lavender, softly washing any color out of the rock, the sky, and Mirko, who lies spreadeagled on a dark slab of stone. Only the sea still sparkles, milk of a magical mother.

I feel exhilarated, and I want to dance — but the few twirls I take on the stony beach make me dizzy, and I stub my great toe. So I sit down in the wan, grainy light, and look at Mirko. Even drained of color he is good to look at. Even in his modest, somewhat baggy bathing trunks. A tall, strong man, his hair shot with gray, also his moustache and the curling hair on his chest. His hands and feet are long. He raises his head and wrinkles bracket his mouth. "You are looking at me."

"I'm looking at an official poet, off duty."

"I am never off duty. Rest quickly — we must be going back."

"I feel as if I could fly back."

"You enjoyed the swim?"

"Very much."

"I tell you little secret. Because I am knowing these tides for many years, we were able to catch the current going out. Now, in one minute or two, we will have our friend the current coming back in."

"That's wonderful. Are you a fisherman?"

"Sometimes. For pleasure only. You understand, for these people, fishing is serious business." He sits up and looks at me. "I don't know about you. You are not like other women."

A stream of white birds like torn paper beat the air over our heads. "Have you read my poems?"

"They are very musical, but — is a different music. Is hard for me
to hear."

"Listen, Mirko — " So many kinds of difference lie between us, I want
to say, but I don't want this moment to end, or to change. "This is a
magical place. I want to write about it."

"Is very famous. Very beautiful."

"I think perhaps there are voices in the island winds."

"As in the play of Shakespeare, you mean?"

"Yes."

"Is perhaps a childish fancy." He groans, bored. He doesn't want to
know what I have heard, what message the winds have borne for me.
He doesn't care that I have had a vision of an ancient queen, something
has spoken to me of women's heroism and the worship of the mother
goddess; and I'm reluctant to spend my gorgeous vision on someone
who isn't going to love it. He might not even think I have a right to such
a vision on his island, in his sea, in his hard-fought, precious country
where day care and washing machines have so improved the lives of
women.

"I've been reminded of my childhood many times in the last few days."

He squints. "I try to imagine you a child."

"I was a solemn little girl."

"Ah."

"What sort of little boy were you?"

"Frightened." He must be about my age. He would have been a child
during the war — the Nazi occupation, then the long struggles that
followed. I feel intimidated by the misery, treachery, and martyrdom
that have marked this man's life, and I don't want to ask any more questions, but I'm powerfully drawn to him, sitting so close I can smell him.
He pushes himself up on his elbows. "What was your father?"

"A schoolteacher. And yours?"

He is silent. The birds still flutter past, screaming fragments. Between
us the air has a grain like the surface of a photograph. The darkness
in its texture deepens. Lights on shore look far away. "My father was
hero of Resistance, of the partisans. I have never know him. He make
my mother pregnant and then he die, in torture and glory."

"Did the Germans kill him?"

"The English." We sit silent and the soft eager air laps our bodies.
"My mother came from rich family but is good Communist, she worked
as bureaucrat in department of transport in Béograd. Now she live here,
with my wife and me."

The grains of darkness have burst. The air is soft and cool, scented
with herbs. Rosemary and lavender grow on this island, too. "Tell me
about your wife," I say.

"Is good woman. Good cook. Good mother. She kick me out of bed sometime, when I take too much covers." I can barely see him now, close as we are sitting, but suddenly I feel his hand against my back, warm as brandy. He strokes me. "You are cold. Tell me: Do you ever make love to a man?"

This isn't fair. Perhaps I have wanted him, but I feel tricked. Who has tricked whom? "Mirko, I'm anxious about the others. We should get back."

"Is no problem. They will go into workers' club, drink beer, slivovic. *Nema problema*. We can do what we want."

His other hand cups my shoulder. Between his hands I feel protected and lovely. The stone beneath us has kept the sun's warmth, I feel it against my thighs. His big head comes forward and he licks my throat. "You taste of the sea," he says, and growls at the bottom of his voice.

Well, yes, we can do what we want, and no, we can't — since what I want is several incompatible things. I want to tell him all about me; I want to go on hearing his deep voice say curious, affectionate things. I want to slip down his damp trunks and lick the taste of sea from his hardening penis. I want to swim back on the incoming tide. I want to join the others; I want to complete my vision of Téuta; I want to wind my hands in his thick hair and hold him deeply inside of me; I want to have a drink; I want to leap up and achieve the shore in one long movement, like an arrow. I want to take him and refuse him, to give myself and keep myself. I want to assert my own vernacular.

"No, Mirko, not here."

"Where?"

"On the stage of Petar's theater," I say, and I lift his head from my lap.

His hands loosen in surprise. "Do I just swim toward the lights?" I ask, and plunge in before he can answer.

The others are in the game room of the workers' club shooting pool, half drunk and very hungry. Of course they make assumptions. "*C'est infâme*, " hisses Stéphany.

"All right for some," sniffs Charlie.

"So — you translate from *hrvatski*?" Joszef is bound to be urbane. Mahmoud says nothing, smiles sadly.

Mirko looks grim and tosses down slivovic, barely glancing at me. . . .

We are very late coming back to the Palace. Zlata has been frantic, trying to hold off the cooks, the waiters, the singers. Chris and Paola, dressed up and drunk, have been dancing to the dreadful wurlitzerist, slipping and falling and laughing. Guli sits at the smart little bar in his derby, with two blondes, a Swede and a Dane. "*Mes invitées*," he introduces them, and the women say, "*Prego*," and giggle. Julian and Darko have put on long aprons and are helping in the kitchen.

The elaborate dinner is spoiled. What was meant to be cold is now warm; what was to have been hot is cooled. The crisp has wilted, the firm has slumped. The cooks treat us with bitter politeness. I don't care. We eat and drink, and the Hvar village singers perform for us between courses.

Their singing is wonderful. They stand in a circle, Darko among them. He has taken off his apron and he is very beautiful in a dinner jacket. The bass voices are deep, the tenors high and clear; their harmony is true but strange to my ears — sevenths, fourths, octaves.

Most of the songs follow a pattern, like the ballads Matilda has read to me, set to music, their patterns of rhythm and sound reinforced now with melody and the blending voices. They sing a verse in close harmony, then a chorus; sometimes a solo; then a climax, with spread octaves, the tenors soaring high and the basses diving deep below them. Zlata acts as compère. "This is song about a donkey and wagon." "This is love song." "This is homesick song of sailor far from his native village."

The long swim exhausted me, and the wine makes my head spin. I see double and triple visions in the candlelight. Mirko drinks heavily and ignores me. Most of the other poets are also seriously engaged with strong drink, although Joszef and Stéphany, who has changed for dinner and dazzles the eye in a tight dress of green glittery stuff, seem to be holding a seminar — in politics? aesthetics? After the singers finish, to long, loud applause and calls of "Encore!" from Chris, the vile organist comes back and plays "I Get Ideas."

Tomorrow I will be far from here. . . .

Nicole Dillenberg

COMING OUT IN LONDON AND BEYOND

When I was twenty-one I went to Europe for the first time as an "adult," armed only with gooey memories and a brand new Bachelor of Arts in Film. I'd developed a crush on a local boy named Nicholas during my school years in England and now that I was out of university and "grown up," I had a mad desire to marry him and work as a film producer in London. The following pages have been excerpted from a journal documenting my naiveté, megalomania, consternation . . . in short, my adventures seeking this goal.

—NCD
Los Angeles, 1990

England, 1985
The negativity of London is getting to me and I'm beginning to feel really paranoid. Everybody from the print shop girl to my so-called best friend backstabs me and calls me an idiot behind my back. Are their lives truly that boring? You'd think they'd find better things to do. I no longer feel obligated to socialize simply for the sake of socializing, though. Why underestimate the quality of my life when I can accomplish more on my own? I'd gladly trade 15,000 evenings with these two-faced jerks who feel compelled to talk about me behind my back for a sole hour with Nicholas. It's rare one finds people who are truly whole. Thank God I'm finally beginning to understand this.

* * *

I'm back at the library. It feels safe and wonderful. It's late night tonight. 8:00 p.m., so I can write away. Lately I've had sporadic feelings of culture shock/extreme isolation — mostly when I'm with people I don't trust. I feel tons better though, now that I've decided to move on regardless of whether or not we shoot Ella's film in Germany this winter. I haven't told my flatmates yet — I'm kind of reluctant to. I'll take everything in my room but leave Henry and Caliana two months rent which will give me plenty of time to decide whether to go back to L.A. to write the script for "Exiled" or come back here.

Cal's had a super week. She's temping for a friend of Henry's who runs a magazine and likes princesses (I guess he created a job for her; good P.R. to have an exiled princess on board). Anyway, Saturday I met Cal at the park where one of her Yugoslavian countrymen was photographing her. I decided to play "stylist"; barged over and insisted Cal and I trade coats, since mine looked better with her headband. Then we started trading jewelry and I made her borrow my lipstick. Afterwards I took several pictures of Cal with the photographer — he was amused, I think — asked me lots of questions about what I do, what I want to do. Then we sat in his car afterwards and he pulled out a briefcase full of Prince Charles, baby Harry, the Queen . . . turned out the man was from the *Daily Telegraph* and a very major photojournalist. I was so embarrassed I could have died. But I think the photos are going to be really great.

* * *

As for the dinner party of my life, I'd only been in love with Nick for . . . what? Nearly a decade? I came back to England expressly to track him down. My oldest friend, Greg, was house-sitting for this photographer named Allen. He has a great flat in Chelsea so we decided to throw a dinner party for eight, at which Nicholas, object of my affections, and I could be reunited in a non-threatening manner.

I never understood during my school years here Nick's social standing. It just never meant anything much; it still doesn't, but I find now I'm bombarded with class trauma/mores/rules. I should have taken it as an omen when I crossed the threshold of Allen's flat and saw all the society photographs covering the walls, many of which were portraits of Nick's relatives. Greg and I took them all down and hid them under the bed, but we then, of course, had the problem of nails sticking out of every wall so we started hanging coasters and pot holders and things at random, whatever we could find, to cover the blank spots.

I was stirring the broad beans when I heard the doorbell. Everyone else had arrived so I knew it was Nick. I made Greg go to the door. I was fully prepared for Nick to have become a geek and thought myself particularly mature to have realized that I might find myself disappointed.

When he finally stepped from the hallway into the main room it was like a bolt of lightning shot through me. I've never felt such an attraction for anyone before or since. Without even thinking about decorum I threw myself into Nick's arms, and the next thing I remember, I was still holding Nick but his arms were at his sides and all six people in the room were dead silent. Apparently, I was so nervous I blacked out. I've no idea how long we stood there — two seconds, ten minutes. All I know is I was so embarrassed I hid in the kitchen for the rest of the evening. Even when Nick spilled the turkey I couldn't relax. Before he left though, Nicholas did ask me to ring him. I wonder what that means?

The next day this weirdo showed up while Greg was replacing all the royal mags., photos, etc.. Apparently he used to polish Earl Blountbatten's boots or something equally important, and he asked Greg why Allen's stuff had been taken down. Greg said it would have been offensive to some of my friends —blah, blah, blah; to make a long story short, this guy, who had not even bothered to stand for me when I walked into the room, is suddenly my best pal. Out of work, you see. Tells me all about how well he knows Nick's older brother Sebastian, but of course Nick is the nicest of the bunch; "So Nick and you are good buddies, huh?" Greg's crawling under the table now and I'm screaming with laughter inside — "Sebastian's so serious. . ." this man says. "Yes well, I expect Lord Bromley has a lot of responsibilities now," I replied, thus politely employing the title he had no right not to use. . .

* * *

Went down to school for the popular music conference my favorite tutor, Mick, invented when I was studying there. Lots of Sociology students raving about Marxism (I never knew one had to be schooled in Marxist theory in order to discuss popular music). I found myself making some really good points. Had forgotten what an intellectual groupie I am. Had also forgotten how pretentious students can be — and how narrowminded. Mick invited this amazing Russian woman to come; she married an Englishman and has lived here for five years. This woman really put her foot down with those Marxists; she knocked 'em dead. Long live the Queen!

It started to blizzard; I couldn't get a taxi to come up the hill and get me to my train. Ended up in a Greek taverna with these music conference people. Some of them were stuck in the sixties but it was a refreshing experience just being with them.

This Russian woman made such an intense impression on me. I felt especially drawn to her because last April I dreamed a Russian woman predicted my future. In my dream I begged her to tell me what would happen with Nicholas but she spoke in riddles I couldn't understand. I woke up an absolute mess. Anyway, as we were walking to the taverna she began asking me various astrological questions — what was my sign, etc.. Much later in the evening I asked her when she was born. She told me to guess. I said April on the off-esoteric chance there was some connection. She said yes. It took a good five minutes for her to convince me she was telling the truth.

Later that night we caught the train together to London. Because of the snow, the train broke down in Gillingham and we had to take a bus for an hour to the suburbs of London, where we caught another train. We talked for hours about Englishmen in general. Her husband works in Saudi Arabia nine months out of the year. Apparently it's a great strain for all women to deal with Englishmen because they're so oppressed and grow up with no emotional freedom — they just follow the many rules laid out for them; and the more "upper class" they are, the more rules there are.

I didn't think I had enough money for a cab once we got to London so the woman invited me to stay at her flat. Somehow I knew if I did, she would approach me physically and I wouldn't resist. So I borrowed some money from her and went home.

As odd as it was, I'm grateful to have met this woman; it's such a relief knowing perhaps it isn't me, perhaps it's their society which makes it so difficult to communicate beyond a purely superficial level. I see it in Henry as well: how smooth and charming he is in public, how often he sulks at home and simply won't talk, how much he reads into the trivial words of the women he dates. Everyone here is so exhausted trying to interpret one another's motives it must take years to develop any real trust that can lead to true friendship.

Caliana and I had a long talk last night about much of the same stuff. She wants to pressure Nick into befriending her while I'm gone; once a bond is forged it won't dissipate (or so she says). This is for my benefit — to keep some sort of connection going. Apparently, they don't even start dating (the English boys en masse) until they're nearly thirty and considering marriage. I asked her what they do in the meantime. She told me how common homosexual affairs are and how oftentimes a family will have a select mistress they go to, as they would to a stockbroker or a lawyer.

I don't know if I can deal with this. Granted I'm not making any assumptions or accusing any of my friends of being bisexual — but I am simply trying to understand this progressively complex culture. Cal's never had an English lover. That speaks for itself.

Friday night Henry invited a bunch of people to have drinks at the flat, then we trekked over to the restaurant where Caliana works as of yesterday. Henry was in a foul mood for various reasons, not the least of which was that one of my American friends opened a bottle of 1963 port without his permission (I didn't intercept in time and felt really, really guilty). At the restaurant we sat at a long table and had chewy rabbit stew in little casseroles. I guess I started to absorb Henry's mood because by dessert I felt completely depressed. As we were leaving I pulled on my St. Laurent cape and all of a sudden Henry's date, the honorable Miss-searching-for-money-to-go-with-title-girl present was my best friend. Her saving grace is that she's unaware of this (actually I sound bitchy about it because she's breaking Henry's heart). Henry and I rode to Annabel's by ourselves, which gave him a chance to rant and rave both about the port and about her. Then suddenly he has to go and change the subject and ask me if I've seen Nicholas lately. I felt the rabbit coming up in my throat and couldn't answer. I rolled down the window thinking I might puke, but Henry thought I just needed air because I was upset and he started giving me this pep talk about how Sebastian had 1000 guests at his wedding last year and who needs that kind of pageantry bullshit in family life. I am so sick of hearing about Sebastian's goddamned wedding! Honestly, I think Henry talks more about Nick's brother than Nick does!

When Cal got off work at the restaurant she met us at Annabel's. Lots of Eaton snobs were there, and Henry kept going up to the Harrow boys and saying, "Harrow. Harrow you? I'm fine thanks." Some of them wouldn't even talk to me because I got a punky haircut last week. I'm miserable about it but at the same time I feel somehow strengthened — like I'm being true to myself. Cal looked beautiful in her red dress and danced happily. In the end I forced myself to do the same.

* * *

I missed my tube stop — bloody Circle line. I feel like I go through my life looking for a loo these days. The disadvantages of walking. Somehow in a car, in 75-80° weather, one doesn't notice the forces of gravity.

* * *

I feel so awake. So scared. It all seems pointless. Why? Why? Why? Jesus Christ I feel like a jerk. I hardly know where to begin. But I'll try.

I finally stopped procrastinating and began research on the fall of Caliana's family for the Yugoslavian script. I was so afraid the material would be bland and overused. Much to my joy, the straight factual material alone was brilliant. And never before used on the screen . . . It triggered all sorts of ideas and I told Cal how excited I was — but I immediately started to feel like I was raping her past. She's been acting weird lately and I don't know if it's because I'm definitely leaving or she's sick of me or what. Sometimes I can't help thinking that if she had money she wouldn't be caught dead with me. I see it when a friend in her social "station" rings her up — and I become inconsequential. She's colder. And now I feel like I can't ask questions. And I've got to interview her father about the assassination of the King if this is to go anywhere. But I feel like I'm exploiting our friendship. I told her before I began that she inspired this story. Damnation. Fine. If Cal's against it I'll just have to use more fiction and less fact. And I'll still dedicate it to her. Maybe the "Exiled" script is the only true fruit of this trip — and even "Exiled" may not ever go anywhere, but at least I can write it off as another fucking learning experience.

* * *

Caliana and I spent all night talking about Yugoslavia and lots of scary stuff came out. She doesn't think I should go, because the embassy watches her every move and knows who she lives with. I'd most likely be followed and may not be able to get a single roll of film out of the country. I want to believe we're being paranoid. I've heard it all my life, but I suppose I've never really believed cultures without freedom exist. Growing up in the old Anglo-American bubble, it just seems so odd people should ever have to watch their actions.

* * *

Today I went to the Yugoslav embassy and applied for a visa. I wanted our fears to be unfounded. I figured it was better to be honest so I explained I was compiling research on Yugoslavia's war history for a fictional film. I was immediately told an English journalist had been imprisoned while visiting Belgrade for asking too many questions. Terrific.

* * *

I found a book of King Peter's memoirs. Brought it home to Caliana and I think she enjoyed looking at it. Nick phoned. Cancelled, wanted to reschedule for next week; I told him I would probably already be gone. I felt nothing and just wanted to get it all over with. I told him I had never gotten in touch with his business partner and that I appeared to be failing my duty as social secretary of our next gathering. Then he asked if I wanted to meet for a drink. I was so sure I wasn't going to see him again that it didn't even register at first — he probably thinks I'm spacy as hell. Anyway, now I have to deal with him on a one-to-one basis. Maybe he's playing diplomat. That's cool. We're just friends. And I'm exhausted. I'll need the two months in Austria to refuel!

* * *

Nicholas just left. It was predictably disastrous. My saving grace was that he gave me a few long lustful looks. We never even made it to a pub. Caliana did most of the talking. As a result the fucking ice still hasn't broken. He did invite us to a ball, though, next July. God! Is this to go on forever? You should have seen the looks he was giving Caliana. Poor Nick — wondering how on earth he got into this. I had so little to say. And yet you just know I'll be at this ball in July. I'm absolutely hopeless. This is my last entry for England — au revoir — ou peut têtre, adieu.

Austria, 1986
I can't remember flying out of Heathrow. I can't even remember arriving in Vienna or taking the train up to Steyr. All I remember is that a gorgeous Indian servant girl picked up my suitcase from the platform and escorted me to Ella's car.

I first saw Schloss Nebligglied from a gravel bridge at the base of the greenest mountain on Earth. The "schloss" is medieval and massive, with a flower-filled park, beautiful stone cottages and a tower. The walls are so thick that when the Nazis occupied the tower in '37 it took them 5½ days to drill the hole for a single latrine toilet.

I spent the night on a narrow horsehair bed smack in the middle of a grand hall the size of a football field. Ella was in the next room, sleeping in a little girl's bed, again set in the middle of a huge hall. When I got up during the night to go to the toilet, the stairwell was so black I felt like I was walking into a cave, and I almost decided to hold it. When I came running back into the suite, heart beating a thousand miles a minute, Ella laughed delightedly and proceeded to tell me about the White Lady, the Von Stepnauer family ghost. I was thrilled to learn the White Lady only appears to family members. Oddly enough, though, I have since met other families who claim the "White Lady" is their family ghost. Must be some sort of Austrian/urban myth; either that or all these families are related and have the White Lady as a common ancestor.

The next morning was the Austrian equivalent of Thanksgiving. I slept through church, but went with the Von Stepnauers to Ernte Danksest, the Harvest parade at the Enns River. There were floats and folk costumes and lots of singing. We had a quiet dinner (lamb, I think) at Nebligglied and then left for Vienna early the next morning.

* * *

Vienna is so spectacular — it fills my heart in a way no place else ever could — a true city to fall in love in, constructed solely for the purpose of going to parties and balls. . . . I treated Ella to Die Derkaufte Braut at the Opera House, and then we met Ella's father and some others for a midnight supper on the Hotel Ambassador terrace. That's when the bank across the street from us blew up.

A window shattered in Ella's film studio, and the following day she was quite upset because the glass man never turned up to fix it. (The glass man had a backlog of work that day, you see.)

No one ever did claim responsibility for the bombing.

My last night in Vienna we went to the Artist's ball. Lots of porno stars were there which was a definite drawback but the women were beautiful, the dresses were beautiful, and lots of flashbulbs went off. Click, click, click.

February 25 — Belgrade, Yugoslavia
For the first time I have the energy to write. Have been so sick with this stupid flu! Seeing Vienna and Ella again was like emerging from anesthesia to find the world's still turning, your mother still loves you, and you're not such a bad person after all. I was so freaked out by the time I left London — God! Have realized so much about myself in the past week. It took five minutes with Ella for me to feel like my old self again. Why did I allow myself to be treated like a worthless bimbette? I made myself out to be such an idiot — I merely wanted to be nonthreatening but I should have threatened the pants off Nick because underneath I am capable of so much — as much as Ella. It's embarrassing; I'm two years older than she is and she's advising me on how to repair my life. She says my life fascinates her; she wants to write my story and I hers; I'm still entranced with the Yugoslav project. . .I'm here.

Everyone told me I'd hate it but the people are extraordinary and I'm beginning to understand some of the rare advantages of a Communist country. Everyone bums cigarettes from each other — no problem — and people here smoke like crazy. I went to the Opera house last night for free, and got to sit down for most of it. People trade chairs and climb on the seats. "The workers take over the arts." Only in a communist country could one go to the opera and climb on the seats.

The women here are shy but ask a man for directions and an hour later he's proposing to you. My first night in Belgrade, the hotel sent one of their staff down the street with me because I asked at the desk how to get to the cinema. I ended up having cappucino with the guy (not that I wanted to), and then dinner (not that I wanted to), then I had a terrible time because he got down on his knees and begged me to sleep with him. I had to deal with all this on 12 words of Serbian! The man polished off a pack of cigarettes in 4 hours and then bummed more from all sorts of people for the rest of the evening. His name is Rada — like the Royal Academy of Dramatic Arts in London. Yesterday I asked for directions in a Bureau de change, and they sent a teen-aged boy down the street with me — Pledzay. Soon we were fast friends and he became my guide. He'd make a perfect production assistant if they'd let me film here. There's a film festival every year so I know there's a production process in Belgrade but I haven't a clue what it is.

After the first day, I felt quite safe. There is indeed a non-working light fixture in my room (a bug), but I guess they're not interested. On the train, though, a Yugoslav man wanted me to hide a suitcase's worth of new clothing in my duffle bag before we went over the border. I had to be simultaneously vague and polite — tried to tell him I wasn't exactly in a position to help. I distracted the customs officer from my hard-won visa by acting real American.

* * *

After meeting Pledzay and going to the cathedral with him, where I took a ton of production stills, we met up with two of his school friends. They are so cool — still so righteous and everything. God! Pure! So I met them for dinner tonight. It was great fun. Tomorrow I go on to Bled, which is where the summer palace was. Belgrade hasn't been too helpful in the history department. A little one-sided. But I've gotten a feel for the people and the look of the place. Very Western for a Socialist Republic. Everyone really does seem happy, except the young kids who say life's just grand until they get a taste of the West, and Yugoslavians can travel pretty freely. Amazing I can sit here and write like this. Only time it got weird was when I went to the library and they wouldn't let me in because the hotel still had my passport. So I gave up and now there's this man trying to pick me up. Jesus. Well now, where was I? Oh, yes. Tomorrow I go to Bled and then back to Vienna to help Ella. I think her film project is going to be superb — really down to earth stuff. Dad is thinking about flying over for a long weekend — I wish this guy would leave me alone — which would be cool as long as we are indeed going into production (budget dilemmas). I can't think clearly because this man is leaning over me. I am thinking but nothing is happening in my brain. My first night here, the fog was in and everything came up grayer than any gray you've ever seen. Your first night in a new country often brings strange dreams not your own — lonely, fearful dreams — but the more

I get to know this place the warmer it becomes. I just wish this guy would leave me alone. Oh hell. Oh hello. Good-bye. Ick!

So now onwards — I wonder if these kids know anything about Caliana? I daren't say a word, though I've thought about it, being as talkative as I am. It just seems safe enough, you know? Even so I spent four hours on the train censoring all my notes, address book, etc., just in case.

People do stare at me a lot and the military are everywhere but so are the tourists, so it's okay. I even saw a magazine in a window with Princess Stephanie on the cover. If that's not bourgeois, I don't know what is. Went to three museums today — this guy's still bothering me. At the Museum of the Revolution the guard found me such an interesting comrade he gave me a hammer and sickle stick pin and pinched my cheek. Hvala. Kokosee? Dobro? Dober. Dobrejenya. I'd like dessert but I think I'll give up now and go to bed since this guy won't stop bugging me. I still think of Nick so much, but God, the strain of it all irritates me and I'm sick of feeling uncomfortable with him. The English make life so difficult sometimes. I still want to take up Henry's invitation for Ascot, though.

How am I going to get my career off the ground?

* * *

Am trying very hard to breathe right now; not having much luck. So many cigarettes — nearly unbearable. It's snowing again. My boots soaked through yesterday, so I had to buy some moon boots in order to make the walk back to the hotel. Cost me the equivalent of 10 Pounds. Cheap! I walked through the fortress and went back to the National Museum. Am waiting for Pledzay and the others in a cafe where the cappuccino is loaded with syrup and the staff are nasty. As a result, it's a youth hot spot. We're going to Filmtown now to find out (hopefully) what kinds of permits are needed to shoot here.

Saw some terrific Renoir sketches in the National Museum. Was surprised at the quality of their collection, but the display was tragic. Fluorescent lights. Ugh! Reflects off the canvases so much all you can see when you look at them head-on are cracks in the paint.

They had a trio playing Bach on the ground floor. Excellent idea for a museum. We should do it in America. They do it in London, too. Makes the whole art-absorbing experience more complete.

Yugoslavian kids drink Coca-Cola like we used to drink beer. It's their ultimate drug. They're only just discovering Punk here; the Sex Pistols are huge. Amazing what they'll allow. There are still those moments though, where you don't look behind you — and you don't stop walking. I can't define the strange, dark quality out there — it has nothing to do with street crime so it's hard to explain. I've never felt it before. Lots of stores here. The mannequins rival 1965 Barbie dolls. Everyone crowds around the shop windows and looks and looks. Especially electronics stores and pharmacies. Most of the women have gorgeous skin and huge hands. Everyone wears fur hats. I'm going to stare off into space now.

* * *

I swear to God I should be an ambassador's wife. Bled has been absolute magic. I've managed to lock down the entire town as a location — including the original summer palace! I'm beside myself. The story just solidified overnight. The teenaged children of an exiled Eastern European monarch sneak back into their motherland on fake passports when their dad is knocked off by a terrorist faction. Or something like that. I don't know. What I do know is that for the first time since graduation I'm sure what I want. And it definitely doesn't involve working as a secretary. Because if you ask any producer/director/writer how they started, they'll tell you they simply got a great idea and made it happen. So now all of a sudden I'm making things happen. God! I've just locked down an entire town! In a communist country! And they'd be happy if I shot the whole film here.

I suppose I should backtrack and explain some things. I took the bus up from Belgrade on Friday and immediately found a terrific, dirt cheap hotel right on the edge of the lake at Bled, which is frozen solid — in fact, on Sunday, six little old men in a sleigh went sliding across to the medieval church on the center island, playing brass horns the whole way. Their songs echoed off the shore and throughout the whole village. I've spent a lot of time drunk in my room writing poetry and walking alone in the snow. This is how the "Exiled" plot came to me. I made an appointment to see the local commissioner about renting out some of Bled's landmarks and then that night I saw "Summer Lovers" (with subtitles) at the little old stone cinema. Afterwards, as I was walking back towards the hotel, I heard this little voice several feet behind me cry "Nicole." I didn't even bother to turn 'round, sure the person was speaking to someone else. After all, how could anyone in a tiny village on a foreign continent know me? But again, the voice called out "Nicole." This went on so many times I started to get really spooked. The voice was always the same distance behind me, as if I were being followed, and it was dark and quiet except for the footsteps. I headed towards the hotel as quickly as possible, all the while remembering the embassy's threat back in London and Caliana's apprehension about my coming here. Finally, right before the entrance to the hotel cafe, where the sole culinary offering is Yugo pizza with egg in the center, I heard "Nicole" again. This time, I whirled around, furious and petrified. It turned out to be the secretary from the commissioner's office. Apparently because I asked about making a movie here, I am now a local celebrity.

You see, to most Slavs, socialism is merely an economic issue — and as far as investment goes, they're gung ho. Plus they appear to talk freely about everything. It was very dramatic my last day with Pledzay, though. I finally broke down and asked him if he knew anything about the falling of the Monarchy and suddenly his English vocabulary crumbled. He didn't understand, or at least pretended not to understand: palace, princess, throne or coup.

Bled is truly breathtaking. "Sound of Music" territory. I'm opening the "Exiled" script with some establishing shots which are going to be great for Yugoslavian tourism. The summer palace is now a superb hotel. The two managers and I talked for hours last night, while a waiter poured me sherry after sherry. Then I had dinner in their restaurant at midnight. I'm so happy about this.

There's an American woman here who looks at me with hatred. Maybe it's because her husband slipped me his business card and asked me to call him if I ever get to Indiana. Nothing infuriates me more that being treated like some weirdo/slut/terrorist by people from my own country!!!

* * *

I arrived in Ljubljana satisfied but worn out from the continuous isolation. Good for the soul but not the kind of medicine one can tolerate for too many days at a time. Had planned to meet Greg Zabec (the Yugoslav filmmaker) but after boarding my luggage at the station, I found out the only train back into Austria was at that moment. Was already two days late so I decided to split. 'Twas pleasant on the way back up to Vienna. I barely made the train, though; I hyperventilated myself into a blue stupor.

Brigitte and Ella weren't home when I got to Vienna, so I went to the Sacher for dinner to test out the best of Capitalism while the best of Socialism was still fresh in my mind. I was very unimpressed with Capitalism. Not only were they rude to me because of how I was dressed (moon boots and traveling clothes), but they wouldn't even let me use the phone.

I arrived at Brigitte's late in the night and she started complaining about everything, including Ella's grandmother, whom she refers to as the "Schloss Vierge"; in English, "castle virgin." Sounds benign, huh? Brigitte means it as an insult, though. (I wish I had a cigarette. Haven't had one for 2½ days.) I scared myself so badly that night. Brigitte taught me all about "automatic writing" (she thinks I'm what they call a scripted psychic) and while she listened to a meditation tape, I took a pen to my Air Mail stationery. All of a sudden I started writing the same name over and over. It freaked me out so much I won't even print the name here. Anyway, I guess I sort of screamed and then Brigitte came over and held me and told me my godmother was my guardian angel. I'm getting sloshed and it feels terrific. I am also, unfortunately, getting too drunk to type. On to longhand . . .

England, 1986
I just flew in for Nicholas' ball. The first thing I did was flip through my mail — no invitation. Caliana came home after work and we fell about the flat laughing and hugging, then she dropped the bomb. Her invitation came months ago. I am so pissed Cal didn't say anything. She knew how important all this was to me. Befriending Nick on my behalf . . . etc.. I asked her if she'd seen him while I was gone. She said once, in passing, at a party. This whole thing leaves a really rotten taste in my mouth — I feel like something's gone on, but I don't know what it is.

Well, Henry's decided to marry Miss-Honorable-searching-for-money-to-go-with-title, or rather, she's decided to marry him. Henry's living in her flat and selling this one, which means the innards of our little home will probably be relegated to the rag and bone man's cart. The Estate agent has one of our front door keys, which means Cal and I have to share. Mega pain.

✳ ✳ ✳

Today Prince Andrew married Sarah. I helped Cal get dressed (we decided on the red hat and matching blouse afterall) and then we took the tube to St. Paul's. Excellent idea on Cal's part as traffic was hellatious! We managed to get through the crowd without Cal's pass (that was a miracle — thank God she remembered her invitation). The police allowed me to escort her all the way to the main entrance, which meant I was right there with the paparazzi and had a perfect vantage point of the procession. The service inside was broadcast over loudspeakers and we all sang along with the hymns. It was very English and very moving.

Greg's house-sitting for someone new, so I went to visit him after the wedding. We hung out together the whole day and then watched the ceremony on T.V. Greg got mad because he thought I was making a pass at him when I touched his knee, and we had a bit of a tiff about that; of course it's a ridiculous accusation; I knew even before he did that he's not into girls. Finally, we both calmed down and cooked some macaroni and cheese for dinner. Then, when I went home to the flat, Del Smith's wife wouldn't buzz me in. I tried to tell her Cal was at the royal wedding ball but she wouldn't even let me finish. She said she'd absolutely had enough and was never buzzing either of us in again! I didn't know what to do, so I went to Garfunkel's for coffee. Then I got a great idea. I'd simply phone Claridge's and have the concierge slip a discreet note into Cal's hand asking her to leave our front door key with the porter. Well, the next thing I know, Cal's on the phone, blaming me for breaking up her future love match with Prince Hubert of Monaco (Henry's only told her a million times he's gay). Anyway, if Hubert really was maybe, perhaps, just about to ask her to dance, he would have asked her to dance. Right? The real fact of the matter is, Cal couldn't stand having a commoner burst her royal bubble in mid-fantasy. Still, I couldn't help feeling badly about it. Henry says he can see why Cal was upset but honestly, if Del's wife hadn't been such an utter slag. . .you'd think she'd give Cal and me a break on Royal Wedding day!

* * *

I told Henry about not receiving an invitation to Nick's ball and he suggested I phone Nick's secretary and casually ask what address it had been sent to. Henry seemed to think it was not bad form to handle it this way, but he sort of cocked his head and looked at me and said "you really have got a thing for him, don't you?" Then Henry told me he'd heard from Nick's brother, Sebastian, that Nick had been dating a girl from Texas! I was so upset I thought I'd die, but I got out the Martel, instead.

The next morning, Nick's secretary, Miss Laycock, phoned to say Nick would be delighted to have me and that I should just come on Caliana's invite. That's when I knew Nick hadn't intended to follow up on his original invitation. I had decided in advance to tell Miss Laycock I couldn't come, but suddenly I didn't want to be victimized by Nick, plus, I wanted to see all our mutual friends again, so I said, "yes, fine, I'll go." I decided at the last minute I'd better not wear black since there'd be royals there so I made a beeline for Old Bond Street. This sleazy salesgirl at Chanel tried to sell me a long-sleeved black velvet gown I couldn't begin to afford, convincing me it would be a great choice because summer nights were cold in England. Then, when I uttered the definitive "no," the salesgirl whispered a snide "bad news" to her fellow worker. Believe it or not, until that moment I never knew salespeople got commissions. I ended up with a Belleville Sassoon gown which is both fine and dandy, even though I hate it.

* * *

When I walked in with Cal and Nick said "glad you could make it," I knew he'd not only neglected to send an invitation, he was peeved I'd railroaded him into giving me one. I never would have known about it if he hadn't asked me to come in the first place, the jerk, and as far as Cal is concerned, she may be well-born, but the fact remains Nick's sole connection to her is that she happens to be my flatmate, so, under the circumstances, I find his contemptuous attitude rather ridiculous. He didn't even kiss me "continental" style (both cheeks), so I'd know for sure I was being punished. I'm pleased to say that I didn't run for a taxi or the roof or something. Instead I started to have a grand time — and too much champagne — had to sneak through the kitchen (escorted by my dashing young tablemate, of course) to the toilet so no one would see me getting up during dinner, which would be a huge no no. During dessert I felt a hand grab my shoulder and then disappear in the wake of a rather strong breeze. I looked up and saw Nick beating a fast retreat from our table. So he's snubbed me but he just has to touch my shoulder? I mean my dress was strapless but please! I kept looking for the girl from Texas and felt quite frankly, numb by this point. Nick danced quite a lot with this blonde girl wearing the same green tafetta gown as Helen of Windsor, who looked bored out of her mind, incidentally. In a polite effort to avoid Nicholas and the girl, whom I guessed to be the one from Texas, I went into the park outside with some of our old schoolmates. We barely got out the door when Nick waltzed up with her, threw an arm around each member of our little group (me excluded, of course) and said, "these are my good friends." The girl, who responded politely, turned out to be the actress Jodi Foster (definitely not from Texas). Then Nick split, leaving Jodi, me and my drunken girlfriends next to this stupid helicopter named "Z Nuts" that no one, not even the Prince of Wales, would claim responsibility for. "It's impressive," Jodi said, sounding just as alienated as I felt.

Of course the guests had no idea Nick and I were feuding, and it was the guests who made the party. The rigid, sweet Prince of Wales worked the room like a lovable wooden toy. Lady Sarah looked incredible, sans make-up or jewels in a lilac 19th century gown. The girl's el smarto — such a keen eye and sense of style. Everyone smirks about her taking photos on movie sets but I'm sure she's going to be as good a photographer someday as her father, Lord Snowden.

Speaking of people's parents, Nicholas' Mummy had these sole words to impart to me: "I believe your coach is leaving." What can one say in response to such charm? A mutual friend of Nick's and mine stole a bottle of something from the bar and we drank it all the way home — riding under the prettiest pastel dawn sky you'd ever want to see.

Los Angeles, 1986

It struck me — the truth of the situation — as I was listening to the Seranata Notturna for the 303rd time while driving under the overpass of the 5 freeway. And so I am actually not so embarrassed after all (or ashamed) for having loved Nicholas.

Quite frankly, from a purely objective standpoint, there is no one anywhere in America who comes close to Nick — and knowing this, I have come to accept that no matter how formal, how relaxed, how warm or down-to-earth or how aloof I may have been, there's no possible way I could have bridged the gap any better than I did. There is nothing else I could have, or should have done. I have forgiven myself; I honestly know I did the best I could under the circumstances, with the limited knowledge that I had.

I hope I'm not getting Poison Ivy.

A Postscript, 1990

"Henry" won a constituency in the west of England and became a backbench Member of Parliament.

Princess "Caliana" married a financier and continues to live in London.

"Nicholas" and I no longer speak. I haven't a clue what he's up to.

"Greg" moved to Greece and has not been heard from since.

"Ella" is now a Hollywood film producer.

The author wrote "Exiled," which was abysmal, but went on to a screenwriting career with her second script, a punk-rock version of the story contained within these pages.

Nancy Raeburn

TWO NUNS
From *White: A Memoir*

For the Hopi Indians of the Southwestern U.S., there is no word for "time" in
their language, because time as we understand it has no existence. So it seemed
to me during the years I lived and painted on an island in Greece. I had discovered
Mykonos on my first trip to Greece in 1967. In 1970 I returned and secured a
house for the summer, but as the hot winds of August and throngs of tourists
began to subside, the island became so tranquil and beautiful, I longed to stay
through the winter. With the help of a small inheritance, the good exchange rate
and painting sales, I knew it would be possible financially and made arrangements
for storage of my things back in the States. I settled in with a propane gas heater
and endless mugs of hot tea to curb the chill of the house, gone damp and cold
in that first bleak and rainy winter without central heating and other comforts
of the American lifestyle. A year later, still with no inclination to leave, I was
able to find a house near the edge of town. My landlord was an old farmer named
Manolis. After a year I moved again, farther out in the country, this time to a
small farmhouse with no electricity or plumbing. Just as the island always changed
in September, my life slowed down, became simple, and I too felt tranquil and
beautiful. When the time came to leave, it was in response to a clear need to reconnect with my roots, my country and to detach enough to somehow shape my experience into a form that could be shared. Two chapters of the resulting memoir
follow. Time for the Hopi doesn't exist. Little did I know in 1970 that the decision
to stay the winter — so casually arrived at — would herald a sojourn of a little
over ten years of my life.

"Who hears the dragon's roar now? Perhaps, after all, humankind will inherit
everything that shines. For all night God enjoys laboring song sung somewhere
with artless abandon."

—Anagram

TWO OR THREE kilometers inland from the main town, a sprawling cluster
of small farms, linked by a labyrinth of unpaved roads and paths,
culminates in the central square of the tiny village of Ano Mera. The
large flagstone square, surrounded on three sides by restaurants and
cafes, is flanked on its fourth by the imposing white wall of a monastery,
where a few monks live away their days. If the cafes form the heart of
village life, the monastery serves as its soul, for the simple reason that

it houses the village church and provides, through its abbot, the parish priest.

Another monastery — a convent for women — sits a short distance outside the village limits, high on a hill near the ruins of an old fort. As I approached the village, walking from the main town along the winding paved road cutting through the center of the island, I could see the convent in the distance. It sat white against the brown hillside, tilting slightly toward the sea, as if it had been pushed off balance by a shifting of the foundation. Or perhaps it was from spending years leaning into the prevailing north wind that troubles the peace of that side of the island for several months of the year; leaning into the wind, resisting it, unlike the olive trees that bent in acquiescence, or like the monastery in the village, upright and protected by the piety of the villagers. From my vantage point on the winding road, the whitewashed convent resembled a patch of wild daisies leaning toward the sea, the blue dome of its chapel emerging like a morning-glory out of their midst.

A half-hour later I was walking through the entryway, a small opening in the thick iron door, that was locked every night with a rusty key large enough to knock any intruder senseless. Inside the gate, a single eucalyptus tree chattered in the wind and shaded part of the large central courtyard, which was bordered by a double tier of cells. The convent had been built a century ago to house thirty or forty nuns. But only two lived there now: Sister Seraphine, a wizened crone in her sixties, and Sister Kyriaki, about to turn fifty, and round and as tightly packed as an onion. Except for the windswept convent they shared, these two were devoid of any common ground upon which to sustain a relationship, except conflict.

Never still for long, Sister Seraphine swept around the convent grounds, her long habit flying in the wind, muttering to herself in her dark, whiskey voice, low and beady as a duck's. Short and wiry, she careened into her tasks like a bent torpedo, or on quieter days, simply leaned into them, as the convent leaned into the wind.

Watching her fly about reminded me of when we kids fed loaves of Wonder Bread to the flock of ducks that swam up and down the shore of the lake where we grew up. The ducks would grab a piece of bread, shake it violently, swallow some and be off to another before finishing the first. Seraphine dashed around the courtyard, bent over her short-handled broom, leaving no corner or crevice in the flagstones untouched. But before she could sweep the pile of dirt into the trash, some other thought would take her, robes flying, into the chapel, where she began to fill the box near the doorway with a new supply of beeswax candles; then, leaving it teetering on the edge of the table, she dashed to the oil lamps and refilled them, but without putting in new wicks, because she had suddenly spied some tourists dressed in shorts, or too-short skirts,

or with bare shoulders, who had just entered, and she unceremonious-
ly swept them outside, raising her voice, telling them that they could
not enter the Holy Place naked, and that besides, it was closing time
thanks be to God, casting a menacing eye on them as she quacked her
orders. With the startled tourists sufficiently cowed, she rushed back
inside to dust the icons, to wipe off the greasy marks of kisses, to clean
first the glass protecting the Holy Mother, then to kiss it and clean it
again. On she moved to St. John the Baptist, unabashedly holding his
own severed head on a plate, and last she cleaned the glass protecting
Christ Enthroned. Even in her obeisance, the icons seemed to be more
pieces of Wonder Bread, and she barely paused to touch the glass with
her lips before she was off to the next, all the time quacking to herself,
to the icons, to the miscreant tourists, and to the insufferable wind howling outside, which at that very moment was causing great eddies of dust
to rise up from the pile of undisposed debris she had left in the courtyard, swirling it smack up against the closed door of Sister Kyriaki.

Sister Kyriaki was a painter and the one I most often came to see, although visiting with Kyriaki meant a visit with Seraphine as well, who
always just happened to drop by shortly after my arrival. Kyriaki was almost as wide as she was tall and, like Seraphine, was covered entirely,
except for her round moon face, in a long black habit and wimple, on
which a small red cross was embroidered just above her brow. Her confined features seemed to have emerged out of a mighty block of marble,
while Seraphine's had been painstakingly carved from a piece of gnarled
olive wood. They were a strange pair to be rattling around in this old
convent, just the two of them: stone and stick, moon and Mars, queen bee
and drone; milk, not quite warm enough and wine, aged just a bit too long.

Kyriaki kept her door shut most of the morning in order to discourage
Seraphine from disturbing her painting. Word had spread among the
tourists, that the nun out at the village painted pictures that you could
buy for a song, and lately her sales had increased so much she had to
work constantly to keep up with the demand. Her paintings were
primitive in a sophisticated sense. That is, she had studied painting
before becoming a nun, and had earned her DEE-ploma, as she called
it. I asked her once how she ended up in this convent, all alone except
for one other nun with whom she didn't get along. Why hadn't she been
assigned to live in one of the flourishing convents — like the one on the
neighboring island of Tinos, that attracted thousands of visitors each
year? It was impossible for her to be in an active community, she said,
because she did not fit in with the life. Still, she loved God and wanted
to devote her life to his service. But she wanted to paint as well. It was
agreed then, that she would come to this small convent where she could
work freely at her art, provided she limit herself to painting religious
subjects. So she had begun to paint small icons of the saints, figures

with underdeveloped limbs and large heads with enormous eyes that stared impassively out at the viewer in identical, blank expressions.

She worked in a small space at the end of the room that served as her kitchen. There she had set up a rickety field easel facing the light from the window of the closed door. At the opposite end of the room, beyond a divider, was the simple kitchen with a two-burner gas plate and small sink. With the exception of the kitchen area itself, paintings were propped all over, paintings of all sizes, some obvious duplicates of others. There were St. John the Evangelist and St. Nicholas with his white hair and beard. And over on another wall St. George on his white steed, reared up over the emerald green dragon with white teeth bared and red forked tongue flickering as it writhed upward in its last throes.

Passing into the main room through a low archway, one came upon even more paintings, which gave the room a cluttered feeling with its heavy mahogany table and paper doilies. A folding screen closed off one end of the room, whose shadows revealed only the foot of a narrow, uncomfortable looking bed.

One day I saw a painting I hadn't noticed before, a painting completely different from all the rest. It was larger, for one thing — almost a meter in length — and it showed the Virgin Mary "asleep" on her bier with all the saints, angels and heavenly host gathered around her. There were mortals present too, the only mourners, judging from their pained expressions. And above the bier, the head and torso of the ascended Christ rose out of a radiant cloud with hands extended downward to receive his mother's soul, depicted by the figure of a tiny, naked baby rising aloft. The entire painting pulsated with color, color caught in the pattern formed by figures of the multitude gathered to witness the event of Mary's Assumption.

I was interested in buying the painting and asked her price. Ten drachmas, she shrugged, indicating by giving the price of a loaf of bread, that the painting was priceless, a treasure inspired by God that she would probably never part with. I was disappointed, but she was firm; Kyriaki was sorry, but she would not sell this painting. I didn't pursue it; I knew how it was when I didn't want to sell a painting of my own.

The next time I visited, about a month or two later, the painting was still there, and Kyriaki was still unwilling to sell. Again I didn't press the issue. But a year later, when I went to see her just before Easter, it was gone. Someone had finally found a price that Kyriaki couldn't resist. And it must have been considerable, because behind the folding screen I noticed a thick, new mattress and box spring, and in the kitchen, the two-burner gas plate had been replaced by a full-sized range, complete with oven. In the corner, a small refrigerator hummed, and on the counter the remains of a joint of meat sat on a white plate. The meat perhaps was the strongest emblem of Kyriaki's growing worldliness.

Eating meat during Holy Week is forbidden by the Orthodox Church.

The painting had been freed from the stifling home of its birth. And Kyriaki, its mother, having been compensated for her loss, went back to her icons and waited obediently, albeit dispassionately, for another rare and transcendent coupling with her Lord.

Before I left, I paid a visit to the convent chapel. Inside, Seraphine was chanting in a high parched voice, pecking at the leaves of the Psalter on the revolving wooden rack before her like an enormous cormorant. I remembered how she had once elbowed her way into a store where I was just paying for my purchases and, not waiting her turn, asked Ioannis, the proprietor, if he had any frames for photographs. When he asked her what she wanted to frame, she seemed embarrassed and then, with some reluctance, pulled out of her black satchel a five-by-seven photograph of a rather severely smiling young woman. It was, of course, Seraphine herself. Seraphine wanted a picture of herself to look at, a picture of her youth, which had vanished long before the day she had taken her final vows and become a bride of Christ.

The villagers snickered at her eccentricities, made jokes and gossiped about her. For it had been said more than once that Seraphine drank. I found that hard to believe, considering her unflagging energy. But I supposed that she could have pulled it off by allowing herself only a drop at measured intervals throughout the day; that could explain why she moved so fast, I reasoned, and left so much unfinished. I could just imagine her with so many icons dusted, one thimbleful of Metaxa; four lamps cleaned and filled, another thimbleful; Psalms one hundred twelve through one hundred thirty chanted, a quick gulp in the damp shadows of the pews from the brandy bottle hidden in the folds of her long habit. But nobody I knew had actually seen her in a state of intoxication, which indicated this story might be nothing more than idle gossip. On the contrary, Seraphine did everything she was supposed to do, followed all the rules, even though it seemed she did so more out of love for the letter of the Rule than for its spirit.

One day I was invited to attend a memorial service for the wife of a friend who had died the previous month. The service had to be held in the convent chapel, because the main church in the village was being used for something else that day. A priest was summoned from the main town, and the nuns were to act as cantors. The whole affair was very somber, and the two women entered easily into the spirit of the occasion. Even though they had no personal attachment to the dead woman, their faces, like those of the mortals in Kyriaki's painting, registered in stylized sadness the words of supplication they intoned. Later, outside, a lighter mood prevailed. The men lit up cigarettes and downed cognac passed by the family of the dead woman. Then we were all invited upstairs to the Abbess's quarters for coffee.

The Abbess didn't exist, but her rooms remained ready in case one should ever be assigned there. There were so many people, I had to join the overflow in the bedroom, where I sat on the impossibly hard mattress of the Abbess's bed. Beside it a wooden table covered in a faded cloth displayed a small brass crucifix, a candle, and a bouquet of dried weeds stuck in an empty Gilby's Gin bottle.

I was glad to be there in that strange room and not in the parlor, where they were all taking care to be on their best behavior, and where Kyriaki and Seraphine, with all the formality and dignity of the non-existent Abbess, (who, from the uncharacteristic gentility of the expressions, I surmised they were both secretly pretending to be), had begun to pass the sweets and thick coffee.

Even at the most somber of occasions, such as this memorial, however, it is hard to squelch the humor of the Greeks for long, and in the relaxed atmosphere of the Abbess's bedroom, the wisecracks flew back and forth with muffled laughter as each tried to top the other. One farmer, half serious for a moment, wondered aloud why humankind feared death so much. A woman next to him, her thick, brown hands rocking the top of her cane, said that she definitely thought we should greet death gratefully; because life calls for so much hard work, a good rest is welcome. Another farmer, her husband and accustomed to using her as a foil, said that, on the contrary, he thought people were so afraid of death because they suspected there would be much more work on the other side! Recognizing this truth in the unending toil of their lives, the bedroom exploded in guffaws.

So, there I was in that obscure little convent on an island in the middle of the Aegean Sea on the globe of the world, itself a mere speck in the relentless wheeling of the universe — there, surrounded by Greeks laughing at death, and I was laughing too.

And we were all being served by two nuns putting on airs in empty rooms. I wondered which of them in the end would be greater in the kingdom, at the same time understanding the meaninglessness of such a question. Like the figures in Kyriaki's painting, we all — the farmers and their wives, the bearded priest, the nuns and I — were gathered there that day in supplication for the "assumption" of the dead woman's soul. What a colorful and rich pattern we presented with all our foibles, secret pains, triumphs and failures.

In a moment of shared hilarity, a kind of Grace had bound us without our even knowing or understanding it. At that moment death had seemed to me to be less a fearsome separation from the world, than an inevitable and celebratory invitation to unite once again with the source — the very ground — of our being.

We had laughed at death. Perhaps our creator laughed at death too, though not out of mirth, as we had, . . . but joy.

Nancy Raeburn

BARBA MANOLIS
From *White: A Memoir*

"How shall the heart be reconciled to its feast of losses?"
—Stanley Kunitz

WHAT PROPELS A MAN in that final hour back to his childhood, to the one place out of all those experienced in a long life, where he had known nothing but the unquestioned integrity of his own imagination? What sense tells him, so that he knows without doubt that his "being in the world" is about to fragment into its most infinitesimal parts; that the place where he had once stood, under the sun of his own certainty, would soon resound with only the reverberating atoms of his own final breath — and then, nothing? What is that something inside us, which is not us, that tells us this: to go home?

From the Journal — August 24, 1977
Barba Manolis was buried yesterday. A week ago he had attended the panagiri honoring the Assumption of the Virgin, a lavish feastday, second only to Easter. For the first time in years, to the delight and awe of everyone, he had danced the Zembékiko — with feeling and surprising agility, considering his eighty-seven years. The next morning back in his house in town, he had wakened feeling ill and, without hesitating even for a coffee, he mounted his donkey and set off up the long, winding road out to the family farm. He just managed to get through the gate when he collapsed on the terrace. Somehow, his daughter-in-law Flora got him into bed. But he worsened as the days passed and refused all food, despite sometimes heroic efforts to get him to take some nourishment. Of his six daughters, the five who lived on the island ministered to him in shifts. The sixth, Anna, was to arrive later from Athens. I learn that he is ill, and late one afternoon I set out on foot to see him.

* * *

"You're going to like your new landlord," Hugh said, as we climbed aboard the bus, a dilapidated Mercedes of unknown vintage. Hugh was an American living on a few drachmae earned from odd jobs. When he wasn't working, he was usually found sitting barefoot in cafes, drinking proffered coffees and smoking cigarette stubs while perusing old copies of *Barron's*. Hugh, a friend and tutor in the simple life, who spoke passable Greek, came along to do the translating.

We were on our way to a farm midway between the main town and the village of Ano Mera. Our mission was to find an old farmer, Manolis Asimomitis, whom everyone called "Barba Manolis," or "Uncle" Manolis, the familiar term of respect for all men past fifty. We wanted to talk to him about my renting an old farmhouse that belonged to one of his daughters who was temporarily living in the United States.

I paid the four drachmae fare while Hugh asked the driver in Greek to let us off at Barba Manolis' farm. We settled into a seat near the front. It was four-thirty, nearing the end of siesta, and the bus was almost empty, a fact for which I was grateful as the screaming engine labored in protest up the steep, winding road leading out of town. Ten minutes later with the brakes squealing and clouds of dust billowing around us, we came to a sudden, shuddering halt.

"You, Barba Manolis, here!" the driver offered in English, flashing two gold bicuspids and pointing first at us, then to the left and finally to the door as he swung it open for us.

The house, which sat low to the left, about a hundred yards from the road, looked deserted. We were perplexed. Everyone had said he would be out at his farm that day — but where? We set off about two hundred yards farther down the valley to ask a neighbor, an old woman sitting on her terrace stringing beans.

"He's there, in his field, plowing," she smiled, pointing to the northwest. Sure enough, we saw in the distance, over several fields and walls, lilliputian figures criss-crossing a triangular field. We thanked the woman and set off immediately down the donkey trail she had pointed out as the quickest way to get there. After about ten minutes we arrived at the triangular field. Three faces, one middle-aged and wimpled, another old and weathered, and the last, bovine with a white star on its forehead, turned in curiosity to greet the two foreigners.

Hugh introduced me to Barba Manolis and his daughter Marseau, and explained our quest. Not knowing the language, there wasn't much I could say, so I just stood there, enthralled with my surroundings and with the old man who, up to a minute ago, had been guiding a ridiculously primitive plow through rocky soil behind a docile Holstein that was ready, I noticed, to be milked.

I guessed that Barba Manolis was in his early eighties. He had a thick bushy moustache and wore his hat perched backward on his head to keep the hot sun off his bare neck. He had secured his plaid flannel shirt inside his trousers with a striped apron, rolled up and wound around his waist like a cumberbund. His thick, bare feet were sunk up to the ankles in the newly turned soil. But probably his most remarkable feature was the expression in his eyes. They smiled at me out of deep tracery of wrinkles with such friendliness, that it was as if they perceived in a glance every thought I had ever had in my life, and it didn't matter, no, not a twit.

"Welcome," he said. "You mean Vangelo's house up the road? Fine, fine. How long would she like to stay?"

"Tell him for the summer," I said, "but maybe longer."

Our negotiations completed, Barba Manolis and I shook hands on our agreement of seven hundred drachmae rent a month, roughly twenty dollars.

* * *

I arrive at the farm. The curtain in the door to the kitchen wafts out over the whitewashed terrace. The small, stooped figure seated on a chair welcomes me. He is in his long woolen underwear, and someone has draped a flannel shirt over his shoulders. After so many hot days unbroken by wind, he says he is enjoying the opportunity to sit outside. From the parlor door I can hear the familiar canned laughter of an ancient I Love Lucy re-run, and I have to shout above it in order for him to hear me. His granddaughter, Maria, about thirteen years old, emerges from the snare of the sitcom to see who belongs to the strange voice that is shouting at her grandfather. When she sees me, she shouts as well: Yiá soú, Anna! How was I and I had come to see Barba Manolis, eh? Then Flora, her mother, returns from milking, hears the commotion and joins in.

"Welcome, Anna! " she calls shrilly. "How are you? You came to see Barba Manolis? He's doing all right, but he won't eat, will you, Babá? Tonight you will have some chicken and macaroni, eh? Anna, tell him he must eat, or he won't get well."

I imagine that the noise from the television, the raised voices all speaking at once, must be as harrowing to Barba Manolis as they are to me. But he looks off over the fields, withdrawn into his own thoughts. I ask Maria to turn down the television. She nods and disappears. Flora chatters off into the kitchen, and we are left alone.

We sit a long time without speaking, just listening to the sounds of the country, the frogs chirruping in the remnants of the pond below the house, the cows lowing to each other across the fields. He smiles and points out a few things, but that's all. It seems right, the two of us here on the terrace, quiet, watching the light change.

* * *

Early evening as the sun set was the time to stop work and relax with an ouzo on the terrace. From this terrace, I could see the four large islands rising from the sea in the distance, under a sky that stretched unbroken to the horizon in three directions. And it was from this terrace on the rare sleepless night, where I would note that the diaphanous cloud of the Milky Way arced directly over my house, or so it seemed, in that mysterious place of the heart where everything was benevolent, everything protected, connected and harmonious.

Some evenings at sunset I would sit with my feet up on the parapet and be quietly roused from my thoughts by a gentle creak of the gate down by the road. I never even had to look to know who it was. I greeted him and went to the kitchen for bread and another glass and poured him an ouzo, adding water, which exploded the drink into a milky liquid.

I spoke only a few words of Greek then, so these visits were forced into becoming language lessons. He'd start out by pointing at something nearby: "*Piáta*," and I'd repeat "pee-AH-ta." Then he'd ask for the word in English, and I'd say "plate," to which he'd respond "PLAI-eet," adding with a nod, "*Kondá*" — close.

The next one: "*Piroúni.*"

"Peer-OO-ni," I'd parrot.

"*Stá 'Angliká?*"

"Fork."

"For-k" he repeated, softly rolling the "r." "*Óhi kondá,*" he added.

"Not close at all," I agreed.

Then we'd clink glasses and sip the strong anise flavored aperitif until it was time for him to untether his donkey and continue into town. Always before leaving, he'd lay bunches of grapes or tomatoes on the old yellow table, or perhaps some new potatoes he'd just dug up. One evening he left a cucumber that was close to a foot long and almost four inches thick.

"Life is a cucumber," he informed me, his eyes crinkling in a smile and his thick eyebrows bobbing up and down, something he did unconsciously, I noticed, whenever he was pleased with his own joke.

It was Barba Manolis who gave me the name, Anna. He had trouble remembering my real name, and since he could neither read nor write, he couldn't picture it in his mind either. "NEHN-si," he'd say, the last syllable barely pronounced. But the foreign sound wouldn't stay in his memory for long and, after several frustrated attempts to remember, he said one day, with an air of finality, that my name would be Anna. Anna, a common, easily remembered Greek name. One of his daughters was named Anna, and Anna was the name of the mother of the Blessed Virgin. A good name, Anna.

Another evening, on the subject of names, I had expressed surprise that he hadn't named his donkey, other than calling it "the donkey." I took the matter in hand and came up with another good Greek name, Maria, forgetting about the Blessed Virgin and not learning until some time later, when my Greek had improved and we were able to converse more easily, that his dead wife's name had been Maria.

"Maria?" he frowned.

"Maria," I said. "It's a wonderful name for a donkey!"

He shrugged with a smile, barely visible beneath his thick mustache, and crossed himself.

* * *

Flora returns to ask if I would like a plate of chicken, winking toward the old man and making me an unwilling co-conspirator in the unending battle to get him to eat. I know he won't eat, and I tell her politely, no thanks, but I must leave, that I must meet someone in one hour. Barba Manolis says something to her that I don't catch, and she disappears into the kitchen. I linger a few minutes more and then, unable to say goodbye, I tell him that I'll be back in a day or two. I step off the terrace just as Flora rushes out of the kitchen with a burlap sack she presses into my arms. Inside I see about four kilos of potatoes, some zucchini and tomatoes, three round, white cheeses, two small watermelons and a corked wine bottle full of goat's milk: Barba Manolis' final gift to me from his farm.

* * *

He had asked me several times to come to his house in town for dinner, but there always seemed to be other conflicting concerns. One night, though, I made a point to go, afraid that after so many refusals, there would be no more invitations.

He welcomed me at the door and ushered me in. His house was tiny by American standards, but not so unusual on this island, where everything, from the harbor to the single molehill of a mountain, was pared down to human scale. There was a narrow bed to the right as I entered, and to my left, an armoire and large wooden steamer trunk. On the wall above, the flame of a small oil lamp cast a warm glow on two icons, one of St. George and the other of the Virgin. We stepped down once into the kitchen in the back, which was located under a sleeping loft and lit by a single bare light bulb. Another narrow bed was tucked beneath the stairs leading up to the loft. I guessed he could shelter three or four friendly people, if the need ever arose.

"*Kátse.*" he said, indicating one of the chairs next to the cluttered kitchen table. I asked him if I could help. Pointing to the dish rack near the sink, he said I would find everything I needed to set the table. I took out a couple of forks and plates, two glasses, but with momentary disgust, I discovered that everything was coated with a thin film of grease. Noting that there was only a cold water faucet I guessed the culprit. I tried to overlook it, but the grease film was too much for even my less than fastidious nature. I tried to reason how to handle it. I could quickly rinse off everything, but more cold water wasn't going to help, and if I proceeded to get a towel and wipe off the water-beaded film I might offend, or worse, embarrass my friend. The only alternative, I realized, was to ignore it and proceed as if everything had just come out of a steaming dishwasher. The choice was clear: in a little act of faith, that never disappointed me, I decided that no bad thing could ever pass from Barba Manolis to me, regardless of the circumstances.

In the meantime, it was easy to see where the oily film had come from. He stood at the small gas stove frying some of the sausage his family had made at the November pig killing, and I watched, fascinated at the half-inch of hot olive oil and pork fat that bubbled up suddenly around the edges of the eggs he had just poured in. The omelet was soon firm, and he scooped it to a plate, pouring the sizzling pan oil on top! Then he put the eggs and sausage on the table near another plate piled high with black-eyed peas and poured half a cup of olive oil on *them*. Well, never mind, I thought. We were hungry, and ate heartily from the same common plates, washing it all down with homemade country wine he had poured into the two cloudy glasses.

With our hunger and thirst satisfied, he started telling stories, how at the end of the World War I Greek soldiers returning from Germany had to get to Athens by any means possible. Many, like Barba Manolis, had to go most of the way on foot, a distance of some three hundred miles.

Then he married Maria, and they lived on the farm where he had lived as a child. His other brothers had left Greece to seek their fortunes — one to France, the other to the U.S. There were children — first a son, Yiorgos, then six daughters, and with them, six dowries to provide. Life was difficult, but when World War II exploded on the continent and both Italian and German troops occupied the island, it became precarious indeed. It was during this time that Maria became ill with tuberculosis and died. Manolis, then fifty, was left with seven children, the youngest, three years old.

Survival was paramount. The occupying troops confiscated all livestock and produce. There was no soap and worse, no oil, except in the dead of night when contraband shipments arrived at remote beaches from larger neighboring islands. Manolis managed to secrete two or three sheep on the northern side of the island. Two of his younger daughters, then six and seven, tended them, sheltering themselves with the steaming animals in crude stone hovels. The eldest sister, Marseau, traveled once a week out the dirt road in order to replenish their meager supply of bread and cheese, a few tomatoes. When these ran low, they survived on the rich sheep's milk alone. After the war, his large brood still intact, Manolis cooked, cleaned, worked the farm and earned extra money as a stonemason on the side. They all survived at a time when starvation took many lives. And somehow, as the money came in, he purchased a field or a house in town, and in time provided a dowry for each of his six daughters. Once I asked him why he had never remarried. He'd often thought about it, he told me, but hadn't done so for two important reasons: he knew there would be another large batch of children, and he was afraid that when they were all grown, the two factions would feud over property. And two, he had genuinely loved Maria; there could be no one to replace her.

Sometimes as the hour ripened and we sat sipping wine, the conversation blended into the realms of religion and spirituality. He often talked about the Bible stories he heard in church. Since he had never learned to read, the only knowledge of the Bible he had was from the verses read in the Orthodox services every Sunday — all visually aided by the numerous icons and paintings that adorned the church walls. His understanding of the New Testament parables was on a literal level, and if he had any doubts that the events in Genesis occurred just as he was told in the scriptures, he never voiced them. He didn't make a big thing of it either, and simply accepted the parables in the manner they were offered. I sat in fascination, listening to the old tales of Adam and Eve, of Moses , Abraham and the prophets, of the Sower and the Seed and the Wise and Foolish Maidens — people who to him were not symbols, but who had been almost as real as I was sitting across from him. And for those brief moments, they came alive for me too, as their stories were passed on to me in the fresh voice of the original oral tradition. Uncluttered by learned theorizing, these had simply been live, flesh and blood people who had gone before us and who, through their own experiences, had been chosen by God to show those who came after how to live good lives.

"Have you lived a good life, Barba?" I asked him one night. He shrugged and pointed to the ceiling. God would judge.

At the end of these evenings he'd ask me to make the coffee. I'd get the copper *bríki* out of the dish drainer and measure out the coffee, sugar and water as he directed. While the brew came to a boil, I stood at the stove behind him, keeping an eye on the contents of the *bríki*. Every once in a while I'd glance at the top of his slightly balding head as he sat quietly thinking, hands folded loosely in his lap. It was at those times that a strange warmth would catch me up, and I'd realize how much I loved this old man. Later, I understood that the intense love I felt for him was the love for grandfathers I had never known — and for the father who had died when I was fifteen.

After coffee and the time for departure approached, he filled a small sack with a few tomatoes, some onions, zucchini — whatever was in abundance and in season. Occasionally, he would slip in a bottle of that very special homemade wine. Always I left with burdens, happy ones, to carry up the hill and out the country road to my house.

* * *

I protest all the attention I am getting, Flora's time that I am taking, which already is overburdened with work. But no, she says, it is a small thing, they have so much, and I am their friend. I thank them, and before I can even begin to wonder how to get it all to my house on foot, she adds that her sixteen-year-old son, Manolis, will drive me and the huge bag to my gate two kilometers away on the back of his new Honda scooter.

Two days later I decide to visit some friends near Ftelia and stop at the farm on my way back. Visibly weaker, Barba Manolis is seated sideways on the bed, his back to the wall, while two of his daughters, Dina and Vengelo feed him some dark liquid in a glass with a spoon. He had vomited all the previous day, they inform me; I am surprised that they are still trying to feed him. Finally he lies down. He seems glad to see me, and he says a few things, but his words are hard to understand, because his false teeth are out, and he is very weak. Dina cries quietly on and off, and a roll of paper toweling is passed around. Flora, intent on her role as cook and keeper of the farm, comes in with a large plate of freshly-fried meatballs and passes them, demanding that each of us "eat, eat."

Marseau arrives in her son-in-law's taxi, with bundles. I take one and glance inside: the black lapel and white striped dress shirt — Barba Manolis' burying clothes. Marseau enters the room. "How is he? No, you're not going to die, you're just sick, that's all," her voice a little hysterical with the effort of the lie she is trying to convince herself is true. "I'm going to die," he tells me. "I know, Barba," I say quietly. I am holding his hand, which is warm and dry. Marseau interrupts us, "No, you're not going to die — you will soon be up, and Anna will paint another portrait of you." The old man and I exchange glances. "Yes." I say. "I haven't forgotten. I am starting to paint it now." He says a few more words and then kisses me goodbye with the multiple tender smacks the Greeks reserve for their small children. I want to say more, but haven't the words and get up to leave.

"Go with the good," he reminds me.

I hesitate. "And you," I respond, and he smiles. I leave the sickroom and the farm and set off down the road, noting the strange dampness in the air.

The next day, the south wind has begun to blow, an unusual phenomenon for August, when the prevailing wind is always dry and northerly. I go to the carpenter and order a board cut in the shape of a small oval for the portrait.

* * *

One evening Barba Manolis had dropped by on his way back to town and spent a good deal of time looking at my paintings stacked in corners and hanging on the walls. What all this uncharacteristic attention added up to was that he wanted me to do his portrait. At that point, I had only been painting a short while, and had never once done a portrait. But I accepted the challenge and we struck a deal: for one oil portrait, Barba Manolis would give me one month's free rent.

I needed about three one-hour sittings at a time of day when the light was still good. Since he was almost always busy in the mornings, he usually came by about three o'clock, siesta time. For the first fifteen minutes or so, he managed to stay pretty alert. But then he'd begin to nod off, and I would have to whistle to perk him up again. After this happened repeatedly, I realized he needed something to do, and I turned the easel so he could monitor the progress of the work. This proved to be a good solution, except for his disconcerting changes of expression, which I guess gauged his faith in the outcome. I forged ahead, trying to ignore this, grateful he was awake and his eyes were alert.

The portrait was completed, and it was a respectable job too, even though his face was slightly too fat and the folds in his jacket a little wooden. Barba Manolis was pleased, except for one small change he wanted me to make: I hadn't gotten the curl in his mustache right. But his mustache didn't curl, I protested; it went straight down like a walrus'. He wanted it to curl anyway and demonstrated with the hairs between thumb and forefinger just how much. I made the small adjustment, and Barba Manolis was happy, maybe even proud, for he hung it opposite his bed next to the armoire, where everyone coming to visit couldn't help but see it and where it was the first thing he saw, after St. George and the Blessed Virgin, upon waking in the morning.

That was the first portrait, but not the last. I decided to do another one for myself, and this one proved to be the better likeness of the two. He wanted to buy this one as well, but I decided not to sell it to him or to anyone else. "For me to remember you by," I told him, and he seemed satisfied, maybe even a little flattered. I showed the portrait at the "Montparnasse," a fashionable bar/expo where I had my first exhibition on the island, and he came to the opening in his Sunday suit and sat by his portrait the entire evening, as the jet-setters awash in French perfume sailed through, so they would know who the distinguished looking man in the portrait was and could compare the likeness.

One day a few years later, he asked me to do a miniature portrait, so that when his family removed the bones from the graveyard four years after his death, there would be a color portrait instead of the usual fading black and white photograph hanging in the family chapel near the marble plaque sealing the niche where his bones would have their final rest.

* * *

I return home with the board for the portrait, and the day passes uneventfully until four, when an American friend comes by. He says he has just been to see Barba Manolis and suspects he won't last the night. The sixth daughter, Anna, has finally arrived from Athens on the three-thirty plane. Later, down at a cafe near the harbor, I sip an ouzo as the sun goes down, and Costas, the owner, comes by the table to ask if I'd heard the news, that Barba Manolis had died at four-thirty.

Out at the farm later the terrace is filled with people. All his daughters are gathered around this strangely small blue box, supported by two chairs. Inside, the corpse is wrapped in a white shroud, the face hidden at sunset. I offer my condolences, as Dina tells me of his final moments, how her father had waited for the last daughter, Anna, to arrive. The two shared about a half hour together. Then he closed his eyes, and soon there were two or three sighs, and he was gone. With his last breath he had cried out for Maria, his wife, dead thirty-seven years. I listen with a curious detachment, nodding absently, unable to relate to the shrouded thing in the box.

The next afternoon I return to the farm to join the procession into town. The family and supporting women friends are gathered on one side of the coffin. On the other side, friends and neighbors come in and sit a few minutes to pay their respects and then depart for the terrace. Barba Manolis' granddaughter, Maria, sits on the lap of her godmother. They both gaze sadly at the old man's face, which is unshrouded now, the body from chin down bowered in astors and chrysanthemums interspersed with large clumps of sweet basil. The room is filled with the smell of burning wax, basil and the sounds of sighing and weeping, which accompany the tender ministrations of Marseau, whose unofficial duty as eldest daughter and chief female mourner is to stimulate and direct the outpouring of grief.

A certain amount of theatrical finesse is necessary in this delicate task, for it is easy to go overboard into melodrama and stimulate hysteria, where hair is torn and clothing rent, acceptable behavior when it is the untimely death of a young person, but which might be considered out of place for this eighty-

seven-year-old man. And so Marseau sits stroking his head softly, calling up memories from years past.

I can't see his face — just the top of his head, where the sparce, grey hair is getting smoothed, disarranged and smoothed again in a gentle, continuous cycle by Marseau's work-roughened fingers. I can see just the top of his head, but it is enough to cause my tears to flow finally —hot, big drops that spash on the floor in spots the size of ten drachmae pieces. I have no chair, so I sit at the end of Barba Manolis' bed, which is covered from head to foot in a clean, white counterpane. No one objects or says a thing, and it isn't until later that I learn I was probably seated on the feet of the dead man's spirit. Barba Manolis would have enjoyed it, I consoled myself for the faux pas. And even if it had been uncomfortable — if spirits can be uncomfortable — I suspect that, in his great courtesy, he had solved the problem in a most unique way.

As I sit listening to the sighs and laments, the movement of a small object under the corner of his pillow catches my eye. I lean closer to see what it is and recognize the silvery shape of a moth nestled in the folds of the pillowcase. Perhaps Barba Manolis had indeed risen, I thought later, succumbing to the phantasy, not in the glorious panoply of a colorful and majestic butterfly, but as a simple, grey moth tucked under the fold of pillow beneath the left ear of the body he had so recently deserted.

I leave the death chamber and walk into the fierce, white heat reflecting off the walls and terrace of the house. A steady stream of people arrives to pay last respects. Flora and Maria pass around cold water and sweet liqueur for the women, cognac for the men. The small parlor is filled with people trying to escape the sun. It is three o'clock, the hottest part of the day; everyone here, under ordinary circumstances, would be taking a siesta. We try to ignore the sweat. Barba Manolis' son Yiorgos stands pale and shy in his unaccustomed role as official greeter, responding with averted eyes to the countless "zoí sé sás" (life to you), the accepted expression of condolence.

When the two priests arrive, the chairs are removed from the death chamber and the final prayers at the house are chanted. The lid is placed on the coffin, and, with five neighbors and his son acting as pall bearers, Barba Manolis is taken for the last time from the home he was born in, where he spent his childhood, where he raised his own seven children and where, after four years, his bones will return for their final rest in the family chapel, to await the resurrection he had heard about from the scriptures.

Vangelo, the daughter whose house I rented when I first met Barba Manolis, calls out in one tearful, melodramatic moment "Kaló Taxídi Barba Manolis," (Bon Voyáge), verbalizing the thought of many of us, too prudent to say it ourselves. Maria, his granddaughter, begins to cry and I hold her; I am comforted by being the comforter, I realize, as I give in to the overwhelming urge to touch and hold these people whose loss I share.

The procession begins to town. The casket sits in the back of a neighbor's pick-up with the black-clad figures of the seven grown children surrounding it, a dark tableau sihouetted against the relentless, bright sky. Two buses, numerous trucks and cars take us the ten minute drive to the hill overlooking town. We disembark there and walk slowly in a long procession behind the small blue casket into the embrace of the narrow, winding streets. It is nearly four, still siesta time, and the town is deserted. The few tourist shops that are open quietly shut their doors out of respect.

The church is filled, and we all stand tightly packed and swaying against each other, steaming in the smell of incense, burning beeswax and sweat, as the ancient chants of the Liturgy for the Dead rise up above us to the dome, and reverberate there against the immense icon of Jesus, who gazes down in wisdom and compassion at the teeming, suffering creation.

I don't hear the liturgy, don't register it; I am still thinking and remembering. I stand facing the head of the casket, but a good distance back by the door. Still I haven't seen his dead face — only the top of his head; still the tears come, though gently now. I keep remembering that view, the top of his head, when I had gotten up to make us coffee in the copper bríki at the end of those many meals I'd eaten in his rough little home — how as many times I had looked down at that head with love. How sad and unreal it is to be saying goodbye.

We move out into the fresher air of the square and assemble for the final procession to the cemetary. A bent and deaf woman of nearly a hundred years, who had been a neighbor of mine that first winter in town, gives me a wide, toothless smile and asks if she can lean on my arm during the walk. I must bend down to her in order to support her, and by the time we reach the cemetary ten minutes later, I feel about ninety myself. But it is nice to be asked, to be so accepted, so cheered by that cavernous smile.

At the cemetary the coffin is uncovered one last time, one last look for the family, the final goodbye, and then the strange, high-topped black shoes are removed — shoes that have never walked the whitewashed streets of the town, shoes the dead wear, but are not buried in, on the celebration day of their last great rite of passage on earth.

WESTERN
EUROPE

RAMONT HALL

I SUPPOSE THERE are less comfortable experiences than driving a leaking tin-can of a car into London in a rainstorm, but I don't want to know about them.

It was June, 1973. I was twenty-five and intimidated by big-city driving. London was ring roads, road works, and roundabouts. My car, an Austin Mini which I had named, in a burst of originality, "Mini," was ten years old and as water-resistant as a colander.

For Mini this was a homecoming. I had bought her three weeks before from a Cockney named Barry. "Tyke the tube to Seven Sisters," he had told me on the phone. "Ring me up from the stytion, duck, and I'll come fetch you." But when, a few days later, I rang Barry as instructed, it was his brother Bob who answered. "Barry's not 'ere to-die," said Bob. "On account of 'e took a car down to Margate, see, and smashed it up."

I said oh, and added that I was at the station with fifty pounds of luggage and ninety-five pounds in cash. Bob said he'd come pick me up.

"Barry was going to give me a driving lesson," I told Bob as we drove to his and Barry's house. "Explain the rules of the road. Do you think you could do it instead?"

"Well," Bob said, "fact is, I dunno 'ow to droive a Mini. Shouldn't be driving this car 'ere, come to that. 'aven't got a license, see?"

I saw. At the house I gave Bob the ninety-five pounds, got a receipt and Mini's key, and stowed my luggage in the back seat. ("I don't roightly know what Barry's done wiv the key to the boot," Bob said.) I got in, said a prayer to whatever gods may be, and drove away.

Other travelers brave rapids, scale mountains, walk on the moon. I drove across London in a strange car, during rush hour, on the wrong side of the road, on the wrong side of the car, without insurance, in what began as a drizzle and became a downpour. It may have been my finest hour.

Now, on my way back into London after three weeks in the country, I decided that Barry must earn his living by driving cars to Margate, smashing them up, and selling them to American tourists.

In the White City I made one of those innocent decisions that quirk into Fate, or Karma, or an Act of God, depending upon your convictions. I didn't want to drive to the American Express office, not down Haymarket in competition with two-layered buses, taxis like overgrown beetles, and trip-footed tourists (most of them American), so I parked Mini under a drooling tree and took the Underground to Piccadilly.

At American Express I collected eleven letters from home and wandered blissfully back into the rain, clutching the precious hoard to my bosom and tripping over my dangling umbrella. I decided to go round the corner to the Stockpot, a quick and filling cafe in Panton Street, and eat while I read.

I saw him through the window as I approached: a tall young man, pale-skinned, rusty-haired, dressed in a three-piece dark brown suit. But I wouldn't have joined him had the waitress not waved me to his table, which sheltered the only empty chair in the restaurant. He watched with a smile while I settled my cape, handbag, and umbrella, and gestured toward the last. "I expect that's been a real friend to you today."

In fact, the umbrella and I were only casual acquaintances. I had jammed it shut somehow, and the handle had fallen off in Westminster Abbey. I carried it, but I couldn't use it. My breast-length brown hair had erupted in full frizz, and my lavender jeans were corrugated with damp-set wrinkles.

But what did my less than appealing appearance, or even this good-looking man, matter now? Eleven letters! I ordered Spanish risotto without asking what it was and grinned toothily at my companion. "Mail from home!" I said, waving the bundle.

"You're American."

It seemed pointless to deny it.

We introduced ourselves. His name was Michael Ross and he was a university student from Yorkshire. I was an American tourist (that much, he assured me, was blindingly obvious). But I wasn't a typical tourist, I told him. I had bought a car and was seeing Britain, not just London.

"What've you seen of London then?"

"Everything!"

"Trafalgar Square?"

"Got splashed by an incontinent pigeon."

"Curses!"

"That's what I said."

"Have you seen Greenwich?" I shook my head. "I'll show you, if you like. That's my part of London. My university's nearby."

"Is it near downtown?"

He was amused at this Americanism. "What makes this 'downtown'?" he asked.

"The Am. Ex. office, of course!"

"I see. Ethnocentrism, like charity, begins at home."

"I'm not enthnocentric!" I protested. "I just like getting letters!"

"Am. Ex.-centric," said Michael.

After I'd consumed something sticky and caloric for dessert, we went out to White City and collected my dilapidating Mini. Michael folded his tall, crane-thin body into the driver's seat and we splashed across the great gray city, over the rain-blistered Thames, around the Elephant and Castle roundabout, past the Frog and Nightgown pub, to the ships and boats at Greenwich.

It wasn't much of a day for sightseeing. Even I, a devout and practicing tourist, couldn't thrill to rain-soaked SE 10.

But in England there is no escaping history. Whenever I looked at Michael's long sea-colored eyes, red hair, and high wide cheekbones, I saw the Viking invasion: men with faces like Michael's, with horns on their helmets, sailing to England in their dragon-prowed ships. A few days before, I had seen the Roman invasion in the brown face of a doe-eyed boy in Cornwall, who, true to his dual ancestry, had tried to seduce me on the village cricket pitch.

"Spark spark danger danger," said Michael in a Captain Kirk voice, swerving Mini between a round-shouldered bus and the snout of an encroaching Jaguar. Star Trek on the BBC, the Old Kentucky Pancake House in Piccadilly, Safeway in Chelsea: the American invasion.

"Americans used to come to my school," Michael said, "to watch the Sunday parade, and point at us and laugh. 'How cute!' 'How quaint!' As if we were animals in a zoo."

"Well, it's difficult to avoid being a spectator when you're a tourist. I mean, you've come to look at things. Anyway, I bet the Germans and the Japanese are just as dumb and tactless. It's just that you can't understand them. But we speak the same language, more or less, and I guess our voices carry."

"Carry me back to Old Virginny," Michael agreed. "By the way, if you've nowhere to stay in London tonight, I think I could find you an empty room in my hall. It's end of term, and a lot of the lads have left."

"Okay," I said.

* * *

Ramont Hall, Goldsmiths College, University of London, isn't listed in the guidebooks, and as a bed and breakfast place it left something to be desired, namely breakfast. Michael signed me up for two dinners, after which I was happy to skip the other meals and snack on yogurt and Garibaldi biscuits in my room.

It was a men's hall of residence. There was a dining room on the ground floor and above that, fourteen stories of rooms, one room per man, each furnished with one desk, one chair, and a bed as narrow as a monk's.

Michael nested in his room like a great untidy bird, splashing through scattered books and papers as he stalked from the piled-high desk to his rumpled unmade bed, moving a sticky mug from the chair to the floor, moving a record onto the stereo. In any room with Michael and music, the music will be on. If he were really a bird he'd sing to himself all day, songs to soothe, songs to lose himself in.

Lads drifted in like leaves gone to gravity, following the fall of sound. They moved to the music, nodding to me when Michael said, "This is Rhiannon. She's American." I was accepted without question or comment. I was young. I had long hair. I liked rock music. In 1973, that was enough.

I sat on the floor and swivelled attention between the lads and my letters from home.

("For some reason your Dad packed a bottle of wine in the trunk and it got so hot in Sacramento the cork blew off and we got wine all over the car. . .")

"Vish comes tomorrow!"

"She going to cook for you, Tom?"

Tom was sturdy, green-eyed, deeply dimpled, with a smile that flashed like water in the sun. He was engaged to an Indian girl who cooked curries for him on the floor's stove, wafting hunger-making scents all down the hall.

"It's been awhile," said Tom, intense with happiness. "It'll be good."

("I finally broke down and bought a 10-speed bike to upgrade from the 3-speed I bought at the Palo Alto police auction years ago, which has never been the same since Vickie ran over it with the jeep. . .")

In drifted blonde comical Andy, a wild bearded Welshman called Chico, and dark-eyed, black-haired Bob. "You've got to hear this new record," Bob said. "It's superb!"

"Put it on then, old boot."

"What's it called?"

"*Dark Side of the Moon.*"

"Pink Floyd's latest?"

"Right."

("How's it going over there? Are you meeting any English people? Aren't they awfully reserved and stuffy? 'Stiff upper lip,' etc. I can't imagine that you're having any fun. . .")

"Hey, Rhiannon," Tom said, "pass the wine."

That evening we all went down to dinner together. Two hundred male eyes looked up, saw me (the only female present), then shifted away.

English courtesy? Probably not. My hair looked as if bats lived in it, and I badly needed a bath.

Our group sat at one of the long narrow tables and Michael trotted off to fetch the soup, which was a vague brown color with yellow bits floating on the surface. "Cor," said Bob, peering wrinkle-nosed into the tureen. "Last night's gravy."

"Conservation of resources," I pointed out. "Recycling, you see."

"I see it all right. Rather wish I hadn't."

"Bit nasty," said Tom.

"We used to have this jam at school," mused Michael. "It was green. Bright emerald green. What sort of fruit is bright green?"

"Mint jelly," I suggested.

"But it had seeds in it. A bright green fruit with seeds."

"What did it taste like then?" asked Andy, slurping soup.

"It was school food, twit. It didn't taste."

I said, "Perhaps it was a mutant."

Light flashed in Michael's long eyes. "That's it! Of course! 'Take three mutants and a pound of sugar. . . .'"

"Andy, old bean," Bob said, "you've got soup on your nose again."

"Soup of the evening, beautiful soup," Tom muttered as Michael bore away the bowls and tureen. "What next, one wonders?"

It was a mound of vaguely meat-like stuff with wet glop on it. After some discussion, the lads decided it was soybean loaf, "in last night's gravy, thickened," Bob said. "Diluted for the soup, thickened for the gravy. Clever devils."

"At my college," I said, "we called this 'mystery meat.'"

"Right," Tom said. "It's a mystery why we eat it."

There was ice cream for dessert. English ice cream does not contain cream, except for Cornish ice cream, which comes in one flavor: vanilla. I don't know what non-Cornish ice cream is made from but I suspect the worst: hydrogenated cucumber fat.

Despite the food, I stayed for five days. The lads and I went to the college bar, which was wall-to-wall blue jeans and four-letter words. We went to a party and danced on the lawn. "Look at the stars, look look up at the skies! O look at all the fire-folk sitting in the air!'" said Tom, quoting Hopkins, in lines that still capture for me the magic of an English summer night.

I worried because Michael wasn't studying, but he didn't want to study. He wanted to finish his exams and join his girlfriend in France. His last year at university was almost over, and he didn't know what to do next.

"What can I do, Rhiannon? I don't want to work at something I hate just to keep alive so I can go on working. Without money you can't be free, but if you have to work for money you lose your freedom. What's the answer?"

I had no answer to give him. I had graduated four years before, spent a year in graduate school, and gotten a job in San Francisco. By going without a car, buying my clothes at factory outlets, and walking a mile to work to save a quarter on cable-car fare, I had saved $2000 in two years, a quarter of my salary. I had bought a one-way charter flight to England. I had bought Mini. If I was frugal, I could travel for five months. And after that?

I didn't know. I was in England, and that was enough.

I still listen to *Dark Side of the Moon* sometimes. When I hear the heart-beat at the beginning of Side One, the present dissolves and I'm back in Michael's room, twelve stories above London. The room smells like Jeyes fluid, books, and cheap red wine. Rain slashes at the window. I sit in half-lotus position, my lap full of letters. Tom gazes down at his clasped hands. Bob and Andy and Chico wrap their arms around their blue-jeaned knees, press their backs against the wall. Michael lies on his bed, staring moodily up at the ceiling as if he sees the future in it and does not like what he sees.

Our faces are unlined. There's not a white hair on our heads. We have no jobs, no bills, no mortgages. But we have almost run out of time for dancing on starlit lawns and listening to music with friends on rainy weekday afternoons, and we know it.

I would never again make a friend in a cafe. I would never again go home with a man I barely knew, sure of my safety because in those days, there was them and there was us, and we could be trusted. In trusting Michael I had trusted us, and it had been all right.

It had been more than all right.

When I left, Michael said, "If you get as far north as Yorkshire, come and stay with my family."

"I will."

"I mean it."

"So do I."

I got into Mini, and, befriended, drove out of London.

Rhiannon Paine

A WALK ON HADRIAN'S WALL

IT WAS JULY when Mini and I reached Yorkshire. I called Michael from a phone box outside York Minster. "Come to Marske," he said. "My mother wants to meet you."

The Ross's house was called "The Limes" although there were no limes in the neighborhood and never had been. The street was called Lavender Court. There was no lavender either. The English are good at wishful naming.

The village was named Markse-by-Sea, and that was accurate enough. If Markse were any more by the sea, it would be *in* the sea. The North Sea, this was, and not a patch on the sky-blue Pacific back in California. It was gray, and the red-brick village looked grim and inhospitable as I drove into it.

I parked Mini in Lavender Court, a no-through-street of small brick bungalows, and walked to the front door. I knocked, the door opened, and suddenly I was in the house and surrounded by large red-headed persons who asked me questions in bright English voices and immediately answered them. I was told I must be hungry, led down a hall, pushed onto a sofa, and given a plate of salad to eat while more questions were asked and answered. Small round people sprang into the room and uttered sentences that tilted up at the ends. Two medium-sized people came in and the red-headed persons rushed at them shrieking, "Condick, Condick!" From somewhere above my left shoulder, a choked soprano voice kept asking querulously for Peter.

The plate of salad was whisked away and a raspberry pie was dropped in my lap. More questions flew past. Had I enjoyed York? Wasn't it beautiful? Of course I knew that the Romans had built a fort there, Ebacorum. "Peter?" Had I seen the remains of the fort? Weren't they fascinating? And had I see the wall? Of course I knew that it was one of the best-preserved medieval walls in Britain. "Pretty Peter!" And York Minster, founded (as of course I knew) in 1172, containing the largest stained-glass window in Britain — had I see the Minster? Had I seen the window? Wasn't it glorious? "Peter! Pretty Peter!" Would I like more pie? Would I like more cream on my pie? Would I like a cup of tea?

"Tea," I gasped, and Michael went to put the kettle on. Gradually it dawned on me that there were only two red-headed persons: Michael (six feet two inches tall) and his mother (five feet ten inches tall). But in their similarity they seemed to multiply each other; it was a case of one plus one making a basketball team.

Condick, it emerged, was a couple, Connie and Dick, friends from Leicester. The small round people, actually normal in size and shape compared to anyone but Michael and his mother, were Julie, a schoolteacher like Mrs. Ross, and former pupils named Pat and Keith. Peter was a budgerigar with a limited vocabulary and an inflated opinion of his appearance.

Absent from the scene that day was Michael's sister, Karen, who was staggering across the moors on a school field trip. At fourteen, Karen was already five feet, ten inches tall, but at least she didn't have red hair.

"We shall take you to the Wall," Mrs. Ross announced.

"Which wall?" I ventured, equally prepared to hear "the Great Wall of China" or "the one in our back garden."

"Hadrian's Wall. You know, of course, that it was built on the instructions of the Emperor Hadrian in 122 A.D. as a defense against the Picts."

"Of course."

"You can walk on it," said Michael.

I said that in that case, it sounded more like a floor than a wall.

"It's a wall," said Mrs. Ross. "There are seventy miles of it."

"I can't walk seventy miles!" I cried.

"We needn't do all seventy," said Mrs. Ross, looking at me pityingly. "We'll go tomorrow."

"I'll coom too," said Pat Briggs, whose Yorkshire accent turned "book" into "buke" and "get off" into "gare off." She was familiar with my accent, though, from "fill-ums."

We set off early the next morning. Michael drove us, but once we got there he announced that he was going to stay in the car and read. He had, he said firmly, already seen the Wall.

"Besides, it looks like rain," I said.

"Nonsense, " said Mrs. Ross. She had been a teacher for many years. It was plain that to her, I was just an oversized and more than usually pig-headed child who talked funny.

She told us educational things about the remains of a Roman hospital which had been left lying around, and then we trudged across the pale green turf, mounted the Wall, and started walking. "We'd better not go too far," I said. "I'm sure it's going to rain, and we didn't bring umbrellas."

"We've got to walk as far as the next car park," Briggs said cheerfully, "'cause that's where Michael's picking oos oop."

"How far is that, exactly?"

"A couple of miles."

"We're going to walk two miles in the *rain?*"

"Can't you just see this landscape in Roman times?" Mrs. Ross enthused. "The green fields aswarm with horses and soldiers, the woad-painted warriors advancing from the North, the scrape of the chariot wheels against the rock..."

"And all of it getting wet," I said.

In the distance, a Land Rover's brakes squealed and a woman shouted, "Nigel, you climb out of that lavatorium *now* and bring your sister with you!"

"Isn't it exciting?" said Mrs. Ross.

"It's raining."

"Misting," she said.

"Mrs. R., is that Scotland?" asked Briggs eagerly, peering into the misting distance. I peered too, though I was almost sure we weren't that close to Scotland.

"It's *toward* Scotland," said Mrs. Ross judiciously. We stopped while she told us some educational things about Scotland. "It's raining," she remarked.

At last, even the English admitted it! Water was running off Mrs. Ross's aristocratic nose. It didn't look so aristocratic when it was wet, I noticed. She followed my gaze and went cross-eyed. "Should I dry it or blow it," she asked and rummaged in her handbag for a hankie.

After blowing her nose, she put the hankie back in her handbag. She took off her scarf and wrung it out, holding it away from the Wall so as not to drip any water on the historical stones. Then she tied the tortured object back onto her head and, upper lip stiffening visibly, pointed east.

We plodded along. "Mrs. R., I'm *wet*," said Briggs forlornly.

"I'm wet too," I pointed out. "'Me skin's soaked through clear to the skin.'" It was a line from the second Beatles movie, but Briggs was too young to remember and Mrs. Ross was too old to care. "Rain, rain, go away," I brayed, and that was better. The English joined in, and one of them could even carry the tune.

Singing and braying, we reached the point where the Wall slid down and buried its nose in Northumberland mud. It dragged itself out farther on, but it had shed pounds in the effort and was no longer wide enough for walking. As we squelched along in the mud, I expressed the opinion that we'd walked two miles already.

"Not yet," said Briggs.

"How will we know when we've gotten there?"

"There's a footpath leading down to the car park," Mrs. Ross said. "We won't be able to miss it."

"I can," I said. "I can miss it easily. You don't know me very well yet, but I promise you, I'm good at missing things."

"We'll find it, Rhiannon," Briggs said pluckily.

"Just think," Mrs. Ross urged. "We're walking where the Romans once trod!"

"I hope they had better shoes."

"And after all these centuries, the Wall still stands!"

"If you can call that standing. It's more what I would call leaning."

"There's the footpath," Briggs cried. Sure enough, we weren't able to miss it. It was three times as wide as the Wall, paved with mud, and encumbered with sheep who bleated mournfully at us as we splodged along.

"We could drive on to Chesters," said Mrs. Ross hopefully. "It has the finest remains of a cavalry fort in the country."

"Oh wow," I said.

"Baaa," said the sheep.

We reached the main road at last, but there was no car park and no sign of Michael's Cortina. It was now raining heavily. I was wearing the charmingly impractical blue tweed coat I had bought in London. Indeed, this was the first opportunity I had had to discover just how charmingly impractical it was. It reached halfway down my thighs; in 1973, that constituted a coat. It did not keep me warm and it did not keep me dry, but it went right on looking charming.

"Michael, row the boat ashore!" I sang, using my full range of four notes.

"Hallelujah!" shrieked Briggs. I thought she'd spotted the Cortina, then realized she was just continuing the song.

We stumbled down the skinny, ditch-lined road in the direction of the car park which Mrs. Ross assured us was "right around the corner." There weren't any corners, but I had run out of sarcasm. Cars splashed past, their passengers staring at us through the rain-streaked windows.

"They moost think we're daft," Briggs said. She was trying to pull her foot out of a patch of sticky mud.

"They have a point."

Mrs. Ross began to hum "Singing in the Rain" under her breath.

"Gare off, you stoof," Briggs said, addressing the mud.

"Here comes a lorry!" cried Mrs. Ross, and jumped nimbly into the ditch.

Briggs pulled her foot out of the mud and leaped in too. I stood my ground. "It's wet in there," I said. The lorry roared past, and the resulting wave, upon which a Briggs-sized person could have surfed, broke over my head. The English were still laughing at me when the Cortina pulled up.

As we drove home, Mrs. Ross and Briggs told Michael how I'd refused to jump into the ditch because it was too wet, and they all had a jolly good laugh about it.

Their climate drops water on them almost continually. Their houses are named after non-existent plant life. Their countryside is littered with old falling-down walls and castles and cathedrals. Their ice cream is made from hydrogenated cucumber fat.

The way I see it, they need all the laughs they can get.

It's just as well I am able to take such a philosophic attitude, because to this day, when Mrs. Ross, Michael, and Briggs get together, they laugh about the day they took the poor daft American to see Hadrian's Wall.

Jennifer Holt

EXCERPTS FROM A EUROPEAN TRAVELOGUE

6/3/87. I am on my way to Europe, flying into Amsterdam, then to my destination — Wales. I am making this trip all by myself — I, who have never even taken a camping trip alone. I have traveled this far once before, but with a lover, Michael. God, how we fought, but still, he was a backbone to lean on. I was so proud that he was my lover, sitting in a little cafe on the island of Naxos, Greece, drinking wine. Too much wine. . . . Michael is at least partially why I am here ten years later, trying to find a comfortable position in my seat on this plane. I am determined to do this on my own, without anyone else to look at the map, change the money, order food, find a reasonable place to stay. But fear is crouching in the back of my neck and shoulders, and I feel like the only solitary traveler on this charter plane, crowded in with a huge party of people becoming acquainted, laughing, drinking cocktails to pass the time. No longer in my protected corner of two years' sobriety, I want to reach out and steal a sip of amber, to quell the anxiety and loneliness already leaking in. My nose hurts from dryness and tears unshed.

"You are going back to the place of your first birth on earth," a psychic told me before I left for the trip. "This is the place where the scenarios in succeeding incarnations were first played out. It is, in a sense, a homecoming. At three separate times, you will be aware of a bell ringing in your psyche. Hold on to these moments."

I have read all the informational books on Wales, have steeped myself in the tales of King Arthur, and the druids' mysterious religion. The mystical bent of the Welsh people fascinates me, since I am a dabbler in pantheism, and new age spirituality. I have danced around fires with women and a full moon shining, our naked bodies reflecting the glow. Yet I have never been entirely comfortable with the rituals — they seem so superficial, ungrounded in any true historical sense. But perhaps part of me, at least, responds to an ancient summons, a call back to my ancestral roots. What is the relationship between a group of self-conscious women attempting to connect with the earth, and worship of the druids? I want to know, to know why these things attract and repulse me at the same time.

My grandmother spoke Welsh, with a strange spitting and cawing, a clearing of the throat on every other word. It is one of the clearest memories I have of her. She was no-nonsense and terse, her hair blue-black until the last few years of her life, and she cooked reluctantly, like my mother. She was the first woman at her college to bob her hair. I am proud of that. I think if she had been born in my era, she would have been a feminist. As it is, she managed to graduate from college in the '30s and become a teacher, fiercely wearing the short haircut in spite of the chagrin of her principal, no doubt. When she married my grandfather, she quit her job like a good wife, and resigned herself to cooking haphazard meals and keeping house for her husband and five children. When he died, she never fully recovered although their relationship was not ostensibly close or affectionate. Six months after his funeral, she followed him, dying in her sleep. Hello, grandmother, wherever you are. I think you would be glad I am doing this, going back to your homeland. I know I was your favorite, the grandchild with eyes like chunks of coal, she used to say, Welsh eyes.

* * *

6/4/87. Amsterdam. I am staying in a dorky Christian youth hostel on the recommendation of a friend at work. She didn't tell me it had such a strong religious affiliation, but I guess if you're into Jesus, it might seem comforting to be handed Bible tracts at the front desk along with your locker key. The price is certainly reasonable, but the curfew is at midnight, which is ridiculous considering most nightlife just begins at 11 p.m. in this city. I am also admonished to be out of bed by 9 a.m. and told not to return until 2 p.m., due to cleaning. What do I do about jet lag??? I am seven tired hours behind their Christian briskness.

After checking in, I am immediately shooed out so I walk around Amsterdam, ending up in a park with gnarled trees and crumbling buildings overgrown with ivy. Just as I spread my coat out in a secluded area by a small lake, a seedy looking man begins stealthily approaching me, shuffling closer and closer, until I can see his unnaturally darkened eyes. Drugs, I figure. Amsterdam is supposedly the drug mecca of Europe. Either he wants to steal money or sell me something, and in either case, I'm not interested. Unnerved, I give up my turf, settling at a spot closer to other people. He does not follow.

On my way back to the hostel, I am approached again, this time by a bearded, well-dressed man with fair hair and glasses. I am walking slowly down a street crossing a canal, and as he passes by me, he stops.

I deliberately swivel the other way, edging over to watch a boat slide underneath. Then I hear him say, "Nice view, eh?" How would Michael handle this, I wonder, and realize he would not encounter such an experience. This is a female condition, being approached by men. Would the sophisticated, well-traveled woman respond and make light conversation? Before my mind has time to consider, my legs have trotted me off in the opposite direction, as I give a vague reply. I hope this afternoon is not an indication of what my entire trip will consist of. Is it so unusual to see a woman alone? Or am I so obviously a tourist, a scared, uncertain, female tourist, and perfect prey for males tuned into that type of radar?

My first day here and I already feel anxiety rising inside, a knee-jerk response to dealing with men after seven years of knowing my lesbian identity and wearing it proudly. I don't remember men so boldly approaching me back home, or was it just that I always had my arm around another woman, a convenient shield? Michael was the only man I ever loved, the only person I have ever loved with total abandon, willing to crawl on my hands and knees across entire continents to gain his love, only to watch his head tip back with yet another drink. Am I truly a lesbian or one by default to this silhouette man?

I feel like I stick out, like everyone can tell what I am thinking, can sense my fear, is noting my American clothing with disdain. How I dress has always been too important — at home I often change my outfits four times a day. The very generic clothing I packed, with the intention of blending in so as to avoid being labeled American, still seems inappropriate. I know this is pathetic, but I can't get the two previous encounters with men out of my mind, and the sense of being fair game. I saw a wildlife show on television a few months back, with a pack of hyenas hunting down a zebra, worrying at the galloping animal's heels and flanks until it fell, thrashing wildly, fighting for its life, even as its entrails were being gouged out with frenzied sets of teeth.

* * *

6/5/87. I have not adjusted to the time change yet. My internal timing refuses to reset itself, in league with my dream state. Father lies on my bed, waiting for me like a cat for a mouse, his smile reminding me of, of something I cannot place. I am very young, perhaps six, with a flannel nightgown on, my hand over my mouth to stop the silent scream. The bed looms in front of me and I am sitting, submitting. Then, with sudden clarity, I see an opening, I am a drowning body crawling up for air, struggling, coming to.

Waking up, there is sweat on my bedsheets, and my right calf is cramped from kicking him into memory.

At 7 a.m. I've had enough and decide to go for a run, slipping out of the hostel as the workers begin to congregate in the lobby, their young faces shining with the certainty of the saved. I have seen that same look of smug certainty on the faces of rich women, walking swiftly into the next store, furs and wrinkles hugging their flesh. Jogging, I head up the block, crossing tiny cobblestone streets more narrow than American alleys. At rush hour, bicyclists fill the streets instead of cars. I am amazed at the natural beauty of the Dutch women I see pedaling by, their hair short and shiny, their clothes bohemian. All manner of objects are transported by bike, apparently. One man pedals through the intersection with several two-by-fours swaying precariously under his arm.

The canals are everywhere, for the most part having sunk into a state of disuse, the water brackish and filled with garbage. House boats are lined up along the banks, each with a set of rickety steps leading from the street to a swaying deck and front door. Such vulnerable homes — anyone could break in, I think, as I watch them rocking silently.

The condition of the sidewalks is much the same as the canals, with garbage and litter overflowing the gutters, particularly dog shit. Everyone has dogs, large dogs, which are allowed to go in restaurants, post offices and stores with their owners. The presence of so many huge dogs seems paradoxical in such a tiny island city, already filled to overflowing with human bodies.

Returning to the hostel, I strike up a tentative conversation with a woman named Françoise, a college student who has been traveling for a year with her boyfriend. Eventually she asks off-handedly, "What do you do back home? You're too *old* to be a student, right?" I inwardly wince, feeling her unconcious patronizing. The knowledge that I am growing older suddenly descends upon me and remains, no matter how many affirmations I patiently write out on page after page of this journal. I hear a persistent whisper: I am getting old, I am getting old. I am galloping as fast as I can, the pack a black and white swirl just in front of me, pounding the ground into dust devils. I stumble, I am falling behind, I can feel nips at the tendons above my hooves...

Back home I am a professional musician, and I have always prided myself on being the epitome of cool, using punk music as a vehicle to trash ideals set by an older generation. But nearly thirty years have crept up on me suddenly. My music means nothing over here — no one knows me except as another tourist, and I no longer have even the beauty of youth to flaunt. All the attractive women and men around my age I have seen on the streets of Amsterdam in groups of two or more do not seem to notice me — only the less perfect, lonely ones, hunting for a connection.

I watch the co-eds at the hostel chatter and fluff their hair in mirrors, and I grieve for my own youth, which slipped away while I was busy committing slow suicide with alcohol, drugs and bulimia. I have no desire to re-live my own painful years — I want to slip into one of their carefree bodies and make my way across Europe, meeting other bohemians, sharing pot, wine, stories and sometimes sex, wearing gypsy clothing, traveling by ferry to exotic islands for naked sunbathing, renting bikes and pedaling through the French countryside.

I say to myself, 'Quick like a fish, Jenni, what's your first memory of your early twenties?' and an image appears of my body on its knees, arms hugging the sides of my oven, shoulders pitched forward into its yawning mouth, the gas seeping into my nostrils. My face and hair are filthy from the burned and greasy remains on its surfaces, and I grimace with distaste, then feel angry with myself for caring.

The position is familiar. I crouched over my toilet in a similar style for years and years, vomiting myself into numbness, offering junk food sacrifices to the porcelain goddess. The oven has become another kind of sacrifice — a prayer for a permanent ending to my pain.

I hold my awkward position at the oven's door, inhaling gas fumes determinedly. Then suddenly I recall a gruesome cartoon I had seen years earlier. A man, holding a gun to his head, stands ready to shoot, with several shadow bodies in identical poses littering the floor around him. Head in the oven, I suddenly understand its meaning — the bodies are past selves, and the message is, what one does not learn, one is doomed to repeat, in lifetime after lifetime. I drily thank the powers that be for the insight, and slowly pull my head from the oven, turning off the gas. Sighing, I go into the bathroom to wash my hair.

I suppose this moment was the beginning of my upward climb, a path I have no desire to repeat. I am sure each one of these hostel college kids has their own grief, their own dark journey to work through. But in my jealous eyes, they seem as pristine and innocent, dammit, as happy, as the scenes of peasants portrayed on the Dutch tile.

* * *

6/6/87. Amsterdam is not getting any better. Thank God I leave tomorrow. The highlight of the day is an experience at a city swimming pool, which I stumble across during a frustrating zigzag walk through the circles of streets surrounding the city's center. It is a long, brick building with windows stretching from floor to ceiling on the side facing the street. Approaching the glass, I note several people swimming vigorously up and down the pool's Olympic-size length. A friend back home told me that many homes in Holland do not have baths, so the city pools, which are built with an adjoining bath house, serve the dual function of cleanliness and exercise. I watch the swimmers mournfully from my vantage point, wondering if negotiating a trip to the hostel and back to retrieve my swimsuit is worth the effort.

At the end of the day, I decide to make the attempt, surprising myself by finding the pool with little difficulty. I pay and blithely enter, changing into my suit. A gaggle of Dutch grade school girls makes no secret of their contempt for my leg hair. So much for my vision of the hairy European woman. In spite of western culture's indoctrination, I have retained my body hair. It is something I find appealing and sexy. When I was younger I deplored the thick black hair on my legs and under my arms, which Mother matter-of-factly said was evidence of my "simian" roots. These days, at least under more favorable circumstances, I am proud of its abundance. I would feel naked without it. But in a city pool in Amsterdam, where it is apparently not exactly de rigeur, I suddenly wish for a razor.

As I enter the pool area, my faltering spirits sink further. Every inch of the pool is teeming with children of all shapes, colors and sizes, doing more in one minute to the pool and flotation devices that I've ever seen kids get away with in American pools. In the States it seems we are obsessed with safety, or, more accurately, the threat of a lawsuit.

Two children run past, jostling me as I approach the pool's edge, and I feel every pair of eyes on me as I slowly descend into the blue, hiding the blackness on my legs. Once in the water, I swim cautious laps around wildly kicking extremities, and it isn't long before a group of adolescent boys targets me for cherry bomb practice, hurling their curled-up bodies vigorously into the water five inches from my head.

At length, a lifeguard approaches the side of the pool I am by now defiantly clutching to, telling me in broken English that I might want to come back tomorrow during lap swim time. Sighing, I hoist myself out of the water, and self-consciously head for the locker room. Retrieving my clothing, I step into one of the not-very-private half-stalls and begin dressing. All at once I am aware that a man in a dirty tee-shirt and jeans is watching me. He slowly saunters over and begins spraying the floor of the half-stall adjacent to my own with a hose, between puffs on a cigarette and baleful glances in my direction. At first I'm so shocked at seeing a man in the locker room, I forget to be mad. Then I glare at him, snorting back tears, furiously gathering up my belongings to scuttle into the bathroom.

Lying in the relative safety of my bunk in the hostel dorm room, I remember my mother's fear of everything foreign — her assumption that

all strange men who so much as look at you want something unspeakable. I am my mother's daughter after all, battling back constant fear
and paranoia. When I reluctantly told my parents of this trip a week
before I left, her reply was, "Write a will; you never know what might
happen over there." I wrote one. Mortality, immortality and posterity
are issues I am beginning to worry about, along with loneliness and
whether or not I will ever have the "good things" in life, namely, the
ideals of my parent's generation. As a teenager on acid, I used to walk
around the streets of my small South Dakota town and look in at the
houses. They seemed like toy houses, or sets for a play, and I could see
comfortable scenes through windows, of a lamp, a sofa sagged from use,
and always a television on, children with wet hair fresh from the bath
seated in front of it. This, in a nutshell, is what I was taught to strive
for: a home with a mortgage, a television set, a husband, children, a
job I hated but held on to, to make ends meet. But somewhere along
the line that vision went haywire, I didn't buy the halcyon image behind
the glass; I could feel discontent lurking underneath. Instead I live in
an apartment in a big city with only a cat for company, and a string of
unsuccessful lesbian relationships behind me. I am no happier by com-
parison; that's the irony. Perhaps my definition of the "good things" will
have to shift again.

'You will never be taken of,' grief insists, curled into my stomach like
a small, mourning snake, an omnipresent traveling companion. 'It is
too late, you are too old, the chance is too long gone.' I am being forced
to confront something that until now I have managed to keep hidden:
a tidal wave of old pain, devastating almost to the point of incapacita-
tion. I try holding back the flow, try rallying myself into good moods,
but the pain seeps into my dreams. I am holding the shaft to my father's
penis, he is angry, he wants it back. I am struggling to hide it behind
my bed, awkwardly, it is as big as my torso, and I can hear his footsteps
in the hall. In the aftermath of this dream, the serpent is wound so tightly
I cannot breathe.

I am anxious to leave for Wales, for a place that will feel more familiar,
hopefully more like home. My body yearns, physically and psycho-
logically, for my own apartment, my own friends, my own little life, as
I toss and turn on my bunk. I feel trapped in a surreal college dorm atmosphere, pretentious, travel-wise co-eds blocking every escape.

* * *

6/7/87. I am here! I can see Cardiff, the capital city of Wales, in all its
glory out of my bedroom window this morning, and I am in bliss. What
a luxury — my room has its own color television set, and there is a

bathroom down the hall I can bathe in alone. At the hostel, the women bathed in gym class unison, all bodies exposed. Twice I got to the door of the group shower room, then turned away, unable to bear the inevitable stares at my body hair.

Postcards are spread out on the bed, and memories of what I have left behind swim into focus in this new-found privacy. I am crying several days' worth of stored-up tears. Turning on the television to hide the sound, a caricature of the ugly American is momentarily soothing. It is the film *Caddyshack*, Rodney Dangerfield's arms around two blonde vixens as he saunters across the country club golf course, lime green polyester golf pants hitched up around his pot belly.

I am missing an ex-lover, C., intensely, although our relationship was destructive and too passionate, bringing out my worst qualities and a ferocious, cat-like sensuality, claws constantly out, marking her. Violence was at the edge of every encounter. We talked through clenched teeth in public settings, leaving abruptly as embarrassed friends looked away. I made furious love to her in the tiny, single bed of her thin-walled apartment. An affair that took place behind my current lover's back, it careened through a year of lies and intrigue. We were bad for each other and knew it, but a core part of me craved this very badness.

On a postcard to her I write, "I am a pregnant woman straining to deliver, carrying the still birth inside like an embryonic torch." Then I masturbate as tears pour down my cheeks, and Rodney Dangerfield's voice intones, "I don't get no respect."

* * *

6/11/87. After two days in Cardiff I decide to move on. A disturbance in the middle of the night prompts this. Around 3 a.m., I hear the door bell ringing, again and again. I can't imagine why the caller would ring so long without giving up, and why no one in the hotel is answering. In the morning the proprietor reeks of booze, no doubt from a very bad hangover. I suddenly have no interest in staying. It has been long enough since chemical dependency treatment for me to have given up such self-righteous posturing but I still can't stand to be around anyone I suspect of over-drinking. God, I feel so easily rattled, a bird flying to a new roost at the slightest provocation.

I am on my way to a seaside village called Swansea. Looking out the train window, I can see rolling hills and valleys, occasional glimpses of unkempt yards along the tracks the only blight in the scenery. The houses are very drab, junk littering the ground around them instead of grass. They form a curious contrast to the surrounding mountains.

* * *

6/13/87. At an ocean-front B&B I choose impulsively for its red-striped awning, the people are pleasant but the first room I look at is shabby and unappealing. Sensing my hesitation, the young woman in charge takes me up two more flights of stairs to the attic, saying, "Well, I think you'll like this room. This is where I go, when I can, to get away and have a fag."

She opens the door to a little bit of sky — a huge, rectangular window at a slant overlooks the sea and I can see a lighthouse down the beach. The room's angled walls are painted light blue like the water on a fair day, a small bed and nightstand the only furniture. I promptly say, "I'll take it," and put down my backpack as she leaves. Running down the four flights of stairs, I fly out the door and across the street to the ocean. Once my feet hit the sand, I kick off my shoes and begin approaching the sea reverently, slowly. For the first time in my life, I cry with happiness. The sea is like a giant mother welcoming me home with wave after embracing wave, and I sob in time with their entry to the shore.

* * *

6/15/87. Today I have the pleasure of witnessing a Welsh marching band. I am shopping, visiting small stores and boutiques tucked into streets angled haphazardly against the ocean front, when I hear the strains of an eerie melody. It doesn't sound like anything I've ever heard marching bands play at home — it is haunting, atonal, and played with deep emotion.

Running out of a shop and around the corners of a few streets, I find a small group of middle-aged musicians, smartly marching in uniform. Suddenly the music ceases as they near the open double doors of an official-looking building, and march inside. There is no parade, no festival, just the marching band. I was in fact one of only two onlookers, the other a small boy strutting along the sidewalk with an imaginary trumpet jutting out of his pursed lips. In Wales small bands like this seem to be a commonplace thing.

This is a land of musicians, who, like me, feel song coursing through their veins as strongly as blood, and honor its call. On the street in front of the building, I wipe my eyes, feeling intense kinship. A nation of singers, Wales has been called. Now I understand how accurate the phrase is.

* * *

6/18/87. I have just arrived at Llanurtyd Wells, a very beautiful little village perched up in the mountains of southern Wales, an hour and a half by train from the ocean and Swansea. There is lush countryside everywhere, dotted with a constant pattern of sheep. A myriad of stone fences crisscrosses the hills, and I marvel at the amount of work it took to heave the stones out of the earth and cart them to the fence. The houses are very well-kept and clean, surrounded by hedges which enclose flower gardens of all sizes. Rose bushes line the borders of every garden, and I imagine Welsh women chatting up their roses' foibles over pots of tea.

I am finally beginning to relax, to allow myself to sink into my feelings, regardless of what they are. I have had the strangest sensation on this trip, of my emotions not really being 'mine' at all, but each an entity in and of itself, rising in an ancient rhythm, moving slowly through me in wave after wave, engulfing me, then retreating.

I decide to take a walk down a path by the resident "river," as the locals call it. Actually it is not much more than a brook with wire-encased stone walls for sides, to protect it from further erosion. The evening air is beginning to mist up from the water, and I hear a tinkling sound, like fairies frolicking so near that I can almost turn my head and see them. Not another soul is in sight. At a boulder overlooking the water, I stop to sit down, then spontaneously begin singing, feeling like a channel between the brook and the heavens has just opened up inside of me. The words go something like this, "Evening comes, my spirit soars above me. Evening comes, my spirit now is free. Evening comes, I feel the mists surround me; from within I know I hold the key. Daybreak comes, I fall back to my body. Daybreak comes, I reel my spirit home. Daybreak comes, I hold onto the memory, till the evening when I'm free to roam." Afterwards, I am holding my breath. Is this what I think it is? It feels too subtle, such an ineffable state that if I breathe, the feeling will vanish. Is this all there is? I want something tangible to hold onto, real validation. I don't trust myself. Am I just making up the experience, is it only my imagination? Sighing, I get up and return to my room.

* * *

6/23/87. I have been on trains all day, trying to find the site of a supposed festival. Even though I felt more comfortable and at peace in Llanurtyd Wells than anywhere so far, something propels me onward. I have this feeling that I am missing out, and decide I absolutely must see some genuine Welsh musicians at work. That was, after all, one of my main reasons for taking the trip. In small villages, like Llanurtyd Wells, the only nightlife is the town pub, and I have not wanted to join the locals, sitting by myself at the counter, or worse, refusing friendly offers of beer and ale. So I go to bed early and rise by 5 or 6 a.m., in time to watch the snails and slugs promenade across the lanes while I jog past. Yesterday evening the innkeeper gave me the name of a town having a festival this weekend. But when I arrived today, the train station was deserted and the streets bare except for a handful of strangers. The worker at the station shook her head doubtfully at my query and with a yawn told me the name of another town I could try. Two and a half hours and several train transfers later, I arrive at a town in the midst of a festival. Everyone, including the children, is dressed in Victorian garb, and I feel more than usually out of place, walking through the crowds in American clothing with a huge back pack weighing down my shoulders. I am dismayed to discover that the festival is, however, winding down and all the musicians are packing up. A search for lodging is futile — every room has been rented. In total defeat, I drop my pack and slump to the street corner, tears beginning their descent down my cheeks. I am too tired and at odds with myself to care. I do not know what to do — I simply do not know what to do. Eventually two bobbies (police officers) take pity on me. An off duty officer wheeling a stroller is rounded up and he promptly deposits me in his car along with his child and the stroller. We drive for an hour to surrounding villages, until at length a room at a farm is secured. As I hoist my backpack out of the trunk, the owner of the farm, a man in his late sixties, approaches me from behind and offers to help, his breath too close to my face. I bristle, yet I don't know why. He and his wife seem very nice and I shrug off the distaste, figuring it must be from the stress of a difficult day.

I am crying in my room, the comforter clutched in my hands, when the door to my room opens, and it is him, asking me to join them for supper. I politely decline. A few minutes later, he returns, and again opens the door without knocking, asking if there is anything he can do to help. I am getting unnerved, but I don't exactly have a choice about leaving, so I say, "No, I just need to be left alone," and go into the bathroom to take a bath. I am undressing, when I hear someone at the door, and the doorknob is turning and I sharply say, "What is it?"

"I just thought you might need fresh towels," a male voice replies. Him again! I tell him in a tight voice to leave them outside. There is no lock on the door and I bathe quickly, then return to my room, putting out the light and hiding under the pillows.

* * *

6/24/87. This morning I am up very early, determined to get the hell out of the house before I have to see the man again. But he has beat me to it; as I descend the stairs from my room on the second level, he is waiting for me, smiling, offering to help me with my pack, standing too close to me. I refuse and begin to leave, but he insists on giving me a ride to the train station, explaining that since the farm is not on a bus route, a taxi would be extremely costly. Reluctantly I agree, and on the way there, he talks about a daughter he has about my age. I reply with terse sentences, wondering to myself if his behavior is just Welsh friendliness, this lack of boundaries and personal space. Then at the station, after depositing my backpack against the wall, he comes up very close to me to say goodbye and kisses me on the lips. I quickly back away, I am stunned, repulsed, he is waving a cheerful goodbye as he gets into his car. What just happened? Can he possibly think this is appropriate behavior? I feel sick to my stomach. Shaking, I sit down on my backpack to wait for the station to open. I long to be going home. Just a few more days.

* * *

6/30/87. I am finally flying away from this trip. Held in limbo above the earth, my journey over, I feel no sense of completion, no sense of a job well-done or worth doing. Instead, I am empty inside, immensely grateful to be sitting on this plane flying away from a month of unfulfilled expectations and incredible despair.

But yet, I think I got what I came for after all. It simply doesn't look like the tourist pictures in my head, and it doesn't feel nearly as enchanting as the stories Michael used to tell me about India and Europe as a solo traveler.

First of all, I was hoping for some mystical connection, a bona fide psychic experience that would confirm my pull to Wales and justify my need to be here. And that didn't happen. In fact, coming to Wales in the month of the summer solstice seems to have been a waste of effort. I had planned to visit Stonehenge on solstice eve. But I was told that the ancient site, now a popular tourist attraction, was specifically closed to foreigners on that particular night due to "the proliferation of hippies getting soused," a purse-lipped Welshman told me, arms crossed.

But I did have three moments that I could qualify as the "bells" mentioned by my psychic back home. Crying with the ocean at Swansea was one, the marching band another, and last, singing the evening song in Llanurtyd Wells. These were joyous moments, spiritual experiences in the loose sense of the word, when all my fears and jaded preconceptions fell away, at least momentarily.

Beyond the mystical, in a deeper sense I made this trip to "find myself," to claim my strength and self-reliance at traveling alone for a month. And I did find myself. She simply is not the resourceful, independent,

capable person I wanted her to be. Instead, she turned out to be a snivel-
ling crybaby. But now I know she is there, and I will no longer turn my
head away at her tears, as my mother always did. I am tired of
avoidance, I am tired of running. I have let the pain catch up with me
at last.

Ah, Wales, I visited no ancestral grave, made no bosom buddies or
even passing friends, participated in no holy rituals. I crept and crouched
my way through, slinking along with my back against a wall, constantly on guard but not knowing what I was defending.

The trip is over; I have spent $2,500 to return without a recognizable
trophy. I have only postcards and de-pedestalized images for memen-
tos. But I survived; I lived through the fear, the stares, the miscalcula-
tions, the night encounters with my father. A small voice tells me maybe
someday I will be proud of what I have accomplished. At this point,
I am only glad to be flying home.

Judith Barrington

OF CATALANS AND KINGS

I MUST HAVE been about thirteen when we went for our first family holiday to Spain. I had traveled abroad before, motoring with my parents for three-week trips here and there, so I was familiar enough with the journey to dread only my recurrent car sickness. But Spain was something new: not in the way Switzerland or Austria had been new and unfamiliar, but new and familiar in the way that it is when you go to a parent or grandparent's childhood home, a place that is part of your history, woven through the threads of your family life.

My parents had lived in Barcelona for much of their married life, though I never knew precisely why. My father's family, though English, lived in Cartagena, where they owned tin mines. My father and his brother had been sent off to English boarding schools, and then my father returned to Spain, though why he ended up working as an electrical engineer in Barcelona and not in the family mining business, I never thought to ask. (Ours was not a family that encouraged curiosity about the past: we had no storytellers.)

When my mother married my father, she married into a life abroad, which apparently agreed with her, as her love of Spain was fierce. They lived right next to the beautiful old monastery in Pedralbes, a peaceful district on the outskirts of Barcelona. Although they both spoke fluent Spanish and Catalan, they had mostly English friends in a community that must have been just like any expatriate British colony: they played tennis and bridge, and left the city in the summer for a beach house or some fishing up at Montseny.

My older brother and sister were born in Barcelona, and were just seven and three when the Civil War broke out, causing the whole family to board one of the last boats out of Barcelona, abandoning a house full of possessions they never saw again, and a way of life.

For twenty years, my mother refused to go back. At first, I imagine it wasn't really a possibility, since they had little money, and my father was trying to establish a business in London. Then there was World War II to endure, with heavy bombing along the south coast where they lived. I was born right in the middle of an air raid at the end of the war.

Soon after that, however, when the more immediate effects of the Civil War, but not the rubble of the second war, had been cleaned up, the British started to look south. They were eager to enjoy themselves after years of crisis and rationing. My father wanted to join the crowds that began to flock to the Costa Brava, but my mother, from whom I must have inherited my deep attachment to places, held out staunchly: she knew it wouldn't be the same. From time to time, she would produce as proof some picture in the travel section of the Sunday paper; Lloret de Mar, or, worse, Tossa, the tiny fishing village she had once loved, which was now a center for "package tours." Its shoddy hotels and fish-and-chips shops now catered particularly to the British.

I don't know what finally changed her mind. Perhaps my father's insistence wore her down, just as it did a few years later when she reluctantly agreed to go on the Christmas cruise ship that caught fire, killing them both. Or perhaps it was the fact that the Kings, who had been good friends in their Barcelona days, were also planning a holiday in Caldetas, a small place on the coast north of Barcelona. My mother knew this place well because many of the wives and children in the British colony used to spend their summers there, while the men worked in Barcelona and commuted out to their families by train on the weekends.

At the time of our first holiday back there, I had only the vaguest sense of their previous life in Spain, and a teenager's lack of imagination about the separate existence of parents. Later, I realized that Caldetas was a perfect choice, however much it deviated from the standard image of an attractive Mediterranean resort.

The town, at the time of that first holiday, was an unruly mixture of the old and the new, with the old giving up very little room to the new (which was why it suited my mother so well). Built along a straight stretch of beach, with no pretty coves or rocky inlets like those that occur further north, Caldetas, in an odd way, reminded me of my home town, Brighton. Both had a lively, rough-and-tumble center unconnected to the tourism that flowed around it. Both had areas of decaying grandeur, stately architecture, and wide esplanades where crowds of people strolled. If Jane Austen had written about Spain, it would have been Caldetas to which the flighty young woman ran away with her handsome young officer, for both Caldetas and Brighton were *watering places* at heart, no matter how hard they tried to become university towns or tourist spots, or conference centers.

Caldetas was hardly peaceful, even in the fifties. The coastal highway, which later became a six lane freeway built up on concrete supports sprouting right out of the park, even then intersected the town in such a way as to shake every building, as huge lorries trundled from France to Barcelona and points south. Trains, too, whistled through, following the straight line of the coast on rails that, outside the town, were dangerously unprotected. Every year a few unwary locals or tourists were killed as they hurried home from the beach or took a short cut to the shops. In the town itself, each time a train came through, traffic on the maze of narrow streets would be halted, as railway crossing barriers descended with a din of warning bells that could be heard five miles west in the hills. Yet despite all this commotion, despite the sense of being built in the middle of a journey from somewhere to somewhere else, Caldetas retained a certain dignity — an untouched core of old-fashioned tranquility.

Nowhere was this more apparent than at the Hotel Colon, a massive off-white Victorian structure, with curved balustrades around its huge terrace. It was situated exactly in the middle of the seafront, with nondescript sandy beaches stretching away in each direction, all backed by the huge boulders that protected the seafront from encroaching tides and winter storms.

Right behind the hotel was the park, a shady, gravel area with a couple of small fish ponds and palm trees, flanked by the municipal tennis court, miniature golf, and an open-air bowling alley. From the back of the Colon, you could cross the park where nannies sat together on benches in the afternoon, while their charges, babies of the affluent Spaniards who still owned some of the grand seafront villas, slept in prams covered with white gauze. Just a few steps away, between the miniature golf and the bowling, squatted a rowdy bar, patronized in the afternoons by tourists waiting for the alleys to open after siesta, a few gray-shirted workmen, and unemployed teenage toughs.

But the Hotel Colon, despite its proximity to Caldetas low-life, was grandly elegant. You had only to walk up the semicircular steps from the esplanade, on to the black and white tiles of the terrace bar, to find yourself moving back in time. Although it never, as far as I know, had an orchestra playing at tea-time, it had the shady gentility, the reliable aspidistras, and the haughty staff that called for old violinists in moth-eaten morning coats. The usual clientele of business men and retired British and German couples was interspersed with very old, apparently very rich, regulars. There was the ninety-year-old who sat at her special table overlooking the beach, peering critically at the label on her bottle of wine over an enormous hooked nose. And there were old men too, carrying polished canes, one even wearing spats: Germans, Spaniards from Madrid, and an occasional Italian, all regulars for who knows how many years?

That first year with my parents, I don't think we set foot inside the Colon, though I could see enough from the esplanade to form an accurate picture of the clientele. Years later, after my parents' death, when

I had a job about fifty miles north of Caldetas, my mother's friend Germaine, one of the prolific King family who had been with us that first year, stayed at the Colon with her friend Mary. Germaine was sad: her good friend, my mother, was dead, our large family holidays were over, the children of my generation married or dispersed. So the two old women sank into comfortable nostalgia at the Colon, where I went many times to visit them and ate dinner in the dining room with its straight-backed, carved chairs.

But that first summer, my parents and I stayed at the Hotel Titus, a solidly respectable family hotel on the northern outskirts of town. Caldetas, whose proper name was Caldas de Estrach, had developed as a spa town, with mineral springs emerging from the hillside and its own bottled water that was sold around the region. The springs still bubbled up, right on the grounds of the Hotel Titus, which had rooms in the basement where elderly people could "take the waters," whatever that meant. The swimming pool, too, was fed by mineral springs that smelled of sulphur and made the water too warm for anything other than languid immersion.

We went back to the Titus year after year, but I never spent much time on the premises, preferring as I got older, to hang out at the park, or to swim at the beach with a crowd of teenagers drawn from the King family and other English friends who still lived in Caldetas, as well as some of their Spanish buddies. The last summer we all went there, when I was sixteen, I conducted a number of torrid romances all at the same time, ranging from chaste and proper dates with the King's son Norman to illicit encounters under some scrubby pines with Thierry, a Frenchman who seemed very old. He was perhaps thirty or forty — I wouldn't have known the difference — and was intent on getting his head up my very tight, straight skirt, while I wondered what he so badly wanted to look at. Looking back on all the inept sex I suffered in the years that followed, I wish I had let him succeed so I could have given those English boyfriends a few helpful hints. But I trod a dangerous path between fascination and repulsion, as I made secret assignations with Thierry and an assortment of young Spanish men, danced in basement nightclubs with "my English boyfriend" (more of a fantasy than a reality), and then staggered back to the Titus, often quite drunk, at dawn, to be greeted by the night porter, exposing himself from baggy blue pants and threatening to tell my parents what time I had returned if I didn't stay and look at his eagerly erect penis.

All that was when I was sixteen, but the first time I was in Caldetas I was more interested in tennis and bowling than in boys. That bowling alley was the highlight of our social life. Every evening after dinner my father and mother and I would walk along the seafront to the park, where we would meet the Kings and various other English and Spanish friends and acquaintances.

The Kings were not actually all "Kings," but we thought of them that way. Germaine, for example, was actually named "Barnett," a name she had acquired from a husband who was rarely mentioned and never seen. She operated a telephone switchboard for the Brazilian Embassy in London, where she plugged people in and out rapidly, chattering at full speed in five or six different languages. It was her older sister, Mona, who made the whole family regal by marrying a man twenty years her senior: Sir Norman King, who was a British Consul in Barcelona during the years my parents lived there.

Germaine and Mona had grown up in French-speaking Switzerland, and still usually talked together in the perfect French which Mona passed on to her three children. Norman was one of these children. He was known in the family as "Toto." I was also friends with the youngest King daughter, who went by the nickname "Foufou." (I found these French names distinctly embarrassing at the time, though none of the Kings seemed to find them unusual, not even later when Toto soared up through the ranks of the British Navy and Germaine kept a photograph of him in uniform in her tiny London apartment, fondly captioned "Toto at his promotion to Lieutenant.")

We used to sit in a huge circle in the little outdoor bar next to the bowling alley, my mother and Germaine drinking large quantities of *Anis del Mono*. Germaine's continental background had allowed her to escape my mother's thin layer of British good manners, so she carried a small bottle of *Anis* in her handbag, from which she filled their glasses after they had bought two each from the bar. Mona, whose marriage to the British Consul had endowed her with greater propriety, tut-tutted at her sister. Germaine, however, insisted that the drinks were grossly overpriced and continued to carry her own supply. In fact, the Kings were always hard up, and only managed these holidays by staying in cheap lodgings — a delightfully haphazard *pension* next to the railway station, where they woke up each time the level crossing came down for a train.

The bowling alley had six lanes. Some were claimed early each evening by means of bribes, because they had fewer potholes in their cracked concrete — or, at least, potholes that skillful bowlers could avoid. The chipped wooden "pins" (which we called "skittles") stood on little round markers in the exact formation of modern American bowling alleys, but in the pit behind each set perched a small boy, chewing gum and swinging his legs until the ball came crashing down with the pins. Then he would throw his legs to one side or the other before climbing down to reset the pins and sending the ball back down the wobbly, wooden conveyer. Every hour or two, a boy would get hit by a stray pin, sometimes just bruising a leg, but occasionally cracking him in the eye or head. If he had to be carried off to the *farmacia*, another eager boy would take his place.

The patrons of the alley were forever screaming at their pin boys, who sometimes appeared not to notice that a ball had trundled into their domain, and at other times stood the pins back up in such disarray, so far off the little circular guides, that the customers would bellow and gesticulate, while the boy shrugged and grinned, as if to say "what can *you* do about it, eh?"

These boys, most of whom were less than ten years old, were paid only in tips from the customers at the end of the evening. Any exasperated bowler who tried not tipping simply could not get a boy the next time he appeared. No amount of arguing with José the bartender, who owned the alley, could produce a pin boy in the face of a boycott. There was solidarity among these workers.

Our party had no problems however. Mona spent hours talking to the boys and knew all of their names and most of their relatives' names too. My mother, who was very tall, quite intimidated them, but endeared herself by occasionally handing out sherbert lemons, and by continuing to bowl every evening despite her inability to hit even one pin. When we arrived at the park, hoards of little boys would run up to us begging to be "our boy" for the evening, clowning for the privilege. Three or four would run backwards in front of my mother, shading their eyes with one hand and looking up with awe. "*Qué alta! Qué alta!*" they would say reverentially, as if my mother's statuesque presence were somehow an indication of sainthood.

It was the women in our party who laughed. Germaine and my mother wove fantasies into a zany humor that was unlike anything I had encountered in my proper British upbringing. In fact, my mother in her new relaxed form was like a different person, and I began to understand the extremity of her pain at moving from this balmy Mediterranean atmosphere to our English life. My father, always quiet in social gatherings, sat next to Sir Norman and drank a beer or two, smiling benignly at the liveliness of our party, which often grew to twenty people.

Once in a while, Mona thought that the hilarity went too far and would gently reprove the guilty party. One night it was Germaine, aided and abetted by my mother, who was chastised after someone bet her she could not climb one of the ornate wrought-iron street lights in the park. Germaine and Mona were both under five feet tall so it made sense to Germaine that my tall mother should boost her up the pole; she would then swarm up like a monkey. Mona, however, found this activity unbecoming for a bunch of fifty-year-old women, and put a stop to it with a few gentle words.

It's hard, even now, to capture the essence of those gatherings — the ingredient that made it such a charmed group, but I know that everyone who was there looked back on it the same way I did. Indeed, we all corresponded for a few years, with letters that perpetuated the mythology of "the group." One year, I painstakingly created a spoof newspaper, with articles that described the carryings-on of a strange "sect," observed, of course, in Caldetas. Right in the center of the patched-together page, I placed a photograph of myself as "Queen of Bowling," holding a ball aloft — a triumph of cut-and-paste, which provoked a spate of admiring correspondence, and a rival "newspaper clipping" from one of the Kings.

Those evenings would go on until two or three in the morning, our party talking animatedly in English, French, Spanish and Catalan, the moon often brilliant above the dusty trees that divided the park from the railway. Then, at last, we would separate and set off for our various hotels. One night, when it was particularly warm, six or seven of us decided to go swimming, and plunged into the water in a burst of green fire, leaving a wake of phosphorescence behind as we paddled around under the stars.

Another night I remember very clearly, my mother and I walked back alone, past the grand old villas that stood back from the esplanade behind high walls and intricate wrought-iron gates. As we passed one of these houses the sound of music drifted out: a melancholy song that was popular that year called "Green Fields." Still to this day, that tune conjures up the mansion with its pungent oleanders, its vine-covered terrace, its old blue tiles surrounding archways and patios. My mother's sadness seemed almost to form itself into words that night, but she held back from explanation and stood instead for a long time outside the gates, looking across the coarse, manicured grass, while the music hauntingly insinuated itself into my memory. Later, I would think of that night as something intimate; a moment shared with my mother in which she told me something about herself without words.

Travel in those days was romance to me. I knew little about Spain or the other countries I traveled through, and nothing about politics. In Caldetas, the poverty, the danger of typhoid from the open sewers that ran down to the beaches, and the Civil Guards who clearly engendered terror in ordinary people, disappeared behind the foreign charm that seduced my fourteen-year-old self along with the music, the sunshine, and the brilliant landscape. I barely knew what Franco stood for, and certainly had no opinions about him.

Looking back, it's hard to know if my parents thought about it either. They never discussed politics, though I knew they voted Conservative in General Elections back home. Still, there must have been at least one discussion of Franco's government since I remember my mother's caustic comment that "at least he's built some decent roads and got the telephones working." Some years later, when I finally began to think, I understood fascism for the first time, and took my mother's approval of Franco's roads to reveal an appalling lack of sensitivity. Now, however, I think it more likely that she was simply reaching for anything positive she could find among the massive changes she encountered in "her" Spain. She hated the invasion of tourists, but could applaud the absence of potholes in the roads; she loathed the modern hotels that disfigured the wild coast, yet somehow felt glad to nod approval at the telephones which linked them to the outside world.

I couldn't help thinking she had exaggerated this improvement in telephones when, in 1965, I was settled into life and work in Figueras, from where it often took three days to place a call to England, and where locals knew it was quicker to drive the 400 miles to Madrid than to wait for a phone connection. How bad could the telephones have been back in the thirties, in my mother's golden era, if she found this state of affairs to Franco's credit? It made sense only when I realized how desperately she needed to like the Spain she rediscovered after her long absence: if that meant ignoring atrocities, turning her back on politics, and clinging, instead, to a few symbolic "improvements," to vivid memories of her past, and to selective interactions with mostly poor Spaniards who never mentioned the war, then that was what she had to do.

As is so often the case with parents who die young, mine continued to haunt me in the conversations we never had. I wanted to ask my mother what she meant about the roads and phones; I wanted my father to explain why he left for good, while his friend Freddie continued as a businessman in Barcelona. Was there some political explanation? Was my father secretly a hero who wouldn't do what it took to co-exist with Franco? I wanted to argue with them, to declare that if I had been born earlier I would have fought with the brigades or driven an ambulance. I needed to witness their parental shock but it never happened. I was too young, too little educated to the world, and they were not the kind of parents who initiated such discussions.

So I remember only the personal things: my father fishing off the pier at Arenys de Mar, wearing his black beret, his white skin reddened and freckled by the sun and his crumpled linen jacket looking like some remnant of his colonial past; my mother turning up her face and hands towards the blazing sun in near ecstasy, or stooping from her great height to converse in fluent Catalan with Pedro, the one-armed car-park attendant, waving her hands and seeming like a stranger to me. And, of course, I remember the place itself.

Only now, over this past year or two, looking at the poems I write, have I realized that places co-exist with people in my emotions. Perhaps it was another, more significant, move to a new house that made this clear; perhaps it was a more general shift away from dependence on people. In any case, I have finally admitted my love of places, an emotional stance I certainly learned from my mother. Though she never articulated it directly, her eloquent use of the Spanish language in our British home and her defiant sun worship in our suburban back garden clearly demonstrated her enduring relationship to that place.

At thirteen, arriving in Spain, I embarked on one of the major relationships of my own life — a relationship with the place. Like most relationships, it began with vacations and falling in love. It moved on, much later, to the nitty gritty of daily life — of knowing and understanding.

Susan A. D. Hunter

ALONE AND FOOTLOOSE
IN THE SOUTH OF FRANCE

LAST SPRING, circumstances pushed me to try traveling alone for the first time in my life. I was living in Paris, studying at the Sorbonne, and had two weeks free during the Easter vacation. I wanted to take the fast train to the south of France, rent a car, and head off for parts unknown, staying at inexpensive hotels and eating at least one very good meal each day. None of my classmates were even remotely interested in such a trip, though I *was* invited to squeeze with ten others into a tiny beach house near Biarritz, travel with a warm-hearted Hungarian and her parents to Budapest, and tour the Normandy invasion sites with a charming German fellow who looked and was built like Arnold Schwarzenegger. All these invitations were appealing, and I must admit I was especially tempted by the German. In the end, though, I decided to do what I wanted most to do: travel through the south, even if it meant traveling by myself.

I wasn't happy about this. I'd always traveled with lovers or friends — not because I'm dependent or lack a sense of adventure, but because I enjoy the companionship and sharing. Although traveling with others is sometimes stressful, the rewards can be immense: by sharing new and difficult experiences with someone significant, you learn more about yourself, about the other person and, most important, about the relationship that exists between the two of you. Traveling by myself, I thought, would deprive me of what I loved the most: a comrade in another of life's adventures.

As I began to put my plans together — making train reservations, renting a car, studying the atlas and arranging a vague itinerary — I realized that a great deal of my reluctance to make this trip alone had to do not with lack of companionship but with fear: *I was afraid to travel by myself*! That last sentence is in italics because, until then, I'd never thought of myself as particularly fearful about anything. But the time had certainly come. I was duty-bound now to get on the road and face up to my fears whether I wanted to or not.

I left Paris with a heavy heart: the weather had been gloomy for over a week, drizzling and dreary when it wasn't raining or snowing or hailing, and all forecasts promised more of the same. I tried to be optimistic, but the continual spatter of droplets hurtling against the speeding train didn't bode well. I noticed a difference in traveling alone almost immediately: rather than talking, I took time to observe the world around me. I spent a lot of the journey watching France speed by, watching the north become the south. The tall and slender chestnuts and elms gradually diminished in quantity, replaced by bushier, fatter varieties; then gnarled trees, growing low to the ground, appeared. The land grew rockier and craggier as the houses became angular, evoking Cézanne. Despite the drizzle and somber skies it was easy to imagine summer's heat and piercing clarity.

Soon enough we pulled into Avignon and within ten minutes I sped away in a bright red Renault 5. My destination for the night was Aigues-Mortes, the walled town from which, in 1248, 35,000 crusaders sailed under the flag of St. Louis for Cyprus. Though once the Mediterranean surrounded Aigues-Mortes, today it stands amidst a lonely landscape of ponds, salt pans, and marshes (hence its name, which means *dead waters*). The town is tiny and — considering it's a minor tourist attraction — hasn't changed much. Aside from a few restaurants and a couple of stores selling T-shirts, the commercial establishments are geared toward the people who actually live there: it's a working, apparently thriving, village.

To celebrate my first night on the road, I splurged on an especially nice hotel, the St.-Louis, housed in a building dating from the town's earliest days. The rooms are cozy, comfortable and warm. From my bed I could gaze through the glass French doors to the town's ramparts and largest tower. I lay there for quite a while, putting off the inevitable moment when I must leave for dinner.

Bold I might be about so many things, but at that moment I was filled with anxiety at the thought of entering a restaurant alone. Oh, sure, over the years I'd eaten out alone — usually a hurried lunch in an unassuming dive — but I'd never in my life entered a very good restaurant, at night, with the express purpose of dining by myself. As I lay on my comfortable bed, I wondered *how* one dined alone: what did one look at or think about, to whom did one address comments about the wine? Wouldn't the waiters find me odd, a woman with an American accent and no traveling companion? Wouldn't everyone in the restaurant stare at me, feel sorry for me? At one point I tried to talk myself out of my dinner reservations: "Why don't you," I argued, "buy some cheese and a baguette, a nice winter pear and a good bottle of wine, and eat in your room?" When I found myself wondering what was on television, I headed out the door.

In the end, it was all pretty easy. The waiters were friendly, even helpful, and the patronne came to my table for a conversation about the differences between life in the States and in France. While I ate I watched a langouste at play in the fish tank beside my table: I've probably never observed another living creature so closely. Even now, almost a year later, I can vividly recall its appearance: vibrantly striped red-and-white feelers atop its head, smaller feelers beside its mouth, five pair of long legs on its underside; the front top half of its shell was knobby and gnarled, reddish-green in color; the back portion red and smooth. If I had been dining with someone, I'd most likely have passed a cursory glance over the fish tank, instantly forgetting its presence. Instead, I got to know a langouste in a way I'd never thought possible!

The only drawback to the evening was the unshakeable feeling of being stared at by other (coupled) diners. Convinced it was my imagination, I delivered silent lectures to myself about self-consciousness: "What makes you think you're so wonderful," I asked, "that people would rather concentrate on you than on each other?" Over time, though, and after many discussions with other women who've traveled alone, I've come to believe that people really *do* stare at the solitary woman diner; she is still, unlike her sexual opposite, an unusual sight. Whereas a man dining alone captures the imagination of few, a woman in the same situation seems surrounded by mystery: Where is she from? What does she do? Why is she here? And, perhaps most intrusive, isn't she lonely eating by herself? By my fourth day of travel I was oblivious to the stares of others, real or imagined, but on that first evening I found such attention rather trying.

All in all, though, a splendid first attempt. In facing up to my fears I not only dined extremely well, but made friends with a langouste and expanded my newly-learned French while exchanging cultural viewpoints with the patronne. One of the waiters, a tall willowy fellow in voguish baggy pants, walked me well out into the street when I left and stood watching as I turned up the Rue St.-Louis. He waved a final good-bye and went back inside. As I walked toward the hotel I glanced at the cloudy sky, wondering, but not worrying, what the next day would bring.

* * *

I was at the town museum bright and early the next morning, soon exploring its famous Constance Tower. Built in 1240, this massive, circular tower is 20 feet thick and still surrounded by its original moat. A gigantic bread oven is housed on the bottom floor, and from there I climbed a steep spiral staircase to the watchtower with its immense panoramic view of the surrounding salt flats and marshes.

A wooden walkway leads from the tower onto the ramparts surrounding the town. Here the sense of history is so strong it's almost palpable. Not only did the Crusaders embark from Aigues-Mortes, but heated battles during the Hundred Years War and the Wars of Religion were fought here as well. During the siege of 1418, when the Burgundians were in possession, the dead were salted so they wouldn't rot and then stacked for months in the small tower (now called Burgundy Tower) awaiting burial. Because I had no one to talk to, I found myself imagining battles and stacks of pickled cadavers, which brought the place alive for me if not for them.

From the ramparts I could look down into the village with its red-tiled roofs and simple facades, observing town life. An old woman poked her head out of an upper window to water bright red tulips in a flower box. A stout old man with a black beret biked lazily down a side street, a long baguette tucked tightly beneath his arm. Two young matrons stood gossiping in the sun-dappled street. I could have stayed for hours, but I had much to see; toward mid-morning, I climbed back in the car and took off with my trusty Michelin atlas to explore the Camargue.

Many consider the Camargue to be the most romantic spot in France. Bound by the Rhone River on one side and the Mediterranean on the other, the Camargue is a wonderland of high white sand dunes, salt marshes and lagoons, and home to wild white horses and black bulls. Migrating flamingoes and egrets are found in abundance at certain times of the year, and the waters contain everything from perch to eel.

First stop on my day's outing was Stes.-Maries-de-la-Mer, where, according to legend, a boat containing Mary Magdalene, Lazarus, and a few other saints washed onto shore one day in 40 A.D. Three of the saints remained in the Camargue and were buried in the church, including Mary, the mother of James, who later became patron saint of the gypsies. Today the town hosts an annual celebration in May honoring Mary; gypsies arrive a week ahead from around the world, setting up traditional encampments and adding lively color to the festivities, which include a running of the bulls, horse races and a dance.

Unfortunately, nothing much was going on the day I visited. What I *did* find were countless tourist shops selling every geegaw imaginable, and dozens of restaurants with the same menu. Whatever Stes.-Maries may have been in the past, it's a tourist town now. The only thing of interest was the rather simple 12th century Romanesque church. I was particularly taken by a dedicatory wall showing photographs of local people who had died. One unusual display was a frame containing two photographs. The first showed a dark and handsome Camargue *gardian* (cowboy, or more accurately, bullboy) in his late 20s, standing beside a white horse; he wore the traditional, oversized felt hat of the *gardians*, which cast a slanted shadow across half his face; the second showed what had been his small car, now scrunched to the size of a trashcan.

I found a shack called Café Camarguais on an obscure and badly-paved road far from town and decided to give it a shot for lunch. The proprietor, with his long scraggly beard and black clothing, was a cross between Charlie Manson and a gone-to-seed Jesus freak. He tended bar while his wife — a practical, Germanic-looking type — waited on tables and tended the kitchen. When I asked if the café offered an exemplary regional dish, she suggested the Camargue specialty, gardiane, a stew made from bull's meat, rough red wine, onion, garlic and tart black olives. I hesitated briefly, confusing the word for bull with that for bullboy; to reassure me she kissed her fingertips and gracefully blew the kiss toward the kitchen. "*Il serra merveilleux*," she promised.

And it *was* marvelous, strong and pungent like the Camargue itself. While I ate, two men came in and sat at a table already set with wine and two first courses; they were daily visitors. One of the men, a handsome fellow in his late 50's , came to talk to me. His first question was: "What are you doing alone?" When he learned I came from California he grew quite excited, extolling first the virtues of all Americans he'd ever known, and then the virtues of the Camargue and its people. He insisted on buying me a small pitcher of the local wine and then he rejoined his friend, a very short and stocky man in farmer's clothes. They proceeded to enjoy, with a good deal of enthusiasm, a large meal of many courses.

After *un express* I headed onward in search of the flamingoes who reputedly feed in the nearby waters. I didn't have far to look. The little dirt road on which I found the café led me right to them and, as I traversed the area that afternoon, the graceful, coral-colored birds seemed to be everywhere.

The day had become quite hot, comfortably so, and the sun never wavered. It was wonderful breezing along by myself. The road changed constantly. For a while I drove through marshland, upon which I spotted bulls, white horses, goats, sheep and shepherds, a thousand flamingoes. The few houses were pale-colored with faded red-tiled roofs, structures molded to the land. After a while the terrain grew lush with tall grasses and bushy trees. I skirted the east side of a lagoon; to my left were tall, impenetrable grasses; to my right, the large body of protected water. Eventually the paved road came to an end and a dirt road continued on.

No debates with my partner about whether we should take the road or not: only I made the decisions now. Not giving it a second's thought,

I journeyed straight ahead and found myself on one of the strangest roads I've ever taken. The road, large enough for two cars traveling in opposite directions to squeeze by one another, led straight across the shallow water. The sides of the road banked steeply downward, protected from erosion by boulders. I drove for almost 30 minutes, passing only one other car. I had no idea where I was going. I was surrounded by water as if traveling atop the sea. Just as I decided to turn back, I spotted an advertisement for a restaurant further up the road; I found this so unbelievable that I traveled on.

After a while the land grew up around the sides of the road, flatter, wider and sandier; further still and the road ended, becoming nothing but a bare track across hard-packed sand. Sand dunes skirted the edges of the sea now, and dune grasses waved gently. There *was* a restaurant there, a tumbledown wooden shack which looked like a palace compared to the rest of the tiny community. It was a very back-of-beyond kind of place, with burned-out busses, hovels — not what you expect to see on a French beach, no matter how remote. I had a small coffee in the restaurant and then headed back the way I'd come.

* * *

The morning was extremely windy and very overcast, and as soon as I hit the auto route, headed toward Spain, it started to rain heavily. As the hours went by it just grew worse: a strained, tedious trip. I hit Collioure, a popular vacation resort, around noon. I didn't like it — too many new buildings, too much traffic — and so I continued on. In Port-Vendres I spotted a heavenly-looking restaurant on the other side of the bay. It was wooden, painted light-blue and white, the kind of place you'd see in Alexandria or Crete rather than in France, with a big sign atop its roof that said "L'oasis." It just *looked* right, somehow, so I decided to have lunch there. The owner saw me coming and held the door open so I could step in quickly from the rain and cold. He was black, formal and polite. A large table of men were having a quiet and discreet lunch; an old couple in the rear, a young couple toward the front. I took a small table before the roaring fire. The view was truly great: in one direction I could see the picturesque town, all white stone buildings and red-tiled roofs, facing the bay; in the other I looked across the storm-tossed water into the sea. A wooden porch ran across the front of the building and I imagined how nice it would be to sit there in summer. Warm and safe from the rain and wind, I felt happy and content with my lunch of cold, raw seafood and hot fish soup.

Drove on to Cerbére, four miles from the Spanish border, where I found a cheap, unheated room in a hotel perched high above the sea.

302 / The House on Via Gombito

From my bed I could hear the ceaseless crashing of the waves, and I had a good view into the small town. The owners were so nice that I decided to eat in their hotel (I was the only guest), where I had a truly nothing meal — some poor firm-bodied fish they'd wrapped in tin foil and dried out mercilessly in the oven, calling it, in the process, *"en papilotte."* I didn't really mind, though: I was happy, I was content. From the dining room I had a terrific view across the water. The rain had abated and the clouds looked as if they were breaking up. As I ate I had every hope that tomorrow would be sunny and bright.

* * *

It was. A lovely *petit dejeuner,* a long hot shower, and soon I had passed over the border and into Spain.

Almost immediately you're in a different place: different terrain, different architecture, certainly different language on the signs. The road led straight up and I was soon skirting the sea atop a high mountain. The sun glinted magically on the water far below; everything so blue — the water, the sky! The land itself held cactus, fields of bright red poppies, vineyards. A morning freshness still held the air and the road stretched empty above and below me. I had no particular destination, and I felt quite happy.

Found a charming bay town called El Port de la Selva, with a couple of small, inexpensive hotels. It was the kind of place that was wonderful to discover mid-week in early April, but I could picture it in a few months, over-run by tourists and college kids, frantic with noise and excitement. On the outskirts of town I found a large parking lot, big enough for maybe 500 cars. There weren't even a dozen that day.

I took a table on the terrace of the cheap hotel, the only place in town that had any other diners. I sat in partial sun; below me to the right lay the bay, stretching onward into infinity; to the left were the old houses of the town and, behind them, the pine hills.

I felt utterly content as I ate this meal, probably the first time I experienced total unselfconsciousness eating by myself. I thought about nothing in particular, just watching the bay, watching the pines; I noticed how similar to the 1930s designs of Frank Lloyd Wright were the traditional houses perched on the hill, and sometimes I paid attention to the people around me. One of the fattest men I've ever seen in my life sat nearby with his sweetheart, a slim and very nice looking woman; they held hands between courses. She had only a salad, but he ate two appetizers, two main courses, two desserts, and drank more than a bottle and a half of wine.

In a way I kind of envied him: whenever I enter a new country and look at its menu I want to eat everything I see and learn everything possible about the cuisine; I'm overcome with curiosity and desire. Here I was having my first paella in Spain and there were so many other things I wanted to try — zarzuela, for example.

I sat there eating my paella, staring blandly at the water, wondering if Frank Lloyd Wright had ever eaten here and noticed the houses, thinking about the cuisine of different countries, wondering what zarzuela was and why the Catalan mineral water was so good. Then I realized that the sun had dimmed and that the clouds, which had been slowly gathering themselves in the distance, were rapidly moving toward the coast. Toward *me*. I took the coming gloom as a message to hit the road again.

This time I headed straight north and was soon in the countryside, caught in a heavy — some would say torrential — downpour. But I was on a small road with very little traffic and enjoyed the experience. Thick groves of tall, leafy green trees and towering pines surrounded me. I repeatedly saw an unusual tree that shot straight up and then sprang out like an upside-down umbrella. (I later learned it's called a parasol pine.)

Suddenly I was in the Pyrénées: I could see mountains all around me, faded purple shadows that disappeared far into the distance. The road began its climb, higher and higher, and soon lost itself within a heavy pine forest. Small purple flowers grew in profusion. The rain stopped and the sun came out, and heavy steam rose from the road which shortly began a descent. Soon I left the forest and drove beside huge meadows covered with yellow dandelions. In the distance I could see forests of tall trees and then, beyond, the mountains. I had begun to think about finding a place to spend the night and thought I'd check out Camprodon, a village not too far away. In my mind's eye I pictured a tiny inn on a quiet road, something removed from the hustle and bustle of life.

Camprodon was not the place to realize this dream. It's an almost-ugly little place whose entire reason for existence, from its inception a thousand years ago to the present moment, was to bed and feed those who, like me, were traveling through. A glance at my map revealed that I had no hope of finding a place for hours if I continued on — not until I reached France — but I decided to take the chance.

I'm glad I did. A few miles outside of Camprodon I took a small side road which for some miles traversed flower-strewn meadows hemmed by birch trees. I passed no other cars. After a while the terrain grew rockier and rugged, though still flat enough to support herds of cattle. I drove through a 12th century village, Rosabruna, which consisted of three buildings. After this the road abruptly descended. It was a dangerous, lonely road, quite steep at points, very curvy. Finally, after what seemed like forever, I caught a glimpse of red-tiled roofs: I'd stumbled on an isolated 12th century Catalan village, Beget, of immense beauty. It contained an early, primitively-built, Romanesque church; a fast-rushing, fairly wide creek that tumbled over stones; and, almost unbelievably, a hostel.

Beget is so small it contains no roads — you park on the outskirts and walk in. But it's no Sienna, no large, car-less town with broad walkways; it's a peasant village plain and simple, lost far from anywhere in the bottom of a valley.

I knocked at the hostel but no one answered. A middle-aged man with a gigantic belly, a burgundy-colored sweater and a vacant expression walked by holding his hands clasped tightly behind his back. We had a sort of conversation, me in French, he in Spanish, in which he managed to indicate that I should keep knocking. I did but had no luck, so I took a walk.

I saw no one. It was very cold — though still light, the sun's warmth had long disappeared from this deep valley — and perhaps the coldness gave this place such a crisp, clean, sparkling air. The village was built long ago on rocks perched far above the creek — integral in the design is a high, arching stone bridge connecting the few buildings in the lower village to the even fewer buildings in the upper village. All the buildings are made of cut stones and most have flat slate jutting from the grout above or below the windows; here their owners place pots of colorful, succulent flowers. There were no stores of any kind. The church, like everything else, was in absolutely immaculate condition, but, since it was locked, I couldn't get inside. The pathways were ancient: cut rocks worn smooth by a thousand years of use; they hadn't been modernized or even kept up in any way that I could see. I walked beside the creek for a while, a friendly dog scampering after me.

Finally I roused the hostel owner who spoke no French or English, but of course you manage to communicate. I spoke in French and he responded in Spanish. The languages are not as similar as one would think, but anyway it worked. I took a simple room overlooking the creek. Every once in a while the man with the burgundy sweater walked by but other than that I saw no one. Unfortunately the electricity was off — further up the road the men from the electric company had been working. This meant no heat, no hot water, no lights except for candles. They would cook me dinner at 8:30, so, the evening having turned bitterly cold, I snuggled into the narrow bed under four blankets and read.

I had brought three books with me: a French-English dictionary, a grammar called *l'Isogramme*, and Zola's *Nana* (in French). This latter choice was a bit foolhardy on my part — I'd been studying French for less than six months, after all, and Zola is intricate and worldly — but it wasn't the first time I'd made a rash, wildly optimistic decision about my abilities and it probably won't be the last. The result was that my nightly reading was, though enjoyable, far from relaxing. I lay in bed surrounded by my dictionary, a notebook to record new words, a red pencil with which to record them, a chartreuse highlighter for grammatical questions, *l'Isogramme*, and — oh yes, *Nana*! I spent far more time with the dictionary than the novel, but still managed to make reasonable progress through the suffering and sufferees of its amoral namesake. Occasionally I wished for a good Dashiel Hammett, in English, but *Nana* managed to keep my solitary evenings lively.

Dinner at the hostel was Catalan Rabbit, which apparently means rabbit that's been deep-fried to oblivion. It wasn't great, but it was interesting to sit in the large empty dining room lit by candles, surrounded by stuffed foxes and pheasants, watching the lady of the house shuffle in and out of the kitchen in her fuzzy pink slippers. We smiled nicely at each other but conversation was impossible. I must have seemed very strange to her: a woman alone, thousands of miles from home. . .yet seemingly content. Her husband came in after I'd ordered my meal and poured me a sherry from an old bottle with a faded label. He poured one for himself, toasted my health, and then he left, not to be seen again until the next morning. After eating I returned to my room, read some more Zola, opened the windows, put a few more blankets on the bed, and slept beautifully in the blissful silence of a remote Catalan valley.

✳ ✳ ✳

The morning was cold but invigorating, breakfast simple but good, the coffee great. I felt a bit lonely this morning so decided to get some exercise — always good for what ails me. After breakfast I walked into the country surrounding the village, passing fields of mustard, thick groves of pine, a tiny walled graveyard and, high on a hill, an old stone building with a cross on top. From afar the village was dominated by the high arched bridge, a graceful work of sculpture balanced between two unmatched halves. Surrounding everything were the mountains. Soon I felt better and walked along with a light heart, the bubbling creek echoing my mood. The sun broke through the clouds now and again, but otherwise the morning was overcast, albeit lightly, and the air held a clean, virtuous crispness.

I drove out of the valley a short time later and entered the Pyrénées. The peaks were snow-covered and the day cold. There weren't many trees here and I could see far into the distance, see the road stretching miles ahead of me through the stark terrain, gradually wending its way upward. I had stopped using the radio days ago so all was silence, just me alone with my thoughts and the surrounding beauty. There were no villages, but occasionally I spotted a flock of sheep or caught a shepherd's wistful glance as I drove past. At the very top, swept by strong winds even on this now-sunny and peaceful day, I found the border station, the entry into France. No one came out or even looked to see who had driven up, so I parked the car and went inside. The three border guards were clad in T-shirts and suspenders, laughing, sitting in the kitchen around a solid oak table with their just-cooked, typically French gourmet lunch and a bottle of burgundy.

The terrain didn't stay stark for long as I began my descent. Soon the mountains dissolved to hills and I moved beside a river. The terrain grew slowly less hilly, then became flat and dry until Cénet, the legendary home of the Cubists: here had come Braque and Picasso in the years of their collaboration. Cénet is the hippest town I've seen yet in France. Small as it is, it has a decent museum of modern art, antique stores, an historical society, a bullfight arena, and quite a few artsy characters playing boules or sitting outside the cafés. I had lunch in the pleasant Place Picasso and then decided to move on.

I'd heard about a restored, privately-owned, 15th century peasants' village, Bardou, where one could stay for a week or more: though it was out of my way, I decided to check it out with the possibility of spending time in the coming summer. By six that evening I made it to a town close to Bardou, Lamlou les Bains, searching for a hotel. In the old Hotel Mas I found a huge room with high ceilings and floor-to-ceiling french windows opening onto a garden for something close to 100 Francs ($16) per night. I cased the town reading menus and finally made myself a reservation at the Belleville.

The Belleville's dining room is the kind you see in movies like "Death in Venice," a large, old-fashioned hotel dining room with waiters and waitresses scurrying madly to and fro. The wall-sized rear window overlooked a garden bursting with spring flowers. The waiter brought me to a small table where, with my back against the wall, I had an unobstructed view of the room. A very old French couple sat beside me eating and drinking discreetly; a younger couple on my other side recommended nearby scenic attractions. I had an excellent meal of oysters and *gigot de la mer*, followed by a salad and accompanied by a half-bottle of the region's spicy white wine. I took my time with this meal, absorbed with my thoughts and the pleasure of eating, and then I took myself off to bed and my nightly romance with Zola.

* * *

I rang for breakfast when I awoke and it appeared, presented by a motherly, clucking type, almost instantly. The same ol' stuff: croissant, baguette, preserves, butter, honey, juice, an apple, a plate of brown sugar cubes and two white ceramic pitchers — one for strong coffee, one for steamed milk. I collapsed with it onto the bed and luxuriated.

It was late morning before I was dressed and on my way to Bardou. I'd heard about the place somewhere, written to the owners asking for information, and had received a nice letter welcoming me to come by. They were frank about its limitations — no electricity or running water, outdoor latrines — but said that's how they wanted to keep it, that they'd worked hard to restore the place from its ruined condition, slowly bringing it back to 15th century standards!

The directions were a bit vague — get to such and such a village "and it's a three-mile walk — you can also drive in by automobile on a dirt road." The village consisted of two buildings with an intersection of two minor (and completely untraveled) country roads, so that you could go in four different directions, all of which seemed to lead nowhere. I finally got on the right road after I'd unsuccessfully driven down the other three. I was surrounded by terraced grape fields, the gnarled vines just beginning to show life; fruit trees dotted the land here and there, their branches heavily laden with blossoms. The day was cool but pleasant, cloudy but not overcast, with the sun making frequent appearances. Every now and then I saw a picturesque old stone building, but no people. The tiny road forked constantly. I took a fork that leveled out, then realized I should be climbing. When I turned the car around, I ran straight into a ditch. Unable to reverse, I climbed out to stick a log under the wheel and found that I'd gone in at a severe angle; the right rear tire was about five feet off the ground.

I stood there a moment wondering what to do: I could see nothing nearby but grapefields and the village was a good three miles down the road — no walking distance, really, but it would all take so much time and I wanted to get to Bardou. Unbelievably, about fifteen seconds later two police meandered by in a little blue car, stopping when they saw my predicament. One of them called for a tow truck while I talked with the other, a woman in her twenties who'd studied psychology at the Sorbonne. She found it tough, she said, being a woman and a gendarme in this remote region of France.

"The people are very conservative," she said, "the men as well as the women. It's difficult to be taken seriously." She added that her partner treated her well and that she had no problems within the police force itself.

We had a pleasant wait for the tow truck, sitting on the roadside looking across the green, vine-laden valley while making halting but interesting conversation. In short order the driver pulled my car from the ditch, checked for damage (none), took my 100 Franc note, and with a lot of best wishes all around the four of us went our separate ways.

At last I found myself on the right road: a very tiny, very old, hand-lettered sign pointed the way. Up and up I went, winding around and around until the poorly-paved track became hard-packed dirt and disappeared into bushes. Suddenly I emerged from the bushes, turned a sharp corner and there, below me in a tiny valley all its own, lay Bardou.

My first reaction was laughter: I thought I'd entered the realm of childhood fairy tales. A large body of water lay to my left — a dam, I later learned. The dwellings, with their casual, meandering architecture, resembled nothing so much as gnomes' cottages, the walls of whitish stone and the roofs of interlocking slate tile. Woodsmoke emerged lazily from one or two chimneys and a peaceful silence filled in the edges. Nearby a handsome young man shoveled dirt into a wheelbarrow and I asked him, in French, where I could find Dean (the person who'd written me).

"You must mean Jean," he said in English, still smiling. He had a cockney accent. "Just continue on into the village. You'll find 'er."

I crossed a wooden bridge, under which a small stream bubbled lightly over stones. A beautiful sheepdog trotted up and nestled against my legs, begging to be petted. I knelt and put my arms around him. Just then another boy, same age as the other, appeared — he too, had a cockney accent.

"Need some 'elp?" he asked.

I said I wanted to find Jean and he pointed out the right cabin. Just keep knocking, he said, she might be upstairs doing something, but she'll answer the door eventually. We stood together a moment, silently appreciating the tree-laden hills, the tiny cascade of water beyond the bridge, the sheepdog, the smell of woodsmoke, and, dominating everything, the beautiful old stone buildings.

"This place is magic," I said.

"Oh, yes. It *is* that." He smiled knowingly and moved off.

Jean turned out to be a woman in her early or mid-fifties, with a beautiful and kindly face, soft voice, gentle mannerisms. She said, oh, yes, the writer, and invited me to stay for lunch. "Why don't you wander around and get a feel for the place before we eat?" she asked.

In the courtyard before Jean's cottage two male peacocks strutted about; nearby half a dozen black cats stretched lazily in the sun. The cottages were all different from one another, some with enclosed patios, one with a terrace; all had walk-in fireplaces and one even had a bread oven, no longer used and fallen to ruin. One or two had running water, a modern improvement to the ancient sinks carved from huge stone blocks. The nearby hills were heavily covered with chestnut trees, a big crop in the fall, and further down the road acres of cherry trees were almost ripe.

I met Klaus when I came to lunch, a tall, very handsome German about the same age as Jean (who is American). They met in France in the early sixties, married, and then traveled around Europe and Africa in a VW bus for ten years with their children. When this grew tiring, they looked for a place to settle down. The minute they laid eyes on Bardou, they knew they'd found their home.

It was then a ruin, but they both saw the village as a lifetime project, and that's what it's become: they've now lived here for twenty years. They raise sheep for money, as well as renting out cottages to "a certain kind of person," by which they mean those who love the simple life, who are content to read, write, contemplate, hike, or swim in the natural pools and falls dotting the countryside. I left with a promise to return in June.

Back in Lamlou I sat at a café with a *citron presée*, watching the world go by. Lamlou is famed for its medical baths, attracting people who suffer severe physical complications; thus sitting in a café here is wildly different than sitting at the average Parisian bistro. Two dwarfs engaged in an intense conversation rolled past in matching wheelchairs. Three very old ladies tottered to a table beside me and ordered Orangina, then lifted their glasses and toasted one another: "*Sante!*" they exclaimed simultaneously, to your health. Dozens of people walked by on crutches, most old, some young. A very good-looking woman pushed a wheel-chair containing a man whose legs were encased in braces; three children marched alongside. A child with Down's Syndrome walked by hand-in-hand with her father. Then two 13-year-old girls, quite healthy and lovely, obviously townies, meandered past. A healthy, happy-looking mother and her five-year-old twins took the place of the old ladies at the next table; the girls were full of life, ordering their sodas with tremendous excitement and flashing eyes. Then came a studdly young man with a punk crew cut and a tight fitting T-shirt showing off his heavily-muscled shoulders; he lurched badly when he walked due to his prosthetic legs. A handsome couple zoomed down the street on a motor scooter, a man drove back and forth in a sleek sports car, two sophisticates in matching sweats peddled along on their sleek bikes.

Everywhere around me were wheelchairs, crutches leaning against tables, metal braces holding bodies together. The street itself was quiet, tree-lined. Dull really, but for the fact that one could see all of life and death here, bad luck and good luck, the results of some celestial being's haphazard throw of the dice.

* * *

After an early *petit-dejeuner* I threw my things into the Renault 5 and
headed toward Provence and a place I'd long waited to visit, Les Baux.
I'd heard so many conflicting things about the place that I had no idea
what to expect: it's an ancient city fallen into ruin, it's a relatively modern
village; the food's awful — no more than tourist fodder, it's got one of
the world's truly Great Restaurants; you'll come away from the experience happy, you'll come away sad. In the end it turns out that all
of these things are true.

Situated on a stark and steep rock spur towering above the gently
rolling Provençal countryside, the land that constitutes Les Baux is about
half a mile long and an eighth of a mile wide, completely invisible from
below. Riddled with grottoes and caves, Les Baux was a natural refuge
from marauders and the elements in neolithic times; by virtue of its steep
site it was a fortified stronghold as early as the Iron Age. It wasn't until
the 11th Century, however, that Les Baux came truly into its own. From
this point on — for more than five centuries — the Lords of Les Baux
were among the strongest in all of France, ruling from their warrior's
aerie over more than 80 towns and villages, dominating all of Provence,
owning Sardinia, winning throughout Europe princely titles and
duchies. This is particularly remarkable when one considers that, at its
height, Les Baux contained no more than 5,000 inhabitants; that they
were a fierce and warlike people seems to be a moot point.

Les Baux eventually went the way of all great warrior societies: it
softened with time and success. In 1483, Louis XI, tired of Les Baux's
great power, conquered the village and destroyed the fortress. Despite
this, Les Baux maintained some of its former greatness until, in 1632,
Louis XIII ordered Les Baux completely destroyed. It was, and the inhabitants dispersed, never again to be a problem. A new Les Baux, built
on the outskirts of the ancient village, rose in the 1700s.

Today Les Baux is divided into two parts: the "new," living town, and
the dead town. If you seek unspoiled travel experiences, you'll find the
living town, with its pizzerias and carnival-like atmosphere, ex-
asperating. There's a bright side, however: you can find a passable hotel
here and at night, when the tourists are gone, the new town is a quiet
and lovely place to be.

But you come to Les Baux for the dead town, the town destroyed by
Louis, among the most haunting and mysterious ruins the world knows.
Atop the rock spur the winds are fierce and they — together with time,
rain, snow, avalanche — have sculpted and welded together ruin and
mountain until it is often impossible to discern the difference between
the two. The streets, the fortress with its ramparts, the castle: all have

become fragments sprouting from the dry and scrubby earth. Here, says the guidebook, stood the imposing west wall of the castle or the main entrance to the fort, but all you see is a broken foundation or a gaping window, a fallen chimney, half of a stately arch. There is not enough left to make a statement, but enough remains to excite your imagination: as you wander around you find yourself stretching mentally to envision homes, ways of life, epochs. The only true signs that people lived here are the holes carved into the rock, "closets" and storage space for the fallen stone buildings which abutted them. Here had ruled a race of people so powerful that it became necessary to destroy them completely; and yet today the only remaining signs of their existence are negative: holes, hollow spaces, emptiness. The extinction of this ancient place was complete and final, obliterating its history; its memories, as Henry James once said, are buried under its ponderous stones.

I spent a few hours wandering about the ruins, and then I sat on the southern edge of the spur and ate a simple picnic lunch: some cheese, a baguette, an apple. From here I had a magnificent view over the southern part of Provence, clear to the ocean, encompassing Arles, the Camargue, even Aigues-Mortes. When I finished eating I stretched out and looked at the dead city behind me. It was true, what I'd heard: at that moment I felt both happy and sad.

The mystery of the Great Restaurant was easily solved with my travel guide: down the hill was L'Oustau de Baumaniére, brought to life after World War II by the celebrated chef Raymond Thuilier. During the '50s and '60s this restaurant was considered the finest French country restaurant in the entire world, and has counted among its past guests Princess Grace, Queen Elizabeth and Prince Charles, and the late Shah of Iran. Messr. Thuilier is dead, but his son carries on his work and the restaurant — as well as the small hotel in which it resides — continues to earn the highest possible marks from Michelin, Gault-Millau, et. al.

However, with my budgetary constraints, such a place was not for me. Instead I spent the night in St. Rémy de Provence, a nearby town with an air of decayed bohemianism. Found a truly great place away from the center — an inn on a dirt road, very quiet — and went back to St. Rémy for dinner. The town's center is a circular medieval village, very small; the "new" village — one street wide — surrounds it. The wooden/brick chateaux of the new village, formerly splendid, are now hotels, fallen to ruin but incredibly charming, draped with wisteria and lavender trees. A few restaurants are located on the ground floors of some old chateaux, and my inn's proprietor had recommended one in particular, the Bar/Hotel/Restaurant des Arts. St. Rémy, it turns out, has had quite a history with the arts and with artists; among its former inhabitants: Gertrude Stein and Alice B. Toklas, Van Gogh, Cocteau.

The restaurant still trades meals for paintings, so the walls were crowded with art — most of it very bad. The proprietor, a small, dapper man dressed in a loose jacket, white shirt and ascot, seated me ceremoniously and oversaw the serving of my meal with diligence.

Had a good night's sleep, drove back to Avignon the next morning, turned in the car and spent time wandering around the old town and the pope's palace until my train left. Soon enough I was back in Paris, meeting with friends, sharing gossip and stories. My travels through the south had become a thing of the past.

I knew, though, that I would travel alone again. I liked the ultimate freedom of making decisions by myself, of traveling down any road I chose, of uncovering my own adventures. I liked being able to watch the world around me without distractions. I liked spending hours struggling through Zola without someone else feeling ignored. I liked having the time to think deeply on matters both important and irrelevant. I even, after a while, liked eating alone. My initial fear — that traveling alone would deprive me of a comrade in one of life's adventures — had neglected to take into account just one thing: I have a good friend in myself. I never really understood that until I spent a week alone and footloose in the South of France.

Jennifer Ochtrup and Monica Ochtrup

ROSENTHALLOHNE 8
An Exchange of Letters

These letters were written during two separate trips Jennifer made to West Germany in 1988-89. In October of 1988, she set out with some small savings and a few addresses in her purse, to visit first Frankfurt and Bavaria, and then, as it turned out, Norden, where she found a "home" at Rosenthallohne 8. She came back to Minnesota in November, as planned, but with an invitation to return to Norden for a stay, which she did from January through May of 1989. What follows is a selection from our correspondence over the period of these two trips, with some editing and supplementary material having been supplied in the service of the reader.

-Monica Ochtrup

Saturday morning
October 8, 1988

Jennifer, Dear Jennifer,

It is just after your phone call to say you are there in West Germany and I am remembering to write. Maybe I am supposed to say mother things. What Are They? I don't know any.

This morning in America I am drinking coffee. It is not quite awake around here yet. Kate sleeps so I woke her to say you called and how it is with you. She repeated each thing: Jennifer cried all they way to Chicago? She freaked going through the security check? She had one hundred bucks ripped off in the German airport? She has a cold? I nodded yes. Yes. Yes. Kate said: Oops.

Right. Now I have one daughter in Frankfurt, one daughter in Cottonwood and one daughter in bed prior to hairspray and I am smoking and drinking coffee.

So. Banks. You say Frankfurt is full of banks and good beer. And you will go to Bavaria. Oh, Jennifer. I cannot help but think you will settle in there; into each part of every experience. Store it up. Send us post cards. Wear yr. hat. I send you all my

Love,
yr. mother

October 20. Norden. Boats. Cows.

Hello Mom, Dad, Kate, Heidi, Katz,

It's 3:00 a.m. and Alex is throwing his shoes at me to get me to shut off the light. This house is run by a woman named Hildegard who is 65 and full of more vigor than anyone I've ever met. She and Michael (Alex's grandpa) are both artists.

The house itself is a masterpiece. From the outside it appears to be nothing more than a three-story brick box covered with unkempt vines. Rosenthallohne (which translates Rosenthal Lane) is just that: a lane. The street is brick and barely wide enough for a car. Houses are lined up closely on either side, many with their yards hidden behind rows of high bushes. So it is at Rosenthallohne 8. Bushes cover the length of the yard and form an arch over the gate which is (and probably always will be) in need of oil. The yard is full of life, with a gnarly tree at its center. I am told that in spring, flowers of every kind are in bloom along its perimeters, including roses in the vines. Doves live in these vines, too. I hear them cooing outside my window in the morning.

There is only one door to the house. It is heavy and colored a rich bluish-green. The top half of it can be opened in warm weather. There are no screens, nor are there storm windows, which makes the house drafty, particularly because of the wind coming off the sea — blowing with such force it whistles through cracks at a consistent pitch.

Even though there are many windows that run from the ceiling nearly to one's knees, I have the impression that the house is dark. Most probably this stems from the thickly varnished woodwork. In the hallways, where the only light comes through stained or fogged glass, the walls are adorned with small paintings of Michael's, each a variation on the same theme. My guess is they were inspired by the sea, all painted in intense shades of blue.

On the first floor there is a small but full library adjoining the living room which serves as a studio, office, and parlor for Hildegard. Some of her work and more of Michael's hangs here. Then there is the kitchen, which is large and sunny. The counters hold lemons, tomatoes, onions, and the cakes for that day's tea, in brightly painted bowls and baskets. Through another hallway is the eating room which is as small and crowded as the rest of the house. There are two huge picture windows facing out onto the garden. Two walls hold bookshelves full of dusty paperback copies of war novels and spy thrillers, many in English. Any space left is covered with rows of small paintings purchased at flea markets.

Upstairs there are four bedrooms, each with its own sink. This is apparently because someone originally intended for the house to be some type of hotel or boarding house. A second staircase spirals up to the third floor where there is storage space and a room which Jörg has built for himself.

I mentioned the sea and that wind. I am two miles from the North Sea. There is a dike here. When the tide is in, it is violent, much more fierce than the ocean. With the tide out, the water goes six miles away. Literally. There is a windmill here. It works, too.

Alex and I will be taking a ferry from Nordeich where the harbor is, forty-five minutes out to sea, the North Sea, to an island called Norderney, where Hildegard used to teach. There are deer on that island.

Today I walked with Jörg to the park which is a little more like a well kept jungle. There were swans and gazebos. It was exquisite.

I'm dying for a good movie in English, and popcorn, neither of which they have here.

So anyway, Hildegard is in charge of an exhibition at the school and she has hired me and Alex to watchdog it for three hours a day. The work is by four young artists from Paris. Mostly we sit, read, and play the guitar (I'm learning). Oh, I'm crocheting something, too. With German yarn. Black and purple.

I do plan to get to the town of Ochtrup. It is in the region called Westphalia where Hildegard grew up. We feverishly combed a map for it one night, (although she does everything feverishly), and it is a good-sized town. Darfeld (where Grandpa Ochtrup lived) is not. Darfeld is smaller than a closet. And yes, it is approximately 60 kilometers from Ochtrup.

Also I will be going with Alex and Jörg and Hildegard to Amsterdam and then to Paris for a few days. Amsterdam is about four hours from here. We will stay with Hildegard's daughter for a day, then it's on to Paris for the weekend, with Jörg, Alex and I driving the exhibition back home. I don't give a flying screw about seeing the Eiffel Tower, but I have no intention of going to France without seeing Chartres.

Love,
Jen

January 1989
I honestly don't know what day it is.
Weds. Or Thurs. Something.

Hallo! An Meine Familie,

This time my plane hung around in Chicago for 2½ hours waiting to take off and we arrived 3 hours late to Amsterdam. The airport there has won awards for how easy it is to deal with and believe me, it was. Huge room. Baggage carrousels. Customs with a handy dandy 'Nothing to Declare' line where you can bypass the other lines 20,000 tired people long. And then, too, they manifest respect for the Divine Concept of Communication, or at least being able to see your rendezvous on the other side of customs. This is accomplished through a simple glass wall, with the lovers, relatives, children, acquaintances, employers and Jörg all pressing their noses to it, waving their arms and signing out messages.

Due to bad weather and delays the luggage got all messed up, so I sat there bouncing my knee and biting my nails. Two sisters from Uganda shared their lunch with me, and one of them gave me a back rub while telling me various Ugandan theories of relaxation. So then, the room emptied and the carrousels stopped and *none* of my baggage was there. Freak!!! A very nice brother and sister (about age 16) who had just arrived from Sydney (they were Dutch) told me what to do. I signed through the wall to a giddy Jörg that I would be right back. Off to the KLM office to fill out forms given to me by a nice fat woman with a tremendously pointed nose. Miracle of miracles there would be a second flight in from Chicago that day (usually there is only one) and it would be arriving within the next two hours. Possibly my luggage would be on it. Who knows? She gave me a temporary pass for customs along with a pat on the shoulder assuring me that most luggage is eventually found. Off to Jörg with hugs and kisses and giggles: "My luggage is completely lost." Hee Hee Hee. "Yes, I know." Hee Hee Hee. He promised me we would not leave Amsterdam without it, or appropriate compensation; but sure enough it came off the next flight. Dusty, bruised, but there.

We stayed two days in Amsterdam. It is not nearly as scary to me now. There is such a feeling of energy — creative energy— there. It has its destructive side, too, but not as much as I originally thought. There is a massive artistic community, a mix of Orientals, Portuguese, Jamaicans, Africans and expatriate Americans who have mingled and formed various neighborhoods. The streets are small and dark, all meeting at a center which is a park, usually. They smell of perfume, curry, marijuana, and dog shit. There are a lot of dogs in Amsterdam. A lot. A lot of pigeons, too, who are so used to the city they usually won't go into flight until you trip over them. I insisted , once, that we walk through this nice cluster of them in one of the central parks. I was hoping to make them all go into flight, but instead they kind of shuffled out of our way. When we got to the other side, you could clearly see the path we had made.

Then, too, there are the bicycles, which are *all* old and rusting. No one can explain this phenomenon to me, and everyone rides one.

The temperature has been in the 50's or 40's. There is no snow and the grass is green. People are worried by this, and books on ozone depletion can be found everywhere. Yesterday's headline in the newspaper said the ocean has risen another 2.5 centimeters, which means the polar caps are melting. Imagine how much water it takes to make the entire Atlantic Ocean rise that much.

In one of the cafes (coffee shops by day, pubs by night) we ran into Michael's old friend, Bepe, a stout dutch woman with silver hair, cut short. She is terrifyingly real and vivacious and friendly — a lot like most folks in Amsterdam.

Now I am in Norden at Rosenthallohne 8, feeling newly arrived and somewhat anxious. Hildegard's daughter, Linda, is here and also her friend, Paul, from Amsterdam who has come to do lithography for the next four weeks. I watched him and Jörg clean the stones yesterday. Jörg is fantastic; fine and sensitive, a good friend. He gave me fifty colored pencils, soft water paints, and this paper for Christmas.

Oh! Also when I arrived here I discovered, to my dismay, the leather bag with all my tapes in it is missing! Did I leave it in the living room? If so, could you please, please send it? If not, could you please write me that I didn't forget it? Could you please write me anyway? Soon?

Jennifer

An Meine Jennifer,

We received your letter and it made my heart feel better to hear you say each thing. The glass wall in the airport; the lovers, relatives and children; the path through the pigeons; the lithograph stones; the terrifyingly real Dutch woman — all of it — each word as I read it on the lovely paper made me feel better. This is good paper from Jörg. It feels good in the hands.

I write this quickly, between obligations, to say that the leather bag, dear Jennifer, is not here. I have looked everywhere and found two cats but no bag.

Just now I returned from going with Heidi to have her cast removed. Arnulf, you know that Dr. Svendson, did it and there was a leg inside. Heidi's. Her leg. Whole again.

> Love,
> yr. mother.

More later. Soon, soon as I can. I promise.

Tuesday, a morning
January, 1989

So then, Dear Jennifer,
The sun is just coming up here, with the sky heavily layered and near the horizon line, shot with light. This makes the trees available in detail, especially toward the top where branches thin and shoot out.
We have not yet received any more writing from you since the first (wonderful) letter. I long to hear how it is. Have you walked again outside the town? Which cows and how many? What trees?
Here I have found the book, *Twentieth Century Watercolors*, which contains reproductions of Emil Nolde's work. I have not before seen any of his work in the original or otherwise and these quite take my breath away. Landscapes and seascapes. The storm. The peasant. I suspect Nolde is the man on whom Siegfried Lenz based his character, Nansen, in the *German Lesson*. In fact, I feel sure of it. The character, Nansen, is an artist who lives in and paints the North (where you are!) − the land, the sea. His paintings are confiscated by the police during the war and he is forbidden to paint. So, too, Nolde. Of course, Nolde (as did Nansen) continued to work in secret, making, while in confinement, hundreds of these small, brilliant watercolors. Nolde called them his "unpainted pictures."
I miss you. How you hang around. And say things.

> Love,
> yr. mother

February 8, 1989

Dear Family,

It's warm here. Like bathwater. One has the feeling buds will start appearing like maybe tomorrow.

Jörg and I framed an exhibition and hung it. Hildegard works ceaselessly on organizing these, bringing in paintings, prints and occasionally sculpture from people in various parts of Europe in an attempt to enrich her surroundings with culture — a thankless job in a town of farmers, sailors and bricklayers, many of whom seem not to have the time or the passion for it. This current exhibit is linoleum block prints. Forty-seven pieces. Half of them script and the other half illustrations. All of them are black on white. They form a story, old and folk, that dates back to the thirteenth century, about Ostfriesland — the farmers there who made a break with the Church. This is in book form also, but we framed the originals, printed on a kind of rice paper. It's thick and feels handmade. We'll be hanging another exhibition in about a week. Two women artists. German. I met them.

So, I am learning to use Jörg's tools and help, especially in building frames. Also, I continue my study of German and sometimes summon the courage to speak it. It's getting hard now, not to be home. Very hard. I have dreams about it and at times I get sad.

Everyone here is industrious, and when the day is done their true talents shine in the beer halls. This is a nation of hard-working, domineering, by-the-book perfectionists, who allow themselves playfulness only when they have a few pints under their belts. I ride a bike. I walk. I listen. I'm learning about what is called art these days. I do the dishes. I sit patiently through conversations in German, being spoken at a phenomenal speed, that probably wouldn't interest me much even if they were in English. And I read. Oh God, do I read. Michael has accumulated a life-long collection of paperbacks in English. I've done Virginia Woolf, cleaned out Saul Bellow, read and re-read all the Vonnegut in the house, and paged through for the umpteenth time the small collection of Carl Sandburg you gave me for my sixteenth birthday. This has accompanied me on all of my travels and is ragged almost to the point of dust. However, I have always found that "Chicago, Hog Butcher for the World" provides a temporary but sure cure for homesickness.

The dike flooded in Greetsiel (the place with the fishing boats) from heavy winds. There are a lot of black cats in Norden. Sea cats.

Now. What about this? Dali died and I was (and still am) in Europe when he did it. Did you know that both Dali and Picasso came from the Catalan region of Spain? Yes, you probably did. I wonder if it's something in the water? Dali's house is in Caraques, a small white village on the coast in northern Spain (another northerner) and the house Jörg and I will stay in is fifteen miles from there. I think Dali died in Barcelona. I could be wrong. (I wonder what he thinks about death; what is he doing now. . .?) I am sending the article from the newspaper here.

I miss you all very much.

Love, Jennifer

A Friday
February, 1989

Jennifer, Dear Jennifer,

And some of the time, now, you feel sad. Do you know, there is a way in which you don't seem very far away at all. No, you don't. In fact, I am sure you are not because I looked and there you were: right under my left rib, Heart. So, hush now.

Today the skies are low and close. If this were summer, the air would be heavy with the smell of rain not yet come. A day with all the promise of thunder. Odd, I should think of thunder in February.

These mornings Heidi comes down into the kitchen for a cup of tea. Some toast. She is moving toward Montana, getting ready for her trip there. Kate stays muffled way down under her covers, mending. She is recovering from the flu. I can feel the healing going on. I can feel Kate healing and Heidi being partly gone.

Yr. father goes out the back door, leaving for work. He puts on that coat, the camel-colored one that always looks to me like it belongs to someone else. Someone who buys Italian shoes and sends his suit out to be pressed. *That* someone. But it doesn't belong to him, it belongs to yr. father who keeps meaning to polish his shoes but doesn't, and hurries into his coat, a little too tired and not waiting for it to settle onto his shoulders and then: is gone. I always miss him. I do.

Evenings come long and early. We spend them together in the company of cats and books.

I cannot put aside the headline from the German newspaper: Salvador Dali ist tot. Here, in America, we don't say that. It might say: Salvador Dali *Dies*, a word that implies action — something still going on. But never: ist tot. Is Dead. Finished. Done. Somehow we can't quite face that. Also, the photograph. Here, all the photographs in the newspaper were of Dali as a young man. Not old. Not scraggly hair jumping out from under some seedy hat. Not the face sagging. We don't want to look at: Old. No. And we can't face: Dead. So it is just revolutionary to see that headline and that photograph.

On Tuesday we drove to Sleepy Eye to bring your grandfather here for a visit and check-up with his doctor. On that drive there is always some thing. This time it was horses, the dark of their bodies dense against the snow.

Love, yr. mother

March, 1989

Dear Mom, Dad, Heidi, Kate, Cats,

It rains here constantly, with every now and again a sunny day, warm as summer. The town is full of cherry blossoms and in the park there are small fields of daffodils. The air and the light have shifted entirely into spring. Sea air. It feels good just to breathe. Eases everything. Medicine.

I go on a lot of walks. I finally found the graveyard. They really did a good job of hiding it away. It is very fancy. Each grave has a marker and even the ones that date from the 1800s are clean and legible. Each plot is marked off by brick or stone and is filled with flowers and plants, like a garden. I think the old graves are so new because markers were replaced after everything got blown to bits during the war.

I found the river, too. I was totally shocked because no one told me it was there. That, too, seems hidden. On the bank that borders the town there are many trees and a path that has been laid which Jörg says was not there when he was growing up. Neither was the wooden arched foot bridge. When he was young the only place to cross the river was the train bridge, which was fairly dangerous because it was very active. A lot of Jörg's boyhood naughtiness centered around this place. Jens's, too.

Jens (the older brother, by 16 months) has a wife and two angelic blonde daughters who hide behind Jörg's leg whenever we come to visit. The littlest one — Anja — was terrified of my big red hair when we first met. She asked her mother if I was a Hexe, a Witch — and wailed until I finally put my hair back.

Jens is in the process of building a house in Hage (a town that is more or less connected to Norden). I have watched it from the foundation up, with all the masons in their dungarees and fisherman's caps with ruddy, cocky faces speaking Plattdeutsch and drinking Flensburger beer until they come home drunk at dinner. Plattdeutsch is a kind of

German slang, closer to Dutch than German. It's Ostfriesen and is used by handworkers, sailors, trainmen, and jocular old women, including
Jörg's grandmother, whose house is full of tea sets, doilies, plastic flowers,
and a parakeet that never shuts up. She is funny and smiles a lot and
Jörg loves her. Jörg is privy to Plattdeutsch because his family belongs
to the handworking caste. He is the first from among them to go to
college.

Two weeks ago there was a party held at the house site to mark the
halfway-done point. This is traditional and during the party everyone
helps to build a wooden cross (not religious) which is nailed to the roof
beam so they can hang empty bottles of Corvit (a corn liquor that tastes
like Hell) from it.

The cat — Pauli— is pregnant. I like her fur. It's short and black (white
feet) but very, very thick. Sea-North Cat. Her belly is getting big and
she's losing her sleekness. When she stands or sits up, she has to spread
her feet far apart in a stance our Rimski sometimes takes that reminds
me of an Italian hustler in a pool hall.

I enclose pictures of me and Jörg taken by a man named Dieter, while
we were sitting around his kitchen table. Dieter is a little man with elfin
tendencies and is one of the few people I feel truly comfortable with
here. I send as well the picture I took of him and his little daughter, so
you can see their faces. She is ten times as elfish as he and they love
each other dearly.

Jennifer

Saturday
Dusk
March 11, 1989

Actually, Dear Jennifer —

We had quite an extraordinary day. It was so sort of mild with that
March wind and some kind of dispersed fog in the air making the light
and everything you see through it look: softened. We were up early,
determined to walk, and began at Minnehaha Falls in which there is
a small trickle starting to the left toward center. You can hear it. So we
talked to the Falls — yr. father and I — wishing it well in its melt and
a full run for the summer. We walked a long time on all that land around
the creek and the river, and we could see the lay of the land as we went,
because of the snow cover and the strange light on the mild day, and

also because the trees did not stand out separate and black as they do in winter, but were softened and merged in their new spring grey. Something is happening in them. I think it's Sap.

Love, yr. mother

Hello Dear Family,
    This is Saturday, April 1st. Jörg and I did the drive to Ochtrup. Perhaps because it bears our name I was expecting something spectacular, or at least interesting. In reality it's quite common. It is a farming town, just like all the other towns in Westphalia where it is located. It has its meadows and pastures, its sheep and black-spotted heifers, and, of course, the pointed steeple of the church as its center. The only original place I found is in the park. Standing in the middle of this rolling green there is a mansion which now houses a restaurant, among other things. It is said to have been built by the founder of the town. (Could this be an ancestor?) The drive was pleasant, but sad because I will be leaving in a handful of days.
    As I began to pack my things, I found this card I meant to send with its print of a street in old Norden. You can see the church in the forefront. It's a church that isn't there anymore. Long gone. But there are other churches. (There are always other churches.) Two, that I know of. The large, grand one (which never seems to be open) is Episcopalian or Evangelical or Something. Funny how I always assumed it was Catholic. Anyway, it has a bell that wrings (rings) out the time. It hasn't got much of a tone. No ding or bong. It's really kind of a clang. Rings the note of G, I think. Not majestic or musical or even pleasant. Just a big old bell that rings out time. I like it. The other church is Catholic and smaller. It's about a block away and has a ton of bells. It belches bells. They all ring at once and create this echo — this vibrating after-tone, that makes one's teeth sting.
    I'll write my dates home as soon as I get them. I love you all.

Jennifer

•

An afterward . . .

Our daughter, Jennifer, comes home from her trip to West Germany. She has spent much of it, having found a home, in Norden, a mile and a half from the North Sea. Norden. Norddeich. Norderney. It is a music that continues. The town. The harbor preceded by the dyke. And the island in the sea. Cows. Boats. It does not stop. The town goes into the land goes into the sea comes into the land comes into the town and the people make a life by it.

In a house in Norden a child is born midwifed by his grandmother. He grows up, leaves the town for schooling, comes back. He will leave town again, but meantime has his tools. With his father, the carpenter, he builds houses. The tool box he keeps near his bed. It is elaborate. Pulls up into many trays. His good friend the sculptor has also done his schooling and now for the past eighteen months looks for an apprenticeship. While the American is there, he finds it. The celebration that night in the Borka is noisy. The American lights her cigarette from a candle on the table. People look up. Conversation stops. When you take light from the candle a sailor dies at sea.

Sharon Chmielarz

A LOOK AT BORDERS

Travel to Schleswig Holstein and Berlin, 1988
In western Iowa, in Ida County, lies a town named Holstein, of interest mainly to buffs of German-American history. Holstein is a point to which many Germans emigrated from Schleswig-Holstein, the northernmost state in the Federal Republic of Germany. It is a place of attics and trunks and sepia-colored photographs in albums. Turn the thick, black leaves and find a young woman in long brown dress, with mock orange flowers in her bridal cap. She stands with her hand on the shoulder of the groom. He sits, tense, ready to bolt at the Midwest's alarm words — hail, fire, snow, love.

One of these wedding pictures is of my maternal grandmother, Margarete Speck. When she was eighteen she boarded the *Gross Bismarck I* with her cousin, Marie Neumann, sailed from Kiel to New York, took a train out to Holstein, Iowa, and in 1894 married a man twelve years older than she. For the rest of his life, she took care of him, raised their seven children, worked and lived on one rented farm after another. When her husband died she settled on her own small farm in North Dakota.

Materially Marie fared better. She stayed in New York, became a dressmaker, and when she was considerably wealthier than my grandmother, sailed back to Germany, moved into a posh hotel and announced to her relatives that they could come and visit her. But it has been my grandmother, Margarete, who has been my impetus to travel to Germany.

Through my mother's stories she became a mythic-sized figure. I've tried to write poems about the emerald ring from Columbia, sent to Grandmother by her sister's, Amanda's, husband, the coffee merchant, who regularly sailed from Kiel to South America; a ring given to my mother, then to me; a ring I thought I'd lost once, but found again, like ties to family or tradition.

As a girl I loved imagining my grandmother at her farm, Three Pines, finagling enough egg money to buy a ticket to Minneapolis, 400 miles away, where Madame Schumann-Heink was singing on her 1926-27 U.S. concert tour. . .or was the story how Grandma could not afford the trip?

Over the years her disappointments fade like palimpsest into a scene of Grandma weeping in the yellow farm kitchen on an afternoon in 1941; the Kaiser had died, the Kaiser who had married Princess Augusta Viktoria of Schleswig-Holstein, ending an era, the world she came from.

With a group of *Germanisten*, students of philology, a heavy word we used on the bus to refer to us, an amalgamation of plain, high school and junior high school German teachers, I visited Schleswig-Holstein in the summer of '88. I slept where the group slept, in the dormitory of a police academy, below deck on the sailing ship *Passat* in Travemunde, at an exquisitely clean and comfortable retreat center in a northern, owl-song drenched woods where I would gladly return alone. I gawked with them during our daily scheduled *Stadtbummel* — city walks — through historic centers. I took notes elbow to elbow with them at conference tables in beech-panelled seminar rooms. I posed with them in snap-shots for local newspapers (a group of Americans who could speak German). I even found a place among the cliques on the bus — not in the back where the younger teachers were on the make, nor in the front where the chronic complainers huffed — but towards the middle, among the second or third generation German-Americans, warm-hearted (they made room) but tunnel-visioned in their quest to be 'more German.' I probably even looked (and do look) like them. And at the time I real-ized that all of these people were sharing with me, for better or for worse, an experience I'd not likely have on my own. But my secret motive, the one I used their agenda for and gave up my privacy for, was to ride in their comfortable bus, at a bargain price, letting someone else expend his energy on procuring meals and lodging, while *I*, the eight-year-old from my childhood, watched from coach windows for scenarios which matched the pictures in my mother's stories.

I would see first hand the docks of Kiel Great Uncle Johann had sailed from and Kiel's rain-wet cobblestone streets Grandmother had shopped with her sisters, Amanda and Helen. *I* would ride past the park, the row of flats, the canal where maybe, 100 years ago, my grandmother had strolled on Sunday afternoons.

My *I* looked in vain out the bus window for that Germany. Grand-ma's Germany is long gone, not only because of the border, the two Ger-manys. There had been artificial borders long before. In the heart of Europe political borders have been shifting for centuries, tumbling the citizenry about like jacks. A fateful hand draws — as a result of treaty or victory — a new border and the people in any house or village that sits in the way must suddenly wear a different regional or national allegiance. What is stable is the collection of taxes; but to which lord, which country this year?

A treaty made in 1648 recognized more than 300 independent duchies where the people spoke German. Three-hundred borders to be crossed or broken, all waiting in various states of squabbling for eventual unification under Otto von Bismarck, the Iron Chancellor, in 1871.

In Schleswig-Holstein, an area somewhat smaller than New Jersey, the border has been hoisted up or down, north and south, many times. In 1243 the Danish King Waldemar II seized Holstein, Mecklenburg and Pomerania. Holstein still "moved in a Danish orbit," writes historian Geoffrey Barraclough, in 1466. In 1648 the northern provinces became spoil again for the kings of Sweden and Denmark to divide. In 1659 Friedrich Wilhelm drove Gustav, the Swedish king, out, but by 1762 the north was in Danish hands again, and the border became a problem for the German Friedrich Wilhelm's successor, Friedrich. And so on.

In his water castle, Glücksberg, a contemporary Friedrich Ferdinand addressed our group. When we were all neatly seated in his family's chapel on the ground floor, when we were all properly whisperingly attentive, Friedrich Ferdinand strode down the aisle under the light of colored windows. He looked like a German businessman on his day off, wearing a white Brooks Brothers button down shirt. He carried a riding crop under one arm, and in his left arm the Prince of Schleswig-Holstein carried two books which he thought would be interesting to us *Germanisten*. They were from his library, now museum, and they were, of course, commissioned by and written for and about his family.

The concerns of his family make the history of the whole region — their wars, their borders, their castles, their children, their operas, their books, their dogs, their past. I could read forever and never find the name of my grandmother on their pages. Unless, of course, she had overstepped a social border; then her name might have been in a footnote to a footnote; peasant, maid, seamstress, tradeswoman, Margarete Speck, convicted of trespassing on. . .

Look, Grandma! I'm in the Glücksberg! Sitting on a royal pew, the Prince so close I can reach out and touch his riding britches. Suffocatingly close. I think he's come down to the kitchen to give the help holiday packages. At least, he's passing them around, giving us a chance to touch them.

How did my grandmother retain her love for the Kaiser? Was it pure nostalgia? Homesickness for the family and landscape she'd left? Was it like loving a religion, loving the Bible but cringing at the interpretation given it by some clergy?

After the Prince had gone, we toured his family castle, saw the china, the tapestries, the parquet floors, the paintings, the *klos*, the little closets the royalty stepped into before modern plumbing to relieve themselves (their feces slid daintily down an outside chute into the moat around the castle.) Today the cost of our admission helps pay for upkeep, just as the sweat of our physical labor used to. Still, we can take it or leave it; that's progress: no one forces us to buy a ticket.

After the tour our group leader, Yogi, took the obligatory photo, in color, of our group. Twenty-six smiling faces; three tiers of commoners invited onto the Prince's property, red blood on blue soil, poaching on the past by shooting at it with a lens and taking away a piece of it to hang, acting like royalty who have always had their faces hung like trophies to the past on living room or work room walls.

The present, Grandma, is also a border; into whose space I freely step back.

In Schleswig-Holstein you will hear a joke told by every local historian: "Our history is so complicated only three people have ever been able to understand it. One has died, one gone insane, and I, the third, have completely forgotten it."

Before the flood of what the historian *does* remember, this quip comes as a friendly, non-aggressive opener, a slightly humble pie joke, though one you may have to crank your mouth open to get a laugh out for. A glass of German beer in the hand helps; two even more. And at the long tables in the Germans' library in Apenrade, Denmark, there was plenty. Over the bottle-necks we faced each other — a delegation of Americans, Danes who live in Germany, and Germans who live in Denmark. We smiled over islands of beer slightly chilled and thoroughly delicious and barge-like platters of open-faced sandwiches: cheese, curled slices of sausage, raw egg on raw steak, caviar, black and rye breads spread with creamy sweet butter. We ate, drank, listened. Dry jokes were not so hard to laugh at. Raw facts, delivered civil-service style, were not so hard to ingest. Did we know, a voice droned, that in Denmark and Schleswig-Holstein minorities are taught in their mother language? Did we realize these rights are a tax-paid, fundamental part of the regional laws for Danes in Germany and Germans who, when the border shifted, found themselves citizens of Denmark?

That's very nice, I thought, enjoying the golden smoothness of the beer. Problems solved without war. Swimmingly well done. I tried to imagine this scene in the local Brooklyn Park library, the boardroom's cookies and coffee cleared from the tables for beer.

More interesting was trying to remember where I had seen the faces of these Danes and Germans. . .

"After centuries of warfare, compromise," Peter Iver Johannsen, General Secretary of the Federation of German North Schleswigens was saying to our group, grinning broadly.

Where had I seen this wide-toothed grin, the broad nose, the low forehead? Where, the pudgy man sitting beside him, in the olive-jacket, the Bürgermeister-like medallion on a chain around his neck? Where these breadbasket figures?

Where, but in paintings! Medieval, 16th century, 18th century artists preserving forever the faces of contemporary peasants and guildmen, the step-and-fetch-its of history. And here we all are, again, live reproductions in the 20th century!

"...leaders," Peter Iver was saying, "have surrendered to the idea of working out solutions at tables, not on battlefields. And we've agreed with them on minority rights not on paper but by word of honor." Then he laughed, both rejoicing in his minority rights and revealing the tip of his security's underbelly, "And if we didn't keep our word, the Germans were stronger anyway; what could the Danes do?"

Lucky you, ancient peasant, current civil-servant-leader! Lucky you, Peter, to live today in peace, with your own clean library, clean school, clean house and friends who speak your own language at your table on the 'wrong side' of the border!

I don't ever remember any mention of Danes in my mother's stories. Denmark was a country I became acquainted with through books, a chance encounter on a page with a mermaid on a rock in a copper-green turreted harbor. Then, at General Beadle Elementary in a small South Dakota town, Denmark had looked pure fairy-tale, a step beyond my mother's stories about Uncle Johann's travels from Kiel's harbor, or about her life on Grandmother's farm, Three Pines, a harbor in a sea of North Dakota fields.

Only when our group visited a German farm did I feel as if I were getting closer to the source of nostalgia, Grandma's homeland. Barns, duck ponds, the shoescrape at the door for encrusted cowshit. Not to mention the smell. And beside the farmhouse, gardens. But, ah! As we walked closer my feeling of coming home withered. Unlike my grandmother's garden, where tumbleweeds and love-lies-bleeding — pigweed— strained the sagging gate, Frau Philipsen's gardens were unfenced and sculpted with rocks and fountain. You could strain your eye, but there was not a weed in sight.

Nor did she look like my grandma, the archetype I'd kept through childhood for grandmothers and women, the aproned Amazon with the breadbasket belly. Walking down the brick path to greet us, Frau Philipsen looked much more like the photo of my grandmother I'd found when I was much older, my grandmother on her wedding day, August 25, 1894, the twenty-two year old woman with an eighteen-inch hourglass waist.

Both Herr and Frau Philipsen laughed when I made the comment that North Dakota farmers were fatter. "Oh, we have that variety, too. Retired. They sit and drink coffee all day."

Without question Frau Philipsen's house was the cleanest I've ever been in. "You could eat off her floor," used to be one of my father's measures of a woman's worth. In Frau Philipsen's dining area, though possible, even the thought, uttered, would have been shocking. 'Eat? Off the floor?!'

Tiles, wood and brick, style influenced by Danes, Dutch, Deutsch, softened by lace curtains, focused the rooms' cleanliness and order. As did the computer in the farm office. As was Herr Philipsen's concern for the environment, the seas of fields, butterflies at flowering time and a field-lake he had to plow around.

That landscape was Grandma's Schleswigen normalcy, too. It never included fields that run into a border with the German Democratic Republic, fields with watchtowers, barbed wire fences and armed soldiers. A field lake where on one side a German may not come close while on the other a German may sit and fish; where a bridge falls asleep as if under a spell and stands useless, half in East, half in the West; the border, a barbed line of unseen dots and poisonous dashes under it.

We drove on to Berlin. Grandma, to my knowledge, never visited Berlin. Never saw the woods — der Grünewald — in this city, or Sophie Charlotte's summerhouse, or her husband's hunting palace, its casino, and not far away, the Glienicke Bridge, as gracefully lovely today as it was in the Golden Age when Kaiser Wilhelm's coach rolled over it.

Grandma never dreamt of movies much less Hollywood's and Berlin's directors using the Glienicke Bridge for filming spy stories, or, as exciting, for real exchange of political prisoners and spies between East and West.

Grandma never used force or cunning. Never hit her children. She would have been appalled at a theme like Bertoldt Brecht's in *Caucasian Chalk Circle* where two women pull at the arms of a child to establish possession of that child. Ownership, its rights, and justice are briefly recounted on a carved lintel in the medieval Rathaus in Lübeck. The true mother, fearing harm for her child, lets go of its arm in the tug of war for possession. And does she lose her child? Or gain it with the knowledge that it may at least live. And does this kind of justice also apply to a divided country?

On this latest in a string of imposed borders in Central Europe I imagined the soul of the German nation, a ghost-like apparition appearing in a foggy field in Schleswig-Holstein or on the Glienicke Bridge. Two beings now, doppelgänger, both one-armed from war casualties, meet the Other Self in the mist around the bridge. Would they not be restless with the need to transform the naughty child or the evil man, their dark side, never quite made whole? Would they not want to be treated neither as child nor tyrant, but simply as (hu)man?

In West Germany the striving for wholeness is placated by material satisfaction, stability and acceptance by the other Western partners as an inferior country politically, but as home of Die Deutsche Bank, a superior banking and economic system. The Western influence is reflected in language; words like *Strategie, Opportunist, patriotisch, Sex, Job, interviewen, Rolex, Technologie, detailliert, prüde, Bestsellerautor, Who-is-who* abound in magazines.

In contrast, the one-armed soul of East Germany tries to keep its language free of Western influence; its vocabulary, truer to Goethe's, is a purer German. (If one could only say that about their air!)

Now, in '89, with the '88 trip decades away in time when compared to the flood of events which have washed this fall across Central Europe's borders, I watch on T.V. at home what Grandma personally experienced with her emigration: a non-violent uprising, a voting with one's feet, a raising by footfall of protest against old, unsuccessful social and economic structures. A place — Holstein, U.S.A. — becomes a destination; a place — "golden" West Germany — becomes a home to go to. The young one-armed soul wants what is in the other arm of its doppelgänger (and the West German's artificial arm is made so well, sweethearts can hardly tell it from the real).

To Grandma the spirit of the U.S. was wild and new, beckoning to her across the ocean with its arm in rolled-up sleeves (looking more appealing than the braid on the Prince's), and its thumb held up.

In 1989 the closed Glienicke Bridge has become an opened border crossing, alive and useful again. Leipzigers demonstrate shouting, "Gorbi! Gorbi! Wir bleiben hier!" Berliners picket, "Wir wollen freie Wahl!" (We stay here. We want free elections.) History repeats itself in that borders are again changing. The border-eased Europe of 1992 will also be busy making routes through the rubble of an Iron Curtain which is falling, creating joint enterprises in and freer access to states in a no-man's land which has been unavailable to the West on a passport. Again, it's the young, as my grandmother was, who have had *"die Nase voll,"* have had it "up to here," who are emigrating, stirring the stew of discontent. Anonymously and without weapons, they are changing the course of governments. In the future, the frontier may be the East, land of new economic possibility and opportunity.

Like my grandmother, East (and West) Germans may find democracy at times baffling, but never do they mistrust their yearning for freedom to travel (inbred, ancient as Germanic pagan worship of the spirits in free-running brooks in the Thuringian Woods or Harz Mountains) or to live in their house and town as they wish.

What is dead is one German-American's nostalgic creation of her ancestor's homeland. RIP. What is very much alive, stupendously awakened and heart-moving, is the spirit that led my grandmother to emigrate, to look for a new future, to find at least the promise of compromise like that worked out by Danes and Germans along the Schleswig-Holstein border. (Could similar compromises relieve the tensions between Poland and Germany over Silesia-Poland's western front, land given her after WWII? Or to the pockets of Germans in the U.S.S.R.? Would they be less inclined to vote with their feet, try to get back to Germany *when* it's possible to get a visa, if they were given more rights as an ethnic minority in Russia?)

No more fiats by duke or Parteikomittee. No more artificially imposed borders. No more political black holes.

Borders are shifting. Seismic-like seizures are shaking the imagination, making history at another border between two centuries. Can we cross it, toting our stories and experience, but this time insisting on a fair crossing for all?

Emily Meier

JOURNEYS IN THE HIDDEN WORLD

IT WAS SNOWING when they came home from school. After her brother said she'd gone over three minutes on the egg timer for her "Minute Waltz," the girl stopped practicing and knelt on the window seat, her face against the pane. She watched the snow drifting hump-backed over the trees. In the fading light, the lilac bush reminded her of pussy willows. The branches were gray, and the fat parts she thought were dried-up buds had swollen into glassy sacs that had the shape of lemon drops or tears.

"Did I hear your father?" her mother asked, coming into the living room. Around the chin and eyes, she was more like the girl than the boy, but all three of them had a dark sweep of eyebrow beneath lighter hair, and their noses were nearly the same, a thing they'd discovered early and still confirmed, when they thought of it, front and profile in the hall mirror.

"I didn't hear him. I didn't see any cars."

"I hope he didn't get stuck. David, did you put the lid on tight when you took out the garbage? There. Maybe that's him now."

The woman went to the window. The car lights she was looking at went on past the driveway, and for a second she leaned against the window frame. Then she turned around. She switched a lamp on. "Leah, you'd better set the table. You've finished your practicing?"

"Yes."

"Do you have homework, David?"

The boy was lying on the rug with the cat going up and down on his chest. "No," he answered. He shook his head. He rolled over and the cat fell off and sat up purring and the boy scratched its ears.

"He never does. *I* had homework in third grade. Even in second."

"Set the table, Leah."

They were all waiting now. They didn't say it to each other, but all of them were listening and all of them kept glancing out the window into the snow and falling darkness.

"Hibbards are home," the girl said from the table. "I just saw their lights go on." She put the silverware down at the last place and went back to the window seat. The lilac branches were lost in the shadows but she could see dim house shapes all along the street, the bright rectangles of windows and lights dimming as curtains were closed. Then everything blinked. The refrigerator stopped. It made a coughing start and went quiet again and the whole room, the whole house and street were dark.

"I didn't have the toaster on," the boy said.

"It's not the fuse." His mother ruffled the back of his hair. "It must be the snow. It looked like wet snow. It must be heavy. Maybe there's a break somewhere in the lines. Maybe there's a problem at the power station."

"So how long is this supposed to last? How can I do my homework when it's so dark in here?"

"You told her you didn't have any."

"Well if I did."

"David, you're a lunch bucket."

"Light the candles, Leah. You can light all of them if you want. At least we can still eat." Their mother was down on her hands and knees starting a fire in the fireplace.

"Are you going to cook on that?"

"No. The chili's already done. But we should eat it before it gets cold. All right, David. I know it's always hot. You got me."

"We could pretend this is *Little House on the Prairie* and we live without any electricity at all and that we're waiting for Pa who's lost somewhere in a snowstorm. You could be Ma."

"Mom is fine. And I'd prefer actually, Leah, to think your father will be home any minute and that the lights are about to come back on. You can put the chili on the hot pad and, David, set the milk out. I'll get the salad."

"I bet it was like this outside when Vladimir got lost on his way to get married." The candlelight was flickering on their faces while they ate, and the girl turned the spoon over in her bowl while she talked.

"That dumb story?"

"It's not dumb. It's Alexander Pushkin. He's a very famous writer. Or he was. Is he dead yet?"

"Very. For a long time."

"Didn't he live in the Bahamas?"

"I think your father might have detoured him there when he told you that story. But he was Russian. Like Vladimir."

"I like the part where Vladimir's in a panic and his droshky keeps tipping over and he gets snow way down inside his collar and he's so cold he can't feel his face."

"It's getting cold in here, too. Is the furnace electric?"

"The starter is. Finish your milk. We can sit in front of the fire if you're cold."

"I still think it's gross the bride married the wrong man and that Vladimir died."

"Well at least he finally got to the church."

"I never figured out how the peasant's son was able to find his way in the storm when Vladimir couldn't."

"Wasn't the storm over by then? You can ask your father when he gets home."

"Remember I get to tell him first."

"Tell him what?"

"About the cow those guys at the meat locker were strangling that got loose and came to school and threw up all its guts."

"You are *so* gross, David. Who'd want to tell him that anyway?"

"They were all chasing it."

"We could make animals on the ceiling from the firelight."

"All you can make is a crocodile. That's boring. This is boring. Mom, could you tell us a story?"

"Yes, I suppose that I could." The woman had gotten up from the fire. She was standing at the window, but she came back again and sat down on the rug. She leaned her back against the girl's and the boy put his arm on her knee.

"Let's see. How many different kinds of coins do you have, Leah?"

"I don't know. A bunch."

"Well how many countries have you been in?"

"Was it ten?"

"Close."

"Twelve."

"Right. And it happens that's just the number of countries the people in my story have been too — all on one trip. There're four people — a man and a woman, a girl and a boy."

"It's a story about us."

"They took a trip on a shoestring."

"We took a 747."

"They did too."

The woman leaned forward and pushed a log back with the poker. "Eventually anyway. They started on a DC9, though, and they went on from there to trains. And then they wound up on ferries and cable cars and ponies and vaporettos and a double decker bus that shook so hard their giggles broke. . ."

"That was in Rome. It *is* us."

"The thing is these people seemed restless. It was as if they were looking for something."

"We sure found a lot of stuff. Remember those snails by the beach in Ireland after the storm? Where was that?"

"On the North Atlantic."

"But there weren't as many snails as there were bees when we climbed up Tornado at camp. There must have been ten million! Really. *Bees!* And six girls said they were allergic and Jenny Kidder's even got medicine she has to take if she gets stung plus she has to get to a doctor in fifteen minutes but her mother made her leave it at home so she wouldn't break the bottle. We had to keep going to the next clearing and boy were we hungry. That's when I got the blister on my foot."

"I bet the people were looking for a T.V. How come we didn't stay longer in the room in Barcelona that had the T.V.?"

"Actually these people were always in a hurry. They flew to Reykjavík, to Luxembourg City — all right, Luxembird, David — and they went to sleep in this dark skinny hotel room with carved beds and when they'd slept twelve hours to get over their jet lag, they got up and ate a sausage and caught a train to Germany."

"You can skip Germany. I didn't like that part."

"I was going to — except for the Moselle. Except for Karl Marx's house since it looked so impressive. So clean.

"And these people rushed off again as a matter-of-fact. They went to France and the woman had her birthday with strawberries and *croissants* for breakfast and in the evening they ate dinner in an old-stone-walled restaurant with the sun slanting in golden and warm at the windows, and the tables set with green glassware and giant vases of flowers."

"They should have stayed there."

"They went on. They did Switzerland in the blink of any eye — Basel, Lucerne, a walk down a mountain for another birthday dinner — for the boy this time — a cake with ice cream and whipped cream and more strawberries — enormous ones — and two inch tall barrels of chocolate."

"David, remember that cake!"

"They went farther, deep into the Alps, searching to the end of the train routes until they ended up in — *voilà* — some little subdivision of a ski resort. They stayed in a room in a brand new house with two featherbeds for four people. There were bare white walls. The featherbeds were white and there were white crosses in the cemetery by the graves and pictures of soldiers who'd died in the wars. They left and went to Vienna and in the night were awakened roughly on the train by men in uniforms. The passport control."

"It wasn't the Gestapo?"

"It wasn't. There is no Gestapo now, Leah. Vienna frightened them, though."

"But the English bookstores, the coin shop. . ."

"Yes. And the Rembrandts and Brueghel. They went on anyway. They went to Venice, to the wonderful light, to the pink buildings swimming up out of the Grand Canal and a beautiful, brown grandmama of a hotel owner who smiled and cried *Ciao!* every time they came in the door. It rained and they went to San Marco's and the children played tag in the Doge's Palace and were scolded by a guard in a language that was clearly not up to the task. He looked at them. He almost smiled. *'No, no, bambinos,'* he told them.

"But even that didn't keep them. They rode on to Ferrara. They shared the fruit they'd bought with an Italian who talked to the children by folding paper hats. They raced through the treasures of Florence and then remembered Rome for a beautiful umbrella they saw in a shop window on the *Via Venetto* and for the papist takeover of the Pantheon and for an enormous orange moon over the railway station.

" '*La luna!*' the woman pointed to the ticket seller, and he nodded back, perfectly calm, perfectly placid, as if there were always such a moon — always such a tourist to announce it.

"Still they hurried. They took a rushing train ride up the white beaches of the Mediterranean coast and stopped at Nice for an afternoon, an evening. There were fishermen on the shore casting lines for squid far out to sea.

"Then Antibes. The covered market, the villa where Picasso lived for a moment after the war. They walked among the rooms — among the sculptures and chunky plates, the rising walls. They listened for Picasso as people wait for God in church. And then, in Avignon, a man ate fire.

"It was after that that something changed. They kept up their frantic pace — it was not that that was altered. Slowly though, imperceptibly, the impression that they were running toward something was replaced by the notion that they were running away instead. In Barcelona, puzzling out trains, they passed a sign so often — *A Tarragona* — that they dreamed of it at night, and two and a half weeks later in a tent in Ireland, they learned that a lorry on the coast road in Spain had careened in flames into a campground, igniting sunbathers and campers with a chain reaction of explosions from their own cookstoves."

"A lorry's a truck?"

"*A Tarragona.* Yes, it's a truck.

"*A Tarragona.* There on the coast of Spain a disaster that was only one of many they skirted now with the random charge of their travel — the bomb at Versailles which they missed by a day, the fire in the British Rail sleeping car in the south of England when they were heading north, the arrest of terrorists in London at a cultural center they'd toured the day before. They were in a minefield, somehow, its perimeter drawn by their trip the way cities are linked by routes sketched out on a map."

"Mom, I don't get it. I don't understand. Anyway, this is getting scary."

"Is it? I suppose it is."

"Did all that stuff really happen? I don't remember it. What about Scotland and Wales?"

"I remember the roosters and burros and cows in the field next to us when we woke up in Ireland. And the old man with his bucket of milk."

"I remember when it stormed."

"Yes. And we could hear the waves crashing all night and the wind shook the tent so hard it was like sleeping in a great big bowl of Rice Krispies."

"Mom, what were they looking for? What were those people in such a hurry about?"

"I don't know. I'm not sure. Maybe they wanted to get their money's worth on their rail passes." The woman stretched. "Maybe they weren't really sure themselves. Maybe they didn't even know if they'd found what they were looking for, so they should go again. Maybe they need another shoestring."

"At least the kids would be old enough. How come you took us when we were so little?"

"You were as old as you'd ever been."

They were all stretched out now, their toes reaching toward the fire. They were quiet and in awhile the boy's breathing grew huskier.

The cat jumped them then. It landed square in the pack of them with its tail up, and they were laughing and tussling when they heard the banging at the door.

"What's that?" The girl was sitting upright and the boy held onto the cat. Their mother stood up.

A Tarragona. Avignon. London. Versailles.

Her heart was throbbing at her temples and at her wrists, but when the banging came again, she was in front of the door in the darkness.

"Yes?" Her voice was a question that settled in her throat.

"For godssakes open up, Laura." The sound was broken apart. It was put back together as it came through the wood, and she had the door unlocked and wide open.

"Oh Zack. Oh Zack, you're a snowman. Where were you? I was worried to death." She was helping him with his coat, with his gloves. They were iced like his whiskers. She kissed the snow from his face onto hers.

"We've got a fire." She put a log on, and the children had him then. They were blowing on his face and on his hands.

"Get him some chili, David. Zack, what happened? Right, David. I know it's still hot."

"Maybe the alternator. There isn't a light in the whole damn town. Leah, are my boots frozen on?"

The girl was tugging at them. She was pulling at the laces, and they were like the branches somehow. They were the lilac twigs wrapped in ice.

"There." She had one boot off and then the other, but she kept on at the laces.

"And *there,*" she said finally. She lay the shoestrings on the rug in the darkness. "We've got two, Mom." She looked up, the firelight caught in her eyes. "We could take another trip again and miss the scary parts. Maybe we'd even figure it out.

"And we'd come back safe again. Like Dad from the storm."

"What's she talking about, Laura?"

"Ask her. Well a story. About traveling. Maybe about coming home. Have you gotten any warmer?"

They were lying there, twisted up in a family way and watching two feet defrost. They were watching the fire burn, too, and thinking that any moment now, the lights would come back on.

ITALY

Chitra Divakaruni

THE DRIVE

OUR FIRST EVENING in Italy and we're careening down Via Appia Antica in Uncle's rickety Fiat, the windows down, the hot July air flooding our skulls with the smell of field dust and manure and drying sunflowers and the crickets crying in the grasses. Uncle aims for the center of every pothole. The car lurches and shudders and Aunt, sitting in front, shrinks into the worn plush of her seat and clutches at her face. Your fingers are gripping the armrest, white, but floating in the last of the brassy light I note them only vaguely. *A Celebration*, Uncle yells, *because it's the first time you and your husband are visiting Rome and me!* Yes, yes, I call out. The signs stream past us, Catacombe di Domitilla, Tomba di Cecilia Metella, a few olive trees with sparse silver leaves, large empty fields of barbed wire, exposed bricks, ruins of pillars, towers, the gates of a hidden villa.

Uncle points. *See where the armies marched in triumph.* Yes, yes. And it is a night with sudden fireflies exploding against the windshield, the sweet-sour smell of old wine drifting through the car like a suspicion, the car going too fast, flying through the potholes and years, is it forward or back, someone crying in the front seat, and your voice with the shaking in it saying shouldn't we be returning to the city. Breathing is hard and wonderful. And it's my father's voice now, rising like bells out of a lost time. *Imagine the emperors at the head of the procession, Augustus and Trajan and Nero.* Yes, yes. The road slippery as a snake twisting, trying to throw us off and alien stars hurtling across the inky sky just as in my childhood. So I am ready when the tree looms up, a mad lunge of thorns straight at us, ready this time and laughing above the screams. Is it aunt or my mother? Ready for the jagged glass, the black splatter of blood, yes, yes, the ambulance's red whirling eye, the pale slits of mouths at the funeral, the relatives saying *we knew, sooner or later, this would happen.*

The brakes screech, the car jerks, I fall forward, hit my forehead, it doesn't hurt, I'm still laughing in great gasps that can't be stopped. You make a harsh sound in your throat and slap me across the mouth. What are *you* doing here, in this car out of my childhood? Thorns scrape metal as you throw the door open and pull Uncle from the driver's seat. Aunt is bent over, crying soundlessly. I want to touch the thin ridges of her shoulder bones, but where are my hands? You shift the gears, reversing, getting us back onto the road, towards the city, away from the fireflies, the past. I read the short stiff hairs on the back of your neck. It's going to be one of those nights. Then he leans toward me, a conspirator, his breath sweet and grape-red, my father's. *Remember the gladiators with their shining tridents, the slaves and Christians naked in chains, behind the chariots the wild caged bears.* Yes, yes, I whisper back.

Chitra Divakaruni

TOURISTS

THE HEAT is like a fist between the eyes. The man and woman wander down a narrow street of flies and stray cats looking for the Caracalla Baths. The woman wears a cotton dress embroidered Mexican style with bright flowers. The man wears Rayban glasses and knee-length shorts. They wipe at the sweat with white handkerchiefs because they have used up all the kleenex they brought.

The woman is afraid they are lost. She holds on tightly to the man's elbow and presses her purse into her body. The purse is red leather, very new, bought by him outside the Uffizi museum after a half-hour of earnest bargaining. She wonders what they are doing in this airless alley with the odor of stale urine rising all around them, what they are doing in Rome, what they are doing in Europe. The man tries to walk tall and confident, shoulders lifted, but she can tell he is nervous about the youths in tight levis lounging against the fountain, eyeing, he thinks, their Leica. In his halting guidebook Italian he asks the passers-by — there aren't many because of the heat — *Dov'e terme di Caracalla?* and then, *Dov'e la stazione?* But they stare at him and do not seem to understand.

The woman is tired. It distresses her to not know where she is, to have to trust herself to the truth of strangers, their indecipherable mouths, their quick eyes, their fingers each pointing in a different direction, *eccolo, il treno per Milano, la torre pendente, la cattedrale, il palazzo ducale.* She wants to go to the bathroom, to get a drink, to find a taxi. She asks if it is O.K. to wash her face in the fountain, but he shakes his head. It's not hygienic, and besides, a man with a pock-marked face and black teeth has been watching them from a doorway, and he wants to get out of the alley as soon as he can.

The woman sighs, gets out a crumpled tour brochure from her purse and fans herself and then him with it. They are walking faster now, she stumbling a bit in her sandals. She wishes they were back in the hotel or better still in her own cool garden. She is sure that in her absence the Niles Lilies are dying in spite of the automatic sprinkler system, and the gophers have taken over the lawn. Is it worth it, even for the colors in the Sistine chapel, the curve of Venus' throat as she rises from the sea? The green statue of the boy with the goose among the rosemary in a Pompeii courtyard? She makes a mental note to pick up some gopher poison on the way back from the airport.

They turn a corner onto a broader street. Surely this is the one that will lead them back to the Circo Massimo and the subway. The man lets out a deep breath, starts to smile. Then suddenly, footsteps, a quick clattering on the cobbles behind. They both stiffen, remembering. Yesterday one of the tourists in their hotel was mugged outside the Villa Borghesi. Maybe they should have taken the bus tour after all. He tightens his hands into fists, his face into a scowl. Turns. But it is only a dog, its pink tongue hanging, its ribs sticking out of its scabby coat. It stops and observes them, wary, ready for flight. Then the woman touches his hand. *Look, look.* From where they are standing they can see into someone's backyard. Sheets and pillowcases drying whitely in the sun, a palm scattering shade over blocks of marble from a broken column, a big bougainvillaea that covers the crumbling wall. A breeze comes up, lifting their hair. Sudden smell of rain. They stand there, man and woman and dog, watching the bright purple flowers tumble over the broken bricks.

Chitra Divakaruni

A TRIP TO THE HILLS

THEY HAD BEEN planning to go to Fiesole before they had the fight. The hills would be greenish-gray and there would be pink flowers in the grass. The city with its domes and spires would float in the distance, an airborne Atlantis. They would bring a picnic lunch, perhaps a bottle or two of red wine, a white tablecloth to lie on under the cypresses. She would read from her copy of *The Divine Comedy*. Now of course they weren't going anywhere.

The fight had started in the Piazza della Signoria, right under the statue of David. Or had it been in the Sistine Chapel last Monday when he complained of claustrophobia? Perhaps it had really started at home, with her arguing they couldn't do it all in one week, Rome and Pompeii and Pisa and Florence and Venice and Siena and Naples, and him saying, wanna take a bet? He had been right, of course, and they had done it all, even when she had dragged herself each morning from a different hotel bed with a pounding like stones inside her skull.

Now they are sitting on the balustrade of the Ponte Vecchio, the marble warm under their thighs, each staring in a different direction. There are fish in the water, large and silver where the sunlight hits them. She briefly considers throwing herself off the bridge, pictures his agitation, running up and down, shouting for help (he can't swim), the police, the tragic drowned body with its Ophelia hair being dragged from the river bottom, his lifelong guilt. No. There must be an easier way of making him suffer.

"My legs hurt," she had said in the Piazza. "I just want to sit here for a while and look at the David."

"But the Palazzo'll close in half an hour."

"Let it."

"Whaddya mean, let it. We only have today, tomorrow you want to go to that place Fesole or whatever it's called, did I spend all this money to come sit under the trees, no, but O.K., anything to make you happy, but at least today let's see all we can."

"Why don't you go ahead. I'll just wait here for you like you did at Dante's house."

"And you sure took your time there. What were you doing, kissing the steps? Besides, I can't leave you alone with all these weirdos hanging around. You know what these Eyetalians are like. Look at them, that one looks like he's on drugs for sure."

"O.K., O.K., let's go."

"Now what're you sighing about? Don't you think you could act a bit happier, all these places I'm taking you to see? Most women would give anything for it. I should've just left you at home and come by myself."

"Maybe you should have."

"Next time I will. You can bet on it."

There had been nothing to say after that. Now they are sitting by the water, by the little shops with their trailing window boxes of red geraniums, and night falling. A young tourist in a skintight tanktop and white shorts walks by, and he makes a big deal of watching her, even turning around, all to get his wife angry. Stupid, stupid. And yet she can't stop the burning that speeds up her spine and explodes behind her eyes, the nails that dig into her palms and leave little red arcs. Maybe she should push *him* into the Arno, maybe that would be it. She can almost feel the satisfaction of the push, the moment his body takes on its own motion away from her fingertips, the splash of gray, the fish swarming around with their tiny, sharp teeth. But no, she knows she can't do it that way.

A song spirals through the darkening air, tantalizing, the words escaping her. At the foot of the bridge the black-haired singer is playing a guitar of some sort. Swallows skim the water, the color of smoke. Then she thinks of it. She'll wait until he falls asleep, take her passport and all her traveler's checks. One overnight bag with a change of clothes and her books. Catch the night train to a small town somewhere, go up into the hills with their hot brown smell, the olive groves opening around her like slender fingers of light. She would lie under the orange trees and read Petrarch as long as the money lasted. Maybe she would never go home.

Above her the sky is a brilliant crimson. The river, too, has picked up a pale sheen of the same color. The singer is still there by the water, but now he's turned so she can see his face. And all of a sudden she understands the words. *All things are possible in Italy when your heart is young.* He's smiling directly at her, his teeth like silver in the last of the light. Everything, she knows, is going to work out O.K.

"Let's go for dinner," she says brightly. "We can go to that place near the station that you liked, the place with the hamburgers." He peers at her, a bit suspicious, through the glassy haze of the streetlamps, but she has already turned away and he doesn't see how her eyes shine like bits of fire.

Chitra Divakaruni

TERMINI

WE'RE IN AN immense hall lined with black — black walls, black floor, a roof that recedes into black. A fitting end to this vacation. The smell is of steam and sweat, of fear and time running out, and barred ticket windows spilling out words that run together in jittery letters, *prenotazioni, oggetti smarriti, biglietteria*.

In front of each window endless lines twist around each other. Men in black fedoras and bowties, girls in spiked eyelashes, stiletto heels, coats with huge black padded shoulders. Shriveled beggar-women huddled in gypsy shawls that smell of smoke. Over the entrance an enormous banner dances out *Bienvenito a Roma*. You run from line to line with your pale papery voice, from face to blank face, *Per favore, scusi, is this where I get a ticket to Venezia*. I hate the apology in your shoulder blades, your watery smile. I want to walk from your life into the yellow Roman afternoon outside, opening for me like a sunflower.

But I am trapped in my own line, a caterpillar that inches its sections up to a neon sign which announces, dispiritedly, *Ufficio Cambio*. The neon has burnt out in parts, leaving black holes in place of the o's, and as I watch I feel their dreadful suck at my sleeves. They siphon the air out of my lungs. They pull disheveled hair over your eyes. So that you don't see them coming, the four boys that spring up out of the cement, the desperate thin bones of their hands going for your pockets, throwing you down onto the streaked floor. As through a magnifying glass I see the moving shapes of your lips, *polizia, polizia*. But a whirlwind sucks the words away and the people go on standing in their lines, the women in midnight skirts, the men in their buffed leather jackets. An elbow rammed against your breastbone, a flash as of a knife, your mouth opening like a wound. *Aiudo, aiudo*. I am trying to go to you, pushing, but they stand dense and faceless, a forest of bodies. So hard to get past them, past the cement buckling around my feet like the years we've been together.

The boys are gone now but you're still on the floor. The lines coil past you. Gleaming Bruno Magli boots flash by, transparent Luisa Spagnoli stockings, a heart on a thin gold anklet chain. Is the roof swaying, or is it your voice? I have to bend low to hear, against your thudding heart. *Nobody tried to help. Nobody even looked around.* A bruise on your forehead the color of a rain cloud, the lines of your mouth smudged with disbelief. I put my arms around you and we're both shaking, the floor and walls also, they rush at us like dark glass. The letters are falling off the welcome banner onto our heads like dying stars. They sizzle in my hair. I can't brush off the burning. Is this what love is, this harsh need, this fear clamming our palms, why I can't leave you? *Let's go home,* you say against my shoulder, your whisper white as the Alyssums that grow in our yard. *Let's go home,* I reply.

Patricia Hampl

ITALIAN TWO-PART INVENTION

Venetian Winter

WINTER HERE IN Minnesota is so radical that it seems not a season, but a foreign power marched in to occupy us. The mustard-colored snow-plows that lumber through our white streets might be tanks raking rub-ble onto the boulevards. By January the population has been reduced to the guerilla action of trying to start the car at 25 below.

To be fair: Our winter is a great beauty. At night, cascades of snow-flakes cast tiny ghostly rainbows under the street lights; these prismatic arcs, hardly the width of a hand span, are bled pale except for a lunar aura of silvers and blues.

And each winter that lonely sound, first heard in childhood — and understood even then — returns with its uncompromised sadness: the rasp of skate blades cutting across a freshly flooded playground rink, saying, *solo, we are solo, solo, solo.*

Once experienced, these moments of winter beauty retain a gravity that causes them to *seem* like travel even though they occured just down the block. They go into the album of foreign places where we have ven-tured, caught our tantalizing glimpse, and moved on.

However. There is such a thing as going soft on bad weather. At a Christmas party last year, for instance, a perfectly nice man standing by the buffet launched into the subject of winter camping without the least provocation from anyone. A man who, moments before, had been mopping up his baked brie in phyllo with the best of them was sudden-ly nattering on about a sleeping bag "good" to 30 below. Nothing is good at 30 below.

Travel, too, suffers from the siege mentality. The true spirit of travel is adventure, a quest, not an escape. But in a harsh climate, winter travel gets vulgarized into a getaway scheme. The idea is: Find a stretch of ultramarine sea and a sand beach the color of ground glass. Lie there. Sweat yourself into reassurance: Winter is elsewhere.

This seems to work for a lot of people, but I'm not sure it's travel. Sounds more like a jailbreak. But I may be bruised. The only time I went south for winter, to Savannah Beach, it snowed in Georgia for the first time in 23 years.

I watched from the window of our rented beach house as, every day, a couple in their 50's gamely set up deck chairs on the deserted, cold sand. They drank steaming coffee from a thermos and stared at the metallic sea. Their beach towels hung like oddly cheerful shrouds from their chairs.

I met them trudging back to their car one day. "Where you folks from?" I asked. Looking at their happy faces, I had a sinking premonition. They were faintly blue, stiff from the salt cold.

Sure enough, their name was Lundquist, and by the time we parted they had reminded me three times that, no matter what the Georgians were saying about the weather, it was a hell of a lot warmer where we were standing that minute than "back up there," as Mr. Lundquist put it, referring to our mutual home state.

"We just have to escape winter," Mrs. Lundquist said, obviously satisfied that they had. She sounded a little guilty.

Somewhere between these opposing fantasies of island beaches and aloof snowfields lies the winter trip I want to take. In fact it's one I've already taken. Maybe thinking of it now means it's time to embark again.

What I have in mind is a winter visit to Europe some years ago. There were many winter moments that year as I moved from north to south. In Prague, my northernmost point, I encountered a man dressed up as St. Nicholas (not to be confused with Santa Claus). He leapt around the tatty second-floor *kavarna*, shaking a pine branch before the nonplussed patrons of the place. Then he settled down near the bartender with a shot of slivovice, suddenly as morose as the other habitues of that time-warp cafe.

The next morning, after a heavy snowfall, I was rewarded with the rare sight of the black statues lining the Charles Bridge cloaked in white, as if they were emerging from great chunks of moist cake. I ate caviar at the Hotel Intercontinental with (I decided) a couple of black-market traffickers and their demure, madonna-faced mistresses who drank only mineral water.

Later, on New Year's Eve in Vienna, I heard Beethoven's Ninth and watched the Viennese step into their glittering ball season. I spent a gray afternoon contemplating the wintry Breughels in the Kunsthistorisches Museum. Finally I passed into Italy via the Brenner Pass, sharing a compartment with holiday skiers whose cheeks were all roses.

I had all that northern winter. But it wasn't until the train left the station of the industrial town of Mestre, and we started across the causeway, the spit of land connecting the mainland to the Venetian lagoon, that I was swept into serious winter, as into sudden, but decisive, love.

Nothing new can be said about Venice. Even that statement is a steal (from Mary McCarthy, I think — and she was probably quoting someone else). It's all been said. Venice not only floats on water; it's also sunk in mud. And all descriptions of the Serenissima (the vain nickname it accords itself) ooze out of an emotional response whose substance is just as primal. That primal substance, I think, is wonder. Can this place really exist? From the first instant, it's the city of the unadulterated gawk, the slack-jawed stare.

Venice doesn't feel foreign because it's Italy — it might just as well be Pluto. "Streets full of water," Robert Benchley cabled home on his first visit. "Please advise."

Venice is never "empty." It's been a tourist town for hundreds of years. The Venetians, inhabitants of the world's most improbable city, haven't been alone at home for centuries. Perhaps for that reason, as much as for the famous summer light, Venice clearly pines for summer. That's its professional season, when the tourist industry revs to a pitch, and the violin-rich orchestras play (against each other, it seems) at Florian's and the other cafes that spill onto the Piazza San Marco.

Venice is less visited in the winter. There's a certain cachet in that. A Texas heiress whose apartment on the Grand Canal is near one of the gondola crossing points has developed a method for gauging her escape from the tourist season. Venetians, she says, always ride in a gondola standing up; tourists invariably choose to sit. When, sometime in June, she looks down from her balcony window and can count more people sitting than standing, it's time to go back to the ranch. She returns again in October, when the standers outnumber the sitters, and waits for winter, the real and private Venice season.

The Venetian winter is not kind. Nor is it exactly cruel. There is more grief than malice in the cold clutch of its dampness. It allows you that most romantic of emotions — sadness.

In summer, Venice offers itself to be seen. It presents itself as a gift of light, shimmering and reflecting, full of poses that keep the eye busy. In any season it is a city too grave merely to wink, but it does certainly glint and flirt in the spreading June sunshine.

But in winter, Venice permits a greater intimacy. It can be touched. The mastery of the Venetian fog pulled me through the streets my first evening there. I felt held by the hand, led. The only other fog I knew, the enveloping mistiness of Superior's North Shore, has no body. Unconstrained by architecture, the North Shore fog remains a huge, impersonal weather system, inducing a desire to snooze rather than explore.

But that first January night in Venice, the fog was a lithe body. It darted down a dark *calle*, ducking into a bleak, withdrawn *campo*, where it puffed itself momentarily into a thin gauze that filled every corner, before dodging again down a narrow passageway, where I felt compelled to follow. It paused at a turn where a lantern was hoisted over a doorway. It seemed, hovering around the globe of light, to cause the lantern to glow more richly.

I was led from the train station, over bridge after bridge (there are more than 450 of them). I was without a map in a city I didn't know, a city more mazelike than any other. Yet it didn't occur to me that I might get lost.

And of course I didn't. I was held firmly in hand by the fog. A most paradoxical fog — fine and misty, but utterly certain of a course. The embodiment of travel itself. I have never wandered so freely, not even in a dream. I went where the fog led, and I saw what it wished me to see, lifting its veil by a *menu turistico* cafe, where plates of calamari and mussels sat on beds of seaweed surrounded by eggplants and tomatoes and cut lemons. I looked at this display as at a great tank in a dark aquarium.

In the days that followed, the fog lifted, and the peculiar romance — more truly, the erotic certainty — of that first night gave way to bone-cracking cold. The profound, knowing cold that only dampness conveys.

My (crummy) hotel was cold. The vaporetto rides down the Grand Canal were cold. My rib cage was caught in a permanent shivering con-striction. I fought bitterly with my companion — over which of us was suffering more from the cold. Standing at a zinc bar near the Accademia (where the lighting had been too poor to see the art, and where — naturally — it was cold), I knocked back a double tot of cognac and didn't feel a flicker. It might have been poured over ice instead of my mouth.

I spent one night perched on the narrow radiator of the hotel room, trying to leach some warmth out of it. No good. Venice held me in its romantic, clammy hands.

I did not wish to be released — that was the funny part. Or maybe that was the romantic part. I kept hanging in there for more, no matter how miserable I was. I wandered along the cold canals, shivering and ecstatic.

The garbage barges floated serenely down the canal early in the day; they looked noble as gondolas to me. The ambulance speedboat, the Arab wedding party, the long, low skiff full of vegetables docked by a restaurant, the discerning gray cat judging me from behind a diamond-mullioned window, the great stone palaces furred with moss: I loved the whole daft, unlikely business.

I discovered a confectionary shop where two elderly brothers, bald and pink, wearing spotless aprons, whisked heavy cream and powdered sugar together in copper bowls they held in the crook of their arms, close to their plump bodies. They sold great dollops of this *panna* in paper cones. It was thick, unctuous and cold. Only in Venice would something cold seem comforting. I walked around the canals every day, carrying one of these cold white torches.

I came to understand that I was in love with Venice because I was so damned cold in it. The coldness was a relationship more intimate than any warm-weather sightseeing would permit. I was shaking in my boots, literally vibrating with the waves of the city. It overpowered me.

As I meandered the canals with my wand of cold whipped cream, for once I had no complaints about this life of ours. Bring on the trouble, bring on the heartache. The world is beautiful — Venice is in it.

Water, of course, is the Venetian element. But even water is only the circumstance that makes possible the city's deeper identity. Venice not only gives the sensation of floating. It presents itself as a floating thing that is complete. In spite of its age, Venice is not static, not brittle. Nothing so intimate with water can commit the sin of perfection.

On a *fondamenta*, looking up at a proud, filthy palace where even the lank red mohair draperies looked evil, I felt that what is sinister must be here amongst us too. It all fits.

No, Venice is not perfect. It is simply complete. Entire. It is full of itself, enclosed and artificial, as a garden is — and as vulnerable to the elements and as dependent upon them. The grandiose palaces, squalid with the sludge of the ages, tack the lagoon down to earth as best they can — as best as wealth and power, avidity and greed ever can. But the winter fog, which can go anywhere, reclaims the city every year. It puts its cold hand everywhere, touching.

On the last *vaporetto* ride, which took us the length of the Grand Canal back to the train station, past the Palace Mocenigo, where Byron's mistress, in a pique, had thrown herself into the drink (no harm done; a gondolier fished her out), I was overwhelmed by that pathetic impotence at the heart of tourism: All I could do was look, and leave. Remember this, I told myself sternly, like a teacher instructing children on a field trip as they clamber back into the charter bus for home.

As I stared and stared, reverent with tourism, one of the water taxis, a dandyish speedboat, streaked by, its brightwork gleaming with fresh varnish. The driver stood on the back deck, as at home on the water as a New York cabbie in heavy traffic on 5th Avenue. Inside, the cabin glowed with cream paint and mahogany.

A strikingly handsome man, about 45, sat on the white leather cushions. He was dressed in a rich gray topcoat and was reading, with absorption, that morning's edition of *Il Messaggero*. He never looked up. How can he *do* that, I wondered, aghast at such a waste of prime viewing. He's in Venice, and he's reading the newspaper as he goes down the Grand Canal. What kind of person would do that?

A Venetian, no doubt. Not because he was jaded or cynical. Simply because he, too, was *it*, was Venice. It's not always necessary to look. The most private things happen in the dark.

In the dark season, you don't need to pretend travel is only for the eyes. The cold touches you as if it wants to love you, leading you forward, down the most hidden corridors, along quaysides where tethered gondolas, shiny black and empty, slap gently in the water. You stand there, you close your eyes, and you see it all.

Umbrian Spring

At one time, the little mustard-colored room in my high school where I was sent after lunch to practice playing the piano had been a dormitory room. Years before, farmers and bankers as far away as the Dakotas had sent their daughters to the nuns in St. Paul to be finished — as the rather sinister phrase of the day put it.

But by 1964 the boarders were long gone. We were all day pupils, studying trig, hoping to score high on the SAT's. Most of the old dorm rooms, opening onto a long, dim corridor, had been turned into practice rooms. One, used for storage, was filled with Singer treadle sewing machines from some ghostly home-ec class of yore. And one room, always locked, at the darkest end of the corridor, remained a mystery.

The room was next to a door on which a white cardboard sign announced in stern block letters: ENCLOSURE.

It might just as well have read STOP. No girl was allowed past this door or past any other "enclosure" signs posted throughout the building. Such markers indicated the border, strictly observed, between school and cloister.

The whole place, even the big, walled courtyard, was divided in half like that. Them and Us. "I'll fetch it, dear," a nun would say affably when one of us lobbed a tennis ball out of range into the cloister garden behind the tall hedge called The Maze. It was unthinkable that one of *us* might trespass Over There.

The building was romantic, made of red brick and laid out in an L-shape, with a great bell tower from which the Angelus tolled. There was an arched walk, a reflecting pool, statues, a grotto — the works.

Though it was only a few blocks from my own house, it seemed — and was — foreign. The design of the building had been taken from that of an old French monastery. The fact that the nuns casually referred to their own rooms in the cloister as *cells* only heightened the romance, the oddity of the place. There is something tantalizing about what can never be seen, especially when it's nearby. Even more so when those deadpan "enclosure" signs were posted on every floor, teasing.

So complete was the injunction against entering the cloister that no one flirted with the idea of a raid. It was impossible to imagine putting a hand on the doorknob of an enclosure door.

Yet, the cloister calm reached us. I loved the cramped, yellowed room on the fourth floor where, truth be told, I did precious little practicing. After a few swipes at "The Jolly Farmer" and "Für Elise," I threw myself on the flowered daybed behind the black grand piano (said to belong to the archbishop, who stopped by at times and spent an hour playing things like "Begin the Beguine" and "Sweet Georgia Brown"). The long window rattled in its sash, and I stared down upon the courtyard. I was so high up that no enclosure sign could deny a view of the cloister garden below. It proved to be disappointingly ordinary.

I lounged on the daybed in my blue serge uniform and brown oxfords and considered my future. I had many airy castles in mid-construction. I would travel, I would see the world. It was some kind of oversight, a mistake, that I'd been born in St. Paul, Minn., in the first place. I was really destined for. . . .

One afternoon, emerging from the practice room and my fine plans, I saw that the door to the always-locked room was open. A shaft of light fell across the dark corridor. There was a window in the room, south-facing, and the sun was flooding in.

It's strange, the places that strike one as perfect. They needn't be beautiful. But they must somehow *register*, must touch a core of harmony. A room, after all, is an *interior*: it speaks to the inner self.

The floor was maple, golden, highly polished. Nun's work. There was a small, blue rag rug, a plain table meant to be a desk, a chair. No crucifix; instead, a print of a painting of a ship at sea. Behind it, someone had stuck a dried frond — from Palm Sunday — that curled around the wooden frame.

But it was the bed, I think, that did it. The narrow, white bed, the candlewick spread, the great wafer of sunlight cast upon it from the window.

I wanted to go in there, lie down and sleep for maybe a hundred years. The entire cube (it was tiny, another former dorm room) was engulfed in the light. It seemed not part of the school, not part of the cloister, but belonged to some middle ground of utter serenity.

Sister Marie Therese was placing a vase of lilacs on the table. She had a bundle of bedding under her other arm. She gave the white bedspread a final flick as she came to the door. What was this room for, I asked.

"This room dear? This is for visitors."

"Visitors?" Who, I wondered, ever came here to visit.

Sister Marie Therese took a final look around the little chamber; it seemed to pass inspection. She stepped outside, near me. "Strangers, dear," she said, closing the door, which left us suddenly in the dark again. "We must always have a room for strangers."

Then she opened the enclosure door and went on her way into the cloister, out of my part of the world, the bundle of laundry balanced on her hip like a baby.

Hospitality is one of the oldest missions of the monastic life, one largely forgotten by the modern secular world. We tend to think of monasteries, reasonably enough, as places apart, hidden, off limits. And it's true: The primary work of a contemplative monastery is the *Opus Dei* — the Work of God. That is — pure and simple — prayer.

But the tradition of monastic hospitality is an old one, providing lodging for "pilgrims and strangers," as St. Francis of Assisi called himself and his followers. There was a lot of wandering about during the Middle Ages, much of it by pilgrims and itinerant monks attached to no specific monastery. Such wandering monks, called *gyrovagi*, were a social embarrassment, trading on the commitment to hospitality that governed the great monastic houses. "Concerning their miserable way of life," St. Benedict wrote, "it is better to be silent than to speak."

Today's monastery inns can be anything from a few rooms along a convent wing to a great monastic complex with a separate visitors' *auberge*. Maintaining some kind of hostelry is an obvious way for monastic communities to earn some money. But when Soeur Ste. Agathe at Santa Coletta in Assisi handed me the change from my American Express travelers check after I had spent three nights (private room with breakfast), I knew — if I'd ever doubted — that something besides a healthy entrepreneurial spirit was running the show there.

Italy — no surprise — is especially rich in monasteries that take in travelers. In Umbria, "the mystical province," home of St. Benedict, St. Francis and St. Clare, it seems easy to find convents and monasteries offering hospitality in the little hill towns.

Late last spring, on a hiking trip in the region (destination: Assisi), I stayed one night at the Benedictine monastery in Bevagna. The entrance faced a dark, cramped street littered with cars parked every which way. The place looked as unpromising as the front of a warehouse. Once inside, though, the blank facade gave way to a labyrinthine series of white, hushed hallways that — best of all — formed a square facing a flagstoned courtyard covered with vines and bright flowers. At the center was a fountain. Tucked under one portion of the arched walk was a cash bar tended in the evening by a novice who bore down forcefully on the chrome handle of the espresso machine and urged me to try the local liqueur, made from truffles sniffed out by dogs trained for that purpose.

In Todi, the most beautifully situated of the medieval towns I visited, I stayed at the Hotel Bramante — not a monastery but a *former* monastery.

There again were the mustard-colored walls, a foot thick, the un-mistakable solidity that is a feature of monastic architecture, as though the work of prayer, being so effervescent, requires especially fortified housing.

In the morning, I swung open the inner louvered wooden shutters of the casement windows. The room, which had been dark, was pierced with sunshine. The sharp black-white of a southern landscape. The keen distinction between cloister and world. Outside, the mist that gives Umbria its mystical reputation strayed over the distant hills and the camel-colored medieval towns clinging to them.

After trekking through the region, the final hike brought me into Assisi. From Spello, up and then steeply down Monte Subasio, was a glory of wind and wildflowers. The wind was fierce — not cold, but as if a part of the sun had detached itself and become all blast, no heat. Easy to imagine St. Francis tearing around this exposed exultant spot.

The wildflowers clung bravely to the rocky soil of the sheer rise, then grew lush in the greener, protected dips. A lot of screaming orange from poppies in great profusion. Also wild gladioli, convolulus, grape hyacinth, and a lovely china-blue flower with black markings called, in English, love-in-a-mist. Here and there, lizards sunned themselves on the gravel path; the bleached white pebbles made a dry ticking sound as they were dislodged and skittered down the path in little landslides.

Assisi presented itself, finally, as part monastery, part carnival. The twisting streets leading to the Basilica of St. Francis were chockablock with concession stands selling souvenirs. I looked up from a plaster beer mug made in the shape of a friar to see, walking by, a sandaled friar in the shape of a beer mug.

I stayed at the Poor Clare monastery of Santa Colleta on the Borgo San Pietro — a community from France; the language of the house is French. The monastery has a strict cloister as well as common rooms (a pleasant, shadowy lounge and library with easy chairs and a piano, and a breakfast room with many small tables).

The bedrooms, each named for a saint or some part of the liturgical year, are located in a wing of the main monastery and in a separate building that overlooks, on one side, the convent garden and, on the other, the Plain of Spoleto and Church of Santa Maria degli Angeli. That was my view from L'Annunciation — the Annunciation, my room. Next door, in La Joie (Joy), a man I never saw coughed a racking smoker's cough most of the first night and then was gone — or dead. I never heard him again. I seemed to have the whole suite of little rooms to myself the rest of my stay.

At breakfast I sat with a once-beautiful woman, a retired professor of French literature from Nice. After our first *cafe creme* in the breakfast room, she said she could tell that I was well trained. Trained? I felt like a dog.

"*Chez les soeurs,*" she said. "By the good sisters." Oh yes, that.

I wandered around by myself, in between the proper sightseeing of churches and Franciscan places. I bought a pair of shoes and tried, without success, to use my phrase book to get enzyme tablets to clean my soft contact lenses. I drank coffee at an outdoor cafe by the Temple of Minerva, a refreshingly pagan site in the middle of town — a building that proved, however, to have been turned into a Catholic church. I lit a candle for world peace in the dark interior and again wandered out into the sunlight.

But the truth was, I wasn't much of a tourist. I spent most of my time not viewing the Giottos, guidebook in hand, but sitting on the little balcony of my room, gazing down at the nuns who were cultivating the garden, dressed in their heavy habits, which were hitched up slightly. They had broad straw hats over their veils. Birds dipped and paused, twittering and scolding, very busy about their own business.

I read. I slept — maybe a small version of the hundred-years sleep I wished for that day in high school when I saw, briefly, the flood of light coming from the locked room for strangers.

I was content. I had bought some ham and cheese, a loaf of crusty bread, some figs and wine, and a bar of chocolate at a local store. "*Bien sur, bien sur,*" Soeur Ste. Agathe said. Of course I could have a picnic in the garden. I stayed all afternoon. The light began to fade, going toward Vespers. At five, the bells started up all over town, from church to convent to monastery, a wild cuckoo-clock-shop effect.

I could hear the nuns' voices coming from the choir, chanting a long, wavering line of a psalm in French. I had no desire to go anywhere.

I gathered up my picnic things and turned toward my room, where the simple bed with the white spread, the plain table and chair and the long French window were waiting, just as they'd always been, just as they would when the sun would come flooding in. Just as I would be, letting the bright light fall on my face, clear as a ringing bell.

Mardith Louisell

TOCCATA AND VARIATIONS ON VENICE

VENICE, Venezia, Serenissima.

Serenissima, the name with which the Venetians christened her, most clear, most bright, most fair. Glittery but grounded. The word most like Venice, so long, so slow, so many s's, a little m, a little r, but mostly the s's swishing along, gently, gently, like the lagoon.

"It is truly a city of appearances." Mary McCarthy. Vistas everywhere, but small, tiny, limited vistas, narrow passageways, crooked, broken spokes at the rim of a "campo," the small plaza of Italy, literally "ground." If you stand on any one of the dozen openings at the edge of the "ground" and peer nearsightedly down a corridor, you see a church across a square with what appears to be a false front, then follow a gnarled alley until, after many knottings and twistings, you're on the fondamenta, the long breezeway of the city, sinuous turns behind you, limitless water before you, and islands floating like cakes in a swamp. Space and nagging closeness at the same time.

Line and surface. Things in their proper place. "Please do not touch the fruit," arranged just so — red, orange, red, orange, red — nor the window. I can with persistence prevail upon the shopkeeper and lightly brush the fruit, but not the window.

Glass. Blue, pink, coral, ruby, translucent Murano glass, crafted on the island across the lagoon, echoing itself. Medallions, necklaces, earrings arranged in stores to create vistas and halls of mirrors so that the shops reflect the maze of cramped narrow alleys in which Venetians pace their days.

Lost always. Today the other side of the Rialto, so far west that the buildings actually looked new and then I knew I was too far. Lost is a more or less permanent state here, a turning around to an "aha" of found only to twist again and lose oneself. No whisper of a grid wafts over this city. A short man in his seventies, dressed in suit and tie, finds me one evening after I have followed a trail of people, thinking they stroll to the center of Venice, to find instead I have followed them home to their little doors and large smells of dinner. Frederico walks me out of his neighborhood, over a large bridge, under a cramped archway, up a higher bridge, under brick walls, through umbrellas, in the dark and rain of a Venetian night, murmuring a soft misty hello to people he knows. He knows the whole city. When, after a time that is like dream time, forever and an instant, I find a place I know, he bows, nods and smiles, and turns to track back the miles to the smells of basil pasta and wine where I found him.

Do not bother to talk about directions in Venice. Do not bother to tell a friend where the Filippi poster shop is, the roasted red peppers, the Pesaro family. It is not possible. Talk submerges quickly into surrealistic patter and you find yourself in a Beckett play. Even guidebooks limpidly succumb to the futility of directions. "Off Piazza del Frari" is as specific as you get. Then you're on your own and you can't remember if the Frari is the place where you found the love of your life or where you collapsed with exhaustion because you couldn't find your cappucino.

Room XX, quite by chance, as I race through the stone maze of the Accademia, a drowning woman gasping for breath, guards closing the gates behind me, turning out lights as I run around curves, into rooms and out, under paintings, around sculptures, voracious, American to the core, my eyes devouring what art they can scan in seconds. Against the will of the guards who are crying silently, "Leave them, leave them alone, home, go home," I am running from imprisonment in the 12C. when I trip upon whole rooms, whole walls, frescoed, painted, temperaed, with scenes of Venice as she was when other merchants lived here, parading in their pageants, costumed in their long carnelian and cerulean gowns. Carpaccio, Bellini, two minutes to gobble it up, Veronese, Giorgione, Vivarini, della Francesco, Mantegna, Tintoretto, Memling. Memling? How did he sneak in here?

Constant angles, here, there, under, over. The one-oared boats must navigate canals as angular and tricky as the sidewalks. Changing directions is hard; whether maneuvering a gondola or hobbling home it demands preparation, split second timing and care — no simple turn to the left and switch of lanes. Venetians are accustomed to making quick turns, to moving deftly in small spaces. Even in the arts. The Last Supper, crafted by Veronese, in the face of Church opposition to the secular appearance of the tableau and the presence of Germans in the scene, turns into The Feast in the House of Levi. An about face. Nothing wasted — a few strokes here, a few strokes there and the masterpiece is useful once more. Venice is, after all, a city built on commerce.

Clarity of sound. Metallic tinkles. Every so often a song or a prayer heard through streets from the next campo, around a corner, down an alley, clearer for being so far. The boats lap, footsteps trudge or scurry on bridges. I sense the ups and downs and distinguish them from level clips. Gates close, wooden doors shut, brass knockers ring, arguments echo. No wind here — wind lacks clarity — through leaves or grass. No leaves or grass.

Rainy season. "Aqua alta." 30m high at 7:00 a.m. The Venetians turn out in one body with their brooms and sweep the water out of their stores. First floors are tiled, not carpeted, part of the Venetian's precautionary respect for the Adriatic. They sweep, swishing as the water obeys the shopkeepers and does what it's told — out to the street, into the canals. After all, this is a city where people and water have struck a truce. We will stay here and you will stay there except for the aqua alta. We allow you a tirade every year or so but then get out.

It's during the aqua alta, "high water," that you see rubber boots in unequivocal color, yellow, red, and blue, hanging from the tops of hardware store windows, a gay laugh in the face of the routine swampings. Fashionable Venetian women are up to their knees in color, above the knees their torsos swathed in suede coats. Ugly and rough wooden swampwalks appear in the night — the snowplows of Venice, they allow commerce to continue. Venice, always pragmatic, always in touch with the necessity of accommodating the elements, knows that there are times when beauty cannot prevail and it is prudent not to argue.

Water protocol is finely developed. Umbrellas, at least one million of them, float through the narrow streets, bobbing along, disembodied. Hold them straight up, straight across, do not slant. If I tilt my umbrella, the whole city loses its balance. Balance is everything, analyzed and synchronized centuries ago. Like the gondola and the harmony of life in death, the rainy season has been sorted through. When I make a mistake, when I angle it sideways like *Singing in the Rain*, a chorus of Italian erupts and I quickly get in line.

Please use the umbrella stand in caffes. When I neglect water protocol the owner points to the umbrella stand with his long fingers, and a peremptory nod indicates what I should do. When I lay a wet blue umbrella on his chair, with a cigarette in his hand, he picks it up silently, puts it in the umbrella stand, then wipes the offending chair. I feel as though he would wipe me if he could. I am trailing water into his shop, water which the Venetians agree belongs in the lagoon. As a tourist I have not understood. Everyone should help.

A huge puzzle, Venice. Thousands of islands creaking on piles, temporary artificial legs, approximately the size and shape of pieces in a jigsaw puzzle and as easily separated. A soggy jigsaw puzzle sitting on poles. The stones "strain,/ Crack and sometimes break,/ Under the burden,/ Under the tension, slip, slide, perish/ Decay with imprecision, will not stay in place,/ Will not stay still." T.S. Eliot.* You see how precarious it is.

Restoration is the business of Venice. Memento mori. Although everything is passing, peeling and patched, the city plods along, preens and on occasion drops off a bit. Craftspersons work for restoration, commemoration and magic. A Jewish artist at work in the ghetto says, "I work from the Bible and from my imagination." From form and image. The imagination, always present in Venice, near the surface, intruding, extruding, suffusing, stretching its tendrils into reality, making us pay attention. In Roeg's movie of DuMaurier's *Don't Look Now*, the husband won't admit that whether he believes in seances and spirits or not they affect him here, and because he doesn't admit this he is caught, fatally, unaware. The city is a phantasmagoria, insinuating the imagined whisper, the word left unsaid, the boat, almost seen, slipping around the corner.

Controlled passion and imagination — that's what Venice is. It's also what obsessiveness is all about. "The things of this world reveal their essential absurdity when they are put in the Venetian context. In the unreal realm of the canals, . . .the real world with its contrivances, appears as a vast folly." Mary McCarthy. Venice is funny, a cackle, like an obsessive is funny when you make a movie of him or her but not so funny to live with.

The algae of course have upset the balance for now. The gnats nibble as Venice dehydrates, swarming, constant, overwhelming the brain with sheer numbers like the paintings and the churches, the Byzantine tiles, the lace and glass silhouetting the air, Escher and Gaudi magnified to city size. The frenzy that is me finds perfect recourse in Venice. I run tearing through the stone streets, rubber tennis shoes on my American feet. There is still more.

No cars, no busses, no bicycles, nothing on wheels. My bicicletta sits on its haunches in the car park adjacent to the train station outside of the city, waiting to whiz off through Mestre, a less silly place, towards Ravenna, Bologna, Firenze. What could you do with a bicycle in a city where a bridge interrupts your straightaway every few yards? The specter of a ten speed careening around Venice is funny and horrific at the same time.

I visited Venice once with a friend. She was paralyzed and claustrophobic, the confined streets, the cramped canals, the constricted landscapes, and then the water nibbling away at us, the destructive devious water trapping us, forcing our slow pace, our inability to flee quickly.

---

*Subsequent unidentified quotations are taken from T. S. Eliot, "Four Quartets."

To her it was a nightmare of running down corridors to dead ends and resounding gloom with disaster chasing a few steps behind. It was *Don't Look Now.*

I am never dropped at my door, always at the vaporetto dock. From there I must walk. I wonder, what happens to the old, the infirm, the wheelchair bound, the dying? Where are the ambulances? Even what Venice lacks stimulates obsessive thought, worry, and giggling. The hearse I can picture but not the ambulance. In a city of death, a hearse appears often, the ambulance is silent. Or maybe I have it mixed up with the movie.

Because there are no cars, no street needs to be broader than the widest human being. There are few street lamps, no traffic lights and no stop signs. Everyone uniquely free and confined.

No one can see where they are, who is with them, or where they are going. I certainly can't in the dark streets, snaky walkways, and deluge of umbrellas. I think Venetians find their way with radar, bats after sunset, not too fast and hurried, not too slow, at the water's pace.

At night in the mist, muffled voices, the clackety clack of shoes on pavement, I light upon a restaurant and feel I have discovered a hut in the middle of a night in the Alps. I am grateful, crazy with warmth, bubbling from wine.

There is a regularity even for tourists. I go to the same caffe bar, Piccolo Martini, whenever I can find it, three times to Malibran's for ham and marinated red peppers on white bread, to the same pasticcerias where the same people serve me. To Harry's Bar in '83 and '87, the same waiter both times. Obsessive sameness, infinitesimal changes. I return to the same places inevitably. I must concentrate with all my might to find them, but I do because even I need the certainty they provide, that I am here and haven't floated off into some interminable eelshaped alley leading infinitely to nowhere.

Confinement on islands constrains. "Isola," the Italian for island. Walking up up up and then down down down, go a few feet and do the same, go further, again up and then again down. "The way up is the way down, the way forward the way back." Now I've crossed into the Jewish ghetto after a walk over a bridge, "Sotoportego de Gheto novo." The world's first ghetto. In the sixteenth century, the first naming of the act of isolating, the Venetian love of clarity again. How fitting that these island livers would turn to isolation as a solution.

"Ghetto" seems to have meant a foundry for artillery when the Venetian Republic placed the Jews here in 1516 having forced them to leave the fertile Ilse of Giudecca due to the usual real estate imperatives — the land was beautiful and more powerful people wanted it. The Jews were plopped down here in limited space. Venice doesn't expand but the Jews did — their buildings grew higher and higher. In the ghetto the height between floors is smaller than in the rest of Venice — more people had to squeeze in so there wasn't room for the luxury of air or tall people. Guards watched the bridges at night to ensure no Jew leaped out the windows to passing gondolas.

The Campo Ghetto Nuovo is very small, women in black, children so tiny they pass unnoticed. The memorials to Venetians boated away during the Second World War never to return hug the northeast wall. Seven small bronze reliefs, each the size of a painting you might hang on your den wall. A small tumor growing out of the wall, mottled and chipped, white and brown and beige and ash in decay.

"Old stones that cannot be deciphered." What is compelling, mysterious, eerie, what we love about old places is the sense that many lives have passed through, millions have been here before, and they are watching, rising up from the water, their spirits hovering, slightly damp and wrinkled, an eye lost to the fish here and there, but clearsighted, thoughtful, attentive.

The city lends itself to the neurotic. The water, its hypnotic changes, the labyrinthine besotted alleys mirroring the waves, always changing, always the same.

I obsess in Venice. I must. I can't not. This is Venice, this trying every which way with slight variations, losing yourself so deeply that you don't remember where you started from and where you hoped to end.

I too like to get lost. I like to get lost in my mind. I like to follow each path around and down and over to dead ends and multiple choices leading to more dead ends and more multiple choices. I like to take a question, big or small, and tease it to its very marrow, chew it down to its skeleton. An Irish friend tells me this is the essence of Americans. We devote the same attention to everything whether it's a funeral or buying a pair of shoes. Lack of perspective makes us dizzy.

Like remembering, reexperiencing, retelling a drama of love. Each time I relive it in my mind I find a new detail, a nuance neglected in the previous telling, a reminiscence with new meaning, or have I perhaps fabricated the whole affair? If I returned to the place, could I find it again? Can I be sure? All the obsessions that slither and slime around in my mind, that slosh in and out of the blood vessels in my brain, are externalized in Venice.

Every so often a square opens up, lets in the light, gives me breathing space before I am off again to the mire, the subconscious elucidating just long enough to keep me above water. The next step and I am plunged again into the subterranean landscape of my soul.

But to prove they know the beauty of light in space and form against sky, in addition to glass, water and lace, Venetians give us Piazza San

Marco. A huge square where the light never stops, where there is more space than there is any right to be in a city. The orchestras, the caffes, even the millions of tourists don't fill it up. The pigeons in San Marco's square, millions of them, as many pigeons as there are tiles in the Byzantine mosaics of the story of Job in the Basilica of San Marco, can't darken it. Their millions of shadows, Escher reflections, constantly ebb and flow on the stone floor of the square.

How brilliant to have a square like this, so large, so full of light that it easily accommodates the regularities of obsessive detail and at the same time measures God.

Frame anything against water and it pleases the eye. Laundry hung out between buildings, colored and white, is strung like chunky Navajo jewelry above the canals. I wonder how many pale blue shirts, plum colored skirts, pairs of pink underwear fall into the canal, how you find them, do they smell, do the neighbors know exactly whose they are? Impossible not to be a great photographer in Venice. She welcomes the camera as a good friend dedicated to her reflection, like her glass, mirrors and water. Despite this Venice is always a double or triple exposure.

Portraits of the doges, former presidents of the Republic, lined up on the ceiling in the Palazzo Ducale, look down on me as, my neck cramped, I crane upwards. A veil blackens one painting. A doge betrayed the Republic, high treason, the veil a potent sign of what happened to those who did not fear the Republic. It remains covered today, chillingly clear what these water people can do.

Is Venice a place for lovers? I haven't done it but I think not. Venice is for intrigue, for mirrors, to take a microscope in greater and greater depth to the tentacles and terrors beneath the surface, the crack in the stone, the intricacies of the waves, to plan, plot and perhaps consummate an affair or a liaison, but not a romance.

On the surface it seems a likely place but "seems" is what Venice is about. In no time, with a few steps in one direction, a few errors in another, your romantic notions hit a bridge, or an unknown alley, or a stony dead end, or the perilously seductive water, and the chill and "waste sad time before and after."

The glitter of Venice is built upon its antitheses, water and stone. The tensions of these, the fight as to what will endure, is the lure of Venice. Venice is not a happening, it's carefully planned, diagrammed, and measured. Very real materials constitute the show of Venice, glass, tile, and stone, and the whole chimera wages a constant battle not to lose ground for its existence. That battle is more than any romance could sustain.

Julie Landsman

CHIAROSCURO

Stresa on Lake Maggiore. First night in Italy
Money in Italy sounds like a song. I trade dollars for lire, francs for lire, marks for lire. There is no other country that has the kind of currency that sings to you, that says: quatrocento mille lire − wings of gold.

* * *

Perhaps what is wonderful about traveling is that for a while I can remember my mistakes, the things I said to my mother. I can remember them with accuracy. They are smaller, contain the detail of miniatures, the precision of cut glass.

We are in Italy, yet I see places from my past. I see porch lights, the Adams' field, boarding school. They are caught in stop frames so that I can turn them over, examine them for a moment, move on. I sit in small apartments or hotel rooms and remember my mother's softness, trips to New York, Lesley and I in identical blue and white dresses, a grocer in a building full of dark wood, handing us oranges.

I never satisfied my mother with my scattered hair. My clothes, however, were always well kept. I came home from school without a scuff. That was one of the compliments she paid me: I could go into a school building and come home without looking wilted.

At forty-two I am already separated from her by time. Now, I am separated by distance.

Stresa, a restaurant by Lake Maggiore
It is raining and I have bought an umbrella which stands dripping on the deep red tiles in the corner. It is ten-thirty and we are drinking cappucino in a small restaurant. A man and his wife are sitting next to us. They are from Belgium. None of us wants to go outside. We talk about Belgium and America, "Dallas" and "Falcon Crest."

Then in a long pause, the man says: "They are all guilty, you know."

The woman who has served dinner comes back to offer fruit and pecorino cheese.

"The Germans, they are all guilty still," he repeats, his wife smiling at his side, nodding her head. "You wait and see after you have been here. Wait and see how they are with their money." He tears some grapes from the large bunch the woman has set before us in a wooden bowl. "Even the children are guilty." The rain pounds harder and we become silent.

Maury and I had two weddings, a Protestant one for my mother and father and later, a Jewish one for his parents. I remember my Uncle Clayt at the first reception. He was a New England farmer, always working over rocky soil, determined to make grass grow for his cows grazing. Later he would go mad, come after Aunt Alice with a hatchet at midnight, just after reading Shakespeare. But now, I see him at my wedding, his round glasses resting on his lined and windblown face, holding her large hand, his diminutive body resting next to hers, almost childlike at her side. I see my mother, moving among the guests, sitting next to Maury's Uncle Jack, explaining that the hearth in the music room was actually a gravestone, from some New England patriarch named Stoddard.

I see the second wedding, three weeks after the first, this time in D.C. Four stern men stand at the corners of the chuppa. With his black leather shoe, Maury grinds a glass under a white napkin. Aunt Sylvia, dressed in red, passes out, drunk on the blue satin couch. Uncle Jack carries her into the back bedroom. My parents are not there.

Bologna

Bologna is a fierce city until the first person smiles at you. It is full of pigeons and small children in yellow slickers.

We sit at a table in the piazza. We are in love with stone and the way the old women bend, coming out of churches. They walk out of the huge doorways, backwards, crossing themselves the whole time. And I walk backward into another time.

At St. Margaret's boarding school in the spring, old women in silk dresses walked past swans. In winter, old women in long wool coats hurried around campus, going from science lab to math class, to the large dining room where we sang grace and missed our brothers, missed the crooked rooms of our houses, the imperfections of our summer afternoons.

Every night we were taught how to handle rows of silver on each side of our plates; we were taught about white linen table cloths. Waitresses with gray hair, incongruous in girlish uniforms with short skirts and frilly aprons, stood along the side of the dining room, ready to bend over our left shoulders with heavy platters full of meat.

We walked around the old rooms in the afternoons while the sun came through the ivy on the patio. We were held for years and then were let go, out of the ornate doors of boarding school, with such suddenness that the streets were too full too soon and we stumbled onto faces we didn't know were there, behind doors, on rooftops, in the hallways of our own apartments. We were not prepared.

Florence

Maury says, at dinner, "I notice centuries, you notice details."

He is right. We walk around the city and I notice a small boy dressed in yellow near the Duomo. One sock is up to his knee, the other is down around his ankle. I notice a girl dressed in red. She is about eight and her mother stops to arrange her sweater so it falls exactly right over her shoulders. There is a clarity about the girl's face that is rare, even in children.

Maury reads about castles and how families sold towers to each other when they needed money. He talks about age and the dates of churches.

Walking around the hills I point out the flowers. He smiles. "Details," he says. "You notice red."

* * *

The next day we visit the synagogue in Florence. A middle aged woman who guides tours through the building says to us after all the others have gone, "They took four hundred up on a hill and shot them, all at once, the men, the women, the children. And now that I give tours of our synagogue I have to speak German for the Germans coming in and I find that it hurts, you know, my throat." She says this as her mouth trembles, and speaking about it, she begins to weep.

"You are so lucky," she turns to Maury, who has put on a yarmulke, "to live in America where there are so many Jews all around you. Here there are only hundreds left in all of Florence. Before the war there were thousands."

I am silent. I think of my own father who has never wanted to say my son's name because it sounds "too Jewish." So he calls him A.D. instead of Aaron David. I love Aaron's name. And now I want my father to sing it, shout it, chant it, repeat it like beads on a rosary, Aaron David, Aaron David, Aaron David. Like a Jewish chant, a part of the Torah, a chorus to a song, the repeat lines of a hymn: Aaron, Aaron, Aaron.

Later, as we leave the synagogue, we read the names of the men, the women, the children, on stones in the garden outside the heavy wooden doors.

History. The details of history: Ana Levin, 1932-38, Maurizio Stein, 1926-1938, Rachel Goldman, 1936-38.

Bibbiena, a small town in the Appenine foothills
We are in Tuscany. We are watching rain, the same rain that creates porcini mushrooms, the kind we eat at midnight in Siena. We have bought food and wine, even coffee and milk. We need bread and some lettuce or spinach, maybe vinegar, too. There is oregano. The doorways are small. I notice: the dark wooden beams across the kitchen ceiling, the veined marble of the table, the red tile of the slanted floors, hand stitched quilts on each of the twin beds and the blue figured tile in the bathroom.

I notice Maury's back, the way it bends, the way he walks.

I sit in a restaurant. On my right are geraniums and through the same window where I see the geraniums, I also see the mountains, castles, and old buildings. A man comes to wait on us, sets down containers of vinegar and oil, so the light shines through them. I am sleepy with too much red wine, late afternoon. I am falling in love these days, and wish Maury and I could lie down in the middle of this restaurant.

A day in the mountains
Last night I dreamed about a man with a knife who told me I had to perform fellatio on him or he would kill me. I knew that even after I did what he ordered, he would kill me anyway. I could tell this by the way he smiled as he unbuttoned his shirt and began to undo his belt. I woke up from the dream at 2 a.m. and walked to the bathroom, across the old, polished tiles of the apartment. Later that morning, just a few hours before we drove up to this restaurant, I told Maury about the man, the knife. He asked me if I knew why I had the dream now, here, Italy. I said it happens a lot around the middle of June. Maury stood in the small doorway, light on his graying beard, a slice of melon on the table next to him. He was remembering the day I was raped, twenty years ago, June, Washington, D.C., and the summer afterwards.

It was August of that summer when Sarah my friend, was getting married. The night before her wedding all of us who lived together in the same apartment sat around and helped her decide on a nightgown. Sarah was the one who was a real virgin. She was the one who had waited until a certain day, a certain time, to give up something extremely secret to Joe McDonnell. We watched her try on negligees and decided on pale yellow for her first night. It had rosebuds on the shoulders and an extra lining of white. When she twirled around the living room a cigarette resting between her slim fingers, the orange glow a streak in the darkness, we clapped.

After that summer: of Jeanie's abortion, Stacy's miscarriage, my rape, we needed to see Sarah pirouetting in the D.C. midnight, wondering about the scar on her stomach, worried about the size of her breasts. She was our ballerina, on the top of the music box, twirling in front of us, drifting by our bodies, her cigarette making circles, like a child's sparkler on the fourth of July. We needed her then the way women need women who have lived their lives well, who have not caused their mothers' heads to bow with disappointment.

Sarah walked around the room, bending over us, kissing the tops of our heads, taking our hands in hers before she went to bed, telling us thank you, thank you like a small child in yellow rose buds on Easter Sunday, her father smiling as she walks down the green and blue morning.

And now, it is good Maury and I have taken this trip to Camaldoli just hours after my dream, my memories of the summer. It is good we came here, to this place, that in the middle of a perfect meal I hear someone singing "Oh My Darling Clementine" with a country western twang. We are going to visit a monastery. I hear echoes of America while I look out on the mountains. Maury places a cappucino next to me, offers his pen when mine runs out.

In a few minutes we will leave to visit the place where men, because they were not willing to face the world, or even each other, lived in twenty separate cells. They rubbed their hands together in the middle of cold stone, looked out, waited for summer. These men, along with Maury, along with the man who brings me vinegar and oil. These men say: "Not all of us are in your nightmares."

* * *

It is easier, seeing old scenes, caught from this distance. I am not sure what lessens the pain, whether it is the fact that twenty years have passed, or that no one speaks English and there is safety in such separation. I feel like a photographer with a zoom lense. I close in on something that makes my heart ache, yet concentrate on the shadows, the light, what the man wore, how the sun moved on the blade of his knife so that the light bounced off the walls of my room as he waved his thick arm. I feel like a war correspondent, cannot turn away, but must catch this now: Maury's arms that day, and for years after that. From Italy I can hold my lens steady, details clear, the policemen's pink necks fringed with white hair, the dark stitches in the dog's head where he had kicked her. On this trip my hand is finally steady, photos finally unblurred, emerging clear from the wash of memory.

Always back to our apartment in Bibbiena
I begin to be aware of dates again, and that is a bad sign. I keep wondering if we should skip Venice. For two weeks I have allowed myself to fall in love with the man I have been married to for twenty years, to blur over any imperfections, the same way I did with the food, the bread that was a little tough, the cheese a little old. I see now that the orange is shriveled, that the man at the wine store is not the dear old Italian that I thought he was, but is young and a little lecherous. The kids in Siena pop water balloons in front of tourists. I see groups of young girls fighting and recognize the cruel tone, the same way I recognize it in the halls of any junior high school in Minneapolis.

We go out to the corner store and I see details I never saw before. Dust has settled on the boxes of crackers. The woman at the bar looks really more tired than angry. A baby in a stroller frets for a nap while his mother talks excitedly to an old woman who waves her hands in the air. The women touch, shrug shoulders. Maury is impatient, eager to get back to the apartment, doesn't know what to do with himself once we are there.

Suddenly, I know too much to keep him or this country at a distance.

Siena
A blond girl, about two years old, runs up and down the piazza carrying a huge Italian silk flag, waving it, wrapping it around her body. No one notices but me and the couple behind me. Maury is busy talking to an American man about cameras.

Always, I want to ask, wherever we go: "What did you do about the Jews?"

Morning in Siena
The sky is gray, the city has not changed to rust yet. The birds are swirling back and forth in the morning fog. Because Maury woke last night, I woke too. I went over to his bed and wrapped myself around him until he fell asleep. He has done this for me many times at home. "Money anxieties," he said, but I know it is really that he has admitted for the first time that the vacation is ending.

When I was six, a boy on the playground poked his finger in my ear. I still have a hole in my ear drum with a membrane stretched over it like bongos. On some days, when the wind is just right, I can feel the membrane beating. Today it vibrates as I walk through a flea market outside Siena.

It is amazing what we carry around with us in our bodies. We carry the anger of our father, our escapes, the wind in our heads, the flat stones on the playground.

Monterchi

We walk into the chapel and see the Madonna del Parto, the pregnant madonna, by Piero della Francesca. Our bodies shift, recognize something from our past. I remember that one evening my mother was taken away in an ambulance. The blood wouldn't stop after Claudia, her fourth child, was born. I crouched behind a chair, watched the men lifting her out the door and down the steps, her face as white as the sheets, her hair darkened on the pillow.

We stand in front of the Madonna and I can see my mother in blood, going out the door like a raft in the middle of a jungle.

Last night in Bibbiena

Every evening, women in long black dresses and scarves follow the bells of the town, the bells that seem to speak across hills to each other. The women walk into the tiny church. Yesterday, in that same church the years became dark and silent around me: all the years, all the minutes of the past were still. Resting there, my entire body was still. A relationship, whether to some God or to silence or love or the animals in the hills across the way where St. Francis bent on thin bones, was all that mattered. Even old pictures receded, left me alone for awhile.

Now, while the bells repeat themselves and the women trudge up narrow streets again, I iron clothes. I concentrate on one small place on a pair of Maury's slacks, the ones he got from Lesley, my sister, after Walter, her husband, died. I sit and look at the hills changing in the light and remember that Walter's biggest regret was that he'd never see the places in the world he really wanted to see. He wanted Hawaii and never got it, but died out on the unbroken Indiana farmland where the fields flatten with stiff corn. Walter wanted some place new, the deep pink of jungle, a tropical importance. He wanted mist walks in the morning, the path disappearing as part of the grass, a parrot asking unusual questions in the hot afternoon. All this is what he did not have. He died withering into bone and anger, the heat lighting up his inadequate house, the heat burning his lips, his fury in the face of pain pushing him toward that garage, pushing him toward his last and most important walk, the radio playing in the pick-up while the canoe moved down the wall from the force of his gunshot.

And I think, Italy. I have not died too soon.

* * *

The mynah bird on the veranda below sounds so human this evening. The old woman, Eva, waters her geraniums and talks back to the bird. Later she will probably fight with her daughter.

I go around the apartment and open all the windows. This lets the hills in on the wind.

I wish that Maury had stayed home with me instead of going to the last day of his conference. I wanted him to choose me over those wonderful people from all over the world. I realize that he is drawn to people more than I am and this surprises me. I am worried he will try to drive home from Siena after too much wine, taking the curves, lights flashing, just like an Italian.

This moment, Maury on his way home, the women answering those bells that ring from the mountains, this moment when all that death means, comes to me quickly on the wings of evening, on the breeze from the hills, in the silence of that church, this moment is curved like a bell itself, holding a tone.

The Lake District
Now we are back in Stresa for our last day. The man from Belgium is not here. We go for a tour of the island in the middle of Lake Maggiore, wander in the garden around a sixteenth century palace. We take pictures of Carlo, the smiling Italian boy who tries to speak to the pure white peacocks who are strutting around the squared hedges. Later, Carlo leaves and after we stay with the British couple who feed goldfish at the end of the garden, we walk out to one of the cafes for a glass of wine. There are the Germans, singing their songs.

Everyone in the cafe is listening silently to one group of people singing in their harsh language. Maury says, "I can't listen to this right now." He walks away. For the first time in a month, the muscles in his neck tighten.

We find a different cafe, at the other end of the island, where we can hear, only faintly, the voices, the accordion, the dark singing at the end of the garden, the Germans.

And while we sit, I remember the night, a few weeks back when we were in Siena. A young man sat out on the campo near the Toacana Hotel and played the guitar. The music was as gentle as the city itself and its sound carried all the way to our room. Later when he stopped for a moment to speak to his girlfriend, I heard his German accent. I was disappointed. Yet, his fingers worked quietly on the strings. I must remember such contradictions: the night in Siena, the boy playing flamenco, classical, American jazz. The boy, speaking in his own tongue. I must remember him, understand the disappointment I felt when I heard him speak, his sweet voice, the white throat of his girlfriend. I turn toward Maury, remember that he said to me, that night in Siena, "Even that language, when whispered, can sound soft."

On the boat back from the island is a woman from Scandinavia. She wears a beautiful blouse that reveals her naked breasts whenever she leans over. A young Italian man in front of her turns around and looks inside her blouse the whole way across. Her husband relaxes at the end of the boat and plays with their children. The woman wears a thick gold chain and lots of bracelets. Her breasts are so lovely I suddenly understand Maury's desire to touch mine.

Last night in Italy
Rain. We are blessed by the man at the bar in our hotel. He pours Campari into tall glasses, adds ice and a twist of lemon. At this age, when we are sent to bed with someone else's approval, his easy smile, all is fine in the world.

Usually in sex, we never really get through to each other. There is a wall of skin and we don't make it inside up into the center of the other person. But in the best sex, the best times, rain or wind, an unusual ease at the end of the day I feel that what happens is this: it is safe to let Maury reach up into my body, almost to my heart.

Tonight is like that.

* * *

I lie in bed. Maury is asleep. I can remember how, twenty years ago, another body was over mine. I can remember that while the knife lay next to my head in the summer heat of the attic room, while his knees pressed in on either side of me, I willed myself to forget. For years I only remembered the terror, muscles tensed for death, my body open to pain.

These past weeks, new details have come back: the harsh cloth of the pants he wore, the fact that he never said a word, the whimpering of the dog, how she turned circles for days after that, around and around the kitchen while a blonde child chased her, toddling after her, laughing at her confusion, the stitches dark in her head. These things come back now, details: the plastic radio he had me put in the suitcase, the knives on the sideboard, the women in the police car, driving me to the hospital, talking about a barbeque they were planning, what to serve, whether to drink beer or soda.

Details are coming back now when I am ready for them: the smells in the room, the children outside on their tricycles, yelling at each other in high voices all the while he was over me. I am ready to hold all this next to me, to learn to understand it, to take it into the outline of my life, fit it there, just after the civil rights marches and just before the trip to Maine.

Maybe the pain becomes touchable, now that I can wrap words around it because, after twenty years, I have learned to accept it as a part of the succession of my days.

* * *

This is what we do when we leave the places where we were hurt, where we were loved. We begin to see the contradictions, the juxtapositions. We allow moments to become separate from others. We stop, still, hold the focus clear, our hearts at ease.

Lying here, next to Maury, I can remember bodies, lights, my father's room above the ocean. Lying here I see the names of Jews who died, the man who stood in the room with a dangerous light in his hand. I hear the German boy in Siena, saying something to his girlfriend. I remember Maury's words, "Even that language, when whispered, can sound soft."

Margaret Todd Maitland

THE HOUSE ON VIA GOMBITO

Poetics

The year my husband and I spent in Bergamo, we lived in a medieval building held together by small-scale feats of ingenuity. Modern conveniences had been installed during the last century, but the building, enjoying a dignified entropy, never wholly accepted them. In the uneasy partnership between old and new, the pipes, wires, and hoses had to make all the adjustments, turning at odd angles, emerging through thick stone walls in unexpected places. Needless to say, things regularly went wrong. The task of fixing, which really meant rigging up another temporary compromise, fell to the repairmen we came to know well.

We arrived in Bergamo in September, during the first year of our marriage. The town, settled in ancient times by Etruscans, was perched atop a green hill facing the foggy plain of the Po River and was encircled on three sides by the Italian Alps. We had come to Bergamo so that Dan could attend the Istituto Montessori Internazionale, and while he learned how to communicate the wonders of Maria Montessori's cosmic education, translating tales of dinosaurs, ice ages, and volcanoes for the minds of nine- to twelve-year-olds, I was on my own in a language I had yet to learn.

For several weeks after our arrival, we suffered a dripping faucet, plugged sink, slow seepage from the kitchen wall, and a strange odor from the bathtub every day at noon. I sat down with the dictionary, collected the words I needed, and prepared a speech for our landlady, Signora Agazzi. She came to inspect the problems and promised to call the plumber. He arrived on the day — though not at the time — I expected, wearing a suit. Apologizing for being late, he explained that when he'd opened the morning paper, a photograph of his cousin had jumped out from the obituary page, so he had put on a suit and rushed to the funeral. Then he'd come directly to our apartment. I gave him a towel to protect his wool trousers, and he knelt down to work on the stopped-up bathroom sink.

He dismantled the U-shaped drain pipes and dug out a dripping wad of muck, some hairpins from about 1930, and five red toothpaste caps.

When he reassembled the pipes, the drain ran free, but water gushed out around the joints. He unscrewed and inspected the worn threads, rescrewed them more carefully, and when they still leaked, he pulled from his tool box a shank of long, brown fibers: horse-hairs, he said. He wrapped a few of these around the inside threads, and when he rescrewed the pipes they were perfectly sealed.

The house itself was difficult to comprehend. Built during the 1400's, it appeared to be one thing from the outside, and from the inside another. The blank face of the building made with its neighbors a continuous wall broken only by an enormous wooden door tall enough to ride through on horseback. Passing through the door, you first entered a red-tiled courtyard with a stone fountain in the shape of a lion's head (symbol of St. Mark) and four or five motorcycles on which a one-eyed cat dozed. Craning your neck, you could see five stories of arched porticoes and a jumble of balconies with laundry, hanging bird cages, and bobbing geraniums. Stairways zig-zagged in all directions, and there were many mysterious doors.

We never saw whoever lived two floors above us, where a basket swung outside a window, though we'd hear shouts from the courtyard, watch the basket descending on a rope, see the relatives filling it with bread and packages of cheese. We never saw the cats that raced all night in the attic above us. Our bedroom walls gave off the smell of cat urine, which seeped through the ceiling boards. We heard that former tenants were awakened one night when the cats crashed through a sky-light and landed fighting and clawing on the bed.

In our early flush of enthusiasm to make the apartment our own, Dan and I stripped the living room wallpaper. Anything would have been better than the discolored orange flowers, 1950s style, that puckered across the wall. To our great surprise, underneath the wallpaper we found a fresco. We pulled each strip of paper carefully, liberating garlands of leaves, vines, and flowers. At the very end a girl appeared, her breasts bare, her arms upraised as if holding the garlands in a dance.

There were big gouges, lots of nicks and scratches. From cataloguing works of art in a museum in Minneapolis, I was acquainted with two philosophies of painting restoration: one method is to camouflage repairs and repaint the work so that it looks as it did when new; the other is to leave the work as untouched as possible, making repairs obvious so that the effects of age and damage remain part of the work. We decided on the latter, and limited our repairs to filling in the holes and painting out the orange streaks. The paint I bought at an art supply store, tubes labeled "Burnt Sienna" and "Umber" matched exactly, and I stood with my brush in hand thinking about the artist who five hundred years before ground up pigments from the earth of nearby places — Siena and Umbria.

One day we noticed a black cloud growing around a hole high in the kitchen wall and realized we were waking up with soot in our noses. After much puzzling, I discovered that the exhaust pipe from the tiny space heater, our sole source of heat, conducted soot from the dining room into the kitchen. We called the landlady who sent the *muratore* — the mason. He immediately ran into a problem. Even after crawling around in several of the attics, he couldn't tell where the exhaust pipe was supposed to connect with the main chimney, which was buried somewhere in the walls between other apartments. Signora Agazzi brought an architect, and they stood a long time on each landing, pointing and peering up at the top of the chimney, which emerged from the many-angled tile roofs. Then she consulted her older relatives who knew the building better. (Her family had lived there for centuries.) Unfortunately, the only person who had dared in recent years to climb the steep, slippery roofs was a young nephew, Roberto. He'd been an adventuresome twelve-year-old but wasn't inclined to risk his life again at twenty-two. He didn't remember anything about the chimney.

It was incredible to me that no one understood the building, that knowledge of its structure had been completely obscured as generations had added and subtracted sections, and that there was no way to imagine the relation of the parts to the whole. This building had become inextricably, unexplainably connected to the buildings closest to it.

In the end, the muratore and Signora Agazzi decided on an attitude of humility in the face of a problem too old and complex to be thoroughly understood. If it was impossible to route the soot into the chimney and out of the building, it could at least be channeled to land somewhere else. The muratore extended the exhaust pipe a few feet, and twisted it so that it opened into the attic and deposited the soot there. This was an improvement. Maybe the soot would at least discourage the cats.

The dictionary gives the word "repair" a hopeful definition: "to restore to a sound or good state after decay, injury, dilapidation or partial destruction." But this naively assumes that every problem can be isolated and treated in its entirety; it ignores those difficulties that lie embedded in their own complex contexts. The Latin root seems more realistic. It means "to make ready again." Our repairmen didn't sell perfection.

In *The Poetics of Space*, Gaston Bachelard laments the advances of domestic architecture. He abhors the efficiency and predictability of the modern apartment and suggests that people need to live with dark, secret spaces (basement, root cellar), with forgotten spaces (attic, stairwell), with intimate spaces (kitchen). The human spirit needs physical metaphors for itself. Bachelard especially disliked electricity.

In the days of candles and hearth, every room had a physical and emotional focus. To enter a room was to move from darkness to light, from cold to warmth, from things unseen to the seen. Electricity, spreading an even bath of light, banished mystery. The condition we call comfort, Bachelard regarded as a state of dulled sensation and diluted emotion.

Reading the views of that French philosopher in the bright light of a library some years ago, I was ready to leave the bland twentieth century for good. But to live in Italy, in the kind of house that inhabited his dreams, was to step inside a kaleidoscope and find myself among huge chunks of glass whose sudden shifting was both beautiful and violent.

Damage

It was the evening of our fourth day in the apartment, before we had become acquainted with the peculiarities of the space. Those were the early days of shins bumped in tight spaces, toes stubbed on steps the wrong height, eyelashes singed because each burner of the stove flared differently. The building demanded that we, the modern visitors, make many compromises, and our early partnership was uneasy. We made the compromises in our bodies.

At about nine o'clock Dan was fixing dinner. We'd had an argument, but night was quieting the courtyard. As he washed a piece of glass he'd used as a cutting board, it slipped out of his hands and smashed against the wall. I heard a sickening crash and rushed into the kitchen. Dan slumped on the floor as if he'd been shot — he'd slid down the wall into a sitting position and clutched his left hand to his chest.

"I think I've cut my finger off."

My mind raced out the door, down the stairs and into the street where I tried to imagine a phone booth. I couldn't remember having seen one and knew that even if I found a pay phone I wouldn't be able to read the instructions to operate it. My Italian was so rudimentary I wouldn't be able to summon help or follow directions to a hospital. My mind went blank. I stood staring at Dan, gulping. "Go get Signora Cerutti," he said. I ran out in my bare feet.

I had forgotten Signora Cerutti, a neighbor we'd met the day before. She had been watering plants in a window box and had greeted us from her window across the courtyard. She had lent us her vacuum cleaner.

I wasn't sure where she lived. I ran down three flights of stairs in the dark, then groped my way toward what I thought was her stairway, found the tiny light that illuminated her doorbell. After a long time she came to the door and opened it as if expecting guests. Her smile changed to a look of alarm. I said *"dottore,"* hoping that was something like the

Italian word. She understood. I ran back and helped Dan down the stairs. Her son, Roberto, pulling on a shirt, met us at the door and led us to a car. Someone who seemed to be Roberto's girlfriend came too. He drove to the hospital, a dizzying zig-zag down the steep hill on which the medieval city was built, the lights of the modern lower town coldly flashing. I had no idea where we were going.

The emergency room was quiet and empty except for a woman with a little boy on her lap. She looked up grimly as if she'd been waiting but hadn't dared ask for help. No hospital staff were in sight. Benches lined the smudged walls, and we sat Dan on one of them. His face had turned pale gray. My feelings of panic had collected in a small ball at the top of my stomach, and I felt drained and weightless. I paced, listening at the doors that led to examining rooms. There were voices behind one door. No one came out. We could do nothing but sit and wait.

I began to notice Roberto and the girlfriend. They fidgeted and sighed, and I felt bad that we had dragged them here. Neither of them spoke any English. Dan held his hand in a towel, and reviving a bit, tried in a hoarse voice to talk with Roberto who gallantly nodded and smiled. He seemed the pleasant kind of boy who would do whatever his mother asked, but was not about to call attention to himself by knocking on one of the doors and demanding a doctor.

His friend, a girl of about nineteen, had dull blonde hair, a colorless face and funny teeth, which I kept noticing because her vague smile turned to startled giggles whenever I spoke. The smile seemed to be an attempt at helpfulness, and for some reason it really aggravated me. She was dressed in pink, with earrings and a matching bracelet of fat pink balls which she kept twisting and rearranging on her thin wrist. These two teenagers were our only allies. Her bracelet drove me crazy.

Finally one of the doors cracked, and a doctor in wrinkled whites and a two-day beard shouldered his way through. I jumped. The doctor looked up and, saying nothing, led us through one of the doors. He gestured toward an examining table. He unwrapped the dish-towel around Dan's hand. After looking a little while, he said in Italian, "It's nothing. A few stiches, and it will be alright." His tone implied we were idiots for getting excited. I didn't care: the finger was still attached. He handed me the blood-soaked towels. Then looking more closely, he changed his mind. "No, you must remain in the hospital for a week." We caught the words, "*in ospedale*" and "*una settimana*," but not why.

"Una settimana!" Dan cried. He was beginning to get loud, and I realized later that he must have been going into shock.

Perhaps the doctor explained the situation to Roberto, but neither of them tried to make us understand what exactly was wrong with Dan's finger or what would happen next. A nurse walked us outdoors, through a vast courtyard and into another building. We rode up a freight elevator and walked along a darkened corridor that opened into a forlorn waiting room. After a while a pair of white doors opened and a tired-looking nurse summoned Dan inside. Our only hope of communicating in Italian was to do it together, so I marched toward the examining room too. The nurse closed the door sharply in my face. Roberto had disappeared. I sat down on one of the molded plastic chairs, in the dimness, with the girlfriend.

After half an hour, a wedge of light crept across the floor as the door opened. This time I was invited in. Dan lay on his back on a sheet-draped table. I stood by his head and held his shoulders, wishing someone would hold mine. A young nurse motioned me to a desk where she asked me to spell Dan's name, but it was German and incomprehensible to her. Because I hadn't learned the Italian names for letters, she never got it right. I stumbled over his birthdate. I could manage the month and day, but from our five Berlitz lessons I only knew numbers up to twenty, and had no idea how to say "nineteen-fifty-one."

The atmosphere eased when a male nurse appeared, ambled over to where Dan lay and said in a hearty voice, "*Salve!*" At the time I was sure it meant "Health!" or "Salvation!" and I took it quite literally, the way someone not used to "God bless you" after a sneeze might feel an actual blessing bestowed. He had thick black hair and a smile that reached back to empty spaces where teeth were missing. He wore white clogs.

Introducing himself as Giorgio, he shook Dan's good hand with exclamations of "Danny, Danny, che disastro!" He waited with us, teasing, making us laugh. Then a second miracle occurred. Roberto returned with Kay Albani, the agent who had found us our apartment. Kay, a Canadian fluent in Italian, was the only person we knew in Bergamo besides Signora Cerutti. How Roberto knew her or knew that she knew us was a mystery, but we were so relieved at her magical appearance that we didn't ask.

"*Poverino!*" she said to Dan — poor thing! — and immediately quizzed everyone in sight. She drew the doctor aside and argued with him. Finally she explained the diagnosis to us: the wound was very deep, a main tendon and several nerves had been severed, and two operations would be required. One was to be performed the next day to repair the torn skin, the other in three weeks to reconnect the nerves and tendon. Dan would stay the night in the hospital. She would meet me there the next morning and arrange for us to be allowed to see him.

Roberto and the girlfriend drove me home. As we walked through the enormous doorway into the black courtyard, the girlfriend stopped, felt along the wall, clicked a button, and suddenly lamps appeared in the passageway.

"*La luce*," she said in her soft voice. "*La luce*," I repeated, amazed. We hadn't known there was a night switch for the courtyard and had been creeping up the winding stairway, cupping hands around matches that always blew out, trapping us in the darkness. La luce. I thanked them both as many times as I could and walked up to the apartment.

I went into the kitchen. The floor was covered with glass, and blood, and the spaghetti Dan had been making. I picked up the large pieces of glass with washcloths, mopped up the shards and the spaghetti.

All night the building was noisy, something scratching at the kitchen window grate, creatures scurrying through the walls. I dreamed my parents came to visit, and as we climbed the stairs, I described our beautiful, crumbling apartment. Just at the top, the outside wall of the building, a bright ochre color, detached itself, fell in a slow arc, and crashed on the ground. We stood at the apartment door on a ledge, the ruined stairway below.

Hospital

In the morning light the hospital towered like a fortress. A bronze gate controlled the entrance between two huge nineteenth-century buildings, and through it I could glimpse the courtyard of the night before. Roads with turnstiles and sentry cubicles led to twenty other buildings in the rest of the compound. Blue-shirted guards stood by the gate, arms across their chests, pointedly ignoring a group of women who waited with bags and baskets for the start of visiting hours.

I was nervous about finding Kay. Feeling small and completely helpless, I paced in front of a newspaper stand across the street. I bought a paper without wanting to and after some time spotted Kay. She was striding back and forth in front of the gate, glancing around like an irritated hen. Plump and fifty, she had coppery blonde hair and wore a navy blue dress with assertive white polka dots. A Canadian married to a native of Bergamo (her husband was a taxi driver), she had carefully studied the town life. She knew useful people everywhere, at the butcher's and the fruitseller's, in the hospital. She had nurtured and pruned her connections for twenty years until like hardy trees they all bore fruit. While the women at the gate had to content themselves with cultivating *la pazienza*, Kay could get things done. We marched up to the guards. She delivered a barrage of Italian — I caught "American husband" and "anxious wife" — and emphasizing the name of her friend the hospital administrator, she eased me forward.

Six buildings of dull yellow stucco formed a grand quadrangle, several blocks in area. Paths criss-crossed the lawn where women in chenille bathrobes walked slowly on the arms of nurses. Men in pajamas and slippers sat in the sun on stone benches, smoking and talking. They looked like rest cure patients at an out-of-fashion spa, people who did not expect to get well in a hurry.

I was afraid that Dan had been moved in the night. There seemed to be no central information office. What if we couldn't find him? I had memorized the important words, written on a slip of paper by the nurse: "Chirurgia Plastica Sezione Maschile, camera quattro, letto sette." Men's Plastic Surgery, room four, bed seven. Dust coiled along the marble stairway as if the maintenance staff were years behind. A small trail of dried blood, little circles, tiny splashes, led from the second floor to the third.

We found Dan asleep in a long green room. An older man with a tube protruding from his neck peered over his newspaper as we entered and greeted us politely.

"*Buon giorno, signore.*"

Dan's eyes were closed, one arm tucked beneath a very white sheet, the other in a fat bandage that rested on his chest. He looked extremely clean. They have taken good care of him, I thought. I could draw comfort from the whiteness of the sheets, the tightness of the blanket. Someone has known what to do for my husband, and it has been done.

He opened his eyes. Kay and I pulled up chairs. He smiled and reached his hand from beneath the sheet to hold mine. Kay unknotted the handles of a bulky plastic grocery bag and pulled out a large bunch of green grapes, three ripe peaches, and a bottle of wine.

"Later, when you feel better, try this Sassela," she said. "It will restore your strength. I don't like red myself, but it's my husband's favorite."

"You brought all this for me?" Dan exclaimed.

"You need fresh things to recover. I heard the hospital cooks might be going on strike. How are they treating you?"

"I can't tell what they're saying most of the time, but someone found a nurse who speaks a little English. Angelo. He says Italian doctors believe in rest. It may be hard to get out of here."

We talked until Dan grew sleepy. Kay departed in a flurry of admonitions and good wishes, and I sat by the bed listening to Dan's steady breathing. From the corridor drifted the clattering of silverware as tables were prepared for lunch. Through the doorway I saw the other patients in Men's Plastic Surgery emerging from their rooms. Each had a grotesque bandage. Later we would learn about their accidents. A power saw jumped out of control — the stocky white-haired man swayed beneath the weight of an arm-length cast. A motorbike swerved in front of a car — the sallow-faced teenager stared from beneath bandages that bound his head and chin. A firecracker exploded too soon — the twelve-year-old sat very still, his jaw held rigid by a complicated intertwining of wires.

Suddenly, I had to leave. I wrote Dan a note and hurried down the stairs, across the courtyard, and out the hospital gates. I stopped at the first cafe I saw. Sitting in the cool sunshine, I stared at the steam that curled from a cup of cappuccino and tried not to think about the men, the brokenness, the damage that had been suffered by all those hands, arms, faces, the fragility of the spirits that awaited repair.

I felt like crying. Dan seemed safe enough for the moment, and as the worry ebbed I realized how abandoned I felt, alone in a foreign city, agonizingly clumsy without my own language. Bergamo had been Dan's choice, the Montessori training a step toward doing the work he loved, and I had come under protest, deciding after many arguments to accommodate myself to his plans.

But if I felt angry and vulnerable so far from my moorings, a more profound sense of unease gathered like a cloud. It wasn't just that the scene had changed, that every cultural marker had been replaced by something new and enigmatic. The worst thing was that Dan was hurt, that his body had been changed, and the laws of safe passage through the world had been broken.

The laws of safe passage? Isn't it by carefulness that one outwits danger, aren't the people who avoid accidents the smart ones, the ones who know how the world works? I had learned from my childhood to be cautious. The other accident victims in the ward had put themselves in the path of danger, riding motorcycles, using power saws, playing with firecrackers. Dan had simply been making dinner. For the moment, I couldn't forgive him.

The Frescoes of Giotto
Between the first operation and the second, scheduled in two weeks, we took a trip. Our destination was nearby Padua, where I wanted to see one of Giotto's most famous works, the Scrovegni Chapel. Since college art history classes I had been interested in the fourteenth-century master, and during the years I catalogued works of art at the museum, I had grown to love seeing things up close. My job required traversing the surface of each object inch by inch, with my eyes, making maps of flaws and weak spots, scratches and flaked paint, writing long descriptions of the exact condition of the object when it came to the museum, a history of the effects of age and wear: The odd darkening of a still life (had it been used as a fire-screen?), the horizontal abrasion in the same spot on a pair of portraits (had dining room chairs backed into them every evening for centuries?), and the tiny losses whose causes were

unknown — a chip of paint missing from the lace of someone's sleeve. I was, in a way, a cataloguer of damages and repairs.

Though the art history professor made much of Giotto's pivotal position between Byzantine painting and the perceptual innovations of the Renaissance, I remember responding to something the professor never mentioned: Giotto's figures show a strange and beautiful range of feeling on their faces and in their bodies. I had seen the images only in reproduction, and I felt eager to stand before the actual walls that held the frescoes by his hand.

We arrived at noon to find the chapel's massive doors locked, and realized we'd have to wait out the long mid-day break. The building itself was discouraging — an unadorned rectangle with thick, colorless stone walls and a severe roof. A small crowd had gathered by 3:00 when two men in silver-buttoned uniforms returned to open up. We got in line, and when we entered saw the others standing with heads thrown back.

From floor to high ceiling, biblical scenes in Giotto's famous cobalt blues, reds, and golds filled the space with another crowd of people, smaller, more vivid, less restless.

Before the Bible was allowed into the hands of the people, paintings inside a church did not merely decorate: they were the main means of instruction for the illiterate faithful. As I stared up at the walls, I felt I'd just crawled inside an illuminated manuscript. I stood at the bottom of the page in awe.

I dropped a large coin into a metal box, turned the dial, and heard a woman explain in English the iconography of the scenes. The highest band of painting showed the life of the Virgin, a story unknown to me. The most surprising painting depicted the "Meeting at the Golden Gate," in which Mary's parents, Joachim and Anna, first encounter each other. In the previous scene Joachim, an old man with a curly white beard, leans dejectedly against a rock and surveys the surrounding desert. He has waited his whole life to marry, and in the desert a dream tells him that he will find his wife at the Golden Gate. Joachim and Anna embrace, his hand on her shoulder, her hands cupping his face, forehead touching forehead. Giotto paints both pairs of lips as they meet. Most amazingly, the eyes, so close together, are open, as if they must take in everything about the other, as if every point of contact between their bodies is essential and cannot be done without.

Somehow their need becomes a source of strength. Their bodies make a solid unit, backs and heads uniting to form an arch, which Giotto accomplishes by painting them the same size. The arch, I remember, is the strongest of the architectural forms and can bear almost any weight. It is impossible to imagine prying them apart.

Then I noticed a long crack running through the painting. Because the man and woman are so close, the crack enters each of their bodies at the same angle, first one, then the other. Having found each other, they stand under the same tree when lightning hits, they eat the same broken bread.

What, I wondered, did they say to us? Our marriage hardly felt like a solid architectural structure. We too had met one another late after waiting in various deserts. For our marriage ceremony we'd asked the priest to avoid using images of marriage as repose. We'd put red and purple flowers on the altar.

"Most like an arch," writes John Ciardi of marriage, "an entrance which upholds/the stone-crush up the air like lace." Not us, not yet, I think. Better Robert Bly who says, "When men and women come together/how much they have to abandon!"

Reading later about Giotto, I found the scenes of Joachim and Anna described as filled with a "strange absorption, a slow but inflexible continuity of action, controlled by the quiet assurance of a destiny traced by God." The lovers seem intensely aware of what is happening to them. Their solid, bulky bodies absorb the feelings of grief or love in each scene. They appear to meet their fate with dignity and weight, as if with an inner conviction they are capable of suffering their own drama to the last.

Giotto united Anna and Joachim and enclosed their spirits in an image of strength. But some accident cracked them open. Only slightly, but forever.

Repair
Monday morning was cool and clear. I got up knowing someone had opened Dan's hand and was somehow reconnecting the nerves and tendon. A piece of sky, intense, enamel blue, appeared above the courtyard when I unlatched the shutter. As I walked down Via Gombito, the cobblestones were slick with cold dew. A slant of sun cut across the empty street. A man on a three-wheeled motorbike with loaves of bread bristling from a huge basket sped toward me. I flattened myself against the wall of a shop to let him pass. The medieval street was only just wider than a car, the incline steep, and pedestrians had to fend for themselves.

I entered the funicular station, bought a ticket from the sleepy news seller, punched it in a machine, and entered the little car, glad to put myself in someone else's hands. As I waited I studied the metal cable that lowered the trolley-like car down the hill. I had earlier discovered the connection between the cable and the movement of the car, and like the time I rode in an elevator with a hole in the top, I wished I hadn't seen its inner workings. The trembling cables, thinner than my wrist.

The conductor, red-cheeked and wearing a thick wool uniform, emerged from the cafe in the station and guided the car down the hill. After passing through a dark tunnel beneath the city walls, we emerged to a glittering view of the lower town, red roofs, bell towers, church spires spreading toward the plain of the Po. The car moved slowly and silently, not much faster than a wagon pulled by a child. The foothills of the Alps appeared further off, and the blue hills cradling wisps of white morning mist seemed ancient and dense.

Dan's bed was empty. An elderly man in green pajamas told me he'd been taken to surgery early in the morning. It was already 10:30. I waited by the tall French doors in the corridor, jumping at every sound. Eventually I heard metal wheels on the marble floor and saw a cart being pushed by four male nurses. It clattered harshly as if the wheels were uneven or the floor had a grid. Why are they going so fast? Why aren't they being more careful? They stopped in front of me, but the cart kept rattling. Dan's skin was the color of cement, and he was shaking violently, his stiff body banging against the hard surface of the cart.

The nurses were somber. They lifted him onto the bed, tucked sheets around him. Giorgio was there, and I asked how the operation had gone. "*Bene, bene,*" he said, but his grim tone frightened me. They told me not to give him anything to drink for three hours. Then they left.

Dan was very cold and completely unconscious. I held his hand, massaged his forehead, waited. He began coughing. The coughs wrenched his body off the bed, then released it to fall back limp. He opened his eyes and asked for water. I said he couldn't have any. He coughed some more. He realized who I was and tears blurred his eyes. He asked again for water. I explained what the nurses had said. He got angry and coughed and coughed. He talked nonsense, slept, woke, coughed. I gave him a wet washcloth to suck and he spit it out.

The operation had been unusually long, four hours, and they'd given massive doses of anesthesia to keep him under. After several hours two young nurses came to the room. I wanted some reassurance that Dan was alright. One of the girls said "You must bring him pajamas." The hospital provided nothing. The thought of going out for pajamas just then brought a knot of anger and helplessness to my throat. I swallowed hard and said, "He has no pajamas. I will have to buy them." My tone of despair didn't get through. The nurses seemed satisfied and left.

I still did not know how to find the main shopping area or what kind of store to look for. Any exchange of money was humiliating and exhausting. I would have to talk my way past the hospital guards a second time that day. Dan looked scared when I said I was leaving.

I walked out the hospital gate feeling useless. Since the night of the accident I had tried to understand, to speak, to comfort. Today I'd only been able to watch while a violent experience passed through someone else's body.

On the street I asked a teenaged boy the way to *il centro,* and he politely walked with me to make sure I understood his directions. He asked if I liked Bergamo. After a few questions and answers, each repeated two or three times as we tried to understand each other, our conversation faded. I didn't want to tell him I was going to buy pajamas. He didn't tell me his destination. He could not have known what he meant to me then or that I would remember now his tall, awkward presence, his concern that I find my way, the comfort I felt walking silently next to him. Is it true that two boats together quiet the waves, the way a long truck on the freeway makes a windless passage for a smaller car?

After we parted, I found a store with display windows and hoped it was big enough that I could look at pajamas without having to explain myself to a salesperson. I knew that sizes would be meaningless, and that I'd have to hold up the tops and pants to look at them, something that was not encouraged in Italian shopping. There was a selection of pajamas, all expensive, and I bought a blue-and-red pair that looked like a soccer suit. The shirt, I realized wouldn't fit over Dan's bandage. I would have to cut off the sleeve. It was new, it cost too much, and I would have to cut it up to make it right.

Tightrope
Sun streamed through the French doors in the corridor, and the slanting rays burst and scattered in the commotion of glasses and plates, laughter and exclamations that meant lunch in Men's Plastic Surgery. Dan was well enough to eat with the others, and I sat nearby enjoying the scene. The men who had frightened me earlier with their bandages and their silence had become a jovial group (everyone was in for a long stay), and as usual at lunch time they fetched bottles of wine from their nightstands and offered to fill each others' glasses. The nurses ladled soup and pasta from big pots on carts, bantering with the men, then brought around platters of roast chicken and ossobucco. Sounds of high-spirited Bergamasco, the local dialect, filled the corridor.

"*Che è successo, che è successo?*" they asked Dan, wanting every detail of the accident. What happened, what happened?

"*Ah, il mignolo!*" they cried. The little finger. They said the name for each of the fingers, introducing Dan to his hand in Italian. Most knew stories about injured fingers, crippled fingers, fingers that had been cured by miracles. They were hard men, used to physical work, aware of their hands as tools. They reminded me of the men I had watched repairing a section of paving stone on a side street in the old part of the city, with a small pick making rhythmic indentations in the sand, then smoothly setting the rounded stones like a farmer nestling eggs in a basket, then a few more chin-chinks to tap them into place. They used fist-sized river stones, tumbled smooth by water, and they hauled them in large wheelbarrows to the places in the streets that needed mending.

One afternoon as I sat by Dan's bed, I read aloud from a newspaper article I'd been trying to translate as a vocabulary exercise. It described the circus that we had seen during the weeks between the operations. Il Circo Moira Orfei was a family circus in a single tent, with Moira Orfei, the matriarch, who led forty elephants through a stately dance, her teenaged children, who did acrobatics and stood on the backs of galloping horses, a pair of Czechoslovakian gymnasts, a French contortionist, a Spanish sword swallower. But the performer who electrified the crowd was a Bulgarian aerialist, a stocky, ugly man of about thirty-five. He seemed immune to gravity. Or perhaps he knew the air so well that he could ride its currents like a rafter in a dangerous river. Above the ground he somersaulted, flipped, and twisted like a joyous fish.

It was his joy that made me puzzle. Surely he of all people had lived with the daily possibility of disaster, surely he had lost his footing, had peered over the sharp edge of the world. His movements were too powerful to be naive. He reminded me in some way of the men on the ward, victims of violent accidents, but even in their bandages and pajamas full of life. Like him they must have known how hard and how far one can fall. Was there some relief in that, some spiritual composure gained from seeing the tightrope with complete clarity, as well as the abyss on either side?

The newspaper reporter asked the aerialist, "*Da dove viene la sua sicurezza?*" "Where does your safety come from?" seemed an odd question, though I didn't know whether it was because an English speaker wouldn't phrase it that way, or because an English-speaking journalist simply wouldn't ask that kind of question. The answer was even more surprising: "Dal cuore." From the heart.

At the root of courage is the Latin word for heart.

The Woman at the Gate

Dr. Losapio was a handsome man of forty-five, tall and imposing as were all the doctors in the very hierarchical hospital. An aristocrat by birth, education, and position, Losapio carried his authority like a Renaissance prince, one in whose court art and music would have flourished, excellent meals have been served, whose estate would have been protected by chained dogs and guards more eager than skillful in their use of spears. He was Dan's surgeon. The deference with which doctors were treated by the rest of the staff reassured us at first, and the class distinctions worked in our favor. When Losapio discovered that Dan's father was also a doctor, he gave our case new respect and attention.

Losapio understood some English, and could write it fairly well, though he was reluctant to speak, being skilled in the art of avoiding public mistakes. After failing to communicate to us in Italian the details of the surgery, he wrote out a page of explanation. We stared a long time at the delicate blue script and read it aloud point by point, but between the medical terms and the idiosyncratic English grammar, we couldn't understand it. We couldn't tell what the glass had really done, what had gone on for four hours during the operation, what the chances were of the surgery's success. The anatomy of the hand was the first mystery from which the others followed. Dan and I stared at our hands trying to imagine what had gone on inside his, and we were no more successful than Signora Agazzi, our landlady, staring at the chimney, trying to see how it fit into her building.

When the cast was finally removed, the finger appeared pale, stiff, frozen in a hook. It had no feeling and no movement. For two months Dan had been eager to get the cast off, and here it was, a different hand, partly numb, partly shrunken. I don't remember if we cried, but we stood a long time in the cold dining room underneath the cloudy skylight, holding each other, face against face, the way beings who love one another press into the stillness each contains when there is nothing else to be done.

We sat down at the table, and Dan unbuttoned his shirt sleeve to show me something else: a series of precise white scars marched up his forearm. He had no idea what they were. Then we remembered an unintelligible part of Losapio's explanation. A tendon stretches to do its job like a rubber band. When severed, it snaps and retracts, trapped far from its original location. Losapio had been searching for the tendon.

It was so frustrating not to understand! Dan was to return in a month for a check-up, and during that time we talked once or twice about physical therapy. Was this the kind of situation in which people got therapy? Could the finger still be saved? I'd noticed what seemed to be a rehabilitation clinic near the hospital, and I tried to call once to find out if therapy might help. At a pay phone, on a busy street, I couldn't find the right words. The gap between me and the stranger at the other end was too great, and I had to hang up.

When the day for the check-up came, we walked down the ancient stone stairway that zigzagged through fields sloping from the upper town, a walkway laid by hand, parts steep, parts eroded. There had been no bulldozer to grade the hill and make a smooth bed, no machine to spew uniform paving bricks. Instead, the medieval builders, and anyone who had repaired the stairway since, had taken the land as it was — uneven, unpredictable — and had worked from one irregularity to the next. Losapio's job had not been so different. One fork in the path led nowhere. It bent over a sharp incline, but the drop below had been too steep. An eroded gulley cut the rise where the stairs should have been, and a pile of stones lay as they had fallen, broken, caught in a tangle of brambles.

We arrived at the hospital hot and sweaty. I had to sit outside the examining room while Dan and Losapio talked. Losapio came out first, smiled uncomfortably at me, his princely manner shrivelled. He ducked into an office where I could hear him making an appointment with a physical therapist.

Dan emerged furious. "When I asked if physical therapy would help," Dan said, "Losapio mumbled, 'Ah,. . .yes. Do you want physical therapy?'"

Then we ran into Angelo, the English-speaking nurse who had become a friend. We told him what had happened, and a strange look came over his face. "A month after surgery and only now he thinks about therapy? He must be crazy! It is imperative to begin to exercise the finger immediately after the cast is removed, to encourage the circulation, to prevent the tendon from cementing itself to the scarred area." I was horrified. "And you know," Angelo continued, "Losapio does not do many hands. He specializes in faces."

I was so angry I could barely speak. Did this mean the finger was beyond repair? Were we supposed to let it fall into the oblivion of doomed things, hopeless things, rejected things? The ruined stairway, so exposed, so abandoned, had given me a strange chill. I knew no one would ever try to repair it.

I thought about Losapio. For months his judgments, his predictions, even his moods had seemed crucial to Dan's recovery. What happened? Had he failed to plan for physical therapy out of laziness or forgetfulness? Had the operation been a failure, a half-hearted attempt to patch and make do in the tradition of the repairmen who never really fixed anything? Or did the piece of glass invade the internal universe of the hand in ways so minute and complex that no one could have comprehended?

After a month of therapy, Dan's finger remained unchanged. Gianbattista, the blind physical therapist, taught me to do the exercises: rest the hand on a pillow, massage the finger for circulation, bend in, bend back, just a little further each day. But the finger did not respond. It stayed stiff and cold no matter what we did. There was no question of philosophies of restoration. It was not fixed. It was not repaired. The hand could do no more than bear witness to its own experience.

In Giotto's painting of Joachim and Anna at the Golden Gate, there are others who watch the man and woman embrace. They are happy at the meeting, at the new life that waits beyond the scene, but there is one figure who looks away. Her head is covered and her face partly hidden by a dark cloak. She too watches, but her attention is elsewhere. Perhaps she is the girl from the fresco in our house, but older, her garland set aside, the dance slowed. Perhaps she is the necessary presence who gazes clear-eyed into suffering, who contemplates the mystery of losses, who lives with each thing we have tried to mend.

Madelon Sprengnether

FATA MORGANA:
MEMORIES OF ITALY

Now let us, by a flight of imagination suppose that Rome is not a human habitation but a psychical entity with a similarly long and copious past — an entity, that is to say, in which nothing that has once come into existence will have passed away and all earlier phases of development continue to exist alongside the latest one.

—Sigmund Freud

THE ORDER IS that of chance, of travel, of memory, the order of a life. A series of images superimposed, like repeated dreams, the scenes familiar, with small changes in details. Or a pattern of interconnected rooms, so that looking back through arches and doorways one can see the interplay of light and shadow. Nothing is single or simple, however it might appear; there are echoes, mirrors, ghosts in every room, making each point of departure as arbitrary as absolute.

In an off-guard moment I realize that my past is continuous and simultaneous with my present, that only with effort do I suppress this awareness, that the effort itself is tiring, and relief from it, like sleep, a form of release. Perhaps also a form of mercy, or the only kind of tolerance that matters, the acceptance of one's own immutable history and, in an odd way as well, that of one's culture or civilization. This is what I find in Italy at least, where my second husband, Robert, and I travel on our honeymoon.

Rise up, my love, my fair one, and come away. For, lo, the winter is past, the rain is over and gone.

— The Song of Songs

Though we arrive in Rome, our trip really begins at Hadrian's Villa, or "Villa Adriana," as the road sign says, a short distance from Tivoli. It is late afternoon by the time we reach the grounds, leaving the car in a parking lot to walk up a long drive bordered by small wildflowers, sweet-smelling clover, and poppies. There is an olive grove on the approach to the villa and scattered cypress throughout the grounds. Underfoot I find wild mint in places and raspberry bushes along the path, with rough leaves and thorny stems. At the entrance to the estate there is an architectural model representing the villa as it might once have appeared and a colored poster giving an aerial view. I have the distinct impression, as in déjà vu, that I have already been here, that the poster in particular resembles the topography of one of my dreams. The dream itself hovers hazily on the edge of remembrance, but the shock of recognition remains, adding its own golden aura to the afternoon.

Within the walls, the first thing I see is a long rectangular pond, its flat, unruffled surface a peaceful contrast to the restless fountains of Rome. The ruins, a warm, honey-colored combination of brick and cement, some of them quite massive, with pure, rounded arches, are simple rather than heavy in effect. Being open to air and sky, the buildings seem cool, with their white-tiled floors figured with geometric designs, the general absence of clutter. The only rubble consists of pieces of broken marble, fluted columns, cornices. Hadrian, according to legend, tried to reproduce the buildings he most admired in his travels, yet he hardly lived here, dying too soon after the completion of the villa to enjoy it. Poet and aesthete as well as emperor, he addressed one of his last verses to his "naked soul."

* * *

Our room at the Eden Sirene in Tivoli is small, with barely enough space for a double bed. Reflecting the bed there is a full-length mirror on the door of the wardrobe and a window on the opposite wall overlooking a courtyard. We make love toward evening to the sounds of accordion music in the restaurant below, the steady drone of locusts. This hotel is poised on the edge of a ravine and somewhere out of sight there is a long waterfall. We read about the luxurious fountains of the Villa d'Este, tumbling down a series of graded terraces, but we never see them. Through the colored photographs in my book, however, they take their place, like the poster of Hadrian's villa, in my imagination.

At lunch, a long table with families gathered to celebrate a birth, the dessert arriving in a special box, a white confection with ladyfingers and whipped cream, topped with a blue stork. The ruddy tomatoes on my plate — *pommodori, pommes d'or,* golden apples — freshened with mint. The next morning, a pair of newlyweds washing remarks in grease pencil off their automobile.

* * *

In Spoleto we stop at the duomo to view frescoes by Filippo Lippi, a triptych in the sanctuary depicting scenes from the life of the Blessed Virgin, with Lippi's mistress, a former nun, the beautiful stand-in. But it is really landscape that takes the eye in these paintings, the Umbrian hills softly disappearing in a blue haze, a gentle rebuke to the drama of foreground, to the featureless triumph of heavenly coronation. It is the sensation of depth that gives these scenes their dreamy intensity, against which all the richness of gold leaf becomes flat and indifferent.

Our room in Assisi — a very pale peach with high ceilings, cool at midday with the heavy shutters closed. The accommodations are simple and pleasing, a wash stand in the corner, a bidet, the *bagno* next door. The bed, however, far too soft so that finally, not able to sleep, I put the light mattress on the floor. Also twin beds, not our choice.

The rhythm of the day. Robert wakes, walks around town, has coffee, buys fruit — cantaloupe and cherries, which we eat in the room. We go out together to find places of interest, returning after lunch to read, do laundry, sleep in the heat of the day. Around 4:00 p.m. we go out again for more sightseeing and dinner. To bed between 10:00 and 11:00.

Assisi, owing its current prosperity to the cult of St. Francis, was also a Roman town, with the small round of an amphitheater still visible on one edge and a temple long since converted to Christian use at its heart. Looking a little like Gulliver among the Lilliputians, or some kind of caged lion, hemmed in on both sides by buildings of lesser dignity, the temple of Minerva stands gravely, squarely, at the center of the main piazza. Massive and unadorned, it looks as forbidding as the Pantheon, in contrast to which the Basilica of St. Francis at the other end of town, with its highly decorated surfaces seems fanciful, almost childish. At the foot of the temple, underneath the street, moreover, excavations have revealed a forum. We descend into its cool stone chambers, the antithesis of the busy life in the cafes and shops above us.

Here there is evidence of another life: tombstones, rough inscriptions, and flat slabs of pavement, the remains of steps descending from the temple, an indication of its former elevation above the street. Freud would have understood this doubling effect in terms of the relationship between conscious and unconscious mind. For me it is like the persistence of images from my past, shadowing, interrupting, sometimes usurping the present, a sudden reversal of figure and ground. Below the street, Assisi in all its modern trappings fades, whereas above it, the Roman forum vanishes.

The Basilica is also built on two levels, the lower part embedded in the hillside. The effect of the lower church is fantastic, with multi-colored frescoes, the low, wide arches banded with geometric designs —like walking through giant illustrations from a child's picture book. For 300 lire we can purchase a brief illumination of each chapel. And, by descending another narrow staircase, we can view the tomb of St. Francis. I am no pilgrim, however, and the life of the saint, figured in exemplary stages by Giotto in the upper chapel, perplexes me. The story on one level is simple: early conflict with the father (a prosperous burgher with no use for his son's charitable abandon); progressive withdrawal from society; growing asceticism; the stigmata; a longing for death. Along with fasting and mortification of the flesh, a conviction that he understood the language of birds, like that of the chittering sparrows in the evening outside my window. Toward the end he spoke fervently of his desire to be laid on the "*terra fredda e nuda*," waiting for "*sorella morte*." All in all, a saint's life, but no more comprehensible than that of the elusive Hadrian, as indecipherable as the conversation of birds.

Giotto's frescoes themselves in the long nave of the upper church are brightly surreal, with their flat colors, conflicting perspectives and sharply delineated forms. They remind me of landscapes by de Chirico, of Escher prints. Even Chagall must have learned from him — his flying creatures owing their serene pose to the figure of St. Francis ascending to heaven, his legs and feet dangling stiffly behind him. This series of panels, as open as a hand of cards, is visually as hieroglyphic as a Tarot pack.

Our last evening in Assisi we encounter a group of Americans gathered at the temple of Minerva, singing. Moving from the upbeat tempo of Broadway musicals such as *My Fair Lady*, they drift in a kind of nostalgia to "Shenandoah," "The Ash Grove," "The Battle Hymn of the Republic," and finally to Negro spirituals, "Swing Low Sweet Chariot," and others. I feel that the temple through its centuries of transformation is still exerting its influence, reminding all travelers of time, of loss, of home. The last song I hear consists entirely of the refrain "Amen," repeated softly over and over again against the silent backdrop of stone.

* * *

One evening in Siena. *Il campo* full to overflowing and it begins to rain. Slipping and sliding over the cobblestones, we dash over the expanse of piazza into a side street and the Bar Onda operated by a large, smooth-faced black man who plays American rock music on his stereo. On one wall there is a comic poster of the sort one can buy in ghost towns in the west with the logo "Wanted Dead or Alive: Steve the Black." On another wall, Rolling Stones posters and two African photographs. The owner's accent is British, not American, his small cubbyhole of a bar like everything else here bespeaking a mixture of origins.

My lessons in art history are equally jumbled. One afternoon in Perugia a seemingly endless series of madonnas with infants, their expressions nearly identical, Byzantine in aspect, with stiff elongated torsos and staring eyes. In this prim procession, spanning nearly two hundred years, the slightest modification of attitude, of gesture — the crook of a finger, the shift of the child from the right knee to the left — seems revolutionary. I understand this as a form of claustrophobia, there being only one story to tell. At the same time I wonder how many stories have been compressed into this one. What does this goddess, fixed in gold leaf, owe to the ancient pantheon? Only later, in the Vatican museum, will I encounter the terra cotta image of Isis with the infant Horus on her lap that reminds me of her.

Traveling north from Rome toward the Renaissance city of Florence, I see forms in art and architecture merging, almost metamorphosing before my eyes, like time-lapse photography. The long succession of madonnas fuses briefly into a single moment, a pause, a subtle stabilization of elements, in themselves heterogeneous and resistant to form. I begin to see each work of art in terms of captive restlessness — the duomo in Siena, an example of Italian gothic with pointed arches, adorned with a profusion of medieval looking animals and figures of saints against a bold, zebra-striped facade. Inside, with a kind of crazed consistency, it is also striped, the deep vaults painted black with large gold stars, as if to represent the night sky. Such a style, somber, idiosyncratic, vaguely schizophrenic, has no name. It is a collision of influences, curiously bonded, as real and ephemeral as individual history or personality.

In Siena I am also aware of space, of what seems to me a confusion of narrow, winding streets, widening unexpectedly into small piazzas, then bursting into the great central space of the "campo" with its imposing civic building, its beautiful tower rising easily, like some long-necked bird, above the city. Looking down at the piazza, I notice the pattern of streets spilling into it, one down a long cascade of steps. From this height, as in a draftsman's design, the baffle of buildings and passages becomes comprehensible, whereas the effect from below is forbidding, defensive. There is a quality of brooding inwardness to this city with its thick-walled, heavily shuttered facades, its archaic fortifications. In painting too, there is something witheld, medieval, with the exception of two small landscapes by Ambrogio Lorenzetti, one portraying a ship on a cool, green sea, the atmosphere calm and gay. In it I glimpse another world, seemingly accessible, like the sleepy farms and hillside gardens outside the city.

Other glimpses: a man carrying flowers toward the *neonatologia* across from our hotel one morning; a street vendor pushing a cart piled high with gladiolas, singing his wares.

* * *

Arriving in Florence. An enormous volume of traffic, no lanes to speak of, drivers weaving all over the road with little warning. The noise stupendous, mainly because of the small scooters and motorcycles, of which there are many. Our first night in a stifling hot room with the worst traffic din I have ever heard. No plug for the drain in the bath down the hall and no cold water. It is hot and humid on the streets, all of us tourists jammed together at the Piazza della Signoria, the Uffizi, the Academy where we queue up to see Michelangelo's David. A strong smell of horse piss outside the Palazzo Vecchio at the carriage stand. I have a very bad headache, primarily due to the noise.

We change hotels, escape to the Boboli gardens where the locusts are louder than the cars across the river, spend two afternoons in the long arms of the Uffizi, where the heat penetrates less intensely, but I am disheartened, remembering how much I loved this city, arriving fresh as a student from southern France so long ago. Nothing feels familiar, not the golden palace of the Medicis, the building that stunned me into an awareness of architecture, nor the statue of Perseus poised in an arch of the Galleria, nor Botticelli's "Primavera," which has lost its jaundice, having been cleaned in the interval. Even space feels strange, as though someone had taken the city and rotated it, like a map, 180°. Clearly I have lost my bearings.

* * *

It's 11:00 p.m., and I'm wide awake. I tried lying in the dark so as not to keep Robert awake, but he didn't sleep either, sensing my restlessness. At least two sirens went off in the last hour, one as steady as a heart-beat, the other continuous. The first seemed as though it would never stop, blaring for several minutes.

I suppose I am thinking too hard about Florence and my visit here twenty years ago, puzzling around it, worrying it, unable to let go. The city seems smaller to me now, the way places from one's childhood seem smaller when one is an adult. Also dirtier and more crowded, with stale odors and dank smells that are really unpleasant. It makes me think of decay − anything fresh, like fruit, seeming precious and imported from far off. Nothing is very cold here − no air conditioning, and ice rarely served in drinks, the beer warmish like the soft drinks and the gelati all *semifreddo*. I am feeling some core of North American desire for space, appreciation even of Minnesota's harsh clarity in winter.

But twenty years ago what I felt was an awakening, an exhilaration. Lying here I have been thinking how I turned toward that experience then turned away, afraid of something — of what? I believe I had caught a glimpse, through the window of the Renaissance, into my own history, as though a long-sealed corridor had suddenly been opened to light. I preferred, for the time, the protection of darkness. Intending, when I was still a student to return to Europe within a year, I delayed, beginning when I was thirty-one the exploration of my childhood, my adolescence, that has led me finally to this moment. Only now I'm older, and it isn't the same. I can't look at this city with the eyes of a twenty-one-year-old, as revelation. Unlike the Renaissance in architecture, in painting, with its immediacy of subject matter, its sudden expansion of background, the renaissance in my own life seems slow to emerge, painful, arduous. I feel like Michelangelo's unfinished statues of slaves, still struggling to disengage themselves from their stubborn matrix of stone, rather than his David, fresh, free-standing, and confident.

* * *

And yet it is Florence in a shop on the Ponte Vecchio where I choose to buy a wedding ring. Old fashioned in appearance, it is gold with a small sapphire set in a crown of diamonds, with smaller sapphires on each side. The colors — white, blue, gold — are both blazing and innocent, reminding me simultaneously of western landscapes, of hill, sea, and sky, as well as Giotto's simple palette.

Remembering the wedding ceremony in my garden, lush from the heavy spring rains, I recall the place where I stumbled, where I struggled not to cry, as I read the passage we had chosen from *The Song of Songs*, "For, lo, the winter is past," a phrase with serious meaning for those who live in northern climates, as well as those whose hearts packed in ice have experienced a long thaw.

Dolcezza, I think to myself as we make love one afternoon during the siesta hour. Such a deep sweetness. The beautiful light filtered through the shutters into the darkened room, playing over our bodies, reflected in the mirror on the door of the wardrobe, slightly ajar, the door to the bath with its greenish, mottled glass. There is a stillness to this moment, as self-contained as the clear bowls of fruit, half-filled with water, that we see in restaurants, served for dessert.

* * *

Pompeii. Wildflowers everywhere among the ruins. Cornflowers, very tall dandelions, spiky yellow flowers with red stamens, a kind of ladyslipper or jack-in-the-pulpit, poppies, of course, much Queen Anne's lace. Lovely carvings in marble bas relief around one portal, a profusion of acanthus leaves twining around small animals and insects. I can make out a lizard, various birds, a small rabbit, grasshoppers, and winged insects. In the frescoes too one sees birds, animals, fish, as well as household objects like baskets and peaches. The colors mainly are carmine, amber, a soft black, like charcoal, and a deep watery green.

I buy a book called *The Forbidden Pompeii*, with illustrations of the ancient erotic art, unearthed like the city from featureless volcanic ash. Images of the erect penis are obsessional, even comic, as in the figure at the entrance to the House of the Vetii, weighing his colossally engorged member on a pair of scales. Disembodied phalli and testicles appear on facades of buildings, engraved in outline in the streets. But couples dominate the frescoes, demonstrating with frank enjoyment the various positions for intercourse. Un-selfconscious in their nudity, they are not pornographic, as the title of my book, the product of a later era, would seem to indicate. Instead they look comfortable with their bodies, gazing humorously out at us from the darkened rooms to which we are solemnly admitted by a guard. The phallus, I am told, represents fertility rather than obscenity, which it does in our culture. Playful and inventive in their sexuality, these men and women have survived the devastation of their world to unfold their impudent pleasures before our curious eyes.

The first plaster cast of one of the victims of the eruption, in contrast, takes me unexpectedly. I can see its teeth in an open mouth, the fixed expression one of anguish. Parts too of its fingers and toes, the entire figure enclosed in a glass casket, a perverse allusion to fairy tale where death resembles sleep. Here instead of the impassive features of a Snow White, or even the leathery repose of a Santa Chiara on display in Assisi, we see the twistings of a soul in purgatory under a hot, annihilating rain. This drama immediate, ongoing, alive. In another house we come upon a cluster of them, two in one case, forever entwined. The guide tells us with assurance that one is a husband, the other wife, though gender seems hard to determine and in this case irrelevant. What is compelling is the pose, the head of one, skull showing, buried in the chest of the other, both lying on their side. All of the casts seem small in stature, like children somehow, naked in their catastrophe; vainly I want to protect them.

Everything here is suggestive, tantalizing, but also out of reach, unknowable. The plaster casts are shells, the shape of an emptiness, at the same time that the bits of teeth, of bone, are terrible and real.

Lying open to view, these figures seem vulnerable, confessional even, yet their cries are silent, their language, like that of the Etruscans, without a key.

* * *

Days overcast, hazy, brightening at midday for a very hot sun. The pattern of our trip, very few clear days, muggy weather making me feel sticky and sweaty. A long, rugged drive from Pompeii to Reggio Calabria, the mountains reminding me briefly of California, though rougher in aspect, cool in the afternoon until we descend toward the sea. I feel sluggish most of the day, sleepy and discontent, suffering from a kind of homesickness difficult to describe. This mood darkening into depression as we enter Villa San Giovanni, a down-at-the-heels town catering to ferry traffic, which I have falsely imagined as a beautiful seaside resort. We go on to Reggio, encountering an energetic civic official, who, responding to our questions about hotels, invites us into his office where he phones to make reservations for us. His brother, he tells us with pride, works at the museum (which we must surely visit) across the street from the hotel.

In the evening we walk down to the beach, where the water is so clear we can see through the gentle waves to the multicolored stones. There is a couple kissing ardently on the pier and men fishing farther out, casting lines with lighted floats into the water. Pieces of terra cotta litter the shore, washed up from where? The moon hangs low in an amber sliver, like the rind of a melon, while the water makes a soft rattling sound as it sifts back through the stones.

* * *

All day I have been harboring images of disaster, half- submerged, barely articulate, of what might happen at home in my absence. Storms racking my house, the great oak tree in the driveway falling across the roof; my daughter Jessica tumbling out of the raft on her trip down the Colorado river with her dad; my mother ill suddenly, unable to reach me. And deeper, my failures, as wife, daughter, mother. Old ruptures, losses, willful abandonments. Doublings: my first wedding, marriage, my curious sleep-walking state. Loss of innocent dreams of the pastoral life along with my first job in Vermont. The long lurch and stagger into consciousness, toward some acknowledgement of my past. Everyone I hurt. Too late for recompense. Most of all, my child.

I have bad dreams, one on the edge of forgetfulness about *Macbeth*. Then, toward morning, another dream, lucid and disturbing.

Dream of a Gap in Memory

*I am in a kind of bar or restaurant where I order breakfast: coffee, orange
juice, cereal. I am served some tepid milk instead. Then I begin talking with
a young woman, a dancer, whom I seem to recognize from Minneapolis at
the same time that I think she is too young to have known me there. She
leaves and I follow her out to the piazza, leaving my handbag on the floor
next to my stool. When I return it is 10:00 p.m. Slowly I realize that it is
night and that I have no idea how I have spent the time. I worry about
Robert waiting for me at the hotel, but don't know how to find my way back.
I look in the phone book for the address, remembering the name of the hotel,
but I can't find the right section. In a kind of despair, I ask someone for the
name of the city and the answer comes: "Alnuova Porta." At this point I
wake up.*

*Later I remember a dream insertion. In the middle of the phone book
there are brilliant color photographs, like the ones in our tour books, of the
region. I remove them, for reference, on our trip. I think of this, in Freud's
terms, as the "omphalos," the point of opening in the dream.*

The next morning, walking through the civic museum, I juxtapose
the beautiful fragments in the display cases with the enigmatic contents
of my dream. There is no existence, I tell myself, without representa-
tion. The deep past (in one instance Neolithic) lives for me by virtue
of a pile of bones, without which the task of reconstruction, always arduous, and error-prone, is impossible. Without history, or the saving
grace of memory, there is no ground for the creation of that fragile
necessity, a self.

This museum, we discover, owes its fame to a pair of bronze statues,
dating from 5th century Greece, lifted virtually intact from the Ionian
sea near Riace. They are sleek male nudes, wearing military arm bands,
though missing shield and sword, one having lost his helmet as well,
the other with long, curling hair. The display room with the magnificent
bronzes, returned to upright posture from their centuries of ocean
repose, leads into a room full of photographs documenting each stage
of the process of restoration. Some, detailing the nicety and precision
with which the statues are handled, make me think of open heart
surgery. Blurry and thickened from the encrustations of shell and bar-
nacle, the features of the younger man gradually emerge, revealing the
fine eyelashes, the full underlip, the small, perfect teeth, all in shining
copper in contrast to the duller bronze. Slowly the eyes regain their lustre,
individual hairs their spring and curl; a jagged puncture wound in the
thigh is healed. At last, something approximating the original clarity
of contour.

What I see in photograph after photograph is both the delicacy and the sheer hard work of recovery. A careless movement can be ruinous at the same time that the process is tedious, repetitive, time-consuming. Did Freud in his passion for archeology, his collector's eye for the significant artifact, understand this aspect of his own art? And the final paradox. Newly naked and resplendant after their numerous acid baths, their second birth under skilled intstruments, these rare and beautiful nudes are also newly vulnerable, deprived of their comfortable obscurity. Subject now to the vicissitudes of humidity and temperature, the effects of their rude awakening, they inch toward their own decay. The sea in its easy indifference was kinder.

What is known about these bronzes is hypothetical in nature and far less compelling than their presence. And yet we try to find a place for them in the fine web of meaning that constitutes our understanding of history. By giving them a story, however tentative, of origin, of destination, we draw them into the realm of myth, into the kind of symbolic procession we see in the terra cotta images of Persephone, depicting her progress through the underworld. We see her in shallow bas relief: in a chariot with a young man, extending one arm backward in long farewell; in a series of harvesting and dressing scenes, including the presentation of gifts; holding a mirror and wearing a diadem, with a dove or a rooster on her lap; opening an elaborately figured casket out of which springs a child. Later in Sicily we drive through Enna, the city designated as the place of her abduction.

So much of this landscape has been mythologized. We cross the straits of Messina on a ferry called "Ulysse" for the fabled adventures of Odysseus supposed to have taken place here. The water for our own crossing is a deep, silky blue with a frothing as from carbonation where the waves break away from the prow, looking like petticoats as they ruffle outward.

* * *

Much of the countryside on the eastern coast of Sicily is terraced and scorched from the sun, brightened by brilliant rushes of bougainvillaea along the highways and in town. Taormina built on the side of a mountain, the roads steep and serpentine. At our hotel, high above the sea, a beautiful fluted flower called *mongibilia*, native, as the manager tells me, to this region. A clear yellow near the base, opening out like a trumpet into five fine petals folded over themselves, flushed at the tip. *Mongibilia*, the name almost an invocation, like *mongibello*, an Arab word for Aetna — mountain of mountains. *Terra ballerina*, a phrase that describes the fine agitations of the earth.

We try to reach Aetna one morning by the southern route, but the road comes to an abrupt halt, blocked by lava flow, cool enough to walk on, with heat waves rising in a dancing shimmer — like charcoal. Somber from a distance, a dull black crust, the lava underneath my feet glows with lighter hues, a whole range of yellows, blues, reds. Later as we try the northern route, it begins to rain, a heavy fog settling over the road, water running swiftly in narrow channels on either side. Aetna, veiled and ominous, has simply withdrawn from us. That afternoon at lunch in a cafe, thunder and lightning simultaneously, a deluge of rain in the street, as the electricity fails, a sharp current running through my arms, hands, fingers.

Some days, from Taormina, Aetna appears through the persistent haze, long sleeves of smoke billowing from its crest. Some days it hangs in the air, barely visible, a phantom volcano, or *fata morgana*. One evening on the corso we stand hypnotized before a videotape of a recent eruption, watching the massive molten flow, as the people in the film gesture nervously, themselves transfixed.

* * *

Let my beloved come into his garden, and eat his pleasant fruits.
The Song of Songs

Agrigento. The farthest point in our travels from Rome. Birthplace of Empedocles, the philosopher who articulated the theory of the four elements, who believed the world to be animated by the principles of love and strife, and who ended his life on Aetna, returning through air, through earth, to fire.

Agrigento, the ancient Akragas of Magna Graecia, is golden. The drive from Catania, through wheat-colored fields, then a series of rolling mountains, one behind another, like waves, with sudden outcroppings of rock, a landscape suited to dream. The hotel, the Villa Athena, with a fine view of the temples, our building adjacent. Down a dirt road through an iron gate to a farmhouse converted for guests, with a garden outside our window, set with olive trees, grape vines, a fruit tree laden with golden plums. The plums with a translucence as if lit from within, like the flesh of a child whose blood you can almost see beating under the skin. We pluck three and eat them, tangy to the taste, with a full plushy interior, at the peak of ripeness.

Flowers everywhere. Hibiscus outside our window, large, open, red. Geraniums growing like bushes, bougainvillaea like a weed, climbing up pine trees. Blue morning glory vines along the road. Clusters of petunias at the hotel, white with violet centers.

The magnificent temples on a rise overlooking the sea, a pure honey color, the main building material seemingly sandstone embedded with fossils, porous like a sponge and softly eroded. Illuminated by night, they seem to float in the darkness, like the low-hanging moon, the color of old gold.

The hotel one evening hosts a large wedding reception, guests appearing in the late afternoon: the women in gowns of light-figured material, in shades of mauve and lavender, the men in starched white shirts, little girls in frilly dresses with petal shaped collars, little boys in short pants. Gradually they settle among the tables in loose family groupings: parents, children, grandparents, the boys and girls running in twos and threes, with the younger ones, barely able to walk, clinging to their older brothers and sisters, the babies with their mothers, lifted and held, passed from lap to lap. Some of the guests are drinking from glasses with a bright pink liquid, the same with which the bride and groom toast each other, descending dramatically from the upper terrace to a quick reprise of the wedding march. The bride, wearing a full, white dress with several layers of net, is dark-haired and young. She and her new husband pause for the leisurely appreciation of their guests then retreat to the end of the terrace out of our sight.

Later they reappear, the bride without her veil, a sprig of white flowers in her hair, passing from table to table, greeting friends and posing for photographs. We watch the line of waiters, platters held high, form and re-form to serve each course, the ritual so precise that it resembles something out of a fairy tale. I myself feel like a child, peering over the balustrade, permitted for the sake of a party to stay up late. When we leave, they are just beginning to pop the champagne corks, the celebration continuing, with the moon, the temples as silent witness, far into the night.

Interludes of lovemaking. At midday, the slanting light from the shutters. Lying naked with wet linen over our bodies to reduce the heat. The slow, sweet spring of desire. The flesh that answers, the luxuriance and the sureness of touch. The open hand, the grateful heart. No knowledge, as we take and eat, as deep, as good, as this.

* * *

Thus the wish to go to Rome had become in my dream-life a cloak and symbol for a number of other passionate wishes.

—Sigmund Freud

Several years ago, a dream containing the imperious injunction: "You must go to Rome." Toward which all roads. Toward which a longing, after Sicily, for something familiar. The comfort of our reserved rooms, the cool tiled bath, the beds with soft cotton sheets. In the morning the crusty rolls, puffed and hollow, the smooth white pitchers of steamed coffee and milk.

The jumble that is Rome — the labyrinthine pattern of one-way streets, leading us ever farther from our destination as we try to drive to the rental car office, the casual appearance of monuments, a soaring wall, a triumphal arch — now feels less confusing than expected. Here the landscape of the mind is literalized, the dream world made apparent. Consulting our map each morning as we chart the course of our day, we might as well be trying to read a map of the land of Oz. Like looking into the interior of the Colosseum from which the floor has been removed, revealing its subterranean passages, or trying to read a honeycomb. This city, where the kind of ruined past we are willing to call maturity coexists with the curious modern bustle that so resembles hope, is the city of my middle-age. It opens before me, like Dante's beckoning wood, neither ominous nor infernal, but rather human and fallible, offering more roads than I can ever follow.

Margot Fortunato

VICOLETTO:
SCENES FROM NAPLES

ITALY, AS A land and a people, came into my life early with my father's *pizzichilli*, little pinch kisses. Like their sharp affection, my last name *Fortunato* meant good luck but had to be spelled for teachers and shop clerks. More unpleasant was my mother's advice: I had to preserve appearances because loose behavior might connect me to the Mafia. Italy as a place where these facts of my life come together looked like a rugged boot that would never fit me. But I knew someday I'd have to try it on.

Meanwhile it contributed curious bits of history to my childhood. My father, a first-generation Italian-American from Pittsburgh, had studied the violin in Ferrara when he was in his teens. My mother, a German-Scandinavian from North Dakota, had married him because she had a Midwesterner's yearning for hills, history, and life lived with operatic intensity. During the early years of the Depression, she ate oatmeal twice a day so that they could save enough money to travel to Italy. In 1936, a submarine escort ushered them through the Straits of Gibraltar between Franco's insurrection based in Morocco and the beleaguered Spanish government. This dangerous passage on an Italian ship supportive of Franco became in her telling a romantic escape.

When she put "La Boheme" and "Tosca" on the record player to accompany her dusting, I swooned with her and forgot that I lived in Charleston, South Carolina in the 1950s. But my father's request for wine vinegar at motel restaurants where we stopped during summer trips brought me firmly back to American reality. Why did he have to insist on being different?

In South Carolina blacks and Anglo-Saxons knew who they were, but as I grew up I often felt like a foreigner. To escape that, I stopped thinking about Italy, married right out of college, changed my name and moved to the Midwest.

Slowly, my curiosity about Italy rekindled. I studied Italian for three years. Then in 1977 I spent a week visiting Venice, Florence, and Rome.

Now I was pleased to be mistaken for a native. But the minute I opened my mouth, the illusion was dispelled.

Hotel clerks greeted my Italian with disdain and answered in English. When my lost suitcase finally arrived at the Venice airport, I used the most elementary Italian to explain what was inside: *scarpe* (shoes) and *camicie* (shirts). The customs officials took my word for it. How could someone so bumbling be a smuggler?

During the second week of the trip, I met my father at the Hotel Ambassador, the only skyscraper in Naples. He had flown directly to Naples to meet me. We had a magnificent view of the bay where white tankers crossed bright blue water and the chaos of the streets dissolved into a panorama of white-studded hills. He was going to guide me into the hills to the town where our family had started. As he waited for a telephone call from Cousin Giovanna, he railed against modern Italy: the cab drivers who talked like brothers, then swindled him; the waiters who scowled when a tourist ordered only pasta for lunch; the telephones operated by hard-to-obtain tokens; and finally the shortage of coins for which shopkeepers substituted stamps and candy.

He was appalled at the strikes, kidnappings and kneecappings that took place that summer in Italy. He wanted Mussolini to return and make the trains run on time. He praised the U.S. But the minute he hit the street, his mood changed. He didn't care if he got lost. He simply stopped and began talking to the first person who would answer his classical Italian. He introduced me, explained our origins, the reason for our return. Slowly, we made our way down the street, sticking our heads into every grocery store, complimenting the shopkeepers on their wares, picking our way through the throng of gypsies who camped in the main piazza near the marina. He taught me that on the street in Naples, it was *dolce far niente*, sweet to do nothing.

* * *

That week, my father hired a driver to take us the 60 miles along perilous mountain roads east from Naples to Pescopagano, where my grandfather was born in 1880. Set in a mountainside with a limpid valley stretched below and gray hills ringing the horizon, Pescopagano is as remote from modern Italy as a town in the Ozarks is from New York. Many young people have left for jobs in the north or in Germany, but they come back every year for the Festa di San Francesco di Paolo, the town's patron saint.

By coincidence, we arrived the afternoon of the festa, June 30. From the high-ceilinged bedroom where I was napping in Cousin Maria's house, I heard the music of John Philip Sousa. The town band, followed by chickens and children and women pushing baby carriages, paraded through the narrow streets. In my halting Italian, I asked Maria, "Why Sousa?"

"He is universal," she said.

We spent the afternoon going from house to house in search of people who remembered my grandfather. Everywhere we were embraced and served a glass of wine. My father immediately began to converse, and I asked questions about genealogy. One old woman insisted on showing us the house where my grandfather was born. As we stood on the cobblestones, chattering and gesticulating, a short, bald man in a bright blue suit came out on the balcony. Then he disappeared and returned waving a piece of paper. "I have a letter from your grandfather," he called out.

The relatives explained afterwards that he is a little crazy, does nothing all day but sit in his room wearing the bright blue suit. But I saw him as a man of perception and unrecognized talent. Not only did he save the letter my grandfather wrote from Pittsburgh in the early 1920s, but he put his hands on it in seconds. It was the only written proof I had of my origins in the town, for the graves of my great-grandfather and great-grand-uncle had been dug up, if indeed they had ever been there, and the bones piled in an open *ossario* or bone room. As I stared at the mound of skulls, I realized that I had traced the family connection as far back as it would go.

What I had in common with the town was more elementary than a name or a letter from America. Staring into the gray hills with the moon rising above them, I could make sense of the mountain air in my grandfather's demeanor. He was the mountaineer who had looked toward the mountains, and one day traveled to the sea on their other side. Now I understood some of the nostalgia he brought with him — his taste for the local cheeses, *cacciacavallo* and *burro*, the first a soft provolone sold in two balls connected by a string to be thrown over a horse's neck (*cacciacavallo* means horse's catch). And the second, *burro*, a soft mozzarella with burro or butter in the middle. I understood why first my father and then I savored these tastes instinctively, and why we both had what my mother called "itching feet."

✳ ✳ ✳

Back in Minnesota after that first trip, I kept turning over in my mind the small artifacts of family story that had descended to me. I asked relatives about my grandfather's emigration. One said he left because he had fallen in love and could not remain celibate in the seminary. This story contained the dramatic episode of my grandfather stealing across

the rooftops of Pescopagano to say goodbye to his sweetheart, then flee-
ing to Naples to stow away on a ship.

Another version of his leave-taking explained that one day in Naples,
while he and the rest of his seminary class walked in the street, a carriage bearing the shield of the king of Italy passed. He alone of his class
cheered the king and a unified Italy. Hearing him, a group of artisans
raced across the street behind the carriage and lifted him to their
shoulders: they too supported the monarchy over the papacy.

But the seminary was not pleased. As punishment for his anticlerical
sentiments, my grandfather was sent home to report to the bishops of
his region. But he never arrived: on his way he met an Italian Protestant
who converted him during the carriage ride. The Protestant invited him
to America.

This version had the virtue of suggesting why he converted to Prot-
estantism when he arrived in Pittsburgh, then married a minister's
daughter and became a missionary to his Catholic brethren in the slums.
But both stories had appeal, and I had no way of knowing which was
true. My grandfather had died ten years before. Even in his life he had
refused to discuss his motives. Finally at the limits of truth, I began to
enjoy the fictional possibilities of my family story. I decided to write my
own fable of his emigration. Where should I go to discover how to flesh
out its ambiguity and create a lively, believable possibility?

The answer was Naples. Naples and the seminary my grandfather
had attended, and the hospital where, ill with cholera, he'd been visited
by the beautiful countrywoman who perhaps swayed his faith. Naples
Bay, ringed by Vesuvius, Pompeii, and the town where my Cousin
Giovanna lived with her mother, Castellammare di Stabia. Naples and
its monuments and museums and paving blocks made of black lava.
I decided to revisit Naples, this time by myself, and look for a clue caught
between the lava blocks.

* * *

On the mid-September plane from Boston to Rome, three years after
my first trip, I asked the man beside me where he was going. "Home
to Rome," he answered in an American accent. Indeed, he looked
American: tall with a genial full face, he wore a blue knit shirt. But this
turned out to be an acquired look. Fernando was born in Naples, and
his wife spent the war years in, of all places, my grandfather's hometown
of Pescopagano. When we discovered that we had the town in common,
our reticence disappeared and he explained his work as a nuclear safety engineer. As we circled Rome, he insisted that I call his sister Nerina
in Naples. "She will treat you like a *paesana*," Fernando assured me. I

accepted her number and made my way alone to the plane from Naples.

From the air, Naples looked like a soft pink confection, its hills covered with white, beige and tan buildings. But on the ground the purity disappeared. The air was smoggy. Customs officials herded us as if we were guilty of some crime. Taxi drivers, with shirts unbuttoned to their navels, stalked the airport veranda like haughty predators. I adjusted my self-confidence and walked past them to the bus stop. Newly divorced, paying my own way, I had to save money.

Two young Italian men, wearing sailor uniforms and carrying duffle bags, waited with me. When we boarded the bus at the rear, we had to deposit 100 lire for a ticket. One of my companions handed me a silver coin. I stood at the back of the bus, relieved that they were kind and genteel, and I told them why I had come.

As we talked in my classroom Italian and their Texas, merchant-marine English, each practicing an acquired second-language, we swayed and bumped over the narrow streets. A Naples I had never seen before flowed by the windows. Stores opened right onto the street. In one, a blond svelte woman spoke intimately over the counter to the butcher in white coat. They are lovers, I thought: she pays him in gossip. Then a woman got on, staggering and clutching a pole. She had no money to pay. From the front, the driver ordered her off, but she closed her eyes and stayed. We passed a side street where market stalls were set up in the midst of traffic. From one stall rose bunches of balloons, blue, red, yellow, white. Dark green watermelon and yellow crook-neck squash sat under another awning. The streets were mobbed. Hawkers sold coconut halves and bottles of *aranciata*, orangeade. Old men in baggy trousers and straw sandals tipped their chairs against the wall. Children in dull gabardine skirts and tailored blouses ran through the crowd, and old women in black walked arm and arm with younger women in pleated skirts and tailored blouses.

As the sun set, slanting across the pale buildings, I leaned out the hotel window and watched life on the balconies opposite. Families prepared to eat, a woman watered flowers that carpeted her balcony. Further up the hills, the Old Quarter clustered around the famous church of Santa Chiara, with its cloister winding like a ribbon behind it. Tomorrow, Cousin Giovanna had promised to take me to the Old Quarter and the Capodimonte Museum, on top of the hills. But tonight, alone, observing the swarming pink city, I felt restless.

Impulsively, I telephoned Nerina, the sister of the nuclear safety engineer from the Rome plane. The minute she heard who sent me, her voice rose a notch in excitement. "But of course, you must come to dinner. My brother knows I love Americans," she laughed. We would meet downstairs in an hour.

Tall, red-haired, chic, Nerina took charge of me in the hotel lobby. Walking to her car, she pulled the sleeves of her tan sack dress away from her arms. Her English was slightly accented. In the warm night, her voice fell as liquid as the air. Next to her suave vitality, I felt stiff and shrinking. But she took my arm as we crossed the courtyard of the huge, 19th-century palazzo where she lives. By the time we stepped into the elevator, and she called up the airshaft to her mother and son waiting by the door, my courage and confidence had returned.

Her sitting room was lined with book shelves topped with posters all the way to the ceiling. Most of the posters came from exhibits in American museums. For a number of years, she explained, she spent every fall in the U.S. while her husband taught. There at Rutgers she took a master's degree in museum administration. Books in English and Italian caught my eye: *Pentimento* by Lillian Hellman; *Red Brigades* in English; *Un Uomo* (A Man) by Italian journalist Oriana Fallaci.

Although the books suggested otherwise, Nerina said that the American part of her life was over. In a week she would start a full-time job teaching geography in the public schools. She laughed, "You will like this because you are a writer." Fingering a gold chain around her neck, she said that while substitute teaching in the Santa Lucia district — "that's along the waterfront, the black-market area" — she asked students to write about the joys and dangers of the sea. Their themes came back describing the dangers of sailing in darkened boats to collect black-market cigarettes and outwitting the police.

At ease with vermouth and her lively talk, I described my Italian background and asked about the seminary where my grandfather was once enrolled. "It's in the Old Quarter," she answered. "Be careful when you walk there. Don't carry any money."

In a small dining room across from the kitchen, a table was set with green strawberry-dotted cloth and napkins. Nerina's mother ate sliced tomatoes first. Nerina, her son Lucca, and I began with *risotta*, rice made with peas and mushrooms. Then we ate tomatoes, bread, some gourd-shaped cheese and we drank water and wine. Nerina joshed Lucca, 16. Tomorrow he planned to get up early to run: "You've never done this before," she said. He explained solemnly, "I'm going to run the 440."

When I asked about his other hobbies, he pointed to a shelf of American games and said, "In Italy, we play by all the rules." As distinct from real life, I thought, meaning the train strike that threatened and the chaotic traffic. But I said nothing, made easy by the wine, my vocabulary in both English and Italian gone to sleep.

After dinner, Nerina poured *espresso* from a two-cup, upside down coffeepot, like the ones my father had collected at home. We sat in the living room, and she and I smoked German cigarettes advertised as "mild for women." Always *vivace*, she imagined five Americans, expected to arrive for a visit with a friend, stranded by the strike in a provincial station. "It's not funny, don't laugh," I blurted out, making her laugh even more.

"In Italy, everything is always breaking down," she said. "We women have to be foxes to survive." She leaned back against the sofa cushions. "In America, everything runs smoothly. I know, I've lived there. But that ease makes the women boring."

Now alert, I challenged, "What do you mean?" She reassured me, patting my hand with her tanned one. "Not you, *cara mia*, the professors' wives. They're the ones I mean. They're all alike. They have nothing to contend with. They don't even talk to each other. But in Italy we have to talk. We always know each other's troubles."

Her brown eyes kind and sassy, she smiled at me. "Think of the feminists, here and in America," she said. "Many people think they're silly, bra-burning, that sort of thing, but many women in Italy have changed — how do you say, — consciousness?— because of them. The laws in Italy have not been so hard on women as you have in America: here pregnant women have six-months leave routinely on most jobs, all paid. But this is no nirvana," she hastened to add. "Of course, men know that to hire a woman. . ." Her eyebrows implied the danger by rising and flourishing.

As we were talking, her husband joined us, a bit gruff, tired out from the start of fall classes. Nerina patted him on the head and opened a desk inlaid with garlands of multicolored wood. "Give me your address," she asked and sat down. "Then we must go."

* * *

Next morning I ate breakfast at the restaurant atop the hotel, feasting my eyes on the patina of soft colors, noticing how the shutters on every building jack up to let in the breeze. It was a beautiful hazy blue sky, no sign of the islands, but the Carthusian Monastery of San Martino clearly set its claws into the ridge overlooking the bay. When Cousin Giovanna arrived at 11, she wore a white pleated skirt and turquoise silk blouse, but she looked tired after an early morning teachers' meeting. The elementary school where she teaches science wouldn't start for a week, but she was already working. I suggested taking a taxi to the Capodimonte Museum.

Out on the street, in the clamor of noon traffic and pedestrians crowding home for two-hour lunch breaks, we changed our minds. Practical and quick, intent on getting me to the top of the mountain, Giovanna went from bus to bus at the piazza terminal until she found one about to depart. It was mobbed and more people got on pushing us against the windows.

As the bus mounted higher and higher, past a hotel, I spied a child in white T-shirt and diapers sitting in front of a mirror. The air became fresher, and on top of a church, statues of angels and Mary stood out white against a brilliant sky. The museum, which used to house the Neapolitan royal family, is set in a *bosco*, wooded park. To commemorate its past glory, it is still painted dark red.

Invigorated by the fresh air and winding paths, we chattered about trees and plants. Even inside the museum we kept up this scientific prattle. Giovanna stroked a column on the stairs, "From Pescopagano," she told me, "not *marmo*, (marble)." Evidence of royalty — a room covered floor to ceiling with ceramic monkeys, their tails curved over their backs, under their feet, making crooks, curlicues, and then near the ceiling parrots pecking at fruit and looking in mirrors. An elegant, dandified, totally impractical room.

I pestered Giovanna, the science teacher, for names of monkey, parrot, vine, flower, not only to hear them in Italian, but also to watch her laugh at my ignorance. Wanting her to enjoy this visit, I played the eager student.

We were good companions. She established a regimen. Since she had never visited the museum before, she wanted to see it all. We would visit the picture galleries chronologically. Because her devotion touched me, I didn't tell her that madonnas and saints bore me. She could not understand why I stood so long before the "Self-portrait" of Sofonisba Anguissoula, "Woman of Samaria," by Lavinia Fontana, and "Judith and Holofernes," by Artemesia Gentileschi. I told her that I teach about female artisits, but she was more awed by Raphael, Lippo Lippi and Caravaggio. "*Be*," she kept saying as she tripped back and forth on her backless cream sandals, bursting out in enthusiasm to a guard with a huge barrel chest, not much taller than her five feet. "*Be*," she cried, "I was *in ignoranza* of all these treasures."

When we left, she vowed to come back. Then walking back and forth along the gravel paths, she remembered a ceramic factory that used to be here. Finally at the far end of the park where the ground slopes away, dry and brown, cut with gravel tracks, a cream building of Renaissance proportions announced the possibility of a ceramic factory. Like many things in Italy it was closed.

We turned back to the woods and sat in a spot of sun until a strange man, pale and plump, rested beside us. Then we moved to another bench under an arbor of oak trees. Here Giovanna dusted a place for her white skirt. Across the path, a small brown bird with reddish breast scratched in the leaves. "*Pettirosso*," said Giovanna, little red, or according to the dictionary, robin redbreast. I told her about the big American robin, which is not in the robin family at all, it's a thrush. The real one fit the park with its dusty and unpopulated grandeur.

The bus down the mountain was also sparsely populated. The few passengers were sleepy after lunch. I sat in a seat labeled, "*Posto reservato di mutilati di guerra* (Place reserved for the wounded of war)." With this image of the defeated and maimed, I stepped off the bus and into the Piazza Dante in the heart of the Old Quarter. Giovanna, still pursuing my tourist interests, seemed energized by the din and the heat; she spoke faster and faster, taking my hand and pulling me along the narrow sidewalks. I had trouble understanding her, my answers in Italian resistant and sleepy.

We reached the Polyclinica, the hospital of the University of Naples. The building looked like a 19th-century resort hotel, turreted, massive, white. I expected to hear crashing waves and squalls of gulls, but instead, only a line of mimosa trees inside the iron fence separated the place from the narrow streets. We looked up into the trees, admiring their delicate blue blossoms. This is the place where my great-uncle studied pediatrics in the 1890s. Looking up the word for lace in the dictionary, I said it to Giovanna, "*Merletto*." And nodding her head sprayed with sun and shadows, she knew I meant the mimosa leaves.

Like children at a peep show, we proceeded down a *vicoletto*, a diminutive street where no cars pass. Bedrooms and shops opened directly onto the pavement, and we passed quietly for fear of disturbing an old couple having lunch at their sewing machine or of defiling a crucifix hanging above a bed with pink coverlet. Then as we turned into a wider thoroughfare, I suddenly realized that Giovanna was confused. She grabbed the shoulder strap of her purse and felt her throat. She was talking, almost shouting. A man next to her had seen it happen. A kid on a motorcycle had torn the gold chain and cross from her neck.

Now I don't remember what she said as she talked to the man in gray, but I was glad that he was there to understand her anger and loss. She bent her neck for me to see the stress marks where the chain had pressed the skin before breaking. Then holding my arm, she led me along a way to the church of Santa Chiara, famous for the majolica-covered columns of its cloister. "*Chiuso*," said two well-dressed men leaning on their automobiles beside the cloister door.

"Only in Italy is everything closed," cried Giovanna as they shrugged at her anger, anger at the lost chance to see the treasure, but also at the loss of the chain and cross sent by her father before he died in Africa. The only comfort I could offer was promising that, yes, tomorrow I would come back and see the cloister.

* * *

But too afraid of the Old Quarter, I did not return to Santa Chiara, and Giovanna's voice on the telephone rebuked me. "You have come so far," she said. I could not tell her that after only three days, I had to force myself out of the hotel room in the evening to find a restaurant. "But yes, I will vist and meet your mother. Yes, I will take a train and get off at Via Nocera; I will call from the station and you will walk the short distance from the apartment to meet me." After we hung up I wondered if I had understood her: the phone distorted her Italian and made my limited comprehension even more tentative.

Via Nocera Station, on the periphery of Castellammare di Stabia, between Naples and Sorrento — no more than a bare room with a cashier's window. There was a public telephone, but no token box beside it. I tried buying a token from the cashier, but he did not sell them. I must have looked desperate; my accent faltered. Then a large bald man approached and put a token in my hand. I tried to pay him, but calmly he refused and walked outside to the platform.

When Giovanna appeared, tousled and flushed from school, she beamed at the man who had helped me. Then she took my arm, clutching my hand as if I had survived a perilous journey. Her exuberance, expressed in smiles and rushing, bell-toned words, frolicked around me.

From a balcony high in the huge, pink cement building, a short woman in a black dress began to wave. "Ciao, Mama," Giovanna called, "we're coming." Only in stature did Giovanna resemble her mother. When we embraced, Elisa's white-knotted hair reached only to my chin. She held me off to look for some family trait, or to judge how American I looked. Somber yet articulate, this old woman led me to admire their bedrooms, each with a balcony full of plants. Giovanna wanted me to admire the patterns of the tile she had chosen for each room.

We ate in front of open French doors, platters of pasta, chicken, zucchini. Elisa held my hand and answered my questions about her husband who had lived in Pittsburgh and died in Africa.

Giovanna chided her mother, "Mama, don't be sad," as she filled our glasses. But Elisa, her old hazel eyes imperious and insistent, told me that her life has been hard. Her husband had left for America and never sent for her. She had taken care of her daughters, traveled to Naples in the midst of the Second World War, and walked the strange streets while bombs fell. "I don't love America," she said, not blaming me, but speaking the truth. "After the war, he came back and there was no work. He had to leave again, for Africa."

Giovanna placed a frosted dessert on the table. "Now, Mama, don't be sad," she said.

From each balcony, Elisa waved to me, becoming smaller and smaller as I walked away. Sitting on the train as it sped around Vesuvius, I remembered Nerina telling me in her mother's presence, "In Italy, we never get rid of the mothers; we expect to take care of them." As they take care of curious, half-lost American women.

The cross torn from Giovanna's neck was the last gift she had left from her father. Now with it gone, she was cut off from her patrimony, as I am from mine. The father she knew so little had sent her the cross as he lay dying in Africa. None of the family could afford to visit him. The city's white-painted frosting covers old grime and our common loss. The next night, alone on the quay, I dined in an empty restaurant. The solo violinist started up "Oh, Susanna." I knew it was for me. Nervous and furtive, he had been eyeing me ever since I arrived.

Now the violin quavered the song of American loneliness, and I spooned a minestrone into my mouth, giddy and embarrassed to be alone and half flirting with the grizzled Italian, my family as close and as far away as the familiar song in the late, wavering Neapolitan light.

FAR EAST

Linda Woolman Perry

EVENING IN PADANG

WHEN MY HUSBAND, who had experience living in the Far East, told me
I'd grow to love Padang, I didn't believe it. After two months I was still
overwhelmed by one obscurity after another. Meanwhile I tried to create
a haven of comfort, familiar objects and books in our house on *Jalan
Manggis* (Mangosteen Street).

It was evening in Padang, three degrees below the Equator, but I wasn't
susceptible to its charms. A small coastal town in West Sumatra, Indonesia, it is bordered by chartreuse rice paddies, tall, thin palms, and
the Indian Ocean. But the chaos of the town smothered me with its ex-
otica: eerie smells, five people on a motorbike, open drains oozing black
sludge, burning garbage on every street, mendicant lepers, sheets of
dust, masses of people at every hour, unrelenting noise...

David was an agricultural consultant; he'd signed on for two years.
Two years. I would write. All I'd written to date were cheerful letters
home belying my failure to understand.

Our son Sam had impetigo, his second case since we'd arrived. The
few nasty red scabs on his back were not serious, but it meant a trip
to a new doctor for a prescription. The first doctor said it was due to
dirty conditions. I bristled at that: our live-in help, Ida, kept our house
cleaner than I'd ever managed to in California. We bathed Sam twice
a day, but our street was paved with crushed rocks so the dust was rife
and the neighborhood chickens invaded our lawn regularly.

It rained hard on the way to the doctor's — the way it rains only in
the tropics: noisily and persistent until it stops abruptly. I held Sam on
my lap on the passenger's side of the jeep, and we stared out the windows at the melting colored lights in gaudy contrast to the dark night.

David turned the jeep onto a residential street bordered with plumeria
trees whose large-petaled white blossoms briefly reflected the headlights.
As he parked the rain stopped. "That's lucky," I murmured opening the
door and handing Sam to David who stood tall and smiling, ready to
take him. The rain had cut the dust and humidity of the day with a new
and earthy smell.

We walked over a wide concrete slab bridging the open drain at the side of the road and approached the brightly lit front porch of a Dutch bungalow lined with chairs. On them sat young mothers of Padang with well-dressed babies due for their regular checkups. The women wore fresh dresses and red lipstick as if for a special occasion. Everyone's dark eyes were soon on us, and we smiled before turning to each other.

We were used to this. I wrote home that when we were out in the jeep at any given moment no less than ten sets of eyes focused on us. At first it was numbing and made me self-conscious; later I forgot about it and was only reminded occasionally when I noticed someone nudging a friend and gesturing toward us. An outer island and less traveled than Java, Sumatra was not used to *orang barat* (people of the West).

Sam squirmed on my lap, and I put him down after kissing the top of his blond head and breathing in with pleasure his sweet and salty scent. He immediately picked up some gravel rocks and made piles of them on the seat next to me. A few older children, all of whom seemed to sit quietly in their mother's arms, watched him. The mothers were more animated and friendly, and one said in English, "How old?"

"A year and a half," David answered.

"And your baby?" I queried.

"Six years, no, six months," she laughed. Her baby's face was shiny with sweat under the bright porch light which was alive with flying insects. The baby tolerated a thick pink sweater and bonnet in spite of the evening's muggy warmth.

"Maybe she's hot?" I suggested. The woman smiled and said, "Hot, yes. Rain, *bagus* (good)."

There would always be gaps in understanding, I thought, feeling uneasy. I could have tried to explain what I meant — that the baby was overdressed — but where did concern end and interfering begin? All the mothers here clothed their babies in modern synthetic fabrics in spite of the heat. Should I suggest that they dress their children in lighter clothing? They probably wondered why a "rich foreign woman" put her child in a simple cotton T-shirt, shorts, sandals, no socks. When you are in a foreign country some things remain a mystery and you just finally let go.

It was like the time I came home to find Ida and Sam sitting on the cool tile floor holding a small wild bird by a string attached to one leg. It was brown and black and frantic with fear. It kept jumping away from Sam only to be stopped when the string pulled taut. Sam grinned and said, "Look, Mommy, look!"

"Oh, no, darling. It's only a young bird and he wants to go home to his family." This appealed immediately to Sam who dropped the string, which was snatched by Ida.

"Ida," I tried to say in my best Bahasa Indonesian, "the bird wants his freedom." I used the word *merdeka* that I'd heard in the national anthem, unsure of its appropriateness here. I felt foolish and inept as her smile grew. Ida and I stood staring at each other, and I knew that I was unable to bridge the river of misunderstanding that separated us. I smiled now too, but we stood eye to eye for another moment or two before she took the bird outside. I promised myself that I would study the language well: the inability to speak in the local tongue renders you lonely and impotent.

This was our first visit to the doctor's, and we were last on the list that was posted on the door of the office. We did not know that we could have signed up that afternoon, so we prepared to wait.

Someone approached, crunching the gravel with slow, heavy steps. Everyone turned to watch a man in the dark carrying a rather large boy. The man was a young father in simple but clean clothes, his and his boy's hair slicked down and shiny. The boy wore no shirt, and I wondered at that — to see his bare brown back, unusual as Indonesians are rather formal making a trip to the doctor's.

The man set the boy — ten years old perhaps — on a chair and sat down beside him. He smiled and laughed a little, but the boy was quiet, his eyes cast down.

Everyone's eyes moved to the boy's chest, which had a terrible large red and purple open wound. Some of the mothers whispered to each other, and I felt sick to my stomach and looked at David. The two men — David and the father — faced each other. David said something I did not follow in Indonesian, and I understood only one word of the father's — a word I knew from another context: *goreng* which means fried. I felt my scalp prickle. Every morning a boy came down our street, Jalan Manggis, shouting "*Pisang goreng* (fried bananas)."

The door opened and the doctor came out — a short, plump Indonesian woman in a blue batik blouse and black skirt. She looked around at the patients briefly, scanned the list, and then she beckoned us in.

I stood up and turned to David. "But we're last, and surely that boy should be seen first." David said something to the doctor, but she continued to wave us in. David picked up Sam and went into the office and I followed, silenced by my lack of Bahasa Indonesia and the growing certainty that to make a scene would be inappropriate and rude.

I touched David's shoulder. "Why are we next, David? That's not fair, and the boy. . ." David was torn between my questions and those of the doctor who spoke now in rapid Bahasa Indonesia and was prodding Sam's back. He decided to deal with the doctor and with Sam who began to writhe about and whine, and I felt a sudden urge to cry. Tears came and I bit my tongue and read the doctor's chart on the life cycle of the mosquito and its relation to malaria.

Why were we being given special treatment? Because we were American? Was it a courtesy, a kind deference to us as expatriates? And what about that poor boy? The tears started to fall. Why didn't the doctor rush him in? Why did the father laugh? People here laughed on different occasions than we did; I had decided it was often embarrassment or nerves. I rummaged around my purse and blew my nose on a tissue. The doctor looked at me and shrugged. "Why do you cry?" she asked me in English.

"The boy. . ." My throat constricted and I couldn't speak. Should I give the father some money? No, he might be humiliated in front of the others and, besides, why should I assume he hadn't enough? I found a roll of candies at the bottom of my bag and clutched them.

It was time to leave. David held Sam and a prescription for medicine. The door was opened and we filed out. My face was red, my eyes puffy. The women outside stared at me with undisguised interest. I stopped by the father and handed him the sweets. "*Untuk dia* (for him)," I said, nodding at the boy who looked ahead blinking in the lightbulb's glare. The father smiled and bobbed his head saying, "*Terimah kasih* (thank you)." Such a pathetic gesture on my part, I thought to myself.

"What was that all about?" asked my husband, starting up the jeep and peering at me over Sam's round head.

"I don't know, I don't know," I said slightly rocking Sam who was relaxed and limp in my arms. "Let's go home." I longed for the morning when, rested, I would better face the day. Mornings in bed David and I would watch the palms across the way out the high window for a cooling breeze or clouds. Sam would come in drowsy and sweet for a cuddle. Ida would rattle things about in the kitchen preparing our tea and toast, and we would hear the thunk of the knife as she sliced orange-red papaya.

As we drove off, I looked out the open window at the illuminated porch. The father and boy remained in their seats waiting to see the doctor.

Vivian Vie Balfour

TAXI

BELINDA PRINTED the Zen haikus on 3x5 cards. She cut them into shapes to fit around the words, cutting off all the sharp edges. She curled the tape around on itself to make it self-sticking and attached the haikus to the inside of the doors of her built-in closets. The cards stuck out slightly and she pushed them hard against the wood to make them stick, closed the doors, and got into bed. She wondered if Carolina, the maid, read them when she came in her bedroom to hang the washed dresses that she had spread on the lawn in the backyard to dry. It did not seem to matter, and no one ever asked her about them. Having her own bedroom gave her a degree of privacy that she never had before. It was a new room, a single bed, two closets, an air-conditioner, a desk where she did her homework (sometimes nude). The furniture, like almost everything else, had come from AID housing supplies. The floors were bare. The curtainless windows had opaque louvers that were usually kept shut. The Thai cotton bedspread was striped in the deep hues of marooon and orange worn by Buddhist monks. It could have been a boy's room except for the cosmetics on the niche between the two closets. Her family had left a lot behind when they had come here. But she had liked the freedom, the bare floor, the expanse of space, the rows of cotton dresses lined up in her closets, the ink brush from her attempt to learn Japanese brush painting, the absence of personal history. She could be anyone.

It was hot, always hot — always sunny, except when it rained and the streets filled with water and the school closed. It was a land of perpetual light and blue sky. She woke on school mornings at 5:30, turned off the air-conditioner, and opened her windows to let the heat into her cold bedroom — too cold now since her blood was thin. She was on her way to becoming some exotic flower — moving through the days of heat and sun, lying by the pool, and soaking in what Minnesota doesn't have. Even the night was easy — warm and soft. She could feel her body cutting through the atoms — in this hot house of eternity.

That night for the first time, Belinda heard the rats in the walls of her bedroom. A couple of days before, her mother had said that she had heard what sounded like squirrels playing at night between the walls of her downstairs bedroom. But this was a country without squirrels. When her mother had told her about the sounds, she had not been concerned. It had seemed like something in her mother's life and not her own. Now she was afraid and so she told herself that the rats couldn't get through the walls. It was safe to go to sleep. But it was a fact that she was not altogether sure of. She slept and dreamt and saw herself crawling through a network of tunnels, like a gigantic ant farm. It was only now in the dream that she realized they joined her house to her high school. The tunnels ran in layers, some with doors of burlap connecting them. Others had trap doors that led to lower levels. She heard squitching noises but saw no animals. She could finish one series of tunnels and then find herself without having moved, in another one similar to the one she just completed. All were different but essentially the same. She breaststroked through the last tunnel, dragging her legs behind her. And then she was falling forward out of the tunnel onto the floor of the little room above the gym where her English class met. Her feet had dragged the dust with her so that now the wet suffocating smell of earth rose all around her.

She was awakened early by the sunlight flooding into her bedroom on the second floor. She turned off her air-conditioner and cranked open the louvered windows and looked over the wall around Magallanes Village. The houses of the squatters were so close that she could hear roosters and watch their bare-bottomed toddlers chasing each other. She went into the bathroom to shower and when she came back the heat from the day had warmed her room and it was no longer cold.

When she went down to breakfast with her mother, Joan, Carolina looked odd. Her hair which was normally pinned into a small, neat bun at the back of her head, hung down her back to her waist. It was dry and brittle, streaked with gray. And when she walked near the fan, it wrapped itself around her face like a mask. She hadn't smiled yet either, which is something she did sporadically as if she suddenly remembered it was part of the job.

Belinda waited until Carolina padded back to the kitchen and said, "You know those scratching sounds you said you heard the other night. I heard it too in the wall in my bedroom. I think they're rats."

"I'll tell you about rats. Did you see how Carolina looks this morning. She says she can't sleep at night because of the sounds. I told her they were rats and I would get an exterminator in here today. Well, Carolina doesn't think they're rats."

"What does she think they are?"

"She thinks they're the sounds of demons from the Thai temple rubbings I hung last week in the spare bedroom. It's quaint, but that's

Carolina for you. She says it's the demons trying to scratch their way out of the frames. She says she was up half the night saying the rosary which I'm supposed to be grateful for. I don't pay her to do rosaries. I just don't think it's healthy for people to think like that. It's just not good for people."

"That's weird. It's bad enough thinking about having rats."

"God, I wish we had a phone. Do you think they have something like a Yellow Pages here? I could look up Rat Removers and see if there is someone in Makati and drive over there after I drop you at school around noon. You're still tutoring this boy today?"

"Willis. We're doing English. He can give me a ride home."

"We wouldn't have rats if it wasn't for all those squatters living so close. I think the government should clear them out. And Carolina is going to cut out this haunted house stuff or she is out of here."

* * *

Joan tooted the horn and smoked a cigarette while they waited for the school guard to come and open the heavy metal grill that closed off this entrance to the high school.

"I think you should wear a helmet if you're going to ride on the back of this boy's motorcycle."

"I'll be fine, Mom." Belinda said getting out of the car. "He's a really good driver. Really dependable. We might go to the Chinese Cemetery. It's kind of an interesting place."

"Okay. It doesn't sound that interesting to me, but maybe you have to be young to get excited about visiting cemeteries. I'll be busy with the rats," Joan said with a sigh. "I got the address of the company that just did our neighbor's house."

Belinda pushed her sunglasses onto the top of her head and peered through the grill into the darkness of the school's corrridor. She waved her mother on when the school guard was close enough for her to see him.

The corridor felt cool compared to the air outside in the sunlight. A slight breeze moved through the empty school halls. The only light filtered through the ends of the corridors which were open to the out-side.

They walked in even steps down the hall, which was silent except for the slap of her sandals against the terrazzo floor. She looked sidewise at him from the corner of her eyes. He was oldish, maybe forty, thin and gnarled. He wore a military-type uniform, khaki pants, a MacArthur-style hat with a visor and a silver whistle hung on a chain around his neck like a lifeguard's. When she stopped at her locker she remembered to thank him, and spoke in quiet shy tones . He nodded and walked away quickly.

The locker ponged slightly as she opened it. Her small English text was on the bottom of a pile of books. She pulled it out and the rest fell down with a thud.

She had signed up as a student tutor before she had known that it also would involve coming to school during Easter vacation and not just spending an hour of study hall time with Willis once a week. They would go over again the intricacies of sentence diagramming. He was eighteen, almost two years older than her and spoke a nasty Southern drawl and, despite his occasional personal charm, would not graduate, would not go to college, would probably get drafted and end up in Vietnam, if he did not learn some basic facts about the English language.

Willis' father was on the Board of Trustees of the American School and had lived in Manila during the Japanese occupation. He had come one day to her history class to talk about his experience in the internment camps. Near the end of the class, he talked wistfully about the day of his wedding, more than twenty years ago, to a young woman in the camp. He passed around a photo of that day. The bride looked radiant in spite of her gauntness and even held a bouquet; the groom wore shorts that looked as if they would fall off except for the belt he wore, and a shirt that looked two sizes too big. The minister standing at his side held a Bible tightly clenched in his fist.

"We were all so thin from eating the rice rations the Japanese gave us. That was a happy day, though, the best — except for the day we were liberated, and I ate too much and got sick." He laughed, and the teacher thanked him for taking the time to talk to her class. It added a lot to their World War II unit, and she knew that the students really appreciated his talk. She would have gone on thanking him but the buzzer rang for the next class.

The first time she had seen Willis, he had been sitting in the Senior Lounge, a place forbidden to underclassman, like herself. He was leaning into his guitar, playing the plaintive chords to "House of the Rising Sun," singing it as if he personally had been ruined by an experience in New Orleans.

* * *

The double doors to the library stuck together slightly as Belinda opened them. The air-conditioner had been turned off. Ceiling fans swirled above her. The room was empty except for a student named Teresa who was shuffling library books around on a cart. She scowled at the book she was holding. Her hair was blond and lank and hung very straight around her thin pale face. She swung her long hair back to study the call letters on the book she was holding and then she looked up at Belinda without changing her expression. Belinda gave her a half-second smile and sat down. She opened her English text but ended up watching Teresa reshelve books. Teresa stood out. Her plainness seemed forced: the clean but drab hair, the solid color shifts that she wore, all cut out of the same pattern, that hung loosely on her body. But mostly it was that Teresa had crossed a cultural boundary, like a Christian who marries a Jew and converts and thereafter celebrates only Hannakah and never again has Christmas.

The story was that a long time ago, like in kindergarten, the American kids in the class didn't want to be friends with Teresa, so she made friends with the Filipino kids, and she became like her friends. She spoke fluent Tagalog, spoke English with an accent, ignored American kids, and, despite her blond hair and pale skin, looked and seemed Filipino.

Belinda was sorry now that she had waved her mother on so quickly. She was stuck here with Teresa. She opened her English book and started working out the sentences for herself. She liked putting the pieces in their proper places, looking at the balance like mathematical equations.

She liked tutoring, but she was not so sure how she felt about Willis. At first, he was sullen and slow and unhappy, and she felt strangely guilty even though she barely knew him. He answered in monosyllables, barely acknowledging her presence. She grew tired of staring at the side of his face while he sat turned away from her. The sound of the ceiling fan whirring and whirring made her sleepy. The boy made her sleepy. It was just too elementary, this slicing up of the English language.

The last time they had met, Willis had given her a ride home on his Honda. She had never been on a motorcyle before. At first she had leaned away from the curves instead of into them. In her mind she saw the bike losing the edge of the wheel that it balanced on; both of them falling, the bike landing on top of them. And she leaned away.

"You're screwing up my balance. Lean the same direction I do," he had yelled. She followed his lead and the machine did not spin out from beneath them.

"I want to take you somewhere. "

"Somewhere?" she said. What did he mean by "somewhere"? "Maybe I should just go home."

"No, this is a really neat place."

"I'm not going to go with you to some dive and drink San Miguel beer all afternoon."

"No, it's the Chinese Cemetery."

"Where's that? "

"Just hang on. I'll show you."

He maneuvered through the traffic between the lanes. She clung to him and pulled her legs as close to the motorcycle as she could to keep them away from the traffic. The air was heavy with the smell of diesel fuel. She shut her eyes so the dust wouldn't get into her contacts.

When the air smelled fresher, she opened them. They had stopped at an ornate wrought-iron arch. A man came up to them, a groundskeeper. Willis spoke in Tagalog, fast and smooth, and the man nodded. The air was cleaner than it had been in the streets. They were away from the traffic and the people. The cemetery was lovely. A suburb for the dead. Each family had its own miniature house/tomb proportioned like a child's backyard playhouse. The streets were impeccably clean and rose in a hill above Manila. Inside the houses were photographs propped on altars. The faces and writing were Chinese.

"The Chinese are afraid of showing their wealth by living really high so they save their money and build these. I like this," he said.

Then he had driven her back to her house and said, "Next week around noon, meet me at the library. You can tutor me and I can give you a ride home. Maybe we can go back to the cemetery if you like." He putted his motorcycle away slowly and softly as if not to bother anyone.

It was then that she began to wonder about him. What he was like. Who he was. What his life had been like. And she saw herself for a moment, in his life, touring cemeteries.

* * *

The longer she sat there in the quiet of the library, the stronger that hollow feeling grew that she was in the wrong place at the wrong time. That, despite the words, there was no agreement, no understanding to be here.

"Teresa, has Willis been here?"

"No one has been here all morning. I don't even think anyone is supposed to be here now."

Belinda said, "Thanks," and heard the sound of her own voice. She listened to it. It was as if she was picking up some accent that could only be described as "American living abroad." She guessed that there were people living all over the world with the same accent, the same carefully enunciated speech, not specific to any region of the United States, but rather beyond the pale.

She gathered her books, ripped a piece of paper out of her notebook, and wrote, "Willis, I was here, and I shall not return." When she reached his locker, she folded the note and slipped it through the slot until just a tiny section of it stuck out. She walked away, stopped, and then went back to the locker and with the tips of her fingernails pulled it out again. The principal was walking quickly towards her.

"Teresa just told me that you were here looking for Willis."

"I thought we were supposed to have a tutoring session. He's not here."

"His mother just called me. He didn't come home last night. Do you know where he might have gone?"

She shook her head. Where would he go? Get a job on a freighter? Enlist in the Navy? Run off with a girl? It was the blackheads in his ears that convinced her that he had not run off with a girl. Where would they go? There was no place to go. Those pale blue eyes. That Southern accent.

The principal opened the gate for her and thanked her for her help. She knew that she had not been that helpful. She sat down on the bench outside. She leaned against the rough stone walls of the school. Then she stood up, unsticking her dress from her back. She felt a slight breeze fill the new space. She picked up her books and headed up the hill past the sari-sari store.

Heat lines shimmered off the concrete ahead. It was too hot to walk through one cement suburb of Manila and then another and then across the highway, and still be only at the gate of the village. Besides it wasn't proper for a woman to walk down the street by herself — to be stared at by men. Neither was it proper, and maybe not safe, to take a taxi by herself. But a taxi would be quicker.

She raised her arm and flicked her fingers up and down to signal the taxi. It wasn't a Yellow Cab but she didn't want to wait for another. He pulled up and stopped with practiced efficiency. She got into the cab and said, "Magallanes Village." He looked back at her, and then turned around again. He breathed in sharply. She did not understand the meaning of this double take. He looked puzzled, surprised. Americans had been in Manila a long time. She was not so unusual, blond, pretty but not unusual. She repeated "Magallanes Village." He said, "Okay," as if coming back to himself. She sat next to the door with her hand clutched on the handle, thinking of the scenes in movies when spies and heroines jumped from speeding cars or high off of box cars, leaping hand in hand to freedom and safety. There was nothing soft out there, hot pavement and more cars. She knew she would not jump. But her father's words came back to her: "Having a white woman, that is a real big deal to men in Spanish cultures."

The taxi driver was young. His taxi wasn't. It smelled of oil and musty old leather. Like a cave. The dashboard was decorated in a trinity of religious statues, and a rosary hung from his mirror. Jesus bumped along. The driver's fingers were long and sinewy and his thumbnail was three or four inches long, so that it started to curl at the tip. Yellow and thick, like an old man's toenail with wavy lines of black grease patterning it. She had first noticed it when he flipped down the meter. She stared at his hands on the steering wheel. To be stabbed by such a thing would be death by infection.

A Manila newspaper lay open on the seat beside her. It showed a photo of a man who was crucified every Holy Week in the countryside. The photo was a blurry kind of pieta, the man collapsing among his friends, an old woman at his side. She wondered about the nails, whether they used them or not, and why he did not die. She wondered what it felt like. To be a scapegoat. The sun looked harsh and ugly in the picture, the man's face exhausted, his body slumped. She slid the paper away from her.

The taxi driver was going the right direction. She relaxed her grip on the door handle, and pushed her sunglasses up on to her head and tried to read his ID card.

They reached her village. The Magallanes guard waved them through as they slowed up at the gate. She watched the driver's eyes in his rear view mirror. "Go straight," she said. He nodded.

"Turn here," she said. They stopped in front of her gate. The exterminator's truck was there, and she felt happy that the rats would be gone, that the noises at night would stop.

She pulled some pesos out of her purse. They had scribbles on them — phone numbers, slang words. She handed them to him. They were all crumpled up and she was glad to get rid of them. He took them from her carefully, touching only the money and not her fingers.

She was home. The look meant nothing. He looked at her again and she saw that his eyes were milky and yellowed, his skin slightly pocked. His tone was of a man speaking in confidence, low and soft, and the whole sentence sat in her brain before she understood what he meant. "Mary, I thought you were Mary."

In that instant he seemed like himself, not a Filipino, not a man exactly, but someone who had slipped out of his role because he was touched by something extraordinary, even though it was only a very common thing. For just a flicker of a moment, she too felt touched out of herself.

Not American. Beyond herself. But not quite real. Nothing.

BELINDA

THE CAR WAS HOT, even though it had been in the shade of the carport. Belinda opened both doors, unrolled the windows, and sat on the rattan chair on the small covered patio in front of her house to wait for her mother.

The gardener, and sometimes chauffeur, who said he had studied mechanical engineering, was bent close to the ground, sculpturing the plants that rose in a slight mound against the concrete wall separating their yard from the one next door, where a two-story house was being built. He was thin and short, young, slightly pockmarked, but pleasant-looking. He wore a short-sleeved white shirt, hemmed at his waist-line, and tight black pants. He was a fearless and aggressive driver who could argue fine points of religion with his employer, while battling downtown Manila traffic.

Belinda raised her hand to shield her eyes from the sun and watched the Filipino workmen walking on the stick-like scaffolding. One of the them nudged his friend, said something loud in Tagalog, and laughed. The gardener looked up for an instant and then went back to his pruning.

Annoyed, Belinda turned her back to them. She rummaged through her carry-all containing her swimsuit, towel, her twelfth grade English text (a suntan lotion-stained copy of *Paradise Lost*) until she found her father's most recent letter from Saigon. Although he worked for the Agency for International Development and not the military, all of the references to events were in military time. She translated them on her fingers. At 1800, or 6:00 PM, he was going to his first Vietnamese language lesson. He liked his apartment, joked about having a room-mate, and planned to buy a motor scooter through the PX. He closed by saying, "Tell your mother that Manila is a much more dangerous city than Saigon." Belinda folded the letter and put it back in her bag.

Carolina, the recently acquired maid, came out of the side door to unlock the gray metal driveway gate.

Belinda's mother, Joan, came through the carved, Spanish-style front door, not bothering to lock it because the maid would always be there. Belinda and her mother got into the car. Joan lit a cigarette with the car lighter. Belinda stared at the short black hairs on her mother's bare legs.

"Belinda, roll up your window. The air-conditioner doesn't work at all with it down, " Joan said, as she started the car and carefully backed out of the driveway.

Carolina stood patiently in the street, waiting to close the gate.

The guard at the entrance to Magallanes Village nodded to them as they left. They drove past the lines of people squatting on the road waiting for busses and jeepneys. They went past walled yards until they reached Roxas Boulevard, which curves along Manila Bay.

By this time, the air-conditioner started to cool a small area of the front seat. Belinda moved over slightly so that the cool air blew up her skirt.

The Filipino guard at the entrance to the U.S. Embassy/AID compound stepped from the shade to check the sticker on the car before he waved them through. They parked in the lot in front of the club, gathered their swim things, and headed for the dressing room.

The attendant was crocheting hats out of plastic yarn.

"Three pesos, only," she said, offering them to Belinda and Joan.

"Maybe later," Joan replied. "After we shower."

A woman in her late thirties waved at them when they came out of the dressing room, their new beach hats in hand.

"Joan, you and Belinda come and sit over here," Madge said.

"Oh, Madge, we'll have to get some more chairs," Joan said, looking at the empty ones at the table next to Madge's. The man who was sitting by himself there looked up from his magazine.

"Help yourself," he said. "I'm not expecting anyone."

They thanked the man for his chairs, and settled in. He smiled at them. It was a rather nice smile, thought Belinda, as she looked up from *Paradise Lost*. She smiled back.

Madge lifted her arm and waved her finger up and down, "Pss Psssst," she said in the direction of one of the poolside waiters.

He nodded to them and hurried over.

"What would you like, Mum?"

"A Calamanici Collins, please."

"Sounds good to me, too. Belinda, a coke?"

"Coke, please," Belinda said to the waiter, and went back to her Milton.

Madge watched the waiter as he walked away. "Elaine's baby is quite dark," she said. "It's obviously not her husband's or even American."

"Well, it has to be at least half."

"We were all so close I don't know how she could have let this happen."

"Obviously not as close as Juan," Joan said.

"Do you know what Elaine said to me?—this was before I even knew about this thing with Juan. She said that she liked being friends with me because I was so respectable. She was half-smashed at the time."

"Sort of innocence by association. Listen, Madge, I don't think she meant it like that. How did you find out about the baby, anyway?"

"My kids heard the maids talking."

"You know the baby will probably just blend in after awhile. Things like this happen in wars," Joan said.

"Well, I don't think of Vietnam as a war exactly."

"We could get another opinion." Joan turned to the man that they had taken the chairs from and said, "Oh, sir, excuse me."

"Yes?"

"You were very kind to let us use your chairs."

The man looked as though he was going to dive back into his magazine.

"You're not anybody's husband are you?"

The man frowned at Joan with a slight quizzical look.

"I mean you're not anybody we know, or we would already know all about you. You don't look like intelligence either, so I would guess that you're a soldier."

"Well, yes, I am," he said. "I'm stationed in Nam and I'm here on R&R."

"I'm Joan Evans and this is Madge Bradley," Joan said, extending her hand to him.

"Nice to meet you, ladies. I'm John Monroe. Lieutenant Monroe."

"We were talking about the war," Joan said.

"What about the war?"

"Just whether it really is a war."

"I wouldn't know what else to call it."

"Won't you come and join us for a drink?" Madge asked.

They discussed the finances of the club, brands of scotch, the C.I.A., and the price of pearls in American cigarettes on the black market. At least Madge talked about pearls, until Joan hinted that this wasn't the best place to bring that up.

Belinda read *Paradise Lost* and made notes in very small print in the margins: Eve is wondering how high heaven is and whether or not God is watching her and Adam.

The Lieutenant leaned over to see what Belinda was reading. The book was propped against her knees. "Oh, Milton!" he said. "How do you like him?"

She extended her foot over the side of the chair, dipped it into the warm water on the patio, spread the puddle out as far as it would go, and said, "He makes me want to convert."

"To what?"

"A college English major," she said.

"I used to teach English in the States."

"I could have been one of your students."

"That would have been pretty distracting," he said, very softly.

Just then her mother and the others decided that Lieutenant Monroe, because he didn't have any other plans for the evening, would come to Joan's house for dinner.

He protested only slightly that he didn't want to be any bother.

* * *

Joan honked the horn as they pulled up to the house. They drove in while Carolina held the gate open with one hand and the dog's leash in the other.

"Brownie's always so excited to see us," Belinda said.

"He's not brown, though."

"He's a she and she was named after another dog who was."

Carolina locked the gate after them and started for the kitchen with the dog.

"Carolina, what on earth have you done with these plants?" Joan said to her retreating figure.

Carolina pivoted herself and the dog around and said, "Mum, I didn't think that they looked so good, so I brought them outside."

Joan touched the leaf of her favorite dieffenbachia and said, "These plants don't belong outside. We must get them in right away."

"Yes, Mum, I'll move them right in."

"Come in, Lieutenant Monroe, and sit down. Such a hot drive. I'm bushed. Carolina, bring us some cokes. Lots of ice. Then take care of those plants."

He stepped over the threshold, with the air of a man returning to his own home after a long absence.

"Your house is very nice. Please call me John."

"I have tried to make it look more individual," she said. "We had our choice of covers for the cushions on all the furniture from AID housing. I really like the ones I picked."

The Lieutenant scanned the room. His eyes stopped on a batik buddha. "Now that certainly didn't come from Housing, did it?"

"We got that at the PX and had it framed," Joan said. "It turned out very nicely, don't you think?"

"We used to have these wonderful pictures in the spare bedroom," said Belinda. "Temple rubbings from Bangkok, very nice blues and greens. It was a picture story of these evil creatures that kidnapped this beautiful maiden. She's rescued by a prince. We had them hanging in the spare room, but Carolina had a fit. She said they were evil. At first, it was just that she wouldn't go in there to clean, and then she said that she wouldn't stay in the house if they were left up. She said they were giving her bad dreams."

"So what did you do?" he asked.

"We took them down and put them in a box," Joan said.

Carolina padded into the living room, her slippers slapping the terrazzo floor with each step.

"Just put the tray down, Carolina."

"We haven't any curtains. I miss curtains," said Belinda.

The Lieutenant looked at the frosted louvered windows.

"Oh, Belinda, you know they're always closed anyway." She turned to the Lieutenant. "We have air-conditioning, which you have to have in a climate like this, except for the maid's room and the kitchen."

"Sometimes I open my windows upstairs in the morning because I get so cold from the air-conditioner," Belinda said. "I can look out and you know we're at the edge of the village because there's the wall with all the broken glass on top of it. Beyond the walls, there's all these little huts with corrugated tin roofs and all these little babies and kids running around with no diapers or anything on. Just T-shirts."

"Belinda, you *know* you really shouldn't open the windows like that."

＊ ＊ ＊

They ate dinner in the dining room. Although the kitchen was huge, no one ever ate in it except Carolina. She served them a dish she had learned to cook from Joan's Betty Crocker cookbook.

After dinner, Joan, Belinda, and the Lieutenant decided to go to the dance at the club.

The club was at its very best! The tablecloths and the jackets of the waiters had recently been changed, candles were lit at every table, colored lights were strung outside and reflected off the pool, and the band–to which Belinda and John now danced, was okay.

"You slow dance like an adult," Belinda said, as her foot collided with his shoe.

"O.K., Belinda, you teach me how to dance."

"Pretend you're in junior high school. Try shuffling back and forth or something."

He laughed.

"You don't act like a soldier," she said.

"How exactly do soldiers act?"

"I don't really know. I sort of thought that I was supposed to avoid them."

"You don't seem to be avoiding me."

"What did you do before you came to Vietnam?"

"I taught school for awhile and I traveled."

"That's right. You said that. So you'll go back to teaching?"

"I suppose so."

"You don't sound very sure."

"And what will you go back to?"

"College in Minnesota," she said.

"Do you want to go out by the pool, Belinda?"

They sat on the edge of the children's pool, dangling their bare feet in it and watching the colored light reflect in the still water.

"Do you want to walk around?" he asked, rubbing his feet against hers.

They walked toward the tennis courts.

"They show movies outdoors here sometimes," she said.

"But you have to wear white."

She laughed. "Did you use to tell jokes like that to your students?"

"Never. You play tennis?"

"No, I never could hit the ball."

"We could take care of that," he said, pantomiming a backhand to hit an imaginary low ball. "Just hit the ball back to me. You can't miss," he said, running to the other side of the court.

He arched his body, mimicking the perfect serve.

She threw her sandals into the empty court and ran to return his ball.

* * *

They were sitting on the bank of grass, laughing.

"I'm glad I finally missed before anyone saw us."

"You were pretty good out there. So, what else is here?" he said, rising and taking her hand. "Let's go that way." He swung her arm with his.

She was reminded for an instant of Dorothy and the Tin Man.

"That building there has something to do with embassy communications, like between Saigon and the embassy here. I was only in it once. A friend of mine's father worked there and he needed to borrow a typewriter for a paper for school. I went with him and you like walk in and there's this reception area and a Marine guard. I would think it would be a real boring job guarding buildings. My friend thought it would be a real prestige job. His father wanted him to join the Marines."

"And what did you think?"

"I thought it would kill him," she said. "I'm talking a lot. Let's go back."

"Tomorrow night, Belinda, do you want to go out with me?"

"I'm sorry. I can't."

"You don't have to be sorry. If you can't, you can't."

"I have papers to write. I'm sorry. I wish that I could."

"Why do you keep saying you're sorry? What's there to be sorry about?"

"Nothing, of course."

In the pool of light by the tennis courts, they saw Joan approaching.

"Yoo hoo, you two. Well, John, Belinda needs to be going home."

"Thank you for having me over for dinner."

She shook his hand, wished him good luck, and announced that she had to run back to the club for a moment.

"Belinda, I'll walk you to the car."

"The air is so soft here."

"If I write to you, Belinda, will you write back?"

"Of course."

* * *

Belinda turned to watch the swaying of the plants against the latticed walls of the church. She fanned herself and wiped a drop of sweat off her leg.

The front of the church was dominated by a life-size cross and the minister, who was still talking, although Belinda had timed his sermon at over twenty minutes already. She finished filling in all the open letters in the bulletin and looked up. It sounded as if he was just winding up his sermon on the parable about it being easier for a camel to go through the eye of a needle than for a rich man to enter into the Kingdom of Heaven.

"The point of the parable," the minister said, "isn't that there is anything wrong with making money or having it but rather being too attached to it."

"Who does he think he's kidding?" Belinda wrote on her bulletin and put it in her purse as the congregation rose for the closing hymn.

"He was a nice man, wasn't he, Belinda, that Lieutenant Monroe we had for dinner last night," her mother said, as they were leaving church.

"Yes."

* * *

The letters arrived.

She wrote back. Milton was finished. The year was coming to an end. She was going to Minnesota soon. It was probably much colder than she remembered. What would she wear to the prom? Her mother's friend, Elaine, had left for the States with her kids, and without her husband.

From the changes in his return address, she thought John must have been promoted.

"Send pictures," he'd asked.

She didn't send any.

She wrote that she was almost happy to be going back to the States. Brownie had chased a guard in the village and he had pulled a gun on her. The man had threatened to shoot her and the dog. Dumb with fury, she had walked away.

He wrote back that he was upset. She told him not to be — the guard had been whisked away efficiently by AID housing.

She wrote that she was having bad dreams. Her mother was anxious that she would be packed in time. There were things to do, final shopping, airline tickets and traveler's checks to pick up. She had gotten sick from the shrimp the maid had cooked and had tried not to throw up till she made it to the bathroom and had almost choked to death on vomit.

Joan hung the Thai temple rubbings back up in the spare bedroom and told Carolina she could just adjust.

The maid said some very un-maid like things and left in a huff, leaving behind boxes of their waste paper neatly sorted and categorized.

The gardener stayed on, although he made it clear that he was an educated man and planned to get something better eventually.

She sent a picture of herself standing with her suitcase in front of the house, taken with her father's polaroid. She wrote her name and the date on the back of it.

✳ ✳ ✳

The church in Minneapolis was as it had been. The same red and green flowered curtains covered the basement windows. Someone had left a tic-tac-toe game on the blackboard, unfinished, though its outcome was obvious. A half-completed Bethlehem was being made from sugar cubes. The chairs were in less than precise straightness facing an altar.

She went up the oak stairway until she reached the top, through the turn where there was no light until she pushed open the heavy leather doors. The light was softly diffused by the windows. The cross still shown. Jesus the Shepherd stood with infinite patience holding a lamb, and the carved heads of wolves and goblins stood guard on the balcony.

From her pocket she took a packet of matches and lit the two candles on the altar.

And she stood there and said, "I have come to say goodbye. I sat and listened almost all my life here. The answers aren't here. This is a place of my childhood and I love this place, but it's no longer right for me.

The world is crazy. Was the world you lived in crazy? I'm angry at this place for teaching me to love someone who died two thousand years ago. I wanted to be like you and I can't. My mother thinks that you were a sucker. She really said that. I think that you were just different. You know, on Star Trek there was this being from another planet that humans couldn't look at because it would drive them insane. You didn't know if it was because this being was so beautiful or so ugly. So this being lived in a protective box. The church is like that box, a protective covering so that we can't see you because you could drive us mad or maybe even sane. I would ask you for your blessing in this, but I think I would do what I wanted anyway. May the Lord bless me and keep me and make his face shine on me and give me peace. Amen."

She blew out the candles and left.

Deborah Fass

A THOUSAND FAREWELLS

SOMETIME DURING the winter months it began. Like a gradual shift in the light, she became interested. She's endured months of taking tests and writing compositions under the strain of concealing it. She's in love with her Japanese teacher.

He's close to 50 and lives alone; never married. He spends his off hours deep in his old house writing novels that no one ever reads. Linda went to his house once, when he invited the whole class over for dinner. It was a warm house with a fireplace and a bay view. He'd stood by the stove cooking tempura. She'd taken in every nuance of his home, aching to be a part of it.

He tells her about the scholarship. A year studying Japanese literature at a university in rural Japan. He invites her to dinner Friday night. The semester ends Thursday. She's sure about going anywhere but Japan. Across the bridge to his home, yes, but across the Pacific Ocean to his homeland, that's a different story.

* * *

She remembers the room with the fireplace and the view. After dinner there are two glasses of wine and pillows in front of the fireplace. His hands are like frantic animals. They climb her and sniff under her sweater. "I'm not sure what to call you," she says. "I don't want to call you Sensei anymore." He whispers his name and gives her his mother's phone number in Tokyo.

* * *

Linda arrives in Japan a month before classes start. It's cold and snowy and within hours she learns her first word: Mezurashii. "Rare." Like the inches of snow falling around her apartment house. Like her presence in the photo taken in the parking lot.

Linda writes him letters in Japanese: broken descriptions of things that remind her of him. She signs her letters "love." He corrects the letters in red ink and sends them back. "I cannot do more than this," he writes, "but *you* do more. Do more and tell me all about it. Don't revise. I'll be in Tokyo this summer."

* * *

Fifteen foreign students and not another one that looks like Linda. They ask each other, "Why Japan?" Linda answers, "For the full moon." "You've got cherry blossoms in your eyes," they tell her. In the spring those cherry blossoms fall as old dying trees bloom above the trash dump. She's waited months for the blossoms. Neon lights from a Pachinko Parlor distort their color. The flashing petals fall with nobody noticing them. But people notice Linda. Down by the disco a group of college students watches her. Better than TV, she's live. She bends over to scratch her knee, and the whole group bows in response.

In this private society, her every action is public by merit of its rareness. They say, "Aren't you the foreign student that lives at Yumi's place?" And, "I saw you last Thursday on the bus. Where were you going?" They see her everywhere: buying bread, at the post office, in a restaurant ("With a man. Who was he?"). She stands head above the crowd and glows like white light. In front of dark windows she startles herself. Another foreigner, she thinks, excited. When she realizes she's discovered her own face, she feels betrayed by its false promise of companionship.

Linda lives above Yumi's Chinese restaurant, behind the boys' dorm. Yumi's place is usually full of students avoiding their studies with comic books. There's always a hot cup of tea for Linda and Yumi's willing to talk. When the restaurant is quiet, Linda brings her dictionaries. Under Yumi's tutelage Linda learns the rules of women's behavior: always hold a tea cup with two hands, never sit cross-legged, always cover your mouth when you laugh.

At Yumi's house Linda learns survival. At the university she studies literature. Her teacher is an old man. They read novels and poetry. The grammar is difficult but Linda gets the general idea of what's going on. They read a novel by Yasunari Kawabata. Linda has trouble with a passage about bugs crying before the first day of spring. When the teacher realizes she isn't following he says, "I know why you don't understand: because there are no seasons in America. Since there's no first day of spring, you can't understand Japanese literature." He dismisses her with a wave of his hand.

* * *

May brings wild wisteria and the rainy month of June. June opens into humid summer, and vacation. Linda plans a trip south to the beach. Yumi shows her a map. She can take the train there. "Bring a hat," Yumi advises. "And you'd be much more attractive if you'd shave your face."

Yumi's directions lead Linda to a beautiful beach resort. The horizon is panoramic. As Linda walks along the beach and into the water, she thinks of the scenery of Yumi's town. It's an industrial town filled with the smells of melting plastic and steel. Yumi told Linda that it used to be a fishing town with a long beach. About twenty years ago they paved over the beach and into the ocean, filling it to build the factories. The fishermen lost their jobs.

Linda swims far into the sea. Level with the horizon, she washes images of factories and teachers from her mind. She feels solitude and privacy for the first time in Japan. She ponders the colors around her. Out of the turquoise and green sea, a black head emerges and says, "This is a pen." Linda swims back to the shore.

* * *

Back at the restaurant Yumi laughs at Linda's sunburn and gives her a phone message. From him. His first correspondence since the red ink. He used his first name. A name which means "A Thousand Farewells." A name which Linda can't yet give voice to. Yumi voices it in multitudes of questions. "Where'd you meet him? How old is he?" Linda walks to a pay phone to call him. When his mother answers, Linda can't say his name. It sticks in her throat and threatens to overpower her. "Is Sensei there?" she whispers. His mother sounds very old. Linda wonders what she had foreseen when she'd named him. Is it like a cat's nine lives, his thousand good-byes? Finally his voice is on the line. Linda suggests they get together. She could go to Tokyo or he could come to her town. "No," he protests, "I can't do that." "Why not," she demands, "we could get to know each other." "I can't," he says, "and anyway what would I tell my mother?" "Good-bye," he says hanging up.

Nine-hundred and ninety-nine to go, Linda thinks, and returns to Yumi's questions. "What did he say? Will you see him?" The light in Yumi's restaurant is bright. Linda's sunburn isn't the only thing that stings.

* * *

Summer sweats on. Linda walks to the store to buy some juice and a popsicle. At the check out stand she notices pink, delicate razors. The pictures on the packages show women shaving their faces, forearms and underarms. Their faces are dwarfed and jailed by the dainty shavers.

Linda makes her way home through the screech of cicadas. There's no mail and the phone doesn't ring. As she opens her door, a red cockroach the size of a thumb flies through the doorway. Linda sits down by the window, opens the popsicle and looks into the neighbor's garden. She thinks about the hot, dry summers of California. No seasons in America? She pulls on the cotton shirt sticking to her back and licks the popsicle.

* * *

Linda sleeps late in the morning with the window open. She wakes up to hear her name outside. She listens. "That's where the American lives. Is she home now? Look, her window's open. They say she dates a man in Tokyo."

Linda can hear Yumi's laughter through the floor. She has just opened the restaurant. Yumi is constantly laughing. She has the kind of laugh that is obviously *at* someone; something different about someone. Occasionally Linda hears her own name from under the floor.

Linda takes the bus downtown. She walks past the statue of Colonel Sanders to the department store. Among the clothes, she runs her fingers through the fabrics. Synthetic fibers catch on her fingertips. At the counter, next to the cash register, there are stacks of cassette tapes. When she looks closer she sees that they're bootleg tapes of American FM radio. She wonders how, when Japan is struggling to keep American goods out of its market, thses bootleg tapes are in so many shops.

While Linda waits for the bus home, a man approaches her and says, "I know where you live. Above Yumi's, right? Hop in. I'll give you a ride." Linda looks at his face but has never seen him before. She moves closer to a group of high school girls.

When she gets off the bus she can see the second floor of Yumi's building and her one room apartment. As she approaches her door she can see a note on it. It's from Yumi. "Come downstairs," it says, "I have something cute to show you." Downstairs, Yumi's door is open and she calls Linda in. Linda's whole body is shocked when she sees Yumi's "cute thing." It's him. Her Sensei. He's sitting in Yumi's living room drinking tea. They've introduced themselves. "I was in town," he says, "Let's go up to your room." "You could've called," she says, "I haven't heard from you in weeks." "Sorry," he says, "I didn't know I was coming until I was here."

Linda's room is a mess and he comments on it. After an hour he says he's got to go. "Why can't you stay? Where will you go?" she asks. "I can't," he says, "Anyway, what would I tell my mother?" "Then I'll go with you," she says throwing some things into an overnight bag. She catches up with him on the stairs as Yumi's face pops through the back door of the restaurant. "Where are you going?" she asks eyeing the overnight bag.

They take the train out of town and get into a cab. He asks the driver to take them to a hotel. The driver cranes his neck to look at Linda, and he looks hard. Then he drives to a hotel called New Cherry. The driveway is a small hill. The entrance is hidden by plastic curtains. The taxi drives under the plastic.

He chooses a Western style room. It's got bright red shag carpets and velvet paisley wallpaper. There's a plastic bridge connecting the bedroom and the bath. She crosses the bridge to the big white bed. There are condoms and a package of tissues on the night stand. The tissues show a couple in an embrace and a car driving up the steep driveway to Hotel New Cherry. She sits down in a chair. He fills the bath with water.

He calls her to the bath. He's already naked. He takes off her clothes, seats her on a little plastic stool and pours water over her with a shallow plastic bucket. Then he takes the soap, lathers up his hands, and washes her. She's a little embarrassed by the thoroughness of his bathing. She is totally unprepared for him. Her legs and underarms are hairy. He won't let her bathe him in return, and they soak in the hot water together, looking at each other and not looking.

On the bed, in a towel, she is unprepared for him, again, as he fumbles to get inside of her. He's on top of her before she's had time to believe he's really there. She's amazed he is, in waves above her, and then he stops. Separates. "Did you come?" he asks. "Did you come yet? Because I didn't." She is speechless. He is stopping. "What makes you come?" he demands, moving away from her. "Some time. Or your mouth on me," she whispers. It would be easier to call his name, the unspeakable, than to say what she does. But he tries it, spreading her legs and putting his tongue on her. But before she can relax he is stopping again. "I taste urine," he says. "I didn't come and you didn't come so I guess I just don't love you," he says putting on his pajamas. She puts hers on too, numb and aching. She'd had to pee from sitting in the hot bath, after his deliberate washing and before he'd flung himself into her. She'd *had* to go. She feels flattened to the bottom of a deep crater. She feels low. He continues his explanation. He'd come to see her to decide if he loves her, could love her. It was a test, unannounced for his advantage. Great, she thinks, from his pop quizzes to this. What's next? How does one spend the night at the bottom of a crater, next to her ex-teacher who said he smelled urine? She thinks about his name and his mother's prophecy. Or was it a curse? A thousand withdrawals. Curled away from her on the bed he snores safely, halfway through a life sentence of parting.

* * *

Fall brings its red wounds to the hills and its loss to the trees. Linda buries the summer under the falling leaves. When classes begin she devotes herself to her studies. No one can hurt her that lives on a page. She sits down in the back of the class. The woman next to her leans over and says, "I saw you at the beach during the summer. Were you alone?"

Melissa Sanders-Self

NAMELESS THINGS
from *Drawing in the Dark*

Drawing in the Dark *is a story about modern innocence lost. Two young newlyweds, Jud and Claudia, are traveling in the Philippines relaxing on white sandy
beaches and absorbing the incredible culture of the Marcos' regime, when she accidentally gets pregnant. A painful and traumatic abortion costs them nearly all
of their money and much of their romanticism. They have just enough left for
tickets to Tokyo where they have heard money is plentiful for gaijin, foreigners,
who speak English. Jud finds a job teaching. Claudia finds work in a club, pouring whiskey and smiling for Japanese businessmen.*

*The abortion has had a tremendous effect on her personality, but she represses
her pain, referring to the event as something she 'can't think about right now.'
At work she rages against sexism, but in her treatment of the Japanese men she
is unconsciously racist. She sees the differences, rather than the similarities, between herself and others.*

*Jud is a good, sensible man whose primary conflict is his relationship to Claudia.
He has never known anyone quite like her. He is physical and practical, but overpowered by her intensity. Also, she has introduced him to drugs, which are for
her (as they have been for years,) part of her daily existence, while Jud is experiencing their effects like sledgehammers smashing all of his secure perceptions.*

The novel ends with both characters living out their worst fears.

* * *

Outside the West entrance to Ikebukuro station, Claudia watched the
hot pink neon sign of the Marui department store flash on and off. Other
neon twists and sticks, hundreds of them, whirred and flashed, reflecting brightly in the air full of wet drizzle. But the Marui sign was on
the tallest builing, and it was the most interesting color. It assaulted rather
than attracted her eyes, but since Claudia liked to stare as high as possible, searching for bits of sky inside Tokyo, her eyes were fixed on the
flashing squiggles. At head level she would see only drunk Japanese
men, and looking down at the oily pavement like the Japanese women
did was too depressing. So she watched the neon, pretending fascina-

tion, and paced back and forth in front of the station entrance.

Claudia was waiting for Jud. Usually, he was waiting when she emerged from the gray cement depths, ready to hug her and take her arm and lead her home. But tonight, after climbing the too-long flight of stairs, tired but expectant, she had been disappointed to discover Jud was not there. She walked the space before the gates again, her head fixed high, and when her neck grew tired she sent her eyes searching through the crowd around the circle and down the backstreets for the hurrying figure of Jud. She wondered what was making him late. It did not occur to her that he was not already on his way. He was so insistent about meeting her. "At 1:00 a.m. you shouldn't be walking alone even if there is supposedly no crime in Japan," he said. Besides, it gave him something to look forward to all evening.

'So where is he?' thought Claudia, noticing the pink flashing design was in time with her turnings. She was beginning to feel terribly impatient. A drunk Japanese man in a blue jacket stumbled up beside her, demanding her eyes.

"Cute. . ." he slurred, and Claudia glared at him, disgusted by his blurry eyes, his sloping stance. "American?" he asked, smiling a wide row of teeth gone slightly yellow.

"Chinese." Claudia answered sharply, pushing past him, not wanting to be bothered, but a little surprised at her nasty response. 'Chinese,' was something Helga, from the club, might have said. She was a German woman with a sharp, sarcastic wit. Claudia admired her ability to scathe, since it was usually at the expense of the businessmen whose whiskey she poured. It was part of getting even for being paid to be subservient.

Claudia moved nervously and for the first time it occurred to her that perhaps Jud was not on his way. 'Maybe he fell asleep, or got high and forgot the time. Maybe the tiny watch he had pinned to the wall for want of a clock, had stopped ticking? Still, it is so unlike him him not to be here,' she thought, afraid to leave and miss him by crossing paths. She thought she could try to walk home on the path he was most likely to take, but there were so many different routes. . .'I'll wait a little longer,' she decided, turning around. Then she saw the drunk man in blue wavering where she had left him, and thought 'But I can't wait here all night.' She had a sudden feeling that she just couldn't stand it if that man spoke to her again. All night, from 7:00 to 12:00 she stood it. She was nice and polite to man after man who stared at her body and face, asking the same exact questions, making the same comments: 'American?' 'Cute.' 'Very young!'

Her evening flew by like a film in fast motion behind her eyes. Claudia in green silk jumping from one red leather stool to another, inside the mirrored and red carpeted basement club. The other girls jumped and moved about; all of them were involved in an elaborate game of musical chairs. 'Only no one ever gets out. Unfortunately,' thought Claudia. 'The music never stops.' George, the Chinese musician, played his amplified electric guitar in the corner. He drank a lot of whiskey. He backed up the men who came to the microphone, to exercise their voices, good and bad, for an always predictable round of applause.

In her mind she saw man after man in blue, leaning perpetually forward, toward her. She poured their whiskey and water carefully, aware of their scrutiny. If it was a large party she was often relieved to be ignored while they spoke and laughed quickly with one another. If it was a small group, or if the worst happened and she was alone with one man, then they 'talked,' heads bobbing in intended communication. She understood them intuitively. It was rare that she understood their attempts at spoken word after the phrases which every Japanese club-goer could say quite articulately: 'American,' 'Cute,' 'How long you stay in Japan?' Occassionally, a man would say: 'Do you speak Japanese?' Claudia laughed at them when they asked her that.

She reached the drunk and realized she had decided enough was enough; she could not wait any longer. Ignoring him she walked past, but he followed and tapped her shoulder. She winced angrily and turned, "Leave me alone!" she said sharply and the man laughed, seeming to enjoy her irritation. "Ahhh soo." he cooed, smiling, "Cute American!" Claudia turned her back and walked away, questioning, 'Is this what I should do? What if Jud is really on his way?' but she followed her natural urge to escape. The giant digital clock above the circle read 1:35 and Claudia quickened her pace, listening to the tap-tap of her heels ringing out in the slightly less crowded night-time streets. She glanced over her shoulder to make certain the drunk wasn't following her, and she saw him talking with a group of men bathed in neon by the station. She felt a strong urge of hatred for all of them and the strength of her feeling surprised her. 'God, what a night.' she thought, walking fast.

Work had started off poorly. At 6:45 Claudia had rushed in, a little late from taking her time at home getting high on the new stuff Klaus had smuggled in from Pakistan. She had thrown her bag into the tiny coat closet, and, hoping she looked relaxed and composed, she had slipped quickly down on the red leather bench between Helga and Annie. Annie was the English girl Claudia had noticed arriving late during that first interview with Charlie. She lived with Joyce, an Australian woman and the two of them were discussing a man they both knew. Claudia had listened, senstive and aware, as she came down off the hash, to Annie's voice full of innocent passivity.

"But I don't want him to think. . ." she had said and then Joyce had interrupted, her voice heavy with humor and worldly sarcasm.

"If I were you dear, I'd go right to his room and tell him that."

Claudia had been interested and wanted to know what it was Annie didn't want this man to think, but she had missed the details because of Charlie. He had suddenly appeared pointing to her, curling his index finger toward himself, indicating she was to get up and 'report' to him by the bar. As she squeezed out, Claudia had whispered into the silence which had fallen immediately at Charlie's appearance: "What do you suppose I've done now?" Joyce and Helga had laughed very low, understanding, and Annie had smiled with them, but looked very obviously preoccupied, anxious to resume her conversation.

Claudia had gone and stood before Charlie in the narrow passage between the bar, the coat closet, and the bathroom. He had leaned against the bar top and looked down at her from his black height. She remembered the anxious feeling which often came to her in his presence, and she had just barely restrained herself from insolently repeating, 'So what have I done now?' Twice before, the mama-san had instructed Charlie to speak to her about mistakes she'd made.

She rather liked remembering those reprimands; they struck her as amusing now that they were in the past. The first time, she'd done the wrong thing by answering truthfully an unusually articulate customer's questions about what she was paid. The man, thinking her wage was too low, had complained to the mama-san on her behalf. While defending herself that time, it had not occurred to her, being new to club work, that perhaps the customer was right. Rather, she had seen the incident as his mistake. She had said to Charlie; "But I was just being polite. He asked me, so I answered. I didn't tell him to go complain." She had been afraid during that first reprimand that she might lose her job, but Charile had patiently informed her it was against club policy to speak of how much the girls were paid. He had instructed her to tell inquiring customers that if they wanted such information they must ask him, Charlie; he would answer all questions.

Her second mistake had been jointly made with Joyce and Helga. The three of them had been assigned to a large party, a table of nine company men out celebrating someone's promotion. In a magnanimous gesture they had ordered a 'Club Rolapoggi Appetizer,' an extremely rare occurrence. A plate of plastic multi-colored ribbons attached to toothpicks stuck through pieces of pepperoni, cheese and cucumber had arrived at the table. The three women had exchanged excited glances and eyed the western food happily. But then, not one of the men would touch it. The food sat on the table undisturbed for so long, Claudia had begun to wonder if it was really just plastic, like the dishes outside the restaurants she and Jud ate in.

Finally, Joyce, experienced for many years in club work, had picked the platter up, her hand flat under it like an expert waitress, and had cordially offered it round saying "Dozo. . . Dozo. . . ." Meaning, 'please eat, so we can.' But the men politely refused, each one waiting for another one to go first, until one man caught on and repeated "Dozo. . ." politely back to her. This parrot custom was what Joyce had been counting on. 'Dozo' was roughly equivalent to 'If you please.' She had smiled graciously and answered "Domo," 'Thank you,' and lifting a toothpick from the plate, she scraped the food off with her small sharp teeth.

Then she offered the plate to Helga and Vicky who felt free to eat since it seemed the men didn't want the food anyway. In between refilling the glasses with whiskey and water, and drinking their own Kirin beers, they had covertly plucked toothpick after toothpick from the plate, until they had eaten all the snacks but one. The lone food-coated toothpick remained standing in the center of the plate — no one dared to take it — and the many bare wooden sticks, their plastic ribbons crumpled by crumbs, lie like flags trodden down on a battlefield. At the time, the men had said nothing to them, and the women had assumed they were oblivious. But they had not been. One with genuine concern, rather than the nasty sarcasm Helga had attributed his comment to, had remarked to the mama-san on his way out; "Don't your girls get enough to eat?"

So the three women had been reprimanded by Charlie, but only gently. He had stood with amusement in his eyes, a small twist to his smile, as he warned them to eat dinner before they came to work.

This evening, standing before him, Claudia hadn't been able to recall any recent misbehavior, apart from her slightly late arrival. Now, she shivered as she walked home, hunching her shoulders forward against the wet air. She could still feel him looking down at her, not speaking. She had looked down at the red carpet, embarrassed by the intensity of his dark eyes on her. She had felt immediately guilty, without even knowing what she'd done.

She was passing the porno cinemas which lined the side streets near the station, and was distracted from reliving her experience by a life-size neon blond wearing a black bikini. From the corner of her eye Claudia thought the woman was real. A Japanese man in a tux stood by the door. Seeing her look, he whistled and shouted out "Hey baybee. . ." Claudia ignored the doorman, and returned to remembering her evening. She knew only a few seconds had passed while she and Charlie had stood there in silence, but it had seemed like an hour to her. She hated to wait and had felt herself squirming inside against his stillness, when suddenly he had lifted her chin with one hand, then reached out with his other to press a single black finger against her lips. Remembering it made her stomach rise and fall as if she had driven over a bump in the road too quickly, but at the time she had felt almost nothing. He had held the finger tip before her eyes and her mind had memorized the delicate print, the brown on pink swirl.

"The mama-san say you do not wear enough lipstick," he had said, his voice cool and impersonal. "My finger should be red and it is not." Claudia's whole body had gone tight with anger. She did not like being criticized. She did not like being told what to do. And there was more she had not liked; his attitude, touching her lips so intimately, yet remaining so calmly removed, as if she wasn't a real person at all, just a life-sized walking-talking painted American doll.

But when she had opened her mouth to protest, she had seen in his eyes that warm amusement, a friendly shine, as if the whole thing was a silly joke and not only did they both know it, they were sharing it, so she should try to enjoy it. It was a silly ritual no one believed in, which nevertheless must be performed. 'But why?' thought Claudia, wondering 'Why didn't I say something?'

She left the porno streets behind, and passing closed shops she remembered how, at the time, she had felt her anger evaporate under his gaze. She had felt ridiculously guilty and had responded seeking his reassurance, "I just can't do anything right around here." She had smiled, trying to make a joke of her feelings. Charlie had laughed at that, his laughter rumbling and warm. "Ah Vicky. . ." her fake club name had rolled like lava off his tongue. She had stood waiting for him to say something more, but instead he had called over his shoulder to the bartender and then disappeared under the bar, leaving her standing there, staring into the space where he had stood, feeling somehow the interaction was incomplete, yet over.

She had turned and squeezed herself into the closet which was also the dressing room. With her back pressed tight against the hanging coats, her face was three inches from the mirror. To find the red lipstick Maria had given her she had to dig through the junk in her bag, and then carefully, with the uncertainty and clumsiness of a woman who rarely wore lipstick, she had slid the red tube up and down around her lips, rolling them together just lightly, surprised to see the red heart shape which had glared back at her. Usually she put her lipstick on in the flat, with her tiny compact mirror propped against the futon, but she had dropped the compact from her bag, while searching for her key on the way out of the flat to the baths, and it had struck the tile floor cracking inside its case into three jagged pieces. 'Now that's probably the thing which made the whole evening rotten.' She had known immediately it was a very bad sign, but of what, she did not know. 'Bad luck,' she had thought at the time, 'very bad luck, which I don't need.' Now, walking alone, she felt again uneasy. She felt threatened by something she could not name, something she could not remember, some uncertainty of meaning.

While she had stood staring at herself in the mirror, she had thought Charlie was behind the bar, watching her, and she had worried that once again he would think she was just a kid because she didn't know how to put on lipstick. Turning her back to him she had found a piece of paper in her bag, the outside wrapper of the chocolate bar she'd had for dinner, and carefully she had blotted her lips, leaving a very sensual wide strawberry shape, white at the center as if the berry had been pierced with the prong of a fat fork. She had turned to face Charlie with what she had hoped was aloof nonchalance, but he had not been there after all. She had heard him greeting customers at the door. She knew now he had not really been watching.

She frowned, realizing Charlie made her feel unsure of herself and she knew insecurity was an intolerable trait for club work. She remembered how completely odd she had felt when she went and sat back down at the table beside Joyce, Helga, Annie and the Israeli woman Rachel, who had joined them in her absence. They all examined her fresh lipstick and Claudia had felt a rush of self-conscious blush rising to her already artificially reddened cheeks. "Is nice. . .this color." Rachel had smiled warmly, dispensing her judgment with her hands folded neatly on her lap. Claudia had noticed Rachel wore almost the exact same shade of red, but her mouth was flat and thin, a slit between heavy cheekbones. It didn't look the same on her. She was a large woman and older than Claudia, a solidity surrounded her. Claudia liked her. She had responded to the compliment by violently bursting: "I hate it, I really do! What am I? A clown?" And the other women had nodded, sympathetic in varying degrees. They each understood Claudia's resistance to being Vicky. All of them had felt that angry irritation which comes from being forced to look or act a certain way to please someone else, but that was the essence of their job. Annie had offered, "Just don't dwell on it," and compassionate laughter had followed. Helga had tried cynicism, "Think of it as make-up for the stage, Vicky. We are the actresses. The audience is just arriving, and the play is the same play as last night; the Club Rolapoggi. . . ."

"Very profound," Joyce had commented, smiling with amused sarcasm. Claudia had said nothing. But thinking back on it, she saw there was truth in the joke. When she put on her silk dress, her heels and make-up, it was like dressing for a show, transforming herself to play a part. And hearing the sound of her other name, 'Vicky,' when Charlie or the other women or the customers addressed her, was a constant reminder that she was not herself. Vicky was someone else; a character mischievous and worldy, daring after a few drinks. 'I can't think about it.' Claudia shook her head, hoping to shake the thoughts away. 'Why does it even matter if I'm one person with Jud and someone else at work?' Claudia knew she couldn't do what Vicky did. 'I'm not really like that,' she thought, without asking herself what 'like that' meant. And Vicky was becoming as easy to slip in and out of as her clothes. The hard part was now, the time in between work and home she was Claudia and Vicky too. And usually there was Jud to talk to, to tell her evening to, and for some reason it seemed easier to talk it out than think it through.

She was walking down the hill now. The sound of a Japanese woman singing into a microphone drifted out from frosted glass doors. Claudia knew this whole area was full of clubs where Japanese women did the same job she did. The only difference was the class. She worked in the Ginza, the expensive part of town, where businessmen paid to have an American or generic 'western woman,' pour their drinks. But mama-sans were everywhere.

In Ikebukuro, an area Claudia had been told was 'poor' by Japanese standards, (though it certainly didn't resemble poverty in any other coun-try) Japanese men were served by women of their own nationality. 'Women whose jobs are probably harder than mine,' Claudia reflected, thinking that if she was Japanese it would be much worse. 'Then I'd speak the same language as the drunken morons, and I'd really have to enter-tain them, with more than just a smile.' She cringed against those thoughts entering her head with the loud voices and electric music hang-ing in the wet night air. The doorways to the scattered clubs were well lit, contrasting with the canvas flaps of the vegetable stalls which were tied to the ground like the shut eyelids of sleeping people, incongruous, beside the bright doorways where people stayed awake.

The thought of sleeping people reminded her of Jud. She suddenly felt sure that he was home in bed. As she rounded the corner at the bottom of the hill, her pace increased. She had missed him today. It felt like ages since she had seen him. She needed him. She wanted just to touch his hair and hug him. Her heels were clacking faster, now that she was finally on their street. Her mind was already up the stairs and inside the apartment, kissing Jud awake.

A man, crouching in the shape of a frog, sat outside the entrance to the downstairs apartments. He shocked her. She was so absorbed in her thoughts, she jumped when she saw him. He was serenely smoking a cigarette and she recognized him as a tenant of the building. The look he gave her made her wonder if he was the father she had heard yelling and slapping his kids who lived beneath her and Jud. He nodded, acknowledging her just slightly and Claudia said "Kumbawa. . ." politely.

She ascended the steel staircase anxiously; she thought she'd seen a judgment, condemnation on his face. 'So you work late nights in a club. . .' his eyes had seemed to say. 'Well so what?' thought Claudia, 'What's wrong with that? You beat your kids.' She hated going up these steps at night. Her heels sounded into the late night quiet like the giant gongs the monks rang at the temples. They lacked the rhythm, but contained the loud solemnity. 'But I can't help it,' she thought, resigned to her self-consciousness. She felt a person would have to be Japanese to master silent, quiet, footsteps.

At the landing she slipped her shoes off, but did not leave them there with the shoes of the other tenants lined in a neat row. She knew it was silly not to, really, but here was another thing she could not help. She didn't trust her good shoes left outside all night and day. Her sandals, yes. She left them almost as an offering. She saw them, at the end of the row, scuffed and still holding the dust of the Philippines in their leather creases, so unlike every other neat and tidy slip on in the row. She searched for Jud's ripped and dirty, graying sneakers, and was relieved to see they were not sitting out. She thought it sensible that he bring them into the flat; in such bad condition, they were a terrible disgrace.

She hurried down the corridor, disliking the cold tiles under her stockinged feet, but pleased to dislike them since they served as her reminder to jump across the four tiles inside the flat, insuring her good luck. In her head the omen was repeated 'If-you-don't,-something-bad-will-happen.' She dug through her bag as she walked, looking for her key, but when she reached the door she was still searching. It was always this way with her. Once she dropped something in her bag, she might as well have dropped a pebble into a bottomless lake. She turned over loose pens and scraps of trash, a brush, a book, lipstick, a piece of dusty chocolate. All of them tumbled back down without relinquishing the key. Claudia thought of the large claws of garbage trucks lifting and turning waste. She sighed and set her shoes down so she could use two hands. 'Why doesn't Jud answer the door?' she thought, irritated, knocking very softly. 'He must know I'm out here.'

She was agitated by the thought that the witchy old woman who lived next door might need to pee and might come out of her apartment and catch Claudia in her make-up and silk, crouched under the bare bulb in the hallway. 'God knows what would happen then,' thought Claudia.

She imagined a curse would be thrown on her for living a devious lifestyle, or perhaps just for waking up witches at night. With much concentration she finally found the key and swiftly stuck it in the lock. Pushing the door open, she cringed at the grinding squeak that escaped into the hall.

She jumped across the four red tiles and landed squarely on squishy tatami. The whole room shook a little and Claudia felt 'Nothing in Tokyo is really solid.' She went directly to the far end of the room where the futon was and looking down she saw she had been right at the station when she assumed Jud had fallen asleep. He was there, under the harsh overhead light, lying on the bed fully clothed, Koestler's book of essays open by his head. He was just waking up.

"What time is it? What are you doing here? I meant to. . ." As he came into consciousness Jud knew immediately something wasn't right, but what it was escaped him. He looked horrible. His eyes were red, squinting against the light, and his cheek wrinkled in grotesque patterns by the cheap blanket. Seeing him, Claudia almost dropped to her knees and cradled his head in her silk lap. She had the sudden urge to stroke his hair where it was damp on one side from sleeping. Instead she found she was backing away, towards the closet, saying indignantly, "I waited for you at the station, nearly an hour." 'Really,' she thought, 'it was only thirty minutes. What made me say it was longer?'

"Ah I'm sorry baby." Jud was contrite, "I looked at the watch at 12:00, I was going to leave but it seemed too early. I didn't want to hang out there, you know, so I. . .I sat down to read, but. . .I must've fallen asleep. . . ." Jud was slowly coming to life. He'd been smoking hash since he got home from work at 6:30, and it had left him feeling odd. Time seemed confused; he felt he'd been asleep for days, yet only an hour could have passed. With great effort he focused on Claudia and saw she was backing away. "What are you doing?" He asked, "Sit down, tell me about your night. . . ." He sat up slowly, preparing himself to listen.

"NO." She shouted at him. She felt her anger rise once again with unexpected force. "I don't want to talk about my night. Just let me forget it will you?" 'Why wasn't he waiting?' She felt something terrible had happened and it was his fault because he hadn't been there. 'But I didn't step on the tiles,' she thought, her head filling with pressure, as if her thoughts were splintering into bad luck like the broken compact mirror.

"Everyone makes mistakes, Claudia. You don't need to shout." Jud was staring, his haze going, a cold fog settling in on him. Claudia did not look him in the eye, but Jud thought he had reached her as she moved tentatively towards him. But she kept moving, right past him, into the corner at the foot of the futon, where she began undressing. Jud watched her face carefully, and wondered if something was really wrong. He hated her job, and suspected that men frequently hassled her, though she never said they did. He worried that something might happen to her without him around. He felt guilty for not having been at the station.

She silently undid her red leather belt and hung it around the hook of their only hanger which would soon hold her dress. Claudia was careful to keep the dress hanging up, unlike everything else, which she randomly tossed on the floor. But, she thought 'Vicky only has one dress, so it shouldn't be wrinkled. It has to be smooth and pretty.' She peeled it off, smelling the stale cigarette smoke deep in the silk. The smell made her sad. She withdrew the looped ribbons from inside the seams, and wrapped them around the neck of the hanger and then stood on tiptoe to balance the wire on the edge of the molding. Now the dressed hanger would stare down on them, a head and legless figure.

Sometimes when Claudia woke in the night, from confused chaotic dreams she could not recall, she thought the dress was a ghost or spirit, wavering, translucent in the dark corner, half-lit by the lights outside behind the patterned glass. Sometimes in the day when she was high and alone in the flat, she imagined Vicky inside the dress, hanging lifeless, her legs swinging, heels limp, like a waiting puppet.

Claudia sank down on the futon, sighing. She had forgotten all about being angry at Jud. She felt nothing but incredibly relieved to be out of that dress. She realized she was exhausted, and she craved sleep. 'I am so tired.' she thought, unhooking her lacy bra, she felt Jud's eyes on her. 'Damn men. That's all they want,' came raging to her, but then she was confused; 'What am I angry at, really?'

She flopped like a rag doll, face down on the futon and mumbled "There's something wrong with me. . ." into the heavy cotton. Jud heard her and put his hand down on the center of her bare back, meaning to comfort, but she shook him off, moaning "Noooooo. . . ."

Jud removed his hand and inspected it as if it was burned. He had tolerated her anger and her irritation from the moment she walked in the door, but now he was offended. It occured to him that she was 'like this' nearly every night when she came out of the gray subway. A breeze came in from the corner where the window did not shut entirely. The hanging green silk rustled and Jud turned to it, startled by the movement. Looking again at Claudia's naked, inert form he didn't think her job was really worth it, but their choices were so limited. Club work paid even better than his job teaching English and they wanted to earn money as fast as possible so that they could escape Tokyo, and relax somewhere else, maybe Sri Lanka or Thailand.

He wondered if something was happening to them, if the pressure of Tokyo, the mecca of the East for capitalism, was crushing them. But it wasn't like him to dwell on it. He had thought it all through several times, high and alone at night in the flat, and concluded that both he and Claudia suffered from thinking 'If only. . .' too often. 'If only we had more money and could be together all the time.' 'If only we hadn't gotten pregnant when we did.' 'If only the abortion in Manila had been less expensive and less awful.' 'If only we hadn't been forced to come here to make money.' 'If only we could speak Japanese.'

Jud looked again at her bare back and decided not to try again to touch her, even though he wanted to. He thought by morning everything would be all right again. He hoped they would wake up and make love, with the whole day unencountered and nothing between them but skin. He got up and turned the light off, then silently undressed before lying down beside her.

Claudia felt like crying but she could not think of a reason. The phrase 'something is not right.' repeated itself in her head like the Zuki Suzuki tune. She felt lonely and unhappy and angry as Jud's body settled against hers. 'Why doesn't he do something?' she thought. 'But what?' she asked herself. 'What is it I wish he would do?'

She wanted to live in a magical world where wishing something would be enough to make it happen. Money would appear from nowhere, cities would be relaxed places and babies accidentally conceived would vanish painlessly back to where they came from. Touching her skin with his was the man she loved, the man she was sharing her life with, but what did Jud understand about how she really felt? He didn't believe in omens or magic or even in longing for them.

Claudia realized lonely felt worse with Jud beside her than it did when he was gone at work. The emptiness seemed more profound. Squashing her eyes into the dark of the pillow, she thought of White Beach in the Philippines and saw the brilliant stars of the southern hemisphere. Wrapping the pillow around her ears, she listened for the sound of the quiet sea. Claudia felt a desperate frustration, because her feelings seemed not to fit into words, and this inarticulateness depressed her. She thought Jud thought the way to best express herself was to make love. That was why she'd shaken off his touch. The thought of touching in her current state of mind physically upset her. It seemed to Claudia that sex would only drive the pain deeper up inside her, into the very core of her being. She felt she had to keep these feelings on the outside, or she would be lost. She tried to sleep, and it seemed to her the nameless things swarmed around her body, brushing her skin like hands, inquiring, but unable to penetrate.

Constance Crawford

PILGRIMAGE TO ATAGOYAMA

Tokyo, May 13, 1983
The May morning was warm and muggy so I leaned over from the desk, slid back the plastic shoji screen, and opened the window onto my view of the artfully pruned garden. I was lucky to have friends in Tokyo who had arranged for my room and library privileges here. International House is supposed to be for foreign scholars and dignitaries. Did I qualify? A fifty-five year old American woman, a writer of stories, a long-time single mother, a long time on my own, I had returned to Japan to see more of a country I love. I was also poking around the library for clues to the story of my great-grandparents. They were missionaries. Young, newlywed, godstruck, they stopped in Japan, early, during the first months it was opened to westerners in 1853, then spent twenty years of fire and brimstone in China. At mid-life, only she came back alive, with their one surviving child. Who had they really been? What did they see? What had they felt?

I had a big pile of books on the desk, but this morning they were not yielding up anything I wanted. All of Tokyo, that roaring banquet of a city, beckoned to me from outside the garden wall. I am a restless and greedy traveler and after mornings at my desk, I had been cramming much too much into my afternoons and evenings. My gimpy knees were feeling the strain. Today, bent on simplicity, I had planned only one excursion, the 4:30 p.m. performance at Kabuki-za, the Kabuki theater in the Ginza district.

It was only mid-morning, but surely, to sit chained to the desk was a mistake on such a balmy day? A short walk around the neighborhood might clear my thoughts, perhaps a visit to just one new place on my list? I flipped open my notebook.

"Atagoyama," was the first name I saw. "A hill with a shrine on it," my friend had dictated. "Nice walk, not too far from International House." That seemed right for my sensible program: first, Atagoyama, then Kabuki.

I left the desk, put on my good gray pants, a cool pink shirt, and my old Rockport walking shoes. The camera went over my shoulder, two extra lenses made my purse bulge. I wasn't going to be any competition for the elegant Japanese women at the Kabuki-za, though I did put my black patent high heels into one of the chic, colorful shopping bags which abound here. At least the shopping bag part of my attire would fit the prevailing fashion; everybody in Tokyo, man, woman, and child, carries some sort of bag, satchel, briefcase, or knapsack. The women carry, in addition, their Gucci — or at least Gucciesque — handbags. The very toddlers are apt to sport bright, nifty little purses.

I looked up the entry, "Atagoyama (Mount Atago)," in my guidebook. Yes, there was a shrine, *Atago Jinja*. I skimmed the fine print: view not as good as it once was. . .lots of very Japanese carryings on. . .a council of armies that saved old Edo. . .cherry blossom festivals since time immemorial. . .a shogun's retainer rides up 86 steps to hilltop, cuts blossoming branch, rides down *backward*, feat of horsemanship repeated only three times in centuries since. . .site of suicide by hand grenades of five World War II vets in 1945, et cetera.

I have a very detailed map of Tokyo, of course. I spread it out on my desk and took a good look at Atagoyama. A long green crescent shape, surrounded by city streets. I held my pencil against the scale of kilometers and figured my route, two and a half kilometers, roughly a mile and a half, along clearly marked thoroughfares. It should be easy. Then, after a leisurely visit to *Atago Jinja*, I would come down, go to the subway station which the map showed to be nearby, travel to the Kabuki-za, put on my high heels, find my seat, take off my high heels, rest my feet, eat rice crackers and candy and dried seaweed from little bags, revel in the virtuoso Kabuki actors in their gorgeous costumes, and more or less understand the drama, which I hoped would be a bloody one. I love Japanese theater of any kind — the aristocratic, nearly motionless Noh plays, the marvelous strange puppets of the Bunraku, and maybe most of all the histrionic, crowd-rousing Kabuki. It was going to be a great day.

I stowed the map in the outside pocket of my purse, knowing that I would be consulting it at every street corner. At the same time I made sure I had three other vital papers in my wallet: my Kabuki ticket (the date of which can never be exchanged nor the high cost of which — about sixty dollars — refunded), my subway map, and, perhaps most important for all foreign visitors to this maze of a city, a card with the name of and directions to the hotel *written in Japanese* so that, in case of collapse from exhaustion, *sake*, or other causes, a cab driver could at least deliver the body home.

Finding one's way in Tokyo is confusing and time-consuming; the Japanese themselves have difficulty, after all, for few of the smaller streets have names and there are no sequential house numbers. As a traveler trying to find your way you must only surrender to the knowledge that you *will* be lost, repeatedly, and for rather long periods. You must trust that you will eventually stumble on the right place by accident, or, just when you are beginning to sweat with despair, the God of Journeys will put up a sign in western letters or send a Japanese Oxford scholar around the corner to meet you and take you courteously to your destination.

Besides, being lost in Tokyo is safe. A woman can walk here alone, any time, in almost any district. Robbery, mugging, and rape are all rare.

I set out into the soft, bright morning. Ten minutes of walking brought me to the main intersection of Roppongi, "my" neighborhood, a roaring, glittering, polyglot scene. Right in the midst of the bedlam is the paradoxically serene noodle shop where I usually ate my lunch. I was already hungry, but I decided to try a new sushi place I'd heard about from an American diplomat's wife I met at an art opening. This woman had also recommended the noodle shop so I knew her second tip would be worth following up. "It's *behind* the Russian embassy," she had said, gesturing. "You will see the guards. . ." The Russian Embassy was on my way and going around "behind" it should be simple enough. Already I was complicating my plan.

I am more timid while traveling than I like to admit — I knew the new sushi place would make me nervous, with its door that wouldn't look like *the* door, its emphatic, unreadable signs, all the subtle customs and procedures — but I'm really happiest if I challenge my timidity. I could have made it easy on myself, gone to my familiar noodle shop or to one of the foreign-style places which are everywhere in Roppongi. The signs scream at you all too legibly: German Beer Hall (pumpernickel's all the rage now though five years ago not a piece of bread could be found), Mister Donut, Coffee Bar, Pizza Hut, Plaza Bar, The Lobster Pot, Chez Louis, Indonesian Ristafel, and of course, McDonald's. I took a picture of a sign that said "Jack and Betty ('We Love Food')."

But, no, I was committed to sushi. It took twenty minutes to reach the Russian Embassy. Along Tokyo streets the sights throng at you — so much, so modern, ugly, funny, elegant, venerable, garish — a complex and incongruous backdrop to my day's gentle adventure. What a different Japan my great-grandmother must have seen. I hoped Atagoyama would show me something of that country.

The Soviet Embassy, massive yellowish concrete behind an iron fence, was a startling contrast to the trash and splash of Roppongi. The proportionately massive Russian guards carried the only guns I'd seen in Japan. Feeling tired, I shifted my heavy sacks in a way that I hoped the guards would not consider provocative, and headed around *behind* the embassy, as the diplomat's wife had directed. There was a bar, an apartment house, a dead end fence. No sushi.

I retraced my steps, eased past the guards and their ominous van with its huge antennae, walked down the embassy's other side where I again found no sushi but, after a time, came on another enormous building of molded concrete, this one signed "The American Club." I'd heard of this enclave. Instead of guards there were tennis courts. Glossy cars were driving up and well dressed American women were getting out and going in to lunch. I saw a vision: a bacon, lettuce and tomato sandwich on white toast. That's what I *really* wanted to eat.

But at the door there was a sign saying "For Members Only." For a moment I stood there feeling bleak, lonely, thwarted. I considered trying to wangle my way in. If only a man were with me, I thought . . . and stopped. Did I really want that? Did I want somebody to fend for me at these glossy doors, to order my lunch, and help carry my burdens toward Atagoyama? Did I want a man's comments, his sharing in this day's adventure or pilgrimage or whatever it was turning out to be? No, I truly did not.

To mark this realization I set down my shopping bag and took a picture of the door of The American Club. With renewed determination I hiked back under the Soviets' antennae and turned toward Atagoyama again. As I walked I thought some more about changes happening in me. If I had been taking this walk alone a few years ago, particularly in the time just after my divorce, my mind would have been spinning a phantom man to walk beside me. I was then as romantic as an adolescent. If I had a lover at the moment, it was he I would have visions of, or, if there was no flesh and blood man to carry in my mind, a fantasy being would hold my hand through the foreign streets. Now the phantom is gone.

I settled for lunch in the next cafe I came to. It had black padded booths and stale air. To the weedy teen-aged waiter, I said my one sure-fire word of Japanese, "*Kohi*" — coffee — and I pointed at whatever food two other customers, men, were eating from lacquer-red plastic trays. I nodded hopefully. The waiter went to the kitchen and I heard him say, "*Gaijin*," meaning "foreigner" with a touch of "barbarian" mixed in. A cook poked his head out of a hole and grinned. What did he see when he looked at me? A funny-looking foreign lady alone, a cause for ridicule — no, perhaps just mild amusement, really a cause for nothing. I didn't care, I was hungry.

The food was not very good except for the rice which was sprinkled with tasty little black seeds. Much restored, I put down my *hashi*, my chopsticks, and sat back to drink the strong coffee.

Music is loud and incessant in Roppongi places. *Thud-thud-thud* — new rock, punk, whatever it is. "Babee I gotta have youooo," the singer wailed over and over. Lovesick cries of boys and girls. I felt how little the music of desire has to do with me now. My kids' rock music of the sixties and seventies did express many of my desires then — but now I'm different. So is the music, of course. But I don't mean only the cheapness of this music — even at the opera nowadays I observe the desperate pairs of lovers with compassion rather than empathy.

In that cafe I began to think in a new way about my life. I am alone here, yes, but now I do not think of it as only a transition or a preparation for something else. I feel *on my own* in my life, and I believe this will continue whether I happen to find a partner or not. Is all this just the cooling of approaching age? Or is there something else that draws me forward, not as passionately perhaps, but more deeply? Perhaps this kind of aloneness is not an absence but the positive stuff from which must be made. . .whatever is now to be made. The next stage. The rest of my life.

I studied the map. Atagoyama looked to be an easy half-kilometer away. I walked along the wide boulevard contentedly, thinking my thoughts and only tempted outward once when I saw an antique shop plastered with signs in English and a tour bus parked in front. I should be buying antiques! a part of me cried. Oh, no you shouldn't, countered a stronger entity within, and I kept walking.

My shoulders and feet were aching. I took a turn into a back street and set my burdens down for a moment at the gate of a small newly-built Buddhist temple, spic and span in its gravel yard. I did not venture through the gate for there were two dressed-up men in the yard bustling around a glossy black Mercedes. I rested my weight against the stone railing, snapped a picture when the men had their backs turned, and got out my map.

Temples are Buddhist and marked on the map with a reverse swastika; shrines are Shinto, marked with the symbol 卄 denoting the *torii* or gateway that stands in front of most of them. Shrines, from tiny to vast, are everywhere, one of the aspects of Japan I enjoy most. On my map the long, irregular green area of Atagoyama was marked with both a swastika and a *torii*. Dotted lines denoted footpaths across the green but it was unclear what street or path would lead me into it. Above the houses ahead I could see trees rising. Surely the way onto the hill would be self-evident.

Another few minutes' walk brought me to a street at the base of an abruptly rising, greenery-hung stone cliff. This was more of a mountain than I expected — my friend and the map said "hill," and I hadn't taken the guidebook's "*Mount* Atago" literally. I found a set of concrete steps, zig-zagging upwards, and I started to climb. My purse, camera, and shopping bag put on fifty pounds. The steps ended at a row of shabby one-storey houses nestled on a ledge. Long grass, old fruit trees — a charming place to live, but no path up the cliff to the top.

I started back down, and passed a man on the stairs. He stopped and stared at me: what was this *gaijin* doing up here? I might have said: Excuse me, sir, where is the path to the top of the hill? He might have known English, or we could have gestured. Why didn't I? A sub-sense that he might be hostile? A fear of ridicule? I think rather it was a growing sense that the day's task *was* to find my way alone.

So I put on my blankest, most self-sufficient expression, a mask which says: I know what I am doing, I can take care of myself. It preserves my privacy — and sometimes, I suspect, cuts off help, amusement, companionship as well. I developed this mask long ago, in my native territory, but it strikes me now that it is quite like the mask that the Japanese wear to make their crowded life feasible. The jammed Tokyo subway is a study in masked faces.

At any rate, I went down the stairs and the man went up. I worked my way through a gloomy, cliff-shaded neighborhood stretched along the west face of Mount Atago. There were some tangled stands of bamboo, glimpses of family life in modest houses stair-stepped under the rock wall. To write of Tokyo houses perhaps creates a picture of lovely old wood and paper structures of the historical movies. Finding one of those is rare, in the city at least, and it's hard to say what an ordinary residential neighborhood is "like" even immediately after one has seen it. Apartment houses of gray concrete are common — the first postwar remedy to the work of the firebombs. In this neighborhood under the flank of the hill, though, the close-packed houses were motley, nondescript single-family dwellings. Here and there I did glimpse traditional Japanese detail: a sliding window, a wooden gate, a good tile roof.

Always searching for a way upward, I tried several promising paths which led only to private doors. I entered a broad cross-street leading in the right direction, but it disappeared into a tunnel under the hill. I climbed more dusky steps and was turned back by a chain link fence. Atagoyama is long, and I was apparently on the wrong side of it.

I flagged then. My simple walk had become an ordeal, my precious self-sufficiency had backfired. At this point I *would* have asked directions, but the street was deserted. Suddenly the shrine on Atagoyama seemed a silly goal. It probably wouldn't be pretty even if I did get up there, I thought. I had passed not far from a subway station a while back. Perhaps I should just give up, flee down to the Ginza, and get into a department store, where a *gaijin* belongs.

But something in me refused. They say my grandmother was a tireless traveler, a formidable seer of sights. She was born in China at her parents' Baptist mission. She was their third child and the only one to survive in that garden of microbes, perhaps because she was the only one to have a Chinese wet-nurse. As a young child Grandma had visited Japan where she was given a doll she called Japunka. Together they sailed across the Pacific Ocean three times before Grandma was eight years old. When she grew up, it was no wonder that my grandmother had great stamina as a sightseer. By then, of course, she had luggage-bearers and agents from Thomas Cook, but I like to think that she contributed a certain traveler's grit to my gene pool which gave me the energy — the courage, really — to tackle anew my pilgrimage to Atagoyama.

I walked passively then, not searching, but simply wandering along. I made random turnings and somehow — perhaps the angle of sunlight changed as my route turned or perhaps, newly humbled, I was more receptive — I began to notice things that held mysterious promise: a shrub with a dark purple flower, a beautifully veined rock placed by a doorpost, a bent old woman in kimono and apron. Things were silently revealing themselves to me. These moments are the reason I travel. My spirits rose.

I turned into the old woman's street, then into another, deeply shaded by large trees. There were widely-spaced wooden risers in the pavement; then a set of cement steps like the ones I had tried before, only these kept climbing and soon brought me to a paved road, curving upward. I took a steep, leafy side-path, puffing hard, hauling my burdens. The ground leveled and I found myself in a small, shaggy wood. On Atagoyama, at last.

Among the trees there was a tall standing stone, carved with characters. You are never far from a standing stone in this country. I find their unknown messages encouraging. The city had dropped out of sight and nearly out of hearing, too. I heard the sound of trickling water, and, following it, found a bamboo gate and the curved lintel of a gray *torii*, just tall enough for me to go through. Beyond the *torii*, almost invisible amid rocks and ferns, a small waterfall gushed into a pool. Water at the top of the rock! I realized that my tortuous path had led me to the middle of the shrine garden.

By no means all Japanese gardens are carefully raked and pruned. Here it was hard to say where thicket stopped and garden began. A few yellow irises were blooming by the overgrown pool. A small bridge led to a shrine the size of a dollhouse. All this was unspectacular, a little shabby. Few people come here, I thought, charmed and self-congratulatory.

Farther on was a grove of cherry trees. Now, near summer, they were in full leaf, but some of the trunks were still straw-wrapped against the winter cold. Some curvy trees had bamboo props, some were straggling at ease amidst the other greenery.

Like most cherry trees in Japan, each of these bore a white tag with written characters. I guessed the writing told a tree's species, the grower, maybe its grafting and pruning history. I like being among people who keep track of their cherry trees. Atagoyama must be heavenly in blossom time. It was not heavenly now; it was untidy, simple and homey, like somebody's much-loved back yard.

Nearby were some low wooden buildings. As I came around the side wall I realized that I had arrived at *Atago Jinja*, the shrine on Atagoyama. At the front of the shrine and some distance away stood the tall handsome red pillars and tile roof of a free-standing *torii*. I went outside this gate, then turned to get the view of the shrine which the formal approach to it would have given me.

A Shinto shrine is generally a three-walled room open to the view of worshippers who stand outside a low railing. There is always a rope of rice straw looped from the shrine porch or perhaps from the gate or nearby trees. It denotes the sacred space. Usually, folded zig-zags of white rice paper dangle from the rope. These talismans move gently in any breeze and, in turn, move my heart, though I do not know what they "mean." Shinto places and ceremonies appeal to me deeply. In the shrines, more colorful and perhaps less sophisticated than the Zen temples, one still feels the deep attraction of formality within simplicity. Here the natural order of things is honored. Even the tourist is a part of the natural order, and I always feel free to step up to the railing under the wide eaves, send a few coins rattling down into the great wooden money box, clap hands to call attention to my presence before the gods, and, if I'm in an outgoing mood, to pull the rope which rings the bell hanging from a beam of the ceiling.

Then one stands with palms together and head bowed, presenting oneself — one's weaknesses, strengths, failures and hopes — before the holy altar. One does not go any closer unless involved in a special ceremony. From outside the railing, looking deeper and deeper into the inner space, one sees, toward the rear, the basics of life: two jars of rice wine, a pile of rice cakes, and often a small pyramid of fruit. Above hang the sword and the feathered end of the arrow and, between them, the mirror. Standing before a Shinto shrine what one sees, ultimately, is oneself.

At the Atago Shrine I felt too quiet, perhaps too weary, for the bell-ringing and the wish-asking. I watched from outside the pillared gate as people in ones and twos came and went before the low wooden building with its fine copper roof. It appeared to be a well-visited place, after all. A housewife, neatly dressed, her apron still on, paid her respects at the shrine. Her stance paid respect to herself as well — feet together, arms at her sides, hips and shoulders at ease in perfect alignment. I love this in the Japanese. They stand so when they are having their pictures taken. Here I am, as I am, they seem to say, I express no particular thing,

I am doing nothing, I am just standing. I've learned that it takes clarity and even a certain courage to stand as simply that. I tried it then, standing like the housewife.

I wondered, did great-grandfather the Baptist ever let himself stand before a shrine without denouncing it as heathen?

In a few minutes I moved forward to the shrine railing. Over my head a beautifully made banner of white cloth moved in the warm air. It was stenciled with circular light-brown seals, three stylized leaves within each circle. My book of seals tells me these were hollyhock leaves — a homely plant which seems a perfect symbol for this place I came to through the backyard.

But there was nothing of the back yard about the inside of the shrine. Never have I seen a lovelier one. Every lantern was lit, electric but soft as any candle. There were red tassled cords, rice paper pompons, objects of brass and black lacquer. Here and there through the deep room hung strings of lacy golden discs. They twinkled in the dim recesses by the altar itself where the modest porcelain wine jars shone. The floor reflected these gentle lights and shinings. In this serenity my spirit rested and knew itself.

A couple came and threw coins into the box. A businessman, his suit coat neatly over his arm, was coming up the walk. Out beyond the gate, by the stone trough where one purifies oneself before approaching the shrine, several elderly men were dipping water over their hands and chuckling. I had failed to dip into the water, of course, an awkward *gaijin* who came to the shrine by the back way.

I left the shrine and walked through a grove of regularly-spaced cherry trees where the gravel was dotted with bottle caps and food wrappers. Meticulous on their own turf, the Japanese are great litterers elsewhere. I was very thirsty and approached a stand with a few mismatched plastic tables and chairs out in front under the trees. The middle-aged woman behind the counter stared at me expressionlessly. *"Ocha?"* I said, wanting tea. It's an easy word for a readily available refreshment, you would think, but my pronunciation is seldom understood, and, anyway, after repeating the word I usually find out that I am trying to order tea at the wrong time and place. So it was this time. The woman scowled and waved peremptorily toward the soft drink machine behind some piled junk. I smiled cravenly and bobbed my head, trying to save face, I suppose, but the woman didn't give a damn about correct behavior with me. I was a *gaijin* with low blood sugar and she, I thought meanly, was a bitch.

The drink machine worked — they always work — and I sat on a tippy chair in the cherry tree shade and gratefully drank one of the peculiar Japanese soda pops I'm getting a taste for.

Out of the snack bar came an old woman. Her back was bent into a right angle. Lives of toil in the fields have stamped many old Japanese. As she headed toward the shrine, the old woman smiled at me warmly and kept smiling, nodding her head. She looked at me sitting there on one of her daughter's chairs, as though it brought her the greatest pleasure. Perhaps she was apologizing for her daughter's rudeness, but more likely she was just being Japanese. As soon as you decide on one thing about this people, someone comes and shows you the reverse.

A bit rested, my appetite for sights returned. Atagoyama's Buddhist temple was, the map indicated, at the other end of the hilltop. I emerged from the cherry grove and, astonished, faced a huge, modern building with a western lettered sign: "The Museum of Communications." Grandma might have done it but I couldn't. It was already three o'clock, the play began at 4:30, and I had to allow time for getting lost on the way. I let the Buddhist temple — not to mention The Museum of Communications — go unseen.

The map showed a subway station near the eastern foot of Mount Atago. It was no trouble finding the way down. Just beyond the water font a very broad, very long flight of imposing cement stairs descended steeply. Down, down, down I went holding tightly to the railing, pausing several times to quell the shaking in my tired knees. I tried to imagine the shogun's man getting his horse down these stairs.

I reached the foot of the steps at last, went out between two stone lions and through an enormous gray *torii* arching thirty feet overhead. I was on a city street again. I turned to look back. The official approach to Atago Shrine loomed, imposing and magnificent. Going up those steep stairs would be, I now saw, one of the trials demanded of the devout. My knees and I had been spared, coming up through the back yard as I had. There was more than that: it was only on looking back that I could finally see where I had been. The shrine on Atagoyama is one of the great city's lovely and holy places.

I continued on my way to the theater. Very close to my destination I got lost once more — the right subway station but the *wrong* exit — and by the time I found the theater I barely had time to put on lipstick and change into my high heeled shoes. Stubbornness more than fashion made me do this. My sweaty, rumpled clothes were beyond help.

In the Kabuki drama played that afternoon, the women languished, sickened and died after their few courageous moments of passion or bloody rage. The Kabuki audience is made up mostly of women, many of them old, not a few showing the toil-bent back of my friend on the hill. Surely these women have proved tougher than the characters shown by the exquisite male actors in their old dramas.

I felt my own toughness, too, that day, making my way alone, dreaming neither of love nor rescue, exploring what was there, and eventually finding what I sought. I have made my pilgrimage to Atagoyama.

CONCLUSION

Michelle Dominique Leigh

THE BLUE-GREEN SEAS
OF FOREVER

Intimate Matrix

Abandoning oneself to the landscape, seeking the rapture of merging with it, being entered by it, and emerging from the union amazed and transformed, one is in the mood for rapture of all sorts. Breathe the air, smell the wind, drink the water, taste the dangerous wine of wild berries, move to the music, sleep under those supernatural stars on that curious bed made of — what? —, caress the children, bathe with the women, thrill to the touch of a man with whom you share no spoken language, taste his secret skin on your lips, fall into the simplest kind of love.

Love, History

My African lover takes me through his landscape and beyond it, into its ancient past and into its texture and into my own impossibilities. I couldn't have dreamed this world, couldn't have entered it through any old door. In our dark hot room, buzzing with magic and insects, we move on the rhythm of this man's childhood, we receive and know the village priestesses who taught him woman-love, we weaken with the power of his history. Using my body's way of becoming one with this place, this whole other planet, this man who has it all inside him, living in his movements into me.

Woman, Danger

Traveling man: all man. (Explorer, conqueror, hero on a quest, missionary, messiah.) The woman, traveling the same route, say through an interminable blonde desert, over green mountains which shelter coughing antelope and other dark beasts, into jangling marketplaces and sparse villages and monolithic, disease-ridden cities, the woman traveling is hermaphrodite. Hermes, Aphrodite. Unfaithful Aphrodite, lover of all, seer of beauty; Hermes/Mercury, messenger, god of trade, travel, communication, thieves. What is a traveler if not inconstant? Winged, to soar and glide from love to love, place to place, seeking beauty, truth and messages.

Dictionaries, Maps
Hermaphroditus: all in one, self-contained, you travel alone, fertile and unarmed. You need no one. You are an arrow adrift, you float gracefully. You are dangerous, endangered. The traveling woman wants no shoulder to lean on, no strong back to wield her trunks — she has no trunks—, no map-reader to diagram, plot, and point. She has a man in her, a dream-man; she has his power and his spirit. Her style, however, is all female; she is always in danger. (What woman has not walked on the danger-edge, felt the smouldering volatile arousal she provokes, moving exotic, womanly and vulnerable through a place not her own?) She journeys away from her shelter with only her body and its magic otherness — she is innocent to the ways and the contracts and the conversations and the negotiations of the new place. How can she embrace it? What does she mean here? What does the narrowed eye mean, the way it sees her? What are five sets of narrowed eyes; get the dictionary, quick. The dictionary is useless, it answers only the known.

No Meaning, Know Meaning
Can I smile? What might it mean? My own smile is no longer known to me; I cannot predict its result. My body transmits a simple message: *woman.* This is woman, it says. I too feel it — this is my definition, the outline around a mystery. I know a delicate fear. But being woman, I have some skills and wisdom: I sense, I blend, I have a quicksilver method for grasping the new ways, learning the limits of give and receive. I move through the misty landscape and enter into a thousand small communications, engage in a thousand subtle negotiations, often dealing in such goods as life and body. Ownership is a common dispute. I may be perceived as a gift, an item available for trade or sale, a service to be rendered, an offered potential. I learn: to trust my inclinations, to check the shadows, to find friends, to attract protectors (guardians, uncles, grandfathers, brothers), to tread the deep universal human currents, to heed the nuance and music of languages, to know meaning without knowing words. I am never out of danger, but protected by the magic of the very thing which makes me weak.

Getting Around

The main thing about travel is that it is movement. Movement over the surface of the earth, usually, but one supposes that interplanetary and sub-oceanic might be just as likely, merely trajectories of different direction: upper or outer, lower or inner or downgoing types. We become fish, seaborne. We are birds in blue space. Walking is the only form of travel natural to man — swimming too, but distances are a problem. We engage animals — horses, mules, dolphins, giant turtles, elephants — and vehicles that imitate these animals, and with them, we become mythic: Pegasuses and mermaids and lizard-men and gods and goddesses of all sorts.

The Blue-Green Seas Of Forever

Travel is metaphor, too, of the most idiotically simple kind. What are we doing when we travel? Crossing boundaries of reality, enlarging the spirit, exposing oneself to the unknown, discovering, being endangered, being infected, escaping, conquering, getting lost, forging a path, taking on the world, abandoning native origins, freeing oneself, asking questions, looking for something, finding oneself, going native, falling apart, experiencing the multiplicity of existence. Digging a tunnel to China. Sailing off on the blue-green seas of forever. Following a siren's call, following a drumbeat, getting away from it all.

Lost

Traveling, we lose all our possessions. We leave everything behind: vistas, seaside cafes, lovers of one night or one year, memories embedded in the walls and rocks of where we stayed for a time, money lost and spent, good meals with Italian wine, strange quarrels in invented languages, nights of retching, pieces of clothing washed into the sea, tropical dance-music, angry belly-dancers, insane border guards with Russian guns, the threat of cannibalism at dusk. A five-year-old girl named Ama, smoking a cigarette naked, one morning by my bedside, that was once a moment in my possession.

Chiaroscuro

One of the things I try to do: memorize the smallest, most mundane and ordinary, unprepossessing, and virtually invisible of physical moments: the look and feel of a certain wall at a certain time on a certain day. Those walls, those little shacks, those cats in the sun: all that is lacking in self-consciousness I seek to hold in vision, memory.

(Simple composition, color tints, a wash of light, crumbled brick, cold shadow, stillness, rose-color dirt, a twitching whisker.) Not knowing why, but thinking I may want it later, I try to keep it and I never can.

Places I Don't Know

Photographs: moments preserved, often of travel. Who wants them? I have never liked trophies, souvenirs. (Taking a picture, in the moment and decision of that act one ceases to live, saying: this is already a memory; I grasp the present too tightly and make it past, to preserve it for the future, also nonexistent.) I prefer my memories out of whack, confusing, ever-changing, nonchronological. I like the images evanescent. Photographs are fear of death, that's all. I have them, of course, like everybody else. But the ones I have torment me. They puzzle me, shock me; I don't trust them. They make me stare stupidly, like a monkey. They pretend to be memory and remove the soul from true memory. When I think of Ama my mind is trapped by that image, her photograph. The moment, fuller, more fragile, escapes, fades, is obscured by evidence.

I like photographs of people and places I don't know, times I didn't live. I'd like to own a lot of unknown people's pictures, that could fill me with longing. With those as clues, I could make new stories, mysteries.

Stolen Rooftops

Deep night, Haitian hotel. There is a hurricane, and the hotel is immersed in wild tearing sound, a beating beating sky of black wind and flinging water. The sea seems to be rising up into the night, no more horizon, and it sounds like bleating, shrieking pigs and crashing sea-monsters out there. The room we're in is a kind of tomb, small and narrow, all concrete, a tiny iron bed; we lie jammed together in it covered by a plastic sheet, sweating, cold, while the rain flies down upon us from the chink high in the wall (a prison window). Flapping on the window, another sheet of plastic: flapping, flapping, letting in the monstrous sky. Fatigued by the wet and sleepless huddling, we leave our rainy chamber and wander into the dark dining room; it booms metallically. In the midst of the tables and chairs sits the hotel's owner, Madame Sandrine, and she cries. The tin sheets of her rooftop, blown off by the storm, are at this very moment being carried away by thieves. The next morning, in sunshine, we sit; we have bread and butter tartine and black coffee in the roofless hotel.

Ancestral Oranges
On a train in Botswana, on the map a place in middle Africa, a place residing deep in the unconscious, the unknown primal Africa of the imagination. Stopping slowly at a station, looking out the window: small boys sell oranges. At this moment, seeing these oranges held out to me like glowing round suns, seeing these smiling children so real and familiar, so strangely remembered from a time before history, there is something I know. This is the birth of my world, this is my ancestry, this is the beginning and the heart and what the rest of the world has lost. It is fearfully good here; I sink into it. This is the source of the blood in my veins. This is the land of my body, the home of my soul. How gentle you are, children with oranges, ancient land, source.

Noodles, Noise, Light
The street-corner in Tokyo: Shibuya. This future-place, this gourmandise of neon, grand brilliant colors, every color but mostly blues — royal blue, blue-green, violet blue — high nested buildings, hives, lights on and blinking everywhere, giant screens with soundless images, or perhaps, more likely, sounds that insert and bury themselves within the antagonistic rushing harmony. The mass of people is like insect-life. With the absence of danger and the illusion of vitality, there is something else, something harsh, explosive, edged with madness, a collective seething hum. Always, always, it moves. Swarms, multi-level swarms. There are no smells. Traffic is fast and blind. One imagines this to be the confusing dreamed future of primitive man. In this future, we eat noodles. . . .

Pink Soap: Kenya
I am living in this enormous house, many rooms and windows, the walls are thick, carved coral. There is a green breeze that runs through the house like a river, from room to room and down the wide halls. There is no glass in the windows. The rooftop is another large room; leading up to it, steps cut into an outer wall. That cosmic surface belongs to the wild night: stars and full moon give the only light, strange sinuous insects with sharp red legs and horns and secretive shifting movements inhabit that place. In the trees around this echoing dream-house grow cashew nuts, mangos, coconuts. During the night, wild donkeys roam the silver-lit jungle garden, galloping through tall grass, bumping over fallen coconuts, crashing into watermelons, seen only as shadows. Where I bathe, down the hill from the house: a stone bathtub sits by the well.

My pink soap, left in the fork of a tree-branch, is eaten one night by the donkey tribe. Scattered everywhere, teethmarked bits of it.

The Dreams of Crocodiles
In the deep sky of Africa, where at evening the sun spreads molten like scarlet-gold lava, where the full moon gives cold silver light so sharp you can set a desk in the sand and write, in this supernatural sky one is not surprised to consider the spheres as gods. One night, walking through the sprawling sandy village-town of Maun, Botswana, whose edges segue into swamps and then lagoons where crocodiles rest and listen, a place of huts and small wooden houses scattered at random in the sand, where outside almost every shack sits a record player on a little table, playing the music that courses through all of Africa, a music rising from the dark happiness of sex and jungles and beer and never any money, a music that turns breathing, walking, even thinking into a rhythmic hypnosis, a crazy lilting dance, there, all day long, all the different songs float out from all the record players, and all (belonging to the one mother-body of sound) pulse together in a fine way, in a perfectly confusing brimming-over of unreasonable harmony. Anyway — before being pulled away by that music that still runs its melody in my blood, I meant to tell about the night in Maun when I saw the ball of fire; I watched it float down through the black sky far above. A fantastic blazing sphere with a billowing train of flame. I fell to the cool sand, as if my body too was pulled down by the downward-falling vision, magnetized to Earth. Around in the village, mostly quiet then, with cooking fires smoking the air, the sound of a Bushman woman's singing, eerie and punctuated with click-tones, made a fine, cool tremor on the air. This was just one small moment, a tiny rich instant, when I looked up to see a witch's vision, fire-sphere moving through sky, as if a child of the sun had lost its way, visiting forbidden night.

Reptilian Reality
Give me a reality with holes in it, one that fits me loosely, with plenty of negative space, one that crumbles and sloughs off at every opportunity, with the first drop of rain.

Pigs
Travel is magic. Stepping through the doorway to another world, a reality guided and formed by different rules, we encounter enchantments, illusions, multiple realities, strange distortions of the laws of physics —

cause-and-effect, for example. A man I knew in Cape Palmas, Liberia, cooked rice (in that hot, sun-washed town of pastel wooden houses, pigs, and one rusted, fallen traffic-light) every day for more than 20 years, but he never could say how long it might take the rice to cook. On any given day, things might be different. He was not about to presume anything.

Do you know the song?

> Chicken is nice
> Chicken is nice
> Chicken is nice with
> Palm butter and rice.
>
> Don't want no wife
> from Cape Palmas
> Don't want no wife
> from Cape Palmas
> Don't want no wife
> Don't want no wife
> from Cape Palmas. . . .

John Toe

In another little town in West Africa, there was a splendid mansion belonging to the president off in the capital city. He was the one who had put in the traffic light, the only one for hundreds of miles. I was taken to that mansion by a kid called Toe — John Toe — and we walked through every room, through the black-tiled bathroom with 20 shower nozzles (visions of the president showering with his dinner guests), admired the usual dictatorial gold-leaf decor, gazed into the coffin-like freezers at the coldly steaming stacks of white-wrapped suspended animal/vegetable life. Servants made sure that electricity was always running, kept every light on all day, all night, checked daily that the shower nozzles produced the astonishing luxury of hot water on command. The house, kept humming with life systems, thus mystically invoked and enclosed the invisible, powerful emanation of man-symbol, leader as something more than his image, divine force, top witchdoctor whose magical body extended to the country's borders.

Upwardly Mobile
In that same town, I was warned there was human sacrifice after 6 p.m. Not cannibalism, just ritual death for political reasons. The idea was that if you were, say, a post office clerk and you wanted to become mayor or even something higher, you could sacrifice something living, and that life force, with its own status in the hierarchy of power, would then accrue to you. So a goat would be okay, do some good, but a human would be better, and a human with power best of all. It was generally believed that anyone in politics had gotten there by sacrificing some human. What a mystique! I had to curb my inclination to follow drumbeats after dark...I probably could have gotten someone a pretty good job.

Bus-Stop
At dawn in Barcelona, I'm at a bus-stop with the beautiful Nigerian Iffy. Everything seems empty and arid in that particularly Spanish way, with undercurrents of secret evil and baroque ignorance swimming in the shadows between buildings, in doorways. We stand talking vaguely, disoriented, sleep-walkers in a strange city, feeling the white warmth of December sunshine. We are gradually aware that others have joined us at the bus-stop, and we turn to see five men, narrow faces, narrow eyes, eyes sharpened to slits of lightless animal seeing, five sets of male-animal slit eyes in dark burning unison, dream-hunting us in a daydream of desire.

Croissants
I met the Marquis on the train from Paris to Basel. We smoked cigars, both dressed in white. It was hot golden August. We hit it off well in a flippant sort of way, and over the years I visited him at random, sometimes spending weeks in his *hôtel particulier* in the area back of Étoile. He had a quiet manservant; he lived a simple rough life steeped in gloom, tradition, and dust. He opened his mother's trunks and gave me lace chemises, his childhood umbrella with an ebony dog's-head handle, books by Baudelaire, a hand-painted fan made by his grandmother. We ate dinner by twilight on his balcony, I in transparent lace, he shirtless and tanned brown; we ate with knives and forks of heavy tarnished silver. I delicately tortured him; he bought me the finest croissants. I loved his coffee, rich and dark and bitter, which he brought to me in my bed, from a kitchen smelling of pears. He called me to watch him in his bath; he had filled the room with terrifying flowers, those used for funerals, that appear in nightmares, that use up all the oxygen in the bedroom of a sleeping person. I cooked mushrooms for his two

daughters, grown married women with sweet childlike faces. I wandered in his rooms in the darkness, feeling the ancestral gaze of portraits, all with the same cruel blue eyes and haughty noses. I searched the roof-tops of Paris for artistic visions. I wandered the streets and flirted with men, then returned to him. It was no love affair; he couldn't have me. He was a connoisseur of women's bodies, a gourmet of love, an aristocrat of the erotic realm, and he loved me with desperation. I knew, I knew somehow, in some young, shadowy, way, that to him the pain of want-ing was the most exquisite of pleasures, and that pain is what I gave him, beyond his limits to endure. I gave him morsels, little bits, and then withdrew. It was a sweet game we played, those days and twilight nights in Paris, near Étoile.

Hunting for Mermaids
When I found out about the mermaids in West Africa, I went all over the place looking for them. The word for mermaid is mami-wata, water-mother. I used to ask everybody about mami-wata, to get detailed in-formation. I've always liked the idea of mermaids, the thought of something free, beautiful, powerful, a seductress of the deep, dangerous, long hair floating, enchantment, songs, something unknown, creature-like and feminine hidden in the dark salty ocean depths. . . .

It's all so secretive; the men I talked to who'd met one wouldn't say much. One guy told me that a mermaid's voice flowed like liquid sugar, and then he said, "I can't say more." A taxi-driver friend told me that generally you'd meet a mermaid on the beach at night, when you were out walking by yourself. The mermaid would sit in the shallow sea, showing her pointed breasts and swishing her fish-tail, calling out to you quietly and making all kinds of wild promises. Men couldn't resist this – she would give secrets and grant wishes in exchange for eternal devotion to her – and they usually agreed to everything. Of course, that was the end for them; they would never again be free, and they could love no other woman.

I went to a town called Axim in Ghana; people said it was a great place for mermaids and witches. The "x" in the name made it seem true. There was a little island there, visible from the beach, an island pyramid-shaped and of uncertain distance away. Depending on the time of day, it was sometimes near, sometimes impossibly far. A death-swim. I used to watch the island all day long, watching it approach and recede, watching it look friendly and green or harsh and remote. I had a vague plan to swim out there – I'm a strong swimmer, mermaid blood perhaps – but the island was unpredictable, and it seemed essential to time it right. I thought about it so much that finally I had a dream, and the dream took me there, just like that. Once I got to the island, I met the mermaid more or less, and it wasn't long before I'd had enough.

The place was an old shipwreck all turned to ice, with ice-rooms and ice-stairs, and on the other side of the ice-island, out to sea, was black night and raging storms, whipping and sucking and howling, carrying sailboats away at a terrifying pace. I heard, coming out of the ice and the storms and the dark, the sugar-water voice talking to me, so sweet and cold it made my teeth and brain ache. It slid liquidly, musically along, making almost-words with an underneath sense, words I couldn't bear to hear fully, words which seemed to melt and chill my deepest heart. I don't know how I did it, but after a while I got myself out and away from the cold sugary fish-woman and back to bed in my little hut full of fat malaria mosquitos, just in time to roll into the warm arms of my sleek-skinned man, just in time for a little sunrise lovemaking before the plantain lady stuck her head through our window to say good morning and give us our roasted plantains and oversugared coffee.

Cameo Role
Traveling is living stories, entering unknown locales where unpredictably horrific, sweet, dangerous or maddening plot lines await you, wait to incorporate you, weave you into some saga or serial episode or novella, sometimes even tying you right into an epic drama of some sort. These stories might or might not have perceptible narrative consistency, logic within their own bounds, but almost always there are peripheral, illogical characters drifting in and out, proposing their own unresolvable plots, suggesting improbable changes of locale or adjustments to the style of enactment; all these constant wandering possibilities tend to obscure whatever basic narrative might be present. There are no beginnings or endings, just episodes connected to others, just partially perceived, partially participated-in larger, longer stories. The African prostitute walks into a bar and starts a fight with the seedy French expatriate, the lapsed priest, the alcoholic. And then, because you have blonde hair, the Frenchman starts shouting at you. "You wander all over Africa with blonde hair! Who do you think you are? Why is your hair tied up? Are you afraid of your animal, sensual nature?" The drunk prostitute sees you as a kindred spirit and asks you to dance; she strokes your hair like a mother and shakes her round belly against your hips. The guy gets madder than ever and starts yelling at some depressed government official who's talking philosophy and analyzing all of our skulls. The evening drifts on like that, a curious scenario of angry men, rebellious women, dancing, skulls, Catholicism, beer, lust, and blonde hair. What do you think? Good topics? There's a lot there to work with. Anyway,

the evening drifts on like that, with the given themes interweaving in multiple ways. There are some climaxes and some lulls, and nothing is ever resolved. It doesn't end; people get tired and go home. You run into them all again later, and the same topics are taken up again, looking different under a burning sun at noon.

The overall form, all the stories put together in the line of your life, is postmodern Zen, with unfinished bits, broken-down realities, edges revealed, seams unraveled, but still, running through it all is the continuity of you. Don't try to make sense of it; it's all a maddening puzzle with pieces always missing, new pieces always being created from nothing.

The things I remember most, for travel is all vanished remembered stories, story bits, are about food, sex, music, and houses. These things in combination are especially good.

Writing Letters
One night I walked into the dark calm sea at Mombasa; I remember clearly, I was wearing a pair of brown silk panties. The guy who was with me was a very handsome genius, an adventurer, a reckless pursuer of women, an undomesticated Scottish lord. (He kept his lordliness a secret, but I had found out; I kept that a secret.) He was young and strong, with big stocky Scottish legs, Indian Ocean blue eyes, and chopped messy blonde hair. I was addicted to how he made me feel. That's another story. . . . I'll try to stick to the main narrative here. (But tell me the truth: which story would you rather hear? Hmm?) Anyway, he, that glorious Zeus-like creature, was sitting at a desk on the beach, typing a letter by moonlight. Something came out of the night and hit me on the shoulder; I thought my divine lover was throwing rocks at me, some curious sex-game. I got hit by several more of these flying objects, so I screamed a little, but quite soon I saw by moonlight that what was zipping through the dark at me were wild winging flying fish. (A secret god typing a letter by full moon-light, a girl mostly naked in the sea with flying fish: a story about fish, flight, sex, night, salty skin, full moon, letter-writing. A surrealist tale of seduction, basically a mystery, with strong elements of danger and comedy, a suggestion of myth.)

La Tigresse
I am sitting in a cafe at the Marché aux Puces in Paris, I'm probably having my usual café crème. This gray little man comes up to me, whispers in my ear: "I have a woman for you, dressed in leopard. She is a tigresse; I want to bring you to her . . . she will love you." I was terrified by the

tigresse; I ran away but couldn't stop thinking about her, and she lives vividly in my imagination even now. You see, that dim little man was a poet-merchant of desire. Is not the whispered image, doubly feline, predatory, the invitation to dangerous, death-tinged love with woman more seductive for being invisible, yet perfectly, economically, conjured by hissing words?

Moon, Easter, Blood

I once lived briefly in Malta, on a tall ship, a schooner in drydock for repairs. Perverse, to live on a wooden ship, its sails furled, its hull still and dry, gold-gleaming wood of voluptuous form, barnacles clinging. A ship indoors, with electric lights and workmen and machines and vehicles running around. I went to a cathedral there (in Malta the religious fervor is deep and dark and thorny with penance). I went to a cathedral there on Easter Sunday, and when I stood to sing, when the effigies were going by and the purple banners waving, the incense smoking, crimson blood began to flow between my legs, big drops falling red on the marble floor, rivers coursing down my bare legs. Taboo! – this blood, this place, this day! Never before or since have I bled so abruptly and with such vehemence. Running to escape the cathedral, weaving through the singing people, I left a scarlet trail across the marble. Later, I watched the penitents, men carrying enormous timber crosses, wearing hoods, walking barefoot, wanting to suffer, to be seen to suffer. I was not raised a Catholic, but throughout my childhood I had had a terrible fear that I would grow up to become a nun.

Two Fat Brothers

There was once in Paris a tiny restaurant, only two tables inside, one out (where a cat usually slept), called the POURQUOIS PAS? The cooks were two fat brothers who just barely fit side by side in their tiny little kitchen. When you ate your meal they took turns coming out to watch you eat, making sure you ate it all. If you slowed down or couldn't finish, they became most perturbed and scolded you. If there were diners at the other table, the brother cooks would get them involved in the problem, and of course the general consensus would be that you were extremely remiss in your behavior. The cat would sleep through everything; the food was always exceptionally good.

Bacteria

Everyone knows this: when you travel you get sick. It's not a surprising idea, is it? It's that foreign bacteria — we're not used to it — and besides, it's bad, dangerous, and dirty. We Americans think we are the cleanest of all cultures, but just ask any foreigner: he gets very sick when he visits America! The more different the culture is from your own, the sicker you are likely to get.

All Shook Up

In Africa, malaria got so familiar and personal to me that it was almost a friend. I recognized the subtlest early signs of its onset and accepted its coming each time with a mixture of resignation, anticipation, and fear. There is something soul-shaking and transcendent about malaria: you feel worse than bad, of course, you feel like death would be a relief, but you are also aware of being in the grips of a real force, something bigger than yourself, something that runs rampant in your blood like a divine visitation. The heat it brings is supernatural; you become fire. The cold too is otherworldly, lunar ice. The shaking of your shoulders is a possession, a helpless ecstatic frightening dance, the body moving, vibrating, to a perfect relentless beat. You are absolutely, horribly, caught in the here and now, in its depths, no escape. To me, malaria and Africa were one thing — I could not have loved Africa as I did had I not known bodily its deathly suffering, the more humble human place in the balance of nature equation, the intensity of all of its life forms.

Living in Haiku

It's summer: the persimmon tree in my Japanese garden is in full leaf. The fruits are all potential now: hard and green, squared spheres. Like the future, *"furoshiki"* — wrapped in green silk. The sight of the tree puts me into poetry. There are persimmons in my past. The childhood Chinese painting on some long-lost bedroom wall: in colored brushed ink, the eternal lone persimmon, the bare black branch, the backdrop of quiet snow. Seeing no ripe gold-red persimmon now, still I see the color that was, the color that will be, spiritual warm Buddha-orange, the color of monks' robes on a sunset beach in Thailand. A life-force color, sun and blood.

In shadowy parts of my brain, long-ago persimmon conversations are revived; faintly, I taste the memory of the strange flat sweetness of first-tasted persimmon. I see, too: the star-flower when the fruit is sliced. I return to the doorway of a shepherd's cottage in the French Midi, with one persimmon tree, ripe fruits, and a glimpse of the blue sea.

All persimmons gathered and together, the past, present, and future fruits, in the moment when I see this tree. I see it all, from the time now of the green baby fruit knobs which sometimes fall and knock the ground hard, to the fruit-becoming-succulent-and-fruit phase, to the bird-coming time, then the leaf-turning-red-orange-gold time, to the leaf-losing time with the wind tossing it, to the slow cold time when snow drifts down, to the final small sweet long-lingering moment (from long ago, from childhood, from a lost painting, from dreams of paintings, from memories of fruit, from tree-moments since, from a future foreseen): one persimmon, on the bare black branch.

Ink Mountain

In the mountains of Japan: autumn. Far off, gray mountain-forms softened by mist into rounded shadows. A gentle rain, so light it seems to hover instead of succumbing to gravity, makes the nearby hills and rice-fields a quiet, glistening green. Who am I in this? A woman standing, a small human figure in an ancient landscape, listening to the wind.

Kings, Queens

Evening, the outskirts of London. That day, I had run from a tube station with many others: a bomb threat, police everywhere. There had been explosions in the city for weeks; when I arrived, the airport runways were full of tanks, sandbags, roaming soldiers waiting to discover the end of the world. It was the time of the energy crisis. In the backstreets of London, lamps were low, burning yellow, the streets were wet with rain, the row houses dark grim bricked-up secrets. Small clusters of people scurried by, speaking Indian languages. And suddenly, I was inside the real London. I had been in the city many times, but its essence had eluded me (not that I'd noticed its absence) and finally here it was: the echoing past, the history that had been lived, the blood and badness and danger and lowlife and glory, the gloom and the mystery, the repressed scandals and the lilting street rhymes, all this moved in the air that night, bloomed in the shadows.

To know the essence of a place: this is the traveler's epiphany. It is the frontier-crossing moment when the limits of time and present reality drop away, allowing in to consciousness all the lived past, all in one unutterably rich moment.

Here comes a candle to light you to bed; here comes a chopper to chop off your head. . . .

That Night, The Monkey Ate The Pomegranate

In Africa, I was in the habit of following drum-sounds. They were always at night, a tantalizing call through the darkness. Why did I follow them? I like the feeling, when you are close enough for the drumbeats to enter your body, when the pounding vibrations make you have to move, no choice but to dance. Sometimes odd things happened as a result of this habit. I wandered into witchcraft rituals, sacrifices, forbidden ceremonies, strange scenes of possession. Sometimes, too, more mysterious: I followed drums and never found them; the sounds drifting and changing direction and distance endlessly.

One such night was spent in a seaside swamp-forest, a place of twisted stumpy water-sucking trees with roots for branches, stark skeleton-shapes against the sky where they grew out upon the beach and rose from the water for a ways. It was not a place where people lived. The nearest village consisted of a long dock that smelled of dead fish, a couple of poor shacks, and a crazy, bewitched fisherman who lived alone.

After a morose dinner in my curious desolate house — two storeys, one servant-cook, one monkey, rudimentary electricity, an inner courtyard with one pomegranate tree, scavenger birds in the trees all around, I heard faint drums and set out to find them, finally never finding them, but hiked and circled for hours in the swamp-tree forest. The sea, when I saw it, gave off a dim gray light.

Stilts

In La Ceiba, Honduras, there was hunger and violence and sex. A geographical id. The place felt like a careless blend of volatile chemicals, poisonous and sweet, just about ready to explode, sizzling. But there was a dark warmth to this — because volcanic danger was right there outside your window, sitting at the next table in the bar, walking towards you down the street, you felt both aroused by adrenalin and benignly tolerant, fatalistic. Fears were more real, more vivid, bigger than elsewhere, but there was a sense of fate, chance, destiny to it all. The gamble.

We stayed in a house on stilts, no lights, isolated from the town by jungle, a few feet from the waves. One sleeping night, harsh noises. We got out of bed to look: below us, in the space between the stilts, a car was parked. There was shouting, a woman laughing, gunshots. A simple lovers' outing by the sea: inside the car, the woman drunken, sprawling, her legs out the open door, her dress falling to reveal shoulders, breast, fat thighs; her uniformed companion lurching and bellowing as he shot his pistol into the night, the bushes, the sea, the world.

Long-Armed Woman

Sultan, my fisherman friend, my simple wise man, my island sage in a thread-bare red sarong. He brought me gifts: pineapples, fresh fish, fine stories. We often talked about magic; his life was full of it. Genies were his specialty. Men had to be careful, he said, you never knew what a woman might be beneath her veils. A friend of his had followed a woman to her room one night; she had beckoned to him on the street during the night-hour when women came out to do their shopping and their banking. He was still too poor to afford a wife, so when he could be with a woman he was grateful. It was something to treasure – but since all women belonged to someone there was danger in it. . . . They got to the room, the woman removed her veil – she was beautiful, terrifyingly beautiful– and she asked him to come to her. He went to her, lay down beside her, and they began to kiss. But the window was open, and he felt cold. He told the woman; she said "Oh." Then without moving from the bed, she raised her arm toward the window, which was high in the wall on the other side of the room, and her arm stretched and stretched until it had become long enough to reach the window and close it. Although the man could hardly gather the strength to move, so frozen was he with fear and desire, he managed to pull himself up like a sick man and stumble out of the room, away from the long-armed woman. He was lucky he discovered what she was before anything else happened. (I wondered: is this the way to test for genies? When you're about to have sex with a woman, ask her to close a distant window. . .)

Diane Glancy

ONTOLOGY & THE TRUCKER

I wrote "Trucker" in 1985 when I was traveling between 2 states and 2 heritages. But Walking-in-2-Worlds is a common saying for the Native American. I'm still walking between 2 heritages, though I'm now in one place. But making sense of the journey is still a theme. And travel is still something I do as often as I can. There is a "foreign" travel possible right here in our own land. It happens on the backroads of the less-traveled states. It happens in the "otherness" of diversity emerging now in our culture. It also happens in the spirit world that travels just above the road. Follow a trucker for several hundred miles some night and you'll see those round, white road-reflections are eyeballs from the other world.

I AM ARTIST-IN-RESIDENCE for both State Arts Councils of Oklahoma & Arkansas. Across the top of the adjoining states, there are 849 miles. I travel up & down & back & forth. On this particular trip, I am returning to Tulsa from Arkadelphia, some 250 miles. The largest part of my work seems the travel, & the loneliest part of the road is when there is no trucker.

This is a tribute for truckers who like to be followed. They are the ones who, if you show the slightest whit of intelligence about driving, let you know when to slow down & when to go fast. It's like finding broken pieces of my father along the road. Part Cherokee, intuitive, he was the surest guide I ever had.

I don't have a CB to talk to the truckers I follow. I don't want one either. There is something basic in being cut off as I travel. It reminds me I am between the way life was before I was born & how it will be after I die.

The highway is a universe where my car follows the trucks. All of us are migrating by instinct knowing somehow where we are going. Just ahead, the sun crosses an interchange of clouds in the west, soon to exit Arkansas for the day.

I remember once on the way from Oklahoma City, there were three truckers passing, & wind blowing so hard when they passed, it shook the car and blew my papers across the seat. I keep a journal of what I pass & carry books and maps & papers with me. & out of those three truckers, I chose one to follow all the way up the hundred miles of Turner Turnpike. When we got past the toll gate at Tulsa, I turned off on the road to my house. I waved to him as we parted. It has to be that way. There's no permanency here except the highway & toll gates & road construction.

I just think how I had to say good-bye to someone I didn't want to & how everything has to move on & I didn't have any choice. That's the way it is cut off from relationships, left with the memories of them. But these ghosts are always here. I feel surrounded by them yet not really attached.

The trucks & the dotted line on the road are more real than the shadows & dreams that wait in their own world, sometimes breaking thru in poems or the last of the red sky that roams over western Arkansas. & in the dark you see more clearly sometimes if you look off to the side. That's where the poem is. You've been at a school for a week trying to tell them that, talking about poetry & why you do it, & just what it is you do. It's a long haul no matter what you pull. Might as well make it something that counts.

Might as well open this rectangle of the prairie as though it were a paragraph. Light up your truck for the dark. Name your words. Paste your meaning on like mud flaps. That's how you get thru the universe.

Now the car lights come toward you, just as white as the crack of the moon through the clouds, & the trucker ahead of you isn't going fast enough because you want to get home. It's been a long time & the mail is stacked up & the cat is lonely & you have to see how your daughter is getting along because you don't think she's old enough to get along without you all week, even though she says she is.

& you don't want to think of the week behind you because finally it is over. Soon you'll be home safe as long as a trucker's ahead of you & moving about the speed you want to go. I can't keep up with the fast ones. My car is too old & I am not that daring. I leave the slow ones behind. Soon another will come. It always does.

I remember once coming back to Oklahoma from Kansas City. My mother had been sick. & about Pittsburg, Kansas, there was a storm like we have out here — one that sweeps down from the Rockies or up out of the southwest with nothing but a few scrawny trees & a Hereford or two in Kansas or Texas to give it any resistance. I couldn't see the hood of my car for the torrents of rain & was thinking about surgery & pain & the end of life & what do we live for anyway? & thinking that maybe in the storm would be a chariot that would swoop me up to the glory these churches preach & suddenly there was a truck ahead of me & all I could see was his red tail lights across the back of his truck & I held on to those lights for miles through that storm, not pulling off the road because I didn't know what was there. I was on the other side of Pittsburg when I could see the road again & I passed him — went right by like he hadn't done a thing for me. You've got to be tough.

If I had a CB, sometimes I imagine we would discuss the nature of being as we peddle along the road after dark when I am thru gathering images. The prairie is chuck full of them. I fill my notebooks on the seat beside me. Even after dark sometimes, things come — old visions my Indian ancestors left along the road —

Soon I stop at an all-night gas station & buy jelly beans to stay awake those miles across the prairie. I ignore any trucker who might be there. Our road game is a silent one, as though we were lovers who could not speak in public. As though our game did not exist at all. Then I just keep going again on the highway as though I took off with my poems from this prairie out into the skies thru the swinging door of the moon. I can see the trucks up there — their lights like new constellations. I try to tell what color the jelly beans are in the dark. Pretending I'm further along the road than I am.

& those ministers come on the radio with blessed Jesus carrying the burden of his cross. & I think that must be what we are doing right here on this road, carrying our load of words across the Arkansas River with this weight of hope & despair & earning a meager living & not being overloaded for weight stations.

Finally, the Oklahoma border & I'm back in my own state to one toll gate after another. I bite into a jelly bean, & if it is an orange one I don't like, I throw it out for the gophers — careful so the car won't get splattered.

That old black jelly bean sky when there are no stars out — they've all been gathered up & hauled to the roller rink in one of those twinking towns you see along the highway — FINALLY! Two trucks pull onto the road & behind them a whole convoy of trucks signaling to one another, flashing their lights when it's all right to pull back in — mud flaps dancing — War-painted braves! From the back, the trucks look like large ice-cube trays & beyond them you see the skinny line of highway barrels lined up for miles on the road & you know how far you have to go.

Better than one truck is two truckers who want you to follow between them. It's called, 'riding the cradle'. My sister-in-law told me that when we were on our way to Iowa. Just act like you can hold your own on the road & they take you on as worthy to travel with them. How could I tell them they represent the poem for me?— Or the process of the poem — pursuing the organization, the form & energy of it. Or they represent, anyway, what I've found about writing here on the prairie — How much of it is actually a matter of attitude & vision.

& following them, the struggle of migration across the prairie is a little easier. Then the trucks become the ancient herds of buffalo the tribes followed — returned just as the fathers prayed they would — thick & fat — & the buffalo-burger is over the fire, so to speak. & the lights of oncoming cars thru the median grasses flicker, then dance again like a ghost tribe & you hear the words 'Hey yey hey yey' —coming from your mouth & finally, FINALLY, the miles go by.

Soon my turnoff comes & I hate to leave my place between the two trucks. I have the last 70 miles without them & I wave. Goodbye— It's like before you were born when god says, 'see ya', & you can never hear him again in this life but you know he's there with you on the road late at night when you're tired from working & on several hundred miles of your way home. That's mostly the way it is out here following a trucker who wants you to follow — You see him go on west, maybe Amarillo or Albuquerque or even the coast still 1,500 miles away, while you turn north & watch the trucks disappear & you feel that thread, that invisible twine like words that somehow hold us all together—

CONTRIBUTORS' NOTES

BARBARA ABEL has received a University of Wisconsin-Madison Vilas Essay Award, a Loft Creative Nonfiction Award and a Lake Superior Regional Writers Award in poetry. Her poems have been included in several publications, including *The Nebraska Review and Kalliope*. She is interested in meeting potential traveling companions and Spanish speaking friends of any age and either sex. No photos, please.

MIMI ALBERT received her M.F.A. degree in writing from Columbia University; her first novel, *The Second Story Man*, was published by The Fiction Collective in 1975, and a collection of her short stories and poetry was later published by the Shameless Hussy Press in Berkeley. She has won a NEA/PEN Syndicated Fiction grant; a New York State Council on the Arts grant for writing; a Los Angeles/PEN Award for Best California short story in 1986; and a Yaddo Foundation Grant. She currently makes her home in Sonoma County, in northern California; she teaches in several local colleges and is also an active member of PEN American Center West, heading its Freedom-to-Write committee, which works to help free imprisoned and oppressed writers throughout the world. In 1980, having studied meditation and healing with an Indian physician, Dr. R. P. Kaushik, she went to live in his household in India for a year, from which she traveled to various Gandhian communities in northwestern India, between the Himalayas and Delhi.

APATHEE ANANKE says that if she ever grows up, she wants to become a Libyan terrorist, but if that fails, she'll settle for an academic career.

VIVIAN VIE BALFOUR lived for a year and a half in Manila during the Vietnam War and graduated from the American School there. She lives in Minneapolis with her husband and son Jeff, writes fiction and poetry, and does extensive editorial work for New Rivers Press.

BEVERLY BARANOWSKI lives in Minneapolis with her husband and two children. Her previously published work includes poems in *Lake Street Review, Milkweed Chronicle, Sing! Heavenly Muse* and the anthology *Concert at Chopin's House*. Her favorite cities are Hayward, Wisconsin and Paris, France, because of the giant muskie museum and the giant tower. She still has dreams of flying and often wakes with a smile, whispering, "Would you like something to drink?"

NINA BARRAGAN is the pen name of Rocio Lasansky Weinstein. Born in Cordoba, Argentina, she was raised and educated in Iowa City, and received a B.A. from the University of Iowa. Barragan has traveled extensively. With her husband, painter Alan Weinstein, she has lived and worked in an old finca on the Balearic island of Ibiza, in the Dutch village of Bergen-an-Zee, as well as on their farm in southern Ontario. Presently she is back in Iowa City, where she and her husband run an art gallery and pursue their work. In 1988 they collaborated on *The Egyptian Man*, a limited edition, large format, fine art book. Barragan has four children, ages 20 to 7. In her rare spare time, she bakes bread and occasionally travels to Argentina. She has published short fiction in several reviews, including *West Branch*, *The Antigonish Review*, and *The Long Story*. She has also published under the name of Emily Hollis McIver.

JUDITH BARRINGTON is a poet from England who has lived in the U.S. since 1976. She is the author of two collections of poems, *Trying to be an Honest Woman* (1985) and *History and Geography* (1989), both published by The Eighth Mountain Press. She is the founder of The Flight of the Mind, an annual summer writing workshop for women writers, and she teaches in the Arts Education Program in Oregon, Washington, and Utah. From 1964 to 1966, she spent most of her time in Cataluna, working for a wine company based in a castle near the French/Spanish border. She has also been a secretary at the B.B.C., a public relations executive, a furniture mover, and the director of a heating and ventilating company. She now lives in Portland, Oregon, with her woman partner of twelve years.

SHARON BROWN has spent most of her life being pulled by two very separate interests: visual arts and the psychological field. She would somehow like to combine the two. She writes "I never believed I would add writing to my professional interests. But it somehow fits into my love of books and my interest in the dialogue between written and visual images. I have done journaling for years, but I have rarely brought the writing and the images together. 'Borders' was my first formal attempt to integrate the two. My next task will be to incorporate my social work background with my art and my newfound interest in writing. And I have a feeling that will be truly a lifelong project."

SHARON CHMIELARZ says in her spare time she washes windows, vacuums, has hip operations, weeds, loads (or unloads) the washing machine, cooks, swims, dreams, meets her husband Tad in passing on the stairs — two ships in the night —, lets the cat, Fritz out (or in), telephones friends, teaches, reads, but otherwise, she's fully engaged in writing. New Rivers has published one book of her poetry, *Different Arrangements*, and another is forthcoming in the fall of 1990. An escapee from South Dakota, she now lives in Minnesota.

HELEN DEGEN COHEN is the recipient of a National Endowment for the

Arts fellowship in poetry for 1988, two Illinois Arts Council Literary Awards, and a special award from the Indiana Writers Conference, among other prizes. To date, four sections of her novel about the war, *The Edge of the Field,* have been published, one of which received first prize in *Stand* magazine's International Short Story Competition in England, and another an Illinois Arts Council award last year. Her work has appeared in numerous journals, such as the *Partisan Review, Another Chicago Magazine,* a recent interview and poetry feature in *Spoon River Quarterly,* and in *Concert at Chopin's House* (New Rivers Press). A graduate of UIC's Masters "Program for Writers" and for the past six years an Artist-in Education through the Illinois Arts Council, she has also taught for Roosevelt University and co-edited the journal *Rhino.* She writes, "I spend as much time as I can in the woods, literally and metaphorically. Before I injured my ankle my favorite name tag said 'Folk Dancer.' Years ago when people asked me, 'What do you do?' I would say, 'I suffer.' Now I tell them I write."

KATHLEEN COSKRAN was born in California, grew up in Georgia and, following four years in East Africa, has lived in Minnesota with her husband and five children since 1974. Coskran is attracted to the shock of other cultures and writes to learn the ordinary details of other lives, how an Ethiopian woman bathes her child, for example, or infuses her cooking with the sharpness of turmeric and coriander, or sustains belief in magic and mystery. When Coskran travels, she dutifully visits museums and monuments, but her real goal is to see how life is lived on other squares of earth. Her first book, *The High Price of Everything,* a collection of short stories, was a 1987 Minnesota Voices Project Winner and was selected for a Minnesota Book Award in 1988. She is currently working on a novel set in Ethiopia. "The Cook's Child" is a chapter from that work in progress.

CONSTANCE CRAWFORD is a native Californian who considers the few years she lived in other parts of the world to have been broadening though they did not cure her California habit. She spent five years in Minneapolis around 1960 and loved the place and the people notwithstanding the fact she was carrying many babies up and down forty icy steps to reach the house. She is a graduate of the Creative Writing Center at Stanford. Raising four kids, with a long stretch as single mother, and a span as a therapist have not cured her writing habit, either. In addition to short stories, she has published an autobiographical "cookbook," *Muse of Menus: Stories from Life and Cooking.* When not traveling — another habit — she now lives in San Francisco and writes away on what may turn out to be a novel.

NICOLE DILLENBERG, Libra, grew up in a tiny New York art town and spent her childhood along the banks of the Hudson, wiggling her toes in the polluted water, much to her mother's dismay. She studied humanities at the University of Kent, in England, and holds a film production degree from the University of Southern California. Dillenberg has worked as a screenwriter and actress — credits include "hob-knobization" with the famous and infamous, some great paychecks, and a couple of actual films (one in which she co-starred took the L.A. Critics prize last December.) Her poetry chapbook, *Man Ducks Down in Front of Movie Screen*, was published by Jamar, Inc. in 1988.

CHITRA DIVAKARUNI is originally from India, and now lives in the San Francisco Bay area. Her work has appeared in several anthologies and magazines, such as *Woman of Power, The Beloit Poetry Journal, The Colorado Review, The Indiana Review, Kalyx, Chelsea, Folio, Three Penny Review, Primavera, Occident*, and *Kingfisher*. Her work was nominated for a Pushcart Prize in 1989. She is the author of a book of poems, entitled *Dark Like the River*.

DEBORAH FASS was born and raised in Los Angeles, California and currently lives in San Francisco. Her poetry and fiction have been published in anthologies including *New Directions* and *Home to Stay* (Greenfield Review Press). As an undergraduate she studied Creative Writing and Literature at San Francisco State University and the University of New Mexico, and received a B.A. degree from the Poetics Program at New College of California. In 1984 she went to Japan with a Japanese Ministry of Education Research Fellowship. Fass lived and studied in Japan off and on for the next six years. She has an M.A. degree in Teaching English as a Second Language or Foreign Language. She currently is working with adult immigrants and refugees in the San Francisco Bay area.

MARGOT FORTUNATO (GALT) was born in Pittsburgh, PA, after a midnight ride which almost made her parents name her Paula. When she was four, her history professor father took a teaching job at The Citadel in Charleston, SC, where she lived until going to college at Goucher in Baltimore. Moving on North, she attended Columbia University (M.A.) and worked at Doubleday Publishers. She married, dropped Fortunato and followed her physician husband to Kansas City, and finally to Minneapolis/St. Paul. It seemed she'd never finish studying — she wrote a novel about the Civil Rights movement for her Ph.D. thesis in American Studies (University of Minnesota). Finally, with her daughter Helena in first grade, she declared herself a writer/teacher and got a divorce. Poet, memorist, playwright, student of Italian and felines, birds, wildflowers, and trees, she now lives in St. Paul with second husband

Fran Galt, two permanent cats Bad Bart and Fluffy, and three intermittent children. She teaches creative writing through COMPAS Writers-in-the-Schools and an occasional class of women-in-the-arts for local colleges. She is writing a book on using creative writing to teach history. During the summer of 1990 she will return to Italy after a hiatus of ten years.

DIANE GLANCY, after writing for 100 years, in the first half of 1990 won an NEA; a Minnesota State Arts Board Fellowship; a Jerome Travel Grant; a Blandin Foundation Fellowship; an NEH Summer Institute Fellowship to the Newberry Library in Chicago; a Diverse Visions Fellowship for collaboration with Harmonia Mundi for an experimental musical/verbal composition; the Capricorn Award from The Writer's Voice in New York for *Iron Woman*, a poetry manuscript published by New Rivers Press; The Nilon Award from the University of Colorado and The Fiction Collective for *Trigger Dance*, a collection of short stories; a letter of acceptance from West End Press for another poetry manuscript, *Lone Dog's Winter Count* to be published in 1991; and a Borderlands Theater award for *Stick Horse* with a week's residency in Tucson and a reading of the play.

PATRICIA HAMPL is perhaps best known for her memoir *A Romantic Education*, the story of her Czech family and of her travels to Prague. She has also published two collections of poems, *Woman before an Aquarium* and *Resort and Other Poems*. Her prose meditation on Antonin Dvorak's 1893 visit to Iowa, titled *Spillville*, was published in 1987 with engravings by the artist Steven Sorman. Ms. Hampl's next book, a memoir about her Catholic girlhood with reflections on contemplative life (no title yet) will be published by Farrar Straus Giroux. She is also completing a collection of essays titled *The Need to Say It: Essays on Memory and Imagination*. And to come full circle, she will be returning to Prague in 1991 in order to write an afterword to *A Romantic Education*. Patrica Hampl was born in St. Paul, Minnesota, where she still lives. She reviews regularly for the *New York Times Sunday Book Review*, and her work has appeared in various magazines and anthologies including, *The New Yorker, Antaeus, Best American Short Stories*, and *The Writer on her Work* (Vol. 2). She has received awards and fellowships from the Guggenheim Foundation, the National Endowment for the Arts, the Bush Foundation, the Ingram Merrill Foundation, among others, and has just received a MacArthur grant. She teaches at the University of Minnesota.

JENNIFER HOLT is a 33-year-old Leo, and a completely self-supporting artist, who makes her living as a voicework specialist, a singer/songwriter, and a writer. After surviving 21 years on the flat plains of South Dakota (she is an honors graduate of Augustana College in Sioux Falls), she lived a gypsy lifestyle, traveling with bands across country for two years before settling down in Minneapolis. As a musician, Jennifer founded and led a critically acclaimed all-women band Têtes Noires (French for 'dark heads'), who garnered favorable press from such sources as *The New York Times*, *Village Voice*, London's *NME*, Germany's *Spex*, etc. Since the band's demise, she has been pursuing a solo career and expects to have a record out by 1991. As a writer, Jennifer served as the managing editor for *Equal Time*, a gay/lesbian bi-weekly, and worked as an editor at *City Pages*, an alternative weekly, both in Minneapolis. When Jennifer grows up and/or gives up trying to become rich and famous as a singer/songwriter, she would like to become rich and famous as a feminist fantasy/science fiction writer. Her hobbies include competing in triathlons, traveling, learning 100 ways to cook seaweed (macrobiotically speaking), and pursuing a path to wholeness through 12-step recovery, therapy, affirmations and consciousness-raising work.

SUSAN A. D. HUNTER, the classic Air Force brat, can't remember a time when she hasn't loved the stimulus and the unexpected revelations that come from travel. Over the years she's hiked the Andes, studied at the Sorbonne, had all four tires stolen off her rented car on a Caribbean island, ridden camels across the endless sand dunes of Egypt, eaten a basket of sautéed locusts in Japan, and caught her own fish dinner in the waters of the South Seas. In between jaunts she's graduated from Stanford University, edited a computer journal, written for a wide variety of general-interest magazines. She loves to sail, ride her bicycle, work out in the gym, fish, hike, run, forage for wild mushrooms and chit-chat. She is a passionate reader and currently totters right on the verge of speaking fluent French. She is presently at work on a non-fiction book about Americans in Paris in the 1920's.

MAUREEN HURLEY lives near the Russian River, where she is California Poets in the Schools Area Coordinator for Sonoma and Napa Counties. She's recipient of several artist in residency awards from national, state, local and private agencies including seven California Arts Council grants, and has led workships in public schools, a mental institution, universities in California, the Bahamas and the USSR. She is director of Poetry Across Frontiers: Sonoma Heritage in Santa Rosa, a program that exchanges student poetry and art with Soviet sister city, Cherkassy, in the Ukraine, USSR. Hurley is a visual artist and photo-journalist as well as poet. Her poems and photographs have appeared in numerous publications. Her poetry has been translated and published both in Spanish and Russian.

JULIE LANDSMAN is married to a man obsessed with Italy. Thus, she feels obligated to accompany him to such places as Florence, Siena, Pisa, etc. It's a tough job, but.... When she isn't staying in an apartment near the Boboli Gardens or having coffee in Venice she teaches at the Minnesota Center for Arts Education and at the Loft. Then, if she has some more time she writes and publishes personal essays and poems in such periodicals as *Clinton Street Quarterly, Sing Heavenly Muse, Anna's House*, etc. She also has a teaching memoir in the hands of an agent and is waiting patiently for good news. Her Sheltie Max is now hinting he would like a walk by the river. She must go.

GRETCHEN T. LEGLER was born in Salt Lake City, Utah, and lived there until she moved to Minnesota to attend Macalester College, where she got her B.A. in political science and journalism in 1984. After her first job as a reporter at the Associated Press in Minneapolis, which she was dismissed from for misspelling the word 'carp' in a story about a local carp festival, she spent two successful years as a soybean, sunflower seed, and features reporter at the *Grand Forks Herald* and Agweek Magazine in North Dakota. She is currently finishing an M.A. in creative writing at the University of Minnesota and also pursuing a Ph.D. in English with a minor in feminist studies. Her freelance writing on such subjects as barber poles, slipcovers, cowboys, goose hunting and trout fishing, has appeared in the *St. Paul Pioneer Press* and other local and regional magazines. When she and her husband, Craig Block, are not fishing, picking blueberries, or hunting mushrooms, they reside in an old house with a huge vegetable garden in St. Paul.

MICHELLE DOMINIQUE LEIGH is a writer, illustrator, and jewelry designer. She is 37 years old and lives in Sendai, Japan with her husband Bruce and children Gabriel and Amber. Her writing and artwork have appeared in *The Village Voice*, M.I.T.'s *The Drama Review, Winds, Mothering, Seventeen*, and *The Japan Times*. She is currently at work on her first book, *The Japanese Way of Beauty*, which is to be published by Lyle Stuart in 1991.

MARDITH LOUISELL grew up in Duluth, MN, on Lake Superior. She has lived on Vancouver Island, in Toronto, New York, San Francisco, always near large bodies of water. Now she lives in Minneapolis and has to content herself with a large puddle called Lake Calhoun which isn't nearly enough water. She seems to be the only person living there who prefers the damp cool fog to the too bright sun. She has never lived in Venice but wishes she had. Louisell was supposed to grow up to found a new order for nuns or marry a professor and entertain him with piano sonatas. Times being what they are, neither of those fatherly fantasies came to pass. Instead she manages a staff development department in a large public service agency. She'd rather be a painter, she says, because it's hard to be obsessive and write — you have to keep making decisions — what to put in, what to take out. An artist can do the same scene over and over and, with sunlight in this one, moonlight in that one, not bore the viewer. But a writer can't tell the same story over and over in 100 different ways without losing the reader.

JANE MAEHR, wife and mother, reader and listener, people watcher, teacher, dreamer. The animal has not been born, the historical event has not been recorded, the fossil formed, the children's book written, and the wildflower identified that would not stir her interest. Currently living in Ann Arbor, MI, she shares two recurring dreams — visiting the homes, palaces, coffee houses, and churches where Johann Sebastian Bach wrote and performed music. And, she would like to retrace the journey of Alexander the Great. Conquering Persia is optional.

KATHERINE MAEHR came home from studying in Florence, Italy, to discover her parents had plans to move from their home in Urbana, IL. Refusing to be daunted, she decided to make St. Paul, where she graduated from Macalester College, her new home. She is inspired by cross-court backhands, dinosaurs, family, friends, a cat named Camille Claudel, and the idea of travel to new and far-away places. This year she saw the onion domes of Trump's Taj Mahal, the silos of Hastings, NE, and the garbage left on the streets after the Boston Marathon. Hardly lacking in inspiration, or material, she continues to write as much as she can. This is her first published piece.

MARGARET TODD MAITLAND has published essays, poetry, and articles on art, architecture, baseball, birthdays, and book collecting. She has received a Bush Artist Fellowship in creative nonfiction (1989) and grants from the Minnesota State Arts Board. She has worked as a crisis counselor, art teacher, editor, museum cataloguer, and, currently, freelance writer. She lives with her husband and son in St. Paul.

SHARON MAYES, beginning in the hill country of Tennessee, has spent forty years traveling the world, first across the United States, then at the age of five, settling on the foggy coast of Suffolk, England. Two years later she was living in the exotic city of Ankara, Turkey. Coming back to the U.S. at age nine was the most depressing experience of her early life. Since then restlessness has been a permanent condition. Sharon is currently in love with sub-Saharan Africa, the first place in the world that upon arrival felt like home. She recently completed a new novel, *An Unlikely Terrorist*, set in Zimbabwe. Her first novel, *Immune* was published by New Rivers Press. She has published eight short stories and ten poems, plus numerous academic and journalistic articles.

Momentarily, she is resting in a town on the West coast she calls "Mental Park."

EMILY MEIER writes novels, short fiction, and occasional non-fiction pieces, and has had a novella and numerous short stories published, including one in *Threepenny Review*. She has been a *Passages North* Fiction Prize winner and a Pushcart Prize nominee and a winner in the 1990 Lake Superior Contemporary Writers Series. Under severe duress, Meier does passable sheet rock finishing.

LINDA MATHIASON NORLANDER was born and raised in several small towns in Minnesota where her father edited various newspapers. She spent her senior year of high school in Caracas, Venezuela and her freshman year of college in California. Other than a bicycle trip from the west bank of the Misssissippi to Boston Harbor and an ill-fated trip to England and Ireland (where she ran out of money, lost a lot of weight, and broke out in a rash), she hasn't traveled much. (She writes "I get motion-sickness sitting in a rocking chair which sort of squelches any adventuresome nature.) She currently works in a hospice with dying patients and their families.

JENNIFER OCHTRUP lives in Minneapolis. In the move there she packed the wok in the hat box with the kitchen clock. She continues in the struggle to find the balance between passion and objectivity. This is her first published work.

MONICA OCHTRUP has decided the approach to fifty is good. This is when your children turn into people, leave and (yes) write letters. Twice a winner in the Minnesota Voices Project competition, she is a poet and author of two New Rivers books: *What I Cannot Say/I Will Say* (1985), and a new book of prose poems, *Pieces From the Long Afternoon*, available November, 1990.

RHIANNON PAINE has made many trips to England since the first in 1973. From 1975-78 she was married to an Englishman, an officer in the British Merchant Navy, and went to sea with him on gas ships and an oil tanker, calling at such exciting ports as Santos, Brazil, and Umm Said, Qatar. After the marriage broke up, she earned her M.A. in Victorian Literature at the University of Liverpool, where she introduced the high-brow crowd of university lecturers and Ph.D. candidates to the delights of hanging out in pizza parlors. All these people, including the ex-husband, are still good friends. Mrs. Ross, from the stories printed here, visited Ms. Paine in California in September 1990. It was her first trip to the U.S.

LINDA WOOLMAN PERRY, a graduate of Stanford University, is an editor at Stanford's Food Research Institute; wife to Doug, economist; mom to Tristan, actress, to Ben, cubscout and baseball player, to Sally, buff cocker spaniel. An American born in Lima, Peru, she has lived in France, England, Switzerland, and Indonesia, but longest in Palo Alto, California. Her enthusiasms include the garden, books, family travels, friends, India tea, and walks with the dog. Having contemplated writing for two decades, she has been writing fiction for two years. "Evening in Padang" is her first published short story. She has lots more stories to tell.

NANCY RAEBURN grew up in Mahtomedi, MN, a small town near St. Paul on the shores of White Bear Lake. She attended the University of Minnesota for three years before moving to Cambridge, MA, where she worked at Harvard. She later enrolled as a painting student at the School of the Musuem of Fine Arts in Boston. Her travels to Greece led her to the island of Mykonos, where she lived and painted for ten years. Her writing side blossomed back in the U.S. when in 1984 she completed her B.A. in English at Macalester College and was the recipient of the Wendy Parrish Poetry Prize and the Academy of American Poets Prize from the Associated Colleges of the Midwest. She has written a memoir about her experiences in Greece, and is currently painting from sketches of the New Mexican landscapes and writing short stories in Northfield, MN.

NORA REZA moved to Minneapolis in 1986, after having lived in Palo Alto, CA, where she studied painting and psychology at Stanford University. In painting, fiction, and real life she has sought to explore, among other interests, the complexities of her Persian-Irish background. She is currently writing a novel which reflects some of her experiences as an adolescent visiting Iran. She lives with her husband and two daughters.

MARTHA ROTH, kidnapped from her gypsy parents by well-meaning social workers, felt dull, stuffy, and out of place through her formative years. On being reunited with her people she joyfully embraced the role of an itinerant bunkum artist. Early in her second life it dawned on her that women's experience of travel is different from men's; her first published story, "Mediterranean Outlook" (*Nugget*, April 1957), dealt with this curious fact and she is dealing with it still. Educated in the streets and academies of several continents she has worked as an actress, waitress, sycophant, concubine, and editor (founding editor of *Hurricane Alice: A Feminist Quarterly*). In the evenings she enjoys early music, late movies, and playing with her husband and their cats.

MELISSA SANDERS-SELF is a writer who lives in Santa Cruz, California with her husband and two sons. She is currently working on a piece about the 1989 earthquake which devastated her home. She teaches creative writing to teen-age mothers, and also works as a SPECTRA artist-in-the-schools. She is busy looking for a publisher for her novel *Drawing in the Dark* and is hard at work on her second novel *Living*.

MADELON SPRENGNETHER used to dislike her name because not only could she not spell it when she was small, but she could hardly even say it, it was such a mouthful. This is how she acquired the nickname "Mimi." Now, however, some forty odd years and one divorce later, she has a different take on things. As the clerk in downtown Minneapolis said to her when she applied for a license to marry Robert Grayson Littlejohn (whose name she likes): "Honey, you can call yourself anything you want." After sifting through a number of imaginative possibilities, she settled on her own given name, because, as she figured, it was almost certainly unique.

CATHERINE STEARNS is a poet and teacher of creative writing and American literature. She has lived, worked, and wandered abroad on numerous occasions. On her first prolonged trip, to Belgium at age six, she recalls with fondness the lambic beer served with her school lunch each day. Whether taking the midnight bus to Cuernevaca or walking in the mists of Victoria Falls, Catherine explores and records the inner as well as the outer journeys. She is a regular visitor to Paris, Land's End, Cornwall, and Minneapolis. Her current jumping-off point is Wellesley, MA where she frequently travels in the company of sons Nathaniel, four, and Samuel, one, to the grocery store and back.

SARAH STREED lives in Tucson, AZ with her husband Roger Luhn, a physician, and their three-year-old son. She has an M.F.A. degree in Fiction Writing from the University of Arizona, and a B.A. in Literature from Wheaton College. Much of her adult life has been spent abroad: She was a Peace Corps Volunteer in Morocco, North Africa, and for part of that time, lived and worked in the American Legation Museum in Tangiers. Prior to that, she had been a summer student in Oxford, England, after which she worked as a governess for a family in Geneva, Switzerland. Sarah and her family are looking forward to the fall, which brings both the publication of her memoir and the birth of their second child.